1995

Scholarship on the West African kingdom of Asante is at the leading edge of Africanist research. In this book, T.C. McCaskie gives a detailed and richly nuanced historical portrait of pre-colonial Asante. His delineation of state and society in Asante in the eighteenth and nineteenth centuries is centred on an extended analysis of the crucial ritual of the annual Kumase *odwira* festival. It is at once a profound historical reconstruction of an African polity, and a deeply informed meditation on key Asante concepts and ideas. Throughout the book, the Asante experience is consistently discussed in relation to a broad range of historiography and critical theory.

State and society in pre-colonial Asante

African Studies Series 79

Editorial Board

Professor Naomi Chazan, *The Harry S. Truman Research Institute for the Advancement of Peace, The Hebrew University of Jerusalem*
Professor Christopher Clapham, *Department of Politics and International Relations, Lancaster University*
Professor Peter Ekeh, *Department of African American Studies, State University of New York, Buffalo*
Dr John Lonsdale, *Trinity College, Cambridge*
Professor Patrick Manning, *Department of History, Northeastern University, Boston*

Published in collaboration with
THE AFRICAN STUDIES CENTRE, CAMBRIDGE

A list of books in this series will be found at the end of this volume

State and society in pre-colonial Asante

T.C. McCaskie

University of Birmingham

CAMBRIDGE
UNIVERSITY PRESS

Published by the Press Syndicate of the University of Cambridge
The Pitt Building, Trumpington Street, Cambridge CB2 1RP
40 West 20th Street, New York, NY 10011-4211, USA

10 Stamford Road, Oakleigh, Melbourne 3166, Australia

First published 1995

Printed in Great Britain at the University Press, Cambridge

A catalogue record for this book is available from the British Library

Library of Congress cataloguing in publication data

ISBN 0 521 410096 hardback

VN

For Lynne

'God say, "You can do what you want Abe, but
The next time you see me comin..."'

(R.Z., 1967)

Contents

Illustrations

Maps

Plates

All of the plates, with the exception of Bowdich's *The First Day of the Yam Custom*, are taken from the R.S. Rattray Collection deposited in the Pitt Rivers Museum, University of Oxford, and are reproduced by permission. In each case the author has given the catalogued Pitt Rivers Title and Classification Number of Rattray's original negative.

Preface

This book originated in a paper commissioned by the late Trevor Aston for publication in *Past and Present*. My thinking and writing swiftly outgrew the bounds of a journal article, but the ideas that first animated Aston's request and my agreement to it survive in the structure and content of the present work. *Past and Present* wanted two things. First: an analysis of Asante that described the historical complexity of an African polity in all of the detail – and with a sophistication – that would bear comparison with the endeavours of contemporary historians of any society and time. Second: a discussion that remained anchored in the specifics of the Asante historical experience, but that faced outwards from it in constantly engaged dialogue with ideas and concepts that command an interdisciplinary attention across the community of scholarship. This book is shaped accordingly. The text is addressed to Asante specialists and to those academically interested in Africa and its history, but also, I trust, to those who come to the subject with a passionate curiosity but little prior knowledge. It is written to be read by anyone with the intellectual commitment to that task, for it is an argued essay in which the main themes are consistent throughout, and in which I have tried to keep asides, digressions or distracting impedimenta to a minimum. The notes, as is customary, serve to document the text, but they are also in many cases intended as supplementary argument. It is here that those readers who wish to pursue matters beyond the text itself will find dialogue with and reference to that broader range of ideas and concepts already noted. Simply put, on the estimable principle that light is preferable to dark, I have tried to open the – all too often shuttered – disciplinary house of (in this case Asante and African) history to as much external illumination as possible. A confident intercourse with ideas – judged only by their significant relevance, and not by a plodding, timid literalness about disciplinary points of origin – is at once an acknowledgement of complexity, an enrichment of analysis, and a signal that a given field of study has passed from childhood to maturity. Thus, very much later, and in a different context, I have tried to meet the objectives generally set out in my original commission. I thought then and think now that these are exemplary, if very demanding, goals. I have tried to provide a rigorous analysis of the Asante past, and to place that Asante past in a wider intellectual perspective and before the largest possible constituency. My success or otherwise in realising this is for the reader to judge. That said, I enter an additional plea for the enterprise itself, as distinct from what I may or may not have made of it. To address the history of Africa at the highest sustainable level of analysis is, I fear, more urgent now than ever it was. Recent years have seen the lamentable remnants of patronizing attitudes towards Africa resurrected, in the academy as in the world, into a complaisant *bien pensant* cynicism about that continent and everything to do with it. Disappointments about the aftermath of Africa's independence in the 1960s – outrageously experienced by many outside of Africa as *their* failures and *our* disappointments – have engendered a widespread ignorance and apathy. Fundamental to this is complicity in the continued (if often unvoiced) denial of an African past. From there it is the shortest and laziest of steps *mutatis mutandis* to condone Africa's present marginalization, and to condemn its future out of hand.

Books do not emerge *ex nihilo*, and this one is no exception to that rule. My debts, scholarly and personal, are legion: first, to Trevor Aston, of course, and to various members of the editorial board of *Past and Present*; to Robin Law and Larry Yarak, who in 1988 coaxed from me a conference paper of such Brobdingnagian dimensions that I was incontrovertibly confronted with the evidence that the Rubicon had been crossed, and that I had a book on my hands; to Terry Ranger, who made some valuable suggestions at a critical early stage; to John Peel and Richard Rathbone – friends as well as scholars – who read the entire draft text with acuity, sympathy and exemplary patience; and to David Cohen, who read the final chapter on an autumn day in Evanston with an understanding and enthusiasm that carried me over the finishing line. To all of these persons I owe a very great deal. I owe debts of another kind to Robin Law, David Anderson, David Henige, John Peel, Murray Last, Karin Barber and Paulo Farias. These forgiving souls were the editors who patiently and skilfully brought papers of mine (written in part to keep the present book down to manageable proportions) to successful publication, and in the process uncomplainingly put up with and otherwise endured the vagaries of an author whose attention was distracted by the writing of this book. Arguments that have found their (modified) way into my text have been variously aired over the years at conferences or seminars in Birmingham, Cambridge, Oxford, London, Stirling, Barcelona, Chicago, Madison, San Francisco, Kumase and elsewhere. I am grateful to all who participated. An especial mention must be made here of the postgraduate students that I talked with in the course of a visit to Northwestern University in 1992. In seeking out my own thoughts as I was finishing this book they contributed their own, together with their manifest enthusiasm for the African past, and all unwittingly benefited the final draft.

I have worked on Asante since the 1960s, and have published extensively on that society over the years. In the course of this long involvement, I have accumulated broader debts within the field of Asante and Akan scholarship that I wish to acknowledge here. In various ways and at different times I have benefited from the writings and talk of Jean Allman, Ron Atkinson, Gareth Austin, René Baesjou, Tony Berrett, Adu Boahen, Wilhelmina Donkoh, Tim Garrard, Michelle Gilbert, Paul Jenkins, Norman Klein, Tom Lewin, Malcolm McLeod, Donna Maier, Stephan Miescher, Claude-Hélène Perrot, Sandy Robertson, Emmanuel Terray, Albert Van Dantzig, Ivor Wilks, Selena Winsnes and Kwesi Yankah, and the late Kwame Daaku, Ray Jenkins, Marion Johnson and Alex Kyerematen. The late Edmund Collins gave me insights into the evolution of Asante historiography in the 1950s and 1960s that could have come from no other source. I also wish to acknowledge a unique debt to the late Meyer Fortes; simply, this book would not have been possible without him. Finally, in the field of Asante and Akan scholarship, I acknowledge three people who have both inspired me by their work and sustained me by their friendship; they are Kwame Arhin, Ray Kea and Larry Yarak. Others who are not directly or primarily engaged with Asante have aided and supported me in the writing of this book. These include many individuals, but I owe particular thanks again to Richard Rathbone, to Phyllis Ferguson and Frank Longstreth, and – last and certainly not least – to Jeff Rice and Truman Metzel, who somehow manage to preside over what I can only describe as a stimulating moveable feast of a *salon* in the very best bookshop that I know. The Centre of West African Studies at the University of Birmingham has furnished me with congenial colleagues, and it has unstintingly funded no less than five research trips to Ghana. In 1990 I worked in Kumase as a consultant to a joint UK-USA television series (since broadcast in Britain) on dance. Geoff Dunlop, the director of the segment on Asante, provoked me to think some things afresh by asking the kind of basic or fundamental questions that are proverbially the province of intelligent outsiders. My final debt – already acknowledged in a narrower context – is to John Peel, an extremely close and valued friend and a model of scholarly excellence. Highly specific debts to some among the foregoing are gratefully acknowledged as appropriate in the footnotes.

I first went to Asante in 1967, when I was a very Junior Research Fellow in the Department of History at the University of Ghana at Legon. My most recent visits there, but I trust not my last, were on two separate trips in 1990. In the many times that I have been in Asante I have unfailingly come away with new insights (some making exciting sense only years after the event), and with warm memories. On my first visit I was introduced to the late *Asantehene* Osei Agyeman Prempeh II, who was considerate and tactful in dealing with a very young – and nervous – apprentice scholar. During my most recent visit the incumbent *Asantehene* Opoku Ware II displayed the same qualities of kindness in dealing with the importunate excitement of my four-year-old daughter Anna. Apart from these two most distinguished occupants of *Osei ne Opoku sika dwa* I hardly know where to begin in acknowledging all of those who, in one way or another, have facilitated my work in Asante. My footnotes indicate specific debts, and to all those not mentioned here by name for reasons of space I say *mintumi menna wo ase da*. That said, I should like to record certain obligations that – gratefully incurred and impossible adequately to discharge – command mention. The late *Akyempemhene ɔheneba* Boakye Dankwa and I. K. Agyeman not only shared their profound knowledge of Asante with me, but also pointed me in the direction of a host of individuals who deepened my understanding. In the essential matter of arranging and effecting discussions on different visits to Asante I owe thanks to numbers of persons; these include *inter alios* C. Osei-Bonsu, J. Agyeman-Duah, Anthony Kwadwo, Michael Adjaye, J.F. Opoku, I. Donkoh, Osei Bekere, Thomas Djang, and Isaac Kwarteng. Joseph Agyeman-Duah was a patient guide to the resources of the Manhyia Record Office in the days before it reached its present level of ordered efficiency. Kwame Arhin – or, as I should properly refer to him in this context, the incumbent *Nifahene* of Bare-Kese – is author of a Kumase guidebook and a fount of great knowledge, generously shared, on the places and people of that city. As anyone who has worked in and on a society for quarter of a century must know, increments of understanding come, not simply in the formalized interviews that compose what M. Fortes named 'the rites of fieldwork', but also (and perhaps even more so) in the innumerable exchanges of human sociability. Africanists are generally too reticent in giving this important aspect of experience its due; it is woven into what they write, just as, for instance, his experience of French society is a tangible and enriching presence in the historical writing of Richard Cobb. I remember here (gratefully, but alas only representatively, for this listing can be no more than a ruthlessly curtailed sampling of memory) enlightening encounters with the Asante *habitués* of the Phobia Base, Boatengs, Takoko's and Chop-Chop; with T.K. and V.O. and their families and friends, with whom the Christmas and New Year of 1975–6 became a long seminar on Asante customs and *mores*; with classes of schoolchildren at Edweso and Kuntanase; with Eddie and his intimates at Brodekwano by Lake Bosomtwe; or with the outstanding musician Koo Nimo, who informed as he entertained on a Sunday at his house at UST. To all these, and to all the others, heartfelt thanks. Finally, to get to Asante from outside Ghana means first flying to Accra. At Kokomlemle in Accra on several occasions I have been the grateful recipient of the hospitality of Mrs Emily Asiedu, a family friend; I thank her and her household for the twin blessings of care and comfort. In Accra too I have benefited from long talks with Professor Adu Boahen (of Dwaben, Asante), who was my Head of Department at Legon in the 1960s. Adu is retired from academic life, but is now of course a very prominent figure in Ghanaian life and politics. Notwithstanding these commitments, his interest in the Asante past is undimmed, and his devotion to thinking about it unswerving.

It will be apparent from my Guide to Sources and Materials Consulted that, over the years, I have incurred many debts in exploiting archival and other institutional resources. In every case, I have met with unfailing kindness and assistance from the custodians of the materials in which I was interested. I thank them all for their efforts on my behalf, and would like to make particular mention of two. First, like anyone interested in the Ghanaian past, I owe an immeasurable debt to Paul Jenkins, Archivist of the Basel Mission. A historian himself, he is famously generous to fellow scholars with materials and insights that he has gleaned from the very important (and dauntingly large) archive of which he has charge. This book owes much to his selfless help. Second, in 1983, when life in Ghana was the reverse of easy, the staff of branches of the National Archives there proved endlessly helpful in circumstances of notable difficulty. I have always found them thus, but in that trying year they excelled themselves. I thank them. Lastly, Wendy Guise and Jessica Kuper, my editors successively at Cambridge University Press, have been patient with an author whose instincts are for researching and polishing, rather than saying enough is enough and writing *finis*. But that point has at last now been reached, and both deserve my thanks for going the distance with me.

1 Varieties of the Asante past

Asante historiography and its discontents I

Africanist historiography has a very distinguished but incontestably short ancestry. Intensive scholarly investigation of Africa's precolonial past dates only from the 1950s. First, without doubt, among the leading themes that have emerged from over three decades of academic endeavour is ongoing discussion of the structure and characteristics of the precolonial African state. Scrutiny and analysis of this issue are contentious. This is most especially the case when the problem being adumbrated is refined to a close consideration of the precise nature of the historic relationship between given African states and societies. Thus, for instance, in 1981, in a very compressed but still lengthy survey of the literature then available on states and social processes in Africa, Lonsdale prefaced his observations with the cautionary disclaimer that his essay could 'only be one historian's view of a large and controversial matter'.[1]

The matter has indeed remained controversial, albeit in an inconclusive and generally unsatisfactory way. The chief reason for this state of affairs is that our analyses of state and society in precolonial Africa, and of the nature of the relationship between the two, are at once notably skewed and imbalanced. As a direct consequence of this state of affairs there exist very substantial gaps in our understanding.

In part at least this situation has arisen from recalcitrant problems with the data. It must be conceded immediately and without reservation that for large tracts of the African past conclusions are reduced to the tentative or the speculative by severe limitations in the historical record. This factor is undoubtedly important. But it can be overstated. For the more privileged parts of Africa's past the data are no worse and in fact are often very much better than comparable materials used in the reconstruction of, say, the 'ancient economy' of the Greco-Roman world, or the history of popular ideas and attitudes in medieval or early modern Europe.[2]

Evident lacunae in our comprehension of the most fully documented African states and societies have arisen, not from an absence of information,

1

but from the sedulous application of limited – and limiting – strategies of approach, analysis, method and reading. The problem can be adduced with the greatest economy by focusing now on the precolonial state and society that are the subject of this book.

The Asante (Ashanti) are a Twi-speaking Akan people long situated in the Guinea-zone tropical forest region of what is now south-central Ghana in West Africa. Asante society slowly crystallized in its historic form in the course of the sixteenth and seventeenth centuries. The Asante state came into being around the close of the seventeenth century and the beginning of the eighteenth (the conventional *annus mirabilis* is 1701, when the nascent Asante state liquidated the rival Akan power of Denkyira at the battle of Feyiase). Thereafter, throughout the eighteenth century and far into the nineteenth, the Asante state was imperially enlarged and spectacularly elaborated; and despite a period of British colonial overrule (1896–1957), the Asante state and the society over which it presided still exist in vital if modified form as a discretely identifiable component of the independent Republic of Ghana.[3]

Extremely dense Asante historical traditions are complemented by voluminous eighteenth- and more especially nineteenth-century European reportage, and by intensively detailed twentieth-century ethnographic investigation. It is arguable that the sheer abundant wealth of the historical record is quite without equal in sub-Saharan Africa. This plethora has enabled the generation of a very considerable historiography of which one commentator has remarked as follows: 'Nowhere in Africa – perhaps in the world – has a precolonial polity been more thoroughly researched than the kingdom of Asante, political center of Ghana's Akan peoples.'[4]

The nature of the state, the state as practice, is absolutely central to the discourse of Asante historiography. Equally apparent, however, are the gaps and deformities already referred to in general terms. In fact, because of the volume of scholarship dedicated to it, Asante is a supreme instance of the difficulties of approach, analysis, method and reading discussed above. Let us now enlarge the theoretical framework of the argument by way of brief introduction to the specific historical disfigurements of the Asante case.

The disfigurements in Asante historiography have arisen primarily because of an approach to the evidence that has the effect of combining a seriously miscalculated partiality – a blinkered tunnel vision – with a relentlessly mechanistic and ultimately self-validating analytic application. That is to say, existing readings and interpretations of the bases of state power tend overwhelmingly to favour two perspectives or lines of argument. The first of these is defined by its choice of subject matter; the second is circumscribed by its intellectual presumptions. These perspectives are intellectually distinct, but they are not mutually exclusive, and in point of fact or achievement they often go hand in hand.

The first perspective or line of argument concentrates fixedly on the idea and nature of the political superstructure. At first glance this appears to be perfectly understandable. Elite political behaviour is of clear and quite obvious significance in any complex polity. And for precolonial Asante, as elsewhere, the historical record is most detailed and least ambiguous where it pertains to the historical facts of institutionalized office holding. The difficulty with this approach in practice is that it has created a species of hermetic or self-referencing analysis. In reconstructing and anatomizing in maximum detail and as chronological narrative the 'history' of an elite political order – a self-validating procedure not so far removed from Ranke's *wie es eigentlich gewesen ist* – there is a very real danger, most unfortunately realized in the Asante case, of detaching and virtually isolating the history of the political superstructure from the history of the society over which it presided and in which it was embedded. The social order – society itself – is reduced almost by default to a passive, inert or 'given' status. It is presented as existing only in as much as it is susceptible to interventionist regulation by a seemingly autonomous political order. This issue will be addressed more fully below. For the moment let us simply note that even if we concede Jacques Le Goff's widely discussed point that politics remains the 'backbone' of history, then Asante political history is still very, very far from being the integrated, totalizing *social* history of politics that he and his antecedent *annalistes* had in mind.[5]

The second perspective is characterized by an adherence to what is perhaps best termed a crudely or vulgarly materialist mode of analysis. In this construction all motive is circumscribed by, and all action is determined from within, the simplistic boundaries of a quasi-logic of perceived material advantage. The sheer consistency of this quasi-logic through time is guaranteed by its mechanical single-mindedness. That is to say, the evolution and movement of the historical process are understood to be determined by evident success in translating imperatives, drawn from an unswerving reading or appraisal of self-interest, into the arena of coercive capacity or will. This is very obviously an elite perspective (and a rather Hobbesian one at that), for it simply differentiates rulers (or the ruling class) as being those most successful in the pursuit of a self-evident, self-replicating and objective range of material goals shared in by all. This is history with the ideas left out. In consequence, this perspective is directly linked to the history of the political superstructure by a host of instrumental but extremely facile behavioural presumptions.

This second perspective is grounded in a totally misleading sheen or patina of rationality. People – Asante people – are construed as acting in and within the 'commonsensical' parameters of their lived, sensory, here and now material existence. And the material bases of advantage and power, in collusion with the history of the political superstructure, are of crude instrumental significance in all of this. Examined closely, however, the chimera of rationality dissolves into rationalization. Asante historiography constructs lopsided archetypes by distilling all of social reality down to a usable, mechanical framework of 'rational', materialist explanation.

The principal casualty of this second perspective is also the history of Asante society, and more precisely the history of cultural practice. This is either neglected, rationalized or marginalized in an epiphenomenal way. When indigenous concepts of belief, religion, knowledge, custom and habit, and patterns of thought – the leading elements in cultural practice – are discussed at all, they are either rationalized in materialist, instrumental and 'commonsensical' terms or, if refractory or otherwise resistant to such redefinition and reduction, they are consigned to a residual category. In the latter case, they are presented as being at best passively contemplative, and at worst exotically irrelevant. This is unfortunate, for meaningful reconstruction requires an integration of the materialist perspective with cultural specificities taken on their own complex terms.[6] This issue will also be addressed more fully below.

Gramsci, *annalistes* and others

Helpful in enlarging our understanding of the problems inherent in the two perspectives adumbrated above, and illuminating in terms of the history of society and of cultural practice and specificities, are Gramsci's remarks *contra* Marx, or more exactly his observations in refinement of 'classical' Marxist historical materialism.[7]

A Gramscian reading *sensu stricto* would argue that existing interpretations of Asante state power imply differentiation and the existence of objectively situated Classes *in* Themselves; that is, classes in unmediated relation to the means of production and the appropriation of surplus. Simultaneously, however, the argument would continue, Asante historiography (like Marxist historical materialism) is poorly equipped and even evasive when it addresses the much more intractable problem of Classes *for* Themselves; that is, classes in relation to the acquisition and articulation of consciousness.[8] A strict Gramscian reading is not attempted here. For a variety of reasons it is inappropriate to historic Asante society. Nor is this very surprising, for precolonial Africa was not twentieth-century Italy. Gramsci's *conclusions* are suggestive at best. However, the *procedures* or *lines of argument* that led to the formulation of these conclusions are of direct relevance to the Asante case.

Underpinning Gramsci's interpretation and definition of Classes *for* Themselves was the construction of his master concept of *egemonia* or hegemony. This was developed from his perception, by no means novel to himself or to his century, of a very widespread, even universal dichotomy in political practice between what he termed *direzione* or consent (with the sense of collaboration or subscription to leadership) and *dominio* or coercion (with implications of domination and force). He went on to posit a necessary balance – what he called an equilibrium of compromise – between rulers and ruled in any evolved or mature polity.

The point itself is commonsensical. The problem is, and always has been, how and by what means is this necessary balance secured and maintained? Fundamental and indispensable to this balance, argued Gramsci, was the operation or articulation of hegemony. And hegemony, he concluded, must always be a supremacy attained primarily by means of consent. Coercion, he urged (in elaboration of others, and notably Hume), was in and of itself a *necessary* but not a *sufficient* condition for the effective articulation and implementation of hegemony.[9] He went on firmly to root or locate the articulation of consent in the institutionalized practices – belief and religion, knowledge, custom, habit, patterns of thought – that together comprised what he termed civil society.[10]

The historiographical marginalization of Asante society and cultural practice is directly related to our present very limited comprehension of the historical determinants of Asante civil society. We have already taken note of the severe limitations that ensue from a fixation on the history of the political superstructure. And by the logic of its line of inquiry, as discussed above, the materialist perspective – in Gramscian terminology the implied identification of Classes *in* but not *for* Themselves – has also virtually nothing to say about the practices comprising civil society. In fact, the very concept of Asante civil society remains historically *in vacuo*; in as far as it exists it is anchored in a permanent ethnographic present, and bereft of historically situated ideas or precepts.[11]

Gramsci's insights are employed at various points in this essay where and as they seem appropriate. His concept of hegemony grounded in consent, as a number of scholars have remarked, is a most useful tool for generating a dialogue between the history of structures and the history of cultures, and for relating social and cultural practices to their mental, intellectualist and ideological representations.[12] His treatment of the articulation of consent has the virtue of liberating cultural practice and/or discourse from ossified, synchronic definition, and instead situates the meaning of that discourse in contingency and in the shifting kaleidoscope of particular or discrete historical circumstances.

Gramsci's concerns, procedures and insights, together with elaborations and variants of them, are increasingly widespread among certain historians, sociologists and critical commentators on cultural practice and civil society. Gramsci's influence in general stretches very far, although choices of locution and language sometimes serve to mask the debt.[13] This is because Gramsci addressed himself, with sustained and formidable acuity, to deliberating on a series of problems that have come to be recognized – but only recently – as being of crucial importance in a number of disciplines.

Let us restrict our remarks to history and historians. In recent years historians of many areas and periods have tried to tackle the problem of relating cultural practice and its representations to the historically revealed structurations of social reality. In part this was a rejection of the norms of intellectual history as it was traditionally understood and practised. Intellectual history was (and is) concerned with the autonomy of cultural practice; its field is the phenomenology of culture, and because of this orientation it has no interest in any relationship of mediation or determination between cultural representations and social reality.[14]

The critique of this particular type of idealism was led by materialist historians (Marxist, *marxisant* and otherwise), by those interested in the history of *mentalités*, and by mavericks like Norbert Elias.[15] But to a greater or lesser degree all of these approaches were characterized by the same besetting limitation that we have seen in the materialist perspective on Asante history, and that we have noted as being central to Gramsci's critique of Marx. That is, cultural practice was marginalized as an epiphenomenon, and cultural representations were always reduced to some other classificatory category – social class, material conditions, the politics of coercion, or in literate societies (and as a dependent function of any of the foregoing), socio-political distinctions between the production and consumption of cultural representations (texts).[16] In varying degrees, many historians were bound to these categories by personal conviction; and those concerned with the history of *mentalités*, influenced by Braudel's promulgation of the successive economic, social and cultural levels of serial history, frequently utilized the same or similar benchmarks to reduce cultural practice to the statistically quantifiable.[17]

The beginnings of a more fruitful historical critique can be traced back through the historians of *mentalités* to the work of their mentors. In very significant measure the foundation of the *Annales* school was undertaken in conscious repudiation of idealist intellectual history. Febvre and Bloch were much concerned with the history of cultural practice, and with the insights regarding it that might be gleaned from other disciplines: social and cultural anthropology, literary criticism, folklore, psychology.[18] But as has been noted above, subsequent generations of *annalistes* tended to 'scientize' or to reify cultural practice, or otherwise to reduce it to some other category.

Other scholars went (and still go) too far in the opposite direction. They isolate cultural practice from social, political and material reality, often adventitiously, by means of an uncritical framing of its representations within the synchronic vocabulary of symbolic anthropology.[19] Thus, even if we accept the notion of a world saturated in symbols and substantively lived through them – as for example in Geertz's sophisticated treatment of the nineteenth-century 'theatre state' of Negara in Bali – then we are still left with nagging diachronic questions concerning the evolution of relationships in and through time. Not just symbols, but symbols of and for what and when? Theatre by and for whom, and when? Representations in what context, and from whose perspective? And how and by what means, and with what effects, does all of this transmute in time as it is lived through by individuals and groups in relation to the evolving conditions of material reality?[20] At its most extreme, presumptions about the special status of cultural practice – its isolation, its autonomy – translate all of its representations into the vocabulary of a master symbol, and frame historical interpretation accordingly. Sahlins' reading of eighteenth- and nineteenth-century Hawaiian history as 'a political economy of love' (in which 'love is the infrastructure' and 'the erotic is the pragmatic') is a supremely elegant instance of this tendency.[21] Less dazzling examples of the same kind of myopic particularism are to be found in what has been called the 'new history' in the United States.[22]

Historical process cannot be reduced to crude materialism, but neither can it be entirely displaced onto a shadow world of symbolic performance in which, at one or more removes of representation and with presumptions of diverse or unitary intent, it *enacts* itself.[23] As Febvre and Bloch recognized a long time ago, historical process *expresses* multiple realities in symbolic and even theatrical terms, but it is not itself *realized* as a performed simulacrum of its own content. Thus, as we shall see, execution and human sacrifice in Asante were transacted as symbolic performances or ritualized texts; but to the state that prescribed them, and to the victim or oblate who played the leading role in them (terms absolutely precise in their ambiguity), performative enactment was a reference to and a corroboration of the actualities of historical process. Meaningful reconstruction, as has already been stated in other terms, requires an integration of material circumstance, action and consequence with the realm of cultural practice and representation.

This brings us back to Gramsci. His objective was class analysis, and it was undertaken in conscious enlargement of Marx's contribution. Although he strove to universalize his conclusions in the Marxist manner, Gramsci's field of historical study, to put the matter in his own terms, was bounded by the evident disintegration of Italian 'feudalism', and the concomitant emergence and consolidation of Italian (and European) capitalism and mass society.[24] The precolonial state successfully constrained the emergence of capitalist production in Asante. This is discussed more fully below. To reiterate: rigorously to apply a Gramscian class analysis to precolonial Asante society would require a misplaced leap of faith. Gramsci's relevance, as has been argued above, lies in his procedures, his lines of argument and his insights, rather than in his uncompleted and often haphazard attempts at systematization. His propositions concerning hegemony and the articulation of consent in the institutionalized practices of civil society were intended to put cultural specificities back on the materialist historical agenda. He recognized the interdependent explanatory significance of both perspectives, and sought to effect a reconciliation between them. Something of the same sort of reconciliation is attempted in this book, and the themes introduced here are further refined in direct relation to the Asante material discussed on pp. 19–23.

Cultural practice and civil society

At first sight the failure to provide any adequate historical account of Asante cultural practice or civil society seems puzzling on a number of counts. First, an understanding of the relational balance between consent and coercion is evident in remarks attributed to some of the state's rulers, the *Asantehenes* Osei Tutu Kwame (1804–23), Kwaku Dua Panin (1834–67) and Mensa Bonsu (1874–83), and in nineteenth-century European observations concerning Asante.[25] T.B. Freeman, a Wesleyan-Methodist missionary who visited Kumase, the Asante capital, four times in the 1830s and 1840s, stated his perplexed view of the matter at some length.

Indeed the Ashantees seem to pride themselves in the cruel and sanguinary despotism of their government: and hence, as the King of Ashantee parades the streets of his capital on the great *Custom Days* the women crying his strong names add 'Long may you live and be strong to kill us at your pleasure'; and the masses of men seem to take delight in the horrid scenes of cruelty which too often transpire; as though they would say 'Our King is a great despot and kills us as he pleases, and we all imitate him in our way and our sphere as much as we can'; and hence the wild dance of the public executioners before their victims ere they strike off their heads, or, in any other way despatch them: and hence also their occasional parading of the streets of the capital with pieces of human flesh in their mouths... In Ashantee despotism is seen *Out of Doors* as it were, without any concealment, at high noon, asking who cares? Who is afraid to own it? In any little village the visitor may as it were stumble on a human sacrifice, or in the capital an executioner may rush past him in the street and nearly brush his dress with the human head streaming with life's warm current and laugh at his surprise and disgust.[26]

Freeman went on to contrast these paradoxes of participatory subscription and consent in Asante with the draconian system of state oppression that he had observed further to the east in Dahomey. There were, he noted, 'strange antitheses' between the two polities; Dahomey was 'despotism in the entire extreme', and Dahomean society was 'stagnant as the silent waters of a pool'; but in Asante, the state was 'more open' in its exercise of power, and it was mystifyingly 'sustained as such, by the peculiar prejudices, manners and customs of the people'.[27]

Second, despite very notable achievements, the precolonial Asante state simply lacked the infrastructure and technology to command society solely by coercive force. Historians have presumed a great deal concerning the instrumental efficacy of late eighteenth- and early nineteenth-century processes of Asante 'bureaucratization' (an issue which is discussed more fully below), and they have made much of the state's supposed adherence to a rational decision logic in, for instance, the implementation of foreign policy.[28]

But set against these putative advantages were massive, recurrent and often intractable limiting factors. Literacy was virtually non-existent; it was viewed with grave suspicion by the Asante state, and only achieved anything approaching widespread dissemination well into the colonial period.[29] The possibility of dissension at the centre was endemic, and intra-elite conflict was not infrequent and sometimes disabling; this culminated in a murderous internecine civil war (1883–8) in which the state's office-holding cadres did severe and irrevocable damage to the political superstructure, materially bankrupted themselves, and in the process lost much of their capacity to persuade society, let alone to command it.[30] Provincial rebellion and divisional secession punctuated the eighteenth and nineteenth centuries; the defection in the 1830s and again in the 1870s of the ɔman (pl. aman) or territorial division of Dwaben – one of the five core Asante akan aman nnum, or historically oldest and largest constituent divisions of the first rank – is the most serious but by no means the sole instance of the second of these tendencies.[31] Peasant rebellion, concerted or inchoate, was not a feature of precolonial Asante history; and this was the case despite the fact that the Kumase ruling elite systematically exploited a numerically huge rural underclass – both slave and free – that could never have been held in check by repressive coercion alone.[32]

The nature of the forest environment was the basic fact of Asante life, and the ultimate infrastructural and technological constraint on it. The core of the polity was situated in an ecological niche that was inimical and resistant, difficult to manage, and ultimately hostile. An important illustrative instance of this factor is the issue of communications. The *ŋkwantempɔŋ* or 'great roads' that radiated out from Kumase were the channels along which the state's coercive capacities flowed. Two views can be taken of the *ŋkwantempɔŋ*. On the one hand they were triumphs of muscle power, organization and ingenuity. On the other hand they were a fragile, technologically underdeveloped communications system, subject to recurrent seasonal disruption and to very rapid deterioration if and when they were neglected.[33]

Let us take as a single example the vital governmental, military and commercial artery that ran south from Kumase to the Bosompra river, and thence onwards to the European settlements on the Gold Coast littoral. In May 1817, Bowdich found the road north from the Bosompra river to Kumase to be well cleared (by order of the *Asantehene* Osei Tutu Kwame), and in places it was 'frequently eight feet wide'; on his southward return in September, however, 'the rainy season had set in violently', and this same road was 'almost a continued bog' along which his Asante escort was reluctant to travel because of the 'aggravated difficulties' caused by torrential rain.[34] In the course of the civil war(s) of the 1880s this road virtually reverted to forest through neglect; Terry-Coppin (1885) and R.A. Freeman (1889) both commented on this, the latter describing stretches that were cripplingly obstructed by secondary undergrowth, fallen trees and swamps.[35]

Furthermore, no technological innovation was introduced to maximize speed or carrying capacity. The tools used in clearing the forest remained essentially the same throughout the precolonial period; although the Asante were familiar with oxen and horses, the widespread use of draught or riding animals was precluded by the disease environment; and while the principle of the wheel was understood in the nineteenth century, its deployment in the Asante forest would have required a road system of a type that simply could not be constructed.[36] Thus, the reach of coercive capacity depended for its effectiveness on a most fragile equation. To function at its upper limit of efficiency – that is, so to speak, to stand still – the Asante communications network had to be relentlessly maintained and renovated just to sustain operational viability; but a lot of factors, environmental and otherwise, could radically upset even these relatively modest performance standards, and intermittently, and most notably from the 1870s onwards, they did.

Third, the discipline of social anthropology, or more precisely the practice of British structural-functionalism – a tradition in Asante scholarship older than the historiography – did much to illuminate those very issues of belief and religion, knowledge, custom, habit and patterns of thought that are central to cultural practice, to civil society and to an understanding of the articulation of consent. Two commanding figures – R.S. Rattray and M. Fortes – have dominated the anthropological enterprise in Asante. Rattray was a colonial official who carried out an extensive programme of research and publication on Asante, mainly in the 1920s.[37] Essentially he was a romantic folklorist, but he was also a structural-functionalist *avant la lettre*.[38] Rattray was 'so scrupulous, and sensitive an ethnographer', noted Fortes, 'that he did in fact contribute data that still lend themselves very well to functionalist and structuralist analysis'.[39] Fortes himself, who worked in Asante in the 1940s, was perhaps the leading practitioner in his own generation of British structural-functionalist anthropology. The guiding principle of this analytic method, he remarked towards the close of his career, was 'to trace out how things hang together consistently in a given social system'.[40]

Structural-functionalism has been severely criticized, but only one major point need be noted here. Fortes explicitly traced structural-functionalism's intellectual genealogy, or at least one of its major lines of descent, back through the work of A.R. Radcliffe-Brown to Lewis Henry Morgan's seminal and immensely influential *Systems of Consanguinity and Affinity of the Human Family* (1871).[41] But Fortes' view of Morgan was extremely partial. The matter at issue has been trenchantly summarized in the most recent treatment of Morgan's work.

Fortes says in effect that Morgan is a much better anthropologist when we leave the history out, and he says so from the vantage of a tradition that has endeavored to do better anthropology by leaving the history out... Fortes avers, however, that Radcliffe-Brown got much of his structural-functionalism from Morgan, specifically from deeply reading the *Systems*. This interpretation of Morgan's anthropology is a consequence of the decision to assess it from the vantage of one of its descendant intellectual lineages... It is at one and the same time an assessment of Morgan and a description of the shape of current anthropology – or, at any rate, one version of it. Morgan's structuralism with the history left out is what anthropology has become.[42]

Structural-functionalism as practice concentrated on the nature of social relations within the framework of a permanent ethnographic present, and paid virtually no attention to historical process.[43] Freedman, himself an anthropologist, has summarized structural-functionalist practice in the following succinct terms.

Concentrating on the study of primitive societies for which the historical evidence appeared (in the absence of any appetite for it) to be lacking or grossly deficient, practitioners of the mode created, often quite unconsciously, the fiction that they were dealing with timeless entities which upon analysis would be demonstrated to consist of an intricate mechanism of interacting parts.[44]

A great deal of Asante (and Africanist) historiography has been written in more or less conscious repudiation of the structural-functionalist tradition. It is highly unfortunate that in Asante historiography the rejection of the intellectual premisses of structural-functionalism has been extended to encompass most of the subject matter of social anthropology. We might say that any historical study of cultural practice, civil society or the articulation of consent has been damned by association. This tendency must be reversed. The concerns of the anthropological tradition need to be engaged and located in historical perspective, and not simply passed over in silence.

Asante historiography and its discontents II

In order to understand the foregoing lacunae and omissions in relation to existing historical perspectives, we must look at the corpus of Asante historiography in more detail. Let us start by examining the historiography as a historical artefact in its own right.

The very recent emergence of modern Africanist – including Asante – historiography was profoundly influenced by the intellectual and political circumstances surrounding the decolonization and independence of Africa. On the one hand, elite nationalist aspiration sought a source of legitimation in the history of the precolonial state and its ruling class; in 1957, the very choice of the name Ghana for the newly independent Gold Coast made deliberate if extremely tenuous reference to 'Ghana the land of gold', a sophisticated and wealthy Western Sudanic state first mentioned by the Arab geographer al-Fazārī as early as the eighth century.[45] And concurrently, on the other hand, liberal scholarship – which identified itself with nationalist aspirations in general – saw in the analysis of precolonial states and governments, and in the rationality of their performance, a rebuttal of the sceptical Hegelian dismissal of an indigenous African history; this was a necessary and very timely corrective, for as recently as 1965 Hugh Trevor-Roper, then Regius Professor of Modern History at Oxford, infamously and ignorantly dismissed the very notion of African history as being nothing more than the study of the 'unrewarding gyrations of barbarous tribes'.[46]

Africanist historians urged, therefore, that African history was part of global history by virtue of its complex state structures, its rich political and material past, and above all its own coherent rationality. It could be reconstructed along received and understood historical lines. However, as we have already noted, in the precipitate but understandable rush to prove legitimate sameness and belonging certain perspectives were very much privileged at the expense of others.[47]

Asante historiography is a paradigmatic example of crucial aspects of this intellectual trajectory. Let us begin by considering the most substantial contribution to that historiography. In the very carefully phrased preface to Ivor Wilks' monumental, 800-page *Asante in the Nineteenth Century: The Structure and Evolution of a Political Order* (published in 1975, but researched in the 1950s and 1960s), which is widely acclaimed as a landmark in the Africanist historical enterprise, we read that:

throughout this study I have been less concerned with those aspects of Asante society which are unique to it, and more with those aspects which it has in common with other complex societies whether on the African continent or elsewhere. Accordingly, I have felt no hesitation in applying such terms as 'bureaucratization', 'mercantilism', 'modernization' and the like to those aspects of the Asante experience which invite comparison with similarly identified phenomena in other societies. To critics on this score I reiterate *my belief* [my emphasis] that only thus can the Asante past be viewed within the wider perspectives of human endeavour and its place within comparative history ultimately be assured. The alternative, always to stress the unique and unrelated and to reject the use of concepts developed in geographically and temporally different contexts, can lead the scholar towards the morasses of a nationalistic or 'tribal' mystique and an underlying historical solipsism.[48]

It is difficult to imagine any historian of, for example, Europe, Asia, the Americas or the Middle East engaging in the 1970s in such an elaborate, circumspect and cautiously worded vindication of his or her chosen subject matter and treatment of it. But Wilks' book, and much of his other writing on Asante, is rooted in and takes its cue from that era of liberal scholarship that sought legitimacy and acceptance for the very project of African history, and that strongly identified with aspirant African nationalism.

What Wilks in fact attempted was to incorporate the Asante past into the historical mainstream – to give it legitimacy, sameness and belonging – by substituting for the discredited 'nationalistic or "tribal" mystique' a more rational, dynamic and progressive nationalism derived from acceptably familiar European models; nineteenth-century Asante, he noted elsewhere, 'moved toward what in a European context is conveniently if ambiguously termed "nation-statehood"'.[49] Hart, a not unsympathetic critic, has accurately summarized this aspect of Wilks' work in the following terms: 'His [Wilks'] account of Asante is rationalist, stressing the *real politik* of interests at the state capital and thereby lending to Asante protonationalism an air which would not seem out of place in eighteenth century Europe.'[50] In short, Wilks concentrates on the history of the political superstructure, and on the 'rational' logic of material advantage, here rationalized to a progressive nationalist aspiration. His arguments for the legitimacy of Asante history and for the rationalist components in his nationalist model of it are underscored by the use of broad conceptual analogies couched in comparativist historical terms. But again, the wording is careful, and not fully explicit. Thus, 'bureaucratization' *et al.* are applied to those aspects of

Asante history that 'invite comparison with similarly identified phenomena in other societies'.

Let us confine our observations to 'bureaucratization'. Over many years this theme has held a consistently central place in Wilks' interpretation of the Asante state. Thus, he has discussed 'aspects of bureaucratization' in nineteenth-century Asante (1966). He has urged the case for the late eighteenth-century emergence in Kumase of a 'centralized and largely appointive bureaucracy', a development which he has associated with initiatives taken in the reign of the *Asantehene* Osei Kwadwo (1764–77), and which he has characterized as 'the Kwadwoan revolution in government' (a locution that echoes, and surely consciously, Elton's 'Tudor Revolution in Government'), (1967).[51] Subsequently, he has 'assume[d] that extant studies demonstrate' that in Asante, and in Dahomey as well, 'a degree of bureaucratization of the organs of administration' was achieved such as to make Asante 'essentially comparable' with those 'historical bureaucratic polities' identified by Eisenstadt as being intermediate between 'traditional' and 'modern' societies, and as being characterized by the presence of *inter alia* 'elaborate bureaucratic administrative organs' (1970).[52]

Finally, in 1975, Wilks explicitly associated his findings with the classic, but problematic, formulation of rational bureaucracy as expounded in Max Weber's posthumous *Wirtschaft und Gesellschaft* (1922). He wrote of the Asante *asomfoɔ* (der *ɛsom*, 'service'; those charged by authority with a duty; those holding appointive rather than hereditary positions) in the following terms.

The distinctive features of the *asomfo* of Asante are so significantly alike to those identified by Weber in his general model of a bureaucracy that there can be little hesitation in characterizing the 'Kwadwoan revolution in government' as a bureaucratic one.[53]

There are major flaws – theoretical and historical – in Wilks' construction of Asante 'bureaucracy'. That these are obscured and sometimes camouflaged by Wilks' careful, shifting and occasionally equivocal use of language can be gleaned from a close reading of the materials cited above, and are more fully evidenced (in this and in a number of other contexts) throughout the entire body of his work.[54] This is an extremely important issue, for nowhere does Wilks explicitly conceptualize or theorize Asante 'bureaucracy' in detailed relation to the Weberian model with which he identifies it. Indeed, a recent critic has called attention to Wilks' highly selective, partial and 'peculiar use' of Weber.[55]

Let us go directly to first principles. The term bureaucracy is derived directly from the French *bureaucratie*. This in turn was itself derived from the French root word *bureau*, which originally meant the baize used to cover writing-desks (old Fr.: *burel*; a coarse kind of cloth). The word *bureau* came to mean the writing-desk itself, or a chest of drawers with a writing board, and was subsequently extended to define that unit of space where writing-desks were assembled together. This space was the French (and Anglo-American) *bureau* and the English office, where public and private business, normally of a clerkly kind, was transacted.[56]

Weber was very well aware of this etymology when he conceptualized bureaucracy. Indeed, he accorded writing the primary, defining role in the construction of a model of bureaucracy that was explicit rather than general, and that required the presence of the following essential conditions.

1 Legal rules
2 The conduct of official business on a continuous basis
3 The conduct of official business in accordance with stipulated rules
4 The conduct of official business in an administrative agency with three attributes:
  a specific official duties delimited by impersonal criteria
  b officials to be granted authority necessary to carry out assigned functions
  c officials to have limited means of compulsion, and strictly defined conditions of legitimate appointment
5 All authority and responsibilities to be rooted in a hierarchy of authority
6 All officials to be accountable for resources used in the performance of their assigned functions, but such resources are not the property of these officials
7 All official revenue and private income and all official business and private affairs to be strictly separate
8 The existence of a salaried officialdom (see 7 above)
9 All authority to reside in the non-hereditary office and not in any individual incumbent
10 No office to be appropriated by incumbents and treated as disposable private property in the sense of sale or inheritance
11 All official business to be conducted on the basis of written documents, and all such business to be rendered continuous by the keeping of written records[57]

The Weberian model of bureaucracy is characterized by a system of legal domination in which the exercise of authority is promulgated as and in the rational implementation of enacted norms. The political objective of this is continuity in time, and the keys to that continuity – written records – are obviously rooted in literacy.

Wilks presses the contingencies of the matter as far – and as implausibly – as he can. Thus, he glosses the Asante architectural feature of the ɔdampaŋ (pl. *adampaŋ*), or house containing a room with an open front, as being an 'office opening on to the street' or 'the bureau of a government functionary, ward head, village head, etc.'.[58] The implication is that the business transacted therein was essentially bureaucratic business. But the Asante ɔdampaŋ is simply an unstructured forum for airing household matters in public (dwamu), for talking over the news (amanɛɛ boɔ) of the day, for exchanging information, and for a generalized gossiping or social interaction. When confronted with the core issue of literacy, Wilks simply prevaricates. Thus, the haphazard and intermittent employment by the Asantehene of individual foreigners as letter writers (in English, Dutch, Danish, Arabic), which Wilks discusses within the framework of his general model, in no way signalled a process of 'bureaucratization' of the Asante state in the Weberian sense.[59] Those who have incautiously built upon Wilks' premises without rigorously scrutinizing their shaky conceptual underpinnings have taken analysis to insupportable extremes; Adjaye, for example, talks of the aforementioned letter writers in terms of a 'chancery' constituted as 'a bureau responsible for the maintenance of diplomatic communication' with foreign powers.[60] In sum and plainly, the Weberian essential of an institutionalized officialdom trained to record keeping, and through it to the maintenance of the other bureaucratic practices, objectives and conditions enumerated above, was absent from the precolonial Asante experience.

Wilks' construction of Asante 'bureaucracy' is ultimately grounded in the spurious intellectual dichotomy that he erects between comparative relevance and cultural specificity. To make Asante (or African) history a respectable constituent of global history, Wilks imports bits and pieces of usable theory and employs them in a purely descriptive, largely tendentious manner. But applying such items in so opportunist a way hardly qualifies as theorizing from the record of the Asante past to any satisfactory form of comparative relevance. In essence, Wilks' history has no real place for ideas.[61] It seems at once breathtaking but entirely predictable that – following criticisms of his ill-thought-out use of Weber – Wilks simply shifts intellectual ground. In his most recent treatment of the Asante political superstructure (1987) he announced,

I intend this paper as neither a defense nor a retraction of the views I previously expressed for I believe the problems that have arisen warrant not so much solution as dissolution. Specifically, I suspect that the Weberian concepts we have all used have led us somewhat astray, enmeshing us in an evolutionary model of administrative change in which one (ideal) type of system, the patrimonial, is seen as not only logically but also chronologically prior to another (ideal) type, the formal rational. In this paper I shall be concerned less with a taxonomy of the Asante administrative system than with the emergence of an Asante administrative class. I shall ... prefer a Marxian to a Weberian approach while entering the caveat that

Weber himself was never insensitive to the fundamental importance of class formation.[62]

Anyone reading the carefully nuanced wording of this in the light of Wilks' previous work might be forgiven for presuming bad faith on the part of the author. Be that as it may, the passage simply confirms his adventitious relationship to theory, and his selective use of ideas as interchangeable props, situationally convenient or inconvenient by turns. His work, it would now appear, had little to do with Weber, for 'the problems in which I was primarily interested were those classically defined in the writings of Marx and Engels'.[63] But Wilks' project is even less rigorous as a Marxist analysis than as a Weberian one.[64]

Let us now look at the wider consequences of the foregoing. Implied in the 'alternative' between comparative relevance and cultural specificity is an irreconcilable antagonism or choice between a masterful, instrumental rationality and an alien (ir)rationality held to be deeply subversive of it. The mutual exclusiveness of these opposed explanatory modes may be simply illustrated. The military reasons for the Asante defeat by the British in 1873–4 have been very comprehensively and rationally analysed. But a principal contemporary Asante explanation for this catastrophe – the loss in the Bosompra river of the *Anantahene* Asamoa Nkwanta's invincible war charm – cannot be integrated, or rationalized, into 'rational' argument.[65]

The quasi-logic underpinning this polarization is one major reason why Wilks consigns to silence any direct discussion of Asante cultural practice – belief, religion, knowledge, custom and habit, and patterns of thought. His very superficial engagement with civil society as an entity veils the subject in a philosophical idealism reminiscent of Croce (or Collingwood); and specific cultural practices are introduced only when they can be rationalized in an instrumental or quasi-logical way.[66] Law has pointed out, for example, Wilks' habitual assimilation of human sacrifice to the jural category of execution, and his avoidance of discussing it as a practice related to or permeated by belief.[67]

The subject of religion in general – which has no entry in the comprehensive index to Wilks' 800-page book – is treated very indirectly, when at all, and in a predictably teleological manner. Peel has divined this fundamental weakness, albeit from a perspective somewhat different from my own. He notes that it

is important, when we recognize that religion serves as an ideology, to stress that it *must* be more than that. There is a danger here of another form of sociological determinism, that 'left functionalism' which embodies a teleology: the ruling class needs an ideology to justify its position, so religion must somehow be on hand to provide one. These teleologies often paper over crucial gaps in the explanation. So Wilks tells us that in late eighteenth-century Asante, 'government *had* to be extended in range ... in scope ... and in proficiency' (1975: 127. My italics). He tells us *how* it was, not how it *could* be so. The 'need' does not suffice to produce the effect; the crucial cultural conditions had to be met. If it 'had' to be ideology to work the trick because purely material conditions fall short – and we should never forget that in West Africa the most segmentary peoples and the most centralized states share the same technological, ecological and physical conditions of existence – there had to be some independent strength in the religious ideas drawn upon. Religion had this power because it was already the shared idiom in which both chiefs and people confronted the pains and anxieties of the human situation.[68]

Despite emphatic differences of approach, Peel is here roundly castigating a 'left functionalism' that is cousin to those disfiguring limitations of Marxist theorizing criticized by Gramsci.

Wilks makes little reference to the articulation of consent in Asante history beyond vaguely identifying it with his own particular reading of nationalism; either it is off stage, an unexamined dependent variable of a nebulous 'Asante-ness', or it is selectively pressed into teleological service. In truth he can do little more than this, for his analysis of the institutionalized practices of civil society in which the articulation of consent is located is virtually non-existent. In response to criticism on this score, Wilks has acknowledged that what he terms 'cognitive systems' are not unimportant, but lamely excuses his signal failure to deal with them in the Asante case by asserting that such matters are 'singularly resistant to satisfactory description and understanding'.[69] This has the authentic ring of platitude, for surely 'cognitive systems' *always* present such challenges to historical reading. Certainly, nothing justifies Wilks' glib and self-serving abrogation of any responsibility in this matter; any integration of 'the material and cognitive dimensions of the Asante experience', he writes, is a 'still unattainable' goal.[70] And that, with hands duly washed, is that.

In recent years, however, there has emerged a body of scholarship on Asante that has begun to question the explanatory value and authority of a history constructed overwhelmingly from the linked perspectives of the political superstructure and the 'rational' quasi-logic of material advantage. There are those, for instance, who have suggested that a close analysis of Weber's concept of patrimonialism – and a deeper reading of Weber generally – might lead to an enlarged understanding of the nature of the Asante state; and certainly, some kind of a case could be advanced for seeing Asante government organization as a more or less direct extension of the royal household (as opposed to a formal-rational bureaucracy, and divorced from Wilks' serious misreading of Weber as situating patrimonialism in an evolutionary succession of ideal types).[71] Unfortunately, work along these lines has been restricted to administrative history, to speculation about the parameters of political conflict, and to analyses of concepts of status and rank.[72] Underlying the focus on patrimonialism, however, is a discernible orientation towards vitally significant, associated Weberian concerns regarding the nature of the state's legitimation of authority; and this, of course, leads directly to the issue of the articulation of consent.[73] Similarly, there now exists some work that has begun to consider a few of the philosophical and cognitive aspects of the Asante past, together with the expressive formulation of belief as symbol and metaphor; this, in turn, opens into an historical exploration of the relationship between the state, cultural practice and civil society.[74]

These insights are unsystematic but they are suggestive. What is needed now is a more systematically rigorous historical exploration of the fundamental articulations that conditioned the relationship between the Asante state and Asante society. In brief, we must examine the parameters of the Asante experience in the light of those basic concerns that inform the crucial theoretical formulations already adumbrated. After all, Gramsci's meditations and propositions concerning the indispensable role of the articulation of consent in the implementation of hegemony address the same basic historical issues as those considered by Weber – from a different perspective and in different formulations – in his deliberations on the nature of legitimate authority and the mechanisms of subordination and domination. Such issues, however construed, lie at the very heart of authoritative historical reconstruction and explanation.

In sum, we must commence with the fundamentals of Asante cultural specificity and then proceed, where appropriate, to matters of comparative relevance. That is, we must reverse the existing, dominant priorities of Asante historiography in order to reconstruct a specifically Asante history. As we have suggested throughout, this is a project that requires a more general implementation throughout Africanist historiography.[75]

Representation and other problems

For the most part Asante (and Africanist) historiography has been written without explicit theoretical formulations. Implicit assumptions or hidden agendas, of the sort explored above, have been masked either by the equivocal use of language or by the fetishization of facts as objects of an erotetic technique designed to build 'objective' narrative via the camouflage of syllogism and inference. The sheer increment of positivistic narrative serves to diguise the underlying premises that inform its very construction. This procedure is akin to the concealment of the author (or, as some would have it, his or her 'epistemological ego') that is now a much debated issue in contemporary ethnography and literary discourse.[76]

In addition to the general historical and theoretical concerns already described, but directly related to them, are three perspectives that inform this book. These are of primary significance, and are explicitly stated below.

First, due account is taken of recent work in cultural history that acknowledges its debts to Gramsci's insights, but that seeks to enlarge upon them in one particular area, and that simultaneously tries to redress the tendency in much existing history of *mentalités* to reduce cultural practice to some other category. At the core of this scholarship is the problem of how to relate political action and social practices to cultural, intellectual and ideological representations. In what follows it is argued that representations are, so to speak, objectifications rather than objects, arguments rather than statements. Representations are never neutral, for by definition they are the products of engaged or interested processes of cognition.[77] They reflect political action and embody social practice, but they are covalent with neither, being themselves active constituents of historical reality. By definition, therefore, they are open to interpretation.

This is why, when we come to investigate representations in relation to the articulation of consent, we must be fully aware of their primary status as arguments. In its attempt to implement hegemony, the state is trying to arrogate these arguments, and forge statements from them; but at the same time, dissenting, oppositional or 'counter-cultural' elements are trying either to keep these arguments open, or to interpret and appropriate them for their own collective purposes. Thus, a prime consequence of the state's success in implementing hegemony, or in legitimating its authority, is a persuasion away from plural argument to consensual statement. As we shall see, this requires unremitting effort, for representations are standing invitations to multiple reading.[78]

Moreover, the act of appropriation is not defined simply by the explicit intentional polarities embodied in the state and in active forms of group dissent from it. In the grey ·area between the two, individuals may appropriate representational motifs that they ostensibly share with others, but in ways that are private, quite specific, and even idiosyncratic. This has been termed the 'history of conscience', and it is an area notoriously resistant to historical reconstruction.[79] As will be made apparent, however, the Asante state was acutely aware of the dangers inhering in any form of self-referencing or self-validating individuated reflection.

Second, the commonsensical assumption is made that those processes of cognition that produce representations are covalent with the spectrum of epistemological address. They define(d) the sentient horizons of *being* Asante. In what follows we will be much concerned with that issue which is central to any epistemological agenda. That is, we will attempt to investigate the various distinctions, such as they are, that the Asante have made between *knowledge* and *belief*, and to explore the nature of the boundaries between the two. Our approach to these matters will be chiefly historical rather than philosophical or linguistic, for our focus is on the Asante conceptualization of knowledge and belief in and through time.

The cognitive processes out of which representations are constructed, and by means of which structurations of knowledge and belief are generated, may best be understood as a 'text' or framework. This 'text', as Gramsci, Weber and many others have understood, is to be construed as *the* crucible of ideological discourse. Thus, periodically in any society, ideological tensions (contradictory appropriations of arguments in the 'text') can threaten, if unchecked, not only immediate conflict, revolution or dissolution, but also immense and quite unforeseen consequences.[80]

In any society where hierarchies of differentiation and control are presided over by the state, a fundamental object of that state must be to impose ideological definition on knowledge and belief, to regulate the boundaries between the two, and to exercise an absolute discretion in shaping both of them. The capacity to dictate the fundamental conditions of epistemological discourse legitimates control over the social expressions of power, and it is part of the same imperative that seeks to transform representations from arguments to statements. Laxity in these areas invites an interrogation of the epistemological agenda, and once again exposes representations to plural appropriation. This is the prelude to dissenting intellectual criticism, and ultimately to direct assaults on the state's authority. To survive and to prosper, any state, including that of Asante, *must* strive to encompass the arena of epistemological possibility.

Third, it is proposed that we proceed with the following consideration in mind. In recent work I have urged the relevance of seeing the Asante view of the Asante past in hermeneutical terms.[81] This is a complex issue, and disentangling its convolutions requires some explanatory clarification. Since the seventeenth century the dominant Cartesian and Kantian tradition of Western thought has both shaped and been shaped by empirical science's methodological imperative towards the uncovering of universal laws. Accordingly, it has presumed that the objects of concern and reflection are more or less the same in all human cultures; that the pursuit of these objects is characterized by generic principles and ideas; and, most significantly, that these last might be established for any and all societies through the identification and application of a universal criterion of evaluation. In strictly philosophical terms, the pursuit of this goal has taken the form of a quest to construct a foundationalist or universalist epistemology.[82]

As is well understood, the precepts, procedures and objects of this 'scientific method' were internalized to such a degree in nineteenth- and twentieth-century Europe that they came to assume a virtually unchallenged supremacy. They were duly imported into Africa as triumphalist certainties in the mental baggage that accompanied European imperialism. In the colonial period and beyond they were embedded in African consciousness through formal education and a host of other means.[83]

The adherence to the concept of a foundationalist epistemology was part of this process of colonization. Thus, most contemporary African philosophers continue to investigate the historical framework of thought in given African cultures for specific evidence of orientation towards and fit with European discussions of the foundational premises of this putative, universalist epistemological model. Some, indeed, have gone so far as to pursue a chimerical abstraction called 'African thought'.[84] At the same time, numerous African intellectuals have written pessimistically about the evident lack of consonance between the thought of their own societies and the demands imposed by an alien, incredibly powerful epistemology with pretensions to a sovereign uniqueness. Such discontinuities are most often addressed in terms of the quest for a 'usable' epistemology, but in many cases this is patently a mask for the despairing legacy left by a long process of political victimization and cultural self-denial.[85]

It must be accounted something of an irony that while the derived concept of a foundationalist epistemology continues to hold sway in African philosophy, it has been severely and perhaps fatally criticized from within the tradition that first imposed it on Africa. Moreover, that criticism is hermeneutical, historical, pragmatic and pluralist, and it is argued here that it has parallels with and speaks directly to the identifiable premises of Asante (and African?) thought and cultural practice as these existed prior to European colonization.

The thrust of the European hermeneutical tradition (from Dilthey, say, to the contemporary expositions of Ricoeur, Gadamer and Rorty) is that interpretation, the act of the *hermeneus*, resides in the reading of cultural practice, tradition and historicity where these are defined as 'the horizons of existence'. Veracity is to be located in the disclosure of events as these are *historically* encountered within *specific* cultural horizons, and not in metaphysical speculation on a universalist canvas. In reviewing the signal failure over three centuries of the Cartesian and Kantian tradition actually to substantiate the concept of a foundationalist epistemology by formulating a universal criterion of evaluation, this reading rejects the concept itself as being at best ahistorical and idealist, and at worst an instrument of European power and an exercise in bad faith.[86]

This is *not* an argument against the universality of epistemological concerns. But it is an argument *against* doing ahistorical violence to such concerns by reducing them to the non-existent categories of a foundationalist epistemology, and *for* interpreting them as they occur historically within a discrete cultural formation. This is a commonsensical approach, although its pluralism flies in the face of what we might term, philosophically and historically, Europe's received image of itself. It is an argument for taking cultures on their own historical and intellectual terms. It permits us the latitude to inscribe items like knowledge and belief on the agenda, but it does not commit us to situating them in relation to spurious epistemological absolutes.[87]

It will be argued throughout this book that historical Asante society manifested basic epistemological concerns about knowledge and belief, but that it had no imperative towards pursuing a foundationalist epistemology in the manner of the Cartesian and Kantian tradition. This was because Asante singularly lacked certain characteristics – for example, a tradition of literacy, or a sustained exegetical theology; thus, Asante society was spared wars of religion, but at the same time it had no continuous tradition of dissent grounded in the rigorous or sustained examination of alternative epistemological possiblities.

It will be argued instead that in the crucial arena of epistemology historic Asante society was particularly fertile ground for hermeneutical reading, and that the Asante state constantly sought to arrogate to itself the role of ultimate *hermeneus*. The state tried to subordinate and shape the possibilities in the spectrum of knowledge and belief, just as it attempted to convert representations from arguments to statements.

The Asante state's intentional project was the promulgation of a master reading of experience; this ordained the careful monitoring or exclusion of external influence. And underpinning this project, as we shall see, was the state's own ideological construction of Asante as a society comprising only two orders, the division being determined by membership in or exclusion from itself, and the distinction being maintained through a dialogue – or a Gramscian equilibrium of compromise – in which coercion played a supporting role to the state's primary objective of securing the social order's consent in its own subordination.

Summary of contents

The concerns and arguments outlined above are explored in historical detail in the four chapters that follow.

In the next chapter our concern will be with the bases of power among the office holders or members of the Asante state. Particular attention is paid to the distinction made between Kumase, the capital of the state and the seat of government, and the remainder of Asante society; to the agricultural and labour factors upon which that distinction rested; to the crucial concepts of accumulation and wealth; and to the articulation of all of these features in the history of the eighteenth- and nineteenth-century polity.

Chapter three is devoted to a consideration of the relationships that existed between the state, society and the individual. This is a complex matter, and it is approached from two broad perspectives. Attention is paid to the ideological bases of the relationship between the state and the organizational principles of the social order. Discussion then turns to the badly neglected issue of belief. This is considered historically, in terms of its ideological relationship to knowledge and cultural experience, and in relation to its central role in many areas of Asante life.

In the fourth chapter we locate and investigate all of the foregoing in one crucial and richly detailed historical context. This context is the annual Asante festival of *odwira* (also known as the 'Yam Custom'). The *odwira* was the single most important 'event' in the Asante historical experience. Its central significance is fully acknowledged in all of our sources, but it has never been the subject of detailed historical analysis.[88] This is a very major lacuna. The Asante construed *odwira* as a calendrically determined, performed meditation on epistemological concerns in the contexts of polity, society and human existence. It has the greatest relevance, not least as a distilled enactment of the issues of ideological structuration with which we are concerned. Again, this is a complex matter. Our reading of *odwira* presupposes an understanding of the Asante conceptualization of time. And the performance of *odwira* unfolded as a bewildering series of episodes or sub-texts embedded in a master text. These issues are fully discussed in their historical context, and in relation to comparative insights derived from the work of historians, anthropologists, cultural critics and semioticians.

In the final chapter we offer a summing up of our findings with respect to the nature of the Asante state and Asante society, and of the relationship between them. We also offer a number of reflections on the broader implications of our argument for the history of Asante and of Africa generally.

2 State and society in Asante history

Introduction

Analyses of Asante oral histories and traditions of origin in relation to evidence contained in contemporary European records have furnished a broad portrait of the materialist evolution of the Asante social order and the Asante state. The crucial enabling factor in this general model is the existence of substantial, accessible deposits of alluvial and shallow reef gold in parts of Asante. The pivotal development in it is the inception and establishment of a rural economy based on subsistence agriculture. The significance of both of these elements is richly and diversely documented in Asante tradition. Both are matters that we will return to below. The evolutionary model in summary outline – from the fifteenth century to the beginning of the nineteenth – is as follows.[1]

Gold-producing Akan, including the 'proto-Asante', were inexorably drawn into the world economy of the fifteenth and sixteenth centuries by the European mercantile presence along the Gold Coast.[2] Gold was exchanged for slave and otherwise unfree labour, much of it imported into the Gold Coast by Europeans from other parts of western Africa. This sustained demographic increment made possible the arduous, protracted transformation of the mode of production in the hostile forest environment from hunting and gathering to subsistence agriculture. From the seventeenth century onwards, the rural economy was centred in the production of staple crops, and agriculture was supplemented by hunting and gathering activities. Matriliny – structurally the most efficacious system in the circumstances – was the mechanism by which imported labour was assimilated, organized and deployed in work gangs, and through which novel social relations of production based in agriculture were realized.[3]

Asante traditions and European evidence concur in documenting a sequence of developments over time. The embedding of the agrarian order in the forest led successively to the realization of surplus, the emergence of differentiation, and the eventual political institutionalization of that socio-economic differentiation in chiefdoms.[4] Towards the close of the seventeenth century, the nascent Asante state centred on Kumase (Kwaman) achieved a decisive military supremacy among these competing chiefdoms.[5]

In the eighteenth century Asante became an expansionist power. With the agrarian order firmly established as the basis of the subsistence economy, Asante no longer needed the massive labour inputs of the previous centuries. Indeed, it supplied its own diminished requirements by regulated tributary exaction and raiding, and it exported a substantial surplus of captive labour, mainly from warfare, into the transatlantic slave trade in exchange for guns and other European goods. In the first decades of the nineteenth century, the Europeans unilaterally abolished the transatlantic slave trade. Warfare to procure captives became unprofitable – as is evidenced from as early as the 1820s – and thereafter the Asante export economy was successfully modified and restructured into alternative channels.[6]

All of the foregoing is well understood, and parts of it are the subject of highly detailed empirical research. However, by the beginning of the nineteenth century, the political economy of Asante agriculture was in the process of significant but under-studied modification. The changes wrought in food production were a fundamental indicator of major ongoing transformations in the nature of the relationship between the state and the social order.

Society and agriculture: ordering subsistence

Subsistence agriculture was the indispensable basis of historic Asante society. That there is no detailed history of Asante agriculture in the precolonial period reflects the extreme difficulty of any such undertaking. With the arguable exception of certain geographically restricted areas – those parts of Adanse and Amansie lying along or adjacent to the 'great road' (*akwantempɔŋ*) running from Kumase to the Bosompra river, the Mponua towns to the north and west of Lake Bosomtwe, and sections of Asante Akyem lying to the east of Kumase – discrete historical data are extremely sparse.[7] However, some important general observations can be advanced.

First, all of our evidence indicates that the technological and other factors of production remained constant throughout the precolonial period. The axe, cutlass and bill hook were the implements used in land clearing; and for the maintenance of land under crops, as Bowdich noted in 1817, the Asante 'use no implement but the hoe'.[8] The same basic technology was still employed in the twentieth century, and its use continued to depend on large inputs of human labour.[9]

Second, the core crop association was characterized by very long-term invariability and consequent stability. Asante subsistence agriculture was, and is, based on the intercropping of high-yielding bulk foodstuffs; yam (*Dioscorea spp.*: many varieties, but generically ɔde), plantain (*Musa paradisiaca*: ɔbɔdeɛ, ɔborɔdeɛ), cocoyam (*Colocasia esculenta*: amaŋkani), and cassava (*Manihot utilissima*: ɔbaŋkye).[10] Historic variants on this core association have taken the form of limited adjustments to meet changes in specific needs or preferences. Thus, the cultivation of maize or Indian corn (*Zea mays*: aburo), which was mainly geared to the provisioning of field armies, declined between 1800 and 1900 with the military tradition.[11] By contrast, cocoyam consumption has greatly increased in the twentieth century; this is because *Colocasia esculenta*, which contains high levels of calcium oxalate, an irritant of the human digestive tract, has been replaced by the much more palatable *Xanthosoma mafaffa*, a West Indian variety introduced into the Gold Coast in the 1840s.[12] And cassava, which is easier to grow and requires less labour than either yam or cocoyam, has long been used in Asante to make up periodic shortfalls in more desirable crops.[13]

Third, these core bulk foodstuffs were supplemented by other important sources of nutrition. As T.B. Freeman noted of mid-nineteenth-century Asante:

In these bright and sunny regions nature is also bountiful in its supplies of suitable vegetables and fruits – the yam, cassada, Indian corn, sweet potato, cocoa-bulb, or *Caladium Esculenium [sic]*, millet, rice, sugar-cane, ginger, tomato, onion, ground-nut, orange, lime, plantain, banana, sour-sop, custard apple, and last but not least, the noble pineapple, all flourish in Ashantee, under ordinary cultivation.[14]

Sheep, fowls, goats and pigs were kept as domestic animals, but habitual consumption of these in the rural economy was restricted by availability and relative cost. Moreover, sheep and fowls were preferred sacrificial animals, and their slaughter in any number was dictated by the calendar of ritual and oblation.[15]

Although displaced as the dominant mode of production by the beginning of the seventeenth century, hunting and gathering retained a significant role in support of subsistence crop production. Uncultivated vegetable produce – oil palm fruits, palm wine, fungi, wild yams – continued to be gathered into the twentieth century. The sharp twentieth-century decline in hunting has served to mask its importance in former times as a source of animal protein. Nineteenth-century European sources attest to an abundant variety of game, even in central Asante. Thus, in the 1840s, elephants were still being successfully hunted for food along the Bosompra river; and as recently as the 1920s, game hunting was an intensive and valuable economic activity in north and west Asante, in Asante Akyem to the east of Kumase, and still further to the east on the broad floodplain of the Afram river.[16] Freshwater fish, generally smoked,

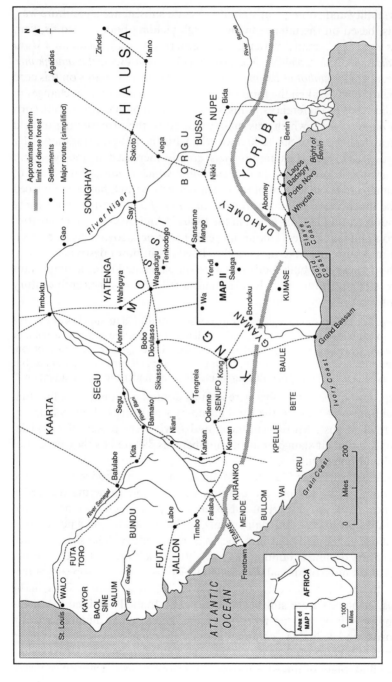

Map 1 West Africa in the early nineteenth century

and crabs were also important sources of protein. So too were snails (ηwaa: sing. ɔwaa). Snails were 'one of the richest kinds of animal food' in nineteenth-century Asante; they were 'found in all parts of the forest country', but in particularly dense numbers in western Asante, Ahafo and Domaa.[17] Cardinall, in the 1920s, gave a graphic account of the large-scale organization and continuing significance of snail gathering in Ahafo; by then, snails were important not only as subsistence food and as items of barter, but also as retail merchandise in the partially monetized colonial rural economy.

Snails are one of the most important articles of food among the forest people. I do not think any estimate has ever been made of the value of the trade in them, but it must be quite colossal. In the district of Ahafo lies one of the most valuable areas for catching snails in the country... The proper season for collecting the snails is at the beginning of the rains, and lasts for about six weeks. Whole villages – men, women and children – migrate into the forest, leaving only the old and infirm to look after their homes... There are a hundred snails on each skewer, and twenty skewers are made into a bundle. Two such bundles make a load of the average weight carried by these people – approximately sixty pounds... The value of this trade to the Ahafo people must be very great. A skewer varies from ninepence to one shilling and ninepence, so that with an average price of one shilling one will get forty shillings for a load. It may seem extraordinary that one could get snails in such quantities. But once one has learned to detect them among the leaves, one will soon perceive thousands.[18]

Fourth, it is clear from all of our sources that throughout the eighteenth and nineteenth centuries fully established rural subsistence agriculture, augmented by the activities just described, furnished Asante society with a basic and generally adequate, if somewhat monotonous, diet. Thus, deficiency diseases recorded in the nineteenth century tended to be related to protein shortages, or to failure to maintain a balanced diet, rather than to absolute calorific insufficiency, malnourishment or starvation.[19] In the entire corpus of Asante tradition and European commentary, the only accounts of severe food shortages, widespread hunger and regional or sectoral famine are associated with the virtual collapse of subsistence agriculture in areas directly affected by the five years of civil war in the 1880s.[20]

The overall sufficiency of Asante food production was guaranteed by a number of factors. Once the laborious task of clearing the land had been accomplished, the growing environment was generally favourable.[21] Rural agriculturalists practised a calculated system of both land and crop rotation; the basic Asante *afuo* or farm comprised the *afuwa*, the land currently under crops, and the *mfufuwa*, the 'non-farm' or land currently under fallow.[22]

Above all other factors, however, was the favourable ratio of population density to available land. There is some dispute over the total size of the

Asante population in the nineteenth century.[23] However, it has been calculated, on the basis of admittedly crude data, that the actual maximum density of population in central Asante in the nineteenth century never approximated to more than 60% of a conservatively estimated critical density, or the point at which the land could no longer sustain the number of people living on it.[24] These absolute figures are speculative and beside the point, but in providing a suggestive scale of magnitude they fully confirm a great deal of informal evidence. In the central Mponua area in the nineteenth century, for example, by no means all available land had been brought under cultivation.[25] Large parts of western Asante remained virgin forest until the emergence of the cocoa and timber industries in the twentieth century.[26] And even in the 1980s, with Asante and the remainder of Ghana confronting a crisis in population growth, the World Bank noted that 'the total area cultivated, as against the potential cultivable area, is still low', and also that average staple crop yields 'are very low'.[27]

Twentieth-century cash cropping gave Asante farmers a heightened sense of the economic value of land. Even so, there still remained a degree of slack in the rural land economy. In the 1940s, a full generation into the cocoa revolution, the *Goasohene* of Ahafo described the impact of change, but within an overall pattern of land availability that showed marked continuity with the nineteenth century. He is cited here *in extenso* as being representative of much informal testimony that is dedicated to making the same points.

Each elder was in early days given a direction – you go and eat there, you go and eat there, etc. Now a new farmer is sent to an elder and first approaches the odekro [*odekuro*: village head] through an elder. The new man gives drink to the odekro and elders – maybe only 7/-, 13/- or more – [it] doesn't depend on the size of the farm, but more on relationship with sponsors, e.g. a man who had lived long in the town will be let off cheap. Then the elder is sent to show him where to farm.

Land is getting scarce now, but the system is as follows: The farmer is shown a place to farm and is told you can farm ahead from here (*wo dɛ wanim*). He is not shown boundaries. Suppose it is all forest. He starts at a point and he farms out in all directions establishing a line. He is permitted to go on farming 'in front of him' as far as he can go. Later other people will come along. Anyone placed in front of him will be placed in such a way as to leave a substantial strip of forest anything from 20 to 30 to 100 yards or even more... The second farmer is told to farm ahead; he must not farm towards the first. A third man may come along to farm on the 'left' or the 'right' of the first man. He would start from the very 'edge' of this man's farm, leaving perhaps just a yard or two of bush in between and he might farm parallel to number one (the first man) or to the 'left' or 'right' of number one. It is these very narrow strips that give rise to farm boundary disputes as one party or the other tries to take them up... It is an offence to 'cut off the head' (*twa ne tiri*) of the farmer behind or beside you – i.e. to enter the unfarmed strip ahead of him.[28]

An additional source of potential conflict was that part of some farms termed *mfufuwa nini*, or 'barren fallow'; this was land belonging to an *afuo* that had once been cultivated, but that had lain unused for some time. Such land has been the focus of much twentieth-century litigation between established farmers and intrusive cultivators. In the nineteenth century, however, it is surely significant that Asante law – usually precise in matters relating to land – was notably vague in defining the length of time that *mfufuwa nini* might remain in the hands of its original cultivator.[29] The presumption must be that disputes between individual farmers over 'barren fallow' were relatively uncommon at a time when there was very little pressure on land resources in much of the rural economy.[30]

The general picture, then, for the eighteenth and nineteenth centuries, is of a mixed rural economy in which fully established subsistence farming was the dominant mode of production. The availability of cultivable land and the productive capacities of agriculturalists guaranteed that Asante society – with the aberrant exception of the 1880s – was not subject to cycles of massive deprivation, and cannot remotely be classified as an economy of generalized want and hunger. This is not to deny the existence of specific cases of poverty and immiseration in Asante society, but it is to argue that instances of this sort must be set in the broader context outlined above.[31]

State and agriculture: ordering differentiation

Thus far, we have discussed the leading features of a successful but largely undifferentiated rural subsistence economy. But by the beginning of the nineteenth century, there is clear evidence of sectoral change, and of an identifiable underlying factor of differentiation in one key area of the political economy of Asante agriculture.

Nineteenth-century Europeans commented in detail and with approbation on the organized intensity of food production in the vicinity of the Asante capital. In 1817, Bowdich noted the following concerning the half dozen miles between 'Sarrasou' (Esereso, on the Oda river) and Kumase.

There are large plantations of corn around Sarrasou, which is a great nursery for pigs ... The soil from Sarrasou [to Kumase] was a rich black mould, and there were continued plantations of corn, yams, ground nuts, terraboys and encruma: the yams and ground nuts were planted with much regularity in triangular beds, with small drains around each, and carefully cleared from weeds.[32]

Elsewhere, Bowdich registered surprise at the 'extent and order', and the 'neatness and method' of the farming system around Kumase; two crops of maize and one of yam were harvested each year, and the yam fields were well fenced in and planted in regular lines.[33] In 1820, just north of Amoafo and only 15 miles from Kumase, Dupuis noted a number of large, fenced fields that had been prepared for the planting of yam and maize.[34] And at

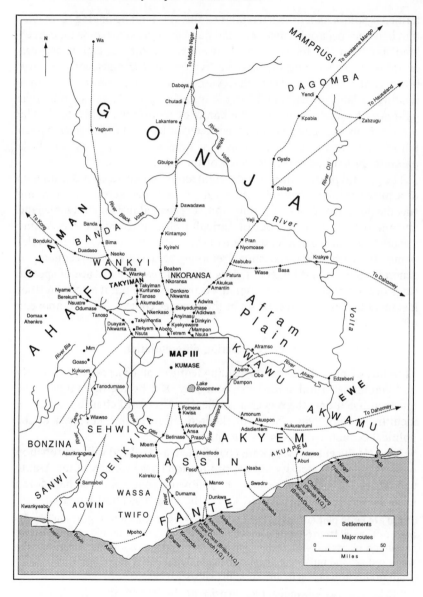

Map 2 Greater Asante and its neighbours in the early nineteenth century

Esereso, which contained some 8,000 'soldiers, slaves, and vassals' of the Kumase *Bantamahene/Krontihene* Amankwatia, he contrasted the 'difficulty of clearing spots, for the reception of grain' with the fact that the 'plantations are extensive'.[35] Hutton, who accompanied Dupuis, recorded that some 6 miles south of Kumase the British mission

passed several plantations which were well inclosed, and in different places there were as much as two acres of ground cleared, and laid out in small beds not greatly dissimilar, or much inferior, to the country gardens in Europe; eschalots, ground nuts, yams, and other vegetables were plentiful.[36]

Agricultural enterprise of this sort encroached upon Kumase itself. 'The grass close around the town', so Freeman recalled of his visits to Kumase in the 1830s and 1840s, 'attains a height of from fifteen to twenty feet, and the farms in the immediate neighbourhood produce the finest crops of corn, yams, and all kinds of vegetables indigenous to the soil'.[37]

The sheer numbers and demographic concentration of peasant cultivators impressed those very few Europeans who were sanctioned by the Asante state to travel with some freedom in the environs of Kumase.[38] In 1848, the Wesleyan-Methodist missionary Hillard visited, by his own estimation, most of the villages in a 5 mile radius around Kumase, and was 'surprised at their number', for 'I have visited above forty – and some of them very large.'[39] Clearly, there existed around Kumase a much more intensive and systemic form of production than the type of rural subsistence agriculture described above, for example, in the words of the *Goasohene* of Ahafo. To European observers, all of this agricultural industriousness around Kumase seemed in very marked contrast to the life of the capital itself. In Kumase, as West typically remarked in 1862, 'the people seem to have but little to do', and 'their time is chiefly occupied in eating, and drinking, public processions, and custom making'.[40]

Observations of this sort unknowingly reflected the fact that with the eighteenth-century growth and elaboration of the expansionist state, Kumase had become significantly detached from the subsistence – and matrilineage – bases of the social order. In effect, it came increasingly to preside over them, with a consequent further weakening or progressive dilution of the older, historic ties of organic continuity between state and society. By the early nineteenth century, the Asante state capital had a permanently resident population of some 20,000 to 25,000.[41] The overwhelming majority of these were fully involved in the transaction of government business; in the time-consuming performance of elaborate state ceremonial; or in servicing the state sector through ancillary functions, such as the production of luxury artefacts.[42]

The office holders and administrative cadres of Kumase, together with their urban retinues, were entirely provisioned and maintained by the intensive agricultural enterprise reported by Europeans. In 1817, Bowdich observed that

the higher classes could not support their numerous followers, or the lower their large families, in the city, and therefore employed them in plantations, (in which small crooms were situated) generally within two or three miles of the capital, where their labours not only feed themselves, but supply the wants of the chief, his family, and more immediate suite. The middling orders station their slaves for the same purpose, and also to collect fruit and vegetables for sale, and when their children become numerous, a part are generally sent to be supported by these slaves in the bush.[43]

The *Asantehene's* household alone daily consumed large quantities of food produced in this manner, together with a leavening of imported delicacies. The *Asantehene* Kwaku Dua Panin (1834–67) took breakfast about 8 a.m.; meat, plantain and yam 'in large quantities' were distributed to the *Asantehene's* wives and children. The main meal of the day was taken at 2 p.m., when the *Asantehene* and his household officials made a selection from 'mutton, turkeys, ducks, fowls, wild game of all kinds, except the buffalo; and fish from the lakes, and adjacent rivers ... also yams, plantains, beans, rice, European biscuits, tea, sugar, wines, liqueurs, etc.'.[44] Immediately afterwards, 'large dishes containing the great family dinner' were distributed, like breakfast, to the royal wives and children.[45]

Gifts of food liberally bestowed upon foreign visitors were a further indication of the privileged consumption patterns enjoyed by Kumase office holders. The Dutch envoy J. Simons, who visited the *Asantehene* Osei Yaw Akoto (1823–34) in 1831–2, scrupulously recorded all such gifts; these varied in size and extravagance, but they were offered on a virtually continuous basis.[46] Obviously, the *Asantehene* made the most lavish presentations. Thus, in Kumase on 15 October 1848, Sir William Winniet, the British Governor of the Gold Coast, received a 'magnificent present' from the *Asantehene* Kwaku Dua Panin. This comprised

2 bullocks; 4 sheep; 4 turkeys; 6 ducks; 20 guinea fowls; 6 pigs; 20 fowls; 20 pigeons; 400 yams; 303 bunches of plantain; 4 dishes [of] native rice; 5 dishes ground nuts; 6 calabashes of honey; oranges; eggs; palm nuts; sundry vegetables; 40 logs of wood; 10 baskets of corn ... [These were] brought before me by 550 men, every one of whom had some share in the work of conveyance. These were accompanied by several officers of the King's household and their retinue, amounting to not less than 300 men. Thus, about 850 men were employed in presenting to me this token of the King's goodwill.[47]

Kumase enjoyed a special status, and this was reflected in the maxim that – with the exception of the *Asantehene* and other members of the royal *Oyoko Kɔkɔɔ* lineage – no one claimed the Asante capital as his or her village (*akuraa*; pl. *nkuraa*) of birth or origin.[48] Everyone, so to speak, came from somewhere else. And they came to Kumase in an attempt to secure the attention or favour of the *Asantehene* or some other powerful individual. Their object was to obtain admission to an office holder's retinue in the ranks of the *nhenkwaa* (sing. *ahenkwaa*: lit. 'servant of an *ɔhene*' or office holder) or *asomfoɔ*, and by performing services, and carrying out designated tasks, to participate as members in the state's powers and privileges. The captive French trader Bonnat gave some account of this process during the reign of the *Asantehene* Kofi Kakari (1867–74). He observed:

Cette énorme importance du roi d' Achanty amène à Coumassie une grande quantité de jeunes gens, appartenant aux meilleures familles du royaume. Ils viennent dans le rayonnement du trône, non-seulement, comme ils disent, pour servir le roi, mais ils sont attirés surtout par l'espoir de se faire venir du souverain, et ils ne négligent aucune occasion pour lui plaire. Semblables aux courtisans des anciennes et nouvelles cours, on les voit continuellement sous les pas du monarque, sollicitant ses faveurs et ses sourires. Tels sont ces *Oinqua* [*nhenkwaa*] ... missions de confiance donnent à ces jeunes gens de grands priviléges.[49]

The Asante capital was the province of the *Asantehene* and of the state over which he presided, and therefore its food supply was earmarked for their upkeep. In essence, the provisioning of Kumase was the provisioning of the state apparatus. Thus, provisioning was substantially determined by command, and effected by redistribution. Producers, office holders, and the latter's kin, clients and retinue, formed a closed system. It is true that office holders possessed of food surpluses might release these into the urban retail market in pursuit of profit; and equally, very wealthy office holders might choose to indicate their substance by marketing the bulk of their own foodstuffs, and by conspicuously supplying their own dependants with the monies to obtain sustenance at market prices. But the market sector was clearly a secondary mechanism in terms of bulk foodstuffs. Thus, the main Kumase market of *dwaberem* had no permanent stalls or fixtures, because the space itself was often commandeered for other purposes by the state; it did contain some provisions, but its principal attractions were imported luxury goods.[50] Freeman intuited something of all this, and was duly puzzled by it. He observed:

Coomassie possesses nothing deserving the name of a market. There is ... a large area in that town called 'The Market Place' (native name – Adjebirim) [*dwaberem*] but nearly all that can be said of it is, that it is a large open space, where a kind of market is statedly held; but there are no sheds or stalls... Pieces of Manchester goods, cottons, silks, velvets, damasks, etc., may be seen ... and lumps of elephant-beef, cow-beef, joints of wild monkey, deer, wild-hog, and all dry articles of food produced in the neighbouring farms, are seen exposed on rude stages or trellises...[51]

A host of ingrained attitudes and practices mirrored the understanding that equated Kumase with the *Asantehene* and the state. Licit or not, the proprietorial assumptions of the *nhenkwaa* – towards food, drink and much else – are fully documented. 'Munis de l'autorité royale', noted Bonnat in the 1870s, the *nhenkwaa* 's'emparent sur leur route de tout ce qui leur plaît; les boissons et les victuailles surtout sont fréquemment l'objet de leurs réquisitions'.[52] As we shall see, the seizure of provisions by individuals acting in the name of the state was of questionable legality. However, the fact that it was a very common practice is significant in attitudinal terms, and it also points to a related aspect of life in Kumase.

Many of those who immigrated into the Asante capital had to wait some considerable time before being recruited into an office holder's retinue. Others never achieved their goal, but remained in Kumase either in forlorn expectation, or because the decisive act of going up to the capital had effectively severed their ties to village and lineage. Moreover, for an individual to return home was to admit failure and, as in other societies, to court humiliating comment.[53] People of this sort lived a marginal life in Kumase. Detached from the rural subsistence economy, but without the official status that guaranteed survival in the Asante capital, they were sometimes forced into stealing in order to eat. It says much about the ruling perception of the *meaning* of Kumase that, in addition to outright robbery and theft, desperate individuals often tried to survive simply by arrogating to themselves the status, attitudes and behaviour of actual *nhenkwaa*. It is equally significant that the state took the most serious view of any such illegitimate usurpation. Thus, in Kumase in March 1845, the Wesleyan-Methodist missionary G. Chapman recorded a not untypical case in which

a youth of precocious genius thought well to adopt the practice of the attendants upon Royalty, and began in the open market to seize upon such articles of food as best suited his fancy, taking care at the same time to announce to the owner that he was of the Royal Household. Certain parties ... who knew the youngster confronted him, and as a matter of course he was taken before the King, where it is said sentence of death would be passed upon him.[54]

By the early nineteenth century, then, the rural subsistence economy had been modified and restructured in one important regard. The intensification of agricultural production around the Asante capital, so extensively noted and commented on by Europeans, was directed at the maintenance of those non-producers, the inhabitants of Kumase, who constituted the membership of a state increasingly detached from and interventionist in relation to the social order. That this increased production was concentrated in a tight concentric ring around Kumase was dictated by the perishability of foodstuffs, the difficulty of bulk transportation, and the need for planning and oversight. No significant technological innovation was involved in this. Intensification of production far above the level of rural subsistence was achieved by a calculated reduction in the length of fallowing periods, and by a systematic rationalization and concentration of labour inputs.[55] Very obviously, these modifications were ordained, mediated and given structural direction by the state itself. How, and on what terms, was all of this effected?

Conceptualizing accumulation and wealth

The preliminary key to understanding what made all of this possible – and 'how it *could* be so' in Peel's phrase – lies in a consideration of the knowledge derived by the Asante from interpretation of the horizon of (their) existence. This knowledge constituted a referential framework of valid(ated) understanding and action that was formulated in fundamental imperatives, *grundnorms* and values, and that underpinned, informed and reinforced the historic and ongoing Asante experience of the social.

Both the underlying general characteristic and the dominant thrust of the experience in question were about the conceptualization of ideas of wealth and surplus, and their historical realization. Wealth and surplus – in gold (the *ur* substance), and in food, and also in people, in goods and in artefacts – were located in Asante experience and so knowledge as *the* engines of insertion, embedding, enlargement and success; they constituted a ready typology or computation of progress. Their metaphorical ubiquity in Asante tradition reflects the *knowledge* that societal and individual achievement was, and historically always had been, built upon assiduously pursued processes of accumulation. Hence, the accumulation of wealth as imperative and as yardstick, and the deeply resonant meaning of wealth as symbol and as mnemonic, were abiding and central features of Asante life, history and self-knowledge.

The state was initiated and entrenched through the aspirant effort and tenacity of the most successful accumulators. In the eighteenth and nineteenth centuries, the state structured and channelled imperative and yardstick, symbol and mnemonic, in order both to mould the idea of wealth in its own image, and to shape the processes of accumulation to its own ends. Its success in attaining these objects certainly depended on coercion, or at least on coercive potential. But it was ultimately rooted in the perceived veracity of an ingrained, undeniable consensus over the drives, norms and values that flowed from and were enshrined in historical knowledge.

The state's structuration of all of this depended upon precision in its especial and particular acts of interpretation. In its role as *hermeneus* it had to work within a vital, pre-existing context of knowledge – one that was the experiential basis of society, and in which its own personnel shared – while at the same time trying to reserve to itself shaping control over emphasis and direction. In attempting to reduce argument to statement by imposing its own definition on the possible interpretations implicit in knowledge, the state, at the very least, had to innovate and promulgate change within a simulacrum of continuity. Its capacity to structure knowledge both depended on and was constrained by the continuing potency and resonance, for society and individual, of that knowledge itself.

Wealth in the eighteenth and nineteenth centuries was measured in gold (*sika*) in all of its forms – negotiable gold dust (*sika futuro*), crude rock gold, and gold worked into regalia and ornaments for display; in investment in subjects (*nkoa*; sing. *akoa*), both slave and free, and control over their and their descendants' labour and services; and in the acquisition, by purchase, usufruct or usucaption, of rights in enough land to enable subjects to support themselves at subsistence level and generate a surplus. At a simple level of analysis all of this was no more than a logical enlargement and situational refinement of the accumulative process, and proof of an ongoing adherence to the imperative to create wealth and surplus. The objects of accumulation – gold, people, land and food – were the same as they had been in the sixteenth and seventeenth centuries. But two things had changed.

First, in the eighteenth and nineteenth centuries, participation in the office-holding structures of the state became the key to accumulation of these resources; membership in the state became the only certain avenue to the possibility of acquiring great wealth. The state sought ways in which to monopolize the (re)sources of enrichment, and means by which to determine access to them. These features are the subject of much research, and will be returned to when we consider illustrative cases.[56]

Second, in the same period, there developed a notable differentiation by value among the objects of accumulation. This may be simply described. In the course of the very protracted struggle to establish subsistence agriculture, people, in terms of their labour inputs into land clearing and food production, acquired a virtually absolute value. Nothing could be achieved by exchanging them for some other good. But with the successful embedding of the agricultural mode of production, and the eighteenth-century expansion of the slave raiding state, a plateau of stability was reached; people remained indispensable as producers, but the new imbalance between need and numbers created a system of relative values. People acquired a novel value as an export commodity, and a greatly augmented value as subjects rather than as producers *per se*; *nkoa* in large numbers, as a following or a train of armed retainers, became an indispensable item in the public exhibition of an office holder's power and prestige. Exchange within this system of relative values was measured against the absolute value of gold. After all, gold was the ultimate basis of the international economy in which the Asante state was enmeshed. Thus, people, and the land to support them, became goods readily convertible against gold. But gold assumed a sovereign position in the processes of accumulation and exchange for a further, very specific reason. By the nineteenth century in Asante, gold – quite unlike people, land or food – was in limited supply.

After the ending of the transatlantic slave trade, all goods purchased by the Asante from the Europeans on the Gold Coast had to be paid for in gold; guns, powder, cloth and other articles were bought with gold that was removed from circulation and lost to the Asante economy.[57] Similarly, office holders from the *Asantehene* downwards took substantial quantities of gold out of circulation in order to convert it into regalia and ornaments.[58] Perceived shortages exacerbated the existing tendency, inherent in the imperative to accumulation, to hoard and to secrete gold; and this simply compounded the problem by taking yet more gold out of circulation. Problems of hoarding and liquidity were still apparent in the colonial period.[59] Thus, in nineteenth-century Asante, the demand for gold exceeded the supply available in circulation.

We can observe the effect of this discrepancy in interest rates. Loans in gold were very expensive. Under *Asantehene* Osei Tutu Kwame (1804–23), the flat rate of interest on borrowed gold was 33% for a 42-day period.[60] Later in the century, the average rate of interest was fixed at 50% per half year. In Kumase, however, 'the rate was higher, and was regarded as extortionate'; in one extreme case 'the charge was 20% every ten days'.[61] The British specified a maximum rate of 50% per year on an unsecured loan.[62] As late as the 1940s, however, illegal money lending was still widespread in Kumase, and the British acknowledged privately that the interest rate on the granting of short-term loans continued to be based on the system that had operated in the precolonial period.[63] They noted that

Short-term loans are usually at the rate of 50 per cent interest for a specified period, not necessarily a year and sometimes as short as three months. In this case, if the capital is not repaid, but interest is paid, the debt remains at the same figure for another agreed period. Failure to repay either capital or interest results in a new loan, the capital now being the sum of the original loan plus interest. It not infrequently happens therefore that a borrower is left with a debt larger than the original sum borrowed, although he has already paid [as] interest over a period of years a sum much in excess of the original loan.[64]

The shortage of gold and correspondingly high interest rates on loans had a direct bearing on the ways in which the state sought to arbitrate access to wealth and to regulate the processes of accumulation. In its application of legal sanctions – fines, imposts, tributes, taxes, levies – the state always insisted in principle upon settlement in gold. But in virtually no case other than the very trivial was payment actually made from accumulated gold resources. The very few who possessed such resources were determined to hoard them; and the great majority, from office holders to lineage segments to individuals, simply did not have substantial assets in gold at their disposal. Two general solutions were possible.

First, other assets could either be sold outright to realize the sum required, or they could be offered directly to the state in lieu of payment in gold (that is, 'sold' to the *Asantehene* or another office holder, who then paid the purchase price into the state treasury). A famous instance of this took place in or about 1785, when the *Asantehene* Osei Kwame (1777–1803) attained his majority. The Kumase *Adontenhene* Kwaaten Pɛtɛ, who had discharged the function of regent, was unable to account for the very considerable amount of 1,000 *mperedwan* (£8,000) of state assets. The office holders of the Adonten *fekuo* or group were held corporately responsible for the debt. Payment in gold of such a sum was out of the question. Instead, five Adonten villages, their lands and people, were surrendered in settlement; the *Asantehene* 'bought' Ahwia and Abira from the *Adontenhene*, and Esaso and Adidwama from the *Amakomhene*, and similarly the *Asantehemaa* 'bought' Krobo from the *Adausenahene*.[65]

Second, assets could be placed in mortgage in exchange for gold. This was a widespread but complex practice. The word *awowa* (pl. *ŋwowa*) connoted surety, pawning or pledging, but it applied equally to land, to groups of people and to individuals. The situation was complicated further by the fact that rights in *awowa* were transferable; an original lender, now a borrower, could pass them on to a new lender, and so on via a chain of such transactions. In nineteenth-century Asante, the pawning of the labour and services of individuals was very extensively resorted to by indebted lineage segments. As small debts were incurred, or some capital was required, an individual might find himself or herself pawned and redeemed several times over. The socio-psychological effects of being alienated by one's kin are well documented. A typical case was that of Kwabena Amponsa, a member of the royal *Bretuo* lineage at Domeabra, who was first pawned at Obogu in the reign of the *Asantehene* Mensa Bonsu (1874–83), and who was put to work carrying kola nuts in the northern trade.

Kwabena Amponsa, my father, had a very bitter experience in his youth, for he was pawned seven times – the first time for [the equivalent of] 30/- when a relative of his became in debt. This experience made a great impression on his character. He became callous, too materialistic, and hoarded money, for he had been taught to appreciate the value and importance of money. He married too late, for the time he might have spent in courtship and love affairs was spent in servitude.[66]

Numerous small-scale debts to the state were settled in this manner. In the case of very much larger debts, financially embarrassed office holders might put land as well as *nkoa* in *awowa*. The advantage of this method of settlement was that pledged land, like people, was theoretically redeemable in law against repayment of the capital loan plus a fixed rate of interest. In actual practice, putting land in *awowa* on any large scale preserved only the fiction of ownership. Some account of the 'inequitable and oppressive' customary system was given by the British.

Though the land is always redeemable, in practice the mortgage is often ruinous to the borrower . . . the lender is entitled to the use and produce of the land (and of the people on it if these were included in the agreement), until the principal money and agreed interest (if any) is repaid. No credit is given to the borrower for such use of produce, whatever their value, against the principal sum or interest. As a general rule the borrower has no other income than that which he derives from the land, and consequently he is seldom in a position to repay the loan or to redeem his land.[67]

Enforcing the conversion of assets by demanding gold in settlement of all manner of obligations gave the state substantial powers of intervention and redistribution. That this was a directed rather than a blunt instrument may be illustrated very concisely from the history of the legal application of the principle of *atitɔdeɛ* or 'buying one's head'. In principle, a range of offences carried a mandatory death sentence in Asante law.[68] In practice, the *Asantehene* sitting in session with the *asetena kɛsɛɛ* (the supreme court: lit. 'the great sitting down together') could exercise discretion, and substitute *atitɔdeɛ* for capital punishment. In tradition, this innovation is attributed to the humane impulses of the *Asantehene* Kusi Obodom (1750–64), but the same sources suggest that many held the practice to be illegitimate.[69] Certainly, the *Asantehene* Kofi Kakari (1867–74), who was habitually in need of gold, is remembered as having overused the device to the point of triviality in order to raise revenue.[70] More germanely, Asante sources suggest that *atitɔdeɛ* was particularly employed in those cases where, for whatever reason, the state wished to ruin a rich office holder and confiscate his assets.[71] This is borne out by the way that the law operated in practice. Unlike the fixed penalties attached to many offences, *atitɔdeɛ*

was any amount the Asantehene cared to name. From all available information it was generally very high. And while the instances of £800 or £1,000 live on in popular memory, it is also known that there were several instances where whole lineages had to be sold into slavery to raise Atitodie demanded by the Asantehene.[72]

It would be naïve to presume that Asante case law was anything other than partial in a great deal of its application. That is, Asante case law was no more and no less impartial than many other codes legislated and executed by a state apparatus. It was inextricably bound up with the political dynamic, and while it existed to reflect Asante constructions of justice, it also served to reinforce the power and interests of the state. It is important to make this point, for the ethnography of Asante law habitually presents a very idealized portrait by collapsing the historical dynamic of the civil and criminal law into the category of immemorial custom.[73] We shall see presently that the Asante distinguished between the categories of the juridical and the immemorial.

State and wealth: the abirɛmpɔn

In the era prior to the emergence of chiefdoms, the most successful individual entrepreneurs had been accorded community recognition of their capacity to accumulate by being called, with accurate simplicity, 'big men' (abirɛmpɔn: sing. ɔbirɛmpɔn). The most tenacious and ambitious among these had eventually institutionalized their wealth in chiefship, inter alia converting their economic clients into a political following of retainers (gyaasefoɔ: der. gyaase, 'under the fire', hearth), and indicating their new political authority through possession of a symbolic spear (pɛmɛ: pl. mpɛmɛ) and other regalia.[74] A number of such abirɛmpɔn were incorporated into the state at its creation, and these retained the dignity of the title; equally, some individuals who had distinguished themselves militarily in the same period were raised to the title of ɔbirɛmpɔn.[75]

In the eighteenth and nineteenth centuries, the Asante state politicized, structured and formalized this crucial appellation. The capacity to accumulate on the largest scale – at different times by commanding the state's armies, by conducting the state's trade, or by being a favoured beneficiary of the state's law – was itself in the gift of the state. Moreover, the state reserved to itself the right to bestow the title of ɔbirɛmpɔn in recognition of an individual's success in accumulating wealth; and only the state could grant the use of the insignia of the elephant tail (mena or mmra), the heraldic badge of the ɔbirɛmpɔn. The state deliberately reinforced the significance of this ultimate mark of recognition by instituting a graduated series of titles that led up to it, and by surrounding the actual award of the title of ɔbirɛmpɔn with very complex ritual and ceremonial.

These ritualized procedures combined public display with public acclamation, and they were punctuated throughout by very deliberate symbolic, mnemonic and historical references. The fullest traditional account of the complexities involved was supplied by the Kumase Akyeamehene and Domakwaehene Kwasi Apea Nuama in 1925.

Those chiefs who were allowed to use elephant tails were called Abrempons. A chief who lives on his own land with his own subjects is known by the King as Abrempon. An Abrempon must exhibit his wealth publicly by presenting £9-6-0 to all the Abrempons in Kumasi; and 10 peregwans (£80) to the King. He would then go to Tafo and pay £1-6-0 to the chief there who would give him an egg to throw against a silk cotton tree. He would then return to Kumasi. He would then go to Essumja Santimanso and buy a carpet (nsa) for £24 (3 peregwans) from the subjects of the chief there. He must only dance on it and leave it after presenting Essumjahene with another £24. Your going and coming expenses (including the £48) will cost you some 20 peregwans [£160]. He would buy an elephant tail from the Assinhene (son of Essumjahene) for £9-6-0. He would tie the elephant tail around the waist of one of his slaves and he must then pass round the outskirts of the town lying on the leaves of palm trees which have been strewn around the town, firing at his slave with blank fire from time to time. The slave falls down eventually and he then cuts the string to which the tail is fastened and takes the tail – then the ceremonies are completed and his people applaud him. Next morning he would get mashed yam mixed with 30 peregwans [£240] and be carried on a litter round the town of Kumasi scattering largesse of the yam mixture. On the following morning he would be carried in a litter with all his regalia, his skin plastered with white clay. Then he would fix up a spear at Dwebirim (the market place) and challenge those of the same rank to remove it. After this he is called Brempon. On the last day anyone who aspires to the rank of Abrempon takes out the spear and appoints a time for performing the same ceremonies.[76]

The state orchestrated this complicated sequence. But the promiscuity of reference contained within these performative acts is such that contingent matters can only be touched upon. Thus, the smearing of the silk-cotton tree (*Ceiba pentandra*: *onyaa*) with an egg was a common ritual; it propitiated the tree's living 'spirit' or *sasa*. Acts of this sort affirmed the historical fact that culture was derived from a hostile nature that constantly needed to be placated or reckoned with. The *nsa* was a coarse covering or blanket, and it featured in many ritual contexts.[77]

The visits by the candidate *ɔbirɛmpɔn* to Tafo and Asantemanso ('Essumja Santimanso') made pointed allusion to crucial passages in Asante history and myth. Tafo was barely 3 miles from Kumase. In the sixteenth and seventeenth centuries it was a flourishing centre of gold production and trade, and the seat of a successful *ɔbirɛmpɔn*. The *Tafohene* Safo Akenten was prominent among those *abirɛmpɔn* conquered by the *Asantehene* Osei Tutu (died 1712 or 1717), and then incorporated into the nascent Asante state.[78] Asantemanso, 20 miles south of Kumase in the territorial division of Asumegya, has a central significance in Asante myths of origin and early history. At Asantemanso 'the first human beings, belonging to certain of their ruling clans, came forth from the ground'.[79] That is, the founders of Kumase traced their origins to Asantemanso. Thus, on 9 February 1832, Simons traversed 'the beautiful open forest' of Asantemanso, where 'in olden times Koemasie town stood, according to the reports of the Assiantijns'; and in the 1920s, Rattray found pottery fragments and other evidence of extensive settlement there, dating from 'some remote period', in what was still 'the most hallowed spot' in all Asante.[80]

The dance or mime of hunting the elephant in order to secure its tail was of central significance. Possession and display of the *mena* was the public mark of the achieved status of *ɔbirɛmpɔn*. Clearly, the mime itself made reference to the remote past of hunting and gathering, prior to the creation of the agrarian order. In that past, the killing of an actual elephant (*ɛsono*: lit. 'the big one') signified heroic individual success, and it was very probably one of the distinguishing characteristics of the first *abirɛmpɔn*. The elephant was both unpredictably dangerous – spiritually as well as physically – and the largest single source of animal food in the Asante forest. The idea of the ɔbirɛmpɔn in his critical historic roles of provider and protector is perhaps best encapsulated in a maxim: *obiakofoɔ na okum ɛsono, na amansam nyina di* ('It is one man who kills the elephant, but many people who eat its flesh').[81]

The symbolism of the *mena* itself is open to two related readings. The Asante classified the elephant as being a supreme animal, not only on account of its size and strength, but also because it had overcome its most evident and anomalous disability. The matter is distilled in an aphorism: *ɛsono dua eye, ode saa ara na epra ne ho* ('The elephant has a short tail, but it can still brush away flies').[82] That is, the elephant's status derived in part from struggle and achievement in 'brushing away' petty distractions. The thrust of the metaphorical association was that the aspirant ɔbirɛmpɔn should likewise pursue the struggle for mastery or supremacy through a single-minded accumulation, and not be deterred from this goal by inconsequential obstacles or distractions. It is also the case that the elephant's tail 'presided' (in a structuralist sense) over the production of excrement, and that this was volumetrically the largest such 'transaction' in the Asante cognitive universe. As has been noted elsewhere, there were clear associations in the Asante mind between wealth in gold and excrement.[83] Both 'substances' were mediated, uncertain and ambiguous by nature; both possessed clearly parallel associations – through evident processes of convertibility – with ranges of other substances or alternative constituents of reality. Thus, food 'converted' to nourishment (wealth) and waste; and gold bearing rock or soil 'converted' to wealth (nourishment) as dust, ornaments and the rest, and left a residuum of dross (waste). The volatility of both wealth in gold and excrement, and most particularly their capacity to transgress and to rupture categorical boundaries by conversion, exists cognitively in cultures other than that of Asante.[84]

In Kumase on 29 March 1862, the Wesleyan-Methodist missionary W. West recorded the imminent 'display of wealth, by an old chief, in order to be entitled to the honour of having the elephant's tail carried before him; an honour to which only the wealthy can aspire'.[85] On the next day, West witnessed the mime of hunting the elephant; his bemused description is the only extant nineteenth-century account of this part of the proceedings.

A very ludicrous part of the anticipated ceremony, 'catching the elephant', came off in the afternoon... A slave had been selected to enact the part of elephant. Besmeared all over with chalk, holding in his hand a small tusk, which he occasionally applied to his mouth, and having an elephant's tail attached by a piece of string behind, he was started off; while some forty or fifty men, armed with muskets, and supplied with blank cartridges, followed in pursuit, keeping up an almost constant fire. His elephantship, as we were informed, made his way, according to usage, to a small kroom [village] not far from Kumasi, where he fell down as if shot, and lay there, until the chief himself appeared to cut off the tail; who, having thus hunted the elephant, and possessed himself of its caudal appendage, was considered, as I suppose, entitled to have it borne in triumph before him.[86]

The piece of land (West's 'kroom') over which the 'elephant' was hunted by the candidate *obirɛmpɔn* was ceded to him for this purpose by a senior Kumase office holder. In 1844, for example, the Kumase *Manwerehene* Kwasi Brantuo performed the mime of hunting the elephant on land granted to him by the Kumase *Akwamuhene* and *Asafohene* Akwawua Dente, who was himself an *obirɛmpɔn*.[87] The land in question was at Adeɛbeba, immediately to the south of Kumase. Such land retained its place as a commemoration and key symbol of an individual's achievement. Thus, in *Manwere* traditions, it is recounted that Kwasi Brantuo used to ride out in a palanquin from Kumase to Adeɛbeba, surrounded by *nkoa* chanting his praise names; and while in residence there, he reportedly used to delight in observing his young granddaughters playing amidst his accumulated gold dust. The intimacy of the association is summarized in the aphorism, 'Where is *Manwere* without Adeɛbeba?'; and as recently as 1951, the then *Manwerehene* Kwasi Brantuo IV observed to the *Asantehene* Osei Agyeman Prempeh II (1931–70) that, 'I am now beginning to take an interest in Adiebeba (Brantuokrom) ... it is the original place you honoured me.'[88] Land at Adeɛmbra, close to Adeɛbeba, served the same function when the Kumase *Ankobeahene* Kwaku Tawia mimed hunting the elephant, also in the reign of Kwaku Dua Panin; this land had originally belonged to the Kumase *Akwamuhene* and *Asafohene*, and at least one other *obirɛmpɔn* – the *Denyasehene* Aduonin – had previously used it for the same purposes as Kwaku Tawia.[89]

Following the mime of hunting and killing the elephant, and securing its tail, the aspirant *obirɛmpɔn* submitted the credentials of his candidacy to public scrutiny by distributing largess, and by making a display of his accumulated wealth in gold. According to West, this phase of the ceremonies 'occupied the best part of three days'.[90] The liberal scattering from a palanquin of pounded yam impregnated with gold dust joined together crucial objects of accumulation, wealth and surplus in one highly visible gesture of actual and symbolic extravagance, and made potent reference to the concept of the *obirɛmpɔn* in direct relation both to history and to continuity. The actual display of wealth was a great public occasion. Gold was worked into new ornaments and regalia, and these were set off amidst gold dust and a host of other elaborate, rare or costly artefacts. In November 1817, W. Hutchison, the British resident in Kumase, witnessed the public display of wealth made by the Kumase *Gyaasewahene* Opoku Frɛfrɛ.

This week past Apokoo and several of the captains have been making an exhibition of their riches... It is done by making their gold into various articles of dress for show. Apokoo, who sent for me before his uproar began, shewed me his varieties, weighing upwards of 800 bendas [1,600 ozs.] of the finest gold; among the articles, was a girdle two inches broad. Gold chains for the neck, arms, legs, &c. ornaments for the ancles of all descriptions, consisting of manacles, with keys, bells, chairs, and padlocks. For his numerous family of wives, children, and captains, were armlets and various ornaments. A superb war cap of eagle's feathers, fetishes, Moorish charms, &c. Moorish caps, silk dresses, purses, bags, &c. made of monkey skin. Fans, with ivory handles, made of tiger skin, and decorated with silk. New umbrellas made in fantastical shapes, gold swords and figures of animals, birds, beasts, and fishes of the same metal; his drums, and various instruments of music, were covered with tiger skin, with red belts for hanging them. Ivory arrows and bows, covered with silk and skins, and many other weapons of war or fancy, such as the mind in a like situation would devise.[91]

The significance of the *Gyaasewahene* Opoku Frɛfrɛ's exhibition of his wealth in 1817 was still recalled in oral testimony given in 1940.[92] Similarly, on 15 July 1844, Chapman conveyed something of the importance of such an occasion, when he observed the following of the public display of wealth made by the *Manwerehene* Kwasi Brantuo and one other office holder.

Two of the principal chiefs have, at the King's command, been 'showing themselves, and their Gold' today. One of them (Brentu) is a treasurer of the King's. The other (Afarqua) is reckoned to be among the most wealthy among his aristocratical compeers. All their people were in attendance, as well as their numerous wives. The King and all the principal Chiefs were seated in the Market. These two 'Gentlemen' whose turn it is to be thus honoured, appear to feel their vast importance. Nor are they at all insensible to the fulsome praises, bellowed forth by their equally vain attendants. At the close of the ceremony a variety of presents were made by each of the two, to His Majesty. It is expected that these will be returned tomorrow, with interest.[93]

It is known from an entirely different source that, following the display of his wealth, the *Manwerehene* Kwasi Brantuo received from the *Asantehene* Kwaku Dua Panin the gift of some *nkoa* confiscated from the *Saamanhene*, and that these subjects were then settled at Adeɛbeba.[94]

In the last of this highly complex series of ritual enactments, the newly recognized *ɔbirɛmpɔn* made public affirmation of his achieved status by planting *pɛmɛ* – the symbolic accoutrement of the original *abirɛmpɔn* – in the soil at *dwaberem*. By so doing, and by challenging his peers to remove the spear, he was linking his personal attainment to the military and other virtues of the original *abirɛmpɔn*, and insisting upon his own achieved right of belonging in a hallowed tradition. He was also simultaneously encouraging other office holders to emulate him in the drive to accumulate, and challenging them to put their achievement forward for public assessment as he had done. Moreover, the planting of a spear possessed resonances and connotations other than the obviously military ones.

In authoritative recensions of tradition, the planting of a spear is symbolic of those facets of accumulation that are embodied in human fecundity. Thus, it is recounted that spears were planted in order to determine whether Opoku Ware or Boa Kwatia should succeed Osei Tutu as *Asantehene*. Opoku Ware's spear, planted in Kumase at *pampaso*, produced *kahire* (pads) containing both harmless and venomous reptiles; Boa Kwatia's spear, planted in Kumase at *asaaman*, yielded nothing. Opoku Ware was duly selected as *Asantehene*, the reading being that only his spear – interpreted as producing a succession of good and bad rulers – guaranteed the continuity of the royal dynasty and of Asante.[95]

The bestowal of the *mena* by the state was reserved to a very small minority of office holders. These were model individuals who had accumulated on the largest scale. That scale was itself notional, because the state left it deliberately unspecified. In effect, this placed the onus firmly on the individual accumulator; it was up to him to initiate his candidacy, and to present his wealth for scrutiny and assessment. Thus, the state both controlled and restricted access to the status of *ɔbirɛmpɔn* by injecting an element of calculated risk into the application procedures. In 1817, Hutchison made reference to this factor when he observed that the public display of wealth 'is generally done once in life, by those who are in favour with the King, and think themselves free from palavers'.[96]

Even in his own lifetime, the *ɔbirɛmpɔn* was inhibited from spending lavishly, or otherwise squandering his riches. The possession of the *mena*, and the enormous social prestige of the 'big man' that derived from it, were indicators that the individual thus honoured was the benefactor of a collective posterity. Such a person was recognized and acknowledged as having added significantly to the increase of Asante society. Thus, nothing was considered more shaming to the name and to the posthumous reputation of the *ɔbirɛmpɔn* than that he died bankrupt – or, in the very precise Asante locution, that he 'boiled and ate the elephant tail' – for such behaviour was disgraceful because it was profoundly and literally anti-social.[97] It was understood as an act of theft from the future wellbeing of Asante society.

The state assiduously reinforced this received construction of the nature and purposes of wealth. The key symbolic artefact deployed by the state was the *sika mena* or 'Golden Elephant Tail', which took precedence – in a sense analogous to parenthood – over all of the elephant tails of the *abirɛmpɔn*. Each *Asantehene*, from Osei Tutu onwards, created his own *sika mena*. Thus, for instance, the *sika mena* created by the *Asantehene* Kwaku Dua Panin was placed for safekeeping in the custody of the *Manwerehene* and ɔbirɛmpɔn Kwasi Brantuo.[98] Such creations symbolized the commitment of each successive *Asantehene* to uphold and to transmit the inheritance of values and practices embodied in the concept itself.

The Asante understood the *sika mena*, symbolizing wealth, as being in an intimate binary relationship with the *sika dwa kofi* or 'Golden Stool', symbolizing political authority and legitimate power. Physical possession of the *sika dwa kofi* was crucial to the legitimation of an *Asantehene*. In metaphysical terms, the *sika mena* was conceptualized as 'enfolding' or 'being wrapped around' (*nnuraho*) the *sika dwa kofi*. This type of metaphorical conceit is common in Asante thought, and it is intended to express notions of support, help and enabling assistance; that is, the *sika mena* was construed as being the 'helper' of the *sika dwa kofi*. This encapsulated the historic perceptions already adumbrated. That is, just as Asante culture and society were held to have been 'helped' into being by processes of accumulation, so it was understood in enlargement that the state's political authority was rooted in and rested upon – that is, was 'helped' into being by – effective controls over the right to amass and to dispose of wealth.

It has been argued that mental representations of the systems of wealth and authority in Asante thought can be read symmetrically as complementary homologues.[99] That is, the *sika mena* was the representation and symbol of the highest level at which wealth could be appropriated (*ogye*); and the *sika dwa kofi* was the representation and symbol of the highest level at which political authority could be exercised (*otumi*). The appearance of symmetry is figuratively or expressively correct, but historically misleading. The very concept of *nnuraho* evidences the lesser or supporting status of the *sika mena*. This representational imbalance was an accurate reflection of Asante thought. That is, the objective value of wealth was always firmly situated in relation to purpose – the embedding of culture, the increase of society, the articulation of political authority.

The concept of *ogye* symbolized in the *sika mena* was articulated through a number of mechanisms. Two of these are especially noteworthy. Death duties or *awunnyadeɛ* were levied by the state on an individual's self-acquired movable property. Similarly, inheritance taxes or *ayibuadeɛ* might be imposed on the immovable part of an estate, and notably land, before the residue was restored to the heirs or successors. These imposts were discretionary, at least in the limited sense that the state determined equity of assessment in each and every individual case. Accordingly, state demands varied, but the principles themselves – and most especially death duties – were very widely and vigorously enforced. There is much detailed evidence concerning the operation of these mechanisms, and their overall significance may be readily summarized.[100]

The implementation of *awunnyadeɛ* and *ayibuadeɛ* underlined the dominant understanding of the purposes of accumulation, not least by denying ultimate rights of disposition to the individual. This was essentially a closed and self-replicating system. By fixing assessment levels in each case, the state was in a position to prevent the dynastic transmission and consolidation of wealth. In consequence, the emergence of a class of hereditary property owners was blocked, and the state effectively retained a monopoly over access to wealth and its redistribution. Tax evasion was construed as being scandalously anti-social, and it was punished with due severity. Instances of it were correspondingly rare.[101]

This system was threatened only when the norms and values underpinning it were called into serious question. In the 1880s, the liquidation of the state's authority and a widespread interrogation of its meaning and role coincided with the exposure of many Asante to new models of individualism and capital accumulation derived from the British Gold Coast Colony. Accordingly, battle was joined over the state's insistence on death duties and inheritance taxes. And, as late as the 1930s, individuals who had accumulated wealth under the colonial dispensation continued to fear that a restored *Asantehene*, with tacit British approval, might seek to resurrect historic forms of appropriation.[102] We will return to these issues below and set them within an appropriate historical framework.

State and wealth: anatomies of power

The beginnings of the system analysed above date from the period of the eighteenth-century expansionist state. Thus, for example, *awunnyadeɛ* and *ayibuadeɛ* are innovations traditionally attributed to the *Asantehene* Opoku Ware (*c.* 1720–50).[103] And, as we have noted, serious disintegration occurred in the 1880s. The system was at the height of its operational integrity between the reigns of the *Asantehenes* Osei Kwadwo (1764–77) and Kwaku Dua Panin (1834–67), or more appositely between the careers in state service of the *abirɛmpɔn Kyidomhene* and *Ankaasehene* Yamoa Ponko (*c.* 1730–85) and *Manwerehene* Kwasi Brantuo (*c.* 1791–1865).[104]

At its zenith this system was characterized by a number of features. As noted, the period described coincided with the ending of the transatlantic slave trade, and a consequent decline in the profitability of warfare. The *ɔbirɛmpɔn Gyaasewahene* Opoku Frɛfrɛ (*c.* 1755–1826) took many captives and much booty in his 1811 campaign in Akuapem and the southeastern Gold Coast, but the majority of his field commands had specifically political objectives, and in 1817 he complained that 'there were too many slaves in the country'; the *ɔbirɛmpɔn* Yamoa Ponko's sole military venture was a punitive expedition undertaken in the early 1780s against the

1 'Two seated men: wicker chair'. The man seated on the right is the Kumase *Akwamuhene/Asafohene* Asafo Boakye (*c.* 1832–1925), a son of the *Asantehene* Kwaku Dua Panin (reigned 1834–67). Asafo Boakye was a leading figure in Asante politics from the 1870s to the 1890s. He married *inter alios* Akua Afriyie (d. 1921), fifth child of the *Asantehemaa* Afua Kobi, and full sister to the *Asantehenes* Kofi Kakari and Mensa Bonsu. In 1896 he was among those arrested by the British and sent into exile with the *Asantehene* Agyeman Prempe. Asafo Boakye is remembered as having sworn that he would survive exile. He did – in Elmina, Freetown and the Seychelles – and he returned to Kumase in November 1924. He died there in April 1925, aged over ninety.

dissident *Mamponhene* Owusu Sekyere Panin; and the *ɔbirɛmpɔn* Kwasi Brantuo never commanded an army.[105] By contrast, legitimate commerce flourished in this period as an important means of accumulation. As a young man, Yamoa Ponko acquired substantial wealth in the northern trade with the Gonja towns of Gbuipe and Daboya, which lay on the commercial route that linked Asante with the Middle Niger; and following the Anglo-Asante treaty of 1831, the southern trade in cloth and other

2 'The chief of Bantama with a war-dress and head-dress with charms'. The Kumase *Bantamahene/Krontihene* Osei Bonsu. Osei Bonsu was a member of the *botaase* lineage of the royal Mampon *Bretuo*, and so was an *ɔdehyeɛ* of the Mampon stool. His elder half-brother was the *Mamponhene* Atakora Kwaku Mensa (d. 1882); his sister's son was the *Mamponhene* Kwaku Dua Agyeman (1931–5). Osei Bonsu fled Asante in the 1880s, prospered in the Gold Coast Colony as a rubber trader, and in 1901 was appointed to the office of Kumase *Bantamahene/Krontihene* by the British. He held that stool for fifteen years, and was then himself made *Mamponhene* (1916–30). In this portrait he is wearing an elaborate protective war coat and head-dress festooned with *asuman* and Muslim charms (inscribed on paper, then folded up and sealed in leather or metal containers). A century earlier, in 1817, Bowdich was informed that the *Asantehene* Osei Tutu Kwame had paid 'the value of thirty slaves' to the *Ya Na* and Muslims of Dagomba to purchase a 'fetish or war coat', similar to that illustrated here, for the *Gyaasewahene* Opoku Frɛfrɛ. A photograph of Osei Bonsu taken at the same time, but showing him standing, is in R.S. Rattray, *Religion and Art in Ashanti* (Oxford, 1927), Fig. 16.

3 'Warrior with fetish-covered smock'. An (unnamed) Asante clad in the same type of protective war coat and head-dress as in plate 2. His garments are richly studded with Muslim charms, and sewn on the left shoulder of the coat is the *suman kwasadwan* ('turning away'), containing a piece of ram's horn. Hunters in pursuit of animals with a dangerous *sasa* favoured protective clothing of a similar sort.

European merchandise afforded retail opportunities and considerable profits.[106]

Access to the possibility of amassing great wealth in either warfare or trade was mediated by the state. By definition, the model or paradigmatic career that led from *ahenkwaa* to *ɔbirɛmpɔn* could only be pursued within the office-holding echelons of state service. All of the successive levels of upward mobility, from insertion through aggrandizement, advancement and reward, depended on having access to opportunities sanctioned by the state. Progress measured as output or visible achievement was highly structured and demarcated. But input or the pursuit of progress combined access and talent with instrumental, opportunistic and adventitious elements.

The operation of these elements can be observed in the beginnings of the careers of successful *abirɛmpɔn*. As a youth, Opoku Frɛfrɛ was summoned to Kumase from his natal village of Anyatiase in order to serve the *Oyoko Abohyenhene* Buapon in the lowly capacity of keeper of the bedchamber door (*dabini*). Buapon buried a quantity of gold dust and, after he had died in the early 1770s, Opoku Frɛfrɛ disclosed this act of concealment to the *Asantehene* Osei Kwadwo. Both the gold dust and Opoku Frɛfrɛ were taken as *awunnyadeɛ*. The *Asantehene* transferred Opoku Frɛfrɛ into his own service, appointing him an *ahenkwaa* to be trained in fiscal matters under the *Fotosanfoɔhene* Esom Adu.[107] Kwasi Brantuo's father was a royal *ahenkwaa* from Atwoma, and a close associate of the *ŋkwaŋtananŋhene* Boakye Yam Kuma. His mother was an *akoa* of the *ŋkwaŋtananŋhene* from Asoromaso. As a young man, Kwasi Brantuo was appointed *mmagyegyeni* (personal servant; 'nanny') in the service of Fredua Agyeman, the youthful son of the *ŋkwaŋtananŋhene* Boakye Yam Kuma by his marriage to the *Oyoko Kɔkɔɔ* royal Amma Sewaa. This association proved crucial. In 1834, Fredua Agyeman was enstooled as the *Asantehene* Kwaku Dua Panin, and Kwasi Brantuo's preferment began with appointment to a senior post within the *ahoprafoɔ* (elephant tail bearers).[108] In the manner described by Bonnat, both Opoku Frɛfrɛ and Kwasi Brantuo succeeded in securing the *personal* attention and patronage of the *Asantehene*. For each, this was the start of a career that led to the award of the *mena*. 'Berantuo [Kwasi Brantuo] was his [Kwaku Dua Panin's] baby nurse', and so, noted a tradition recorded in 1915,

the King promoted him [Kwasi Brantuo] over all his other dignitaries, and consequently he Berantuo became very rich. Only the King surpassed him in elegance. Today, the fortune of Berantuo's family has decreased, but still his children are very respectable. 'Though gunpowder has been fired, it is not (lacking) in Akowua's bottle' [i.e. Though the fortune of the very wealthy like Berantuo may decrease, he will never become a pauper].[109]

The state expected opportunity to be matched by talent and achievement. Bowdich observed in 1817,

It is a frequent practice of the King's to consign sums of gold to the care of rising captains, without requiring them from them for two or three years, at the end of which time he expects the captain not only to restore the principal, but to prove that he has acquired sufficient of his own, from the use of it, to support the greater

4 'Kobina Asabonten before the Tribunal'. This photograph was taken by Rattray in Kumase in September 1921 at the Commission of Inquiry into the Desecration of the Golden Stool. The man pictured (in a mourning cloth, befitting the sombre occasion) is the Kumase *Gyaasewahene* Kwabena Asubonten, who was arraigned and convicted on a charge of culpable negligence, in that the *sika dwa kafi* was entrusted to his care (the *Asantehene* Agyeman Prempe being in exile) when it was defiled, and its

dignity the King would confer on him. If he has not, his talent is thought too mean for further elevation. Should he have no good traders amongst his dependents, (for if he has there is no difficulty) usury and worse resources are countenanced, and though more creditable than a failure, ascribed to want of talent rather than to a regard of principle.[110]

Oral sources confirm these practices. The *Asantehene* Osei Tutu Kwame reportedly entrusted the Kumase *Ankobeahene* Amankwa Abinowa with the sum of 1,000 *mperedwan* (£8,000), and sent him to the Gold Coast with four hundred carriers to purchase guns and ammunition. Amankwa Abinowa was ambushed by the Akyem, but managed to extricate his party and return to Kumase. Because of Amankwa Abinowa's skill in executing this manœuvre, Osei Tutu Kwame 'promised to assist him financially to become a rich man'.[111] Yamoa Ponko kept such a careful accounting of his investments and profits that, when his 'servants returned from trading expeditions, he insisted on examining their boxes to find out what they had brought back'.[112]

The *Asantehene* himself was a participant in and a beneficiary of this system. When Osei Tutu Kwame was preparing to invade Fante in 1807, he received financial assistance from the *Gyaasewahene* Opoku Frɛfrɛ, the *Adumhene* Adum Ata, the Bantama *ɔkyeame* Kwaku Yeboa, the *nsenieni* or court herald (and subsequently *ɔkyeame*) Kwadwo Adusei Kyakya, the *Hiawuhene* Kankam, Oti Panin (son and eventual successor of the wealthy *ɔkyeame* Boakye Yam Panin), and the *Nkonŋwasoafoɔhene* Yaw Kokroko. In 1819, following the conclusion of the campaign against the *Gyamanhene*

Caption for Plate 4 (*cont.*)

gold accoutrements plundered, by Kwasi Nsenie Agya and twelve others. Kwabena Asubonten acknowledged his responsibility in the matter, was sentenced to removal from office and, in accordance with his own wishes, was exiled from Asante. The desecration incensed all Asante, the British feared insurrection, and Kwabena Asubonten was condemned in – and by – this charged atmosphere. Privately, the British minuted that he was greatly esteemed by his stool subjects, and that he was a victim of unfortunate circumstances rather than the perpetrator of any criminal act himself. Kwabena Asubonten was a member of the *gyaasewa mmamma* – the successor in office, as son and paternal grandson, of celebrated figures in nineteenth-century Asante history. His father was the *Gyaasewahene* Adu Bofoɔ (d. *c.* 1883); his father's father was the *Gyaasewahene* *ɔbirɛmpɔŋ* Opoku Frɛfrɛ (d. 1826). Kwabena Asubonten himself became *Gyaasewahene* in 1906, after sustained protest from the *gyaasewa mmamma* and *nkoa* persuaded the British to depose their usurpatory client Kwame Tua from that office.

Kwadwo Adinkra, in which much gold was seized, the *Asantehene* Osei Tutu Kwame acknowledged his obligation by repaying all of these loans with substantial interest. It is recorded that Osei Tutu Kwame particularly rewarded 'Obuabasa ["breaker of arms", a nickname of Opoku Frɛfrɛ, and of subsequent occupants of the *Gyaasewa* stool], to whom he gave very much money which enabled him to exhibit himself (*yi ne ho adi*) to the public as a wealthy man'.[113] The chronology of the tradition is marginally in error; Opoku Frɛfrɛ displayed his wealth in 1817 not 1819. But it is the overall sense of the tradition that is significant, illustrating as it does the factors of lending and repayment, and of reciprocity and reward, in the circulation and accumulation of wealth.

By far the most salient and explicit feature of this system was what I have termed elsewhere a flourishing market in subjects and in the land needed to support them.[114] The use of the term market in this context requires some qualifying definition. It is not intended to imply a commoditization of subjects and land within the framework of a capitalist agriculture. In precolonial Asante, land and labour were not marketable as strictly economic resources within this or any other such rigorous structure of commodity valuation. Thus, anything generally approximating to capitalist agriculture only emerged in Asante with the widespread monetization of land and labour as resources that derived from the insertion of the cocoa-based cash crop economy in the colonial era.[115]

The term market is used here because, as we have observed, the alienation of subjects and land within an exchange nexus based on gold was a principal feature of the precolonial political economy. But the purely economic worth and desirability of these resources, far from being defined by any stringent commodity valuation, were subordinated to a range of socio-political and ideological determinants. The linked attributes of the *sikani* (man of wealth) and the *okanniba* (the good citizen), which were expressed at their highest level in the person of the *ɔbirɛmpɔn*, were understood within a frame of reference that was sociological rather than economic. The possession of subjects and land validated and represented influence, attainment, status and rank. Some indication of the primary emphases and conditional priorities that prevailed within the precolonial market was furnished by the *Akyeamehene* and *Domakwaehene* Kwasi Apea Nuama. He observed,

In the olden days I might have a child and make him an Asafohene [a captain of an *asafo* or company of *nkoa*] controlling slaves whom I would obtain and give him. I might see the entire population of a village being tendered for sale and I might buy them and put them under the Asafohene whom I had created. Such an Asafohene would be my Gyasi [*gyaasefoɔ* or retainers]... It was quite common for them [indebted office holders] to sell their lands, people, and entire villages, and even their rank and become subordinate to the purchaser.[116]

The state arbitrated access to procedures and mechanisms whereby wealthy and influential office holders were able to purchase subjects and land, both around Kumase and beyond, from impecunious fellow office holders, from indebted lineage segments, and from families and individuals in straitened circumstances. We have already taken note of the way in which the endemic shortage of gold and high interest rates in conjunction with state policy exacerbated this situation. Furthermore, powerful office holders were often allocated subjects and land as favoured members of the state apparatus following the sequestration of these items, for whatever reason, by the state's legal machinery. There is much evidence to suggest that seizures of this sort reached a volumetric peak in the reign of the *Asantehene* Kwaku Dua Panin (1834–67).[117]

It is certainly the case that subjects and land acquired in these ways were utilized in the intensification of agriculture around Kumase. But such resources were not commoditized. Labour requirements afforded virtually no distinction in inputs between slave and free cultivators, and the system of intensive production was a form of *métayage* or share-cropping. Cultivators simply surrendered the bulk of their product to tenurial office holders, retaining a one third share (*abusa*) of the crop for consumption.[118] The objectives of this system were political and social. An export economy based on cash crops – or unrestricted commerce in any commodity – was perceived as being inimical to the established interests of office holders. Bowdich, who thought that marketable cotton would grow well in Asante, adverted to this point.

The chiefs are fed bountifully by the labours of their slaves, and sharing large sums of the revenue, (the fines their oppression has imposed on other governments), with incalculable fees for corruption or interference, refine upon the splendor of equipage even to satiety, and still possess a large surplus of income daily accumulating. Were they to encourage commerce, pomp, the idol of which they are most jealous, would soon cease to be their prerogative, because it would be attainable by others...[119]

If the workings of the market in the alienation of subjects and land created no impetus towards strict commodity value, then such transactions did have the effect of accelerating the rationalization of existing food production in favour of already wealthy office holders and their privileged urban retinues. And by liberating urban citizens from production into the pursuit of yet more wealth, the workings of the market contributed – by default at the very least – to the progressive and inexorable monetization of life in the Asante capital. Thus, we have noted the secondary status of food retailing in Kumase. We might add, quite unsurprisingly, that such food as was available for retail purchase was extremely expensive. Bowdich intuited something of the cause if not the underlying reason. 'The surprising exorbitance' of foodstuffs and other items in the Kumase market, he noted, 'is to be accounted for by the relative abundance of gold'; however, compared with these prices inflated by a relatively high level of urban monetization, the commodity valuation of 'labour and manufacture' was static and 'was moderately purchased'.[120]

Rights in subjects and land were quintessential features of the political and social dynamic, and consequently they were of the utmost importance. This is reflected in the sheer volume of the evidence concerning them.[121] Shifts in such rights over time – the movement of subjects and land onto and out of the market – functioned as a ready measure of an individual office holder's wealth, influence and access, and as a highly public indicator of upward and downward mobility. Such shifts mirrored and described major changes in the balance of power within the political superstructure. They also served to define a crucial interface between the state and the social order. The state's interventionist regulation of rights in subjects and land was ubiquitous, and it touched upon and affected the lives of kin groups, families and individuals.

The operation of this market in and over time, and in relation to the system it served, is overwhelming in its historical detail.[122] Succinct illustration and analysis are perhaps best provided by starting with the life, career and achievements of a single ɔbirɛmpɔn, and by then looking at the issues and implications that arise from this within a longer temporal context and a broader explanatory framework. The individual case used here as a basis of discussion is that of the ɔbirɛmpɔn Kyidomhene and Ankaasehene Yamoa Ponko (c. 1730–85).[123] As we have noted, Yamoa Ponko's life and career were coincident with the first stages of that period in which the system we have described reached the height of its articulation.

State power exemplified I: the system ascendant, c. 1700–1840

After 1701, when Denkyira was supplanted by Asante as the principal Akan power, many of its inhabitants migrated northwards to seek the protection and patronage of the victorious Asantehene Osei Tutu.[124] Among these was Yamoa Ponko's father, Gyesi Kuo. Either Osei Tutu or his successor the Asantehene Opoku Ware eventually rewarded Gyesi Kuo's loyalty by advancing him to occupancy of the minor stool of Kra Amponsem in the village of Ankaase; this office belonged to the Kyidom fekuo or division, then under the headship of the Kumase Hiahene. About 1730, Yamoa Ponko was born as Yaw Amoa, probably in Ankaase. Nothing is known about his mother, but he did have two paternal brothers

– Yamoa Asuman and Nti Kusi. We have already noted how, as a young man, Yaw Amoa began to accumulate wealth in the northern trade. His sobriquet *ponko* (horse) marked his commercial success, for the title was current as a praise name among his Gonja trading partners.

In the 1760s, Yamoa Ponko was able to make his earliest known purchases of land and subjects from an indebted office holder. Following the Asante conquest of Takyiman in 1722–3, a number of defeated refugees from there took an oath of allegiance to the *Asantehene* Opoku Ware.[125] He gave one such group as *nkoa* to the *Ahenkurohene*. These subjects incurred a debt of 60 *mperedwan* (by conventional equivalence, £480 sterling), for which the *Ahenkurohene* was held responsible.[126] He was unable to pay. With the *Asantehene's* approval, Yamoa Ponko purchased the defaulting *nkoa* from the *Ahenkurohene* for 40 *mperedwan* (£320); simultaneously, he bought a piece of land at Anyinasu from the same vendor for 30 *mperedwan* (£240).

In the customary manner prescribed for the ambitious accumulator, Yamoa Ponko put his acquisitions to work in furthering his interests. He donated the Anyinasu land to Gyesi Kuo's stool at Ankaase, thereby asserting his own claims to his father's office by enriching it; his paternal brother Yamoa Asuman was given responsibility for the land with the rank of *Asafohene* under the *Ankaasehene*. By reclassifying title to the land from the status of self-acquired, individually held asset to that of stool property, this transfer insured Anyinasu against any possible demands that might be made through the personal tax categories of *ayibuadeε* or *awunnyadeε*. Yamoa Ponko then asked the Ankaase stool for the use by lease of the northern part of the Anyinasu land he had given to it. There he settled the Ahenkuro *nkoa* as traders in the new village of Sekyedumase. This settlement was situated on the road that led north from Kumase to the commercial entrepôts of central Gonja, and it was ideally located for the further advancement of Yamoa Ponko's trading interests.[127]

Yamoa Ponko was duly promoted to occupancy of the *Kra Amponsem* stool of Ankaase, but soon thereafter a much larger opportunity for advancement presented itself. Shortly after his accession in 1764, the *Asantehene* Osei Kwadwo exercised a prerogative of his office in imposing *apeatoɔ*, a special levy on office holders designed to raise revenue for military purposes.[128] The Kumase *Hiahene*, the head of the *Kyidom fekuo* to which Yamoa Ponko's office belonged, was assessed for *apeatoɔ* in the sum of 30 *mperedwan* (£240). He was unable to pay. With the approval of the *Asantehene*, Yamoa Ponko settled the debt by purchasing from the *Hiahene* – in the manner described above by Kwasi Apea Nuama – the headship of the *Kyidom fekuo* and the rank and title of *Kyidomhene*.

Now *Kyidomhene* and *Ankaasehene*, Yamoa Ponko maintained influence and access under the *Asantehene* Osei Kwame (1777–1803); on the instructions of the *Asantehene* Osei Kwadwo, Yamoa Ponko had previously served as guardian to Osei Kwame during three years of the latter's infancy. Thus, in the closing stages of his life, Yamoa Ponko was able to make further acquisitions. He was awarded, for example, *nkoa* from the *awunnyadeɛ* levied on the estate of the *sikani* Akwasiwaa of Domeabra. And he was able to advance one of his own sons to the rank of *Asafohene* to the *Ankaasehene* with a following of one hundred subjects.[129]

It was most probably very shortly prior to his death in or about 1785 that Yamoa Ponko made a public display of his wealth, and was awarded the *mena* and the title of *ɔbirɛmpɔn*. The occasion is very well remembered in oral tradition, for after Yamoa Ponko had 'exhibited all the beautiful things he had made, and declared himself a wealthy man', he made an extremely unusual and probably unprecedented request.[130] He asked, contrary to established custom, that the *Asantehene* Osei Kwame attend and preside over his funeral custom in person. It was presumably in acknowledgement of Yamoa Ponko's especially outstanding achievement in the accumulation of wealth – and perhaps too because of attachment or personal sentiment – that Osei Kwame agreed to this request. Equally, this signal mark of recognition may have been prompted by the fact that Yamoa Ponko was a pioneer in that his method of accumulation – trade rather than generalship – ran counter to the prevailing orthodoxy of the eighteenth century. In due course and for whatever reason, Osei Kwame did indeed preside over Yamoa Ponko's extravagant funeral custom.

In receiving the *mena* and in having the *Asantehene* as his principal mourner, Yamoa Ponko in effect had asserted his achievement and status, at the highest and most public level, not once but twice. This created a new measure of attainment and recognition for the very wealthiest and most ambitious individuals to aspire to. Yamoa Ponko's name has survived as a byword for the accumulation of wealth. It was one, moreover, that Asante traditions have utilized ever since to underscore the norms and values attaching to the concept of legitimate achievement in the accumulation of wealth.

Thus, in 1935, in a case (*Ankaasehene* vs. *Mampon Gyamasehene*) *in re* the issue of the proper allegiance of *nkoa* at Asekyerewa, the Kumase *Akwamuhene* gave it as his opinion that

Yamoa Ponko who was occupying the Ankasi stool was one of the rich Chiefs in Ashanti in those days, and he bought the allegiance of many subjects to make that stool great. I am therefore inclined to agree with Ankasi that the allegiance of these people were bought by the Ankasi stool. In the olden days it was the common practice for poor Chiefs to sell the allegiance of some of their royals to enrich their Stools, and this may be a similar case.[131]

Yamoa Ponko's drum refrain – *kyerɛkyerɛ me wo bɔtɔm, mehwɛm, mehwɛm* ('Show me your coffers, I am looking in, I am looking in') – is still well known. Its sense encapsulates the ethic of competitive accumulation among the *abirɛmpɔn*, for it is said that Yamoa Ponko used to have this refrain played to invite anyone who considered themselves to be as rich as he was to show him their assets in gold.[132] The commonest epithet used of him in modern Asante is that he was *ɔpɛpɛɛfo* – that is given to avarice, but in the admirable sense of being careful in the husbanding and maximizing of his wealth.[133]

As early as the reign of the *Asantehene* Osei Yaw Akoto (1823–34) the *Akuroponhene* Kwadwo Gyamfi, himself an office holder under the *Kyidomhene*, consciously tried to emulate Yamoa Ponko. He buried pots allegedly containing his entire fortune in gold dust. He showed his *nkoa* these sealed pots. He then informed the *Asantehene* that he wished him to preside over his funeral, and so devout was this desire that in return for its fulfilment he had instructed his subjects to hand over the pots containing all of his wealth to Osei Yaw Akoto. Kwadwo Gyamfi died, and Osei Yaw Akoto attended his funeral custom. The pots were opened, but they were found to contain only charcoal and brass filings (*dutu*). Kwadwo Gyamfi's corpse was reportedly disinterred, put on trial, and posthumously found guilty of the capital crimes of trafficking in false gold and of lying to the *Asantehene*. Sentence was duly passed, and the corpse was solemnly beheaded. These events gave rise to a maxim concerning the premium placed on legitimate achievement: *se aturuwhyeɛ sua agyɛnkuku su a ne tiri pa* ('If the thrush [Kwadwo Gyamfi] tries to imitate the cry of the cuckoo [Yamoa Ponko], its head splits').[134]

One feature of the precedent set by Yamoa Ponko – the asking of a special boon from the *Asantehene* on the occasion of the awarding of the *mena* – is known to have been repeated in November 1817, when the *Gyaasewahene* Opoku Frɛfrɛ was raised to *ɔbirɛmpɔn* status. In the course of the ceremony, Opoku Frɛfrɛ was seen to be weeping. Pressed to explain his distress, he stated that his only sister, Amankwaa Yaa, had borne only three female children. Thus, he had no close male kin of matrilineal descent who might hope to emulate his achievement in the accumulation of wealth, and perhaps some day follow him in the office of *Gyaasewahene*. Although individual appointments to the Gyaasewa stool were (and remained) in the gift of the *Asantehene*, Opoku Frɛfrɛ then requested that his own sons and grandsons (*mmamma*) be granted the privilege of corporate rights of preferential access to it. This represented a major departure from established custom. But the *Asantehene* Osei Tutu Kwame granted Opoku Frɛfrɛ's request in recognition of his personal achievement and of the wealth he had bestowed on the Gyaasewa stool, and in commemoration of the personal ties of sentiment that existed between the two of them.[135] The office of *Mmammahene* to the *Gyaasewahene* was then created and vested in Opoku Frɛfrɛ's male descendants. In gratitude, Opoku Frɛfrɛ paid an *aseda* (an offering of thanks) of 30 *mperedwan* (£240) to Osei Tutu Kwame.[136]

It was Opoku Frɛfrɛ – then a *fotosanaani* under the *Fotosanfoɔhene* – who was ordered by the *Asantehene* Osei Kwame to evaluate Yamoa Ponko's estate, and to assess it for death duties and inheritance taxes. The *nkoa* settled at Sekyedumase were taken as *awunnyadeɛ*, and transferred as subjects to the Kumase *Nsumaŋkwaahene* in the *Gyaase fekuo*.[137] One hundred of Yamoa Ponko's other *nkoa* were impounded in the same way, and assigned to the newly created office of *Atipinhene* in the *Ankobea fekuo*; at the same time, one of Yamoa Ponko's sons was appointed *ɔkyeame* or counsellor to the Atipin stool. The *nkoa* who had themselves been acquired from the *awunnyadeɛ* imposed on the estate of Akwasiwaa of Domeabra were retained by the Kyidom stool. However, a number of Kyidom subjects at Mpobi were taken and assigned to serve in the royal *afenasoafoɔ* (swordbearers).[138]

The Anyinasu land was not subject to *awunnyadeɛ*, for it had been gifted outright to the Ankaase stool and remained its property. Thus, although the Sekyedumase *nkoa* were taken as *awunnyadeɛ*, the village itself – built on part of the Anyinasu donation – reverted to Ankaase following the lapse of Yamoa Ponko's personal lease of user rights in the land. Unlike *awunnyadeɛ*, which was a mandatory tax because it involved gold, *ayibuadeɛ* seems to have been a more discretionary imposition. In Yamoa Ponko's case, there is no evidence as to whether or not his personal belongings in land and houses were subject to *ayibuadeɛ* before his designated heirs assumed title. Perhaps, as with the Anyinasu land, he had taken the precaution before his death of transferring ownership rights in his immovable property to his legatees.

Yamoa Ponko was an *ɔbirɛmpɔn* and an extremely wealthy trader. He must have possessed a substantial estate in gold dust. Unfortunately, no accounting of this part of his legacy has come to light. However, some understanding of the scale of magnitude involved may be gleaned from relevant comparisons. The *ɔkyeame* Boakye Yam is known to have amassed considerable wealth during the reign of the *Asantehene* Osei Kwadwo (1764–77) and thereafter. When he died about 1814 his estate included, so Bowdich was told, 'five jars (said to hold about four gallons each) and two flasks' of gold dust.[139] The 'flasks' were presumably the standard containers known as *apem brontɔa* ('bottles of one thousand *mperedwan*'), which were imported one-gallon wine flagons. In all, then, Boakye Yam left an estimated estate of 22 gallons of gold dust. Bowdich's unit of measure was the Queen Anne gallon, which was not replaced by the

Imperial gallon until 1824. Since the density of pure gold dust is in excess of 19 grams per cc, the Queen Anne gallon packed at a less than critical density of 18 grams per cc would comfortably accommodate the equivalent of 1,000 *mperedwan* – 1 *peredwan* being an Asante weight of 2.25 troy ounces. If we assume the maximum case (that the jars and flasks were full, and that their contents were unadulterated), then Boakye Yam's estate in gold dust comprised some 22,000 *mperedwan*. This converts to £176,000 sterling at the conventional nineteenth-century rate of equivalence of £8 to 1 *peredwan*.[140]

In 1817, when the acting *Anantahene* Apea Nyanyo was disgraced for military and other derelictions, Bowdich recorded that 'three jars [of gold dust] were seized' by the state.[141] The implication is that this hoard represented a maximum amount of 12 gallons of gold dust or 12,000 *mperedwan*, with a sterling equivalent of £96,000. Let us set these estimates against one further figure. The display of wealth by a candidate *ɔbirɛmpɔn* involved the conversion of some proportion of his gold into artefacts. In 1817, as we have noted, Hutchison assessed Opoku Frɛfrɛ's 'varieties' or golden ornaments for display as weighing in excess of 1,600 ounces. That is, some 710 *mperedwan*, or £5,680. This was only a small fraction of Opoku Frɛfrɛ's accumulated wealth. Ornaments were displayed as a central focus for the unworked gold that surrounded them, and the number created for a single occasion was presumably subject to the technical constraints on mass production.[142]

The problem of drawing any very precise conclusions from these figures is compounded by additional considerations. First, neither Boakye Yam nor Apea Nyanyo was awarded the *mena*, or indeed ever applied for it. Apea Nyanyo's career was aborted, and Boakye Yam had a specific motive for not exposing his wealth to public scrutiny; it is known that he practised tax evasion in favour of his son and successor, the *ɔkyeame* Oti Panin.[143] Second, some wealthy office holders had reasons other than Boakye Yam's for sacrificing keen ambition and public acclamation to prudent silence. We should recall that the onus of applying to become an *ɔbirɛmpɔn* rested on the individual concerned. Accumulated wealth was the indispensable qualification. But there was no fixed scale. An aspirant had to gauge this indeterminacy in conjunction with other potentially treacherous pitfalls. Was his current political stock ascendant? Was he free from all entangling obligations and expensive claims? Above all, was he secure from pending litigation or even arraignment on charges brought by the state? This last consideration was of the utmost importance, for crimes prosecuted by the state were often 'allowed to sleep for years', in order 'to impose the confidence on the accused that the principal witnesses are dead'.[144] There must always have been a number of wealthy office holders who, for a host of reasons and however reluctantly, would not or could not and did not apply for the *mena*. Thus, it is extremely difficult to determine whether individuals such as Boakye Yam or Apea Nyanyo, irrespective of all other contingencies, actually possessed the purely financial credentials sufficient to support the status of an *ɔbirɛmpɔn*.

Whatever the Asante understanding of the arithmetic of great wealth, it will be apparent that the figures mentioned represent fairly substantial sums of money even by the standards of contemporary early nineteenth-century Europeans.[145] Nor are these figures unacceptable exaggerations. Many accounts assert that at the death of the *Asantehene* Kwaku Dua Panin in 1867, the *adaka kɛsɛɛ* or great chest that contained the state's disposable currency reserves was full. It has been calculated from its known dimensions that when full the *adaka kɛsɛɛ* held in excess of 400,000 ounces of gold dust, or nearly 180,000 *mperedwan*, with a sterling value of approximately £1,440,000.[146]

Let us return to Yamoa Ponko. Whatever the actual value of his estate in gold dust, it was subjected to *awunnyadeɛ* before the state restored a discretionary residue to his brother and principal heir, the *Kyidomhene* and *Ankaasehene* Nti Kusi. There was no fixed scale of death duties, but the state customarily took the overwhelming bulk of the gold dust in any estate. This practice reinforced and promoted the idea that wealth, particularly in gold, resided in individual achievement. It also explains why even the immediate successors of very wealthy office holders were sometimes embarrassed by relatively modest financial demands. Accumulation was also conditioned by changing circumstances, as may be briefly seen from the ensuing history of the office of the *Kyidomhene* and *Ankaasehene*.

Yamoa Ponko, as noted, was succeeded in office by his brother Nti Kusi, who died very shortly thereafter, and was succeeded in turn by Gyesi Tenten, a son of Yamoa Ponko.[147] Gyesi Tenten became blind, and in 1819 the *Asantehene* Osei Tutu Kwame replaced him as *Kyidomhene* with the aged *ɔheneba* Owusu Bannahene, a son of the *Asantehene* Osei Kwadwo. Prior to his elevation, the *ɔheneba* Owusu Bannahene had enjoyed a long and active career, but not one in which he had accumulated great wealth. He had held office as an *ɔkyeame* and as *Adomasahene*, and he had represented the Asante state in its diplomatic and commercial relations with the European authorities at Accra. In 1826, he was killed while commanding the *Kyidom fekuo* against the British at the battle of Katamanso.[148]

Among those taken as *awunnyadeɛ* from Yamoa Ponko's estate was one of his widows. This woman was an *ɔdehyeɛ* (pl. *adehyeɛ*: 'royal') of Gyakye, and she was married by the reigning *Asantehene* Osei Kwame. In the late 1780s this union produced a son, the *ɔheneba* Owusu Dome. As a young man, the *ɔheneba* Owusu Dome impressed the Danes in Accra as being *vredbarn* ('an angry young man'), and he was briefly exiled by the *Asantehene* Osei Tutu Kwame. Restored to favour, he became prominent in diplomatic negotiations with the British, and was apparently appointed as *Atene Akotenhene* within the *Ankobea fekuo* when that office was created about 1816. In 1826, he was taken prisoner by the British at Katamanso. In 1827, following his release, he was appointed *Kyidomhene* by the *Asantehene* Osei Yaw Akoto in succession to the *ɔheneba* Owusu Bannahene. In 1837, about fifty years after Yamoa Ponko's death, he died in office in Kumase.[149]

None of these four successors of Yamoa Ponko accumulated great wealth, and none was awarded the *mena*. Their 'wealth' resided in the fact that they held an important office, and administered the lands and *nkoa* attached to it. But resources such as these were quite distinct from the assets in gold that were the mark of the successful *individual* accumulator. Gold was mobile and fluid, desirable and convertible. It possessed immense social value, conferred the highest prestige, and bespoke purchasing power. It was the currency of the state's taxes and impositions, and it was internationally negotiable. High office, unsupported by personal resources in gold, was hardly an adequate insurance against recurrent liquidity problems.

Thus for example, in or about 1836 the *Kyidomhene ɔheneba* Owusu Dome incurred a relatively small court fine of 10 *mperedwan* (£80). He was unable to meet this modest obligation. In settlement, he sold to the *Asantehene* Kwaku Dua Panin the descendants of that group of *nkoa* that had been acquired by Yamoa Ponko from the estate of Akwasiwaa of Domeabra. In turn, the *Asantehene* awarded these subjects to the future *ɔbirɛmpɔn* and *Manwerehene* Kwasi Brantuo. And in the 1840s, during the incumbency of the *Kyidomhene ɔheneba* Owusu Dome Kuma, Kwasi Brantuo purchased another group of Kyidom *nkoa* and settled them at Ahodwo.[150]

State power exemplified II: the system undermined, *c.* 1840–1900

In ways and for reasons that are well understood – and that are discussed below when and where they are relevant to the argument – the *Asantehene* Kwaku Dua Panin (1834–67) was more interventionist and more authoritarian than his predecessors. During his long reign, the volume of transactions in the market in subjects and land reached an apex. But the same period also witnessed stirrings of dissent, and the hesitant beginnings of an interrogation of the system's legitimacy. Consensus over the historic understanding of the purposes of accumulation, and of the relationship of such purposes to received ideas of advancement and prestige, was disfigured and undermined by a perceptible increase in illegitimate demands, in arrests and confiscations, and in clientage and favouritism.[151]

Thus, the career of the ɔbirɛmpɔn Manwerehene Kwasi Brantuo – by common consent one of the wealthiest individuals in Asante history – was qualitatively different from that of any of his predecessors who had received the mena. Unlike the early eighteenth-century abirɛmpɔn who had forged and enlarged the polity, he never commanded an army; unlike the ɔbirɛmpɔn Opoku Frɛfrɛ, he did not have a long, varied and distinguished career in all of the major areas of state service; and unlike the ɔbirɛmpɔn Yamoa Ponko, his wealth was not grounded in youthful trading ventures. As we have seen in the case of Yamoa Ponko and Opoku Frɛfrɛ, the mena was customarily applied for and awarded late in life, as the formal, public seal of approval on a life spent in the service of state and society. But Kwasi Brantuo was raised to ɔbirɛmpɔn status in 1844, more than two decades prior to his death in 1865. And it was only in or around 1844 – perhaps concurrently with the bestowal of the mena – that Kwasi Brantuo was appointed Manwerehene as head of the new Manwere fekuo, the tenth and last created of the major Kumase office groups. This was his first (and last) office at the highest level, for until then he had held a household post with fiscal responsibilities within the ahoprafoɔ group.[152]

Kwasi Brantuo is still commemorated as Nana Brantuo a otuo sika peɛ, to signify a man of very great wealth, and traditions attest to his riches in gold. His career is known in some detail, and there can be little doubt that his capacity to accumulate wealth and his political advancement were all but totally dependent on the personal patronage of the Asantehene Kwaku Dua Panin. This relationship is summarized in the gloss that is placed on Kwasi Brantuo's horn call: Akyampon Kwasi ɛi, yɛsere wɔ twɛtwɛ, yɛsere wɔ twɛ twɛtwɛtwɛ ('Akyampon Kwasi, you are the subject of mockery, [are] the subject of mockery'; i.e. 'Once I was mocked because I was poor, but [not] now that I am wallowing in wealth').[153] It is argued that the sedulous advancement of Kwasi Brantuo by Kwaku Dua Panin was a surrogate act of assertion by the Asantehene against those who had mocked his own youthful self and denigrated his own dynastic status and position.[154] More bluntly, it is stated that Kwaku Dua Panin fostered the promotion and influence of his dependant Kwasi Brantuo because 'there were many who did not like the Asantehene at all'.[155] Certainly, as a purchaser of land and nkoa from indebted office holders, and as a favoured recipient of commissions from the collection of state fines and fees, Kwasi Brantuo – the erstwhile mmagyegyeni – was afforded seemingly unprecedented access as the most favoured personal client of Kwaku Dua Panin.

Upon his accession as Asantehene in 1834, Kwaku Dua Panin made a grant to Kwasi Brantuo of land and nkoa at Heman; it was here that

Kwaku Dua Panin's *sika mena* was kept, under the guardianship of Kwasi Brantuo.[156] Outright gifts followed, as has already been noted in the case of the *nkoa* surrendered by the Kyidom stool. In the 1840s the *Tafohene* Buadu Kwadwo was fined in the considerable sum of *mperedwan ɔha aduasa* (i.e. 120 × £8 or £960). Kwasi Brantuo was sent to collect this fine. But the amount raised by Buadu Kwadwo was short by *mperedwan aduasa* (£240). The *Asantehene* himself paid the balance outstanding, taking in settlement the Tafo *nkoa* at Drobonso, and gifting them to the recently appointed *Manwerehene*.[157] In the late 1850s, a number of *nkoa* at Apaaso – the property of the disgraced royal Osei Kwadwo – were impounded by Kwaku Dua Panin and transferred as subjects to Kwasi Brantuo.[158]

The *Asantehene's* favour was also evident in court proceedings. Kwasi Brantuo was both an habitual and a favoured petitioner. Thus, in an oath case with the aforementioned Osei Kwadwo concerning disputed authority over *nkoa* at Toase, judgement was given in favour of Kwasi Brantuo; the Toase *nkoa* were transferred to Heman, one of them being given by the *Manwerehene* to the *Asantehene* as a 'thank offering' (*aseda*).[159] Underpinning all of this preferment was the fact that Kwasi Brantuo was widely employed by Kwaku Dua Panin as a fiscal agent, a role from which numerous fees accrued. Entirely typical of such transactions was the occasion in the late 1850s when Kwasi Brantuo presided over the lucrative transfer of Patriensa from the heirs of the *Ntaherahene* Oduro Koko Bereko to the ŋkwaŋtanaŋ stool.[160] Kwasi Brantuo was also given preferential opportunities for purchase, and he invested Kwaku Dua Panin's gifts and benefices in land and subjects. His purchase and settlement of Kyidom *nkoa* at Ahodwo have been noted. In the 1850s he purchased some Tafo *nkoa* in Kwawu and settled them at Drobonso; and he paid 10 *mperedwan* on behalf of Nyameani and Sobonkuo, taking in settlement the *nkoa* of the Nkonson stools of Deduaku.[161] In all of his transactions Kwasi Brantuo fulfilled the imperative of the maxim *wonni sika a, anka wɔfre no nhwea kwa* ('If gold was not made use of, then one would call it sand').[162]

The degree of patronage enjoyed by Kwasi Brantuo may be instructively contrasted with the case of the Manso Nkwanta *sikani* Kwasi Gyani. In 1862, Kwasi Gyani fled into exile in the British Gold Coast Protectorate, after having been accused of failing to surrender a quantity of gold nuggets to the state. His reasons for seeking asylum were stated to and recorded by the British at Cape Coast: 'he is a man of property [*sikani*], and declares that the King [Kwaku Dua Panin] desires only to entrap him, take his head, and afterwards possession of his property'.[163] That illicit seizures of this sort breached the compact that governed wealth and its disposition is clearly illustrated by the outcome of an analogous case from an earlier period. Bowdich reported the following intervention made by the *ɔkyeame* Asante

Agyei – a concise formulation of the agreed rules and objectives of accumulation – when it appeared that the *Asantehene* Osei Tutu Kwame was contemplating an illegitimate act of confiscation.

The King [Osei Tutu Kwame] confessing a prejudice against a wealthy captain, his linguists [*akyeame*], always inclined to support him, said, 'If you wish to take his stool from him, we will make the palaver'; but Agay [the *ɔkyeame* Asante Agyei] sprung up, exclaiming 'No, King! that is not good; that man never did you any wrong, you know all the gold of your subjects is yours at their death [i.e. through *awunnyadeɛ*], but if you get all now, strangers will go away and say, only the King has gold, and that will not be good, but let them say the King has gold, all his captains have gold, and all his people have gold, then your country will look handsome, and the bush people fear you.'[164]

The precedent continuity and coherence of Asante history was decisively ruptured in the 1880s, but signs of accelerated movement towards that point can be dated from the authoritarian reign of the *Asantehene* Kwaku Dua Panin, and more particularly from his death in 1867. External factors unquestionably played a significant role. The burning of Kumase in the Anglo-Asante war of 1873–4 was not only a profound psychic shock, but also the prelude to increasing British pressure; this took the form of an insistent if ill-thought-out meddling in Asante affairs, and it had the effect of exacerbating political divisions and conflicts.[165] At the same time, Asante – hitherto, as we shall see presently, a 'closed' society – was indiscriminately exposed to novel ideas and influences. There are echoes here of the end of the *Tokugawa bakufu* in Japan in 1868, and the beginnings of the *Meiji* era.[166] But in the case of Asante, the problems of a weakened and uncertain central authority were not resolved by a revolution from above. Instead, Asante's rulers pursued a course in which indecisiveness and aborted initiatives gave way to increasingly desperate, arbitrary and punitive behaviour, and ended in a cynical struggle for power and a murderous civil war.[167]

The consensus that framed the historic meaning of accumulation, wealth and the place of the *ɔbirɛmpɔn* was dissolved in the reigns of the *Asantehenes* Kofi Kakari (1867–74) and Mensa Bonsu (1874–83). Both practised and in some ways enlarged the arbitrary tendencies that had existed under Kwaku Dua Panin, but neither possessed that ruler's secure tenurial authority or presided as he had done over a stable and confident society. It is significant that, following the 'generation' of Kwasi Brantuo and Kwaku Dua Panin, there is no very clear evidence of any individual making a public exhibition of his accumulated wealth in order to have the *mena* conferred upon him.[168]

Our best cursory guide to what transpired is the Asante oral sources themselves. Kofi Kakari, it is severally stated, was perennially short of gold, and notoriously spendthrift. He is traditionally given the character of having been *akyɛmpɔ* (a beneficent distributor of gold and largess, with connotations of buying popularity as well as of being philanthropic); he is also described as having been ɔsape (spendthrift, with connotations of duplicity as well as of prodigality). From his palanquin, he freely scattered packets among the Kumase crowd, each one containing a small measure (suru) of gold dust. It is said that he spent his early life in comparative poverty, and that he wept when he saw the amount of gold that had been bequeathed to him as Asantehene by his predecessor. Certainly, he is known to have disbursed much of this inherited wealth – which was state and not personal property – to his individual favourites and concubines. It is said that he justified his behaviour in redistributive terms: 'There is this much gold', he is said to have observed on examining the state treasury, 'while people suffer amidst hunger and poverty.' Whatever the (somewhat unlikely) truth of this, it is the case that his profligacy was compounded by a marked insensitivity to historic norms and practices. Kofi Kakari freely adjusted legal procedures to generate revenue; he tried to shift the entire cost of the Fante campaign of 1872–3 onto the generals and the soldiery; he appointed favourite children to office; and he flagrantly advanced the careers of his personal household servants, without any reference to seniority or to any proven capacity to accumulate wealth, and without the personal authority and will necessary to impose even reluctant acceptance of his wishes. His many fiscal derelictions were among the charges preferred against him when he was removed from office in 1874.[169]

Arguably, Kofi Kakari's illicit practices were expedients prompted by financial incompetence and habitual irresponsibility. No such case can be made for his brother and successor, the Asantehene Mensa Bonsu. Chronically short of revenue, and personally avaricious (for women as well as gold), Mensa Bonsu carried punitive exactions to new and insupportable levels. In mitigation, it must be said that in the early part of his reign Mensa Bonsu's misdirected behaviour was at least partially dictated by the desire to reverse the declining authority of the state. But the situation proved intransigent, and Mensa Bonsu resorted to extreme measures to preserve his personal power. These are well documented, and they were a major contributory cause of his destoolment in 1883.[170]

The popular view of Mensa Bonsu subscribed to by contemporary Asante witnesses emphasized the shortcomings of his character and the corruption of his personal nature.

Anini [Mensa] Bonsu was very mean. He had an unpleasant and frightening disposition. He was not given to mirth. He was huge. He was wicked. He delighted in killing people. He had people prepared for execution while [he was] eating, and as soon as he had finished, the executioners took the culprit away to be killed before Mensa Bonsu went off for his sleep.
An illustration of his wickedness is his attempt to disprove the Asante saying: 'It

takes one day to die, and therefore it is nothing to be apprehensive about'. Bonsu had a man tortured by pushing a knife through his mouth [sɛpɔ]; then the man was put in a room for about three or four days. He started to decay before Bonsu had him executed. People who roamed about at night were often executed. He was so greedy for money that he heavily fined those whose lives he had spared for breaching the ntamkɛsɛɛ [the great oath]; this bankrupted their families. He had innumerable wives, so was unable to pay adequate attention to many of them. Because of this, six of the youths who were in charge of these wives had affairs with some of them. This matter was quickly exposed. The women and the young men involved were murdered so brutally that it caused much consternation throughout the nation.[171]

Mensa Bonsu died in British captivity at Praso in 1896. In 1911, his corpse was disinterred and brought to Kumase for appropriate obsequies and burial. On the occasion of this funeral, the native Twi speaker N. Asare of the Basel Mission recorded opinion then current in Kumase concerning Mensa Bonsu's reputation as *Asantehene*. His account is an indictment, and a telling summary of the widespread belief that Mensa Bonsu had contributed to the collapse of historic norms by subverting them.

This King [Mensa Bonsu] was the most cruel amongst all the Asante sovereigns, he beheaded plenty of people in his time. He was not only cruel, but very wicked and avaricious. He killed many noble men privately because he liked to own their fine looking wives and personal effects. When he saw or heard of a man who was well off in life, he cunningly created false charges upon him, then sent his executioners to kill him by night in order to possess his property... He was a great miser and proud too... The chiefs of Kumase did not mingle themselves much in the funeral as it was expected. The chiefs have still ill feelings against the King because some of them suffered much in his reigning time... Those who saw the golden time of Asante Kingdom mourned greatly and [were] very much cast down.[172]

The testimony of participants indicates that the internecine violence and chaotic disorder of the civil war period (1883–8) were of a severity and duration such as to produce societal incoherence and personal anomie.[173] This catastrophic situation starkly illuminated the ethical and ideological as well as the material bankruptcy of the Kumase political elite, and it all but liquidated the bases of non-Kumase subscription to that elite's historic claims to authority. In the course of the civil war(s) Kumase squandered its coercive power. More gravely, it forfeited its capacity to elicit support and to mediate consensus. At one obvious level of reading, the civil war(s) appeared to be little more than a seemingly endless cycle of destructive struggles between self-interested Kumase dynasts and cynical political factions. In consequence, there emerged two reactions against the corrupt abuse of the system that had regulated and rewarded the accumulation of wealth throughout much of the eighteenth and nineteenth centuries.

The first of these reactions was formulated by Asante refugees resident in the British Gold Coast Colony. In echo of Kwasi Gyani, such men complained of illicit confiscations, of state violence, and of a notable deterioration in the 1880s of general conditions making for the security of life and property. Taking as their model the individual's rights of disposition over wealth in English law, and the low level of taxation apparent in *laissez-faire* capitalism as practised in the Gold Coast Colony, they totally repudiated the fiscal and political authority of the Asante state. In statements addressed to the Governor of the Gold Coast in 1894, they excoriated the *Asantehene* Agyeman Prempe as 'robber King', and all of his predecessors as 'the late thief Kings'; highly significantly, in rejecting the practice of *awunnyadeɛ*, and the very concept of the *ɔbirɛmpɔn* to which it was linked, they called for the abolition of the *mena*, characterizing elephant tails as 'useless and good for nothing'.[174] The ideological descendants of these dissident individuals were the *akonkofoɔ* – a term defying exact translation, but carrying implications of wealth, of capitalist individualism, and of 'modernity' – and the other businessmen of the early colonial era.[175]

The second of these reactions was internal to Asante. It must be seen as distinct from the first in origin and in personnel, although there are clear congruities in the general objectives pursued by both groups. By 1888, Kumase supporters of the two rival candidates with claims to be *Asantehene* – Yaw Twereboanna and Agyeman Prempe, the son of the *Asantehemaa* Yaa Kyaa – had exhausted their resources in years of inconclusive conflict. In that year, Yaw Twereboanna's provincial supporters, the *Mamponhene* and *Kokofuhene*, finally broke the deadlock and gained an apparently decisive advantage. In June 1888, the *Asantehemaa* Yaa Kyaa convened a meeting in Kumase in a last-ditch attempt to rally support to Agyeman Prempe's cause.

In the course of that assembly, provincial office holders led by the *Edwesohene* Kwasi Afrane Kɛsɛɛ, together with the rump of Agyeman Prempe's near-bankrupt Kumase faction, demanded as the price of their military support that Yaa Kyaa take a solemn oath that 'any property that had been seized by Prempeh's [Agyeman Prempe's] predecessors should revert to the original owners'.[176] Yaa Kyaa tried to prevaricate, but she was in no position to dictate terms, and she eventually swore as required. By the end of July, Agyeman Prempe's reinvigorated cause had triumphed, and Yaw Twereboanna and thousands of his supporters were refugees in the Gold Coast Colony.[177] The *Edwesohene* now took the lead in forcing the implementation of Yaa Kyaa's oath. Land and *nkoa* were transferred wholesale from the Kumase office holders to provincial authority; and in the anarchy of the moment, Kumase office holders themselves pressed claims and counter-claims against each other.[178]

An entirely typical transaction involved the Anyinasu land that had been acquired from the *Ahenkurohene* by Yamoa Ponko. Edweso now pressed a claim to Anyinasu, and to all of the *nkoa* living on it of *Asona* lineage descent.[179] The incumbent *Kyidomhene ɔheneba* Kofi Boakye Adwene, a son of the *Asantehene* Kwaku Dua Panin, had opposed Agyeman Prempe and was now, at best, a lukewarm supporter of the winning side. In 1888, the most influential of Yamoa Ponko's direct descendants was Kwame Boaten, a great-grandson on his mother's side, and an experienced negotiator; he was to succeed to the Kyidom stool in 1890, on the death or abdication of the *ɔheneba* Kofi Boakye Adwene. Neither the *ɔheneba* Kofi Boakye Adwene nor Kwame Boaten was in a position to resist the Edweso demand, although there is some evidence to suggest that the *Kyidomhene* did try to retain the land while surrendering the *Asona nkoa*. This ploy failed, and Yaa Kyaa sanctioned the transfer of both land and subjects to the *Edwesohene* Kwasi Afrane Kɛsɛɛ.[180]

In 1889 the beneficiaries of redistribution demanded a further oath in confirmation of the irreversibility of the new arrangements. The oath was administered at *Ahyiamu* ('a place of meeting'), a piece of land near Edweso. The contracting parties were represented by Kwasi Deekye, a nephew of Kwasi Afrane Kɛsɛɛ, and Agyeman Badu, the younger brother of Agyeman Prempe. Kwasi Deekye swore perpetual loyalty to the *Asantehene* on behalf of the assembled office holders. Agyeman Badu reciprocated by solemnly 'drinking the gods', 'to the effect that no one would alter or change or interfere with the properties which had been restored to the fighters'.[181] Evidently – and logically – the *Ahyiamu* oath also encompassed the abolition of *awunnyadeɛ* and *ayibuadeɛ*. In 1930, a group of *akonkofoɔ* commented as follows:

In order to assure Ashanti people of the annulment of this law of taking percentage of any deceased's property, Nana Prempeh [Agyeman Prempe] deputed his sister by name Nana Akua Afriyie and his brother named Nana Agyeman Badu, to Ejisuhene [*Edwesohene*], the then powerful King was to drink fetish that Nana Prempeh should never at any time ask for any estate of any deceased Ashanti man.[182]

The intended effect of all of these proposals and measures was to end the interventionist authority of the historic state presided over by the *Asantehene* and the Kumase political elite. The dissenters in the Gold Coast Colony wanted to pursue accumulation on their own terms, and certainly outside of the definitions and constraints imposed by the Asante state. By analogy, the authors of the *Ahyiamu* oath wished to remove the Asante state's absolute rights of dispensation or regulation over the market in subjects and land. It was indisputably the case that the operations of the historic state – between the early eighteenth and late nineteenth centuries – had favoured and benefited the Kumase office holders at the expense of the remainder of Asante society. This tendency had been set in motion by the phenomenal territorial expansion of the eighteenth century. It was then entrenched by the much enlarged central place status of Kumase, and by the progressive imperial enrichment and elaboration of the state apparatus located there.

The coercive capacity of the state centred in Kumase played an important role in maintaining the imbalance just described, whether in relation to individual accumulator, to provincial office holder or to lineage segment. But, as we shall see, the factors of subscription and consent that we have already adumbrated played the crucial enabling part in the installation, embedding, ideological articulation and long-term survival of the system of control over wealth and (re)production that we have described and analysed in this chapter.

3 Society and state in Asante history

Introduction

It will be readily apparent that there were powerful strands of continuity in the transformations that have been described in the previous chapter. The creation and subsequent intensification of crop agriculture, the principles governing the conceptualization of the good or achieving citizen, and the structurations effected and mediated by the state were all framed within the lexicon of a knowledge derived from a close reading of cultural experience.

It will be evident, moreover, that this knowledge had very high levels of specificity and articulation. The entire thrust of the historical record points to a sophisticated working out or elaboration over time of discrete principles and imperatives that were identified as being *the* instruments of maximization and *the* guarantors of order. All societies, it might be argued, strive for an equivalent success in one manner or another. What is striking about the Asante case, however, is the clearly formulated, precisely defined and tenaciously pursued historical expressions of the principles involved. There is in Asante history a unity of knowledge and belief, of understanding and purpose, that implies very considerable levels of reflective or meditative self-consciousness. The roots and parameters of this – which we have analysed in relation to the crucial structural expressions of (re)production in relation to the state (accumulated wealth in food, gold, people, land and the rest) – are the subject of this chapter.

Clearly, there were areas of potential conflict as well as congruence between the goals of the state and the social order. The intensified mode of production around Kumase – structured by and for the state – was only one among a series of articulations that was forged as an ideological accommodation between the state's discrete purposes and the precedent imperatives, norms and values that underpinned society, and so framed, described and otherwise qualified its ordering. The range and density of this relationship are complex, and correspondingly very difficult to analyse. But it is vital to attempt to understand, as fully as possible, the nature of the historical relationship – the equilibrium of compromise – that obtained

74

between the state and the social order out of which it grew, and over which, in the eighteenth and nineteenth centuries, it presided.

The principle of accumulation emerged organically from the profoundly formative experience of the labour gang in the monumental task, imprinted over several generations of effort and struggle, of establishing the subsistence base of a sustainable crop agriculture in the forest. Culture was quite literally hacked out of nature, and as a result Asante tradition and thought posit a fundamental sense of difference and a perpetual embattled antagonism between the two.[1] The security of the hard-won cultural niche was understood to be fragile, requiring unremitting vigilance in its defence against a vast and anarchically irruptive nature. This cultural niche – the domain of the social – depended for its maintenance, renewal and enlargement on the reproductive increase of the Asante themselves, and that depended in turn, as we have seen, on the viability of the agricultural enterprise.

In consequence, there existed in Asante thought and practice a deeply powerful social imperative towards the historical realization of an aggregated cluster of norms and values: fruitfulness, increase, maximization, abundance, plenitude. Of course, as practical goals for the realization of culture these were open ended, amorphous and unattainable in absolute terms; but then, there could be no perceived completion to the task of defending and enlarging Asante culture.[2] Crucially, however, the unrelenting pursuit of these goals was generalized throughout Asante historical practice. Most precisely, the objective centrality of their status lay at the heart of the expressive ideology through which the social order was articulated. And because of this, they circumscribed vital parameters of contact between state and social order. It was in this arena of fundamental norms and values that the state engaged the social order in the structuration of consent and coercion.

Kinship and state juxtaposed

The structural formulation of the Asante social order was itself a derived institutionalization of the transactional procedures of work efficiency that had been arrived at and successfully implemented in the clearing of the forest. At a significant level, the assimilation of alien labour and the practice of exogamy were techniques of social engineering directed towards promoting cohesive efficiency and the aggrandizement of the group or collectivity. All of this was reinforced and underscored by appropriate behavioural practices that were quotidian distillations of – and references to – the encompassing cluster of norms and values. These behavioural tenets are very thoroughly (and diversely) documented. They included

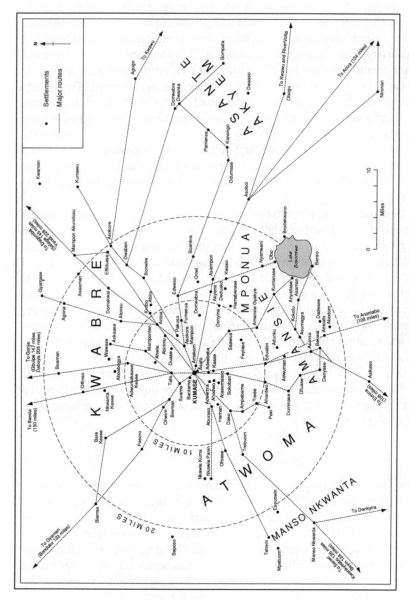

Map 3 Central Asante in the nineteenth century

mutual assistance; cooperative endeavour; mandatory hospitality; sorority, fraternity and other forms of solidarity; the right to arbitration; and collective decision making within an agreed or consensual framework.[3]

By direct extension, as is fully attested to in tradition and in the anthropological literature, the abiding operational premisses of the Asante matrilineage (abusua: pl. mmusua) and the more inclusive but territorially dispersed matriclan (abusua kɛsɛɛ: pl. mmusua kɛsɛɛ) were firmly directed towards the maintenance of jural corporateness, the resolution of conflict by discussion and consent rather than by the unilateral impositions of authority, and the perpetuation of significant degrees of economic egalitarianism. This is why Fortes, in describing from his own perspective the individual and psychological tensions that he observed within what he termed the maximal matrilineage (abusua) and more especially the maximal lineage segment (ɔyafunu koro: syn. (ɔ)fie: what Rattray called the 'family'), still felt able to situate discussion of his findings within an explanatory framework that he grounded in the clear existence of axioms of 'amity'.[4]

The rise of the abirɛmpɔn, the emergence of chiefdoms, and the inception and progressive elaboration of the Asante state increasingly dictated priorities and goals that diverged both from the embodied structural formulation of the social order and from its operational premisses. The factors of differentiation, stratification and hierarchy were implicit in the state's construction. In the eighteenth and nineteenth centuries, as we have seen, these factors were rendered explicit in various ways and degrees by the insistent application of state power to the ordering of Asante existence.

Kinship theorists, primarily orientated towards consideration of the nature of the interactive relationship between structure and function, have confessed perplexity at the ostensible paradox of a centralized Asante state existing in tandem with a segmentary lineage system.[5] This conundrum cannot be resolved, however, by resort to an anthropological interrogation of the synchrony of structure and function, or by an enumeration of the ideational rules of kinship. Thus, both Rattray's and Fortes' anthropological readings of the Asante are more or less thoroughly objectivized ethnographies of such rules. In Geertz's apposite (if somewhat brutal) phrase, Fortes' work on the Asante, like his more fully developed work on the Tallensi of northern Ghana, 'reads like a law text written by a botanist'.[6] The resolution, or explanatory dissolution, of this conundrum does not reside in any such objectification, but in the temporal framework (the horizon) of historicity.

It would be idle to pretend that the Asante themselves achieved resolution in all areas described by this paradox. Certainly, for example, there existed outstanding ambiguities of presentation and assertion in the performative context of social interaction between individuals. In the nineteenth century, the latent or hidden contradictions between some of the goals of state and social order were encapsulated for the individual (as to some degree and in various ways they still are) in potentially competing demands. That is, there was some perception of an anomaly between the differentiation implied by wealth, and the egalitarianism implied by descent. Thus, for example, some confirmation of the uneasy tensions between the moral economy of lineage or descent and the world of the accumulator of wealth is to be found in the contrast made between the concept of *papa* or moral goodness – a principle rooted in consensual notions of sharing, humility and communal wellbeing – and the individualistic behaviour or even hubris that might ensue from enjoying favoured access to the mechanisms of accumulation.[7]

Equally, as we have already seen illustrated in the cases of successive *Kyidomhenes* and of Kwasi Brantuo, there was an evident ambiguity between the norms and values enshrined in the claims advanced by ancestry and lineage and the social perceptions expressed, most pithily, in a number of maxims; thus, *ɔdehyeɛ nhyehye na sika na ehyehye* ('Money not nobility makes a person famous'); and even more pointedly, *ɔdehyeɛ wonnoa woni, na sika ne asem* ('You cannot cook and eat nobility, for it is money that counts').[8] To some appreciable degree, the folk understanding contained in such aphorisms reflected an objective reality. In 1817, for example, Bowdich noted that there were 'only four direct descendants now living of the noble families which accompanied the emigration of Sai Tootoo [the *Asantehene* Osei Tutu]'; the four were exempted from capital punishment, because their lineal ancestors had aided 'the founder of the kingdom', but they were individuals of little consequence, and they were in fact 'all beggars'.[9]

More broadly, the claims of descent might be set aside by the articulation of power in the evolving determination of the state. Thus, the brothers *Dako ne Dako* – members of the *ɔyafunu koro* of Obiri Yeboa, Osei Tutu's uncle and predecessor – lost a struggle for control of the state in the mid-eighteenth century, and their lineage segment then passed from social prominence to perfect obscurity. Indeed, the Kumase ward (*borɔŋ*: pl. *mborɔŋ*) which this lineage segment had founded, and in which its members continued to reside, had its name changed from *asaaman* to *asaaman kwaadane* ('the small, insignificant, subordinate *asaaman*') to signify the fact of historical eclipse in relation to the state and its project. 'Nobility' or 'a great name' survived, but only as a mnemonic of lost power and prestige, and as a shadowy reminder of a distantly receding status. Thus, Kwame Agyem, allegedly the last surviving descendant of *Dako ne Dako*, died in Kumase on 15 December 1908. He was accorded a funeral 'as befits a dignitary', but he – and generations of his lineal ancestors – had lived and died invisibly, outside of and far from that history that took place at the centre of state power.[10]

In Asante historical discourse, the tensions between the values of the state and of the social order, and between the claims of wealth and of ancestry rooted in lineage (and more particularly when unsupported by wealth), were embodied most quintessentially, perhaps, in the concept and individualized behavioural mechanism of *mpoatwa* (pl. *mpoatwitwa*).[11] Etymology is more easily furnished than any adequate translation. The concept was derived from the root words *poa* (pl. *mpoa*), meaning literally verbal defiance or challenge through vilification, and *twa* (pl. *twitwa*), which carries the literal meaning of cutting something down or into pieces. Thus, *mpoatwa* was customarily rendered as a setting at defiance, with defamatory intent.[12] However, in its conceptual role as a descriptive characterization of certain well-understood modes of behaviour, *mpoatwa* implied defiance and defamation primarily by means of an assertion or display of superior social position on the part of the individual practising it.

The practice of *mpoatwa* was often verbal, but not necessarily so; it could be gestural, and it could be expressed via an individual's conduct, bearing or demeanour. The competing claims and pretensions of wealth and ancestry, for example, were commonly articulated through antagonistic formulations or different emphatic usages of the concept of *mpoatwa*. At one level of interpretative understanding, the public display of wealth by an aspirant *ɔbirɛmpɔn* was an assertion of *mpoatwa*. And in the colonial era, the wealthy asserted themselves through all manner of conspicuous display, and notably competitive house building: 'the mere possession of a house at Kumasi', it was noted in the 1940s, 'increases the wealthy man's rank and prestige'.[13] Conversely, those of distinguished ancestry who were in reduced material circumstances – such as Bowdich's penurious 'beggars', or Kwame Agyem – might assert themselves in oblique but subtly unambiguous references to their kin and antecedents. This most commonly took and still takes the form of statements or mnemonic reminders concerning the crucial matter of where and by whom an individual was to be buried; in Asante life, funerals, interment, cemeteries and the constituency of mourners were all key markers of lineage affiliation and social positioning.[14]

The social ambiguities and contradictions inherent in the practice of *mpoatwa* were apparent in other areas of discourse. Thus, for instance, the word *pɔw* connoted selfless values, refinement and personal cultivation within the referential context(s) of a network of lineage affiliations; but its verbal use when applied to an individual's accumulation of wealth made general reference to the arrogance, pride and self-seeking uncouthness of someone who had risen in the world. By analogy, the noun *bakoma* (pl. *mmakoma*) was used of someone to indicate that they were noble and genteel in the sense of being respectable or well born; but the adverbial phrase *di bakoma* (syn. *di ɔdehyeɛ sɛm*) characterized wilful, imperious and arbitrary behaviour – the behaviour, in fact, of a person of distinguished lineage practising *mpoatwa*.[15]

Superficially, there was a ludic element in all of this, an understood irony concerning the comedy of social niceties; Asante perceptions, framed as *contes moraux*, as fables and as aphorisms, all attest to this factor.[16] But folk humour or communal moralizing about the pretensions attaching to wealth or ancestry had circumscribed limits, and only served to camouflage a deadly seriousness and intent. The concept of *mpoatwa* and related practices were safety valves in that they were sanctioned expressions of profound but basically unresolved contradictions in the relationship between the values embedded in the state and in the social order. And quite predictably, such expressions had prescribed limits.

Thus, the persistent, strident or unacceptable exercise of *mpoatwa* was understood as *ahomaso*, literally an exaltation of self, and it was excoriated and sometimes punished in law. The insistent drawing of attention to ambiguities – and notably when speech acts, for example, slid from critical commentary to insult – was identified, quite accurately, as being potentially disruptive and subversive of order. Rattray recorded a case where one Kwame Agyetewa, having been involved in a hot exchange (blows are mentioned) with an *akradwareni* ('soul washer') of an office holder called Kwasi Gyehyene, was arraigned, found guilty, and fined a sheep; Kwame Agyetewa boldly stated that he would go one better, and offered a cow, knowing full well that this animal was forbidden (*akyiwadeɛ*) to the *Bosommuru ntɔrɔ* to which the office holder belonged. He was charged with practising 'poa' (*mpoatwa*) in the form of a directly blatant insult (a quite unacceptable version of 'cutting down to size'), and his ears were cut off in punishment.[17]

On occasion, the historical record affords us glimpses of the underlying gravity of the issues addressed in *mpoatwa*, and of the potential for social dislocation acted out in miniature in encounters and confrontations between individuals. Thus, Bowdich gave the following brief account of just such a confrontation between an *ɔheneba* (pl. *ahenemma*: the son of an *Asantehene*, conventionally a 'prince') and a son of the Kumase *Krontihene* and *Bantamahene* Amankwatia.

A son of the King's [the *Asantehene* Osei Tutu Kwame] quarrelling with a son of Amanquatea's, (one of the four) told him, that in comparison with himself, he was the son of a slave; this being reported to Amanquatea, he sent a party of his soldiers, who pulled down the house of the King's son and seized his person. The King hearing of it sent to Amanquatea, and learning the particulars, interceded for his son, and redeemed his head for 20 periguins [*mperedwan*; i.e. £160] of gold.[18]

Amankwatia was a senior general and politician, and was prominent enough to be ranked in Bowdich's speculative classificatory schema as being one of the four members of the 'aristocracy'.[19] But the stool of Bantama, created by the *Asantehene* Osei Tutu for one of his most loyal servants, was an appointive office (*mmamma dwa*) and not one vested in a matrilineage. Advancement to it was in the gift of the *Asantehene*. Thus, another Amankwatia (Amankwa Tenteŋ), who held the office of *Bantamahene* under the *Asantehene* Kofi Kakari, and who played a leading role in the Anglo-Asante war of 1873–4, was an *akoa* from Akrofuom in Adanse, and was reportedly 'from the lowest ranks of the people'.[20] The occupants of the Bantama stool generally combined very considerable levels of political power and influence with obscure, lowly or provincial origins.[21] The reverse of this pattern was broadly true of the majority of the *ahenemma*. Their dynastic status was somewhat anomalous. The *ahenemma* were not *adehyeε* or royals, for descent in Asante was matrilineal. But they did enjoy the social prestige that attached to them as the children of *Asantehenes*, and they were touchily sensitive and often arrogant in matters pertaining to social status and position. There were very large numbers of them, and only a few in any generation achieved high political office.[22]

The practice of *mpoatwa* framed contradictions, ambiguities, insecurities and antagonisms concerning a host of sensitivities relating to questions of status and social positioning. Such issues were clearly of great and abiding concern to the Asante, and this is reflected not only in *mpoatwa* but in many of the other speech acts, language games and interactionist formulae of Asante Twi. The Asante recognized the social power of words, and accorded no value to reticence. Controlled eloquence or 'dry speech' (*nɔ ano awo*: lit. '[his] lips are dry') was associated with truth telling and the transformational capacity to bring situations under control; uncontrolled utterance or 'wet speech' (*nɔ ano nwoo*: lit. '[his] lips are wet') was equated with the talk of children or the mentally infirm and carried implications of duplicity or evasiveness. In between and qualifying these polar or ideal models of the speech act, however, was a potent battery of mechanisms that were dedicated, revealingly, to indirection in communication. The widespread use of *kasakoa* (idiomatic metaphor), *akutia* (innuendo: most commonly in the mode of traducing someone without mentioning his/her name), and even proverbs or aphorisms (*mbε*: sing. *εbε*), were all conduits of a critical commentary on others that availed itself of third-party analogies and a register of formulaic and well-understood commonplaces. Asante Twi at once reflected and was implicated in the minefield of social comment and interaction. Speech acts took full and complex account of the nuances of social positioning, and afforded subtle opportunities to address and, briefly and interactively, to modify or adjust particular situational constructions of the social.[23]

It might be said that *mpoatwa* and other mechanisms held up a mirror to the state and the social order, and reflected incongruities between the two. However, as practice all of this was individualized, and ultimately interstitial and epiphenomenal. It was transacted on the day-to-day surface of interactive encounters, and represented one form of open acknowledgement or sanctioned expression of that historical paradox – the conundrum of the kinship theorists – that lay at the core of the relationship between the state and the social order.

Ideology and the bases of coercion and consent

The conditions that made the state possible grew out of the same soil, literally and metaphorically, that had previously facilitated the successful establishment of the agrarian and social orders. For much of the eighteenth and nineteenth centuries, however, the mature state was significantly detached from the social order, superimposed upon it, and increasingly interventionist in relation to it.[24] An incremental autonomy of the state's power and purposes added novel qualifications to the precedent, organic nature of its interactive relationship with the social order. Commingled in the consequent series of articulations – including the mode of production around Kumase, and the regulated role of the *abirɛmpɔn* – were the factors of coercion and consent. We now consider each in turn in the context of the eighteenth- and nineteenth-century relationship between state and society.

It should be clearly recorded and understood that the coercive potential of the evolved state was formidable in range; espionage, detention, fining, confiscation, enslavement, mutilation, execution and exile are all abundantly documented.[25] Instances of licit application are numerous, and they evidence two guiding principles. One: a concern with juridical definition of the graduated degrees of coercion allowed and disallowed to particular agents of the state (the death penalty being reserved to the *Asantehene*-in-council, as quintessential embodiment of the state). Two: an equal concern with the explicit enactment of due process. Both concerns were encapsulated in cases where the *Asantehene* was acquitted in adversarial proceedings brought against the dead body of a rebel or criminal notable, sometimes disinterred to stand trial (as in the case already noted of the *Akuroponhene* Kwadwo Gyamfi). The *Asantehene* then sentenced the duly convicted corpse to the capital punishment of beheading.

A succinct illustration of the above is to be found in authoritative tradition concerning the Asante military victory of 1818–19 over the forces of the rebel *Gyamanhene* Kwadwo Adinkra. Following the defeat of Kwadwo Adinkra, it is said that his son Apaw concealed his father's severed head among the slain on the battlefield.[26] The head and the nearby trunk, identified by the gold trinkets on its calves and left wrist, were eventually located by the *Gyaasewahene* Opoku Frɛfrɛ. After Apaw had reluctantly confirmed that these were indeed the remains of his father, the *Asantehene* Osei Tutu Kwame ordered that the head be sewn back onto the trunk, that the reassembled corpse be seated on an appropriate royal chair, and that the surviving Gyaman office holders be grouped about the deceased in the rank order that they had held at the Gyaman court. Osei Tutu Kwame then assembled his own office holders and constituted himself and them as the *Asantehene*-in-council. The Kumase *Bosommuru Fabem ɔkyeame* was instructed to narrate the facts of Kwadwo Adinkra's treachery, and formally to prefer charges against him. The *Gyamanhene* was found guilty by verdict of the court, after Osei Tutu Kwame had gone through the due process of consulting each of his office holders in turn. The *Asantehene* then paid 10 *mperedwan* (£80) as *aseda* ('thank offering') to the court, and waived his right to request the reduction of this sum. The corpse was sentenced, handed over to the appropriate functionary – the *Abrafoɔhene* Kofi Asuman – and beheaded in the prescribed manner.[27]

A reading of the legalist superstructure of the state, and of instances of transgressions against it at the very highest level – as in the case of Kwadwo Adinkra, or in the derelictions of the *Asantehenes* Kofi Kakari and Mensa Bonsu – takes us some way towards an understanding of the basic institutional framework for the structured implementation of coercion. But a more meaningfully textured portrait emerges if we nuance coercive potential to embrace the assumptions and attitudes of all those whose behaviour (or presentation of self) was conditioned by the fact of membership, however lowly, indirect or tenuous, in the state apparatus. Such individuals comported themselves in ways intended to convey an association, presumptive or actual, with the state's powers of coercion, and thereby to impress or otherwise to intimidate their interlocutors. It is suggestive in this context, for example, that successive *Asantehenes* legislated in vain in a forlorn attempt to curtail the widespread seizure of villagers' food and goods by itinerant royal *nhenkwaa* who claimed to be acting in the state's name and with its authority.[28]

The attitudes that underpinned coercion in all of its direct, subtle or even petty guises can be adduced from a very richly documented repertoire of performative, linguistic and gestural signifiers. These even impressed themselves upon otherwise uncomprehending Europeans. In 1871, for instance, the captive Basel missionaries in Kumase gave temporary sanctuary to a royal *ahenkwaa* who had been found guilty of an unspecified crime. They noted in exasperation,

He was a singular man. As he lived the whole day in the yard, we proposed to him to help to pound the fufu [*fufuu*: pounded or mashed yam], not that we needed his assistance, but simply that he might not be idle. To this he replied, 'I am an Ashantee, one of the king's slaves. I have never done such a thing.' My [Ramseyer's] wife then proposed to give him soap to wash his clothes, but this also he considered unbecoming his dignity.[29]

Some thirty years before this Freeman remarked on the 'noisy and often unseemly proceedings' of *nhenkwaa*, and passed general comment on 'their swaggering conduct, shouting, stamping and banging of [the palace] doors'; he added the following concerning the attitudes and deportment of one group of *nhenkwaa* – the royal sword-bearers (*afenasoafoɔ*: sing. *afenasoani*).

The court-messenger in Ashanti bounds along the streets of Kumasi with his gold-handled sword of office, or with the golden plate emblazoned on his breast, or the heavy gold manilla on his wrist, desirous that all should know he is an important personage, and that his master is indeed the King [the *Asantehene* Kwaku Dua Panin].[30]

Tradition and folk memory confirm and amplify the impressions of foreign observers. Thus, it was proverbially the case that *ahenkwaa na ɔma ɔhene ho yɛ hu* ('It is the chief's servant that causes the person of the chief to excite fear').[31] The prevailing or stereotypical folk model of the royal *ahenkwaa* is economically summarized in an Asante oral account of one Sampanne, who was in the service of the *Asantehene* Osei Tutu Kwame (1804–23). The individual case is cast within a knowing field of commonplaces that renders and fixes the type.

A prominent woman from Gyaaman married in Asante. This woman had a son known as Sampanne by her Asante husband. When he [Sampanne] grew up, the King [Osei Tutu Kwame] appointed him his *ahenkwaa*. He was a cantankerous, greedy, and aggressive fellow. He was a typical *ahenkwaa*. He was lazy and a bully, and lived off others. When he had no money to feed himself, he sought the King's permission to visit his mother's people in Gyaaman. Because the people there were cultured but lived in awe of the Asante, he bullied them and took money off them which he carried back to Asante. Part of this loot he gave to the King, and he squandered the rest himself.[32]

Although Akan, the Gyaman were conquered subjects. But it was generally the case that Asante *nkuraasefoɔ* (villagers: sing. *akuraaseni*: der. *akuraa*, a village) and *nkoa* themselves also feared the intrusive attention of the state or of any of its agents. Such unwelcome visitors were identified as embodiments of the coercive power of that state, and as emblems and representations of the distant, hermetic locus of that power – Kumase. The capital was a separate world, and itself served as a common metaphor for the coercive power that resided there. Rural and provincial Asante regarded Kumase as being a remote and forbidding place, a destination 'that it was easier to travel to than to return from [in safety]'.[33] By corollary, the inhabitants of Kumase (*Kumasefoɔ*: sing. *Kumaseni*), as the personnel of the state, were arrogantly dismissive of *nkuraasefoɔ* and *nkoa*, seeing them as fair game for insult, derision and predatory attention. In the everyday speech of the capital, the degree to which villagers were understood to be 'civilized' (*womo ani ate*) depended upon their spatial proximity to Kumase, thus, the people of the Kwabre area were held in marginally higher esteem than the more distant residents of the Mponua towns. In Kumase itself, to refer to some individual as *akuraaseni* was an abusive insult used only in quarrels, for the term connoted rustic uncouthness, implied a stolid stupidity, and, tellingly, was a coded but barely veiled reference to distance, in both senses, from power.[34]

The state signified objective inequities, and employed the (mainly jural) mechanisms of coercive power. But its personnel regularly implemented subjective inequities, relying on assumed status to clothe individual action and illegitimate pretension alike in the nimbus of coercive power that surrounded the state itself. It was in these myriad daily encounters, rather than in great matters of state (*amaŋsɛm*), that a basic pedagogy was imparted. In any social transaction where coercion was invoked, threatened or used, it clearly implied the inequalities that stemmed from inclusion in or exclusion from the state.

Until the civil strife of the 1880s, the Asante just described manifested few signs of those indices of systemic stress and breakdown – peasant and/or slave insurrection, widespread banditry, severe social dislocation – that might be expected to punctuate the history of any regime or system that relied heavily on simple coercion.[35] It would be misleading, however, to assume the contrary case and deduce that the absence of such features indicated a coercive capacity that was unrelenting in its ubiquitous power and application. We have already taken note of the infrastructural constraints on this supposition. It was no less untenable at the level of immediate coercive practicality.

The Asante state possessed no standing army.[36] Although the *Asantehene* retained some stockpiled weaponry in arsenals in and around Kumase, guns were very widely disseminated throughout society.[37] As occasion demanded, a Kumase office holder might mobilize his free and slave *nkoa*; in 1862, for instance (but with ambiguous wording), the *Akyempemhene ɔheneba* Owusu Kɔkɔɔ (*c.* 1820–84) 'exhibited his muskets before the King. Three thousand were displayed on the occasion, each carried by one of his own people.'[38] In fact, free subjects – the great majority in any large-scale levy – were expected to furnish their own weapons, for individual possession of a gun was a more or less mandatory indicator of adult male status.[39] The traditional military system was such that:

A Chief has generally no guns of his own which are supplied to his soldiers when a war is declared. Every individual is expected to equip himself with a gun, but if a man has none he is given one by the Chief during the day when all the guns have to be assembled before the Chief for testing. All guns out of order are repaired at the Chief's smithy free of charge. The lineage has no guns of its own except those belonging to its men. Any gun supplied to a subject by the Chief is not returned to him at the end of the war. They were retained and became the property of the subjects who had to use them in subsequent wars.[40]

Thus, the state's armed coercive power was substantially vested in those very *nkoa* whose labour maintained the office-holding apparatus, and whose commodity value, as items convertible against gold, played a prominent part in defining wealth and in factoring differentiation. Moreover, the state had no reservoir of armed force with which to coerce its own coercive power.

The foregoing dispositions were necessarily characterized by a high degree of consent and subscription. Coercive capacity – whether in the case of the law, the *nhenkwaa* or the army – was subject to very clear and obvious limitations. It was in and of itself a *necessary* but not a *sufficient* condition for the maintenance of the state's authority. The state's ability to coerce society ultimately depended upon society being structurally complicit in, or consenting to, its subjection to the state's interventions. But the bases of consent were not an agenda of neutral agreements. They had to be identified by the state, and then ideologically structured and articulated to serve the discrete objects of power. The ideological structuration of the bases of consent, as we shall see, was indispensable to the ordered temporal reproduction of the precolonial Asante polity.

The bases of consent were situated in the relationship between the state and the operational premisses of the social order. These premisses, enumerated above, were themselves unequal within the logic of their own interrelationship, and hence in terms of socio-historical significance. The premisses of a degree of economic egalitarianism and of conflict resolution by consent and arbitration were contingencies or expressions of the central social fact of jural corporateness or lineage identity. The matrilineage (or maximal lineage segment) and the uterine stirp or group (or 'family'), in Fortes' apt locution, were conceptually understood – each in its own corporately aggregated right – as a single, indivisible 'jural person'.[41] Jural corporateness was the irreducible building block of the social order, and it could not be structured by the state in the same ways, and by the same means, as were applied to its contingent expressions.

We have already noted how the very existence of the state contradicted and diluted the lineage principle of a degree of economic egalitarianism; and then the state weakened this further by applying ideological structuration to the underlying imperative to accumulation, thereby creating and rewarding its own overweening economic model. In a similar manner, the continuing efficacy of the principle of conflict resolution by consent and arbitration was reduced and overshadowed by the coercive weight implicit in state intervention. Most significantly, it was undermined by the state's arrogation of an ideological (re)formulation of the right to arbitration. The adversarial review of a dispute aimed at achieving an agreed decision among peers was preserved as a forensic principle; but the outcome was now subject to imposition by the state's courts, rather than being encouraged to emerge as a consensus acceptable because of its origin in communal deliberation and action.

The fundamental mechanisms that regulated the ideological structuration of these and other contingencies and expressions of jural corporateness were embedded in the practice of legislation (*hye mara*), and were given specific interventionist forms by the promulgation over time of legal enactments and rules (*mara*). Law in the sense of jural custom was constantly under review as the state monitored and adjusted matters relating to discrete aspects or facets of the social order. Thus, nine-teenth-century Europeans commented on the sheer amount of time spent by the *Asantehene* in his judicial role, and the central importance of legislation is emphatically borne out by tradition.[42]

The ideological management of jural corporateness was an issue of an entirely different sort and order of magnitude. This premiss was uniquely essential rather than contingent or expressive, for jural corporateness was, simply, the linchpin of the social order. To have subverted it in principle, or to have fractured its (pre)-expressed realization by interventionist legislation, would have struck at the very root of the organic cohesion of society and culture, and would have threatened dissolution of consensual subscription to the veracity of all underlying imperatives, norms and values.

The epistemological division of the essential from the contingent was expressed in the fundamental, and critically important, contrast made between *amaŋ mmu* (immemorial custom that ordered a community) and *amaŋ bre* (jural custom that might be changed or adjusted by legislation).[43] The principle of jural corporateness was supremely *amaŋ mmu*. As such it implied and connoted completeness. It was not a matter subject to fundamental change by legislative enactment. Thus, in the entire historical record, the only unequivocally reported instance of the abrogation of *amaŋ mmu* was the severe restriction placed by the *Asantehene* Kwaku Dua Panin on the customary implementation of *pae abusua*, or expulsion from the lineage by corporate agreement. And this one very specific intervention, like the same ruler's abolition of the law of *yi adow* (seizure of an individual as substitute for a defaulting debtor from the same *abusua*), was directed towards the curtailment of immiseration and possible vagrancy or banditry.[44] In fact, both of these very precise measures had the overall effect of reinforcing jural corporateness by clarifying its boundaries and so underscoring its central, non-negotiable integrity.

In the eighteenth and nineteenth centuries, the issue for the Asante state was how to mobilize the inviolable principle of jural corporateness in its own interest; or, to put the matter in Gramscian terms, how to locate the articulation of a key item in *direzione* in the institutionalized practices of *amaŋ mmu*. Let us now consider how the state went about this vital problem of ideological structuration.

Identity: citizens, subjects, slaves

Imperatives to consensus and egalitarianism achieved by discussion meant that within the matrilineage framework of jural corporateness – at whatever level of structural segmentation – the potential for a unity of organization and a concerted programme of action was highly inhibited. In addition, both matrilineages and more inclusive matriclans were territorially dispersed, and their principal structural characteristic was a tendency to centrifugal fission. In terms of locational concentration, the basic unit of proximal residence was the numerically restricted lineage segment. All of these features ensured severe disincentives to corporate political action. Indeed, at the level of mobilized political power, the lineage system could not and did not present any serious challenge to the state's project.[45]

The bedrock strength of jural corporateness embodied in the lineage structure (and its ultimate meaning as social knowledge) was passive and inert, and resided in an irreducible definition rather than in any capacity for innovation or interventionist action. That is, full citizenship rights in Asante society were exclusively vested in and defined by membership of an *abusua* and, more broadly, an *abusua kɛsɛɛ*. This was the foundational premiss of social and cultural order, and to alter the definition and construction of jural corporateness in any way would have been tantamount to tearing up the charter of Asante society. Instead, as we have observed in the case of the *Asantehene* Kwaku Dua Panin, the state not only preserved but sedulously reinforced the authoritative integrity of this pre-existing systemic monopoly over the definition of who and what constituted an Asante citizen. Presenting itself as guarantor rather than opponent of this basic definitional feature, the state effectively enlisted jural corporateness in its own interest, and thereby opened the door to a crucial ideological structuration. That is, the state (with the tacit blessing, so to speak, of the politically weak *mmusua*) reserved to itself absolute rights of control and discretionary determination over all other possible avenues to corporateness in Asante society.

Note has already been taken of one vitally important aspect of this ideological structuration in the state's simultaneous encouragement of individual accumulation but prevention of any consequent emergence of a hereditary class of property owners. However, very much broader issues were involved. The entire intentional thrust of the state's ideological structuration in this area was to create a vacuum of non-being outside of itself and the jural corporateness vested in matrilineages over which it presided as guarantor.

Anthropologists have accurately identified and reported the social consequences of this for the ordinary Asante citizen; the severance of lineage ties constituted an isolation that was tantamount to a death sentence.[46] By analogy, for the most heinous political offences the state might impose exile – expulsion from itself – rather than capital punishment.[47] In 1820, Dupuis intuited something of all this from the information he was able to glean in Kumase concerning the isolated villages, forbidden to visitors, that were situated around the crater rim of Lake Bosomtwe.

Many thousands of Fantees, Assins, and Gamans, are there detained prisoners of war. Of the two first nations some are considered free, although narrowly watched to prevent their escape to the sea side: the rest are absolute slaves, having been sold and transferred in due succession from hand to hand ... In short, Echouy, or as it may be also called Bussem Echouy [Bosomtwe], and the territory thereabouts may be considered the Siberia of the Court: for it is also a place of banishment for inferior ranks of insurgents, whom the King may think proper to spare, or reserve for future punishment.[48]

In a survey conducted in the 1940s over half (of twenty-four) lakeside villages dated their foundation to the reign of the *Asantehene* Osei Tutu Kwame (1804–23), and while none, understandably, made mention of any descendants of prisoners of war, several confirmed that they had 'been given charge' of disgraced Asante office holders and other individuals in the reigns of the *Asantehenes* Kwaku Dua Panin and Mensa Bonsu.[49]

By the clear and relentless demarcation of the boundaries of non-being or non-existence, the state ensured that membership in the one sanctioned form of jural corporateness remained the indispensable and mandatory condition of citizenship for a free Asante subject. In effect, it was also the only possible channel of aspiration for a non-Asante slave. An enslaved Asante retained minimal rights in law, including the possibility of redemption from bonded status. But a non-Asante had no lever on jural corporateness, and thus did not exist – fully and legally – as a person. In ultimate definition, he or she was a disposable good. We have seen that in the creation of the agrarian order assimilation to jural corporateness was necessary for the effective incorporation of alien labour, and it was, therefore, relatively open. But in the eighteenth and nineteenth centuries, the achievement of membership in jural corporateness was determined by the discretionary authority of the state's enactments, arbitrations and legal procedures. The state's jurisdiction in this matter was an instrument of immense ideological power, for incorporation was the sole legitimizing point of entry into social existence and its attendant citizenship rights.[50]

The total absence of any alternative form of access to incorporation and legitimation was the most compelling of arguments for acquiescent consent in the received ordering of society. The *nkoa* employed in the *métayage* system of agricultural production were fully aware of this fact. Slave *nkoa* could only establish social identity via their assimilation into corporate status; and free *nkoa* – most notably the indebted or impoverished – stood to lose that same identity by aggravated transgression. There are two points here that require closer investigation and elaboration. The first is the way in which the state's sustained attention to jural corporateness determined the conditions of life for individual Asante citizens in the eighteenth and nineteenth centuries. The second is the way in which the state dealt with the extreme case of the very large number of foreign-born slaves whose status lay entirely *outside* jural corporateness. Let us take each of these points in turn.

In the case of Asante citizens the state acted, on the one hand, as the guarantor of the *principle* of jural corporateness. But on the other hand, the state constantly intervened in the definitions and rights accruing to individual cases and kin networks within the *facts* of jural corporateness. It continually adjusted the parameters of legal status in relation to its own project, recasting people in a succession of more or less privileged roles *inside* jural corporateness, while at the same time retaining final rights of arbitration over the boundaries of incorporation and expulsion.

Two illustrative instances of this are provided below. The first – in the form of a kinship network diagram and commentary – is, it must be emphasized, entirely typical in its great empirical density and legal complexity.[51] It may be construed as the history of a lineage segment, analogous in some ways to the kinship and 'family' histories reconstructed, for example, by social historians of Europe.[52] In specifically Asante terms, however, it presents the state's actions and interventions from the point of view of the *nkoa*, and is therefore the complementary reverse of the office-holding perspective – the state's point of view – explored in the previous chapter. The second, in the form of an annotated oral biography, is indicative of the sheer reach and resilient tenacity of the state in (re)asserting and (re)defining the conditions of jural inclusiveness, even under the most difficult or antithetical circumstances.

A: Yaw Nkyera and his relatives c. 1818–98

I   *The marriage of Yaw Nkyera and Akosua Boadiwaa*

II   *Commentary*

1 Yaw Nkyera was born in *c*. 1818 at Aboabogya in Kwabre. He was taken as a child from his family by prerogative of the *Asantehene* – being a son of a royal *ahenkwaa* – and was given into the service of the *Atene Akotenhene*. Atene Akoten served the Ankobea stool in the Anamenako sub-division of the Kumase *Ankobea* administrative *fekuo*.

2 In the late 1840s, Yaw Nkyera married Akosua Boadiwaa of Aduamoa, a village 2 miles from Aboabogya. The Aduamoa *odekuro* (village head) also served the *Ankobeahene* via the *Anamenakohene*. The marriage produced Kwaku Ntwiaa, and Akosua Boadiwaa died shortly thereafter.

3 Boama, Akosua Boadiwaa's brother, contracted a court debt. He and his brother Beniako went to Yaw Nkyera – their deceased sister's husband – to secure a loan of 1 *peredwan* [£8]. The loan was granted, and as security the brothers pledged (*awowa*) to Yaw Nkyera (*a*) Enieni, one of their own *nkoa* and (*b*) Kwaku Ntwiaa, their matrilineal nephew, and Yaw Nkyera's own son. Yaw Nkyera sent Enieni to trade for him in Salaga, but he died. Having now lost both labour and capital, Yaw Nkyera asked the brothers to redeem the loan, saying that he would return Kwaku Ntwiaa to them. But the brothers refused the return of only one *awowa*, and Kwaku Ntwiaa remained an *akoa* in pawn to his own father.

4 In 1869, *Asantehene* Kofi Kakari gave *Akuroponhene* Kwame Agyepon command of a campaign against the Buem. *Atene Akotenhene* ɔheneba Yaw Ntem held a command in the war, and Yaw Nkyera and (now) Kwaku Ntwiaa – in service to Atene Akoten – went with him. In the course of the war, Kwaku Ntwiaa personally slew the *Buemhene*, and Kwame Agyepon, as overall commander, promised to reward him.

5 The reward was not forthcoming, and Yaw Ntem and Yaw Nkyera, as Kwaku Ntwiaa's superiors, arraigned Kwame Agyepon for default in the *Asantehene's* court. The plaintiffs won, and in redemption of his promise Kwame Agyepon was constrained to give Kwaku Ntwiaa an *akoa* called Yaa Odom, together with her children. In further recognition of Kwaku Ntwiaa's valour, Kofi Kakari gave him *asuaanu + nsuanu* in gold dust (£4.65), and a male *akoa* called Dakakariase. All of these gifts were impounded by Kwaku Ntwiaa's superiors – his father and Yaw Ntem – and they awarded him only the gold as his share. He then begged for one of the two people, and was given the *akoa* Yaa Odom, whom he married. At the same

time, Yaw Ntem disposed of his share in Dakakariase to Yaw Nkyera, his co-owner, for *asuaanu* (£4) and a 2/- *tramma* or sale fee.

6 In the course of the court proceedings against Kwame Agyepon, Yaw Nkyera brought an additional charge, that Yaw Ntem had misused him during the Buem war, and asked to be transferred from the authority of the Atene Akoten stool. The *Asantehene* agreed, and Yaw Nkyera – together with his *nkoa* Kwaku Ntwiaa, Yaa Odom and Dakakariase – was transferred to the authority of Mensa Kukuoni, an official of the royal household and, probably, the Kumase *Oyoko Pampasohene*.

7 Mensa Kukuoni's wife Eyaamami bore him twins. As this was an abomination to his stool, Mensa Kukuoni sold Eyaamami to Yaw Nkyera for *asuaanu* and a sale fee of *ntaku anan*. Yaw Nkyera then gave Eyaamami in marriage to Kwaku Ntwiaa. The union produced three children: Kwadwo Manu, Kwasi Adae and Afua Sewaa.

8 In 1880, Kwaku Ntwiaa was executed for participating in *ɔdomaŋkama* or *abonsamkɔm*, a politically orientated cult with witchcraft associations. The *Asantehene* Mensa Bonsu impounded his wives, children and property. Eyaamami was subsequently given by Mensa Bonsu to the *Akwamuhene* and *Asafohene ɔheneba* Asafo Boakye. Kwadwo Manu, Kwasi Adae, Afua Sewaa, Yaa Odom (and her children) were all awarded by the *Asantehene* Mensa Bonsu to his own wife, the *ɔheneba* Akyampomaa Kwaadu of Kwaso, daughter of the *Asantehene* Kwaku Dua Panin. Akyampomaa Kwaadu gave all the people allotted to her into the caretakership of Nana Saim, the female head of Yaw Nkyera's late wife's lineage segment at Aduamoa. These people were all still technically *nkoa* of Yaw Nkyera.

9 In the civil war between Yaw Twereboanna and Agyeman Prempe, Aduamoa – under the authority of the *Ankobeahene* Ata Gyamfi – opposed the latter and his mother the *Asantehemaa* Yaa Kyaa. Aboabogya declared for Yaa Kyaa, and was assigned to the military contingent led by the *Ofinsohene*. Yaw Nkyera, trying to raise money to fight for Yaa Kyaa, sent to Nana Saim at Aduamoa, saying that she must either (*a*) return his *nkoa* to him, or (*b*) return the original loan of 1 *peredwan* against which Kwaku Ntwiaa and Enieni had been pawned (some two to three decades earlier). Nana Saim demurred, but she did send one of the *nkoa*, Yaa Odom, to Yaw Nkyera as renewed security for the original loan. Alarmed by this development, Akyampomaa Kwaadu removed Kwadwo Manu, Kwasi Adae and Afua Sewaa from Aduamoa, and resettled them at her own natal town of Kwaso.

10 In 1888–9, with the civil wars concluded and Agyeman Prempe installed as *Asantehene*, Yaa Kyaa set about restoring confiscated *nkoa* as she had promised (and as was confirmed in the *Ahyiamu* oath). In the *Asantehene's* court, Yaw Nkyera won restitution of his *nkoa*. Akyampomaa Kwaadu, however, refused to surrender Kwadwo Manu, Kwasi Adae and Afua Sewaa. Thus matters stood for the next few years.

11 In 1894, the *Oyoko Pampasohene* Kwadwo Apae died. Yaw Nkyera was offered the vacant office by the *Asantehene* Agyeman Prempe. He agreed to take the post, provided his claims to the three *nkoa* were once more brought to court. In court, Akyampomaa Kwaadu was ordered to surrender Kwadwo Manu, Kwasi Adae and Afua Sewaa into the custody of Yaw Nkyera, and this time she complied. Shortly thereafter – about 1898 – Yaw Nkyera died.[53]

B: Akuoku of Asokore c. 1875–90

1 Asokore lies between the important divisional towns of Dwaben and Kumawu. It had served the *Asantehene* directly in the eighteenth century, but in the early nineteenth century, in obscure circumstances, the then reigning *Asokorehene* contracted a court fine that he was unable to pay. The debt was settled by the Kumase *Anantahene*, and as a result the *Asokorehene* was made to serve the *Asantehene* via the *Anantahene* in the Kumase *Gyaase fekuo*. In the mid-nineteenth century, the royal lineage of Asokore was temporarily unable to provide males to succeed to the stool. The Asokore stool was put in the charge of the Asokore *ɔkyeame* Buampon, and his nephew Ankra was eventually enstooled *Asokorehene*. The 'true royals' – now possessed of a male heir – challenged this, and with the support of their overlord the *Anantahene* Asamoa Nkwanta, they brought the matter before the *Asantehene* Kofi Kakari. The case was still pending in 1875, following Kofi Kakari's destoolment.

2 In September 1875 the *Asantehene* Mensa Bonsu decided upon military action to settle his outstanding disputes with the *Dwabenhene* Asafo Agyei. Asokore – a scant 5 miles from Dwaben – became divided in its loyalties. The *Asokorehene* Ankra, already in dispute with the Kumase *Anantahene*, declared for Dwaben; the royals and most of the citizens of Asokore supported Kumase. Ankra began recruiting troops for the Dwaben cause. At this time, one of Ankra's *ahenkwaa* named Akuoku, his sons Nimpa and Panin Bɔm, and a number of Asokore stool servants were on the return journey from a trading expedition to Atebubu: Ankra despatched a messenger to Akuoku, summoning him and his party back to Asokore to fight – as rapidly as possible, and on pain of beheading if he failed to comply.

3 Akuoku and his party reached Kumawu at the very time (31 October–2 November) that the main Kumase force, under the overall command of the Kumase *Bantamahene* Kwabena Awua, attacked Dwaben. The Kumase troops suffered initial reverses. Among those killed was the *Anantahene* Asamoa Nkwanta, the overlord of Asokore. But the Kumase forces rallied, Dwaben was occupied and sacked, and the *Dwabenhene* Asafo Agyei fled into exile in the British Gold Coast Colony. In mopping up operations, Akuoku and his party – non-combatants – were arrested by Kumase forces at Kumawu, and taken by them back to Asokore. There the situation was confused, for although the *Asokorehene* Ankra had supported Dwaben he had not actually committed any troops to battle. Akuoku, his sons, and thirty-five others were impounded by the Kumase forces – technically as prisoners of war, on the grounds of Ankra's known support for Asafo Agyei.

4 Akuoku, the other Asokore prisoners, and numbers of Dwaben captives were assembled together at the village of Banko. There they were shared out as booty among the Kumase office holders. Akuoku, his sons, and others from Asokore were awarded to the Kumase *Akyempemhene ɔheneba* Owusu Barempa. The *Asokorehene* Ankra, still in office, made representations to have Akuoku and the others restored, but to no avail. Akuoku, his sons, and others from Asokore were removed from Banko and settled at the Akyempem village of Boaso.

5 At Boaso the Asokore captives were distributed as *nkoa* in the category of prisoners of war (as presumed rebels against the *Asantehene*) among the lineages that lived in the town. They were set to work farming. It would appear that the *Akyempemhene ɔheneba* Owusu Barempa contemplated sacrificing Akuoku and

others in commemoration of the office holders who had fallen in the war against Dwaben. But in the event these people were spared.

6 Between 1875 and the early 1880s Akuoku, his sons, and the others from Asokore served the Akyempem stool as *nkoa* at Boaso. The *Asokorehene* made representations to Kumase on several occasions to have them restored, but Ankra was still out of favour and under suspicion. At some time around 1880, Kwaku Agyeman – a member of the Asokore royal family – swore an oath that (*a*) Ankra was a usurper and should be destooled, (*b*) despite Ankra's equivocal behaviour the Asokore royals had remained loyal to Kumase during the war against Dwaben, and so, (*c*) all Asokore stool servants who had been seized by Kumase office holders – like the *ahenkwaa* Akuoku – should be restored to the Asokore stool. The case was still pending when the *Asantehene* Mensa Bonsu was destooled in 1883.

7 In the confused situation that prevailed in Kumase in mid-1883 one of the most powerful political figures, and the chief sponsor of Agyeman Kofi (the future *Asantehene* Kwaku Dua Kuma), was the *Akyempemhene ɔheneba* Owusu Kɔkɔɔ. In the course of preparing to observe the funeral rites of his 'brother' – possibly the *Akyempemhene ɔheneba* Owusu Barempa – Owusu Kɔkɔɔ sent to Boaso to secure Akuoku, his sons, and the other Asokore *nkoa* in order to immolate them at the funeral custom. At the time, Akuoku and his sons were themselves absent from Boaso, having been granted permission to travel to Asokore to join in the funeral obsequies of one of their own relatives there. Word reached Asokore from Boaso of the arrival and purpose of the *Akyempemhene's* messenger. Akuoku and the others fled Asokore, and hid in the bush rather than return to Boaso.

8 The *Akyempemhene ɔheneba* Owusu Kɔkɔɔ was killed in the course of the civil wars at the end of 1884. As Asante declined into anarchy, Akuoku and his sons led a precarious existence in the rural areas of the Asante Akyem borderland. For long periods they lived by foraging.

9 After the civil wars ended and Agyeman Prempe was enstooled as *Asantehene* in 1888, Akuoku and his sons returned to Asokore. There they became the subject of dispute between the stools of Asokore, Akyempem and (now) Ananta. In this uncertain situation, Akuoku and his sons once more elected to become refugees. They fled Asokore, and settled beyond the bounds of Asante jurisdiction in Kwawu. There they led a precarious life until, about 1890, Akuoku died. His sons remained in Kwawu until after the British annexation of Asante in 1901. They then returned to Asokore. Some time afterwards, Akuoku's funeral custom was celebrated in Asokore, and his bones – carried by his sons on their return journey from Kwawu – were interred in his natal town.

10 A number of Akuoku's relatives and/or descendants were claimed by the Ananta stool when the Ashanti Confederacy was 'restored' under British auspices in 1935. But the Ananta claim was overruled. At the same time, the *Asokorehene* was restored to the status of serving the *Asantehene* directly.[54]

The foregoing examples are necessarily complex, but the sheer mass of entangling detail that makes them so is apt illustration of the myriad ways in which individuals lived out their entire lives in direct relation to the core principle of jural corporateness and the ubiquitous shadow cast over it by the state. Conditional shifts in jural identity – provoked by state action, by quarrels between office holders, by the flow of political events, by circumstance, chance or even accident – constantly drew people into the state's orbit of attention, and mired them again and again in its embrace. This was ineluctable, for the state alone mediated jural corporateness, and membership in that corporateness was the sole guarantee of an identity in law that encompassed objective or prescriptive citizen rights. It was the only valid definition of Asante selfhood.[55]

It should be noted, moreover, that in the instances reviewed above all of the individuals centrally concerned possessed lineage affiliations of one sort or another, and throughout all of the mediated shifts in their status they continued to retain some recognizable (if altered or diminished) form of jural identity, together with some corresponding degree of minimal access to citizen rights. It is notable that in the very extreme case where Akuoku of Asokore faced impending execution, this situation was only made possible by a questionable and partisan reading of his status – rebel, prisoner of war – that chose to construct him as having fallen out of, or having been expelled from, jural corporateness. The unambiguous reality of such a falling out or expulsion was a catastrophe for anyone who suffered it, for it connoted transference to the category of non-existence. The course that the state might then elect to pursue in the matter of someone thus severed from any lien on jural corporateness was unilateral, for there no longer existed any counterbalance of even residual rights on the other side of the equation. A summary view of an important aspect of this was offered by Kwasi Apea Nuama in 1930; his remarks should be read with the case of Akuoku – himself an *ahenkwaa* – in mind.

When an Ahinkwaa [*ahenkwaa*] of a Chief dies, all his belongings should be brought before the Chief, who may select anything he likes and give the rest to the family (i.e. the Ahinkwaa's nearest relatives). I have known cases where a Chief's subject has behaved badly and has been banished and given to another Chief. In such cases the latter has sole control of such a person and has absolute title to his property, and in olden days could kill him if he pleased. If such a person served as an Ahinkwaa, on his death all his property would be taken by the Chief.[56]

Let us now consider the situation of those foreign-born slaves whose lives were lived outside of jural corporateness and the framework of identity that it conferred. Great numbers of foreign-born slaves in eighteenth- and nineteenth-century Asante came from the acephalous peoples of the northern savanna hinterland, or from further afield via the caravan trade of the western Sudan.[57] The generic Asante name for them was *nnɔnkɔfoɔ* (sing. *ɔdɔnkɔ*), a term in such broad use that some European commentators were erroneously led to believe that there existed a specific ethnicity of that name.[58] The etymology of *ɔdɔnkɔ* remains unclear. Rattray, expressing appropriate misgivings, recorded that his informants offered the derivation *dɔ* (to love) + *kɔ* (to go off; to run away); 'i.e. some one whom you love but who may run away'.[59] But it should also be pointed out that the root $d\mathfrak{o}$ can mean to multiply, or to become very numerous, and that the adverbial noun $ad\mathfrak{o}n(a)$ translates as a difficulty in loving, a disaffection or an alienation.[60]

Whatever the case, as is abundantly clear from reported speech and traditions, the term suggested a brute animality to the Asante, and connoted a non-human status. 'The small tribes in the interior', said the *Asantehene* Kwaku Dua Panin in 1841, 'fight with each other, take prisoners and sell them for slaves; and as I know nothing about them, I allow my people to buy and sell them as they please: they are of no use for any thing else but slaves; they are stupid, and little better than beasts.'[61] Dismissive characterizations of this sort were socially precise, for only sanctioned assimilation to matriliny and jural corporateness could confer a legitimate human (Asante) status, and thereby, in theory, emancipate the $\mathfrak{o}d\mathfrak{o}nk\mathfrak{o}$ from an unremitting exploitation that ended in death (and that even precluded burial, for interment was a privilege of citizenship).[62]

Establishing the identity of foreign-born slaves in Asante, as in other historic societies, is a difficult problem. However, some insight into the matter can be gleaned from Dutch records. On 18 March 1837, a contract was entered into in Kumase between the *Asantehene* Kwaku Dua Panin and Major-General J. Verveer, a Royal Commissioner of the government of the Netherlands. Among other provisions, the agreement stipulated that the Asante state was to provide 'recruits' for the army of the Dutch East Indies in exchange for guns.[63] In reality, this arrangement was little more than a thinly disguised continuation of the slave trade. Between 1837 and 1842 the Dutch at Elmina took delivery of nearly 1,000 'recruits' from Kumase, and they recorded the stated birthplace of each of them. Virtually all of these 'recruits' were *nnɔnkɔfoɔ*, acquired by the Asante as tribute, through trade or purchase, or by raiding. Their origins were very diverse. Around two thirds came from the vast hinterland of Asante; from the neighbouring kingdoms of Gonja, Dagomba and Mamprusi, from the Mossi states further to the north, and from the host of acephalous peoples scattered across this entire area. The remainder originated from distant Borno and the emirates of the Sokoto Caliphate; from what is now Togo to the east of Asante, and Ivory Coast to the west; and, at least in one case, from as far away as Zinder in what is now Niger.[64]

Rebellion was never really a realistic option for such people. It is all too often overlooked by historians, among others, that the recognition and articulation of the premisses of disadvantage required phenomenal efforts of imagination, will and tenacity on the part of the oppressed, and that converting all of this to effective action needed a rare unity of identity and purpose.[65] The Asante *nnɔnkɔfoɔ* were ethnically diverse, far from home, stigmatized by a halting or inflected Twi, and often distinguished by cicatrization.[66] Many of them wore clothing that betokened their status; kobɔaka (a striped tunic), kadana (drawers), and a bangle on the upper right arm.[67] Moreover, although slaves were sometimes concentrated together in areas generally distant from Kumase, the more common arrangement was to intermix them with Asante cultivators, and to locate them close to the oversight afforded by local political authorities. Thus, as late as 1883, the Basel missionary Dilger passed through many small hunting and farming settlements inhabited by 'donkos' (nnɔnkɔfoɔ), who were quite unable to speak or understand Twi, in the course of a short day's journey between the major towns of Kumawu and Agogo in Asante Akyem.[68]

The state closely monitored the possibility of slave revolt, and especially after the abolition of the transatlantic slave trade. But its chief weapons in deterring insurrection were physical dispersal, social marginalization, and, above all, the control of consciousness and identity by means of the combination of withholding jural corporateness while simultaneously holding out the implicit possibility of some level of assimilation to it. For the nnɔnkɔfoɔ, the chance of entering Asante society, remote though it might appear, was a far more realistic and encouraging proposition than the hazardous possibility of escaping from it completely. And the only point of entry was the attainment of some level of status in jural corporateness.

Slaves had rights stemming from their status as property, but they were not nkoa, and so such rights were not rooted in any status of being sui iuris; properly, a master (wura) oversaw and exercised such rights on behalf of his property – the ɔdɔnkɔ; disputes between masters and slaves might be resolved by legal action that translated rights in the ɔdɔnkɔ to another owner, but such measures were adjustments in the ownership of a (productive) good, and not status shifts of supposititious personhood in relation to any membership in jural corporateness. Asante views of the issues involved are perhaps best understood by reference to what nnɔnkɔfoɔ actually did, and how this was conceptualized.

At first sight, slaves and nkoa performed the same tasks. But slaves worked very much harder, and they were charged with much of the heavy or dirty labour on farms; ataŋtansɛ nti na yɛ to ɔdɔnkɔ ('we buy an ɔdɔnkɔ because of filthy work').[69] At first a slave worked no food plot of his or her own; slaves were fed by their owners in a direct form of exchange for labour. Subsequently, slaves might be given portions of land for their own subsistence, wives, permission to trade, and a range of other perquisites. But the operational verb is given, for unilateral donations of this sort might be just as readily withdrawn. Bereft of any status in jural corporateness, slaves were denied any rights of control over their own genealogical future. That is, the children of the vast majority of unions into which slaves – male or female – might contract were defined in terms of the rights in property held by a third party in either or both of their parents.[70]

A telling parallel in Asante social practice – and by clear implication in thought – was between slaves and adolescents. Both these categories of persons might do very broadly similar kinds of work under analogous forms of direction and bidding. Neither category had a full autonomy of selfhood or identity within jural corporateness. The crucial difference, however, was that slaves were trapped in the status of being perpetual minors, whereas adolescents might look forward to achieving citizen rights within jural corporateness with the simple passage of time. Bynames, forms of address, objective descriptions and attitudes all reveal the casting of the slave in the role of a minor in Asante perception.[71] Thus, as has been noted, possession of a gun was an indicator of adult male status; slaves went to war, carried weapons and accoutrements in a bag ($bɔtɔ$) that belonged to their master, and might even fight – but they were disbarred from the adult male right of owning or bearing their own gun.[72] The dependence of the minor, and the all but total social isolation that stemmed from exclusion from a belonging in jural corporateness, must have produced atomization, alienation and even anomie in the individual. Of course, we have no direct testimony to this effect, but the conditions that proclaimed such a state of affairs were well caught by Rattray.

The chief danger in which his [the slave's] peculiar status placed him appears to me to lie in the fact that the slave was generally a solitary creature more or less at the mercy of a single individual. Every one around him was in a sense 'the slave' of some one, but persons had always behind them a whole group of relatives, whose numbers and wealth and power were ever at their disposal . . . One outstanding fact, however, remained, i.e. that the status of a slave, i.e. an *odonko*, could never be lost, and, when necessity arose, or the terrible practice of human sacrifice became the vogue, an otherwise kind and considerate master would turn instinctively to the man who had no friend in the world, in order to satisfy the need for money or for a victim.[73]

Even those slaves who exercised high responsibility in the household of the *Asantehene* suffered the crippling disability of not being *sui iuris*. In this they were disadvantaged even by comparison with those relatively few Asante who fell, for whatever reason, out of jural corporateness and into the ranks of bondage (*akoa pa*). An Asante of this status still had precedent ties to jural corporateness, and might hope to be redeemed by his kin and restored to full citizen rights. But – to repeat – a foreign-born slave was in essence a good. No matter how long such slaves survived, or how trusted or favoured they were, their status as disposable property was always negotiable without any reference at all to the premiss of jural corporateness. An *ɔdɔnkɔ* might simply be reclassified at the owner's behest as an *akyere* (pl. *ŋkyere*), or 'one destined to be sacrificed' for a variety of ritual purposes. Nineteenth-century Asante contained entire villages of *ŋkyere*; Konongo, now a considerable town, was founded as an *akyerekuraa* for the exclusive use of the *Dwabenhemaa*. In such settlements people might live for years, have children, and die. But the status of *akyere* was as far away from citizen rights as it was possible to get, and the descendants of *ŋkyere* remained bound by that status without any form of potential redress. Eventually, and perhaps after the passage of a great deal of time, the descendant of an *akyere* might be summoned to be sacrificed in a long-dead ancestor's place.[74]

A degree of assimilation to jural corporateness was the only realistic hope for a slave. It was only after such a person was granted quasi-nepotal status in a family and lineage that he or she acquired any access to jural autonomy and minimal citizen rights. Of course, success in negotiating the very formidable *jural* boundary did not necessarily translate into an equivalent *social* acceptance. The overwhelming import of the premiss of jural corporateness can be seen in this distinction. In effect, the stigma of slave origins in the eighteenth and nineteenth century – the fact of having originated *outside* of jural corporateness – clung to descendants through males of a male slave; and the matrilineal descendants of a female slave might still be kept in a condition of quasi-servile tutelage.[75] Numerous knowing distinctions – between for example the superior 'right' (*nifa*) and inferior 'left' (*beŋkum*) descent aggregates of a lineage segment – preserved the memory of free and slave origins.[76] However, any reference to such matters tended to euphemism or indirectness. Direct public statements about the slave origins and antecedents of lineage filiates were actionable and punishable in law, for even in the second generation the term *akoa* was always employed in describing even the most disadvantaged descendants of an assimilated *ɔdɔnkɔ*. In this matter – and absolutely predictably – the state stood behind the guarantees embodied in any achieved membership in jural corporateness; *obi nkyere obi ase* ('no one must disclose the origin of another'), as was noted in the 1920s, was 'a legal maxim of tremendous import'.[77]

The determinedly relentless ideological structuration of jural corporateness was a primary instrument in the regulation of society, the ordering of servitude, and the forestalling of disruption and anarchy. It was underwritten throughout by coercive power, but that alone could never have guaranteed the continuing integrity of the compact between state, citizen and slave. The importance of structuration is underlined by the fact that Asante slavery was at bottom a system of exploitation and oppression. At a significant level, therefore, the absence of any slave uprising was a tribute to the state's effective mastery over and use of the definition(s) of social identity. It was not, as might be assumed simplistically from that very absence, an indication of the benign character of Asante slavery.[78]

It is important to realize that for most of the precolonial period the state maintained a high level of vigilant control over any indiscriminate penetration of Asante by alien ideas. The introduction or unauthorized use of 'a foreign fashion' (amaɲfrafoɔ yɛbea) – in thought or behaviour – was a capital offence.[79] To all intents and purposes, this was a system closed to the access of unmediated external knowledge. It was not until state power faltered and collapsed in the 1880s that Asante was fully confronted by radically different conceptions of ordering society and interpreting the world. We have already seen something of this in relation to accumulation and wealth, and we will have more to say about it below in the general context of social philosophy and ethics.

We can observe something of the exclusionist power of the state, and of the abiding authority of its ideological structurations and social models, in the history of slavery and servitude in Asante in the early colonial period. The Basel missionary F. Ramseyer had a knowledge of Asante affairs that stretched back to his captivity in Kumase in the early 1870s. In 1904, he complained to the Governor of the Gold Coast that though the British had finally abolished the slave trade in Asante after annexation in 1901, they still condoned pre-existing relations of domestic servitude. The British responded by claiming that with an embargo on the importation of any new nnɔnkɔfoɔ, the institution of slavery would simply wither away with time. Each party was purposely naïve in its reading; Ramseyer wanted converts, and the British were reluctant to meddle with Asante institutions lest they provoke a repetition of the Yaa Asantewaakɔ or uprising of 1900–1. Part of the British argument for retaining the status quo ante was their simplistic view of the benign nature of Asante slavery. As the Chief Commissioner for Asante remarked in 1905 in his rebuttal of Ramseyer's arguments,

It must not be thought from the foregoing proposals that the Ashantis are cruel to their slaves. In point of fact, I have not received a single complaint from a slave against his master. Both owners and owned know that the latter have only to cross the frontier into the [Gold Coast] Colony to shake off the yoke of servitude and the fact that so few slaves avail themselves of the privilege speaks volumes in favour of the good understanding prevailing between lord and vassal, and in spite of Mr. Ramseyer's denunciations, it can be taken for granted that all the slaves who remain with their masters in Ashanti do so of their own free will: because they form a part of the family; because they are well cared for; and because the bond of sympathy uniting them to their masters is based on a community of interests and on mutual good feeling and support.[80]

This agreeable portrait continued to serve the British as explanation when they found it puzzlingly difficult to secure the cooperation of slaves in their own emancipation.[81] But philanthropy, harmony, and 'mutual good feeling and support' were not the real reasons for the slow dissolution of the liens of servitude. Simply, the entire weight of the ideological structuration of historical experience served to privilege aspiration to the most tenuous membership in jural corporateness over an individual 'freedom' that connoted the non-being of exclusion from Asante society. The realization that one could walk away from one's situation was a gigantic cognitive step rather than a simple geographical exercise, and it was correspondingly slow to crystallize into a widespread norm. A slave might run away from a master – and, increasingly, many did – but repudiating the condition of slavery ordained a novel world view that numbers eventually found in Christian conversion.[82]

In the complex of interactions adumbrated above, the state structured the operational premises of the social order in ways that filled the horizon of possibility with a single agendum. This fused together action, ideology and legitimation in an authoritative model of consensus. All of the imperatives, norms and values of Asante historical experience – of self-conscious social knowledge – flowed together in and through the ideological mediations of the state and thence back into their origins in cultural definition. This represented an extremely sophisticated modelling of knowledge, and one that was resolutely integrated and purposefully self-referencing. Structuration of the production of food, the accumulation of wealth, the meaning of matriliny, the content of differentiation, freedom and slavery, and of the sum of related contingencies and expressions, were all locked together in an ideological grid of comprehensive definition, validation and mnemonic.

All of these actualizations were translated from the experiences and observations of quotidian reality, and they were ultimately rooted in the conscious knowledge of a cumulative historical evolution. However, in the eighteenth and nineteenth centuries in Asante the contexts of existence – social and individual – were also defined by a complex of belief(s). As we have noted, the nature, specific content and impact of Asante belief have been seriously neglected by historians. In what follows, the nature of belief is interpreted on its own terms and in its own right, but also in relation to the specifics of its social and individual meanings, and in terms of its interactions with knowledge. Like knowledge, belief flowed from the levels of the social and the individual to crystallize in appropriate representations. As expressive signifiers, such representations formulated and rehearsed the constituents of belief in the public domain, and thereby argued particular constructions of being Asante. And, as with knowledge, the state took measures to arrogate arguments about belief, and to convert such arguments into statements.

Belief I: preliminary remarks

Belief in Asante thought and practice is a subject of immense complexity. It has been rendered even more opaque and resistant to understanding by the habitual reduction of its content, parameters and intentionalities to commonplace or ill-defined categories. Analogy and derivation have ensured that such categories are of the second order of abstraction. Customarily, that is, Asante belief is represented as an agendum internalized and/or practised somewhere on a continuum between formalized religion (however accented in terms of faith, opinion, dogma and ritual) and the individual possession and social enactment of degrees of psychological or intuitive certainty.[83]

In part this situation has arisen because Asante Twi lacks linguistic parsimony in dealing with and describing this and other areas of subjective experience. Belief terms open into a multiple universe of indistinct transitive objects; accepting, taking, asking, demanding, serving, and the rest.[84] In combination with a referencing to second-order categories, this has produced a reading that reduces the contexts of belief – and the expressions of believing – to an unexceptional or mundane ethics of existence. At its widespread worst, this formulation is expressed in a bathetic series of circular tautologies and self-fulfilling pseudo-profundities, of which the following might be taken as a representative instance: 'It may be said without fear of exaggeration that life in the Akan world is religion and religion is life.'[85]

In amorphous ethical banalities, such as the foregoing, belief as an epistemological issue is distilled down to a species of recursive religiosity, in which an equation of identities replaces both subject and object. This is profoundly ahistorical, and adds rather than subtracts mystification. Myopic confusions are also pronounced when, as in twentieth-century Asante, many interpreters produce readings from within the framework of a superimposed, generally Christian orthodoxy. Human sacrifice, to take one example, presents problems of apologetics or evasion no less grave for the Christian Asante than for the historian of 'rational' behaviour.[86]

The propositional framework of Asante belief is adumbrated here in direct relation to the broadest sustainable construction that can be placed upon its historical objectives. Accordingly, the inclusive conditions of belief can be enumerated under the following six general rubrics.

1 A state of mind in which confidence (including faith) is placed in an idea, thing or person.
2 A conviction or feeling that something is true or real.
3 That which is contained in or asserted by an idea.
4 Intellectual assent to an idea.

5 That which stems from immediacy, or non-reasoned acceptance of an idea.
6 That which stems from a deliberately thought-out argument.

This is a calculated enlargement. It is designed to exclude any idealist or syllogistic inference. More importantly, it is designed to include both the intellectual and ideological content of belief items that lay within the all-encompassing received category called Asante religion. That is, belief is construed historically in terms of the force of its *ideas* in lived existence.[87] There is a pressing need for a framework of this sort. As matters stand, even the most sophisticated of interpretations, as we have seen, adduce as historical explanation assertions that there was 'some independent strength' in 'religious ideas' because they were the constituents of a 'shared idiom'.[88] This is just, and it takes us some way forwards to an understanding. But to leave the matter there invites to the danger of a theorizing of formal distinctions without any visible roots in the historical record.[89]

Horton, who has written extensively on the nature of African belief – but from an intellectualist position rather than from any very rigorous or detailed treatment of the historical record – has proposed 'two distinct yet intimately complementary levels of thought and discourse'. 'Primary theory' renders the world in terms of observable categories and spatial and causal connections. 'Secondary theory' references 'hidden' entities and processes, and in transcending the given world of 'primary theory' it proposes explanation of it.[90] Despite Horton's disclaimer, there is the clear implication here – commonly found in Africanist discourse – that belief somehow enjoys a privileged hermeticism; that it is *of* but not truly *in* the remainder of historical experience. In all manner of ways, Asante belief was mired and implicated in the real, lived world of historical experience; that is, 'primary' and 'secondary' theories, in Horton's terms, were not merely 'intimately complementary', but inextricably bound up with and enmeshed in one another. The distinction may seem one of degree, but on closer inspection it is actually one of kind. That is, in order to anatomize Asante beliefs, religious expressions, ritual enactments and the rest, they need to be articulated as *ideas* in direct relation to the historical record concerning the world of state, society and individual. Belief is an *historical* phenomenon, and must be treated as such.[91]

The expressive content of Asante belief – material, performative, symbolic – is well documented historically, and in outline it can be readily abstracted to a hierarchy of order and power. As a result, some commentators have adduced direct parallels between the expressive frameworks, both simultaneously allocative and appropriative, of a supernatural and a human order.[92] The mirror effect is striking, at least superficially. However, it would be a grossly misleading simplification to confine all items of belief to this frame of reference. The descriptive assumptions of an epistemology derived from an identifiable series of upward hierarchical calibrations, leading towards ever more inclusive competencies of affect, direction and control, simply do not meet the case. The arena of belief admittedly contained these features within it. Its principal defining characteristic, however, was the very high degree of plasticity in the range of issues addressed and solutions advanced. Apart from its role in or as structuration in a presentist sense, Asante belief was greatly complicated as an issue by the burdensome impress of cognitive and psychological intentionalities. To make connections and to fill voids by disclosing meaning – metaphorically, liminally, hermeneutically, meta-representationally – was a crucial matter that I have discussed in some detail elsewhere.[93]

To many nineteenth-century Europeans, the Asante shockingly combined an apparent lack of interest in higher theological speculation with a conversationally laconic treatment of it when pressed to any form of considered reflection. The historical sources imply a rudimentary ontology. Creative and/or determining forces – like Kantian *noumena* – were clearly inaccessible to empirical observation, but were held to exist in a seemingly commonplace way.[94]

Onyame (der. *onya*: to get or achieve + *mee*: to be full up or complete) was acknowledged to have created the visible world. Numerous bynames commemorated aspects of his oversight; a Basel Mission list of *Gottesnamen*, recorded in the early twentieth century, is, for example, typically long and complex.[95] The bynames for *onyame* most commonly in use among the Asante included the following (with the attributes encoded or implied in each):

1	*ɔdomaŋkama*	eternally abundant; fecund creator of all; infinite; absolute; boundless; limitless
2	*onyaŋkopɔŋ*	supreme embodiment of the shining expanse of the sky; solitary; alone in grandeur
3	*otweaduampɔŋ*	the almighty overseer; the watching one; the dependable one
4	*otumf(u)o*	the omnipotent one; the possessor of visionary insight (cognate with an appellation bestowed on *Asantehenes*)
5	*bɔrebɔre*	creator; inventor; builder; 'architect' of all
6	*ɔbɔadeɛ*	creator
7	*totorubonsu*	progenitor and bringer of rain
8	*atoapɛm*	final; unsurpassable; beyond which one cannot go[96]
9	*ɔbeannyeɛ*	uncreated; without beginning
10	*tɛtɛkwaframua*	enduring forever (outside of time)
11	*brɛkyerehunnyadeɛ*	knowing all; omniscient.[97]

These attributions were familiar, as is suggested by their promiscuity of referential analogies, and they were neither located in nor supported by a developed exegetics. Historical references suggest a usage at once comfortably intimate, generalized and theologically unpursued. Thus, in 1844, the *Dwabenhemaa* Amma Sewaa typically stated

that they had some idea of a person, generally called '*Dumancuman*' [*ɔdomaŋkama*] who they believed created all things, and was the great originator of everything seen or made. They distinguished him from '*Yaakumpon*' [*onyaŋkopɔŋ*] who they believe is God all powerful.[98]

Reported speech, traditions and *contes moraux* all indicate that the absence of sustained curiosity about *onyame* was due to the assumption that he had removed himself from the affairs of men immediately upon fulfilling his role as demiurge. This explanatory syndrome, sometimes called the 'withdrawn God', is widespread throughout Africa.[99] But in Asante, the specific reasons adduced for the creator's withdrawal were always linked to human duplicity, folly or crime. Thus, Rattray recorded the following folk story, which was 'universally known among the older people' in the 1920s.

Long, long ago Onyankopon lived on earth, or at least was very near to us. Now there was a certain old woman who used to pound her *fufu* (mashed yams, etc.) and the pestle (lit. the child of the mortar, as the Asante word means) used to constantly knock up against Onyankopon (who was not then high up in the sky). So Onyankopon said to the old woman, 'Why do you always do so to me? Because of what you are doing I am going to take myself away up in the sky.' And of a truth he did so.[100]

In the denouement of this tale, the Asante then tried to reach *onyaŋkopɔŋ*, despite his stated intention to withdraw, by climbing skyward on a pile of mortars. But the pile was one mortar short, and when the Asante removed a single mortar from the bottom of the heap to place on its summit, the entire edifice came crashing down and killed many people.

Representations of this sort both fed into and were reinforced by abiding anxieties about the defensible fragility of culture.[101] Implicated in such moralizing constructions were pessimistic readings of historical reality, of situational positioning in the world, of felt limitations to existence, and of brittleness in the edifice of human moral order. The withdrawal of *onyame* bequeathed a reality in which possibility might always be subverted by a ubiquitous and insistent human frailty. We can observe the consequences of this in all manner of belief contexts. Thus, Asante divination was essentially minatory; it dealt in pessimistic texts about the future of individual supplicants. The diviner's pot (*ɛkoro*: syn. *kuŋkuma*) contained water, palm wine and *abo* – a variety of talismanic objects, each of which offered a specific prognostication of the future. The first object to appear after the pot had been stirred by the diviner conveyed the appropriate message. The *abo* and their implicative meanings were:

1 Piece of hoe or digging tool 'You will die; the grave is being dug for your burial.'

2 Piece of sheep/sheep's wool 'The ancestors want a sheep from you'; i.e. the ancestors need to be propitiated.

3 Piece of dog's leg bone 'Your father's spirit wants a dog from you'; i.e. father's spirit needs to be propitiated.

4 Chicken leg 'Your own soul wants a white fowl'; i.e. the supplicant's soul needs to be propitiated.

5 Charcoal 'You are going to confront a grave situation that will make your head reel.'

6 *nyame akuma* (stone axe head) 'God is pursuing you to cut you down'; i.e. you are going to be punished.

7 Knotted raffia 'You are under stress but will toil only in vain.'

8 *hwere* (a kind of grass; cf. *hwere*; to squander, consume) 'You will lose a lot; you will spend much gold in seeking a cure for illness and other problems.'

9 Piece of grinding stone 'You will weigh out much gold and pour it away; you will incur a bad debt and have to pay it.'

10 Egg shells 'God requires twin eggs'; i.e. a need for propitiation.

11 A round stone or 'marble' 'You will be lonely; you will encounter problems and difficulties; you will suffer grief.'

12 *patuwuo* (a kind of bead; cf. *ɔpatwu*; sudden death) 'Maleficence will cause your sudden death; you will not last long.'

13 *ntwemma* (a small white bead) 'Your god and soul have fled from you'; i.e. expect grief or death.

14 *dadwene* (a camwood seed; cf. *ɔdadweŋe*; care, anxiety) 'The spirits want something in order to think well of you'; i.e. you will be worried by something.

15 *asibuo* (a seed) 'Somebody is envious of you; someone wants you to lose something very precious.'

16 *akɔmmeŋ* (a necklace of beads worn by women; said to have magical properties) 'Witchcraft is pursuing you; you are envied and/or loathed; you may commit suicide out of frustration and fear'; (there is an implication in this of infertility or sterility).[102]

Similarly, in the most authoritative recensions of tradition, the secret of immortality remained undisclosed to the Asante because of the precipitate greed of humankind.[103] Analogous *ex post facto* explanations of historical realities might appear as objective rationalizations, but they were habitually clothed in the language and metaphors of a highly subjective relationship with the withdrawn creator. This relationship was fatally undermined by the prevalence of obdurate human foibles, and ensuing disabilities were ascribed to active Asante agency. In 1817, the Kumase *Adumhene* Adum Ata offered the following account of the difference between the Asante and Europeans.

In the beginning of the world, God created three white and three black men, with the same number of women; he resolved, that they might not afterwards complain, to give them their choice of good and evil. A large box or calabash was set on the ground, with a piece of paper, sealed up, on one side of it. God gave the black men the first choice, who took the box, expecting it contained every thing, but, on opening it, there appeared only a piece of gold, a piece of iron, and several other metals, of which they did not know the use. The white men opening the paper, it told them every thing. God left the blacks in the bush, but conducted the whites to the water side, (for this happened in Africa) communicated with them every night, and taught them to build a small ship which carried them to another country, whence they returned after a long period, with various merchandise to barter with the blacks, who might have been the superior people.[104]

In the eighteenth and nineteenth centuries *onyame* had neither priestly servitors nor temples devoted to his worship.[105] As befitted an omniscient absence, his manifestation was ubiquitous, but in a highly diffused and domesticated way. Asante dwellings contained *nyame dua*, simple mnemonic shrines constructed from the forked branch of a particular tree (*Alstonia congensis*). Individual resort was made to these by reflex; sometimes a troubled mind might seek solace or some form of quietus in addressing *onyame*.[106]

There was much passivity, resignation and even scepticism in such familiar practices, as indeed there was in the general lack of interest in speculative theology. *Onyame* was the final arbiter of justice, but in this, as in other matters, he was remote and allocative rather than approachable and flexible. In short, the creator's role in human affairs – in lived existence – was essentially judgmental. It was *onyame* who assigned to a person his or her *nkrabea* (der. *kra*: to take leave of + *bea*: the way of doing something), a component of the human individual best understood conceptually in terms of fate or destiny. The *nkrabea* itself was ontologically unexplored. It might be directly assigned by *onyame* as an ordered destiny (*hyɛbea*), or it might be bindingly approved of by him after being recited in his presence by an individual who was about to be born into corporeal existence. Definition of the essence or essentialist nature of the *nkrabea* was quite unimportant compared with the understanding that *onyame* alone had any say in its dispensation.[107]

The foregoing was a generalized construction. As we shall see, interpretation or comprehension of the idea of predestination, together with the absence of any interrogative or transformational dialogue with the creator, combined in moulding an otherworldliness that lacked imaginative projection. This area of belief – and any possible register of belief items that might be compiled within it – was not the object of a strict quiddity. And in the distinct absence of any defined theological autonomy, ideological structuration moved to fill the gap, peopling the *terra incognita* of a non-corporeal afterlife in its own image. At the beginning of the nineteenth century, Bowdich afforded some insight into this in his descriptive account of an otherworldly differentiation and hierarchy. However, he intellectualized causality, albeit in relation to rudimentary thought processes and the facsimiles or simulacra of reality postulated by a primitive theology. By so doing, he passed over the issue of ideological structuration by domesticating its implications to a species of willed ignorance.

With this imaginary alienation from the God of the universe, not a shade of despondency is associated; they consider that it diminishes their comforts and their endowments on earth, but that futurity is a dull and torpid state to the majority of mankind ... The kings, caboceers, and the higher class, are believed to dwell with the superior Deity after death, enjoying an eternal renewal of the state and luxury they possessed on earth. It is with this impression, that they kill a certain number of both sexes at the funeral customs, to accompany the deceased, and to administer to his pleasures. The spirits of the inferior classes are believed to inhabit the houses of the fetish, in a state of torpid indolence, which recompenses them for the drudgery of their lives, and which is truly congenial to the feelings of the Negro.[108]

Belief II: *abosom, asumaŋ, akɔmfoɔ*

The elaborated representations of Asante belief were articulated most densely – and expressed most potently – at a level of embodiment(s) below that of *onyame*. An immense and fluctuating range of powers, entities and supernatural beings was subsumed in the broad categorical rubric of *abosom* (sing. *ɔbosom*). The *abosom*, variously rendered in the sources as gods, tutelary spirits or 'fetishes', were assigned an anthropomorphic identity as the 'children' of *onyame*. Their origins, crucially, lay beyond human society, and their appearances and manifestations in the affairs of men were unilateral, arbitrary and interventionist. By definition, the *abosom* were powers in and of that nature that had preceded culture. The Asante classified an *ɔbosom* with reference to its source or point of origin within the natural universe. This produced a broad classificatory subdivision of the *abosom* into the following three classes or groups:

5 'Wall painting – elephant, palm, hunter'. The location of this mural cannot be identified with certainty. The original is filed, however, in a series of photographs (including other murals) taken by Rattray in May 1922 at the 'temple' of *Taa Kora* at Tano Oboase near the headwaters of the Tano river in northwest Asante. A vivid depiction shows an Asante hunter (named Kwaku Apea?) taking aim at an elephant (*ɛsono*) with his flintlock musket. The elephant's tail (*mena; mmra*) – the symbol of wealth accumulated at the highest level, and the item of regalia that the state bestowed upon the *ɔbirɛmpɔn* – is drawn with deliberate clarity (and exaggerated size, for effect?). Other murals from Tano Oboase are reproduced in R.S. Rattray, *Ashanti* (Oxford, 1923), Figs. 74–6, and discussed in *ibid.*, 173–5 and 182.

1 *atano*. These were powers that derived from water, and principally rivers. The subdivision was named for the river Tano in northwestern Asante, which was in itself the source of numerous, important manifestations of the *abosom*. Such manifestations, which were disseminated throughout Asante, were popularly known by the abbreviated term *taa* (der. Tano), and were further classified by the day of their revelation; *Taa* (Tano) *Kwabena* (Tuesday); *Taa* (Tano) *Kofi* (Friday), etc. The *atano* protected the community (culture) but were vengeful if shown disrespect.

2 *ewim*. These were powers that derived from the sky (*ewim*). They were commonly understood as being unbending, judgemental, and merciless when crossed. They were very frequently anthropomorphized as *abrafoɔ* or *adumfoɔ* (executioners). They were held to have a special relationship with *sasabonsam*, a forest-being that devoured hunters.

3 *abo. (ŋkwatia ŋkwatia wuram)*. These were powers that derived from the forest,

6 'A *nyame dua* in the modern built house of a paramount chief' (on reverse: 'Boy in white robe with painted body designs standing next to an altar'). This photograph shows *nyame dua* ('God's tree'), the ubiquitous

in the broadest sense of whatever grew wild (*wura*). The word *ɔbo* meant simply a rock or stone (compare the diviner's *abo* – lumps, 'things'), and was a common locus of this class of manifestation. The *abo* were held to have a special relationship with *mmoatia*, small, trickster-like denizens of the forest; hence, *ɔbo yɛ mmoatia bosom (ɔbo* is the *ɔbosom* of the *mmoatia)*. They were particularly associated with the power of healing.[109]

The *abosom* were quite distinct from the numerous class of objects that were termed *asuman* (charms, amulets, talismans; sing. *suman*). Each of these was dedicated to a series of precise and highly circumscribed functions, and was, in essence, an aspectual fragment or derived manifestation of a much larger embodiment of power. In Asante thought, *abosom* made themselves known voluntarily, and could neither be manufactured nor bought. By contrast,

'nsuman' are lower and behave as messengers of a temporary nature. 'Abosom' can give instructions for the making of a 'suman' which is lower order of spirit beings operating through little 'jujus'... 'Nsuman' can be bought. Not so in the case of 'Abosom'... The Ashantis serve the 'Abosom' but single individuals keep 'nsuman' for their own private purposes. Some 'abosom' have 'nsuman' about them which are used as messengers. 'Abosom' generally can explain by oracles certain complicating problems (and 'nsuman' cannot)... The 'Abosom' operate for a much longer time. 'Nsuman' have [a] temporary purpose. They are very revengeful indeed. They borrow their power from lower, lower things which can act without reasoning properly. 'Nsuman' are good or bad. 'Abosom' can be good and bad.[110]

It is important to record this distinction, for although *asuman* were lesser or derived powers, highly specific, personalized, and often very temporary in nature, they were visibly three dimensional and, in their many forms, ubiquitous throughout the whole of Asante society. As a result, Europeans often misleadingly reported *asuman* as being the core of Asante belief, whereas, important as they were, they were actually epiphenomenal to it.[111]

Powers of the three classes of *abosom* revealed themselves most commonly by 'mounting' or taking possession of individuals of either sex.

Caption for Plate 6 (*cont.*)

household shrine dedicated to *onyame*, and made from a forked branch of the actual tree called *(o)nyame dua (Alstonia congensis)*. Various ritual offerings were left in the bowl placed on the top (or put on the skewers, seen in the photograph, that were fixed to project from the forked ends of the branch). The bowl pictured here is a metal basin of modern design (and European manufacture?). Another, similar portrait – but taken in a much older dwelling, with a different boy, and illustrating a bowl of a more traditional type – is pictured in R.S. Rattray, *Ashanti* (Oxford, 1923), Fig. 52. The white clay markings and pectoral discs worn by the boys in both photographs were characteristic adornments of persons dedicated for life to particular forms of ritual service; see *ibid.*, 141–4.

7 'Priest in *doso* with *suman* hat, fetishes, and knife'. Rattray persuaded this (unnamed) ɔkɔmfɔ to describe the *asumaŋ* in his possession, and to don them for this portrait. The hat of woven grass is the *sumaŋ bisakotie* ('ask and turn aside'), which is surmounted by ram's horns with a wooden

Asante seized in this manner then underwent an arduous and prolonged training. Central to this apprenticeship was mastery of *akɔm*, a possession dance through which initiates channelled the intercessionary capacities and prophetic authority of the power that had selected them. The Asante explained *akɔm* in terms of an intervention into human affairs over which, importantly, people had no control, and they framed that explanation in remote time in the maxim, *se Twumasi ammɔ dam antɛ a aŋka akɔm amma.*

Whatever might compose *abosom* none can correctly tell. Twumasi was probably a young man. One day people observed him behaving very much like a mad man. He had been possessed by a certain power but the people with whom he lived did not know that he was becoming a medium of expression of an entity. After a spell of time Twumasi's state got normal. Then the people realised that it must be a new state or condition. *Akɔm* was what they were taught by the power of obsession to call Twumasi's state. So the proverb came about: 'Had Twumasi not gone mad and then normal again, there would not have come *akɔm* or *abosom* worship.'[112]

At the end of the training period – traditionally held to be seven years – the successful adept graduated to the ranks of the *akɔmfoɔ* (sing. *ɔkɔmfɔ*; lit. 'one possessed', but commonly rendered as 'priest').[113] An important feature to note is that the affect, dissemination and reputation of individual powers rose and fell over time. By its very nature, this system was capable of accommodating an endless series of novel revelations within an aetiological and cognitive framework that remained constant throughout.

Belief in this context was inextricably bound up with matters already reviewed. Fundamental to the categorical structuration of all *abosom* was

---

Caption for Plate 7 (*cont.*)

carving of an *afena* (sword) between them. Visible on the man's forehead are the plaited strands of the *sumaŋ ahunum* ('seeing in'), which was used to divine an enquirer's purposes. The *sumaŋ yentumi* ('they are not able'), affording protection, is hanging around the man's neck. Across his chest is tied another *sumaŋ ahunum*, with cowrie shells arranged to form symbolic *ŋkwaŋtanaŋ* (crossroads). Above the right elbow is fixed the *sumaŋ apo*, a specific against the disgrace of falling over while dancing *akɔm*. The iron bangle worn (always) on the right wrist is the *sumaŋ bansere*, commonly made from an old gun barrel and a prevention against assault. The *afena* (sword) in the right hand, the *ɔkɔmfɔ* said, was so that the *ɔbosom* that he served might cut a path during war. Just visible, suspended from the left wrist, is the *sumaŋ kunkuma*, a 'broom' designed to 'sweep away' defilement from all of the other *asumaŋ*. This man is also wearing the characteristic fringed raffia skirt or girdle (*ɔdɔsɔ*) of the *ɔkɔmfɔ*. All of these *asumaŋ* are described more fully in R.S. Rattray, *Religion and Art in Ashanti* (Oxford, 1927), 12–17; *ibid.*, Fig. 8 is another portrait of the same *ɔkɔmfɔ* – less good in many ways, but showing the *sumaŋ kunkuma* more clearly.

insistent concern about managing the relationship between the space of culture and that of hostile, impinging nature. The *abosom*, as noted, were situated as properties of and in nature. By corollary, they were outside human society, ubiquitously surrounding and pressing in on it. While appropriate preparations and measures might assist in conducing their manifestation in culture, the revelatory act itself was effected solely and exclusively by their own unilateral volition. Such powers appeared on their own cognizance from the perilous unknown beyond the domesticated confines of culture and human society. In consequence of this, and quite predictably in Asante terms, they were deemed to be exceedingly dangerous. The management of their interventionist appearance was the hazardous province of highly specialist *akɔmfoɔ*, for they could never be tamed and domesticated by and in culture.

The Asante understanding of these matters is revealed most fully and precisely in specific cases. The following is an indigenous Asante account of the manifestation of the power(s) of *atano* in the form of *Taa* (Tano) *Kwabena Bena*. It occurred during the reign of the *Asantehene* Kofi Kakari (1867–74) in the village of Adeɛbeba, where the *Manwerehene ɔbirɛmpɔn* Kwasi Brantuo had mimed hunting the elephant in 1844.

One evening in the days of Karikari, in the little village of Adɛbeba, a globe of light was seen on a Gyedua tree (Ficus) in the centre of the village. Vultures flew about. There were noises and whistling in the air. The old people then rushed for drums which began to play. Voices began to cry out and a band of musicians set forth *akɔm mwom* (Songs of Fetish Dances). The community was trying to capture an entity that wanted to come and stay with them and protect them. They did not know the kind whether Tanno [*atano*], or Obo [*ɔbo*] or Kobi [*kobi*, a common manifestation of *ewim*] i.e. River or Wood or Sky. The power of something yet invisible was moving like a bird from place to place. The King of Asante [Kofi Kakari] was informed. He sent sheep and long practised 'akomfo' to help in welcoming the new entity that was seeking to come down. A brass pan was procured. A little water was

---

Caption for Plate 8 (*opposite*)

8 'Close view of priest'. This picture is one of a series taken by Rattray when he attended an *apo* ceremony among the Takyiman Bron in April 1922. The man is dressed as an *ɔkɔmfɔ* – which he was – but he was also a hunter, with whom Rattray had discussed elephants a week before this photograph was taken. Rattray met with this 'rather striking-looking man, with a beard' on the outskirts of Takyiman, and photographed him there, when he was about 'to work up the spirit of his god upon him[self]'. He is shown carrying the 'shrine' of his *ɔbosom* on his head, and holding a cow-tail switch (*bodua*) in his hand. This man is pictured dancing on the same occasion in R.S. Rattray, *Ashanti* (Oxford, 1923), Figs. 67 and 68; his performance is described at *ibid.*, 162–3.

9 'Close view of *sasabonsam* figure'. This is one of a number of Asante carvings commissioned by Rattray and displayed at the Wembley Exhibition (London, 1924). The figure pictured is *sasabonsam*, a hybrid (human/non-human), predatory 'creature' of the deep forest, and a servant of the *abosom*. It was deemed to be hostile to human order, and expressed its antipathy by preying directly upon people and/or fostering witchcraft. There are numerous characterizations of *sasabonsam*. In this one the artist has especially emphasized extravagant and disorderly body

put in it. The noise directed this. The old priests called out for his name. He answered he came from River Tanno and was called Tanno Kwabena Benna.

Great ballad singers were then sent for. They extolled the phenomenon in befitting praise. The fetish then called out – 'Are you ready to receive me?' ... At last, after a good number of sheep and fowls had been sacrificed a meteor of light whistling through the air swiftly alighted and fell into the pan. It called out 'Who will come and receive me?'

One man, Kofi Ketewa, went up, embraced the pan to have it covered according to [its] orders. He was scalded all over the body from the chest to the belly. He was reputed to be a very strong man. He did not live long. He shot himself. The fetish then obsessed a woman who died in 1943.[114]

Such manifestations were ubiquitous. In the 1940s, for example, Adeɛbeba had *ayowa* (shrines) to four of them; and the nearby settlements of Toase, Adeɛmbra, Atasomaaso, Konkomaase, Kokoben and Saawua had twenty-two between them, most of nineteenth-century provenance.[115] The shrine of the *atano* called *Taa* (Tano) *Dwum* at Saawua had a great reputation. It was noted for its guidance in the accumulation of wealth, and was consulted in this capacity by the *Asantehene* Kofi Kakari.[116] The most powerful and efficacious manifestations of the *abosom* had prestige throughout Asante, and were consulted by the *Asantehenes* themselves in matters of great importance. Thus, on 22 December 1817, the *Asantehene* Osei Tutu Kwame left Kumase for his war camp near Breman, there 'to make fetish' for the success of the impending campaign against the *Gyamanhene* Kwadwo Adinkra.[117] Among the shrines brought to him for consultation were those of *Taa* (Tano) *Kwabena Bena* from Duase, *Taa* (Tano) *Dwum* from Adwuman, and *Bekɔɔ* (an *ewim*) from Bekyem.[118]

The *abosom* dated from the very beginnings of Asante society. They furnished a basic locational topography of the encompassing natural universe into which Asante culture had been so painstakingly inserted. Simultaneously, they embodied and represented a primary classification of the awesome, untamed, threatening and potentially destructive powers inherent in that universe. The *abosom* were consulted, directly or through the medium of the *akɔmfoɔ*, about baffling occurrences, obscurities of meaning, or in moments of biological, psychological or existential impasse. Thus, at Akyerensua in September 1904, the Basel Mission catechist N. Asare observed three women in the act of unburdening themselves before

---

Caption for Plate 9 (*cont.*)

hair, which was emblematic of a (super)natural force and wilfulness and a concomitant absence of control and restraint. Thus, the figure is cast as the very antithesis of right human (Asante) social order. R.S. Rattray, *Religion and Art in Ashanti* (Oxford, 1927), Fig. 19, pictures this same figurine in reduced scale, but flanked by carvings of two *mmoatia*.

that most potent of all *atano*, the river Tano itself. Two of them spoke of illness and the loss of children, while the third addressed the river as follows:

Good helper, I come purposely to ask you a help, for I have got a bad sore inside my head and throat, being an act of an enemy. I have made several attempts to get rid of same, but of no avail. I now pray thee good helper, assist me and these my grandchildren who stand here presently with me and save us from our bitter enemies.[119]

The resolution of such problems and anxieties clearly lay beyond cultural capacity. That being the case, advice and clarification were sought – often, we must imagine, in some desperation – in and from the natural realm and its immense and anarchic powers.

The prescriptions of *abosom*, generally mediated by *akɔmfoɔ*, might go some way towards dissolving troubled perplexity. But such utterances were always couched in allusive terms. Because *abosom* originated and belonged in the natural realm of unknowing and threat, their prognostications were often calculatedly and spitefully ambiguous. The expectation that they might prove cooperative and consoling when petitioned to assist in human affairs was tempered by recognition of their origin in an antagonism to culture. They were understood to be unpredictable, mocking, duplicitous and occasionally vengeful; some were known to be dangerously fickle. The village of Akyena in Mponua, for example, had two *atano*: a stream called *abrafia* and a pool named *tɔnwora* (*torɔm wora*). But *abrafia* developed a reputation for killing children, and the settlement was re-sited closer to *tɔnwora*. The latter contained numerous fish, the eating of which – after appropriate oblations to the pool – was understood to be a specific against the abhorrent disabilities of male impotence and female sterility. At one stage, to the consternation of the villagers, *tɔnwora* almost dried up. But this calamity was avoided by the offering of a sheep to the *ɔbosom* of the pool, on the advice of its *ɔkɔmfɔ*.[120] As has been noted, the *abosom* in the category of *ewim*, like the *abrafia* stream, were often anthropomorphized as executioners. To some degree of realization all *abosom* were individually anthropomorphized, at least in terms of a general spectrum of powerfully significant characteristics.

The issue becomes clearer if we consider the constructions of cultural meaning that were placed upon the *sasabonsam* and the *mmoatia*. The *sasabonsam* was a negative construct or distorting mirror of social order that inhabited nature. Its projected physicality was a confusion of categories that bespoke the promiscuous anarchy of the natural world. It had the torso of a tall ape, the head and teeth of a carnivore, the underside of a snake, and (sometimes) the wings of a bat. It was said to be covered in long, coarse red hair. These features signified danger and anger (redness) and dirtiness and derangement (hairiness), and together they indicated a selfish excess and an uncontrolled quiddity that stood in direct contrast to the precepts of social order. In sour mockery of the human, the *sasabonsam* was cast as living in a 'social' structure of males, females and children in the tallest trees in the deepest recesses of the forest. Its legs with their hooked feet dangled from the trees to entrap unwary humans, who were then devoured. The *abosom* could direct *sasabonsam*, but the essential nature of the latter was held to be very profoundly anti-human. When the *abosom* declined to control these assistants, the *sasabonsam* revealed its underlying antipathy towards society by encouraging and fostering witchcraft, and by manifesting a particular hostility towards *akɔmfoɔ*. The symbolism is exact. When the *abosom* withdrew their cooperation and became truculently antipathetic towards human society, those in especial danger were their own servitors and interpreters.[121]

The *mmoatia* (sing. *aboatia*) signified unpredictability, mockery and trickery. They are often rendered in translation as 'fairies' or 'goblins', but the Asante understanding was that they occupied a categorical space somewhere between men and monkeys, and functioned as messengers between the realms of spirit and corporeality. Their highly ambiguous behaviour was reflected in their make-up. They were held to be very small creatures, quicksilver in their movements, and red, black or white in colour. Most indicative of their capacities for duplicitous trickery was the fact that their feet were construed as pointing backwards, so that flight away from them in the forest perversely might lead to a sudden encounter with them. And in such meetings, the *mmoatia* might choose either to assist or to attack. Such uncertainties encapsulated in microcosm the extremely equivocal relationship that was held to obtain between the world of the human and those powers of the *abosom* for good or ill that were, in the final resort, autonomous and unbiddable.[122]

Images abounded in the transactions associated with *abosom*. The essence or core of any manifestation was unknowable by definition; most commonly, it fell 'into a container as a meteor and [was] covered by something which grows to fill the receptacle as a dough of bread grows up rapidly and fills the dough-tin or can'.[123] Ancillary or supporting images were furnished by an accretion determined by human agency. The manifestation of *Taa* (Tano) *Kwabena Bena* at Adeɛbeba, discussed above, was entirely typical. It consisted of a brass vessel that contained the revealed aspects of the *ɔbosom*, together with water, pebbles, sticks and other matter; around it were set out *aduro* (herbal and other medicines), figurines, small clubs, animal tails, and other symbolic or mnemonic paraphernalia.[124] Some of these shrines were housed in fairly elaborate buildings called *abosomfie*. Many of these, predictably enough, were constructed on the outskirts of villages, in the ambiguous area known as *kurotia* that marked a boundary or zone of interaction between culture and nature.[125] Thus, the shrine of the *Taa* (Tano) *Abenamu Subunu* on the edge of the village of Abirimu near Kumase was a complex of four buildings, as perhaps befitted an entity that had made itself known as early as the reign of the *Asantehene* Osei Tutu at the beginning of the eighteenth century.[126]

Although such images existed in very great numbers, it has been correctly argued that they had little potency as signifiers and no autonomy as actors. As focus or concentration of power they were haphazard, for whatever lay at their core was merely itinerant from nature – quite literally passing through. This reading is reflected in the fact that throughout Asante history there never developed any tradition of elaborated images that were vested with inherent powers. There was, for example, no masking tradition in Asante, although masks were certainly used in the articulation of cultic practices in Gyaman to the west. This contrast was pointedly noted by R.A. Freeman in 1889, when he travelled from Asante into Gyaman. He saw masks belonging to the *Sakara Bounou* ('Sakrobundi') cult in the Bron village of Odumase, and in the Nafana village of Duadaso near Bonduku in Gyaman. He had seen nothing like these masks before, and observed that he had 'never met with any traces of the worship of this fetish in Ashanti'.[127] The power(s) temporarily resident with the Asante could not be pinned and fixed in this manner, for they were conceptualized as being evanescent in the manner of *mframa* (the wind). In sum, the *abosom* could never be captured, tamed and held against their own dangerously capricious wills.

The *akɔmfoɔ* were the chosen mouthpieces and trained servitors of the *abosom*. The term is often rendered as 'priest', but the sheer cultural weight of that translation misleads to a promiscuous assignation of roles and functions. Primarily, and simply, they were understood to be individuals who had been granted an ambiguously privileged insight into the workings of the dangerous powers inhering in nature. There was no unified intent in this selection process, at least in the sense that its operation implied no extrapolation to the consistency of a theology of causality and explanation. Individual *akɔmfoɔ* simply mediated and expressed – and indeed, in an understood sense, were managed by – the capricious articulations of nature in culture. This identity conferred upon *akɔmfoɔ* a predictably equivocal status in their own right. They were clearly human, and therefore *of* culture. But on account of their apparent traffic or interaction with the supernatural (in the literal sense), they were equally clearly not fully *in* culture. This ambiguous duality in their allegiance and empathy was reflected in difference, in studied exaggeration and in inversion.

The vocation of *ɔkɔmfɔ* was mastered in isolation in the remote forest. Chosen initiates had esoteric knowledge of the powers of the natural pharmacopoeia of herbs and drugs.[128] They abstained from all sexual intercourse during their training, never married thereafter, but were reputedly promiscuous. They lived on the outskirts of villages, and they spent long periods apart from human society. They were reportedly assisted by familiars from nature, including the *mmoatia*. They went barefoot and wore the characteristic *ɔdɔsɔ* (a fringed, skirt-like raffia girdle). They affected the long, unkempt, matted hairstyle of greased plaits that was known as *mpɛsɛmpɛsɛ* ('I do not like it at all'), and that was associated with unpredictable aggression and anti-social behaviour in all of its devotees – including state executioners and itinerant madmen.[129]

The Asante looked to the *akɔmfoɔ* to persuade the powers that inhabited and commanded them to assist with intransigent difficulties; explicating incomprehension, illuminating unknowing, dissolving intractability, defusing threat and assuaging anxiety. Across this vast and problematic range of difficulty, the *akɔmfoɔ* were arbiters of last resort. They offered the possibility of assistance in matters that were amenable to resolution from no other quarter. It is very difficult indeed to characterize and to describe adequately the dynamic of this relationship.[130] The Asante well knew that advice and comforting reassurance might disguise malevolent disinformation, trickery, and even the dismissively cruel hubris of charlatanism. Typical of the perils of this relationship was the case of the aged *Abrafoɔhene* Adu Kwabo, who died in Kumase on 2 November 1843. It was observed that

in connection with the sickness and death of this Chief one of the principal Fetish Priests [*akɔmfoɔ*] has brought himself into trouble. Not suspecting danger he had informed the Old Chief [Adu Kwabo] that 'he could procure him medicine which would be the means of his restoration, or should he happen to die, such was its efficacy, that it would immediately restore him to life.' Giving credit to a statement so absurd, Addo presented the man with a quantity of Gold, two or three sheep, and other valuables, as an inducement to him to use his best efforts in promoting his speedy and safe recovery. The medicine however failed and the old man died. Immediately upon this event taking place the Fetish Man decamped. It is not likely however, that his flight will save him, as the King [Kwaku Dua Panin] has sent messengers to bring him back to Kumasi. De Gowu [Degewa] who gave me this information, says, there is but little chance of his life being spared, as it is almost certain that the King will give him into the hands of the executioners immediately upon his being brought to the Town.[131]

The many accounts of this nature cannot be rationalized to a simple polarity of cynical, predatory *akɔmfoɔ* and credulous victims, although individuals of both categories indubitably existed.[132] Transactions of the sort cited above could only have occurred within a very powerful nexus, at once deeply felt and universally experienced. But a nexus of what? The term belief can be appropriated, but only if it is situated in and qualified by the ideological structurations that shaped Asante historical experience.

Ideology, knowledge, belief

Let us attempt to relate the historical imperative to accumulate to the issue of belief. The *abosom* were independent and autonomous entities, but they were projected by anthropomorphic understanding in and through the categorical filters of Asante social thought. Thus, in one potent reading, they were themselves understood to be devoted to accumulation, even to the extreme point of avarice; *ɔbosom a oyɛ nnam na odi aboadeɛ* ('the *ɔbosom* that is sharp [that is, acute at predicting events and fulfilling desires] is the one that has offerings vowed to it').[133]

As servitors of the *abosom*, all *akɔmfoɔ* were implicated in their fickle and demanding greed – for gold and for everything else. The dominant leitmotif here was once again ambiguity. The *ɔbosom* that might enrich or otherwise aggrandize a supplicant might equally well choose to aggrandize itself at his or her expense. But only a generous – indeed an extravagant – giving by the petitioner might ensure a commensurate reward from the *ɔbosom*. Within this conjunctural relationship (itself an articulation of power), the intensity of the thrust of social imperative confronted the potentially dissuasive ambiguity that inhered in belief. The risks involved were comprehensively understood. And unsurprisingly, they were also generally embraced.

This is seen most revealingly in accounts of the ease with which the widespread practice of 'money-doubling' was perpetrated. The following instance is representative, and occurred in the aftermath of the *Yaa Asantewaakoɔ* or war of 1900–1 against the British. The account is itself British, and therefore presents the phenomenon as being a clear-cut and simple matter of fraud. But particular attention should be paid to the frames of action and reference employed, and to their burdens of historical familiarity and underlying, recognizable validity.

Once ... a gang of men was going around the countryside 'money-doubling'. Their procedure was simple. On arriving at a village they gave out that they were emissaries of the bush gods [*abosom*], who had sent them to help the villagers, and the gods would give them great wealth. They then proceeded to erect a temple, rather on the structural lines of a confessional. In the evening, when all was ready, one of the gang entered the temple to communicate with the gods. The others then announced that whosoever gave money to the gods would receive back twofold as a reward for their faith and trust. An accomplice made a deposit; and the one who was in the temple, taking it, said he would remit the money to the monkeys to carry to the bush-gods, and on the morrow he knew the gods would return it twofold. A villager (why are villagers all over the world so credulous?) followed suit, succeeded by a second, and a third ...

Next evening everyone repaired to the temple; and, sure enough, the money was returned twofold to those who the night before had trusted and believed in the gods' desire to help them. Then many came forward; and only when night fell did the gifts cease.

The following morning the gang had disappeared.[134]

At the most fundamental level of explanation, the *akɔmfoɔ*, as representatives of the *abosom*, uniquely held out the possibility of dissolving the fearful enigmas, anxious irresolutions and disabling imponderables that enshrouded futurity and the most profound questions of existence. That is the principal, indeed sovereign, reason why the Asante persisted in the interrogation of *akɔmfoɔ* and the powers they represented and spoke for, while simultaneously mistrusting and fearing them. There is, too, a clear implication of last resort and desperation in all this. Thus, Adu Kwabo – and innumerable others like him in their lack of any developed theological certainty – clung to *akɔmfoɔ*, and what they purported to represent, *in extremis*.[135]

It seems evident that very widespread concern with the prolongation of corporeal existence was directly linked to the lack of rigorous theological intent and structuration that characterized all speculative belief concerning futurity. The evidence is far too allusive and fragmentary to permit the precise documentation of anything that might be recognized as agnosticism; but clearly – if only at the level of the individual psyche – there were those who harboured a sceptical unknowing and corresponding anxiety about the precise *content*, if not the presumptive *existence*, of the afterlife.[136] It would seem that reflections along these lines, directly related to a mistrustful or suspicious ambivalence about the motives of the powers that uttered through *akɔmfoɔ*, were exacerbated by the state in its relationship with belief. Something of this has already been glimpsed in the state's reaction to the circumstances surrounding the death of Adu Kwabo.

The *akɔmfoɔ* mediated pervasive and terrifying powers. In the eighteenth and nineteenth centuries, however, this did not translate to a commensurate degree of secular influence. One major reason for this, already briefly noted, was that there existed nothing that might be construed either as a consolidated priesthood or as a defined hierarchy of servants of the *abosom*. The individual manifestations of *abosom* operated within a pluralist political economy of belief. This was porously open to novel revelations and accretions, and in consequence it was overcrowded and intensely competitive. The exigencies or constraints of this 'market' militated against any very high level of corporateness among the *akɔmfoɔ*. This is borne out by personal testimonies. Troubled individuals habitually took their problems to a succession of *abosom*. And while certain manifestations enjoyed a popular reputation for efficacy throughout Asante, the more general pattern was for individual choice to be determined by local geography and by word of mouth, in a village or among the membership of a restricted kin group. In the Mponua towns in the nineteenth century, for example, it was rare for people to leave their natal and residential villages to seek the guidance of *abosom* in more distant locations.[137]

It was also the case that the *abosom* were understood in a manner that precluded any sectarian differences arising from theological disputation and refinement. The act(s) of revelation remained opaque. Such an act could be conduced – given the volition of the ɔbosom – but it could not be commanded. The overall meaning(s) of the *abosom* could be debated and interpreted, but not the intentional differences between specific manifestations. The powers addressed were aspects of a uniform totality, and this negated distinctions and stifled the development of conflicting elaborations. In a very exact sense, anything that might be termed 'worship' was a seamless doxology of presentations and practices. In this context, it is of the utmost significance to note that the eschatological tradition in Asante belief – revealed in visions, promulgated in prophecies – remained firmly rooted in first principles, and argued from them. As we shall see, visions of alternative realizations of lived reality were never anchored in any kind of rigorous reformulation of the tenets of belief. Instead, they were always constructed as restorative rather than revolutionary, contenting themselves with restating the fundamentals of the relationship between Asante society and the *abosom*. They castigated the present as error and deviation, but cast the future as a return to the past.[138]

There can be no doubt that the state played an active role in ensuring that the *akɔmfoɔ* remained disaggregated, and disbarred from any corporate unity of purpose and action. Exemplary instances of the state's practice are numerous and unequivocal. Office holders viewed *akɔmfoɔ* as being potentially subversive of their own power, in that they claimed to speak on behalf of and with a hidden authority. Accordingly, *akɔmfoɔ* were under constant surveillance, and stratagems were devised to trick them into error, ridicule and disgrace. The following folk tale – variously associated with the *Asantehenes* Osei Kwadwo, Osei Tutu Kwame and Kwaku Dua Panin – exists in several versions, and was clearly widely known.

A story is told of how a King of Ashanti once heard of a Fetish Priest [ɔkɔmfɔ] in his kingdom. He sent for him. The messengers having departed, the great King killed a sheep, placed it on a royal bed and covered it carefully. The head of an [executed] criminal protruded, but by artifice was screened from close scrutiny. The whole pile was composed to present the uneasy and painful condition of a man about to die. When the Fetish Priest came he was shown in. Little bells dangling in the profuse strands of unkempt hair, powdered white clay all over the body, cow tail in hand, waist high in a cover of raffia strands, the great Komfo looked into the heavens, listened right and left and then smiled. He called for drummers and singers. He then sang: *makɔm makɔm merɛkɔm oguaŋ ti, Barima Agya ma sɛn ni o*, 'In my priestly service I am to serve a sheep.' The King, now convinced of the man's powers, ordered him to be borne out with respect. He was universally accepted as a genuine priest. He established a great fame and his oracles were reputed to be genuine. But what would have been his terrible fate if he had failed to pass this test?[139]

The nature of the relationship between the state and the *akɔmfoɔ* was most apparent in those ambiguous areas where the possible resolution to specific problems might be sought both in items of belief and in legal adjudication. Bowdich observed that the intervention of some *akɔmfoɔ* was requested

especially in cases of theft; when, from a secret system of espionage, and a reluctance, frequently amounting to a refusal to discover the culprit, or to do more than replace the property whence it was taken, they are generally successful. The magical ceremony consists in knotting, confusing and dividing behind the back, several strings and shreds of leather.[140]

The leather instrument described was the *nkɔntwima*. It consisted of strips of the hide of, generally, the grey duiker (*satwe*; *Sylvicapra grimmia*) or Maxwell's duiker (*ɔtwe*; *Guevei maxwelli*), bound together and festooned with cowrie shells and animals' teeth. Thieves were detected by the agitated motion of the leather strips. The *nkɔntwima* derived its power from the *abosom*, although not all manifestations sanctioned the creation and use of one. An *nkɔntwima* particularly noted for its efficacy was in the charge of the *akɔmfoɔ* of the manifestation of the *ewim* called *Kobi* at Gyakye.[141]

Bowdich's view of the matter was far too sanguine. Minor cases of theft might well have been resolved in the manner he described, but serious cases of peculation – and notably those involving gold – were never permitted to remain with the *akɔmfoɔ* for final arbitration. It was standard practice in such cases to seek the ruling of the *nkɔntwima* in the first instance. But thereafter, the *akɔmfoɔ* who had reported its findings were arraigned before the law along with the plaintiffs and defendants. The burden of proof on everyone thus indicted was to disprove their guilt and to establish their innocence or impartiality before the law. Like everyone else involved in such cases, the *akɔmfoɔ* were subjected to forensic investigation, and to poison ordeals such as the swallowing of *ɔdom*.[142] If they were found guilty of conspiracy in the matter, they were subject to mandatory capital punishment, their *nkɔntwima* was ritually destroyed in public, and the manifestation of the *abosom* that they served was henceforth identified as being uncooperative and inimical.

In all such matters, the rulings of the state took absolute precedence over the findings of the *abosom*. Thus, in a case reported from the mid-nineteenth century, a group of *akɔmfoɔ* who served the *atano* of *Afram* at Sɔkɔban were summoned before the *Asantehene* Kwaku Dua Panin to account for a finding they had given in a case involving the theft of gold regalia from the stool of the Kumase *Gyaasewahene*. They were adjudged by the law to have found wrongly, and by implication, with malice. Over twenty of them were summarily executed, and all of their accoutrements were burned.[143]

In its broader interaction with the tenets of belief, the state practised variants of the ideological structurations it had evolved *vis-à-vis* the received premisses and formulation of the social order. But moulding abstraction and sustaining reification in the sphere of belief ordained the most subtle of interventions. By definition, the affect, the resonances and the objectives framed by belief transgressed containment within any materialist structuration of reality. The Asante state, however, effectively turned this disability to advantage by addressing the very root or basis of belief.

This root was the insistent disposition towards belief itself. The aspiration to participate in believing, and thereby to secure some form of explanation, of confirmation or reassurance, underlay all of the elaborated representations described above. This is hardly a matter for surprise, granted the dominant perceptions of a culture that saw its own history in terms of a matrix of highly self-conscious acts of insertion, and that interpreted its accomplishments in the light of the difficulty of their attainment and the existence of abiding challenges to their continuity. We have already seen how the state inserted its own potent structurations and models into a number of crucial aspects of this cultural determination. It practised an analogous insertion into the vital but cloudy area that groped towards resolutions in the profession of belief. And in this case the ideological project of reducing argument to statement was tackled within an explicitly hermeneutical framework of great suppleness and vital energy.

The Asante state's capacity to subsume the epistemological distinctions between knowledge and belief in a flexible hermeneutics was facilitated by tendencies already noted. A precedent, insistent orientation to belief was situated in an unstructured speculation that had no anchor in any tradition of rigorous exegetical theology. Whatever the comforting advantages or threatening disabilities of this weak structuration, it fell very far short of theorizing resolutions to the ambiguities surrounding issues of causality or the question of monads. There were clear openings here that the state filled by forging a purposefully authoritative reading of Asante historical experience. In this ideological structuration, belief was annexed and absorbed into the state's promulgation of the historical record.[144]

This exercise created a unified field of motive and intent that could be expressed, via successive recensions, as a usable master text. In the action of authoring this, the state was presiding as arbiter over the distillation of knowledge and belief into a unitary hermeneutics of experience. This permitted a (highly ideologically loaded) transit beyond metaphysics, and a decisive liberation from foundationalist thought about both knowledge and belief. Structuration away from these extremes imploded any sustained quest for alternatives, although this matter – as we shall see – still required commitment to techniques of careful management. Relevant comparisons are difficult to adduce. However, in a number of ways the ideology articulated by the Asante state was analogous to *pensiero debole* or 'weak thought', in as much as it was resolutely unconcerned with foundations or origins, but instead was fixedly orientated towards the incorporation of contradictions and their defusing and domestication in hermeneutical understanding.[145]

This is not at all a simple matter, but understanding requires that its difficulties be addressed. Let us take a crucial exemplary case. The *sika dwa kofi* (Friday's Golden Stool) was understood as a historical artefact in terms of its supreme enabling capacity in the political realm. In embodying the source of ultimate disposition, it validated all of the state's powers of intervention, instruction and command.[146] Actual physical possession of this peerless item of regalia was indispensable to any individual who aspired to exercise in full the prerogatives of an *Asantehene*. Thus, the enforced abdication of the *Asantehene* Osei Kwame in 1803 was the outcome of protracted and very delicate negotiations; the *sika dwa kofi* was in his possession in his exile from Kumase in Dwaben, and until he agreed to surrender it his successor could not be formally enstooled as *Asantehene*.[147] Similarly, a recurrent theme in the civil war(s) of the 1880s was the battle between the various protagonists for physical custody of the Golden Stool.[148]

But the power of the Golden Stool's historical competence derived entirely from belief in its supernatural origin, and from its identity as the embodiment and repository of the collective *sunsum* (essence; spirit; 'soul') of the Asante people.[149] The state's ideological structuration of these understandings as a historical text proclaimed that upon the appearance of the *sika dwa kofi* – at *the* crucial historical moment in the state's formation – all pre-existing symbols of authority were ritually destroyed, buried or otherwise put aside. In the most authoritative recensions of this text, the chronological appearance of the *sika dwa kofi* is sited or takes place *after* Osei Tutu had rationalized the office-holding structures of the Asante hierarchy, and *after* he had led these new dispensations to decisive victory over the Denkyira at Feyiase (1701). Thus, the *sika dwa kofi* is inserted into the text as culmination and validation of the new historical order presided over by the nascent Asante state. Its actual appearance – its revelation – is conceptualized in terms structurally analogous to the manifestation of the *abosom*, and in common with all such interventions its actual realization in the realm of the human is facilitated by an experienced *ɔkɔmfɔ*.

Komfo Anokye fixed a certain Friday (*Fiada-Fofie*) nine days before *akwasidae* on which the King, the provincial chiefs, the subordinate chiefs and all the elders should sit in state at *dwaberem* to receive the promised supernatural stool. The day came. It was a very cloudy day, and when the King and all the chiefs and the people had sat down waiting, Komfo Anokye was obsessed for a considerable time. There in the assembly, they saw a stool descending from the sky, shrouded in a thick cloud, and [it] lighted gently on the lap of King Osei Tutu. It was acclaimed with rousing and thunderous cheers... When the noise subsided, Komfo Anokye told the assembly that the souls of all of the Asante people had been enshrined in the Golden Stool and that its occupant should be a father and supreme ruler over them all, before whom nobody was to raise a hand in contempt.[150]

The state promulgated and reinforced an incorporative hermeneutics by means of such ideological structurations. In this, items of belief together with components of the existential agenda were subtly and pliantly dissolved into the historical record. And in this resolute ideological process, those lacunae, ambiguities, inconsistencies and hesitations inhering in belief itself could be directly shaped and exploited. At the most reductionist level, the constructions that ensued might be read as historical or philosophical actualizations of the anthropological category of 'divine kingship'. But this would be both incautious and misleading. The category is a descriptive one, and by failing to address process it liquidates complexity and does not relate ideological structuration in any analytic way to the unfolding of a specifically *historical* experience.[151]

The state's most crucial interventions as *hermeneus* are to be seen in the textual assimilation, reclassification and exposition of fundamental epiphanies or acts of revelation. In all of the resulting ideological structurations, belief and knowledge are fused together in and across historical time. Thus, by far the most elaborately detailed substantiation of the ideology promulgated in and through the *sika dwa kofi* is to be found in the mediated understanding of the nature of the *odwira*, and in the series of mandatory enactments associated with it. The intentional meanings involved are the subject of the next chapter. But for the present, comment is restricted to the ideological presentation of the *odwira*, and to the way in which it was integrated into the textual project that united belief and knowledge in the state's master reading of historical practice.

The following passage is drawn from the same authoritative text that contains the account of the appearance of the *sika dwa kofi* that was cited above. The 'author' – that is, the individuation and representative of the historic state's intent – is the *Asantehene* Osei Agyeman Prempeh II (1931–70), here legitimating the findings of a committee of 'authorities' on Asante history that had been convened at his direction and under his chairmanship.

Barikorang, the son of Awere, returned from travel with a fetish called Apafram [*odwira*] and told the King [*Asantehene* Osei Tutu] that he bought the fetish, but because of its methods of worship, he found that only the King could keep it, [and] he therefore wished to transfer it to him.

The King consulted Komfo Anokye whether it was a good fetish which would contribute in a large measure to the well being of the whole Asante Nation, and that it would help the King in all his wars to conquer all his enemies, and that any King whom he would conquer and kill, he should put his skull into it. The King therefore bought the fetish from Barikorang who showed the King how it was worshipped. Komfo Anokye further advised the King to set aside one day in the year for the worship of the fetish. This festival should be attended by all the provincial chiefs in state, with their subjects, in order to give them the chance of paying homage to their King. Every chief who would absent himself from the celebration without a reasonable explanation would be considered as a rebel, and he should be dealt with. This being the case due notice should be given to all the provincial chiefs of the time of the celebration.[152]

Komfo Anokye – who plays the central enabling role in the assimilation of the *sika dwa kofi* and the *odwira* into ideological use and deployment – is located in all authoritative recensions of tradition as *the* demiurgic *ɔkɔmfɔ*. He instructed the first *Asantehene* Osei Tutu in statecraft, in the interpretation of custom, and in the codification of law.[153] In summary conceptualization, he 'made' Asante. Historically, his actual existence is open to debate, but, as I have argued elsewhere, this is a question of the second order.[154] Komfo Anokye's ultimate, indispensable significance – above and beyond whether or not he lived – is as metaphor and representation in the ideological structuration and hermeneutical promulgation of knowledge and belief. He is the conduit in which the ideological fusion of knowledge and belief in a master text is fixed in a historical moment (the beginning); he is the catalyst through which the project of the state in time (history) is given definition and launched on its way. As such, Komfo Anokye's cognitive embrace extended to encompass *all* knowledge and *all* belief in *all* custom, law or history. In the state's construction, he was situated as the quintessential focus and embodiment of all of the polarities (past and future) of the Asante experience. In his personhood – as metaphor and representation – all of the potentially contradictory impulses in that experience were held to be reconciled and *already* resolved. Knowledge and belief, culture and nature, social order and anti-social disorder, and all of the rest, were channelled through him, thereby becoming integrated into the usable ideologies of a master text that explained the past and guaranteed the projection of history into the future. He precluded arguments, reducing them to himself – a statement made by and on behalf of the state.[155]

The sheer totalizing embrace of Komfo Anokye constituted the Asante state's primary line of ideological defence and argument in defining the evils of deviation from custom, law, values, norms and imperatives, and in urging marginalization and validating exclusion for transgressors. This was of basic importance across the spectrum of the discourse of power. Not least, it served to suppress troublesome and dissentient *akɔmfoɔ*, and to stifle the emergence of any putative claims to an autonomous power on their part. Any critical opposition that was grounded in belief – or in assertions that referenced the primacy of the independent authority of the *abosom* – was represented by the state as being the wilful activation of deviant characteristics that Komfo Anokye had already internalized, countered and rejected. Komfo Anokye's reading of belief was projected in the form of a series of totalizing directives that was the code (and the codification) of Asante life, and that was regulated in historical time through the agency of a state conceived in his own image and promulgated through his shaping guidance and masterful intervention(s).

The ideological structurations involved are observable in key metaphors, such as are revealed in this authoritative oral tradition. In its fullest available form, as recounted here, it is again – and highly significantly – drawn from the history 'authored' by the *Asantehene* Osei Agyeman Prempeh II in the 1940s:

1 It is recounted that towards the close of his corporeal existence – in the reign of the second *Asantehene* Opoku Ware (*c.* 1720–50) – Komfo Anokye proposed to secure the secret of immortality for the Asante and to make them proof against death.

2 Komfo Anokye undertook to accomplish this by travelling in spirit – into nature, into belief – while his body remained closeted for seven days in a screened hut in Agona. Komfo Anokye was the chief of Agona, a distinction conferred upon him, at his own direction, when the *Asantehene* Osei Tutu rewarded him for his services.

3 Komfo Anokye left his nephew Kwame Siaw Anim in charge of Agona, with strict instructions that during his seclusion there should be no wailing, mourning, firing of guns, or any of the other customary funeral observances. Komfo Anokye then entered the screened hut, where he lay in a trance-like condition.

4 In the course of the prescribed seven days Kwame Siaw Anim came upon a great deal of gold belonging to Komfo Anokye. He was determined to possess it, and the office of *Agonahene* that went with it, and so he told the Agona people that his uncle had died and would not return to them. Kwame Siaw Anim then ordered and presided over a noisy funeral celebration for his supposedly dead uncle.

5 While the funeral was transacting, Komfo Anokye's spirit was returning to Agona in human form to effect reunion with his body. On the path between Odumase and Agona this (visible) manifestation of Komfo Anokye encountered a traveller from Gyamase. Komfo Anokye asked the man why the sound of firing was coming from Agona. The Gyamase man explained that Komfo Anokye had died there.

6 Komfo Anokye's manifestation directed the Gyamase man to the buttress of a particular tree, and asked him what he could see there. The man found the grey antelope *ɔtwe* (Maxwell's duiker: *Guevei maxwelli*). Komfo Anokye told the man to kill and skin it, and to bring him the hide.

7 Komfo Anokye made strips of the hide into *nkɔntwima*. He then told the Gyamase man that in future, if people wanted to see what might happen, they should consult *nkɔntwima*. He then gave *nkɔntwima* to the man, at the same time charging him with a message for Kwame Siaw Anim and the people of Agona.

8 Komfo Anokye's message – to his kin and subjects – was that he had been successful in his quest, and had secured the means of abolishing physical death. But,

because of the criminal disobedience of Kwame Siaw Anim and the Agona people, he, Komfo Anokye, had decided to withhold this information from the Asante, and himself to go away from them and never return. He then vanished.[156]

As has been noted, the Asante habitually linked deficient unknowing with their own transgressions. But note the specific messages encoded in this tradition. Calamity follows upon a wilful disobedience of Komfo Anokye's instructions. This takes two intimately related forms. One: by flouting prescribed rules of procedure and comportment, the Agona people (i.e. the Asante) are guilty of meddling – ignorantly, and against their own interests – in relations between Komfo Anokye, the *abosom* and the entire supernatural order. This is something they are completely unqualified to do, and a draconian penalty attaches to their negligent presumption. Two: the act of disobedience itself is initiated by Komfo Anokye's nephew, heir and putative successor in office. In effect, in challenging the ordained conditions of belief, Kwame Siaw Anim is also guilty of seeking to subvert the social and political orders, both of which were presided over by the state. He wants and schemes to usurp Komfo Anokye's place – in the kin group, in possession of his property, in succession to him as *Agonahene*. In the tradition Komfo Anokye is an encompassing metaphor of right order. Acts of disobedience towards him are simultaneously violations of belief, disruptions of civil society and rebellions against the state. He is represented as the guarantor (and judge) of the appropriate conditions of integration of belief, society and the state – as, in this account, the Asante, both criminal and foolish, learn to their eternal cost.

The foregoing is underlined by a related tradition that urges the case for equating Komfo Anokye with the apposite rectitude of the dominant ideological structuration of the discourse(s) of power in eighteenth- and nineteenth-century Asante. In a praise poem (*bɛyɛɛ dɛn*) of the *Asantehenes* there are recorded the names of those – chiefs, generals, criminals – killed by the occupants of the *sika dwa kofi* for various acts of rebellion; among these names is that of 'the priest [*ɔkɔmfɔ*] Tuuda'. Extensive traditions surround the personage of Tuuda or Tula of Nsuta.[157] Significantly, for his metaphorical existence is important whereas his actual existence is not, he is variously assigned to the reigns of the *Asantehenes* Osei Tutu and Osei Tutu Kwame. His 'crime' was to claim insight into the secret of immortality – an avenue of aspiration definitively (and justly) closed by Komfo Anokye. For this he was executed by the Asante state. But in death he accreted to himself, in tradition, all of the expressive characteristics of evil. He and Komfo Anokye are conceptualized as mythico-historical individ- uations of the polarity between non-order (nature; uncontrolled supernatural power; anxiety and insecurity) and the right order presided over by the state (culture; mediated supernatural power; integration and security). In cognitive terms, Tuuda and Komfo Anokye are comprehended as being the two sides or halves of one (all) individual(s). The quiddities involved are traditionally expressed via an aesthetics of significant forms and in an explicitly comparative valuation.

	KOMFO ANOKYE	TUUDA
1	'Related' to Osei Tutu and elevated to the Agona stool	From Konya in Nsuta and of 'low' class
2	Tall and lissome	Short and stout
3	Body smooth and comely	Body hairy
4	$kɔkɔɔ$ ('red')	'Mulatto like'
5	Inquisitive/speculative as child	Stubborn/'stiff' as child
6	Whole/complete	Deformed/incomplete[158]

Komfo Anokye was the supreme codifier of custom and giver of laws – Komfo Kwame Frimpon Anokye Kotɔbɛrɛ ('Komfo Anokye ... in whose presence one becomes wearied from kneeling'). He was the eponymous author of 'The Seventy-Seven Laws of Komfo Anokye', a code of binding prescriptions that enshrined fundamental deliberations on the nature of state and society. Taken individually, these laws seem somewhat eclectic and arbitrary, although they were scrupulously adhered to in historical practice.[159] Their true intent and significance, however, may be adduced from their codified number. The number seventy-seven was iconic and resonant, for in many contexts of Asante thought it symbolized both appropriateness and completion. Thus, Kumase itself was often referred to emblematically and with reference to the authority contained within it as being 'the place of seventy-seven wards'.[160]

It is significant in the foregoing context that individual akɔmfoɔ who manifested attachment to any subversive reading or deviant structuration of belief were not simply killed in the manner of other miscreants. They were arraigned, judged, sentenced and metaphorically 'consumed' or 'eaten' (di) in death by the ɔbosom diakɔmfoɔ ('the eater of priests'), a shrine belonging to the Asantehene and dedicated to this purpose.[161] That is, the elimination of any such heinously offending akɔmfoɔ had to be legitimated very strictly within the parameters of their own presumptive sources of power. Their challenge in the arena of belief had to be countered from within that same framework. Thus, they were 'consumed' or 'eaten', rather than being simply executed, with reference to an authoritative ideological structuration of belief that was already possessed of a total comprehension of the sources of their error. And that ideological structuration, as we have seen, was given individuation as Komfo Anokye on the hermeneutical agenda of assertion and counter-assertion in the context of belief. Deviance was understood as being something already doomed to failure in its very inception, for the potency of all of its claims had already been reviewed and rejected by Komfo Anokye.

Some aspects of the foregoing stand revealed in the brief history of *ɔdomaŋkama* or *abonsamkɔm* (*abonsam*: wizard, sorcerer, witch + *akɔm*), an influential cultic movement that arose in Asante in 1879–80. Confronted by a weakened state power, a predatory *Asantehene* (Mensa Bonsu), and an increasingly stressed and disoriented social order – all factors that have already been discussed in the previous chapter – the devotees and adepts of *ɔdomaŋkama* sought to address immediate ills by resort to practising witch finding. They sought out and identified those who were alleged adherents of *bayi boro* ('hot' or maleficent witchcraft) and either killed or fined them; penitent (and impoverished) survivors were themselves then incorporated into the ranks of the *abonsamkɔmfoɔ* by the procedure of 'cooling them down' or converting them to the practice of *bayi papaa* ('cool' or beneficent witchcraft).[162]

The *abonsamkɔmfoɔ* located the source of all of the ills of contemporary Asante in what they saw as the state's deviant and corrupt subversion of and turning away from fundamental prescriptions. That is, they held the state responsible for fatal breaches of the ideological compact that had governed Asante society throughout the eighteenth and nineteenth centuries. Accordingly, the *abonsamkɔmfoɔ* constructed their own alternative to the state in a mirror world of laws, courts and even office holders. All such initiatives were deliberately considered and created elaborations of their central tenets of belief and ideological doctrine. That is, they accused the state of a betrayal of history and framed this as the heinous repudiation of Komfo Anokye by the existing structure of power headed by the *Asantehene* Mensa Bonsu. As a result, they proclaimed a decisive separation between the Asante state and (the individuated metaphor of) Komfo Anokye, and demanded the liquidation of the former in the name of the latter. They announced that Komfo Anokye himself had reappeared in order to validate, guide and otherwise preside over their programme. Thus, in November 1879, emissaries of *abonsamkɔm* carried the following message from Asante Akyem into Kwawu.

Komfo Anokye and his colleagues, Komfo Odomangkama, Komfo Dabe, Komfo Owu, Komfo Kyerekye, send their greetings to the people of Okwau [Kwawu] and say: 'the tree which Komfo Anokye had felled [a reference to the punishment visited on the Asante state in the Anglo-Asante war of 1873–4] he has set upright again and has given life to it. It is he who may destroy a people or give life to them. He sends word to the Okwau people that he intends to visit them. If they wish him to call on them, then he will come in twenty days. If they perhaps doubted his existence, they need only enquire of *Atieyan* and *Buruku* [the Kwawu *abosom*]. They should also know that the star which fell from heaven quite some time ago [the light of a meteor] had been himself, Komfo Anokye. Another sign of his coming was that a hunter wandering lost in the forest had met with ɛfoɔ [*Colobus polykomos vellerosus*; the white-thighed colobus monkey] wearing gold sandals and sitting on a royal chair, who had sent the hunter with a message for Komfo Anokye.'[163]

Whatever the doctrinal inconsistencies and self-seeking contradictions in ɔdomaŋkama, it presented a fundamental challenge to the state's ideological structuration and historical practice by seeking to divorce these from the validating authority encapsulated in the crucial individuated metaphor of Komfo Anokye. It is quite unsurprising, therefore, that the *Asantehene* Mensa Bonsu eventually suppressed ɔdomaŋkama by the wholesale extermination of its membership.[164]

Asante comprehension of the actual *nature* of this conflict was situated within the hermeneutical framework already discussed. The major issue at stake was conceptualized in terms of a polarized struggle that ranged the powers conjured by the *abonsamkɔmfoɔ* against the powers that were supremely embodied in the *sika dwa kofi*. Since the antagonists both claimed Komfo Anokye as superordinate author and guarantor of what were, in effect, conflicting ideological structurations or opposed readings of history, the conflict is understood as a battle for legitimation in and through his person. In the following traditional account, confrontation between disparate avenues of access to the powers of the *abosom*, and to the authority reposing in appropriate structurations of belief, is resolved in a clear reaffirmation of the *status quo ante*. The precedent unity of knowledge and belief in the state's ideological structuration and historical practice is triumphally reasserted through the symbolic legacy bequeathed by Komfo Anokye in the form of the *sika dwa kofi*.

In the history of Ashanti we hear of the purging of Ashanti of a fetish or witch-finding cult called 'Abonsamfo' or 'Bonsam'. This cult had a considerable number of priests and priestesses, who had considerable influence and freedom of speech originally belonging to the most elect in the kingdom. They sallied forth on special days, prophesying, drumming, and sensing out witches and wizards on their way to Menhia (Royal Palace). They adopted an extraordinary way of swearing. They swore seven good times in order to re-confirm that what they said was beyond doubt. The King of Ashanti [Mensa Bonsu] often sent special drums to escort them into his palace. They propounded impossible doctrines. They robbed the laity of their wealth – their health too, for they produced so much fear into them by fostering a woeful superstition among them. Ho! It was intolerable. One day, they fell. They fell because they went into the 'great house' [the *Asantehene's* palace] where inebriated with the strong alcohol of unrestrained freedom they talked and talked until they talked nothing but fudge. The 'Great Stool' of Ashanti had on that day been unveiled. Before 'Asikua Kofi' [*sika dwa kofi*], the greatest of all the great powers of Ashanti, the 'Abonsamfo' lost their power at once.[165]

The *abonsamkɔm* movement flourished in an era of uncertainty and decline. There is no record of any precedent phenomenon of a similar kind. Nor is this absence in any way surprising. Throughout all of the eighteenth and much of the nineteenth centuries, the Asante state very deftly, confidently and assiduously applied its resources to maintaining and refining the ideological structuration of a coherent hermeneutics of knowledge and belief within Asante society. By the earlier nineteenth century, in fact, its most dangerous challengers and antagonists in the ongoing realization of this project were not the Asante akɔmfoɔ, but rather the theologically highly developed world religions of Islam and Christianity.

Islam and Christianity

In the eighteenth and nineteenth centuries, as has been noted, the Asante state censored, quarantined or otherwise filtered all kinds of alien ideas and novel perceptions. This cautious oversight, directed towards the maintenance of an essentially closed and hence controllable society, was most fully evident in relation to the world religions of Islam and Christianity. For a variety of reasons, the conditional access of Islam – historically the earlier of the two contacts – proved more amenable to direction and management.

Much has been written about the specific insertions and the doctrinal flexibilities of Islam among numbers of Asante's northern tributaries, clients and trading partners. The constituent divisions of Gonja, the sister states of Dagomba and Gambaga (Mamprusi), Yatenga and the other Mossi polities, and the Abron kingdom of Gyaman all contained historically influential Muslim minorities and, on occasion, at least nominally Islamic ruling elites.[166] Originally derived from and consistently nourished by Dyula (Juula) and Hausa sources, the guiding orientations of Islam across this area were commercial and quietist rather than political and militant. Contemplative inwardness and public accommodation were the behavioural norms, and there is little evidence of any strong imperative to *jihād*. The militant programmes and ventures of the *shehu* Usman dan Fodio in Hausaland in the 1800s, and of al-Ḥājj 'Umar b. Sa'īd al-Fūtī in Futa Toro, Segu and Masina in the 1850s and 1860s, were widely reported – and even distantly admired – but not emulated in the Asante hinterland.[167]

Some of those peripatetic Muslims resident in Kumase confessed privately to the doctrinal reservations that underlay their commercial and diplomatic motives for being there.[168] They fully understood that while their international contacts and command of literacy were of use to the Asante state, their continued presence and influence depended upon syncretistic adaptation and public adherence to established Asante paradigms of belief, custom and social practice. In nineteenth-century Asante, Muslims carefully avoided translating personal Islamic belief into offensive and hazardous behavioural solecisms. Instead, they prayed for the *Asantehene*, acted as medical consultants, and peddled protective amulets –

derived and composed from the scriptural authority of the $Qur'\bar{a}n$, and from the ostensible possession of esoteric or occult knowledge – that could be readily assimilated to the extant, indigenous, second-order category of $asuma\eta$.[169]

It was only on a single occasion in 1803 that an ideologically charged tenet of Muslim social thought – the egalitarianism implied by a particular exegesis of $fiqh$ as embodied in the $Qur'\bar{a}n$ and $had\bar{\imath}th$ – may have played a significant if obscure role in the highest politics of the Asante state. In 1803, the $Asantehene$ Osei Kwame (1777–1803) was forced to abdicate. This followed his arraignment on a list of charges that, by some reports, included allegations of his personal disposition towards the egalitarian tendencies in Islamic doctrine. This highly ambiguous episode is perhaps best interpreted in the context of charge and counter-charge that characterized the viciously competitive intra-elite politics of the period. It is well nigh impossible to imagine any $Asantehene$ arguing the case for egalitarianism, except as a misguidedly desperate political expedient (an attempt to mobilize northern Muslim – but massively non-Asante – support). A much more significant charge was Osei Kwame's failure as $Asantehene$ to preside over the celebration of the Kumase $odwira$ of 1802.[170]

In Asante, Islamic penetration was confined to a narrowly constrained spectrum of sanctioned practices that could be readily assimilated to pre-existing structural articulations of knowledge and belief. Muslims understood these conditions, and never propounded anything that might be misconstrued by the Asante state as a determined effort at proselytism. In the 1840s, the $Asantehene$ Kwaku Dua Panin appointed 'Uthmān Kamaghatay of Gbuipe in Gonja as $Asante\ Adim\varepsilon m$ (the $im\bar{a}m$ of Asante). He was succeeded in office by his eldest son Abū Bakr, who had been sent by Kwaku Dua Panin to be educated by the $shar\bar{\imath}f$ Aḥmad al-Fūtawi in Buna. Whatever the nature of the religious convictions of father and son, neither ever publicly espoused and practised any form of strict doctrinal orthodoxy. They prayed for and advised the successive rulers of Asante, but they did so from within the assimilated context of being minor office holders in the Asante state.[171]

Christianity was first expounded in a systematic manner in Kumase by the Wesleyan-Methodist mission in 1839.[172] Its very nature, in the Wesleyan-Methodist formulation, was doctrinally evangelical and insistently proselytizing. Unlike Islam, it confronted the Asante state with persistent and recalcitrant ideological problems. From the outset, Christian missionaries gained a highly circumscribed and very closely supervised access to Asante for a number of reasons. First, and not at all always mistakenly, the Asante state believed them to be sanctioned representatives and/or agents under the direct protection and patronage of the steadily increasing British administrative presence on the Gold Coast. Thus, missionaries had a presumptive value as intermediaries in the context of political relations, and as informal channels of contact, communication and indirect influence.[173] Second – and notably during the long and peaceful reign of the *Asantehene* Kwaku Dua Panin (1834–67) – the Asante state viewed the Wesleyan-Methodist mission as a catalyst, facilitator and participant in the burgeoning legitimate trade that had developed with the southern Akan and the Europeans following the Anglo-Asante treaty of 1831.[174] At an early stage of contact, Kwaku Dua Panin had even aspired to use missionary influence to persuade the British authorities to a restoration of the transatlantic trade in slaves![175]

Until the Anglo-Asante war of 1873–4, the Asante state tended to the overall conclusion that the practical utility of missionaries, and their presence as exotic adornments of the *Asantehene's* court, more or less outweighed the management problem of restricting their direct ideological access to the Asante social formation. This last objective was crucial, and it was achieved by a number of stratagems: endless procrastination and delay; deliberate misunderstandings of missionary requests and policies; an absolute ban on unrestricted travel within Asante, and very severe limitations upon its restricted and closely monitored variant; unremitting espionage; and discreet but dire threats to any individual Asante evincing undue interest in Christian ideas or precepts.[176] A number of Asante saw a ready analogy between various attributes ascribed to the Christian deity and some of the aspectual embodiments of *onyame*, but in the conditions imposed by the state the impetus to conversion was individual and clandestine, and adherence had a tendency to be transient.[177]

The insurmountable stumbling block to Wesleyan-Methodist progress in Asante was the mission's espousal of an inflexible doctrine that married together the concepts of a grace and salvation *personally* achieved through faith, and an emancipation and advancement *socially* inculcated through education. In Christian terms, the pursuit and the attainment of these goals implied a referential separation of conscience and aspiration from any precedent habit of allegiance, and an absolutely inviolable priority of the claims of the former over the obligations of the latter. In terms of the Asante state, the ideological articulation of either or both facets of missionary doctrine represented a clear, grave and quite unacceptable challenge. As novel interrogations directed over the entire range of institutionalized practices, both conscience and education evidently had the potential capacity to effect drastic reformulations of the ideological structurations that underpinned hermeneutical understanding; in Gramscian terms, they could and might alter the pragmatics of *direzione*.

From the outset, the Asante state recognized the perilous magnitude of these proposed Christian innovations. It understood the indissoluble unity of personal faith and education in the Wesleyan-Methodist mind. And it saw very clearly that the privileged concept of an otherworldly salvation grounded in individual responsibility, when combined with the reinforcement of an insinuating pedagogy, might well presage a catastrophic increment of questioning, doubt and, in the most literal sense, alienation.[178]

The *Asantehene* Kwaku Dua Panin consistently rejected the ideas in the missionary enterprise in terms that made allusive and sometimes direct reference to the issue of ideological structuration, and to the balanced articulations of coercion and consent that circumscribed the historic niche into which the Asante state had inserted itself. 'If I were to abolish human sacrifices', he opined privately in 1842, 'I should deprive myself of one of the most effectual means of keeping the people in subjection.'[179] In 1849, he justified the state's right to take life in terms comprehensible to any middle-class Victorian: 'White people think that I kill my people for nothing, but I do not. If I were not to kill them when they commit theft and other bad things, they would come to the mission house and steal everything you have, and would even take the clothes from your back.'[180] In 1844, he firmly refused to countenance a school in Kumase, significantly explaining 'that he did not wish to interfere with existing laws'.[181] That Kwaku Dua Panin fully understood the ideological implications of education is confirmed by a cryptic query that he addressed to the Wesleyan-Methodist Chapman: 'Suppose I give a few Negroes [i.e. non-Asante *nnɔnkɔfoɔ*] with the Ashantis (for schooling). Would you instruct them?'[182]

In an important exemplary instance, the *Asantehene* Kwaku Dua Panin was able to argue that Christian education threatened subversion of the social bases of consent embedded in *amaŋ bre* and *amaŋ mmu*. Under the provisions of the Anglo-Asante treaty of 1831, the *ahenemma* Owusu Ansa (d. 1884) and Owusu Nkwantabisa (d. 1859), sons respectively of the *Asantehenes* Osei Tutu Kwame and Osei Yaw Akoto, were baptized and then educated for five years (1836–41) in England prior to returning to Kumase.[183] In 1844, Kwaku Dua Panin complained that these Christian-educated *ahenemma* often committed 'acts of lewdness'; that they were guilty of 'much excess such as criminal intercourse with married and unmarried women'; that they arbitrarily flogged people 'in a most unmerciful manner'; and that their conduct was generally 'scandalous' and 'of the worst possible character'. All of this was far beyond the bounds of any behaviour that might properly be characterized as *mpoatwa*, and it left the *Asantehene* with 'a very unfavourable impression, as to the probable effects of education'.[184]

In February 1874 a British expeditionary force occupied and sacked

Kumase. Asante retained its independent integrity, but increasingly thereafter, as we have seen, it was subject to British interference, imposition and threats. An early instance of this altered relationship was an aggressive attempt by the Wesleyan-Methodist mission to demand from the *Asantehene* Mensa Bonsu all that they had been denied by the *Asantehene* Kwaku Dua Panin. The encounter is treated here *in extenso*, for it says a very great deal about the issues with which we are concerned.

In April 1876, the Wesleyan-Methodist missionary Picot arrived in Kumase with the approval and blessing of British officialdom. At two meetings – on the 13th and 15th – he stated his case. He complained that the *Asantehene* Kwaku Dua Panin had never permitted any Asante to embrace Christianity. He suggested that clandestine, individual converts 'had always disappeared in an unaccountable manner'. He now demanded 'liberty of conscience' for all, and specifically for those Asante who wished to become Christians. He stated further that, in order to achieve such conversions, missionaries must henceforth be allowed freedom to travel and to preach unhindered throughout Asante. And he concluded this stern peroration with the demand that, 'you must allow children to attend our schools'. On the occasion of both meetings, the *Asantehene* Mensa Bonsu pointedly asked Picot to recite and to explicate the meaning of the Ten Commandments.[185]

On 21 April, the *Asantehene* Mensa Bonsu delivered a response to Picot on behalf of the Asante state. In its allusions to the factors of consensual integrity and coercive force, in its promiscuous mingling of references to items of knowledge and belief, and in its appeal to the constructions informing Asante history, Mensa Bonsu's statement may be read as the most concisely articulate summary available in direct speech of the state's ideological structurations and hermeneutical intent. On the same occasion, brief supporting declarations were submitted by the *Bantamahene* and *Krontihene* Kwabena Awua (*c.* 1843–88), and by the *Gyaasewahene* Adu Bofoɔ (*c.* 1818–83), a son of the *Gyaasewahene ɔbirɛmpɔn* Opoku Frɛfrɛ.[186] The words of the *Asantehene* are reproduced here virtually in full.

I am pleased with the friendship you [Picot] have shown towards me, and I will receive you on the same conditions as my grand uncle Kwaku Dooah [Kwaku Dua Panin] received the mission. Mr. [T.B.] Freeman acted as a peacemaker between the Ashantis and the British; so that from his friendship and the wise administration of Governor Maclean [President of the Council of Merchants at Cape Coast, 1830–44: d. 1847] my grand uncle enjoyed peace, and trade prospered in his time. We will accept the mission if you act as he [Freeman] did to help the peace of the nation and the prosperity of trade. As we tell you, so Mr. Freeman, your predecessor, was told by my grand uncle and his chiefs. It was the only condition for the establishment of the Mission House. But you must understand that as my grand uncle did so will we do.

We will not select children for education; for the Ashanti children have better work to do than to sit down all day idly to learn hoy! hoy! hoy! hoy! They have to fan [show respect and obedience to] their parents, and to do other work, which is much better... It is a tradition among us that Ashantis are made to know they are subjects, altogether under the power of their King, and they can never be allowed liberty of conscience. The Bible is not a book for us. God at the beginning gave the Bible to the white people, another book [Qur'ān] to the Cramos [ŋkramo: der. Malinke karamoko, 'one who can read', i.e. a Muslim] and the fetish [abosom] to us. Our fetishes are God's interpreters to us. If God requires a human sacrifice or a sheep, He tells our fetishes, and they tell us, and we give them. They tell us too where the gold is with which we trade. We know God already ourselves, and we cannot do without human sacrifices.

As to the [Ten] Commandments of God, we know that we keep them all. We keep the first through our fetishes. In Ashanti we do not allow people to abuse the name of God. As to keeping the Sabbath we have always kept it. If a man steals we kill him, as the English killed a man in Kumasi for stealing [a Fante policeman hanged for looting during the British occupation of Kumase in 1874]. If a man takes the wife of another we kill him. If a man commits murder we kill him too. But we will never embrace your religion, for it would make our people proud. It is your religion that has ruined the Fanti country, weakened their power and brought down the high man on a level with the low man. The God of the white man and of the Fantis is different from the God of the Ashantis and we cannot do without our fetishes.[187]

Kwabena Awua then corroborated the Asantehene's statement, and added:

The Fantis can do without polygamy, and without slaves, but we cannot. As men differ in complexion so in religion. Your God is not like our God ... if you send in twenty missionaries, you will not get one Ashanti man to be a Christian. It is trade we want, only trade we cry for.[188]

Adu Bofoɔ then concluded the discussion in defiant mood:

... we will never have anything to do with the Christian religion and would stand the results. Where are our fathers? What has become of them? As they did shall we do, and where they are we shall go.[189]

Picot immediately quit Kumase for the coast.

Christianity and Islam both embodied principles, theses and arguments that countervailed and were dangerous to the ideological project of the Asante state. In these two world religions, as they bore upon Asante, the status and role of the hermeneus was paradoxical. On the one hand, it was firmly located in a rooted scriptural textuality that rested upon doctrinally agreed solutions to the problems of monads and ultimate causes. But simultaneously, the tendency to all manner of recurrent hermeneutical exegeses of that textuality encouraged to forms of contravention, and hence – historically – to contentious pluralist heterodoxies. It also proclaimed a separation between knowledge and belief, and privileged the authority of the latter over the former. In strictly practical terms, as we have seen, Christianity presented much more of a problem than Islam did for the Asante state. The Christian enterprise in Asante insisted upon its sovereign right to incorporate all of indigenous reality into its own hermeneutical constructions; the Islamic presence shied away from any such confrontation, confining its own privileged reading of the world to the meditative intimacies that obtained between committed – but mostly foreign – individuals.[190]

The *Asantehene* Mensa Bonsu repudiated the predication that situated the conditional state of belief, as in Christian faith, as being independently prior to, but wholly determinative and explanatory of, an idealized social knowledge and its ideological representations and behavioural expressions.[191] The particular epistemological distinctions between belief and knowledge in missionary Christianity made for an autonomous, hermetic agenda that was inflexibly resistant to structuration by any agency (e.g. the Asante state) external to itself; and so too did the Christian projection of the privileged ideal of faith (belief) as *being* into the subordinate ideological constructions of knowledge as *becoming*. In other societies a collision of iconographies might well supply representational clues to a contradictory evaluation of the relationship between being and becoming. But no such reading is possible for Asante. The *abosom* offered an absolute minimum of three-dimensional dependent statements about themselves for Christianity to seize upon in forcing open the door. The battle – as Picot as well as Mensa Bonsu seems to have realized – was immediately and directly about lived ideologies.[192]

The *Asantehene* Mensa Bonsu's unequivocal rejection of liberty of conscience, and his assertion that Christianity would make the Asante 'proud' (i.e. individualistic, self-seeking, disobedient), were outright denials of epistemological distinctions of the sort proposed by mission theology. To permit any *individual* Asante to appeal to the absolute authority of belief (or faith, conscience, 'pride') in order to validate dissent from the ideological structuration of social reality was simply unthinkable. To encourage *all* Asante to do so was an invitation to the kind of catastrophe that had occurred among the Fante of the Gold Coast littoral, where Christianity had 'ruined' and 'weakened' the fabric of social and political order, and had 'brought down the high man on a level with the low man'.[193]

Did the *Asantehene* Mensa Bonsu believe in belief? Was the lengthy monologue recorded by Picot – in which the terms 'fetishes' and 'God' clearly encompassed *onyame* and the entire complex of *abosom* – the felt testimony of an individual or instrumental rhetoric? It would be presumptuous and quite inappropriate, granted the relative paucity of direct confessional evidence, to offer any firm conclusions about the individual context(s) of believing. But, for the Asante case, it would also be a largely misplaced effort. Whatever the construction of the individual Asante conscience, it was inextricably enmeshed in patterns of belief that were consistently defined with final reference to the nature of historic society. In short, in the eighteenth and much of the nineteenth centuries it was never simply answerable to itself.

Interpreting experience, constructing history

At bottom, the Asante state's ideologies of control – its structuration of belief and knowledge in society – depended upon the blurring of epistemological distinctions rather than on their sedulous reinforcement. By intentionally collapsing such distinctions, and by structuring inquiry away from both precise epistemological interrogation of the definitions of knowledge *and* rigorous theological investigation of the (individual and social) sources of belief, the Asante state arrogated to itself the promulgation of the varieties and the limits of discourse.

The historical construction of the nature of the afterlife is without doubt the most revealing case in point. The overwhelming social presence and significance of ancestors, and the key conceptualization of corporeal death as the point of entry to unity with them (so succinctly stated by Adu Bofoɔ to Picot), were cardinal features of Asante life that very clearly long preceded the existence of the state, and that certainly survived its collapse.[194] In the eighteenth and nineteenth centuries, however, the Asante state compounded this most powerfully embedded (and felt) feature of the aspiration to belief with charged signifiers derived from its own shaping interventions in historical knowledge and lived experience. The resulting ideological structuration, a projected determination of futurity, situated the afterlife as a replication of the lived reality presided over by the state. Existing structures of hierarchy and differentiation would continue to obtain and to apply in eternity. Thus – and note closely the implication of the argument – the standard nineteenth-century defence of the practice of human sacrifice (as presented to European officials, missionaries) was framed with reference to the fact that individuals would continue to require the distinction and the services of appropriate retinues in the afterlife. This was not – or at least not at all simply, as might be incautiously assumed – a crude otherworldly manifestation or coercive assertion of main force. Rather, it was an ideologically structured property of knowledge and belief, for its continuing validity depended upon subscription to its perceived appropriateness.[195]

With reference to all such matters as the foregoing, and to reiterate, it is misleading to attempt to anatomize belief and knowledge in terms of a register of degrees of individual adherence or scepticism. These were not at all recognizably discrete categories, let alone ones characterized by a precisely defined autonomy, and the corresponding processes of reflection and techniques for intellectualizing were very much compromised by this fact. The Asante state combined with society, lineage, ancestors, unborn *et al.* to crowd and press the individual ego away from centre stage. Incautious commentators have adduced detectable forms of a caring – and romanticized – communalism from this historical marginalization of the Cartesian 'I'.[196] But this was very far from being the case (and betrays a regrettable if unconscious lapse into all manner of brittle solipsisms, of which the hoariest traceable ancestor is 'primitive thought').[197] It is to do no more than to acknowledge the vital complexities of Asante thought by confessing the historically obvious – that the individual Asante ego, as much as any other factor, or in any other society, was subject to ideological structuration.

Flexibility, resilience and ubiquity were the characteristic hallmarks, the visible and invisible traces, of the Asante state's hermeneutical readings and constructed texts. In such readings belief and knowledge were maintained in an equilibrium of indistinct or mutable coalescence, and this feature is textually apparent in the formulation and presentation of authoritative tradition(s). And in the shaping and the recall of history the Asante state vigorously preserved exclusivity in its role as *hermeneus*. Pluralist insertions – by any individuals or groups, indigenous or foreign – were actively and roundly discouraged. The uncontrolled, unmediated or teeming emanations of heterodoxy only came to play any significant part in Asante life *after* the collapse of the state. Putting such items on the agenda (or inserting them into the master text) is very largely a twentieth-century phenomenon, and an important but different subject from our present concerns.[198]

4 Asante *odwira*: experience interpreted, history constructed

Addressing *odwira*

All of our ethnographic and historical sources, Asante or otherwise, attest very fully to the central significance of the *odwira* festival in precolonial Asante life. Nineteenth-century Europeans habitually referred to *odwira* as the 'Yam custom' or yam harvest festival. From their bewildered point of view, this was an attempt to reduce the raw sensory data of confused, overwhelmed – even terrified – observation to the cognitive familiarity of a European framework of classification.[1] The characterization of *odwira* as a harvest festival hedged about with incomprehensible rites and rituals had several direct precedents in seventeenth-century European accounts of roughly analogous customs among the Akan of the Gold Coast littoral.[2] But this limited designation of *odwira*, which served to isolate readily understood items or passages in it, and domesticated these to non-Asante categories, was partial, incomplete and ultimately misleading.

By primary etymological definition, *odwira* was a festival that condensed and expressed defilement, and that then transacted a cathartic communal or societal purification (der. *dwira*: to cleanse, to purify). At the level of both society and the individual, it was dedicated to the sustenance and continuity of the indispensable historical, cognitive and ethical relationship that was held to exist between all presently living Asante, their deceased ancestors, and their unborn descendants. Deeply and profoundly implicated in this unity of address were fundamental references to key items of knowledge and belief, and, indeed, to the entire register of concerns that informed the Asante epistemological spectrum. Food, for example, with its unqualified significance for the maintenance of physical existence and the ongoing temporal survival of the social order, was vital to the general equation, but at a secondary or supportive level below more salient determinations of knowledge and belief.[3]

Thus, historically associated with the Asante *odwira*, and encompassed transactionally within it, was a harvest festival dedicated to the first, ritual consumption of new-season yam (*mmɔtɔkroma*: the yam was generically

144

known as ɔde, but numerous type terms were used for the varieties of *Dioscorea spp.*).[4] This association ordained that the agricultural cycle determined the general, but not the specific, timing of *odwira*. With a single known exception, the nineteenth-century *odwira* was celebrated around the time of *adommere* or the second rains (August, September, October), directly consequent upon the ripening, harvesting and then storing of the main yam crop beginning in ɔsanaa (usually August: der. *sanaa*: a store, a treasury).[5] Yam was central to, and the most esteemed component in, that crop association of high-yielding bulk foodstuffs that formed, as we have seen, the basis of all Asante peasant agriculture. Beyond its nutritional importance, yam was the preferred vegetable foodstuff in sacrificial offerings. Agriculturalists believed to have introduced new varieties were commemorated by name. The range of associations of the lexical field surrounding the concept of ɔde opened into a semiological discourse that carried from the strictly agricultural into the social. And, at a mundane level of significance, anyone convicted of the unauthorized consumption of new-season yam was subject to the draconian penalty of capital punishment.[6]

All authoritative accounts ascribe the inception or at least the initial formalization of the Asante *odwira* to the reign of the first *Asantehene* Osei Tutu (d. 1712 or 1717). In 1907, the *Asantehene* Agyeman Prempe observed that his distant predecessor Osei Tutu (with the help and guidance of Komfo Anokye) had initiated the *odwira*, and

published it all through his districts and counties and told them that a day once in a year will be appointed for everyone under Ashanti Kingdom to celebrate the [*odwira*] suman. When the feast is near everyone is informed and they all meet on the eve...[7]

Thus, the formal inauguration of the *odwira* is temporally associated with the inception of the Asante state. This is not at all to say that prior to this the Asante had nothing approximating to a (yam) harvest festival. They almost certainly did. But it is to say that it is from the beginning of the state under Osei Tutu that any precedent festival associated with first-fruits began to become incorporated and integrated into *odwira* as a componential element. By its primary definition, *odwira* was a festival of cleansing and purification orientated towards a ritual meditation on the seamless unity of dead, living and unborn. The eating of new-season yam was an obviously appropriate analogue of this project. The ancestors were thanked for the harvest, and offerings were made to symbolize and to underscore the concept of unity with them; and eating the new crop itself – a cyclical, recurrent opening to futurity – was a marker on the road that led onwards to succeeding generations of the unborn. It should be added here, however, that it is evident from current research in other Akan areas that the Asante *odwira* – over the eighteenth and nineteenth centuries, and under the aegis of the state – came to be more structured, more elaborated, and to serve more directed purposes, than was the case for any broadly analogous events or harvest festivals among related Twi-speaking groups.[8]

The initial determination and elaboration of *odwira* derived in very significant part from the fact that Asante was a state founded in localized warfare, and then spectacularly aggrandized in the eighteenth century by military conquest. Thus, *odwira* came to serve as an annual forum for the mandatory affirmation and renewal of personal allegiance by subjugated or otherwise constituent office holders. Tributaries were expected to furnish quotas of slaves, goods and/or produce; they might also be called upon to offer a symbolic artefact – *ɔserebo* (a grinding stone), for example – that denoted fealty and subordination, in the way of the wife to the husband. This relationship might be further cemented and solemnized in 'marriage' (*aware*) between the *Asantehene* and a 'wife' (*ɔyere*) or consort, in the person of a favoured tributary office holder or ruler.[9] During the course of *odwira* there was also convened the annual plenary session of the *Asantemaṇhyiamu*. From modest beginnings, this developed into a national assembly of office holders, under the headship of the *Asantehene*, that exercised a very broad oversight in fundamental matters of constitutional and state business. At the level of deliberation and discussion, this body might also review or formulate longer-term state policies.[10]

From the early eighteenth century onwards, *odwira* underwent structural modification and emphatic elaboration. The Asante state gave crucial direction to these processes. Successive insertions and palpable metamorphoses cannot be dated with an absolute precision, but the broad evolutionary picture can be readily derived from our understanding of the state's overall developmental thrust. Although we cannot ascribe to it the characteristics of a process of bureaucratization, there can be little doubt that – initially from the reign of the *Asantehene* Opoku Ware (*c*. 1720–50), and more certainly from the reign of the *Asantehene* Osei Kwadwo (1764–77) – the executive (and increasingly even some of the legislative) functions of governing the Asante state became more fully centralized and concentrated in Kumase. In effect, a council or assembly of Kumase office holders presided over by the *Asantehene* took over the day-to-day running of government. The *Asantemaṇhyiamu* (literally, 'the assembly of the nation') became more confined to the broad view; that is, to the annual general discussion of fundamental constitutional and juridical issues, and to the – indispensably important, and very often acrimonious – debate over the affirmation, modification or rejection of specific initiatives, measures or actions that had originated in Kumase.[11]

Simultaneously, and in parallel with these developments, *odwira* was accorded a more precise focus, a more defined intention, and a more instrumental direction by the insertion of a series of discrete ideological structurations that reflected the growing centralized power and authority of the state and the aggrandized place within it of Kumase itself. The central point of all of this was the person of the reigning *Asantehene* himself. That is, within the convergence of an increasing ritual complexity and a more demanding performative rigour, generalized gratitude to the ancestors was articulated by, and communication with them was channelled through, an elaborated dynastic cult of successive *Asantehenes* of the royal *Oyoko Kɔkɔɔ abusua* of Kumase.

In the nineteenth-century *odwira*, the incumbent *Asantehene* profusely sanctified the spirits of his deceased predecessors in office with great and calculated ceremonial, in which wealth, authority and power were constantly rehearsed and displayed. This directed attention to the *Asantehene* as the individuated representation of the state, and as the spokesman, as first citizen (*ɔkanniba*), for all of his office holders, people and subjects. In the marked absence of a corporately institutionalized priesthood, such rites and practices also pointedly underlined the crucial place of the state, personified in the reigning *Asantehene*, in the arbitration and ideological structuration of belief. In a very direct sense too, *odwira* was an ideological structuration of knowledge in that it observed and celebrated the triumphalist history and essential rectitude of the state in the collective person(s) of successive *Asantehenes*. Asante was of course a matrilineal society. But we might say that, in terms of the key symbolic understandings of the embedding and historical enlargement of Asante, the *Asantehenes* were (with Komfo Anokye) the state's own 'ancestors'. And because the cultic rituals involved in all of this constituted an indispensable preliminary to the consumption of newly harvested yam, their very performance cued, and annually reiterated, a densely potent mnemonic that indicated the state's control over food, and through it, over the baseline conditions of all material and social reality. In all of these modes, and with the enabling participation of the *Asantehene*, the *odwira* was a reading, a review and an affirmation by the state of its own hermeneutical master text. It celebrated the received order of history, and confirmed this as the right order of history (here construed as the moment when the past, rehearsed in the present, was projected into the future). The parallels between this specifically ideological statement and the belief continuum of ancestors–living–unborn will be readily apparent.[12]

Unsurprisingly, and tellingly, this formulation of *odwira* flourished in direct temporal correspondence with the authority of the autonomous state presided over by the *Asantehene*. It attained to its apogee of elaboration and impact as ideological discourse between the reigns of the *Asantehenes* Osei Kwadwo (1764–77) and Kwaku Dua Panin (1834–67), and it

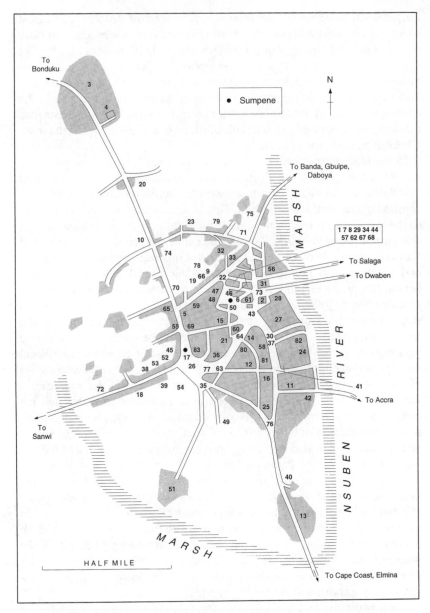

Map 4 Nineteenth-century Kumase (a simplified reconstruction)

Kumase wards, quarters and sites

1	*bampanase*	residence of royal *nhenkwaa*
2	*aban*	'the stone palace'; built 1817–22 by the *Asantehene* Osei Tutu Kwame; destroyed 1874 by the British
3	*bantama*	'the back town'; residence of *Bantamahene/Krontihene*; he and *Akwamuhene/Asafohene* (see 51 below) were the two 'guardian generals' of Kumase
4	*bantama baamu*	mausoleum of the *Asantehenes*; destroyed 1896 by the British
5	*bodomase*	a ward where Komfo Anokye buried 'medicine'
6	*bogyawe*	an open space used for assemblies (see 50 below)
7	*bohenmoho*	residence of royal *ntahera* hornblowers
8	*bonsamoho*	residence of royal *fontonfrom* drummers
9	*abroma(na)m*	'by the way'
10	*abrosanaase*	'by the big thing (money)'; associated with Komfo Anokye
11	*aburaase*	'by the forge'; residence of royal *buramfoo* goldworkers under *Adwomfoohene*
12	*daa(re)boase*	'where the bullets are'
13	*dadeesoaba*	residence of *Dadeesoabahene*
14	*deduak(or)aase*	*inter alia* a place of confinement or prison
15	*(a)denkyem(m)enaso*	residence of *Oyoko Atutuehene*
16	*denteso*	where 'southerners' (Fante, etc.) were given lodging
17	*diakomfoase*	an execution place
18	*adinkrahyefoo(bronoso)*	a pun; residence of *adinkra* cloth weavers; but also where notable prisoners taken in the 1818–19 war against *Gyamanhene* Kwadwo Adinkra were settled
19	*dominase*	residence of *Kyidomhene*
20	*dompem (domponinaase)*	'where the army assembles'
21	*adonten*	residence of *Adontenhene*
22	*dontoaso*	a place where the *Asantehene* sometimes drank palm wine
23	*adonnwe(dena)*	named for the *odom* ordeal ('to chew *odom* tree bark')
24	*adum*	residence of royal *adumfoo* executioners under *Adumhene*
25	*adwaa*	a pun; a public meeting place; but also an execution place ('cutting to pieces')
26	*dwaberem*	'the great market place'; the *sumpi* on its northern side was a key site for assemblies presided over by the *Asantehene*
27	*ahenfie*	'the king's house'; the main royal palace
28	*hiaa(ohenemmam)*	the royal wives' quarters
29	*h(y)iawu*	'if you meet with this (*suman*) you die'; residence of *Hiawuhene*
30	*heman(e)ho*	'do not give offence to the king'
31	*kagyatia*	a meeting place
32	*ankamadewa*	associated with a stick thicket
33	*akan(e)ase*	'the people (us)'
34	*kete*	residence of the royal *kete* musicians
35	*kotoko*	the porcupine; a byname of the Asante
36	*nkraben(nkrammam)*	residence of Kumase Muslims
37	*nkram(u)*	'in the midst of blood'; an execution place
38	*(a)nkra asaaman*	'the real *asaaman* (blood)'
39	*nkuku(w)a*	'a place of pots'
40	*(a)kuoman*	'a place of the *okuo* tree'
41	*nkwantanan*	'the crossroads'; a place where Komfo Anokye buried 'medicine'; residence of *Nkwantananhene*
42	*(a)kyeremade*	residence of *Akyempemhene*

43 *mann(hyi) naho* — 'where the nation assembles as one (for its welfare)'
44 *anamenako* — residence of *Anamenakohene*
45 *an(n)owu (ntannosuo)* — residence of *Anowuhene*
46 *pampaso* — residence of *Oyoko Pampasohene*
47 *apeboso* — residence of *Apebosohene*
48 *apempoa* — 'standing against many'
49 *apetesenee* — a place where dead criminals were thrown for the vultures
50 *apremoso (apemmooso)* — 'the place of the (Denkyira) cannons'; on its eastern side, where it abutted on *bogyawe* (6 above), was a *sumpi* from which the *Asantehene* presided over assemblies
51 *asafo* — residence of *Akwamuhene/Asafohene* (see 3 above)
52 *asaaman* — residence of *Saamanhene*
53 *asaaman kwaadane* — 'the lesser ("enslaved") *asaaman*'; residence of *Oyoko Bremanhene*
54 *asamanpo(w)mu* — 'the bush of the ghosts'
55 *nsansa (sentewosoro)* — 'empty handed'
56 *sanyaase* — a small market
57 *nsenie (nsenea)* — residence of royal *nseniefoo* court criers under *Nseniehene*
58 *sentia(w)* — 'a place for eating and talking'
59 *sereboosakyi* — residence of Kumase Muslims
60 *asikasu (pinanko)* — residence of *Gyaasewahene*
61 *sodo* — residence of royal *sodofoo* provisioners and cooks under *Sodohene*
62 *asokwa* — residence of royal *asokwa* hornblowers (and traders) under *Asokwahene*
63 *asraman nnkyedu(man)ase* — 'where the tree was struck by lightning'
64 *asrampon a(so)* — 'taken unawares'; an execution place
65 *asratoase* — 'where the pipe bowls are lit'
66 *suame* — a generic name (not to be confused with Suame village)
67 *nsuase* — residence of *Domakwaehene/Akyeamehene*
68 *atani (atannaho)* — residence of royal torch bearers
69 *(ni)tibanso* — a place where Komfo Anokye buried 'medicine'
70 *ntommem(mu)* — 'a place marked by *ntomme* trees'
71 *topreduase (tipri)* — 'beneath the *topre* tree'; an execution place; also residence of the butchers
72 *topreman nkwanta* — a (road) site where Komfo Anokye buried 'medicine'
73 *atuatu* — 'sedition'; an execution place
74 *ntuom* — 'taking up guns'
75 *atwereboanna* — a pun; 'the *twereboa* tree'; 'a place of flints (where the guns are)'
76 *wawase* — 'a place of the *wawa* tree'
77 *(nn)ware(m)* — 'marrying together'?
78 *ware(ho)duase* — 'beneath a tall tree'?
79 *wontonase (wanoase)* — a meeting place
80 *worakesee* — residence of *Worakeseehene*
81 *ayakeseeho (dampankesee)* — 'an imposing place of big dwellings'
82 *anyinam asumenam* — an execution place
83 *anyinaase* — residence of *Anyinaasehene*

continued in broadly recognizable form until the deportation by the British of the *Asantehene* Agyeman Prempe in 1896. That *odwira* was essentially articulated by, and served the objectives of, the state presided over by the person of the *Asantehene* may be evidenced by a very simple but significant consideration. From 1896 to 1901, the British administered Asante on an *ad hoc* basis; from 1901 to 1957, Asante was annexed to the British crown and was directly under colonial rule; after 1957, it was incorporated into the Republic of Ghana. Between 1896 and 1935, the British proscribed the office of the *Asantehene*. The position and person of the *Asantehene* were 'restored' by the British in 1935.[13] But, despite this restoration of one of the two crucial actors in *odwira* (the other being the independent Asante state), the festival itself languished in total abeyance between 1896 and 1985. In 1985 the Kumase *odwira* was finally resurrected, but as a result of a generalized cultural nationalism, rather than in any attempt to restore and to reaffirm the full range of eighteenth- and nineteenth-century meanings. This latter objective would be otiose, for the autonomous state to which so many of those meanings attached no longer exists. Instead, the *odwira* of 1985 was celebrated as the central event in a year of thanksgiving dedicated to marking the fiftieth anniversary of the British colonial 'restoration' of the *Asantehene* (and the Asante Confederacy); and its beneficial observance was extended from Asante to encompass, in anticipation of the renewal held to follow purification, all of the peoples of Ghana.[14]

Time and *odwira*: *adaduanan, nnapaa, nnabɔne*

It has been argued elsewhere that at one primary level of significance and meaning the symbolic resonances inhering in the *odwira* were concerned with the Asante conceptualization of time; and further, that *odwira* was construed in this aspect as a calendrical construct that in and of itself commemorated time and marked its passage.[15] The transactional performance of *odwira* – its unfolding sequence of events and epiphanies – was rooted in and defined by the Asante calendar. That calendar was based on the concurrent counting of a six-day cycle (*nanson*) with a seven-day cycle (*nawotwe*). These are reproduced below.

The *nanson* and *nawotwe* cycles of the Asante calendar

nanson	*nawotwe*
nwona	*wukuo*
nkyi	*yawo*
kuru	*fie*
kwame	*memene*
mono	*kwasie*
fo	*dwo*
	bena[16]

Arithmetically, *nanson* and *nawotwe* generated a combinational cycle of forty-two (compound) named days. This was called *adaduanan*. At its conclusion, the cycle began again, the forty-third day being the same as the first day of the preceding *adaduanan*. The Asante *adaduanan* began with *nwona* (from *nanson*) plus *wukuo* (from *nawotwe*); and because of the arithmetical multipliers in the Asante reckoning, *nwonawukuo* (*nwona + wukuo*) was always a Wednesday in the Gregorian calendar. The forty-two (compound) named days of the Asante *adaduanan*, and their invariable Gregorian equivalents, are reproduced below.

The Asante *adaduanan*

1 *nwonawukuo*	Wednesday	22 *kwawukuo*	Wednesday
2 *nkyiyawo*	Thursday	23 *monoyawo*	Thursday
3 *kurufie*	Friday	24 *fofie*	Friday
4 *kwamememene*	Saturday	25 *nwonamemene*	Saturday
5 *monokwasie*	Sunday	26 *nkyikwasie*	Sunday
6 *fodwo*	Monday	27 *kurudwo*	Monday
7 *nwonabena*	Tuesday	28 *kwabena*	Tuesday
8 *nkyiwukuo*	Wednesday	29 *monowukuo*	Wednesday
9 *kuruyawo*	Thursday	30 *foyawo*	Thursday
10 *kwafie*	Friday	31 *nwonafie*	Friday
11 *monomemene*	Saturday	32 *nkyimemene*	Saturday
12 *fokwasie*	Sunday	33 *kurukwasie*	Sunday
13 *nwonadwo*	Monday	34 *kwadwo*	Monday
14 *nkyibena*	Tuesday	35 *monobena*	Tuesday
15 *kurudapaawukuo*	Wednesday	36 *fowukuo*	Wednesday
16 *kwayawo*	Thursday	37 *nwonayawo*	Thursday
17 *monofie*	Friday	38 *nkyifie*	Friday
18 *fomemene*	Saturday	39 *kurumemene*	Saturday
19 *nwonakwasie*	Sunday	40 *kwakwasie*	Sunday
20 *nkyidwo*	Monday	41 *monodwo*	Monday
21 *kurubena*	Tuesday	42 *fobena*	Tuesday[17]

Achieving absolute concordance between the Asante calendar and European chronology is a laborious but essentially mechanical task. It is most simply done by looking at two crucial days in the *adaduanan* cycle; *kurudapaawukuo* (15: Wednesday) and *kurukwasie* (33: Sunday) were also known respectively as *awukudae* (the 'small' or Wednesday *adae*) and *akwasidae* (the 'big' or Sunday *adae*). The two *adae* (lit. a lying down, resting or burial place) were days on which the *Asantehene* – to remain with the leading, illustrative case – made offerings to his ancestors. On these occasions, he also made a public distribution of gifts and drinks to, among others, foreign visitors in Kumase; nineteenth-century Europeans dated in excess of thirty *adae* by the Gregorian calendar.[18] Utilizing these fixed points, it is a simple exercise for a computer to produce an equivalence table of the *adaduanan* cycle and European chronology.

A crucial determinant in the operation of the *adaduanan* cycle was the concept of specific days that were either *dabɔne* (pl. *nnabɔne*: a 'bad' or 'unlucky' day) or *dapaa* (pl. *nnapaa*: a 'good' or 'lucky' day). Those few nineteenth-century Europeans who essayed analyses of the bases of the Asante distinction drew misleadingly facile parallels; in 1817, Bowdich (citing Horace in explanation) equated *nnapaa* with the Roman *fasti* ('consecrated by some good fortune') and *nnabɔne* with the *nefasti* ('condemned from some national calamity').[19] But the matters at issue were more complex than this, and they are subject to interpretation and reading at a number of levels.

Most quintessentially, *nnabɔne* were days devoted to mnemonic reflection on the nature and quiddity of being Asante. This involved ritual communication with – and propitiation of – ancestors; attentive focus on the *abosom*, the agencies and instrumental manifestations of belief; and broader reflection upon the place of Asante culture within nature. All of these considerations were of singular importance. The burden of *nnabɔne* was that they enjoined specific acts and patterns of behaviour, and correspondingly prohibited others; they were ritualized 'interruptions' of daily life. Thus, for example, in nineteenth-century Agogo the following *nnabɔne* obtained in each and every *adaduanan* cycle:

Nnabɔne in nineteenth-century Agogo

1 *kurudapaawukuo* (*awukudae*: 15: Wednesday)
2 *kurukwasie*   (*akwasidae*: 33: Sunday)
           Both devoted to service of ancestors and stools: reigning *Agogohene* leads in offering ritual food and drink to ancestors.
3 *fodwo*   (6: Monday)
4 *nwonadwo*   (13: Monday)
5 *nkyidwo*   (20: Monday)
6 *kurudwo*   (27: Monday)
7 *kwadwo*   (34: Monday)
8 *monodwo*   (41: Monday)
           All *nnabɔne* with respect to the *akɔmfoɔ* and adherents of the Agogo manifestations of *Taa* (Tano) *Antwiaa* and *Taa* (Tano) *Kofi*. The shrines of these *abosom* were ritually paraded ('shown out') and celebrated ('worshipped') on these days.
9 *nwonabena*   (7: Tuesday)

10 *nkyibena*   (14: Tuesday)
11 *kurubena*   (21: Tuesday)
12 *kwabena*   (28: Tuesday)
13 *monobena*   (35: Tuesday)
14 *fobena*   (42: Tuesday)
                    All *nnabɔne* with respect to the *akɔmfoɔ* and adherents
                    of the Agogo manifestation of the *ewim Anokye*. The
                    shrine of this *ɔbosom* was ritually paraded ('shown
                    out') and celebrated ('worshipped') on these days.
15 *fofie*   (24: Friday)
                    A *dabɔne* in that this day was sacred to all Agogo
                    abosom.
16 *kwamememene*   (4: Saturday: and other 'Saturdays'?)
                    A *dabɔne* in that this day was sacred to the River Afram.
17 *nkyiyawo*   (2: Thursday)
18 *kuruyawo*   (9: Thursday)
19 *kwayawo*   (16: Thursday)
20 *monoyawo*   (23: Thursday)
21 *foyawo*   (30: Thursday)
22 *nwonayawo*   (37: Thursday)
                    All *nnabɔne* in that they were days sacred to
                    ɔdomaŋkama and to the 'spirit' of the earth, *asase
                    yaa*. No agricultural work or farming permitted on
                    these days.[20]

The Asante understanding of *nnabɔne* and *nnapaa* was confused, at least
for Europeans, by linguistic usage. In ordinary discourse, many Asante
habitually referred to 'bad' days as 'good' days (a telling instance of the
very common gap between direct translation and cultural understanding);
'good', in this seemingly interchangeable context with 'bad', was simply
intended as an emphatic marker or as a referential qualifier that connoted
the great significance, intentionality, and exclusive or discrete purposes of
nnabɔne. 'Good', in short, meant important when applied to 'bad' days.
Thus, in 1946, Yaw Mensa, the custodian under the Kumase *Manwerehene*
of the shrine of *Taa* (Tano) *Kwabena Bena* at Adeɛbeba, offered the
following remarks on the nature and significance of *nnabɔne*.

What we call bad days, are in reality good days, for they are the best days on which
we can all the better invoke our fetishes, ancestors, spirits, and all unseen creatures
in the woods. We can pour libations to them and exorcize [*sic*] them to help us. They
are holidays. There is nothing so hated in an Ashanti citizen than going to his farm
on any of such days. Naturally the woods are the homes of the spirits, the spooks
[ghosts], the spirits of the earth – *Asase boɔdense*, that of the air – *Mmoatia*, the spirit
of the fire – tall *Sasabonsam*, the ghost hunter – the *Saman bɔmɔfo*, and other

wonderful creatures not often seen. I think, a man who defies the law and goes into the bush will see something he has never seen. He may be shocked to death. Those who observe such days and give food and drink to their fetishes [*abosom*], their stools or ancestral spirits and the spirits of the land, the water, trees and climbers, the air etc. will be blessed.

To these loyal men bad days are good. One of a chief's very greatest duties is the holy observance of these days and the suitability of rites and ceremonies to celebrate them. A chief or elder must know what to say on such days... A prayer will be answered in reality.[21]

The foregoing is a distillation of numerous components of popular belief and folk culture; on *nnabɔne* – 'bad', but also 'good' because important – peasant cultivators were prohibited from farming, and enjoined by law (meaning here *amaŋ mmu* rather than *amaŋ bre*) to consider and to reflect upon other matters.

The Asante state's ideological practice with regard to *nnabɔne* was much more structurally refined and instrumentally directed than can be gleaned from any popular account of the matter by villagers. On such days the reigning *Asantehene* devoted himself to leading both private and public ritual observances connected, at their most elaborated level of performative explication, with his predecessors in office. If he was practising and rehearsing belief, as at one level he undoubtedly was, then he was also engaged in doing so within an explicit framework that served to sanctify the genealogical history and continuity of the state and its authority. The *Asantehene* was devotedly engaged in the repeated affirmation of rectitude and right order, and hence of the state's role in the hermeneutical designation, arbitration, disposition and directed allocation of items composing (historical) reality. At this level of enforceable custom and law, *nnabɔne* did not simply inform the state's construction of the conditional understanding and distribution of the temporal dimension(s) of all of Asante life. Rather, they represented and punctuated the state's degree of interventionist and shaping control over that reality – and its social, political and economic components. As has been noted, agriculture was generally prohibited on *nnabɔne*. So too were – *inter alia*, and with some variations – fishing, hunting, travel, sexual intercourse, warfare, diplomatic negotiations, council meetings, legal enactments, and state business in any public form. Such matters, affecting people both collectively and individually, were customarily reserved to days that were *nnapaa*.[22]

As potent instruments for structuring reality, *nnabɔne* were also characterized by notably high levels of plasticity or hermeneutical flexibility. After all, the state presided over the custom and law that contained and defined them. It proclaimed avoidances and prohibitions in their name, and exercised the discretionary right to punish or even to forgive transgression. Moreover, the state might institute or abolish localized *nnabɔne* associated with particular manifestations of the *abosom*, by the simple expedient of granting or denying legitimation, in the name of Komfo Anokye, to individual *atano*, *ewim* or *abo*.

The *ewim Anokye* at Agogo, noted above, is a case in point. It first descended from the sky (*yɛsɔɔ no ewim*) during the reign of the *Asantehene* Osei Tutu Kwame, and 'announced' that its own particular observance day (*dabɔne*) was *bena ɛda* (i.e. the day or *ɛda*: pl. *nna* of *bena* in the *nawotwe* cycle, or by extrapolation every recurrent 'Tuesday' in the *adaduanan* cycle). The *Asantehene* Osei Tutu Kwame confirmed the welcome or beneficent nature of this manifestation, and *ewim Anokye* was duly celebrated on its (self-) appointed *nnabɔne*. But *Anokye* lost its 'force' at the time of the *Asantehene* Kwaku Dua Panin, and thereafter it gradually suffered neglect and fell into desuetude. Reportedly angry at the neglect of its *nnabɔne*, the *ewim Anokye* manifested itself once more, in the trail from a meteor, during the reign of the *Asantehene* Mensa Bonsu. But this time (and perhaps in the light of the *abonsamkɔm*) the state withheld its sanction. Officials were sent from Kumase to Agogo to suppress adherents of the *ewim Anokye*, and its *ɔkɔmfɔ* fled as a refugee into Akyem Kotoku. He only returned to Agogo following the enstoolment of the *Asantehene* Agyeman Prempe in 1888, when state approval was once again extended to the *ewim Anokye*, and the sanctioned observance of its *nnabɔne* was once more permitted.[23]

Degrees of confusion in both Asante and European sources over the precise number of *nnabɔne* in any given historical *adaduanan* cycle may perhaps be best understood in the light of the state's flexibilities in interpretation and control, and in terms of consequent differences in the highly localized impact of such interventions. In the nineteenth century, moreover, it would appear that *nnabɔne* and *nnapaa* were subject to classification across a spectrum that extended from the most extreme 'bad' days to their polar counterparts – the most wholly 'good' days. Quintessential *nnabɔne* were *fodwo* (6: Monday), *kurudapaawukuo* (*awukudae*: 15: Wednesday), *fofie* (24: Friday) and *kurukwasie* (*akwasidae*: 33: Sunday); the equivalent *nnapaa* included *nkyidwo* (20: Monday), *kwadwo* (34: Monday) and, seemingly best of all, *monodwo* (41: Monday).[24] The middle ground of this system contained a teeming number of specific local variations. It also enabled the state to practise flexibilities in interpretation and to exercise options. Thus, the crisis diplomacy that surrounded the Anglo-Asante war of 1873–4 saw the abstractions of custom in calendrical understanding severely modified in practice to deal with very extreme circumstances.[25] In such grave cases, events ordained an interventionist reshaping of time itself. But such matters were the exclusive province of the state. Certainly, they lay far beyond the competence of the great mass of those who participated (like Yaw Mensa of Adeɛbeba) in an individuated, localized, quotidian and aspectual involvement in the ordering of time.

The state as *hermeneus* gave shape and emphatic interpretation to the *adaduanan* cycle and to its componential *nnabɔne* and *nnapaa*, both across historical time, and in its evolutionary and linear (but at the same time cyclical and repetitive) segmentary expressions. Some items on this agenda were underlined, some were reinforced, some were played down, some were construed as negotiable, and some, we may assume, were ignored, abolished or otherwise allowed to fall into disuse. But each and every one of these hypothetical modifications and permutations was a dependent variable of the crucial social fact of the Asante state's capacity for ideological structuration. Oft quoted proverbs – *tete ara ne nnɛ* ('ancient things are here today': i.e. history repeats itself) or *tete ka asom* ('ancient things remain in the ears': i.e. tradition goes on and survives) – are folk wisdom at its least periphrastic, but most commonplace.[26] That which survived as 'ancient things' (as history or tradition), however, was itself a determination, and one moreover that was filtered through the structured management of time itself.

It was conventionally understood that nine successive *adaduanan* cycles constituted a larger unit of discrete time known as *afe* (syn. *afrihyia*: often translated in the twentieth century as 'year'), after the completion of which a new series of nine began.[27] Clearly, the primordial beginnings of this system lay in the agricultural cycle, and beyond that in the seasonal periodicity of the rains upon which all farming enterprise depended. In the fully elaborated calendar, the state situated the passage from the conclusion (*afedaŋ*) of one *afe* to the new beginning (*afefoforo*) of its successor within the rubric of *odwira* and the associated yam harvest festival; and because of the basic arithmetic of the Asante calendar, these events oscillated historically within the envelope of time defined and described by the European months of August, September and October.[28]

The state alone decreed the precise timing of the *odwira*. The rationale and mechanisms involved were confidential, and as yet are far from being fully understood. Certainly, the river Tano itself and the shrines of selected manifestations of the *abosom* were consulted. Acts of divination also took place, together with the reading of auguries in nature – the way(s) in which fruits ripened, the way(s) in which birds flocked and flew. Under the *Asantehene* Osei Tutu Kwame, it would appear that a key advisory role in these matters was played by the *Gyaasewahene* Opoku Frɛfrɛ, who exercised responsibility over fiscal, demographic and calendrical accounting procedures.[29] And once, in 1871, the *Asantehene* Kofi Kakari arbitrarily altered the observance of *odwira* to the periods of *ɔpɛnimma* (the 'small' dry season) and *ɔpɛpɔŋ* (the 'big' dry season or *harmattan*) between December and January. It has been argued that this was to allow participants to travel more easily into Kumase on dry roads. But we might reasonably ask why this obvious practical solution to a perennial problem was only implemented at this particular point in time, and why in 1872 *odwira* reverted to being celebrated in August and September?[30] The temporary rescheduling had something to do, perhaps, with Kofi Kakari's straitened financial circumstances, for *odwira* (at least in some of its stages) involved the *Asantehene* in considerable expense.[31] But in the end we cannot be certain, because we have no clear understanding or direct record of the confidential deliberations that led to the state's decision in 1871.

Once the state had authorized, announced and publicized the timing of *odwira*, active preparations for its celebration were set in motion. All of the relevant sources – traditional, ethnographic and eyewitness – broadly concur in agreeing that the entire sequence of preliminary, celebratory and concluding phases together extended over a period of time somewhat in excess of a single *adaduanan* cycle.[32]

In what now follows, an analytic reconstruction of the nineteenth-century *odwira* is essayed. Utilizing all of the available data, an attempt is made to furnish a chronological portrait of the Kumase (Asante) *odwira*, and to offer commentary on and elucidation of specific points of detail as these arise. To assist to a comprehension of this reconstruction, chronological subdivisions have been imposed upon it. These are not simply arbitrary. They follow the specifically Asante understanding of the sequence of events, and in so doing they are designed to illuminate discrete evolutionary shifts in rhythm, intensity and purpose, and to highlight the ideological structurations at work in crucial passages. The argument is regrettably but necessarily complex, for the data themselves are exceedingly dense and multi-faceted, and the meaning(s) involved, playing and interplaying across the hermeneutical register, all at once embrace variable intensities and shifting objects of ideological structuration. All of these considerations are testimony to the singular importance of *odwira* in Asante thinking and historical practice, and to the immense subtleties that were directed towards its achievement as performative enactment.

Transacting *odwira* 1: *nkyidwo* to *kwayawo*

nkyidwo *(20: Monday) to* kurudapaawukuo/awukudae *(15: Wednesday)*

The eating of the new-season yam crop was prohibited until the state sanctioned consumption at the time of the performance of *odwira*. Even during periods of fraught disruption, such as obtained during the military crises of the early 1870s, the state consistently sought to assert control over provisioning.[33] In more tranquil times, the theft or unauthorized consumption of new-season yam was construed as a very grave offence. Thus, during the reign of the *Asantehene* Kwaku Dua Panin charges of witchcraft (*bayi*) were preferred against some inhabitants of Donyina; among the accusations, which led to conviction and execution, was the claim that those arraigned had wilfully and knowingly dug up and eaten new-season yams without any authorized permission.[34]

A corollary of state arbitration of the periodicity and timing of consumption was that, during *akitawonsa* and *ɔsanaa* (roughly July and August), the imminence of *odwira* was generally presaged in Kumase by a noticeable decrease in food supplies, and by a concomitant increase in market prices. Office holders experienced some difficulty both in the direct provisioning of their retinues of *nkoa*, or in feeding them from expending inflationary sums on relatively scarce resources. *Kumasefoɔ* quit the capital for their natal villages and farms, there to seek more ready or affordable sustenance, to assist in the preliminary stages of the impending yam harvest, and to prepare themselves for the celebration of *odwira*.[35]

In the course of *ɔsanaa*, the *Asantehene* despatched emissaries to the incumbent of the stool of Amoako and Sakodeɛ (*sɛ odie hew*) at the village of Saawua, some 7 miles southeast of Kumase, there to make formal enquiries into the progress of the yam harvest. This was because the *Saawuahene* Sakodeɛ was traditionally credited with the introduction into Asante of prepared yam as a foodstuff, and because the village had historical obligations in the provisioning of the *Asantehene's* palace and household.[36]

Following receipt of a favourable report from Saawua on the readiness of the yam crop, preparations were set in train by the state's selection of a 'good' or appropriately auspicious *dapaa* in the *adaduanan* cycle immediately preceding the one in which the festival proper was to take place. Preferred *nnapaa* were *nkyidwo* (20: Monday); *kwadwo* (34: Monday), the day immediately following the *akwasidae* on *kurukwasie* (33: Sunday); and *monodwo* (41: Monday), perhaps the most propitious of all *nnapaa*, and the day customarily chosen for the formal installation of an *Asantehene*.[37]

On the morning of the designated day, the *Asantehene* went in state to the royal mausoleum (*baamu*) at Bantama, about 1 mile to the north of Kumase proper, where those of his predecessors who had died in office were interred.[38] There, set before the coffins, each in its own chamber, were numbers of *kuduo* (brass vessels). These containers were greatly valued as *agyapadeɛ* (mnemonic 'heirlooms'), and they were intimately associated with the ritual purification of the *kra* (a spirit or spiritual element that came from *onyame*, and that quit the individual person after physical death, often (mis)translated as 'soul') by the patrifilially determined members of a deceased person's $ntɔrɔ$ group. The $ntɔrɔ$ was understood as a spiritual component of the individual person that was transmitted through paternity.[39]

The *kuduo* at Bantama contained reserves of *sika futuro* or gold dust. This gold was conceptually quite distinct from the capital assets of the state that were stored, pending sanctioned disbursement, in the *adaka kɛsɛɛ* ('the great chest of the treasury'). The gold at Bantama was the property of the royal *asamanfoɔ* (sing. *ɔsamaŋ*: ancestral spirits of the departed: 'ghosts') of the *Asantehenes*. It was exclusively reserved for ritual or emergency use, and in principle could only be borrowed pending its eventual replacement.[40]

At Bantama, the *Asantehene* killed a sheep (*oguaŋ*) – symbolic of peace, innocence and spiritual 'coolness' (*dwo*) – to 'feed' all of the royal *asamanfoɔ*.[41] He then solemnly announced the forthcoming *odwira* to his predecessors in office, requested their intercession and enabling mediation with the *abosom* for its successful celebration, and asked for their protective oversight and assistance for the *Asantemaŋ* in negotiating the next *afe*. The *Asantehene* then borrowed *sika futuro* from the *kuduo* to enable the appropriate celebration of *odwira*. There were fluctuations in the size of this loan, but it was conventionally held and understood that the *Asantehene* might need to borrow some 125 *mperedwan* (£1,000 sterling by nineteenth-century equivalence).[42] The sacred status of the Bantama gold may well have played a role in the *Asantehene* Kofi Kakari's rescheduling of the 1871 *odwira*. It has already been noted that Kofi Kakari was *akyɛmpɔ*, a great and profligate distributor of gold dust, and a spendthrift who rapidly squandered the revenues accumulated by the *Asantehene* Kwaku Dua Panin when these were somewhat reluctantly transferred into his control by his mother, the *Asantehemaa* Afua Kobi.[43] Perhaps for a time Kofi Kakari was unable to celebrate *odwira* because he was temporarily denied access to the contents of the Bantama *kuduo* on account of his well-known habits of wastefulness with regard to gold.

Customarily, the *Asantehene* returned to Kumase immediately after having secured the required loan and having thanked the *asamanfoɔ* formally for it. On the evening of the same day, he, the Kumase office holders and his household officials assembled together in the palace courtyard called *kyiɲiɛhyiamu* (the place of the 'whirling' or 'turning around'). The symbolism invoked here, as in analogous ritual contexts, was protective. The meaning expressed in this courtyard was cognate with ideas of circulation, and of the actual coolness and metaphorical shade or 'defence' afforded by the enveloping shape and agitated motion of the *Asantehene's* great state umbrellas (*ŋkyiɲiɛ*).[44] It was here, in this environment connoting protection, security and calm, that the timing of *odwira* was formally and publicly promulgated, and precise arrangements were discussed.

Messengers were then sent to non-Kumase office holders to announce *odwira*, to command their attendance, and to collect from them any and all outstanding arrears in their prescribed contributions to the forthcoming festival. It would seem that under the *Asantehene* Agyeman Prempe, between 1888 and 1896, various earlier special levies were all finally consolidated into one annual tax, payable at the rate of *domma* (one tenth of an ounce of gold) by every married Asante male, and that this was collected, together with statutory contributions to *odwira*, in the period immediately leading up to the festival.[45]

Between the day just described and *kurudapaawukuo/awukudae* (15: Wednesday) in the ensuing *adaduanan* cycle, in which *odwira* was in fact to take place (a period of 37, 23 or 16 days, depending on whether the *Asantehene* went to Bantama on *nkyidwo*, *kwadwo* or *monodwo*), various preparations for the impending events intensified in Kumase. All items of state regalia – stools, drums, umbrellas, chairs, jewellery, cloths – were very deliberately overhauled and carefully refurbished. 'The royal gold ornaments', observed Bowdich, 'are melted down every Yam Custom, and fashioned into new patterns, as novel as possible. This is a piece of state policy very imposing on the populace, and the tributary chiefs who pay but an annual visit.'[46] The Kumase *sumpene*, or elevated mounds of sun-baked clay – and most notably those at *dwaberem* and *apremoso/bogyawe*, from which the reigning *Asantehene* presided over various ritual and state occasions – were all resurfaced and polished with red ochre.[47] Thus, on 7 December 1871 (*kuruyawo*, 9: Thursday) the public announcement of the impending *odwira* first reached the ears of the Basel missionaries who were captive in Kumase; and on 12 December (*nkyibena*, 14: Tuesday) they observed that the 'public thrones' or 'sitting places' (*sumpene*) were all undergoing repair and renewal.[48] Those *adampaŋ* (lit. empty rooms) which opened onto the main thoroughfares of Kumase, and in which all manner of highly public and visible social intercourse took place, were put in order; bas-reliefs were restored, walls were whitewashed, and red ochre was applied to the floors and dados.[49] All of this busy activity was accompanied by a mounting sense of public anticipation.[50]

During this interval of time, the *Asantehene* continued to carry out the succession of ritual and state duties prescribed by the calendrical evolution of each and every *adaduanan* cycle. Crucial to the punctuation of each *adaduanan* cycle were *kurudapaawukuo/awukudae* (15: Wednesday) and *kurukwasie/akwasidae* (33: Sunday). These two *adae* were the most solemnly observed of all of the *nnabɔne*. More narrowly, their recurrent periodicity served as the primary markers between the hidden and ritual life of the *Asantehene*, and its public and governmental or official counterpart.

In preparation for each of the two *adae* in every succeeding *adaduanan* cycle, the *Asantehene* withdrew from public affairs and retired into the seclusion of the palace. This was done precisely six days prior to each *adae*. That is: on *kuruyawo* (9: Thursday) before *kurudapaawukuo/awukudae* (15: Wednesday); and on *kurudwo* (27: Monday) before *kurukwasie/akwasidae* (33: Sunday). In the afternoon of these two withdrawal days of *kuruyawo* and *kurudwo*, as eyewitnesses observed, the *Asantehene* took his seat in public on the *sumpi* at *dwaberem* or at *apremoso/bogyawe*. There he ritually drank palm wine in the presence of the assembled office holders, citizenry and visiting dignitaries, and then withdrew in state and secluded himself within the palace. There are numerous accounts of these occasions. Thus, for example, about 'half-past four' on *kurudwo* 20 December 1841, the *Asantehene* Kwaku Dua Panin

seated himself in one of the most elevated parts of the town, to drink palm-wine ... the King was seated on a rising ground, under his large umbrellas, surrounded by several hundreds of the people. Boys were standing on each side, cooling him with large fans; and a host of messengers, with gold-handled swords, glittering under the departing rays of the sun, formed a passage up to the place where he sat ... Shortly afterwards his servants arrived, with palm-wine, and a large calabash, partly overlaid with gold, for him to drink out of, and a large silver bowl, to hold under the calabash, to receive the palm-wine which might run down His Majesty's beard. While he was drinking, the large drums were played, and several arrows were shot from the bow, to let the people know that he was still holding the calabash to his mouth. He then sent us a supply of the wine, after which he returned to his residence.[51]

During the consequent periods of seclusion and retirement, all state business, excepting grave or unexpected crises that demanded the most immediate attention, was suspended and deferred; the *Asantehene* neither convened nor presided over any plenary council meetings, took no major decisions, attended no ceremonies beyond the palace walls, and was virtually unavailable to subject office holders and foreign emissaries alike. Thus, in 1820, in the course of difficult discussions over the revision of the Anglo-Asante treaty of 1817, the *Asantehene* Osei Tutu Kwame was confined to his palace between *kuruyawo* (9: Thursday) 9 March and *kurudapaawukuo/awukudae* (15: Wednesday) 15 March; during this period of time, the insistent chief British negotiator Dupuis was admitted to the palace twice for private talks (9 and 12 March), was allowed to enter the palace but expressly forbidden to discuss business once (11 March), and was locked out of the palace on three separate occasions (10, 13 and 14 March).[52] On *kurudwo* (27: Monday) 6 January 1840, the Basel missionary A. Riis was informed that the *Asantehene* Kwaku Dua Panin could discuss no business until 'the time of his confinement has passed and his celebration has ended'; 'the King', remarked Riis, 'does not go out of the locked rooms of his home, sees no visitors and decides no cases'.[53] On *monofie* (17: Friday) 13 June 1873, two days after *kurudapaawukuo/awukudae*, the

Asantehene Kofi Kakari was finally able to perform the ritual of sacrificing a sheep over the foundations of a new dwelling; he had had to defer this ceremony for some time, as 'he could not go out for a week [*sic*] before the Adae'.[54] And in 1882, the British emissary Lonsdale was told that he might not formally enter Kumase until *kwadwo* (34: Monday) 8 May, as the *Asantehene* Mensa Bonsu 'should not be able to receive me until that day, the ceremony of the "Little Adai" [*sic*] keeping him in his palace in the interim'.[55]

Very early in the mornings of *kurudapaawukuo/awukudae* and *kurukwasie/akwasidae* the *Asantehene* performed the mandatory rituals of ancestor worship in the stool house attached to the royal palace. He then quit the palace precinct and presided over a public reception, most usually at *apremoso/bogyawe*. There, in a ceremony that was attended and reported by Europeans on numerous occasions, he distributed packets of gold dust and gifts of alcohol to the assembly.[56] But the two *adae*, being themselves *nnabɔne*, did not mark the definitive re-entry of the *Asantehene* into public life. This metamorphosis occurred on the day immediately following each of the two *adae*.

Early in the mornings of *kwayawo* (16: Thursday) and *kwadwo* (34: Monday), the *Asantehene* paid a formal visit to the Bantama *baamu*, and there saluted his predecessors in office.[57] This progress marked the definitive conclusion of the *adae*; and the return of the *Asantehene* to Kumase after this ceremony signalled his full resumption of public and official state duties. In the *adaduanan* cycle in which *odwira* was to be celebrated, the ending of *kurudapaawukuo/awukudae* – and of the ritual period of the *Asantehene's* withdrawal – concluded the preliminary days of preparation for the festival. The transactions specifically enjoined by the performance of *odwira* began on *kwayawo* (16: Thursday).

kwayawo *(16: Thursday) commenced*

Upon his return from the Bantama *baamu* on *kwayawo*, the *Asantehene* customarily went directly back to the palace. But on the morning of the *odwira kwayawo* this routine was changed. The Wesleyan-Methodist missionary Chapman observed that on *kwayawo* (16: Thursday) 12 September 1844, the *Asantehene* Kwaku Dua Panin:

Instead of returning home direct . . . made a circuit of the Town, going through most of the principal streets. His attendants at the same time poured out occasionally small supplies of rum, as an offering to the Gods [*abosom*]. This survey of the town by the King, as well as the offerings of rum, is a practice of long standing. It seems to be done as a kind of preparatory process against the coming Yam Custom.[58]

One very specific purpose of this ritual promenade was to allow the

Asantehene to inspect the work done in renovating the *sumpene* and the *adampaŋ*. Thus, on *kwayawo* 14 December 1871, the *Asantehene* Kofi Kakari 'went through the Town to assure himself of the renewing of the "Dampans". If the decorations had fallen, or the roofs were leaking or patched, no notice was taken, but the top must be well whitened.'[59] Kofi Kakari repeated this tour of inspection on the *odwira kwayawo* 22 August 1872.[60] 'Tout cela n'est pas ordinaire', opined Bonnat of these proceedings in 1871: 'cette promenade du roi par la ville est pour ouvrir la grande fête ou coutume des ignames, fêtes qu'ils appellent "Apaframe" ou encore "Djura".'[61]

However, this procession had a number of more solemn ritual objectives. Europeans occasionally commented on some of these, but often with only a very limited insight into what was actually transpiring, and no more than a partial comprehension of what they themselves observed. One very important purpose of the *Asantehene's* tour of his capital was to ensure that Kumase was spiritually as well as physically prepared for the celebration of the *odwira*. This took the form of inspecting various boundary markers that defined Kumase – and that signalled the crucial distinction between the spaces of culture and of hostile nature. Thus, the *Asantehene* poured libations at the *ŋkwaŋtanaŋ*, the crossroads that marked the boundaries of Kumase and the beginnings of the major paths that led out of it. The *ŋkwaŋtanaŋ* were themselves concentrations or nodes of great spiritual power; it was at such places on the fringe (*kurotia*) of Kumase, as in all human settlements, that the *abosom*, both welcome and unwelcome, preferred to manifest themselves. It was here too that the Asante believed that any invader, supernatural or human, should be and must be halted; thus, *ŋkwaŋtanaŋ* on the main roads leading out of Kumase had potent medicines (*nduru*: sing. *aduru*) buried beneath them. These were very specifically dedicated to repelling any form of hostile intruder, and it was held that Komfo Anokye himself had played the key role both in furnishing the requisite *nduru* (and *asumaŋ*), and in identifying the *ŋkwaŋtanaŋ* where these were deployed.[62]

Apparently immediately after his belated return from Bantama on *kwayawo* 14 December 1871, the *Asantehene* Kofi Kakari and his retinue proceeded directly to *anowu*, one of the seventy-seven titular wards of Kumase. There, at *anowu*, the *Asantehene* himself alone entered the house where he had been born (in the mid-1830s), and made offerings to all of the blackened ancestral stools and *asumaŋ* contained therein.[63] This dwelling had been the Kumase residence of Kofi Kakari's own recently deceased father, the *Boakye Yam Panin ɔkyeame* Kofi Nti.[64] This was a single episode among many such that together constituted one of the principal significances of the *odwira kwayawo* procession.

Upon returning from Bantama on *odwira kwayawo*, the *Asantehene* first ordered a sheep to be sent to Saawua in gratitude for the new yams supplied by that place for ritual use during the festival. Then, preceded by the Kumase *Nkonŋwasoafoɔhene* bearing the *sika dwa kofi* sheltered by the *katamanso* ('covering the whole nation') state umbrella, and surrounded by the Kumase office holders and the royal *afenasoafoɔ* (sword-bearers), he walked through his capital. His route was firmly prescribed, and it took him to a succession of ideologically and historically potent sites (other than the ŋkwaŋtanaŋ and *kurotia*). At each one of these venues the *Asantehene* offered sheep and libations.

He did this at the residence of the incumbent *Asantehemaa*, the Queen Mother and senior female royal of the *Oyoko Kɔkɔɔ abusua*. He did the same at the stool house, in the *adum* ward, of the ranking head of the *adumfoɔ* (executioners), who was the guardian of the *ɔhemaa dwa*, the blackened personal stool of the first *Asantehemaa* Nyaako Kusi Amoa, and the only pre-existing item of regalia that Komfo Anokye had allegedly spared after the appearance of the *sika dwa kofi*.[65] He did it at the stool house of the *Nkonŋwasoafoɔhene*, the custodian and chief bearer of the *sika dwa kofi*. He did it at the two dwellings, in the *nsuase* and *asokwa* wards, of the occupant of the twinned offices of *Akyeamehene* and *Domakwaehene*, who was traditionally held to have been selected and named by Komfo Anokye to the headship of the *akyeame* ('spokesmen') who served Osei Tutu. He repeated the procedure before the blackened stools of the *Akyempem* and *Kyidom*, whose incumbents were the senior ranking members or representatives of the *ahenemma* (sons) and *ahenenana* (grandsons) of the *Asantehenes*, and hence of the *sika dwa kofi*.[66]

Thereafter, the *Asantehene's* prescribed obligations took him to the buildings that housed the blackened stools of individuals who had fathered those rulers who had died in office; that is, *Asantehenes* who had been accorded burial in the Bantama *baamu*. Thus, for example, on the *odwira kwayawo* 14 December 1871, apart from honouring Kofi Nti at *anowu* – it being an act of *lèse-majesté* to presume that the reigning *Asantehene* would *not* die in office – Kofi Kakari would have offered sheep and libations before the blackened stool of the *Aberenkɛsɛɛhene* Owusu Panin of Nyameani (father of the first *Asantehene* Osei Tutu, d. 1712 or 1717); before the blackened stool, in the *akyeremade* ward, of the *Akyempemhene* *ɔheneba* Kwame Owusu Afriyie (father of the fourth *Asantehene* Osei Kwadwo, 1764–77); before the blackened stool of the *ɔheneba* Adu Twum Kaakyire, *ɔkyeame* to the *akyamfoɔ dumienu* or 'twelve shield-bearers' (father of the sixth *Asantehene* Opoku Fofie, 1803–4); before the blackened stool of the *Asokore Mamponhene ɔheneba* Owusu Ansa Panin (father of the seventh *Asantehene* Osei Tutu Kwame, 1804–23); before the blackened stool, in the *anowu* ward, of the *Anowuhene* Owusu Yaw (father of the eighth *Asantehene* Osei Yaw Akoto, 1823–34); and before the blackened stool, in the ŋkwaŋtanaŋ ward of Kumase, of the ŋkwaŋtananhene and ɔhene of Heman Boakye Yam Kuma (father of the ninth *Asantehene* Kwaku Dua Panin, 1834–67).[67] In addition, a royal ɔkyeame would have been sent with a sheep and drinks to Amakom, the village and seat of the *Amakomhene* Adu Mensa (father of the second *Asantehene* Opoku Ware, *c.* 1720–50).[68]

No such ritual attention was paid to the fathers of those *Asantehenes* who had been removed from office for one reason or another, and who had been interred as a result in the royal burial grounds at *akyeremade* in Kumase or at the *Asantehene's* village of Breman.[69] Thus, Kofi Kakari's 1871 itinerary would not have included ritual visits to the blackened stools of the fathers of the third *Asantehene* Kusi Obodom (deposed or abdicated 1764) or the fifth *Asantehene* Osei Kwame (abdicated under duress 1803).[70] Nor, ironically enough, would the *Asantehene* Agyeman Prempe have accorded any ritual recognition, after his accession in 1888, to the blackened stool of the *Boakye Yam Panin ɔkyeame* Kofi Nti, the father of Kofi Kakari himself (deposed 1874), and of his full brother and successor the eleventh *Asantehene* Mensa Bonsu (deposed 1883).[71]

In the 1920s, Rattray commented that the 'royal progress' just described was 'for the express purpose of informing the ancestral ghosts of all the famous houses in Coomassie of the business on hand'; this was because *odwira* was a festival 'in honour and propitiation of the Ashanti Kings who "had gone elsewhere", and for the cleansing of the whole nation from defilement'.[72] That is to say, the transactions of the *odwira kwayawo* that have just been described were centred on the persons of the incumbent *Asantehene* and his predecessors in office, and on the characteristics that were understood to inhere in paternity, and to be transmitted through male descent. The ideological articulation of these features was of central importance to the state and its definition. The factor of kinship, including royal descent, might be (and was) embedded in and described by the structure(s) of matriliny, but the articulation of political power resided in an *Asantehene* and his fellow male office holders. Thus, the *odwira kwayawo* procession (and indeed *odwira* itself) might freely and openly acknowledge the generic import and social significance of the principle of matriliny, but it also assiduously reinforced the rectitude of received socio-political order as expressed in and through the dominant institutional apparatus of the state and its male elite.

Excursus I: patriliny, matriliny and the Asantehene

In our discussion of accumulation, of *mpoatwa* and of related issues, we have already taken note of some of the accommodations that obtained between the matrilineal kinship structure and the social order on the one hand, and the state on the other. In the vitally important crucible of dynastic politics, the ideological solution to the abiding potential for conflict that existed when the principle of matriliny was subject to intervention and qualification by the competing claims of patriliny was to treat the former condition as *statement* and the latter condition as *argument*. Careful exposition is needed here. Numbers of commentators have been aware of the structural dynamics of this issue, but they have tended to abstract them from historical (and ideological) practice, and then to situate the answer to the problem in propositions concerning unilineal versus dual descent in the operational features of Asante kinship.[73] However, Asante society was not organized around the principle of dual descent, and any satisfactory resolution to this conundrum must be sought in historical ideology rather than in kinship rules. That is, the *statement* – concerning matriliny – was rooted in the fundamental structuration of the social order, and was incontrovertible or given; but the *argument* – concerning the historical succession of competing males to the highest (and indeed to all) ritual and political office – had to be formulated and, as in the highest expression of this at *odwira*, constantly reformulated.

Formulating the *argument* was a matter of intense complexity and application. The matter is here restricted to our crucial exemplary case. That is, the appearance of monolithic unity that the state needed to present, in that such a representation was necessary to ideological articulation and to hegemonic intent, was in recurrent danger of subversion from competition between male royals, and from any ensuing transactional fissions in elite political solidarity. The elements that were involved here required a strict separation. The externally visible body of the state, to reduce things to convenient metaphor, had to manifest the robust health of integrated unity, even if the component organs were afflicted by disabling malfunction or conflict.[74]

The historical realities that underlay the seamless unity of ideological structuration that was displayed in the events of *kwayawo*, and proclaimed all throughout *odwira*, are immensely important, but very difficult to describe with any apt economy. Central to the matter was the convoluted issue of the patrifilial ascription of royal males, and their membership as individuals and historical actors in one or another of the cultic *ntɔrɔ* associations. To begin with, by Asante understanding of the matter, the individual human being was composed of four *essential* elements or constituents. These were the *kra*, the *sunsum*, the *mogya* and the *ntɔrɔ*:

1 *kra* (syn. *ɔkra*: pl. *akra*). This was the essence or 'soul'. It was given directly to each person by *onyame*. It was indestructible, and continued to 'live' after physical

death. The *kra* was the bearer of an individual's *nkrabea*. This was realized on earth as *abrabo* (*ɔbra*), and was an unalterable element in the unfolding of an individual's life; thus, it is generally translated as 'fate' or 'destiny'. The *kra* was in the person, but separate from him or her. Thus, it could give both good and bad advice. Hence, *ne ɔkra di na akyi* ('his *kra* gives good advice and protects him'), but also *ne ɔkra apa na akyi* ('his *kra* gives bad advice and fails to guide him'). The *kra* might also temporarily quit the person in the face of danger. What many commentators have called 'day names' among the Asante were in fact derived characterisations of the names of the *akra* born on specific days. The 'day name', so called, was in fact *kradin*; and each birth day was governed by a *kra* 'spirit'. Hence, a child born on (compound)-*yawo* ('Thursday's child') was predisposed to warfare and heroism; thus, male names such as Yaw Barima (*ɔbarima*: a valiant man, hero). At death, the *kra* returned to *onyame*, and accounted for itself.

2 *sunsum* (pl. *asunsum*). This was an intangible constituent, non-human in origin, and also very often given in translation as 'soul'. It determined the character (*subaŋ*) of a person. Whereas the *kra* was fixed and unalterable, the *sunsum* could be changed or modified by training and application; a 'light' (*hare*) *sunsum* could be cultivated and trained to be 'heavy' (*duru*), that is to be more responsible, reflective, braver, etc. The *sunsum* could leave the body during sleep, was involved in dreaming, and was susceptible to the spiritual malady of witchcraft. But a 'heavy' *sunsum* was regarded – quite predictably – as the best defence against witchcraft (*wo sunsum yɛ duru ɔbayifoɔ ntumi wo*: 'if your *sunsum* is "heavy" the witch cannot overpower you'). A *sunsum* could become agitated and harbour malice; this might presage illness in the individual, and malaise in society. A 'burdened' *sunsum* was encouraged, therefore, 'to speak its mind' and to 'cool' (*dwo*) itself down – often in the purgative context of the *apo* ritual. The *sunsum* was not confined to the individual. Groups or communities could possess a collective *sunsum*; that of the *Asantemaŋ* was contained in the *sika dwa kofi*. Thus, protecting the Golden Stool was in part about defending the collective *sunsum* of the Asante against attack (conceptualized as producing 'illness' in the social order).[75]

3 *mogya* (syn. *bogya*). This was the 'blood'. It was inherited matrilineally, and so it was synonymous in meaning with *abusua*. As we have seen, it furnished and defined citizen membership within the matrilineage (*abusua*) and the more inclusive matriclan (*abusua kɛsɛɛ*). It was the basis of exogamy; no two members of the same *abusua* might marry and have children. The *mmusua kɛsɛɛ* and *mmusua* are understood as the primordial base of Asante society and identity. Traditionalists argue that there were originally seven such matriclans (*abusua asɔn*); but eight – and sometimes more – are commonly listed. Each was composed of complementary moieties; hence, for instance, *Oyoko ne Dako* (Oyoko and Dako). What is of the greatest significance is that *mmusua kɛsɛɛ* – primordial and immemorial institutions though they might be, at least as represented in tradition – were subject to state intervention. The *Tana* (*Atena*) moiety of *Bretuo ne Tana* was abolished in Asante by the *Asantehene* Opoku Ware (*c.* 1720–50), following a heinous offence committed by a *Tana* wife of that ruler.[76]

4 *ntɔrɔ* (syn. *ntoro*: *ntɔŋ*). This was the element that defined consanguinity in patrilineal terms, and it was often used as a synonym for 'semen'. Every Asante inherited his/her *ntɔrɔ* affiliation from his/her father, and through him, from his/her

lineal male antecedents. There is some uncertainty over the precise number of *ntɔrɔ* groups (see below). There is an obscure link between many of the *ntɔrɔ* groups and water, i.e. with the *atano* group of the *abosom*. The *ntɔrɔ* affiliation was sometimes interpreted in relation to group character; hence, members of the *Bosommuru ntɔrɔ* were noble; of the *Bosompra*, stubborn and hard; of the *Bosomtwe*, compassionate, etc.[77]

Very obviously, this quadripartite construction or reading of the human individual lends itself to a structural analysis in terms of sets of binary pairings and oppositions. Such an approach is instructive, although due caution is required in its application, together with a recognition that the insights derived from it must remain speculative rather than conclusive.[78] In Asante thought, the human individual was composed of four elements. Two were human in origin; and of these two, one was categorically male and one female. In numerous contexts of understanding, efficacy of (trans)action was achieved through the pairing of a non-human and a human element. The 'washing' or purification of the male human element (*ntɔrɔ*) was associated, for example, with the 'washing' or purification of the *kra*. Similarly, the female human element (*mogya*) was linked in a direct way to the practice of witchcraft (*bayi*), which was intimately bound, both physically and metaphorically, to the concept and specificities of 'blood'.[79] However, no fixed or permanent binary pairings that cover all cases can be adduced – as for example between *ntɔrɔ-kra* and *mogya-sunsum* – because a host of alternative modes and/or degrees of emphatic linkage is implied in the many combinations that sought to explicate all of the discrete (and overlapping) aspects of human quiddity, behaviour, morality and the rest.[80] It is the entire matrix or compendium of all possible binary linkages considered together that is most suggestively meaningful in its implications. Across the entire range of its explanatory competence, the interpretation of the *nature* of the human individual was actualized via a series of pairings and juxtapositions. These may be construed as being situational 'conversations' in ontology that occurred between elements that were fixed in number and specific in identity. The content and the context of such 'conversations' suggest not only an expected unknowing in relation to *onyame* and the *abosom*, but also an ambiguous opposition, a tension, and an irresolution in achieving any nominated and precisely agreed closure in the definition of the relationship between female and male. Something of this inconclusive dialogue is evident in individual male and female perceptions of the hidden agenda of the 'other' in the practice of sexuality and the representation(s) of gender(s).[81] In an utterly different arena – and one in which the issue of the individual bore directly upon the history of society – it is also evident in the transactional evolution of the royal dynasty of Kumase. It is important to realize that this was a structural feature, albeit one that was often resolved at the level of individuals (and what, for want of any better description, we might call the psychology of interaction between them).

Nine Asante *ntɔrɔ* groups are conventionally listed, and some sources identify as many as twelve.[82] Much of the uncertainty over numbers has arisen because several of the *ntɔrɔ* groups have historically embraced a variable number of discrete, self-referencing sub-divisions, and on occasion some of these latter have been promoted (or laid claim) to an autonomous identity. Members of each and every Asante *ntɔrɔ* shared in common in certain indispensable features that defined the specificity of that particular group, and that described the context(s) of ascribed patrilineal belonging in it. Thus, every *ntɔrɔ* had its own particular salutation and response (*nnyeɛsoɔ*); its own register of avoidances and taboos (*akyiwadeɛ*: generally things that might not be touched, harmed, eaten, etc.); its own totems (*akrammoa*: sing. *akraboa*: animals that were sacred to the members of the *ntɔrɔ*: of course, these were also *akyiwadeɛ*); and, most crucially, its own specific observance day (*kra da*). On such days an Asante performed rituals for his *ntɔrɔ*, the most significant being the 'blessing of the mouth' with water (*ohyira nɔ ano*), and the solemn 'washing', cleansing or purification of his *kra* (*odwareɛ nɔ kra*). All of these observances and ritual practices were exclusively bequeathed to a person by his or her father (and derived from the *ntɔrɔ* identity of that genitor's lineal male ancestors). The Asante *ntɔrɔ*, together with their known characteristics, were as follows:

1 *Bosommuru*	*nnyeɛsoɔ*	(*yaa*) *aburu*
	akyiwadeɛ	*ɔkwaku* (Mona monkey); *nantwi* (ox, cow); *ɔkramaŋ* (domestic dog); *odompo* (wild dog); *asokwa* (a species of bird); *aburo* (maize, Indian corn: not to be eaten on 'Tuesdays'): *nsafufu* (palm wine: not to be drunk on 'Tuesdays')
	akrammoa	*enini* (python); *akura* (mouse)
	kra da	*nwonabena*; *nkyibena*; *kurubena*; *kwabena*; *monobena*; *fobena* (i.e. 'Tuesday')
2 *Bosompra*	*nnyeɛsoɔ*	*anyaado*; *ahenewaa*
	akyiwadeɛ	*ɔkwaku* (Mona monkey); *akokɔ fufuo* (white fowl); *ɔsebo* (leopard); *tamiriwa* (a species of large edible snail); *ɔwansaŋ* (bush buck); *akyekyere* (tortoise); *abɔka/abɔfo* (carcass of any beast found dead); *afasɛɛ* (water yam)

		akraboa	*akokɔ fufuo* (white fowl)
		kra da	*nwonawukuo*; *nkyiwukuo*; *kurudapaawukuo*; *kwawukuo*; *monowukuo*; *fowukuo* (i.e. 'Wednesday')
3	*Bosomtwe*	*nnyeɛsoɔ*	*amu*
		akyiwadeɛ	*ɔkwaku* (Mona monkey); *ɔwansaŋ* (bush buck); *tamiriwa* (a species of large edible snail); *akyekyere* (tortoise); *odompo* (wild dog)
		akraboa	*ɔsebo* (leopard)
		kra da	*monokwasie*; *fokwasie*; *nwonakwasie*; *nkyikwasie*; *kurukwasie*; *kwakwasie* (i.e. 'Sunday')
4	*Bosommram*	*nnyeɛsoɔ*	*anyaado*
		akyiwadeɛ	*nantwi* (ox, cow); *ɔdeŋkyɛm* (crocodile); *nsafufu* (palm wine but no other liquor)
		akraboa	*ɔkwaku* (Mona monkey)
		kra da	*kwamememene*; *monomemene*; *fomemene*; *nwonamemene*; *nkyimemene*; *kurumemene* (i.e. 'Saturday')
5	*Bosommketɛa* (*Asaabreɛfoɔ*)	*nnyeɛsoɔ*	*ɔbere*
		akyiwadeɛ	*odompo* (wild dog); *ɔkramaŋ* (domestic dog); *aburuburu* (dove)
		akraboa	*odompo* (wild dog)
		kra da	'Tuesday'; cf. *Bosommuru* above
6	*Bosomakɛm* (*Akyerɛmadeɛfoɔ*)	*nnyeɛsoɔ*	*anyaado*; *ahenewaa*
		akyiwadeɛ	*ɔdeŋkyɛm* (crocodile); *tweneboa* (a species of tree); *nantwi* (ox, cow); *tamiriwa* (a species of large edible snail); *akyekyere* (tortoise)
		akraboa	*ɔdeŋkyɛm* (crocodile)
		kra da	'Sunday'; cf. *Bosomtwe* above
7	*Bosomdwerɛbeɛ* (*Agyamadeɛfoɔ*)	*nnyeɛsoɔ*	*ahenewa*
		akyiwadeɛ	*ɔwansaŋ* (bush buck); *ɔkaŋkane* (civet); *tamiriwa* (a species of large edible snail); *nsafufu* (palm wine; not to be drunk on 'Sundays'); *akyekyere* (tortoise)
		akraboa	*ɔsebo* (leopard)
		kra da	'Sunday'; cf. *Bosomtwe* above
8	*Bosomafi*	*nnyeɛsoɔ*	*ɔpeo*

(*Ankamadeɛfoɔ*)	*akyiwadeɛ*	*afasɛɛ* (water yam); *adowa* (Royal antelope); *odompo* (wild dog); *ɔkramaŋ* (domestic dog); *aburuburu* (dove)
	akraboa	*kwaagyadu/kontromfi* (baboon)
	kra da	'Tuesday'; cf. *Bosommuru* above
9 *Bosompoŋ*	*nnyeɛsoɔ*	*anyaado*
(*Agyanadeɛfoɔ*)	*akyiwadeɛ*	*ɔdɛŋkyɛm* (crocodile); *mmerebia* (a species of small mushroom; usually found on a dead palm tree); *onyina* (silk-cotton tree); *afasɛɛ* (water yam)
	akraboa	?
	kra da	'Wednesday'; cf. *Bosompra* above.[83]

In Asante thought bastardy in the western sense was a null category. A child's *abusua* affiliation was always known, because it derived directly from the *mogya* of its mother. But in the event that a genitor declined to acknowledge paternity, or there was some question of responsibility in this matter, then a child born under such regrettable circumstances would have no known and confirmed *ntɔrɔ*. Individuals of this category were said to 'lack a whole body' (*wonni mu*) – that is to say, their *ntɔrɔ* was 'missing'. This did not constitute an illegitimate status. For a commoner it was certainly a social stigma, but the actual jural penalties involved could be negotiated. But for an *ɔdehyeɛ* (royal), and in particular for a male in competition for office, it was a catastrophic disability. To be in the status of *wonni mu* disqualified a person as a candidate for any stool.[84]

There were two reasons for this. First: an individual who was *wonni mu* could not 'wash' his own *ntɔrɔ*, and so was disbarred from undertaking acts of ritual purification on behalf of others. *Asantehenes*, it should be recalled, were the indispensable ritual actors in the cleansing of the whole *Asantemaŋ*. Second: the *ntɔrɔ* was both a mnemonic of the past and an affirmation of the future. It served as an instrument for the corporate remembrance and celebration of the lives of all of the distinguished persons – office holders, generals, *abirɛmpɔn*, etc. – in a patrilineal line of descent; these were the 'great names' (*aboadenfoɔ*: sing. *ɔboadeni*) of the *ntɔrɔ*. The admirable characteristics displayed by such persons were understood as accreted properties of the *ntɔrɔ*. That is, they might be reincarnated in descendants in the male line, and various techniques – of propitious naming, for example – were employed to encourage and to conduce this desirable end. Office holders, and the *Asantehene* above all, were looked to atavistically in relation to their *ntɔrɔ aboadenfoɔ*.[85]

The distinction between matriliny (as *statement*) and patriliny (as *argument*), with specific reference to the status of an *Asantehene*, can be adumbrated as follows. The condition of being an *ɔdehyeɛ* of the *Oyoko Kɔkɔɔ abusua* was a fixed expressive feature of an unequivocal and unarguable status in matriliny. That is, any candidate *Asantehene* was *necessarily* royal, in that he was able to trace his uterine descent in the *Oyoko Kɔkɔɔ abusua* of Kumase from the ancestress Maanu, the maternal grandmother of the first *Asantehemaa* Nyaako Kusi Amoa.[86] But the same issue in relation to patrilineal descent was a more flexible, open and arguable feature, for unlike the condition of being *ɔdehyeɛ* it could not be reduced to an either/or simplicity. Thus, Asante traditionalists have sometimes speculated that the *Bosommuru ntɔrɔ* was more 'noble' than any of its structural counterparts. But such statements are assertions of partisan opinion rather than rules *per se*. That is, unlike matriliny, in relation to royalty the issue of *ntɔrɔ* affiliation was a property of actual historical practice and was subject to ideological structuration and debate.[87]

It is the case, however, that opinions framed around the idea of competitive degrees of 'nobility' between *ntɔrɔ* provide a key to the Asante construction of the model of royalty. That is, any candidate to become *Asantehene*, in addition to being *necessarily* royal in terms of matriliny, was also preferentially or ideally, but *not necessarily*, the paternal grandson of a previous *Asantehene* in terms of patriliny. The ideal parents of such an individual were an *ɔheneba* of the *sika dwa kofi* (a son of an *Asantehene*) who had contracted an exogamous marriage with a female *ɔdehyeɛ* of the *Oyoko Kɔkɔɔ abusua*. Any child born of such a union was guaranteed both royal status and an *ntɔrɔ* pedigree that was replete with the most distinguished *aboadenfoɔ*. Arrangements of this type were grounded in the broader belief and social understanding that cross-cousin marriage offered the most propitious opportunity for fathering a *kra pa* or 'ideal (re)incarnation' of a famous ancestor. Therefore, a celebrated grandfather – to take the closest genealogical relationship – might be reborn in his paternal grandson.[88]

The *Asantehenes* Osei Tutu, Osei Kwadwo and Osei Tutu Kwame were all members of the *Adufudeɛ* sub-division of the *Bosommuru ntɔrɔ*, which used the names Osei and Owusu in alternate generations; so too was Osei Yaw Akoto who, though descended through a cadet line, was still a paternal great great grandson of the first *Asantehene* Osei Tutu. The *Asantehenes* Opoku Ware and Opoku Fofie were also members of *Bosommuru*, but in the *Asafodeɛ* sub-division – which alternated the names Opoku and Adu – rather than in *Adufudeɛ*. Wilks has characterized the *Adufudeɛ* and *Asafodeɛ* as being the two original patrilineal 'houses' (of Osei Tutu and Opoku Ware) within the *Bosommuru ntɔrɔ*, from which – preferentially, ideally but *not necessarily* – *Asantehenes* were selected. That is, the model *Asantehene* by this construction traced his agnatic descent as a member of the *Bosommuru Adufudeɛ* (the 'house' of the first *Asantehene* Osei Tutu), or of the *Bosommuru Asafodeɛ* (the 'house' of the second *Asantehene* Opoku Ware). The conceptual model of succession proposed by this, as Wilks surmises, seems to have envisaged a process of serial alternation between these two 'houses'.[89] This is a suggestive and valuable reading, but it requires closer scrutiny and analysis.

In the history of the Asante state between 1701 and 1896 there were thirteen *Asantehenes*. Six of these rulers were members of *Bosommuru Adufudeɛ* or *Asafodeɛ*; seven were not. The first group held office for an aggregated period of some ninety-three years; the second for a total of 102 years. But no *Asantehene* is classified as a usurper, and this illustrates the point at issue. Patrilineal descent in terms of *ntɔrɔ* membership bore upon preference, and partisanship, but not jural right in the selection of an *Asantehene*. The resulting situation may be described in terms that draw a conceptual distinction between processual dynastic politics on the one hand, and the embodied representation of the state in the person of an enstooled *Asantehene* on the other. Dispute and conflict emanating from competitive patrifilial claims, as between *ntɔrɔ*, were anticipated, and were historically endemic in virtually all elections to the *sika dwa kofi*. In effect, *Bosommuru Adufudeɛ* or *Asafodeɛ* could always advance strong historical claims, but because any such case was not enshrined as a juridical right all manner of considerations were liable to vitiate or negate its argument. Candidates from another *ntɔrɔ* might be older, more experienced or better liked; they might possess a proven moral worth or admired forensic capacity; they might be able to muster – through persuasion, bribery or threat – decisive or majority support among office holders; they might have links to a potent *ɔbosom* or to some other supernatural or intangible advantage. However, after the electoral process had been concluded and the succession determined, an *Asantehene* – formally endorsed and enstooled on the *sika dwa kofi* – was an *Asantehene*. He had become a unique, and uniquely different, category of person. The ideology of the state demanded no less, for any continuation of factional warring, in the open and in public, could only serve to subvert the legitimacy, unity and continuity of the image presented to Asante society and to the external world generally by the state itself.

Thus, even in the eighteenth century the preference for rulers drawn from *Bosommuru Adufudeɛ* or *Asafodeɛ* was fractured by political and biological realities. Suffice it to say that the third *Asantehene* Kusi Obodom (*c.* 1750–64) was a member of neither one of these *Bosommuru* sub-divisions; his father was the *Apebosoɔhene* Apaw of the *Bosompra ntɔrɔ*, while his mother was (*necessarily*) the *ɔdehyeɛ* and second *Asantehemaa* Nkaatia

Ntim Abamo.[90] And the fifth *Asantehene* Osei Kwame (1777–1803) only claimed membership in the *Bosommuru ntɔrɔ* through his father the *Mamponhene* Safo Katanka, and not through direct or unbroken patrilineal descent in the dynastically central Kumase-based lines of *Adufudeɛ* or *Asafodeɛ*.[91] Both of these rulers were effectively deposed, in that they were constrained to abdicate – Kusi Obodom on the grounds of his failing health, and Osei Kwame under a variety of political pressures in which the *Asantehemaa* Kwaadu Yaadom played a conspiratorial role.[92] There can be no doubt that, once measures to remove them had gained majority support and an irresistible momentum, their alleged patrilineal faults or shortcomings were added as *ex post facto* argument to buttress the case against them. But neither one was removed from office on the sole and specific grounds of his paternal descent, or uniquely *because* of it. Nor had this factor prevented either one from becoming the incumbent of the *sika dwa kofi* in the first place, or from presiding over Asante for terms of fourteen years (Kusi Obodom) and twenty-six years (Osei Kwame) respectively.

The thrust and emphases of Asante priorities in distinguishing between the processes of intra-dynastic politics and the ideology of the state can be gauged from a close reading of many passages of historical tradition. A representative instance, reproduced below as a narrative of events, is provided by the gloss that is placed on *ntɔrɔ* (and other matters) in relation to key ideological items in authoritative accounts of the selection and installation of Kusi Obodom as *Asantehene* in c. 1750.

1 Immediately after the death of the second *Asantehene* Opoku Ware, the elders of Kumase met together and decided to join his name with that of the first *Asantehene* Osei Tutu in direct association with the *sika dwa kofi*. Hence, the honorific – *Osei ne Opoku sika dwa* ('the Golden Stool of Osei (Tutu) and Opoku (Ware)'). This appellation connoted no proprietorial *right* of succession to the *sika dwa kofi*. The honorific was commemorative; by associating the names of the first two *Asantehenes* with the Golden Stool, the Asante were according recognition of the singular contributions made by Osei Tutu and Opoku Ware to the creation and military aggrandizement of the state, and to the enlargement and adornment of Kumase. *Osei ne Opoku sika dwa* is a historical mnemonic. It memorializes and praises 'great names' (*aboadenfoɔ*). In so doing it acknowledged that the male lineal descendants of Osei Tutu and Opoku Ware would always receive sympathetic consideration in any contest for the office of *Asantehene* – not by any *right* of succession, but in acknowledgement of the lives and careers of their two illustrious male forebears, and in the earnest hope that the sterling characteristics of these ancestors might be reincarnated in any one or other of their male descendants.

2 However, at the death of Opoku Ware, neither *Bosommuru Adufudeɛ* or *Asafodeɛ* had a candidate who could realistically contest the succession; Osei Tutu's grandson – the *ɔdehyeɛ* Osei Kwadwo, who was to become *Asantehene* in 1764 – was no more than fifteen; Opoku Ware's paternal grandsons were even younger, or had

not yet been born. In the event, succession to the *sika dwa kofi* was contested between two (or possibly three) parties. One candidate was Kusi Obodom – an *ɔdehyeɛ* by virtue of his mother the second *Asantehemaa* Nkaatia Ntim Abamo, whose own mother Kyirama was a uterine sister of the *Asantehene* Osei Tutu, both being the children of the *Oyoko Kɔkɔɔ ɔdehyeɛ* (and 'ancestress') Maanu; in terms of patrifiliation, Kusi Obodom traced descent in the *Bosompra ntɔrɔ* through his father the *Apebosoɔhene* Apaw. Kusi Obodom was 'quite grey' (i.e. elderly) by this time; he might have been considered as a successor to Osei Tutu, but Komfo Anokye had recognized the outstanding personal qualities of the much younger Opoku Ware, and had endorsed the latter's candidacy. The other candidates were either of the brothers Dako Panin and Dako Kuma, or by some accounts both of them (*Dako ne Dako*). The brothers were both collateral *adehyeɛ* of the *Oyoko Kɔkɔɔ* – their mother being Akua Ago, a uterine descendant of the royal Birempomaa Pieseɛ, the maternal great-grandmother of Osei Tutu – and paternal grandsons of Obiri Yeboa, the immediate predecessor of Osei Tutu (as ruler of the Kwaman/Kumase area).

3 *Dako ne Dako* asserted a prior claim to the succession, their argument being, (*a*) that they were as 'royal' as anyone else; (*b*) that, as grandsons of Obiri Yeboa, they were direct descendants in a patrilineal *ntɔrɔ* line that contained *aboadenfoɔ* and that boasted a more distinguished antiquity than the comparable male descent lines of Osei Tutu, Opoku Ware or Kusi Obodom; and (*c*) that if all of these factors were given due weight it would be seen that Osei Tutu and Opoku Ware, whatever their personal distinction, had only served as *ahwɛfoɔ* (caretakers, trustees: sing. *ɔhwɛfo*) for the interests of better qualified claimants – namely ⸱hemselves. The Asante office holders discussed the merits of *Dako ne Dako's* case. The consensus was that they were indeed *adehyeɛ*, and that their paternal descent – which included the 'great name' of Obiri Yeboa – was impeccable and laudable. However, it was ruled that Komfo Anokye had said that the *sika dwa kofi* should always be occupied by the best-qualified *individual* candidate, *after* all of the genealogical credentials (*abusua* and *ntɔrɔ*) of all of the claimants to it had been reviewed. The purpose of this preliminary review was only to determine eligibility to compete for the succession, and not to determine the succession itself. The office holders then turned to consider the claims and merits of Kusi Obodom.

4 While these transactions were taking place, *Dako ne Dako* moved to take physical possession of the Golden Stool. They persuaded the Kumase *Akwamuhene* and *Asafohene* Ayirebi to instruct the *nkonŋwasoafoɔ* (stool carriers) to remove the Golden Stool to his own ward of *asafo* for 'safekeeping'. Kusi Obodom realized the implications of this development. Supported by the *Saamanhene* and *Asikasuhene* Kwame Nantwi, he forcibly removed the *sika dwa kofi* from *asafo* and gave it into the (constitutionally correct) care of the *Adumhene* Agyei Kɛsɛɛ Panin in the *adum* ward. In this fraught stalemate, both sides set about marshalling support.

5 The *Anyinasehene* Akyampon Kwasi solicited the mediating support of the *Bantamahene* and *Krontihene* Aprako Yaw – the senior ranking general in the capital – on behalf of Kusi Obodom. Aprako Yaw reportedly asked for and received 1,000 *mperedwan* of gold for his arbitration and assistance. *Dako ne Dako* then offered Aprako Yaw 300 *mperedwan* in their turn. Aprako Yaw accepted, and having received considerations from both sides he proposed to find a solution satisfactory to all parties.

6 At a meeting of the office holders Aprako Yaw outlined his solution. He proposed that – to avoid continuing conflict – Kusi Obodom and *Dako ne Dako* (or one of the two brothers) should rule jointly. He then urged that in implementation of this solution the palace, the regalia and most significantly the *sika dwa kofi* should be partitioned and divided between the two parties. *Dako ne Dako* accepted this arrangement. But Kusi Obodom rejected it, his principal objection being that, by definition, the *sika dwa kofi* was indivisible. The meeting then broke up, with Kusi Obodom saying that he would continue to keep the Golden Stool in safety in *adum*.

7 The stalemate now degenerated into violence. By one account, the *Ofoasehene* Ekye – a partisan of *Dako ne Dako* – brought armed men onto the streets of Kumase. In the ensuing fight he was defeated and killed by Kusi Obodom and his supporters, and his town of Ofoase (near Ohwim) was razed to the ground. By another account, *Dako ne Dako*, realizing their cause was increasingly hopeless, quit Kumase to seek Gyaman help, but settled among the Bawle (Baule) in the west and never returned. By a third such account, *Dako ne Dako* and their supporters were killed in Kumase in fighting provoked by themselves.

8 Whatever the precise course of events, the upshot was that *Dako ne Dako* were disqualified as candidates for the *sika dwa kofi*. Kusi Obodom was now unanimously endorsed as *Asantehene*. Most significantly, because *Dako ne Dako* had acceded to the proposal to divide the *sika dwa kofi* – an abomination in Asante custom – all of their matrilineal (*abusua*) and patrilineal (*ntɔrɔ*) 'descendants' of whatever kind or degree of filiation were proscribed in perpetuity from ever again contesting for the offices of *Asantehene* and *Asantehemaa*. A solemn oath was taken to this effect. And in token of their disgrace, the portion of the *asaaman* ward of Kumase occupied by *Dako ne Dako* was renamed *asaaman kwaadane* (the 'enslaved' *asaaman*, in the sense of being permanently in the dependent status of minors).[93]

The *sika dwa kofi* – very accurately rendered in English by the Asante as 'the palladium of the Asante nation' – was indivisible, and occupancy of it by any given *Asantehene* (Osei Tutu and Opoku Ware included) was conceptualized in terms of custodianship, and not with reference to any jurally formulated proprietary or disposable rights in it.[94] Thus, an *Asantehene* could nominate his choice of successor, but this expressed no more than a personal wish; any such endorsement might assist the recipient in an electoral contest, but it was not at all binding in law and could be, and was, set aside.[95] In a similar way, a particular *ntɔrɔ* affiliation might serve to advance a candidate's claims to office as *Asantehene*, but no question of constitutional right was involved; all manner of other factors – as can be seen in the matter of *Dako ne Dako* and Kusi Obodom – played parts that were equally, or situationally even more, significant and influential.

What then, finally, was the ideological specificity of the *ntɔrɔ* in Asante understanding, and how was this articulated in the contextual arena of competition over succession to the *sika dwa kofi*, and in terms of integration with other spheres of reference and action? For the *individual*, whether an *Asantehene* or a humble *akoa*, the grid of *ntɔrɔ* and *abusua* defined the repertoire of most significant others, and so also the interpersonal forum in which the most intense positive or negative sentiments were felt, engaged and displayed. At a profound level of understanding – albeit one that is elusive and very difficult to reconstruct – the sources afford us rare opportunities to penetrate the carapace of kinship, and to see within it the wellsprings of motive and action in the lives of particular individuals. Because the matrix of issues under review was inextricably bound up with insistent questions about the nature of human (Asante) selfhood, or with the endless making and remaking of the consciousness of self, it is misleading to abstract the quiddity of Asante patrifiliation (or matrifiliation) to the simple uniformity of a series of mandates derived from and dedicated to the systemic advancement of one or another kinship group. Even within matriliny – more clearly mired in and determined by jural structuration than its patrilineal counterpart – the scope for individual initiatives was notably broad. This was where individuals made themselves, and so in their own ways 'made' history.[96]

Thus, for example, broad liens of filiation within the *ntɔrɔ* might well be aggregated and addressed – as on *odwira kwayawo* – in a shared communality of belief, rites and practices. But actors/actresses looked inward as well as outward, to the self *of* society as well as the related self *in* society. That is, action was also subject to a powerful individuation; and this was promulgated in and through a kaleidoscope of correspondences between the emotive, the elective, the situational, the relational and the shifting or, quite literally, idiosyncratic. The revelation of efficacy in the ongoing dynamic of the social required the presence of an active voice. In the case of patriliny – as an *argument* needing to be made and remade – *aboadenfoɔ* conferred credit on an *ntɔrɔ*, but in the end they were one person's ancestors and not another's. When the state rehearsed and affirmed its hermeneutic through an *Asantehene*, he was ideologically distanced from his own subjective status. He was an actor in both senses of the term, for the individual self locked in its own niche of being was necessarily subordinated to the ritual enactment of a fixed and unchanging public performance. The difference between the two was the difference between two kinds of historical consciousness, or two ways of representing historical action.[97]

To illuminate this difference, let us consider the register of speech actions (*ɔkasa*), the importance of which has already been noted, and then consider these matters in a documented historical context. An *Asantehene*, on occasions like *odwira kwayawo*, and indeed throughout the entire course of his public life, gave utterance on behalf of 'something else'. He was the recitative conduit of a ritualized vocabulary. Royalty spoke differently, in the most literal ways. Royal speech (*adehyeɛ kasa*) was transmitted through the mediation of an *ɔkyeame*, but its formulation in the mouth of an

Asantehene was itself an exaggerated mark of a unique status; an *Asantehene* spoke quickly, in a low and measured volume, with a deliberate whistling nasality, sometimes with a stuttering inflection and always with a modulated softness (*bɔkɔɔ*). The *Asantehene* Mensa Bonsu 'spoke through his nose and very quick', his Asante interlocutors said, 'and therefore one could hardly hear him when he talked'; he would then sometimes become 'awfully angry if you wanted him to repeat what he had already said'.[98]

The speech of an *Asantehene* contrasted with and was marked off from the register of ordinary language use (*ɔkasa*). More precisely, many of the verbal modes of expression that were in common use – for example, *ŋkɔmmɔ(bɔ)* (familiar conversation), *obirebire* (unseemly loquacity, loose talk, prattling), *akutia* (in the sense of innuendo), *kasae* (common talk, rumour: *ɔkasafo*, a gossiper), *ntwiri* (talking slanderous lies, splenetic grumbling: *otwirifo*, a slanderer), *ɔkasa guaa* (backbiting), and *nseku* (a voicing of calumny, innuendo, defamatory insinuation: *nsekubɔ*, aspersion or insinuation: *osekufo*, a detractor, insinuator) – were dissociated from the person of an *Asantehene* in two related ways.[99] First, no *Asantehene* would ever have resorted to the public use of such manifestly vulgar formulations of discourse and comment. Second, no Asante would have knowingly cast the *Asantehene* as a subject (*ɔkasa ho*) to be talked about in these offensive verbal contexts; any such act was punishable in law, and aggravated transgression was dealt with as the capital crime of *lèse-majesté*.[100]

However, these formal distinctions applied in public and to the personhood defined by the *office* of *Asantehene*. By contrast, and in regard to any given *individual person* who had become *Asantehene*, covert gossip and rumour of a critical nature – formulated in the verbal modes of expression listed above – were much less restricted, and indeed seem to have been endemic. That this was the prevailing case may be adduced from the fact that, in common with all other matrifilial and patrifilial corporate groups, the *Oyoko Kɔkɔɔ abusua* subscribed to and practised the concept of *afisɛm* (der. *(ɔ)fie*, house(hold) + *asɛm*, matters: literally 'things within the house(hold)': i.e. kinship, domestic or family matters of a private nature: understood as 'secrets').[101] Openly and publicly to discuss one's own *afisɛm*, and more gravely to advertise or to comment adversely on such issues in relation to others, was both an unforgivable breach of etiquette and actionable in law. Knowingly to broadcast *afisɛm* pertaining to the royal dynasty was a capital offence. But, as in every human society, all manner of whispered stories gained currency and were circulated privately. The critical public airing of *afisɛm* concerning an *Asantehene* did not take place; but critical private speculation and even scurrilities concerning *afisɛm* in relation to an individual who was the *Asantehene* were widespread. The distinction between the two proposed an ideological separation between the *office* of *Asantehene* – an embodiment of the state, construed as timeless – and the *individual person* of any one or another successive *Asantehene* – a tenured incumbent, construed as a temporal actor in historical practice.

Excursus II: family, life and times of the Asantehene *Kwaku Dua Panin*

All of the interlocking complexities that have been outlined are rarely recoverable in historical detail (and for numerous societies other than Asante).[102] However, sources concerning the life and reign of the *Asantehene* Kwaku Dua Panin afford an opportunity for reading and interpretation at that very deep level where the construction of the individual self can be observed in detailed and telling interaction with key structurations in (and of) the Asante historical experience. A broad consideration to be borne in mind is that the specific case has resonant and clear implications for our understanding – or lack of it – of other passages of the Asante past.[103]

Fredua Agyeman (born *c.* 1797; enstooled as *Asantehene* Kwaku Dua Panin in 1834; died 1867) was an *ɔdehyeɛ* of the *Oyoko Kɔkɔɔ abusua*, but his matrilineal descent embraced unorthodoxies that were properties in *afisɛm*. The problematic issues pertained to the identity and status of his maternal grandmother, and to kinship relations within the *ɔyafunu koro* ((the offspring of) a single womb: a maximal lineage segment) that traced matrilineal descent from her. In the received genealogies of the *Oyoko Kɔkɔɔ abusua*, Kwaku Dua Panin's maternal grandmother is named as being the Kumase *ɔdehyeɛ* Kwaadu Yaadom (born mid-1750s; enstooled as *Asantehemaa* in *c.* 1770; died 1809). Kwaadu Yaadom is reported to have married the *Mamponhene* Safo Katanka (died *c.* 1767), by whom she bore three children; in order of birth these were Akyaa Kɛsɛɛ (who died in childhood), Amma Sewaa (the mother of Kwaku Dua Panin), and Osei Kwame (enstooled as *Asantehene* in 1777; abdicated 1803; died 1803/4).[104] However, there are grave chronological flaws in this authorized version of tradition.

Amma Sewaa's younger sibling Osei Kwame was certainly born no later than the mid-1760s.[105] Her elder sister Akyaa Kɛsɛɛ was born at the latest, therefore, in the early 1760s. However, when these children were born (by the latest possible estimated date) their ascribed mother Kwaadu Yaadom was only a pre-pubescent child or perhaps, by the middle 1760s, a very early adolescent. Furthermore, Kwaadu Yaadom is known to have died in 1809, in her mid-fifties, as a result of complications that arose from a menopausal pregnancy.[106] Thus, by the authorized account we are required to accept, (*a*) that Kwaadu Yaadom bore children when she herself was a child, and (*b*) that she was able to bear children for the space of nearly fifty years (early 1760s–1809). Since the chronology of Kwaadu Yaadom's last three (of five) marriages is established, together with the birth dates of the eight live children of these unions, then suspicion must inevitably fall on the traditional assertion that she was the mother of Amma Sewaa and her two siblings.[107]

Elucidation of the problem comes from several sources. First: in the most authoritative recension of the *Oyoko Kɔkɔɔ* genealogies there is no *Asantehemaa* listed between Akua Afiriye, mother of the *Asantehene* Osei Kwadwo (1764–77), and Kwaadu Yaadom, who is known to have been made *Asantehemaa* by that ruler in or about 1770. Second: when Kwaadu Yaadom was appointed as *Asantehemaa*, she was enstooled upon a 'new' stool that was transferred from Kokofu to Kumase for that specific purpose.[108] Third: a Dutch account (1758) situates one 'Akjaanba' (i.e. Akyaama) as the 'King's aunt' or senior female *ɔdehyeɛ* (i.e. the *Asantehemaa*) in the reign of the *Asantehene* Kusi Obodom. Fourth: an English report (1766) records an extremely serious conflict between the reigning *Asantehemaa* and the recently enstooled *Asantehene* Osei Kwadwo.[109] If we operate on the Occamist principle of following the line of inference that deviates least from authorized genealogical tradition, then the following suggest themselves: (*1*) an *Asantehemaa* has been omitted from the official traditional list; (*2*) that omission is to be dated to the 1750s/60s, when the senior royal woman was Akyaama; (*3*) the gravity of the conflict of 1766, and the ensuing circumstances surrounding Kwaadu Yaadom's own enstoolment as *Asantehemaa* (*c.* 1770), strongly imply that the *Asantehemaa* Akyaama was removed from office, and that her stool was 'cancelled' (*paɛ din*); (*4*) while the exact nature of Akyaama's offence is undetermined, it was clearly of the utmost seriousness, and it led to her being almost immediately excluded from the royal genealogies; (*5*) Akyaama is ideally situated in time to have been the mother of Amma Sewaa and her two siblings, but because of her genealogical suppression her children have been reclassified as Kwaadu Yaadom's offspring; (*6*) the chronology also supports the conclusion that the *Mamponhene* Safo Katanka was indeed the father of Amma Sewaa and her two siblings, but by a marriage to Akyaama rather than Kwaadu Yaadom. This reconstruction is logical and economical, and, most significantly, it assists very greatly in making sense of key developments in subsequent dynastic politics.[110]

Strictly speaking then, the eponymous founding ancestress (or 'single womb') of the *ɔyafunu koro* into which Kwaku Dua Panin was born was Akyaama, the mother of his own mother Amma Sewaa. But her existence was expunged after her downfall, and it was forbidden (*akyiwadeɛ*) even to mention her name.[111] Initially, this calamity had little discernible consequence for the dynastic prospects of her descendants. In 1777, in one of the most fully reported episodes in Asante history, the barely adolescent Osei Kwame succeeded as *Asantehene* with vigorous support from his patrilateral Mampon connections.[112] Shortly after, in about 1780, Osei Kwame's elder (and only surviving) sister Amma Sewaa was married to the *ɔheneba* Apaw Panin of Apebosoɔ, a son of *Asantehene* Kusi Obodom and a member, therefore, of the *Bosompra ntɔrɔ*. Apaw Panin had been appointed to one of the Kumase *ŋkonsoŋ* stools by his father, and he was subsequently given the more important office of *Gyakyehene*. Although the details are unclear, one authoritative source can be read as implying that the *Asantehene* Osei Kwame advanced Apaw Panin to Gyakye precisely *because* the latter was united in marriage with the former's elder sister.[113] In any event, the marriage of Amma Sewaa and Apaw Panin produced six children. The first five were males, of whom only the two eldest – Kyenkyenhene and Kwame Kusi – survived beyond childhood. The sixth and only female child was Afua Sapon (born *c.* 1787). Shortly after her birth Apaw Panin died. Amma Sewaa, still in her twenties, was left a widow (*okunafo*).[114]

In the words of the *Asantehene* Agyeman Prempe (in 1907), the widowed Amma Sewaa then 'went to a district called In-Kwa-Ta-Nan and (there she) married to Boachie Yam Kuma'.[115] Boakye Yam Kuma – a son of the Kumase *Anyinasehene* Akyampon Kwasi – was the *ŋkwaŋtananhene*, the overlord of Heman in Atwoma (through his matrifilial connections), and the sometime overseer of Asante trade with the Dutch and collector of *kostgeld* at Edina (Elmina).[116] The marriage produced three children, all male: Oti Akenten, Akyampon Kwasi and – the youngest – Kwaku Dua Panin (Fredua Agyeman; otherwise called Kwaku Dua Asamu).[117] The implication of the sources is that Amma Sewaa's second marriage may have been a love-match (*ɔdɔfo*). Certainly, it was unorthodox in terms of the preferred marriage strategies of the *Oyoko Kɔkɔɔ abusua*. Boakye Yam Kuma's ancestry, on both sides, was impeccably sound rather than exalted or even especially distinguished. His steady progress to appointive office from the status of a royal *ahenkwaa* was a meritorious and worthy ascent, but it was far removed from the ascriptive status niche occupied by the sons (*ahenemma*) of an *Asantehene*.[118] Furthermore, Boakye Yam Kuma was a member of neither *Bosommuru Adufudeɛ* nor *Asafodeɛ*, nor indeed of the *Bosommuru ntɔrɔ* at all. He traced his patrilineal descent in the *Aboadeɛ* sub-division of the *Bosompra ntɔrɔ*.

By the time of Kwaku Dua Panin's birth (*c.* 1797), relations between his mother's brother (*wɔfa*) the *Asantehene* Osei Kwame – who was also the senior living male in the *ɔyafunu koro* descended from Akyaama – and his adoptive maternal grandmother the *Asantehemaa* Kwaadu Yaadom had deteriorated to the point of open hostility. A great deal is known about the complex politicking of this period, but the fundamental root of the conflict was that Kwaadu Yaadom wished to see her adopted son Osei Kwame replaced as *Asantehene* by one of her own sons.[119] Osei Kwame was just as determined to resist, and about 1800 – with his opponents propagating or otherwise countenancing all manner of adverse rumours concerning his birth, status and suspect northern and Islamic affiliations – he took a radical and unprecedented step to break the deadlock. He quit Kumase and removed his court to Dwaben. He took with him the *sika dwa kofi*, all of the royal regalia, and the members of his *ɔyafunu koro*: his sister Amma Sewaa (once again a widow, for Boakye Yam Kuma had died shortly after the birth of Kwaku Dua Panin); his sister's daughter Afua Sapon (sixth and only female child of Amma Sewaa's first marriage); and the infant Kwaku Dua Panin. All four of Amma Sewaa's other surviving children – her sons Kyenkyenhene, Kwame Kusi, Oti Akenten and Akyampon Kwasi – perished in the conflict in Kumase, or were otherwise done to death on the orders of Kwaadu Yaadom.[120]

There can be no doubt that Osei Kwame's intention was to re-establish the Asante government at Dwaben instead of Kumase.[121] He clearly planned that he should rule from Dwaben as *Asantehene*, at least until the final resolution of matters with Kwaadu Yaadom. To this end he had taken physical possession of the regalia and the *sika dwa kofi*, the indispensable appurtenance of an *Asantehene*. In all likelihood, he also intended that his sister Amma Sewaa, the senior female of the disgraced Akyaama's *ɔyafunu koro*, should be enstooled as *Asantehemaa* at Dwaben on a new stool, just as Kwaadu Yaadom had been on a Kokofu stool in *c*. 1770. But Osei Kwame's plans failed and then collapsed in a series of complex but well-documented events. Kwaadu Yaadom was able to rally the Kumase office holders to her side, not least to prevent the transfer of state power to Dwaben. Realizing that his cause had now foundered, Osei Kwame decided upon abdication rather than civil war. In the event he elected to commit suicide, and Kwaadu Yaadom's second eldest son Opoku Fofie was enstooled as *Asantehene*. When Opoku Fofie himself died quite suddenly in 1804, he was succeeded by Kwaadu Yaadom's fourth son, the *Asantehene* Osei Tutu Kwame (1804–23).[122]

Amma Sewaa was married in Dwaben to a third and last husband – Okyere Kotoku, a son of the *Dwabenhene* Akuamoa Panin – by whom she bore two further, and final, children.[123] However, with the suicide of her brother Osei Kwame, and the victory of Kwaadu Yaadom and her sons, Amma Sewaa and her surviving children found themselves in the distressing and isolating condition of refugees. The fortunes of the exiled members of Akyaama's *ɔyafunu koro* were now at a nadir. The implication of Asante tradition is that the experiences of this period were crucial in shaping Kwaku Dua Panin. First: Kwaku Dua Panin formed a very strong attachment to his uterine sister, and only surviving sibling, Afua Sapon, who, in her own reported words, 'brought him up'. Second: Kwaku Dua Panin first began to be aware of adverse commentary and even outright fabrications – nseku and the rest – respecting his matrilineal descent (Akyaama), his matrifiliation (a mother's brother who had abdicated as Asantehene, and died 'a bad death' by his own hand), his patrifiliation (Bosompra not Bosommuru ntɔrɔ), and his own parents (a scurrilous story circulated that Amma Sewaa and Boakye Yam Kuma had not been married, and that Kwaku Dua Panin was the result of an extra-marital indiscretion on the part of his mother); throughout his life Kwaku Dua Panin remained very acutely sensitive to such slighting remarks, real or imagined. Third: Kwaku Dua Panin developed close ties to trusted individuals within the numerically highly restricted orbit of exile; Kwasi Brantuo served as mmagyegyeni ('nanny') or instructor to him in Dwaben, with results that have already been assayed. The servant to the boy rose under the patronage of the man – after Kwaku Dua Panin became Asantehene – to the pinnacles of wealth and status.[124]

In what must have been a gesture of reconciliation, offered from a position of very great dynastic strength, the Asantehemaa Kwaadu Yaadom and her son the Asantehene Osei Tutu Kwame repatriated Amma Sewaa and her children from Dwaben to Kumase. Past disputes, together with the problematic status of the refugees, were to be forgotten and confined to or internalized within the afisɛm of the Oyoko Kɔkɔɔ abusua. Afua Sapon, now aged about twenty, was married to the Apagyahene ɔheneba Gyamadua (Owusu Afriyie), a son of the Asantehene Osei Kwadwo, and hence a member of Bosommuru Adufudeɛ. Their eldest child Osei Kwadwo was born c. 1810. The marriage produced eight further children, of whom only six – all of them female (the eldest being Afua Kobi) – survived into adulthood. The Apagyahene ɔheneba Owusu Afriyie was killed fighting the British at the battle of Katamanso in 1826, and the widowed Afua Sapon never remarried. Kwaku Dua Panin meanwhile was awarded his father's stool of ŋkwaŋtanaŋ in c. 1817 (or perhaps earlier), and he greatly distinguished himself in the war of 1818–19 against the Gyamanhene Kwadwo Adinkra.[125]

A series of events conspired to move the ɔyafunu koro of Amma Sewaa (and Akyaama) back towards the centre of dynastic politics. In the Fante campaign of 1807 the designated heir-apparent Osei Badu (Kwaadu Yaadom's fifth son) and his uterine sister Akua Akrukruwaa both died of smallpox.[126] Kwaadu Yaadom's only two remaining sons – other than the reigning Asantehene Osei Tutu Kwame – were Osei Kofi and Osei Yaw Akoto. Osei Kofi had already been passed over as Asantehene in 1804 in favour of his younger sibling Osei Tutu Kwame. Thus, immediately prior to her own death in 1809, Kwaadu Yaadom saw her sixth and youngest son Osei Yaw Akoto recognized as the designated heir-apparent. Osei Yaw Akoto was a member of *Bosommuru Adufudeɛ*, but in a cadet rather than a direct line; his paternal grandfather was a son of the *Akyempemhene ɔheneba* Owusu Afriyie, himself a son of the *Asantehene* Osei Tutu, but by a non-royal woman.[127]

For reasons that still remain unclear, Kwaadu Yaadom's own successor as *Asantehemaa* (in 1809) was her long-dead uterine sister Sewaa Awukuwaa's daughter Adoma Akosua, and not her own surviving daughter Yaa Dufi.[128] In the event, and in a well-reported sequence, the *Asantehemaa* Adoma Akosua was removed from office in 1819 for conspiring to bring about the death of the *Asantehene* Osei Tutu Kwame through *bayi* (witchcraft), in an attempt to secure the *sika dwa kofi* for one of her own sons.[129] The major traditional sources disagree as to who – Amma Sewaa or Yaa Dufi – was the successor of Adoma Akosua in the office of *Asantehemaa*. But the overall thrust of the evidence indicates that both Amma Sewaa and Yaa Dufi in fact became *Asantehemaa*, and most probably in that order.[130] It is certainly the case that in 1819 Amma Sewaa was indisputably the senior living female *ɔdehyeɛ* of the *Oyoko Kɔkɔɔ abusua*, whatever the associations of her name and history within *afisɛm*, and genealogically the most distant from the excoriated Adoma Akosua. It is most probable that she was made *Asantehemaa*, died shortly thereafter, and was succeeded by Yaa Dufi (possibly as a result of a compact agreed in 1819).

In the last years of *Asantehene* Osei Tutu Kwame's reign his younger brother Osei Yaw Akoto was recognized as being his heir and probable successor. Three royals – but all with dynastic disabilities – were next, at least putatively, in the line of succession. These were Amma Sewaa's only surviving son Kwaku Dua Panin, whose antecedents have been discussed; his uterine sister Afua Sapon's son Osei Kwadwo, who was a grandson of the *Asantehene* Osei Kwadwo in *Bosommuru Adufudeɛ*, but who was still only a boy; and Kwaadu Yaadom's daughter Yaa Dufi's son Kwaku Pimpim, who was a member of *Bosommuru Adufudeɛ*, but in the same cadet line as Osei Yaw Akoto (their fathers being paternal brothers). Kwaku Pimpim seems already to have recognized that his own claim to the *sika dwa kofi* was a remote one, and so he accepted the newly created office of *Mamesenehene* in the Kumase *Ankobea fekuo*.[131] Thus, by the time of Osei Tutu Kwame's death in 1823 the male members of Amma Sewaa's (and Akyaama's) *ɔyafunu koro* – Kwaku Dua Panin and Osei Kwadwo – were firmly at the centre of the dynastic politics of the *Oyoko Kɔkɔɔ abusua*.

Authoritative traditions record that, immediately prior to his death, the *Asantehene* Osei Tutu Kwame expressed a preference for Kwaku Dua

Panin rather than Osei Yaw Akoto as his successor, ostensibly on the grounds that the former was the better equipped as an *individual* to preside over the *Asantemaŋ*.[132] Whatever the veracity of this, there can be no doubt that Osei Yaw Akoto entertained strong fears that he would not become *Asantehene*. Accordingly, he seized the *sika dwa kofi* and quit Kumase with his adherents to seek the support of the army and its generals, then on campaign in Fante. He mustered sufficient support to have himself enstooled as *Asantehene* upon his return to Kumase. But his precipitate haste in returning home with the army – after publicly upbraiding the generals for their military dilatoriness – was very widely resented.[133]

After his enstoolment the *Asantehene* Osei Yaw Akoto was constrained to recognize Kwaku Dua Panin – his putative rival, but the obvious candidate – as heir-apparent. Two years later in 1826 Osei Yaw Akoto commanded the Asante army at the disastrous battle of Katamanso. He was slightly wounded in the engagement, and withdrew from the field without the *sika dwa kofi*. All accounts are agreed that Kwaku Dua Panin, who had already distinguished himself in the battle, was instrumental – together with the *Dwabenhene* and *Kuntanasehene* – in preventing the *sika dwa kofi* from falling into the hands of the British and their allies. The *sika dwa kofi* was restored to Osei Yaw Akoto's possession at Saawua near Kumase, where he had finally encamped following his precipitate retreat. The level of suspicion and animosity now existing between Osei Yaw Akoto and Kwaku Dua Panin can be gauged from the fact that, at Saawua, the latter felt compelled to take an oath before the former to the effect that he had taken temporary possession of the *sika dwa kofi* on the battlefield only as a necessary preliminary to restoring it to its legitimate incumbent.[134]

After his humiliation at Katamanso, Osei Yaw Akoto became unapproachable, arbitrary and intermittently violent. Traditional and other sources agree that he drank excessively in an attempt to expiate or obliterate the memory of his defeat and flight.[135] He summarily executed plaintiffs who came before him because they had not been at Katamanso; he contravened the 'laws of Komfo Anokye' by executing a blind man and an albino with aggravated cruelty; he was instrumental in alienating the *Dwabenhene* Kwasi Boaten – driving him to rebellion, and then into exile in 1832. Most revealingly, he had the *Gyakye ɔkyeame* Kwadwo Adusei Kyakya done to death on spurious charges, but in reality because the latter contrasted the *Asantehene* unfavourably with his brother and predecessor, and affirmed the rumour that Osei Tutu Kwame had indeed favoured Kwaku Dua Panin as his successor.[136]

It was in this atmosphere that *nseku* and other forms of rumour and disparagement concerning Kwaku Dua Panin were resurrected and given active encouragement by Osei Yaw Akoto. A fugitive but highly credible tradition gives a telling insight into the matter. Kwaku Dua Panin, it noted,

> was the nephew of [Osei Yaw] Akoto and of Akoto's predecessor Tutu Quahmina [Osei Tutu Kwame], otherwise called Bonsoo or Osai Pynin. The mother of Bonsoo and of Akoto was a royal lady called Coorandoo [Kwaadu Yaadom], descent from whom gave right to the throne. Coorandoo had a daughter of the name of Oseywah [Amma Sewaa], in whose male descendants, after the death of the kings Bonsoo and Akoto the right to the stool ... vested. Quaku Duah [Kwaku Dua Panin] was the son of Oseywah by a man of humble origin, whom the princess had indiscreetly admitted to familiarity in her youth ... His uncle Akoto used to rally him publicly on the possibility of his one day becoming an 'eater of beef', a description of food forbidden to persons of the blood-royal of Ashantee.[137]

The burden of this is that Osei Yaw Akoto was habitually given both to publicizing *afisɛm* and to practising *mpoatwa* – in an extreme, insulting form – by comparing his own exalted status with that of Kwaku Dua Panin. The *Asantehene* reminded Kwaku Dua Panin (by implication, on all possible occasions) of the inferiority of his paternal descent, and asserted the innate superiority of the *Bosommuru* over the *Bosompra ntɔrɔ*; the eating of cattle (*nantwi*), as we have seen, was an avoidance (*akyiwadeɛ*) of the *Bosommuru ntɔrɔ*, but not of its *Bosompra* counterpart. Furthermore, this account implies that Osei Yaw Akoto even countenanced scurrilities – in the related forms of *nseku*, *akutia* and *ntwiri* – about Kwaku Dua Panin's legitimacy; this was a calumny of the gravest sort to direct at someone who was *ɔdehyeɛ*, and it was phrased in a way such as to cast slanderous doubt over Kwaku Dua Panin's actual paternity (the suggestion being that he might be *wonni mu*). It might also be noted that these disparagements were situated within the revised genealogical orthodoxy, constructed within the living memory of some older listeners, that had excised all public mention of Akyaama, and reclassified Amma Sewaa as a daughter of Kwaadu Yaadom.

It was in the late 1820s (and perhaps in 1826) that Kwaku Dua Panin's uterine sister Afua Sapon succeeded as *Asantehemaa*.[138] She was by then the obvious candidate, being the senior living female royal following the deaths of her mother Amma Sewaa and Yaa Dufi. It was about this time that the pre-existing solidarity of Kwaku Dua Panin and Afua Sapon as matri-siblings within the *ɔyafunu koro* began very seriously to erode in structurally predictable ways. In the Asante view, full matri-siblings were themselves conceptually *nipa koro* (one person, of a single womb), a corporate unit in the very narrowest sense. The relationship was held to be (and generally was) the locus of extremely close bonds of intimate affect. In the specific case of Kwaku Dua Panin and Afua Sapon, this structural norm had been fortified and deepened by the mutuality of dependence forced upon them, as we have seen, by the perilous exigencies of their youthful exile in Dwaben. But with the passage of time serious ambivalences entered into matri-siblingship. These were ultimately based in the simple chronological inevitability of consecutive generational succession.[139]

Within an *ɔyafunu koro* an adult male brother (Kwaku Dua Panin) took precedence in the political domain (office being vested in males) *and* in the realm of jural authority. The senior male – mother's brother (*wɔfa*), in his capacity as 'head of the house' (*(ɔ)fie panin*) formed by the *ɔyafunu koro* – was primarily responsible for overseeing the internal affairs of the uterine stirp. Such a brother, therefore, exercised firm jural authority over the child(ren) (Osei Kwadwo) of his uterine sister (Afua Sapon). But sisters as mothers were the indispensable guarantors of the perpetuity of an *ɔyafunu koro* (or, to phrase it differently, of the historic embedding of that unit in a secure niche within an *abusua*). The sister's male child (*wɔfase*) was the jural and political successor-in-waiting of her brother (*wɔfa*), and so Asante thinking cast the uncle (Kwaku Dua Panin) and the nephew (Osei Kwadwo) as antagonists (*wɔfase eye dom*; 'your nephew is your enemy', i.e. a sister's son was his own mother's brother's enemy), for while the first exercised authority over the second, the second was inevitably the heir and successor to the first. Mediating this brittle, competitive and fraught relationship was a woman (Afua Sapon), who was caught between the conflicting ties of matri-siblingship and motherhood, universally recognized as being the two most powerful affective relationships in all Asante kinship.[140]

It should be recalled that Afua Sapon was Kwaku Dua Panin's *only* uterine sister, and that in turn Osei Kwadwo was Afua Sapon's *only* male child. The *Asantehene* Osei Yaw Akoto may well have hoped to exploit the tensions and fissions implicit in these relationships by supporting the election of Afua Sapon as *Asantehemaa*, and then by very deliberately casting her as a dynastic foil – in the interests of her son Osei Kwadwo – against her brother Kwaku Dua Panin. At any rate, Afua Sapon clearly felt a growing divergence between the dynastic interests of her brother and her son. 'Affuah Sappon', so the account cited above very pointedly observes, 'whose father (the *ɔheneba* Apaw Panin) was of high rank, was also accustomed to indulge in sarcastic remarks in reference to the low birth of Quaku Duah's father (Boakye Yam Kuma)'.[141] Be that as it may, it was certainly the case that the structural antagonism between Kwaku Dua Panin and Osei Kwadwo (and the latter's mother) was greatly exacerbated by the specifics of patriliny in quite another sense. That is, Afua Sapon's husband and Osei Kwadwo's father (the *Apagyahene ɔheneba* Owusu Afriyie) had been a son of the *Asantehene* Osei Kwadwo; therefore, and in contrast to the facts – and the malicious rumours – concerning Kwaku Dua Panin's paternity, Osei Kwadwo was not merely heir to the *aboadenfoɔ* in the line of *Bosommuru Adufudeɛ*, but he also bore the name (and the possibility of his being a reincarnation) of his illustrious paternal grandfather.

The *Asantehene* Osei Yaw Akoto died in 1834 and Kwaku Dua Panin succeeded him in office.[142] According to an authoritative tradition, a significant body of the Kumase office holders, and opinion generally, opposed Kwaku Dua Panin's enstoolment on the grounds that he belonged to the *Bosompra ntɔrɔ*, while the alternative candidate Osei Kwadwo, now in his mid-twenties, was a paternal great great grandson of the *Asantehene* Osei Tutu in a direct line of descent within *Bosommuru Adufudeɛ*. It was mooted that Kwaku Dua Panin lacked *aboadenfoɔ* in his paternal background consonant with the status of an aspirant *Asantehene*; it was acknowledged that he was *ɔboadeni* in his own right, particularly because of his part in saving the *sika dwa kofi* in 1826, but that unfortunately he possessed 'a commoner's name'; some urged that his patronymic ('his *ntɔrɔ* group name') was inappropriate, and that the *sika dwa kofi* should 'normally be given to people with appropriate names'; and yet others made slighting comparisons between Kwaku Dua Panin and the 'great names' of *Bosommuru Adufudeɛ* and *Asafodeɛ* – 'if an Osei ascended' the *sika dwa kofi*, then 'he *naturally* [emphasis added] assumed the authority that went along with the office'.[143] Rattray gleaned resonant echoes of all this in the 1920s. He was told by certain informants that the marriage of Amma Sewaa and Boakye Yam Kuma constituted a '*mésalliance*', in as much as the election of their son as *Asantehene* had introduced 'new names into the royal line, "spoiling the *ntɔrɔ*"' (of *Bosommuru*).[144]

Crucial to the election of Kwaku Dua Panin as *Asantehene* was the endorsement, after much prevarication, of his sister, the *Asantehemaa* Afua Sapon. The price of this support was a *quid pro quo*; in return for her assent Afua Sapon and Kwaku Dua Panin's critics asked that her son Osei Kwadwo be recognized as heir-apparent. Kwaku Dua Panin concurred, but with what degree of willingness or reluctance remains unclear. Widespread reservations among the Kumase office holders about Kwaku Dua Panin's *ntɔrɔ* and *ɔyafunu koro* affiliations are the context in which we must situate the unprecedented appointment by him of a *second* designated heir. The individual elevated to this new office was Opoku Ahoni, a son of Ata Sewaa – only daughter of Kwaadu Yaadom's daughter Akua Akrukruwaa – by her marriage to the *ɔheneba* Adu, a son of the *Asantehene* Opoku Fofie (and possibly to be identified with the *Atene Akotenhene ɔheneba* Adusei Kra). Opoku Ahoni, therefore, was a member of *Bosommuru Asafodeɛ*. It is clear that Kwaku Dua Panin was finally elected *Asantehene* because a majority came to feel that he was the *individual* best qualified for the office. But the formal designation of putative heirs from *Bosommuru Adufudeɛ and Asafodeɛ* represented nothing less than an institutionalized criticism of Kwaku Dua Panin's credentials, together with a humiliating public capitulation on his part to the pervasive disquiet concerning his own dynastic status. And in the electoral contest itself, we may be sure, all of the rumours, gossip and falsehoods concerning Kwaku Dua Panin and his filiation were once again intensively rehearsed and widely (if mostly clandestinely) discussed.[145]

A great deal is known about the reign of the *Asantehene* Kwaku Dua Panin (1834–67). He has been identified with authoritarian behaviour and autocratic impulses; with sustained use of instrumental violence to impose and reinforce a personal paramountcy over the personnel of the state; with the advancement to wealth, status and power of individuals who combined proximity to his person with dependence on his will; and with that style of personalized, interventionist rule that mixed what have been called 'sultanist' tendencies with elements of patrimonialism. The overall thrust of this reading is incontrovertible.[146] Thus far, however, insufficient – even negligible – attention has been paid to the ways in which the *Asantehene* Kwaku Dua Panin's exercise of power was conditioned by the factors of his socialization and life experience as an individual actor within the web of kinship relations at the apex of state and society.[147]

Twenty-five years after Kwaku Dua Panin's enstoolment on the *sika dwa kofi*, on 22 April 1859, the Dutch agent Kwasi Myzang of Edina (Elmina) entered Kumase. From there he reported that on 19 June Kwaku Dua Panin's 'uncle and heir Say Kudjoe' (Osei Kwadwo, then nearly fifty) had died, after having been 'for some time in disgrace'. An appropriate funeral custom took place, and 'Kobbena Enien' (Kwabena Anin), 'the King's youngest uncle', was recognized as heir-apparent.[148] On 11 April 1860 the English-educated *ɔheneba* Owusu Ansa, a son of the *Asantehene* Osei Tutu Kwame and a Wesleyan-Methodist emissary, reported from Kumase as follows: 'Many of the Royal Family have met an unhappy end, brought on through opposition to the present King's (Kwaku Dua Panin's) government.'[149]

Suggestive external evidence surrounds the disgrace and death of Osei Kwadwo. It is unfortunate that a deal of it is circumstantial or tangential. It is doubly unfortunate, therefore, that historians have allowed themselves to be misled by it, largely as a result of failing to read it with due care *and* in the light of a specifically Asante reading of such matters. Kwasi Myzang surmised, for example, that between mid-April and mid-June 1859 in excess of a thousand people were killed in Kumase.[150] That a conspiracy of some sort took place is evident, as is Osei Kwadwo's implication in it. In March–April 1862 Owusu Ansa was back in Kumase. He noted,

On our arrival in Kumase I observed to my great sorrow in seeing so many new chieftains' faces, the old ones I knew have fallen by the King's knife, on account of their taking part of the rebellion which the heir apparent to the throne was trying to raise against his uncle the present King, but his ambitious design being discovered he was condemned, transported, and died a miserable death.[151]

Using these reports, together with an undated tradition concerning a rebellion against Kwaku Dua Panin by the *Akwaboahene* Adu Tutu and others of the *Kronti fekuo*, Wilks has situated Osei Kwadwo's fall and the attendant conspiracy within the interpretative framework of a polarization between 'peace' and 'war' interests in government.[152] But apart from a very terse – and optimistically wishful – speculation by Kwasi Myzang that Kwabena Anin 'must have a much more peaceful character' than Osei Kwadwo, there is no clear link in any of the evidence thus far adduced between Osei Kwadwo's death, the conspiracy against the *Asantehene*, and the policy issues of 'peace' or 'war'. In fact, a case (admittedly as equivocal as its opposite) could be made for the pacific nature of Osei Kwadwo's beliefs.[153] Of course, none of this is to say that no office holder conspired (with Osei Kwadwo?) because of opposition to the generally pacific foreign policies of Kwaku Dua Panin. But it is to say that Wilks' inference is not borne out or directly justified by the evidence, and that *primary* explanation of the matters at issue, in this as in all else, needs to be sought in the specifically Asante constructions of knowledge and belief, and not in categories erected upon the ambiguous scaffolding of foreign observation and commentary. These matters are more fully discussed in the final chapter.

Ramseyer and Kühne, Basel missionaries who were captive in Kumase in the early 1870s, gleaned accounts then current in the Asante capital about events in the late 1850s. The phrasing of their report (emphases added) is more significant, perhaps, than the occasionally confused empirical information that they supply.

It is said that in a moment of excitement, Kwakoo Dooah once sent to his sister a silken band, with a message to the effect, that the best thing she could do was to hang herself. She accepted the brotherly suggestion, and committed suicide. Her son Opoku [*sic*] was *then accused of aspiring to the throne*, and was sacrificed, with the honour due to his rank, viz., by having his neck broken with an elephant's tusk. Afua Kobe, the mother of king Kofi Kari [the *Asantehene* Kofi Kakari], is the daughter of Kwakoo Dooah's sister, who committed suicide. *It is said that in his last days Kwakoo deeply regretted his conduct towards her.*[154]

Let us note the following, bearing in mind the history and context of relations between the principals. The flashpoint of these events was a seemingly emotionally charged exchange between Kwaku Dua Panin and his sister Afua Sapon. The *Asantehemaa* is said to have committed suicide, and her son Osei Kwadwo (simply misnamed as Opoku, there being no doubt as to his true identity) was then accused of conspiring to become the *Asantehene*, and was ritually killed in a manner appropriate to an ɔdehyeɛ of the *sika dwa kofi*.[155] Finally, the accounts gathered by Ramseyer and Kühne record that in pondering this crisis in the time prior to his own death some eight years later (27 April 1867), Kwaku Dua Panin gave himself over to self-recrimination about his own part in the death of his only sister.

In the early twentieth century, Sir Francis Fuller, the then Chief Commissioner of Asante, recorded a variant of the foregoing based on traditional accounts, his most probable chief informant being the Kumase *Akyeamehene* and *Domakwaehene* Kwasi Apea Nuama, an acknowledged expert and authority on Asante history.[156] 'Kweku Dua had trouble with his sister, Efua Sapon, the Queen-Mother', Fuller wrote (emphases again added):

Her son, Osai Kojo, was supposed to be scheming to oust Kweku Dua and to obtain the stool for himself. *One of Osai Kojo's domestics informed the King that his master had made a fetish to kill the King.*

A dispute arose between them, and the Queen-Mother tried to shield her son, but Kweku Dua deposed her and appointed her daughter, Efua Kobi, as her successor.

Osai Kojo, who had occupied the Abakumajua [*abakom dwa*] stool (founded by Kwissi Bodum [the *Asantehene* Kusi Obodom] for the heir-apparent), was likewise removed and his stool given to Kobina Enin, eldest son of Efua Kobi.[157]

By this version, rumours of Osei Kwadwo's conspiracy were confirmed to Kwaku Dua Panin by an informer. Most significantly, the enabling agency in the alleged plot is given as witchcraft (*bayi*) – 'a fetish to kill the King' – the classic locus of aggressive enmity among those closely linked by *mogya* in the *ɔyafunu koro*. Afua Sapon is presented as an essentially passive party, although the degree of her personal knowledge and involvement is left ambiguous. She is forced, it should be noted, to a public choice between her brother and her son. Fatally, she aligns herself with the latter against the former. Afua Sapon is caught in an affective or emotional tension between her obligations to her uterine brother and to her son; and Kwaku Dua Panin (as *wɔfa*) and Osei Kwadwo (as *wɔfase*) stand in that relationship within Asante kinship that is a paradigm, as we have seen, of potential hostility and conflict.

The foregoing reports are partial or oblique glimpses into *afisɛm*. Thus, the most authoritative traditional history – that written at the behest of and under the presiding aegis of the *Asantehene* Osei Agyeman Prempeh II in the 1940s – offers no more than the very cryptic comments that Osei Kwadwo was removed from office for practising some variety of 'obnoxious medicine'; that his mother Afua Sapon was removed for giving her son 'bad advice'; and that both were exiled from Kumase to the village of Apaaso.[158] This supports Fuller's informant(s), and its extreme reticence can be ascribed to the Asante precept that the discussion of family disputes was a private matter to be 'kept within the house' (*afisɛm*).

'Within the house' (the *ɔyafunu koro*, and more broadly the *Oyoko Kɔkɔɔ abusua*) this chapter of *afisɛm*, the crisis between Kwaku Dua Panin and his closest kin in the 1850s, was indirectly alluded to by use of the mnemonic euphemism *konnurokusɛm* (i.e. *konnuroku* + *asɛm* or 'matters', in the sense of history or a tale).[159] The word *konnuroku* has more than one contextual meaning, although all of these are linked. Adverbially or adjectivally, *konnuroku* means vile, mean or despicable, and extends to embrace ideas of paltriness or worthlessness and contexts of shamefulness. As a noun, *konnuroku* is used to describe a kind of very inferior cloth; in this context it is sometimes a synonym for *burohono*. But the latter noun is also used to describe maize husks (cf. *aburo*: maize), a useless, residual or nugatory part of that crop foodstuff. In sum, *konnurokusɛm* is a metaphor or idiomatic indirection (*kasakoa*) of a common Asante type, and as such it served as a form of circumlocution or avoidance. That is, it was a trope for defusing a matter of great moment – essentially private to the *afisɛm* of the Kumase dynasty, and therefore hazardous to mention or to discuss openly – into a referential framework that alluded to hidden significances in the very speech act of appearing to downgrade or to diminish their import. Equally, by compressing intent and meaning into such a cursory utterance a speaker signalled knowledge, but without incurring the penalties attaching to explication.[160]

The narrative of the *konnurokusɛm* – as this is understood by the Asante – may be recounted as follows:

1 The *Asantehene* Kwaku Dua Panin was a wise ruler who abhorred war and enriched Asante. The result of his stewardship was stability and harmony. Kwaku Dua Panin presided over the rise to wealth and status of *abirɛmpɔn* and 'many prominent individuals', thereby earning for himself many accolades, and notably *Kwaku Dua Agyeman sika sosɔ* ('Kwaku Dua Agyeman who leaks gold'). His sister, the *Asantehemaa* Afua Sapon was very popular, revered by the people, and notably charitable towards the needy. She was very close to her brother Kwaku Dua Panin, having 'brought him up'; and it was her intervention that was decisive in reconciling the *Asanteman* to Kwaku Dua Panin's election as *Asantehene*. She asked that her son Osei Kwadwo be 'stationed at *Adum*' (i.e. placed on the *abakom dwa*) as the heir to Kwaku Dua Panin. She expected Osei Kwadwo to succeed Kwaku Dua Panin as *Asantehene*.

2 Afua Sapon had, in addition to Osei Kwadwo, six surviving daughters from her marriage to the *Apagyahene ɔheneba* Gyamadua (Owusu Afriyie). The eldest daughter was Afua Kobi, who had married the *Boakye Yam Panin ɔkyeame* Kofi Nti. Kofi Nti belonged to the *Bosommuru ntɔrɔ*, but in the *Anini* sub-division. He lacked *aboadenfoɔ*. He was a grandson of the *Asantehene* Osei Kwadwo, but through a daughter (Yaa Kyaa) of that ruler rather than a son. Afua Kobi and Kofi Nti had five children, of whom the three eldest were sons: Kwabena Anin, Kofi Kakari, Mensa Bonsu. Afua Kobi was a scheming person, and very ambitious for herself and her children.

3 It was Afua Kobi who instigated the *konnurokusɛm*. Her design was to have any one of her own three sons recognized as heir in place of Osei Kwadwo. She

herself wished to be installed in the place of her own mother as *Asantehemaa*. Afua Kobi knew that Kwaku Dua Panin was 'fearful' (i.e. insecure about his own position as *Asantehene*) and that he loved his sister, but was also suspicious of her and her son Osei Kwadwo. Kwaku Dua Panin had already contrived the means of 'losing' (i.e. killing) the second heir Opoku Ahoni out of similar feelings and fears.[161] Afua Kobi proceeded to circulate *nseku, ntwiri* and the rest to the effect that Afua Sapon and Osei Kwadwo were practising *bayi* (witchcraft) in attempts to bring about Kwaku Dua Panin's death and so secure the *sika dwa kofi* for Osei Kwadwo; they were also rumoured to be trafficking with Muslims to achieve the same end. It was also said that Afua Sapon had repeatedly indulged in cursing (*nnuabɔ, nnome*) Kwaku Dua Panin on the grounds of his lack of gratitude towards her for her part in his election as *Asantehene*. Osei Kwadwo was said to have wished his *wɔfa* (Kwaku Dua Panin) dead. Afua Kobi also encouraged the belief that Afua Sapon and Osei Kwadwo spoke of Kwaku Dua Panin as if he was *already* dead – a heinous and treasonable practice. Afua Kobi privately expressed herself as being very troubled by all of this.

4 At first, Kwaku Dua Panin refused to act on these stories. But he became ill. When he recovered he insisted that Afua Sapon and Osei Kwadwo explain themselves before him in open court. Afua Sapon and Osei Kwadwo denied all charges of maleficence towards the *Asantehene*, but Kwaku Dua Panin, with the sedulous encouragement of Afua Kobi, was now disposed to believe the worst of his sister and her son. Accordingly, the court found Afua Sapon and Osei Kwadwo guilty of trying to secure the death of Kwaku Dua Panin through witchcraft. Kwaku Dua Panin was both very angry and very upset. He ordered Afua Sapon and Osei Kwadwo permanently removed from his sight. They were sent into exile at Aboboaso, after having been stripped of their offices. Afua Kobi was appointed *Asantehemaa*, and her eldest son Kwabena Anin (some accounts say Kofi Kakari) was designated heir-apparent.

5 Kwaku Dua Panin became very withdrawn and was convinced that everyone was conspiring against him. In his rage he executed many people – office holders, ordinary citizens and slaves. Once, in a mood of great sadness and anger, he suddenly ordered the death of Afua Sapon and Osei Kwadwo. Accordingly, they were eliminated. But Kwaku Dua Panin now began to remember his sister with fondness, and to have suspicions that the charges against her had been fabrications. In this mood he drank excessively, fasted and had his *kete* band play melancholy songs to him all night long in the palace. He systematically killed everyone who had borne witness in court against Afua Sapon and Osei Kwadwo. He developed a hatred for Afua Kobi and her sons. But he refused to bring charges against them. He remained unsure as to the truth of the matter. Furthermore, having removed one *Asantehemaa* on questionable grounds, he felt that removing yet another – Afua Kobi – would bring his name into permanent disrepute.

6 Kwaku Dua Panin became increasingly alienated from and authoritarian towards the office holders of Kumase. He developed a contemptuous attitude towards them because of the part they had played in approving his decision to disgrace his sister. Whenever a dispute involving close kin came before him in court, and the Kumase office holders pleaded for mitigation for those adjudged guilty, he would insist on the full penalty of the law, and shame his office holders into silence

with the following peroration: 'Kumase office holders, if you understand the matter being considered [so well], then why didn't you plead for mitigation when I had a dispute [*konnurokusɛm*] within my own family, and thereby lost my relatives?' He also deliberately treated his office holders in a high-handed and contemptuous manner on many other occasions. Once, he asked for palm wine to be tapped for him for an *adae*. He drank the wine – which was sour – and pronounced it excellent. The office holders then drank the sour wine, but publicly agreed with the *Asantehene's* opinion of its goodness. On another occasion, he pretended to see a monkey in a distant tree, and pointed it out to his attendants. They complimented Kwaku Dua Panin on his eyesight, and commented on the colouring and size of the non-existent animal. Kwaku Dua Panin upbraided his office holders for hypocrisy in both cases, asking how he could value any of their advice, and saying that he now knew their true nature.

7 Kwaku Dua Panin lived to be very old (about 70). It is said that during his final illness (1867) he was haunted by the *asamanfoɔ* (departed spirits; 'ghosts') of Afua Sapon and Osei Kwadwo. These departed spirits were propitiated by the offering of numerous sheep, but to no avail. As a result, the *Asantehene* Kwaku Dua Panin – still fearful that he had committed a grievous injustice towards his closest matrikin – did not die peacefully.[162]

Aspects or echoes of the complex portrait of Kwaku Dua Panin as a person that is supplied by traditional accounts of the *konnurokusɛm* are to be found in many sources, Asante and otherwise. One well-informed contemporary account offered the following insights (emphases added):

the circumstances of his father belonging to the humbler classes is said to have been not without its effects on king Quaku Duah's conduct both as a sovereign and as the Head of the Royal Family of Ashantee. Princesses of the blood are usually bestowed upon men of power and rank in the kingdom, and Quaku Duah, though the law of the country secured him the throne by right of his mother, no matter who or what his father might be, *felt all through life that his birth was the subject of uncomplimentary remark...*
Osai Quaku Duah was a sagacious and politic prince, reserved in manner, dignified and courteous, not fond of war, shrewd and sensible in administering justice, patient to hear, somewhat severe towards the more powerful of his nobility; withal, *jealous and suspicious of those whose wealth and influence gave them much weight in the state, if they seemed disposed to display too great a degree of independence...* King Quaku Duah countenanced no fools, employed no men of half measures, *nor gave ear to the counsels of those who leaned to the side of mercy.*[163]

Elaboration of the vital continuities between Kwaku Dua Panin as a person *and* as a ruler can be severally instanced, and recognition of this greatly assists to a deeper understanding of the historical record. Thus, for example, in Asante kinship relations patri-siblings (actual or classificatory) occupied a particular niche. They were addressed in the same intimate terminology as matri-siblings (*ŋnua*), and the ties between them were often those of mutual trust, dependence, advice and support; 'one's father's child [*agya ba*] by another wife than one's mother', so Fortes was told, 'is often one's most trusted and loved friend'.[164] The structural or prescriptive reasons for this are clear. Patri-siblings shared the bond of $nt\jmath r\jmath$ affiliation, but relations between them were voluntary and disinterested in ways that were closed to matrikin who were enmeshed in the obligations and duties of the $\jmath yafunu\ koro$. It is indicative of this distinction that $bayi$ could *not* operate in relations between patri-siblings. When we consider this in combination with Kwaku Dua Panin's personal experiences within the $\jmath yoko\ koro$ and the $Oyoko\ K\jmath k\jmath\jmath\ abusua$, then it is a matter of little surprise that two of his closest confidential advisers and executive agents were his patri-siblings Akyampon Tia and Akyampon Yaw, the first an actual son of Boakye Yam Kuma, the second a classificatory one. In turn each occupied the (greatly aggrandized) stool of their and Kwaku Dua Panin's father. Akyampon Yaw also functioned as $Debos\jmath\jmath hene$, enjoyed private access to Kwaku Dua Panin as the 'king's confidential barber', and had the intimate patronage and support of his royal patri-sibling.[165]

The argument being advanced here is that well-documented features of Kwaku Dua Panin's behaviour and actions as *Asantehene* are more fully and readily comprehensible if we take serious account of his formation *as an individual person* within the kinship relations framed by matriliny ($\jmath yafunu\ koro; abusua$) and patriliny ($nt\jmath r\jmath$). Indeed, episodes like the *konnurokusem*, which are central to the indigenous reading of Asante history, are understandable *only* if this factor is constantly borne in mind. This argument does not seek to reduce conflicts over policies to the framework of personalities, but rather makes the case for adding the dimensions of kinship and personhood to the reading of antagonisms that underpinned, informed or expressed themselves in and through such conflicts. At one simple level, it is an argument for the reconciliation of the classic anthropological questions with the record of historical process.

Structurally, it might be said that the nature of relations between Kwaku Dua Panin and his matrikin in the 1850s was rooted in the organization and formulated rhetoric of Asante social relations. This rhetoric was expressed via action, performance and symbol in the unfolding of historical events. Most importantly, it was articulated as a potent ideology governing relations of personhood between individuals at the centre of power in the state. In defining the parameters or the possibilities of actions grounded in knowledge and belief, it served as a vital tool for the person to act out him/herself in history. That such matters cannot always be appropriated to or synthesized within an empiricist model of reconstruction does not mean that they can simply be ignored in a trite positivist manner. The matter might be put in the following way. Granted what we are able to say about the *personhood* of Kwaku Dua Panin – as an ideological self within other arenas of ideology – we can legitimately assume that issues such as have been analysed here hold validity for all other *Asantehenes* (and, indeed, for all other members of historic Asante society). Not knowing the answer does not preclude the scholarly responsibility of acknowledging and formulating the question. Indeed, it is only by the use of such a procedure that the gap between *reading Asante history* and the *Asante reading of history* can be bridged.[166]

As potential occupants of the *sika dwa kofi* – where the Asante state enacted itself – senior *adehyeɛ* were virtually prescriptive foci for the complex clash of personalities, policies, ideas and ideologies. In the 1850s, therefore, those office holders who espoused warfare as a means of maximizing the polity gravitated towards Osei Kwadwo (and then Kwabena Anin and Kofi Kakari) precisely because each was *already* cast in an oppositional role to the pacific *Asantehene* Kwaku Dua Panin. Throughout Asante history, ideological partisanship in the realm of policy has tended to aggregate and to crystallize around the persons of royal individuals who were *already* defined as antagonists by the structure of kinship, and its interpersonal, affective dimensions, in relation to genealogical memory and history. The *Oyoko Kɔkɔɔ abusua*, in sum, was *the* crucible in which interest groups coalesced around actual or nominal leaders, and via which factions might struggle for supremacy in the name of such leaders. That cleavages of this sort expressed themselves by means of adherence to one or another royal was irreducibly predicated upon the transaction of kinship and personhood within the royal dynasty – the very core of symbolic, ritual and actual authority in Asante.

As a concluding remark here, we might observe that the aftermath of the *konnurokusɛm* shows further the extremely complicated interplay between the ideologies governing personhood, kinship relations and political action. It is well known that the *Asantehene* Kwaku Dua Panin developed a pathological antipathy towards the *Asantehemaa* Afua Kobi and her sons. It has been suggested that, in Asante understanding, this was fostered by Kwaku Dua Panin's profound (and even disabling?) regret at his treatment of Afua Sapon, and his tortured suspicion about Afua Kobi's instrumental role in engendering the *konnurokusɛm*. But, as noted, Kwaku Dua Panin did not engineer the removal of Afua Kobi from office, or connive at the death of her sons. It might be suggested that he lacked masterful confidence in his last years; certainly, alienation from his authoritarianism and his convictions intensified in the 1860s, such that 'there were many who did not like him at all'.[167] It might be urged that he lacked personal will in another way; that is, that his recriminations with himself over the death of one *Asantehemaa* – marked by portentous visitations even on his death-bed – precluded or paralysed any initiative by him to liquidate her successor. But, above all, Kwaku Dua Panin responded to the impasse represented by quotidian reality by shifting the contextual grounding of his life from the present into the realm of Asante history. His behaviour in his last years was that of an ancestor-in-waiting.

That is, Kwaku Dua Panin moved, by unrecoverable processes of thought and emotion, to situate his own patrilineal descendants in the *Aboadeε* sub-division of the *Bosompra ntɔrɔ* at the centre of the future of Asante, and thereby to achieve the genealogical obliteration of Afua Kobi's sons in relation to history. Symbolic of this intention was the cloth pattern *Aboadeε* – 'said to have been invented by Kwaku Dua I, for his children'.[168] Practical implementation of this intention took the form of marriages that Kwaku Dua Panin arranged in the 1860s between his own favourite sons and available royal women.[169] These were designed to insert himself and his slighted *ntɔrɔ* into history by producing, for the future, a grandson with overwhelming (and orthodox) claims to the *sika dwa kofi*. In fact, Kwaku Dua Panin's own nominated successor in the office of *Asantehene* was Agyeman Kofi – his eldest paternal grandson who was also an *ɔdehyeε* of the *sika dwa kofi*. Agyeman Kofi's father, the *Somihene ɔheneba* Kwasi Abayeε, was himself a favourite son of Kwaku Dua Panin by his marriage to a daughter of the *Asantehene* Osei Tutu Kwame; his mother was Yaa Kyaa, the elder daughter of Afua Kobi herself. Unless we recall the unborn-living-ancestor continuum of Asante history, then Kwaku Dua Panin's death-bed injunction that he be succeeded by the pre-adolescent Agyeman Kofi (born *c.* 1860), because Afua Kobi's sons would be unable to 'keep his house in order', smacks of wish fulfilment.[170] And so, at the time, it proved to be. In the electoral contest of 1867, the boy Agyeman Kofi was set aside in favour of (the now deceased) Kwabena Anin's younger brother Kofi Kakari of the *Anini* sub-division of the *Bosommuru ntɔrɔ*.[171]

But let us look a little more closely at the context and meaning of this wish fulfilment. It is clear from his name – Agyeman + (the day name) Kofi – that the grandson was named for, and most probably by, the grandfather.[172] That is, in line with Asante thinking about such matters, Kwaku Dua Panin identified his eldest grandson by one of his favourite sons not only with the continuity of the *Bosompra ntɔrɔ*, but explicitly with the perpetuation of his own patri-personality and status in history.[173] We may allow ourselves the speculation, very thoroughly evidenced in the anthropological literature as practice, that when Kwaku Dua Panin, as paternal grandfather, spat in the infant boy's mouth to strengthen his spirit, uttered the formulaic invocation *mε din nyera da* ('may my name never be lost'), and then named him, he had in mind the possible realization of the concept of the pure (re)incarnation or *kra pa*. The process thereby set in motion was finally confirmed in 1884, nearly two decades after Kwaku Dua Panin's death. In that year, Agyeman

Kofi at last – and briefly, before succumbing to smallpox – became *Asantehene*. He adopted the stool name of his grandfather Kwaku Dua. In tradition, grandfather and grandson are now distinguished by the epithets *panin* (the elder) and *kuma* (the younger) – successive incarnations in a patrilineal line.[174]

kwayawo *(16: Thursday)* concluded

All of the complex matters that we have discussed crowded into and filled the horizon of everyone who participated in or observed the *odwira kwayawo*. Following the procession of *odwira kwayawo*, it was incumbent upon the reigning *Asantehene* to participate in the ritualistic defilement of his own *ntɔrɔ* as a necessary prelude to its subsequent purification. This was, of course, a common feature of comparable rites in a widespread number of cultures.[175] But in our long but necessary excursus we have tried to illuminate two things: (*a*) the huge range of meanings – variously perceived, and at different levels of understanding and incomprehension – that found their most exact distillation in that moment, annually repeated, when the incumbent *Asantehene* inaugurated the passage from the past to the future by addressing his royal status to the matter of his *ntɔrɔ*. This was the contextualization of historical ideology in a moment, a mnemonic and an invitation to the most essential reflection; (*b*) the articulation of the self in relation to society and to history that worked through every life in an irrepressible profusion of representations, images, memories, traditions and the rest, and that found quintessential expression – on *kwayawo* and at subsequent moments in *odwira* – when an *Asantehene*, in celebrating history, meditated upon the condition of being Asante on behalf of everyone else by looking into his own selfhood. It is not too misleading a usage to urge that in such moments of seeming calculation, Asante history 'emoted' itself.[176]

The mechanics of defilement may be simply described. Among the avoidances (*akyiwadeɛ*) of the *Bosommuru ntɔrɔ*, as has been noted, was a prohibition against the killing and eating of cattle (*nantwi*). Thus, on *odwira kwayawo* 14 December 1871 – which happened to coincide with the close of *ramadan* among the Muslims in Kumase – the *Asantehene* Kofi Kakari of the *Anini* sub-division of the *Bosommuru ntɔrɔ* proceeded to *dwaberem* accompanied by a number of Muslim celebrants *en grand tenu*. There, he publicly cut the throat of an ox provided for the occasion, and then distributed the meat to those present in attendance upon his person.[177] This was the making of an ideological *argument* about the state in history, in the precise contexts of rectitude and order, but many present, including Kofi Kakari himself in this case, must *always* have silently reflected upon the precise identity of the *Asantehene* who was performing the ritual. The *Asantehene* Kofi Kakari, after all, was given to the private avowal that 'his ascendancy to the throne of Ashantee was like a dream to him'.[178] And on every single *odwira kwayawo* for over three decades in the reign of the *Asantehene* Kwaku Dua Panin, the ritual of defilement had been addressed to the very markedly different *akyiwadeɛ* of the *Bosompra ntɔrɔ*. The immolation, say, of a white fowl (*akokɔ fufuo*), rather than an ox or a cow, was an obviously thought-provoking event for many who witnessed it.[179]

In public, however, the state practised a unitary and ruthless self-censorship on days such as *odwira kwayawo*. Its major purpose on such occasions was to formulate and to proclaim a seamless rectitude of power, and thereby to legitimate, to affirm and to renew its ideologies of control over Asante society in the *statement* furnished by consent in the enactment of public ceremony. Its success may be gauged by the fact that endemic tensions between dynastic actors, of the sort we have seen in the reign of the *Asantehene* Kwaku Dua Panin, only became transferred in full from *afisɛm* to a dominance over public action in the initial stages of the internecine conflicts of the 1880s, when the *Bosompra Aboadeɛ* warred openly with the *Bosommuru Anini*. But by then, as we have already seen, domestic and foreign politics were in drastic transition, and a fragmented elite no longer possessed any clear, unified or even coherently realistic conception of the state.

In the evening of *odwira kwayawo*, the *Asantehene* sat in state on the *sumpi* at *apremoso/bogyawe*. There he formally received the first of the provincial office holders and subject tributaries to arrive in Kumase in response to the summons to celebrate *odwira*. On *odwira kwayawo* 22 August 1816, 'various greater and lesser kings' entered the Asante capital.[180] On *odwira kwayawo* 14 December 1871, a delegation arrived from Kwankyeabo, capital of the littoral province of Sanwi, bearing as tribute 200 barrels of gunpowder and 300 guns.[181] The most spectacular (performative, declamatory) entrances into Kumase on *odwira kwayawo* were made by the *amanhene* of Kokofu and Nsuta, who were forbidden by custom to undertake any travelling on the following day, *monofie* (17: Friday). Thus, on *odwira kwayawo* 14 December 1871, the newly enstooled *Kokofuhene* Kyei Kwame Kuma arrived in Kumase in state to celebrate the *odwira*, and publicly thanked the *Asantehene* Kofi Kakari for attending the recent funeral of his sister the *Kokofuhemaa* (who was also of the *Oyoko Kɔkɔɔ abusua*).[182] These formal, but tumultuous, ceremonies of welcome concluded the events of *odwira kwayawo*.

Transacting *odwira* 2: *monofie, fomemene, nwonakwasie*

monofie *(17: Friday)*

On *monofie* the paths and roads leading into Kumase were densely crowded with people arriving for the celebration of *odwira*. 'Great numbers from all parts of Ashanti' passed through the village of Kaase (then on the Cape Coast road, now within Kumase) on *odwira monofie* 1 September 1843, 'in order to be present at the approaching Yam Custom'; and on *odwira monofie* 5 September 1817, 'the number, splendor, and variety of arrivals, thronging from the different paths, was as astonishing as entertaining'.[183] This huge influx was composed of the retinues and *nkoa* of the *amaŋhene*, such as those of Dwaben, Mampon, Bekwai, Kumawu, Asumegya and Offinso; followers of *abirɛmpɔn* and other office holders from areas such as Adanse, Edweso, Mponua and Asante Akyem; subjects of the Kumase office holders, from nearby villages and from more distant areas such as Kwawu, Ahafo and Manso Nkwanta; rulers and representatives of provincial tributaries and/or clients from Denkyira, Akyem and Assin in the south, from Nkoransa, Takyiman and Banda (Banna) in the north, and from a variety of other locations; and numbers of foreign delegations, and visiting dignitaries with their suites.[184]

In 1817, Bowdich asserted that 'the principal caboceers [office holders] sacrificed a slave at each quarter of the town, on their entré'.[185] The offering of oblates at the *ŋkwaŋtanaŋ* designated by Komfo Anokye was directed towards the spiritual strengthening of the Asante capital. But by the reign of the *Asantehene* Kwaku Dua Panin this practice had been prohibited, or otherwise discontinued. Thus, Chapman recorded that on *odwira monofie* 13 September 1844, 'no person whatever has been killed', and he added, citing Bowdich, that this custom had formerly existed, but that it was now abolished.[186] The reasons for cessation are unclear, but they may well have been connected with Kwaku Dua Panin's well-documented efforts to curtail the privileges of all of the great *amaŋhene*, and to underline the precept that the *Asantehene* alone 'held the knife' (*ɔsekaŋ*) by right.[187]

The great constituent *amaŋhene* arrived from their territorial divisions in considerable state; it was asserted in the 1840s that some among them brought a following of 2,000 armed *nkoa*.[188] Indeed, during *odwira* in Kumase the permanently resident population of some 20,000 to 25,000 swelled dramatically with the influx of celebrants and their attendants. 'The Ashantees persisted', remarked Bowdich, 'that the population of Coomassie, when collected, was upwards of 100,000'; and at the close of the *odwira* of 1848, the population of the Asante capital had risen 'from the usual amount of about 25 thousand to upwards of 80 thousand'.[189] Certainly, the increment was so large that many people had to sleep in the Kumase streets throughout the course of *odwira*.[190]

The formal public reception of these visitors did not take place until *fomemene* (18: Saturday). On *odwira monofie* the *Asantehene* spent much of his time in ritual seclusion, preparing and readying himself for the ceremonies that were to ensue, and in which he was the essential participant. Indeed, *odwira monofie* was a day that was largely devoted to generalized preparation. Ritual efforts were focused on the extremely hazardous business of summoning and placating the ancestral *asamanfoɔ*, in order to secure their full cooperative involvement in the successful performance of *odwira*. Similarly, the departed spirits or the 'ghosts' of those who had suffered execution at the state's instruction were also ritually induced to manifest themselves. Particular attention was lavished on the *asamanfoɔ* of all those who had died, in whatever circumstances, during the elapse of the previous nine *adaduanan* cycles.

On *odwira monofie* 15 December 1871, for example, some 200 royal *adumfoɔ* (executioners), with their characteristic leopard-skin headgear, *ntitabo* hairstyles (shaved in front, long in back), and bandoliers of *kyiɛafaseɛ* knives ('for cutting heads'), met together in assembly in the *anowu* ward of Kumase.[191] There they danced throughout the entire afternoon in a frenzied or possessed (*akɔm*) manner, all the while aggressively brandishing their knives, and with human skulls and jawbones clenched in their teeth. Throughout this performance, the royal *adumfoɔ* cried out – promiscuously intermixing insult, pleading, coaxing, flattery, mock-heroic address, etc. – to the *asamanfoɔ* of those that they had executed since the previous *odwira*. It was understood that the noise and the use of direct speech aimed at named individuals would conduce an initial manifestation or presence (from curiosity as much as any other factor). After sunset – and this was also witnessed on *odwira monofie* 23 August 1872 – the *adumfoɔ* proceeded in a body to *apetesɛnɛɛ* (der. *pete*: to scatter, strew, throw + *asɛnɛɛ*: a place where criminals were killed) or *nsɔre* (a place outside of a settlement where corpses were thrown and/or buried: der. *sɔre*: to part, leave, cease). This was also the location of *asamanpomu* ('the bush of the ghosts': cf. *pɔw*: grove, thicket), on the edge of Kumase south of *dwaberem*, where the corpses of those who had been executed were thrown.[192] 'After a subject is executed for crime', observed Bowdich, 'the body and head are carried out of town by some of the King's slaves, appointed for that purpose, and thrown where the wild beasts may devour them.'[193] That is, the grove of *asamanpomu* – like shrines connected with the manifestations of the *abosom* – was sited in *kurotia*, that zone of hazardous liminality where culture and nature met in uneasy confrontation. At *asamanpomu* the *adumfoɔ* continued to dance, all the while summoning the *asamanfoɔ* of their victims.

Invoking the *asamaɲfoɔ*, let alone those belonging to victims of execution, was a very serious and potentially perilous undertaking. In token of this understanding, the *adumfoɔ* were smeared overall in red clay (*ntwoma*) throughout the *odwira monofie* proceedings. Red (*kɔkɔɔ*: alt. *kɔbene: memene*) was, together with black (*tuntum*) and white (*fufu*), one of the three primary colour classifications in Asante thought.[194] Conceptually, the construction of 'redness' embraced that part of the spectrum ranging from red itself, through purple and orange, to violet and pink.[195] Red occupied a singular niche among the three primary colours. White was auspicious, and was linked to victory and spiritual purity; black stood for death, and was expressive of death and mourning. Both were unambiguous. By contrast, red was full of equivocal meanings. It symbolized both the life and death aspects of blood (*mogya*), together with the potentially volatile mix of feelings that were identified with strongly emotive concepts such as danger, sorrow, impurity, anger and defiance. The common locution *m'ani abere* ('my eyes are red': that is, the bloodshot eye) signified the dangerous confusions that characterized that heightened emotional state which combined extremities of engaged sorrow, despair, anger and aggression. 'Redness' overwhelmed the signal clarities of white and black.[196] To be smeared in *ntwoma* betokened a person in hazardous contact with ambiguous powers, such as the *asamaɲfoɔ* represented. Thus, in the conceptualization of the human, and within the reproductive framework of the *abusua*, *mogya* was identified with life, but in anything other than a life-giving context – execution, spillage, waste, menstruation – it connoted putative danger and implied a deadly specificity.[197]

Red and 'redness' then were replete with highly uncertain, even contrary, significances, and could embrace conflicting ambiguities in the emotional and cognitive expression of ritual action. The *adumfoɔ* were daubed red on *odwira monofie* because they were hazarding themselves in the arena of death, and with all of the degrees of danger, impurity, damage, and sheer inchoate supernatural power that this entailed. Thus, red signified the defiance (*ogyina kɔdom ano*) required to confront their erstwhile victims. But it also united danger with the expression of a sentiment, appropriate in the circumstances, of supplication, of sorrow and regret for past actions.[198]

fomemene *(18: Saturday)*

On *odwira fomemene* the *Asantehene* presided over a formal state reception for those who had travelled to Kumase for *odwira*. This day was the *odwira memeneda* (*odwira* Saturday), and the vast public assembly that dominated and gave focus to the proceedings was a supreme occasion, a quintessential moment, on and in which the Asante state formulated, displayed, promulgated and otherwise acted out the coherent rectitude of its power and ideology. Nineteenth-century European observers had some limited understanding of the intentional meaning of all that transpired before their eyes. But their primary impression was sensory – the noise and diversity of action overwhelmed their perceptions, and reduced some among them to bewilderment and even terror. In this they were unknowing actors in the ritual unfolding of the text of *odwira fomemene*. The very calculated heightening of emotional involvement, and the incremental and systematic overloading of the sensory responses of all of the Asante participants, were intentional or directed strategies that were integral to the performative enactment of the day's events.[199]

The *odwira fomemene* reception was characterized by very dense masses of people, intense noise – drumming, firing, cheering, singing, yelling, crying, debating – and a seemingly chaotic, highly fragmented and relentlessly sustained assault on all of the human senses. Bowdich, who essayed a pictorial representation of *odwira fomemene* 6 September 1817 (see Appendix I), acknowledged that his crowded and intensely busy drawing 'was by no means adequate', but excused the inadequacies of his effort with the pointed disclaimer that, in trying to make any narrative sense of what he observed, a simultaneous rendering in colour and pen and ink – a fixity – offered the closest approximation; his drawing was less than perfect, 'yet more so than description could be'.[200] A century later, Rattray gave it as his considered opinion that the comprehension of individual participants must have been obscured by and dissolved in 'the tumult, the barbaric pomp, the splendid, sometimes ghastly scenes, the marching and counter-marching of thousands . . .'.[201]

In its performative and expressive promiscuity, and in its plethoric multiplicity of sub-texts, the *odwira fomemene* conformed to the art historical characterization of *odwira* as a total work of art or *gesamtkunstwerke*.[202] However, all of the innumerable, overlapping sub-texts were calculated, structured and shaped interventions. The *odwira fomemene* reception was directed power diffused and then condensed for maximum impact to a series of theatrical coups or epiphanies. These filled the sensory horizon of the participants. At the emotional level, they flooded and annihilated the individual's capacity for any form of pause or analytic detachment, and they generated a participatory and communal catharsis on terms defined and orchestrated by the state. The event sequence of *odwira fomemene* worked, sequentially and sometimes conjointly, to structure all of the senses, but especially that of the seeing eye. Participants (Bowdich included) were unable to register and to assimilate all that was transacting before their eyes. Their sight and visual comprehension were reduced to the anaphoric; they gazed upon the unfolding, chaotic spectacle in an unchannelled way, built their own personal connectivities by using metonymy and metaphor, and consistently (and helplessly) referenced cultural inputs to individual experience and ego. Denied panoptic understanding, participants struggled for some form of anamorphism – a channelling of vision to a singular point that might pledge insight and confer meaning. That point or focus to which people clung was the person of the *Asantehene*. He and the space around him were the still eye of the storm, drawing in upon themselves the gaze, and with it the burden of conferring meaning. This was a deliberate ploy, for the person of the *Asantehene* on *odwira fomemene*, as in all of the state's rehearsals of itself, was the key engine of process, and the indispensable embodiment of ideology.[203]

The day of *odwira fomemene* began with the *Asantehene*, the *adehyeɛ* and the *ahenemma* (i.e. the members of the royal *abusua*, together with the offspring of the *Asantehene(s)* – or 'children' of the *sika dwa kofi*), the officials and *gyaasefoɔ* of the royal household, the office holders of Kumase and their combined retinues, all processing together in state from the gates of the royal palace to *apremoso*. This venue was itself a potent mnemonic of the history of the origin of the power of the Asante state; *apremoso* meant 'the place of the cannons' (*ɔprɛm*: cannon, gun), and commemorated the alleged seizure of European-supplied field-pieces from the Denkyira in the war that established the autonomy of Asante at the very beginning of the eighteenth century. In 1817, the British embassy to Kumase was lodged in a house at 'Aperremsoo, big gun or cannon street, because those taken when Dankara was conquered (at Feyiase in 1701), were placed on a mound at the top of it...'.[204] When the procession from the palace had reached *apremoso* and debouched into the open space there, the *Asantehene* took his seat on the *apremoso/bogyawe sumpi*, adjacent to the Denkyira cannon. Meanwhile, all of the Kumase office holders took up their prescribed positions, and,

the assembled thousands of his household, and of the permanent population [of Kumase], occupy the ground on the right and left, the whole scene being made gorgeous by a large display of many coloured cotton, damask and velvet tout-umbrellas, and gold-handled swords.[205]

Dazzled astonishment was the object of this stylized and very carefully choreographed (re)presentation. It was designed in such a way as to draw the vision of the approaching observer ever inward, from the densely packed, extended horns of an enveloping semicircle towards the more distant mid-point where the *Asantehene* sat, above all others, in elevated state. Only the narrowest of paths led through the massed ranks of the seated *gyaasefoɔ* up to (in both senses) the demarcated space from which the *Asantehene* oversaw (again, in both senses) the proceedings.[206] The deployment of the enfolding semicircle was the preferred geometrical and spatial mode in which the state (re)presented itself in all public display. Again, the impact was designed first for the eye. Thus, when the returning army of the *Gyaasewahene* Adu Bofoɔ was officially received into Kumase on the auspicious *monodwo* (41: Monday) of 4 September 1871, it was welcomed by the *Asantehene* Kofi Kakari seated at the mid-point of a semicircle of all of his assembled office holders; Bonnat, who was present on this occasion – and somewhat in the manner of Bowdich before him – supplemented his inadequate narrative powers by sketching a plan of arrangements that were primarily (and consciously) addressed to the eye.[207] T.B. Freeman reminisced about the visual impact of this semicircular (re)presentation (in the 1830s and 1840s) in the following terms.

The positions thus taken by the recipients are extremely favourable for showing a vast concourse of persons at the greatest possible advantage. A continuous line of some 6 or 700 yards, curved or approaching to an angular form, with the Royal group in the centre and the wings inclining forward with the visitor in the area thus formed affords him an opportunity of taking in the whole at a glance, and the line, many yards deep, backed by the sable and frequently beautiful countenances of the females in their gay dresses; the large umbrellas some 70 or 80 in number; together with the vast display of gold-handled swords and other ornaments consisting of, or loaded with that precious metal, such as massy chains round the neck, armlets, manillas, and other trinkets disposed in the most conspicuous parts of the body from the head to the sandals on the feet... That man must be strangely unimpressible who could emerge from a vast forest of so many scores of miles in depth [i.e. between Cape Coast and Kumase], and gaze, all at once on 50,000 pairs of human eyes directed on him with intense interest, and many of them lighted up with such fires as he perhaps never saw before, and not feel strangely impressed and excited.[208]

This visual (re)presentation of the Asante state attained to its zenith of opulent extravagance on the occasion of *odwira fomemene*. Thus, on *odwira fomemene* 2 September 1843, Chapman was moved to an awed description of this semicircular formation by the sheer force of its presence, and by its stunning impact as an exuberant visual metaphor for wealth and power.

O what a display of barbaric splendour. His [the *Asantehene* Kwaku Dua Panin's] attendants were many of them literally laden with Gold, some wrought, others in its pure state. His numerous messengers standing about him each bearing a gold handled sword, and many decorated with large pieces of rock gold. His Majesty himself wore many beautiful ornaments of the same metal, while his stool and many other articles about him, were literally covered with it... I never beheld such a display of barbaric splendour. Gold and Silver have been displayed today, worth hundreds of thousands of pounds. That about the King was of immense value, some of his attendants being laden with it to that extent, as actually to require support from others.[209]

Messengers were then sent off from the *Asantehene* to all of the visiting dignitaries to announce that he was now seated, and was at last ready to receive them. At this point, the *Asantehene* displayed his sovereign capacities for intervening in and ordering the time of others. After having been kept waiting for an indeterminate period, the visiting dignitaries, now set in motion by the royal officials, were constantly harried and impressed with the need for an unseemly alacrity. All of the assembled tributaries and provincial office holders now processed before the *Asantehene* in reverse order of precedence, with those of the highest rank – the *amaŋhene* – bringing up the rear.[210] In the presence of the *Asantehene*, all of these protagonists renewed their personal oaths of allegiance. They swore fealty, the *amaŋhene* most dramatically by taking their oaths on the *afena* (sword) of the reigning *Asantehene's ntɔrɔ* (in practice, *Bosommuru* or *Bosompra*), loudly declaiming while its point was directed towards their persons.[211] The most favoured office holders were singled out for approbation by the *Asantehene* amidst the boisterous acclamation of their retinues. Large quantities of palm wine circulated freely at the *Asantehene's* command. The sustained din of horn playing, drumming, firing, shouting and cheering rose to a series of deafening crescendos as successive office holders approached the royal presence.

Throughout all of this, immense multi-coloured umbrellas were kept in constant, agitated motion (and were contrasted by Europeans with the monochrome green stillness of the surrounding forest).[212] By far the largest and most elaborate umbrellas belonged to, and were deployed around the person of, the *Asantehene*, and each of these had its own name, attendants and observances.[213] The generic term for an umbrella was *kyiŋiɛ* (pl. *ŋkyiŋiɛ*), and this word was cognate with terms that were expressive of whirling, circulation, wind and coolness. The symbolic use of umbrellas was related to one particular typological distinction that was made between the ordered space of human (Asante) culture and that of anarchically fecund and antagonistic nature. Culture was understood to be harmonious and protective, and this was formulated as a condition of coolness (*dwo*); nature, by contrast, was disruptive, threatening, and conceptualized in terms of the antithetical condition of heat (*ahohuru*). The *Asantehene*, as the embodiment of culture, afforded a protective 'coolness' at once physical and metaphorical. The motion of his great umbrellas signified this in a literal *and* symbolic way (supported, as they were, by the lesser umbrellas of ever-diminishing degrees of size and costliness that belonged to descending ranks of office holders), as did the metaphor that likened him to *gyadua* (a large tree offering shade: i.e. *(o)gye*: receiving, acceptance, with the idea of protection + *(e)dua*: a tree). Synonyms encapsulated the idea that the *Asantehene* 'protected' culture by offering a cooling 'shade'; thus, for example, *(ɔ)tew gyadua ahabaŋ* ('he tears the leaves of the shade tree') intended the same meaning as, and could be used in euphemistic place of, *ohyira ɔhene* ('he curses the king's life').[214]

'I never felt so grateful for being born in a civilized country', remarked Bowdich of the *odwira fomemene* 6 September 1817 that was presided over by the *Asantehene* Osei Tutu Kwame.

Firing and drinking palm wine were the only divertissemens [*sic*] to the ceremony of the caboceers [office holders] presenting themselves to the King; they were announced, and passed all around the circle saluting every umbrella: their bands preceded; we reckoned above forty drums in that of the King of Dwabin [the *Dwabenhene*]. The effect of the splendor, the tumult and the musquetry, was afterwards heightened by torchlight.[215]

Chapman was similarly overwhelmed on *odwira fomemene* 2 September 1843, in the reign of the *Asantehene* Kwaku Dua Panin.

And now was presented a scene such as I never before witnessed ... Before us stood an immense concourse of people ... the dense crowd filling the wide streets from end to end, or lost in the distant perspective. Among the multitude stood the large, and splendid umbrellas of the Chieftains, some surmounted by different kinds of animals, others with large gilded balls. The various, and rich colours of the umbrellas together with the gold handled swords held just above the heads of the people, and the beautiful forest scenery in the background, presented altogether a sight not easily to be erased from the memory.[216]

Freeman, a most astute observer, managed to go some way beyond Bowdich and Chapman in intuiting and situating the larger meaning(s) of this extravaganza. His phrasing, with its predictable emphasis on an emotionally charged primitivism, was highly romanticized in the familiar mid-nineteenth-century ethnographic manner. But Freeman did grasp some inkling of the ideological fact that, beneath the bewildering anarchy of its presentation, the *odwira fomemene* reception served all at once to proclaim the unity of society and state, and to reinforce and underline the image of the latter's determining control and authority. Thus, for example, Freeman reflected that the swearing of personal allegiance in such a heightened and emotive atmosphere,

exhibits the Ashantee Chieftain in all the conscious pride and glory in his strength, and of his high position. The heated blood rushes through his veins, with accelerated speed, from a heart swelling with intense excitement, with the sword now seized by the handle, and waved over his head; his countenance is lit up with strange fires of mingled ferocity and dignity; his eyes are dilated, and his very gestures seem to speak aloud – it is humanity in a state of wild untutored grandeur ... the excitement runs like an electric shock among the assembled thousands ... and a nation joins in the general plaudit, and rends the air with barbaric acclamation ...[217]

When this passage of the proceedings was finally concluded, the visitors formed themselves into a shallow arc or semicircle facing the *Asantehene*. Asante was now (re)presented, momentarily but visibly, in the binary equipoise of two complementary semicircles that together formed a whole. The semicircle of *Kumasefoɔ* was mirrored in the other moiety of a rough circle that contained everyone else. Thus, the basic distribution of power in the state was signified in a very fundamental morphology. In turn, this was framed within (and overlaid with) one of the most potent visual metaphors in the Asante register. The completed circle (*puruw*: *puruo*) – as round, globe, disc or cylinder – connoted an aesthetic and morally integrated unity or perfection. It was associated with these ideas in very many contexts, but most germanely in those of the *abosom* and the *ntɔrɔ*. Thus, the circular (re)presentation of Asante that occurred at this moment in the *odwira fomemene* proceedings found one of its many signifying analogues in the *akrakoŋmu* (syn. *ɛkyerɛ*: a gold disc) that was worn on the breast of each and every one of the royal *ŋkradwarefoɔ* or 'soul washers' (sing. *akradwareni*: syn. *ɔkra*; pl. *akrafoɔ*) – individuals who were dedicated to the service, or 'washing', of the *kra* of the reigning *Asantehene*.[218]

The *Kumasefoɔ* themselves – as hosts, and as representatives of the centre of state power – now processed in a reciprocal gesture of welcome (the Asante understanding being that the senior party had the right to the final statement or action in any exchange).[219] The order of precedence exactly mirrored that of the earlier part of the day, with the Kumase office holders advancing in sequence from the lowest to the highest in rank; each was surrounded by armed *nkoa* chanting his praise or 'strong' names, extolling his attributes and his wealth, and reciting the history and virtues of his predecessors in office. Drums and horns played an accompaniment in the same vein. From a plethora of such items, the following brief examples are offered by way of summary illustration:

1 *petepere*: The drum music of the Kumase *Akyempemhene ɔheneba* Owusu Kɔkɔɔ (*c.* 1820–84). The drum itself was a small semi-cylindrical signal instrument (cf. *mpɛbi* below). The *petepere* is a tree with extremely hard wood. The drumming asserted that Owusu Koko was as hard as this wood, and so aggression towards him would end in frustration and defeat.

2 *pɛsɛ kuku*: The drum music of the Kumase *Dadeɛsoabahene* Atobra (*fl.* mid-eighteenth century). This commemorated the victory of that office holder over an Akyem Abuakwa general who had been clad in a war coat sheathed in the quills of a type of porcupine (*apɛsɛ*). The drumming of *pɛsɛ kuku* signified that the *Dadeɛsoabahene* had killed the general with the 'porcupine' smock.

3 *ase ase ayɔ, ase ase ayɔ!*: The horn call of the Kumase *Adontenhene* Kwaaten Pɛtɛ (*ɔpɛtɛ*: the vulture: *c.* 1720–1805). The call meant, 'what was said or proposed has been accomplished'. That is, Kwaaten Pɛtɛ always kept his word and reached his objective.

4 *mɛnya ɔhan kɔse akura o, mɛnya ɔhan kɔse akura o, agyinamoa rɛba o, agyinamoa rɛba o?*: The horn call of the Kumase *Bantamahene* and *Krontihene* Amankwatia Panin (*fl.* early eighteenth century). The call meant, 'who will inform the mouse for me that the cat is approaching?' That is, Amankwatia Panin – a

celebrated general – compared himself to the cat, and his enemies to the mouse. The result of any such confrontation was patent to all.[220]

At the last in this procession came the *Asantehene* himself, seated in a palanquin (*ɔsako: deŋkyedeŋkye*: cf. *ehim deŋkyedeŋkye*, 'to shake to and fro').[221] The music, drumming and calling out around his person reached the highest pitch of intensity. Europeans acknowledged the sheer force of this presentation, albeit as a sort of cacophony of power. But the overwhelming noise was a multi-layered mnemonic and overt celebration of the history of the state. Thus, to take a single example from this kaleidoscopic (re)presentation, the *Asantehene* was preceded or announced by the music of his twinned signal drums of *mpɛbi* and *nkrawiri*. The name *mpɛbi* was derived from the abbreviated phrase *mempɛ bi* ('I do not want any [at all]'); *nkrawiri* was a reference to fate or destiny, although it is sometimes glossed with the sense of life flowing away. The specific historical allusions were to certain orders and actions of the *Asantehene* Opoku Ware (c. 1720–50). That is, Opoku Ware ordered the military reduction of Ataara Finam and other rulers on the Afram plains, and along the Volta river to the northeast. This was accomplished, and much booty was seized from Pran and other areas. In Kumase, Opoku Ware refused to take any personal share of this loot, with the exception of the villages of Bagyamso and Nkaneku, declaring to his office holders: *Pran nniɛma ni mɔnkye nni* ('Here is Pran's wealth, to be shared and enjoyed [by all of you]'). The *mpɛbi* and *nkrawiri* drums were made in commemoration of the *Asantehene's* altruistic largess. Thus, when these drums were borne before Opoku Ware (and every subsequent ruler), the *mpɛbi* played *pran ɔman mempɛ bi* ('I do not want any [at all] of the Pran state'), and the *nkrawiri* replied with *mɔnkye nni, mempɛ bi, mɔnkye nni* ('Share it for your use, I want no part of it, share it for your use').[222]

The *Asantehene* was closely attended and densely surrounded by household officials; by *afenasoafoɔ*, by *adumfoɔ*, and by great masses of *nhenkwaa* from other service groups; by the royal bodyguard; by male and female *adehyeɛ*; and by a representative number of the royal wives. To look upon this last category of women was normally a capital offence for a man, and this was one of the very rare occasions when the *Asantehene's* wives 'passed through the streets, without the men withdrawing'; on the *odwira fomemene* 16 December 1871, some fifteen wives of the *Asantehene* Kofi Kakari (extensively remembered in tradition, it should be recalled, for his love of women) were in the procession. They were clad in silken cloth, and

accompanied by a group of eunuchs [*adabraafoɔ*; *ŋsono*] and small boys passed by with slow steps, looking at the ground, and not looking around at all. They were decked with magnificent gold decorations on their feet, arms, breast and neck, their heads covered with a sort of net of gold chains. The upper part(s) of their bodies were covered with a yellow-green powder.[223]

As befitted its importance, the *odwira fomemene* reception was a very protracted affair. The *Asantehene* usually quit his palace about 10 or 11 a.m., and had finally taken his seat to receive the provincial office holders by 3 p.m. The reciprocal greeting by the *Kumasefoɔ* often took place after sunset – and in pouring rain on *odwira fomemene* 24 August 1872. Tumblers of oil fixed to crossed lathes were used as torches (*agyatɛŋ*), and these were agitated like the umbrellas, and rotated 'like wheels of fire'.[224] The formalities of *odwira fomemene* 16 December 1871 did not end until after 10 p.m., and even then matters were not entirely concluded. 'We left the ground at 10 o'clock', noted Bowdich of the *odwira fomemene* 6 September 1817, and still

the umbrellas were crowded even in the distant streets, the town was covered like a large fair, the broken sounds of distant horns and drums filled up the momentary pauses of the firing which encircled us: the uproar continued until four in the morning, just before which the King retired.[225]

In fact, the formal conclusion to the day was the withdrawal of the *Asantehene* into the palace. This was signalled, as on every other day but on *odwira fomemene* at a much later hour, by the playing of a particular refrain on the royal horns: 'The King's horns go to the market place [*dwaberem*] every night, as near to midnight as they can judge', remarked Bowdich of the normal practice, 'and flourish a very peculiar strain, which was rendered to me, "King Sai [Osei Tutu Kwame] thanks all his captains and all his people for to-day."'[226]

The events of the day of *odwira fomemene* proposed a seeming disorder, expressed in a massively confusing diversity of simultaneous enactments – tumultuous, raucously noisy, densely peopled, and subject to dramatic shifts between fluidity and stasis, movement and inactivity, speed and tardiness. At this level of impact the *odwira fomemene* worked to overwhelm the senses (notably the eye), and to create in participants a sense of fusion with the sequence of events, but in a disorienting and blurred way. But, in fact, this chaotic (re)presentation was punctuated and structured by a series of calculated interventions – or theatrical epiphanies – that revolved around the essential person and the actions of the *Asantehene*, and that celebrated the history and received ordering of state and society. People were exposed to the dense mnemonics of the *odwira fomemene* as a performative sequence, but this took place within a framework in which their receptivity was both manipulated and magnified by the intense heightening of their emotional involvement. The overall purpose and effect was to induce identification and catharsis through a relentless display of condensed essentials over an unbroken period of extremely intense experience.[227]

Throughout all of this, the state was seen to (re)present a simultaneous coherence, rectitude and authority that, expressed as the panoply of power, both invited and commanded adherence. The factors of consensual subscription and coercive power were inextricably mingled one with the other, and promulgated in the ideological structuration of the successive episodes in this kaleidoscopic *mise-en-scène*.[228] The day of *odwira fomemene* deliberately fractured and recast the rhythms of ordinary life. Distilled compression and performative density – the sheer weight of actualizations – combined with mass excitement and lack of sleep to predispose and then to conduce to a suspension of quotidian understandings of time, space and other commonplace gauges of the norms of lived reality. In a number of respects, these features were even more explicitly in evidence on the following day.

nwonakwasie *(19: Sunday)*

The events of the *odwira nwonakwasie* constituted a decisive transitional passage in the overall structuration of the meaning(s) of *odwira*. These events formed a series of enabling transactions that were designed to condition, to manage and to signal transformational movement from defilement towards purification, from disaggregation towards reintegration, and from past towards future. Most fundamentally, on the *odwira nwonakwasie* the historic constructions of the meaning(s) of the relationship between the Asante state and society were articulated and commemorated, the quiddity and ideological conditions of the compact between the two were underlined, and received order – the rectitude of the past – was affirmed and projected into the linear continuity that was represented by the future.

On the *odwira nwonakwasie* critical constituents of Asante culture were profiled and then, literally, deconstructed aspectually, as if in the manner of a hermeneutical grammar, and then these exposed and fragmented elements were reassembled and renewed. Like analogous events in other cultures and times, the *odwira nwonakwasie*, constructed as a transformational hinge, was marked by liminality, and by the excessive disorientation of customary social norms and expressions associated with that condition. Transgressions, pollutions and orgiastic inversions were enacted as representational and highly dramatic antitheses, out of which were created the transcendental theses of purity and wholeness.[229] The (re)emergent ideological text was a triumphalist reintegration of past certainties that proposed (that seduced to?) satisfying and wholly optimistic expectations of the future, confidently and with all due gratitude to ancestors, *abosom* and *onyame*. European eyewitnesses recorded all of this with beguiled puzzlement, but also with a plethora of richly nuanced detail.

The time before sunrise, running on from the *odwira fomemene*, was devoted to a ritualized mourning for the dead that encompassed the specifics of personal remembrance within the context of a valedictory reflection on the past nine *adaduanan* cycles. Customary inhibitions and politic reticences were set aside. Freeman observed that,

in every street and in every house throughout the Town is heard the wild wail of lamentation. Sorrow appears to pervade all classes, from the Sovereign in his palace to the humblest dweller in the hut. This is in remembrance of the evils and distresses of the past year, since the last Yam Custom. Tears of grief are shed to the memory of departed friends removed by death; the survivors of those who have fallen under the King's displeasure, and lost their heads, and who have not dared, at the time the distress occurred, openly to mourn ... can now do so with impunity, and they rend the air with lamentations over the desolation of their families.[230]

At sunrise sheep were sacrificed within the walls of the palace, and their blood was smeared on doors, windows, the *Asantehene's* bed, and other items of his furniture and personal ornaments; on *odwira nwonakwasie* 3 September 1843, the carcasses of sheep slaughtered for this ritual were laid out before the main doors of the palace.[231] The main object of this oblation was to fortify or strengthen the *Asantehene* and to protect him from being troubled by potentially hostile *asamanfoɔ* on a day in which he would have the most intense interaction with these entities. The *Asantehene*, the *adumfoɔ* and the Kumase office holders then went in state to Bantama to secure the protective intervention of all of the occupants of the royal *baamu*. There the *Asantehene* offered human victims to the royal *asamanfoɔ* of his predecessors in office. As each oblate died by the knife, the *Asantehene* uttered a formulaic injunction of parting and farewell. The burden of this was to instruct each and every oblate to serve a particular, named *Asantehene* in the afterlife of *asamandow* ('the land of the ghosts'). For reasons that remain unclear, the *Asantehene* Kofi Kakari apparently restricted the number of such offerings to twelve.[232]

The *adumfoɔ* also performed a single human sacrifice in order to enlist protection and succour during the impending transactions. But unlike the many victims offered by the *Asantehene*, this individual might never be an *ɔdɔnkɔ* or other non-Asante person. The *adumfoɔ* always killed an Asante – whether an unsuspecting individual who had been pre-selected and was now arbitrarily seized, or, more commonly, an *akyere*, or someone already under sentence of death for crime.[233] On *odwira nwonakwasie* 15 September 1844, for example, the victim of the *adumfoɔ* was an Asante man who had perpetrated 'a heinous offence'; and on *odwira nwonakwasie* 25 August 1872, it was a youthful *ɔkɔmfɔ* who had been convicted of the crime of committing incest.[234] The corpse of the person sacrificed was then hacked to pieces and distributed among the *adumfoɔ*.[235] The individual thereby dismembered served to affirm the ideologies of right order, and simultaneously conferred upon the *adumfoɔ* an objectification that detached their 'innocent' personhoods from the prescriptive role and functions implicit in their dread office.[236]

Having completed these precautionary measures, the *adumfoɔ*, now suitably protected, prepared to confront and to deal with the very hostile and extremely dangerous *asamanfoɔ* of the Asante state's most intractable and obdurate historical enemies. Assisted by the Bantama *barimfoɔ* (mausoleum attendants), the *adumfoɔ* ritually took possession of the physical relics – and most notably the skulls (*ntikoraa*: sing. *tikoraa*: cf. *ti, tiri*: head) – of these celebrated adversaries. Each of these skulls (and other surviving bones and/or personal artefacts) was kept at Bantama before the coffin of the *Asantehene* who had overcome and killed the individual concerned. Taken together, these skulls composed a historical mnemonic to the serial narrative of the Asante state's wars, conquests and triumphs. By far the most important skulls kept in this ossuary had belonged to the state's principal foreign enemies, but the collection also included the crania of certain convicted Asante office holders, together with those of other heinous offenders, such as rebel or maleficent *akɔmfoɔ*.[237] Thus, the Bantama *ntikoraa* commemorated the puissant rectitude of the state's authority over its domestic foes, as well as over its non-Asante enemies. No fully comprehensive listing of these relics is extant. However, in the reign of the *Asantehene* Kwaku Dua Panin (1834–67) they included – minimally, and restricting the issue to the category of significant external enemies – the skulls and other relics of the following individuals.[238]

NAME AND DESIGNATION	DATE KILLED	ASANTEHENE
Domaa Kusi: *Domaahene*	1690s	Osei Tutu
Asiedu Papaa Kɛsɛɛ: *Hweresohene*	1690s	Osei Tutu
Ntim Gyakari: *Denkyirahene*	1701	Osei Tutu
Abirimoro: Sehwi/Ndenye (?)	1720s	Opoku Ware[239]
Ofosuhene Apenten: *Akyem Kotokuhene*	1720s	Opoku Ware
Ameyaw Kwaakye: *Takyimanhene*	1723 (?)	Opoku Ware[240]
Abo Kofi: *Gyamanhene*	1740 (?)	Opoku Ware[241]
Ba Kwante: *Okyenhene*	1742	Opoku Ware
Pobi Asumanin: *Okyenhene*	1765	Osei Kwadwo
Worosa: *Bannahene*	1774	Osei Kwadwo[242]
Kwadwo Adinkra: *Gyamanhene*	1818	Osei Tutu Kwame
Sir C. McCarthy: *British Governor*	1824	Osei Yaw Akoto

While all of the above events were taking place at Bantama, Kumase itself was 'in a state of extreme excitement' (*odwira nwonakwasie* 3 September 1843), verging on a generalized condition of 'extreme disorder', as a direct result of, to European eyes, 'the mad proceedings of the people' (*odwira nwonakwasie* 15 September 1844).[243] Chaotic drunkenness, intense noise, hysterical public grief, laughter, tears and disputatious argument, verbal and sexual licence, dirtiness and animality, social inversion, lampooning, insult, and the blurred confusion of all received norms and categories now anarchically manifested themselves in the crowded streets of Kumase. On this day, life in the Asante capital closely conformed to those behavioural features that historians, anthropologists and cultural critics have identified as being characteristic of, for example, the European folk carnival and the *charivari*. In short, the Asante were engaged in the performance of a culturally specific variant of Bakhtin's existential heteroglossia: a promiscuous series of discourses, in which modes of action, utterance and representation were temporarily transfigured by the liminal suspension of customary norms and rules. The streets of Kumase became 'a world turned upside down', and the text of normal life was systematically disassembled and re-presented.[244]

This was a day on which 'all laws were abrogated'; it was 'un jour libre', during the course of which 'on peut faire tout ce que l'on veut sans frisson être repris ou punir' (*odwira nwonakwasie* 17 December 1871).[245] European eyewitnesses censoriously recorded the observable consequences, but, fortunately, in a highly informative, at times almost a predictably prurient, wealth of detail. On the *odwira nwonakwasie* 7 September 1817,

the King [Osei Tutu Kwame] ordered a large quantity of rum to be poured into brass pans, in various parts of the town; the crowd pressing around, and drinking like hogs; freemen and slaves, women and children, striking, kicking, and trampling each other under foot, pushed head foremost into the pans, and spilling much more than they drank. In less than an hour, excepting the principal men, not a sober person was to be seen, parties of four reeling and rolling under the weight of another, whom they affected to be carrying home; strings of women covered with red paint, hand in hand, falling down like rows of cards; the commonest mechanics and slaves furiously declaiming on state palavers; the most discordant music, the most obscene songs, children of both sexes prostrate in insensibility. All wore their handsomest cloths, which they trailed after them to a great length, in a drunken emulation of extravagance and dirtiness.[246]

And nearly thirty years later, in a torrential downpour on the *odwira nwonakwasie* 15 September 1844:

Tens of thousands were in a state of drunkenness, some shouting and singing, others drumming and dancing. Here lay persons of both sexes wallowing in the rain, so far overcome by rum as to be unable to reel home ... Then again, an intoxicated captain, astride, upon the shoulders of his staggering slave attempted to reach his home, but from appearance would not do this in any reasonable time, as both slave and master occasionally came to the ground.[247]

In 1870, the captive Basel missionaries were informed that no less than 400 very large pots of palm wine had been set out in the Kumase streets, on the orders of the *Asantehene* Kofi Kakari, for anyone to drink from freely during the *odwira nwonakwasie* of that year.[248]

In this drunken rout, virtually all ascribed roles were overturned or reversed. Office holders were scurrilously lampooned in song and speech, and their characters and behavioural idiosyncrasies were subjected to criticism through mimicry, pointed exaggeration for comic effect, parodic wordplay and a host of other devices. The *nkoa* gave vent to their feelings about individuals, and loudly proclaimed their views on laws, policies, customs and the rest. Tradition recalls and celebrates the names of persons who were especially skilled in this form of criticism. Thus, the *akoa* Kwame Tua – a member of the *asokwafɔɔ* (hornblowers), who subsequently became the Kumase *Gyaasewahene* under the British (1901–6) – is still remembered for his satirizing of the foibles of office holders in music and song.[249] Similarly, the *akoa* Kwabena Dwetewa of the royal *nsenieɛfoɔ* (court criers) was a noted musician and singer in the same vein in the reigns of the *Asantehenes* Kwaku Dua Panin and Kofi Kakari.[250] At this time, moreover, there occurred the most intimately direct overturning of received social (and gender) roles, for 'each sex abandons itself to its passions, and adultery is sanctioned' – a mode of behaviour that was normally actionable in law.[251] However, at bottom all of this was a species of licensed or contained anarchy that was at once sanctioned and arbitrated by the state. In short, and in common with analogous events in other societies, these reversals of received order constituted a form of ritualized rebellion.[252] Viewed ideologically, it might be said that all of this indiscriminate disorder contained within itself the prediction of its own closure or finitude in time. Its promiscuous reformulations were the simulation rather than the creation of a new order.[253]

Thus, even in the anarchic course of the day's transactional progress, the latitude of expression permitted on *odwira nwonakwasie* was constrained by firmly demarcated and very well-understood boundaries. These were most apparent, perhaps, in the area of sexual licence and in direct relation to the person of the *Asantehene* himself. The wives of an *Asantehene* were kept in close seclusion in that part of the palace named *hiaa* (syn. *hiawa*: women's quarters). They were supervised by eunuchs and by pre-pubescent boys, and the customary restrictions placed upon adult males with regard to contact with these women even extended, as has been seen, to looking upon them during their infrequent perambulations beyond the palace walls. They were kept in the condition of *kyɛŋkyɛsɛm* ('ruled over with severity'), and numbers of them, neglected or otherwise set aside by the *Asantehene*, were privately but widely referred to as being *kyɛansofɔɔ* ('those without a share'). A tradition recounts that, on one occasion, no less than sixty such wives – trapped in their status, but rendered miserable by sustained neglect – committed mass suicide by drowning themselves in the Nsuben river at a site adjacent to *hiaa* and afterwards referred to as *omeneduosia* ('the swallower of sixty': der. *mene*: to swallow, devour + *aduosia*: sixty).[254] Whatever the veracity of this account, there can be no doubt that the wives of an *Asantehene* led narrowly constricted and relentlessly monitored lives. Moreover, it was universally understood that no abeyance or relaxation of this regime was ever permitted, even during the generalized licence that marked the *odwira nwonakwasie*. The following is a vernacular account that reflects this popular understanding (and that was allegedly furnished by refugee slaves among others).

Very soon the whole of Kumase [on *odwira nwonakwasie*] was filled with drunken people, most conspicuous among them young women who could be seen lying helpless in the streets with no one but bad young men to care for them ... It was a licentious day when no one incriminated anybody, for the law was temporarily suspended that day; but in the approaches to the King's harem [*hiaa*], discipline and law were still in force. However drunk a young man might be, he would never forget himself and miss his way to the most dangerous quarters in the capital, where dwelt the King's harem. It often happened that most of these wives were drunk on that day too, and the young ones among them became so wild that they could hardly control themselves. They would start to kick at the main gate to force it open; failing that they would be tapping at any other available gate, trying to get out. But all around, the eunuchs were nearby to push them back into their 'cells'.[255]

In the afternoon of *odwira nwonakwasie*, the *Asantehene* and his retinue returned the short distance from Bantama to Kumase. They bore with them the skulls from the *baamu*. Chapman remarked on *odwira nwonakwasie* 3 September 1843,

In passing along the Bantama road we saw several Chieftains with their attendants who had been to Bantama. They had with them the trophies of victories gained by the Ashantis, over their enemies. Many of the people were carrying in their hands, the skulls of Chiefs slain in battle, and as with naked knives they ran to, and fro, with every expression of men in a state of frenzy, they insultingly taunted these senseless relics, and spoke with the most bitter sarcasm of their present humbled state. One of the Chiefs had with him the skull of the unfortunate Sir C. McCarthy [British Governor: killed in battle at Asamankow in 1824]. This is preserved with great care, and is not exposed as are the heads of African Chieftains.[256]

On *odwira nwonakwasie* 17 December 1871, it took nearly two hours for this procession from Bantama to re-enter Kumase.[257] Some office holders were on foot, others were in palanquins, and 'ils étaient tous, plus ou moins ivre – ainsi que leur suite'.[258] The *adumfoɔ* themselves – 'cet affreux spectacle' – danced with violent, possessed gestures, all the while abusing and extravagantly simulating the eating of portions of their dismembered victim of the morning, while the enemy skulls were all borne aloft in brass basins by the Bantama *barimfoɔ*.[259]

The *Asantehene* then made a circuit of his capital, during the course of which 'his presence in every quarter was the signal for an increasing confusion and riot'.[260] Occasionally, he dismounted from his palanquin and danced – a sign, as in other contexts, of his personal approbation of the proceedings – amidst 'the most tremendous roar of barbaric musical instruments'.[261] According to eyewitness report, the climax of these public proceedings occurred at about five in the afternoon, when the skulls from Bantama were formally paraded throughout Kumase. (Bowdich, alone among our sources, very puzzlingly and seemingly mistakenly assigned the display of these relics to *fomemene* rather than *nwonakwasie*)[262]. Some European observers were clearly much alarmed by what they saw as the extravagantly anarchic and threatening crescendo of this particular passage of the day's events. On *odwira nwonakwasie* 15 September 1844,

The scene at this moment was of an altogether indescribable character. These valued relics [the skulls] were borne by men wrought up to a state of great excitement by the large quantity of rum drunk during the day, and now that they were entrusted with these trophies, every feeling of their savage nation seemed enflamed. Holding high in the air the skulls of the vanquished, and flourishing their long and bloody knives, a deafening shout broke forth accompanied by the most bitter sarcasm. Occasionally, the multitude made a pause, in order to perform some ceremony of a superstitious character. While those whose business it was to attend to these ceremonies were performing their part, the wild and seemingly furious multitude, were with mad gestures rushing to and fro amidst the encouraging plaudits of the bystanders, both male and female. It would not have required any very great stretch of the imagination, for a person to have thought himself suddenly removed from earth, and for the time being placed among several thousand demons.[263]

This was indeed a deliberately structured epiphany, and one that carried a potent burden of meanings and implications.

The public parading of the enemy skulls from Bantama was an exercise in didactic exposition. The insult directed towards them, and the rituals that punctuated their progress, were techniques of pedagogic instruction. In effect, the *adumfoɔ* and *barimfoɔ* repeatedly halted along their route to identify each skull, to address it insultingly with the formulaic preamble *wo (ɔ)se, wo ne!* ('your father, your mother!', with the imprecative and dismissive sense of 'who were they?': der. (ɔ)*se*: a father, but of someone other than the speaker + *ɛna*: a mother), then to recite its history and its heinous crimes against Asante, and finally to describe the precise circumstances in which it had been severed from its body and brought to Bantama.[264] The paraded skulls of major criminals of Asante origin were treated in a like manner.[265] This was a history lesson, iterated and reprised in all of its wealth of circumstantial detail, and delivered before an audience that, by this time on *odwira nwonakwasie*, was in an extremely receptive and susceptible emotional condition ('every feeling of their savage nation seemed enflamed'). The performative milieu conduced to a passionate and self-reinforcing mass identification with a powerful narrative that was, in its essentials and its thrust, nothing less than an unrelenting paean to the ideological rectitude, power and authority of the Asante state.

A military review or display seems to have taken place at the same time as, or shortly after, the skulls were paraded. That this feature is not directly identified in all eyewitness accounts may simply be testimony to the extremes of disordered confusion prevailing at this juncture of the proceedings. 'Towards evening the populace grew sober again', remarked Bowdich of *odwira nwonakwasie* 7 September 1817, and, he added somewhat ambiguously, 'the strange caboceers [the visiting office holders] displayed their equipages in every direction.'[266] But a year previously, on *odwira nwonakwasie* 25 August 1816, the Dutch agent Huydecoper unequivocally observed that the *Asantehene* Osei Tutu Kwame 'held military parades and tested the capabilities of his officers'.[267] Freeman furnished the most suggestively informative account of the matter. 'The King, at the head of his troops, dressed in an ancient native war-costume, with sword and shield, commands in a sham-fight, representing the defence of the throne, or national stool [the *sika dwa kofi*] against an invading enemy.'[268] This too was a didactic performance. It was designed to illustrate the power and triumphant success of the Asante state by means of a highly theatrical re-enactment – including as symbolic props the appropriately archaic weapons of sword (*afena, afoa*) and shield (*ɔkyɛm*) – of its own heroic origins in warfare.[269] This was not the only mnemonic that deployed such techniques. Once a year, for example, the *Asantehene* commemorated the specificity of the economic order that had existed prior to the establishment of crop agriculture, and in so doing he consciously drew attention to history, to continuity and to progress. The device in this case was a symbolic animal hunt in the environs of Kumase, presided over by the *Asantehene* in person. Generally, no game was caught, for this episode was understood as being, in performative terms, 'a mere form in accordance with an ancient custom'.[270]

Some time towards the close of the public exhibition of the relics from the Bantama *baamu*, the *Asantehene* withdrew and retired into the palace. Once inside the complex of buildings, the *Asantehene* seated himself in the *bampanase* or *pramakɛsɛɛsɔ* ('the great court'). It was to there that the *odwira sumaŋ* was now brought and placed before him. The *odwira* itself, it should be noted, was a *sumaŋ* rather than an *ɔbosom*, albeit one of quite unparalleled power.[271] As a *sumaŋ* it was a specifically historical object. Physical possession of it guaranteed a continuity of access to its powers through time. That is, it was fixed in objectification and by ownership in a way that was impossible with the (wilful, evanescent, unilateral) powers inhering in the *abosom*. Its precise beginnings in time and place were vaguely mysterious, but, very significantly, it was understood to have originated at the time of the creation of the state, and 'in some place' far from or beyond the geographical confines of Asante culture. Traditions variously assert that it came from the northern hinterland of Asante, or from Akyem to the south.[272] The vital point is that it was a *historical* object that came from the outside – that is, from beyond the Asante world. As ideology, as a firm determination or focus of cultural address, it is crucially significant that the *odwira suman* was construed in this manner. First, its temporal 'discovery' and earliest articulation (the plumbing of its 'secret' powers) were attributed to the person of the first *Asantehene* Osei Tutu. Second, it might only be activated in its supernatural aspect by worship and offerings, and successive *Asantehenes* were alone understood to be individually qualified to initiate any enabling measures with respect to it. That is to say, its domestication into Asante culture together with its continued historical deployment were conceptualized as functions of an individuated royal power.[273]

The *odwira suman* was contained in a brass-bound, wooden chest. Its chief physical component was a set of massive lyrate horns belonging to *ɔtrommo* or the Bongo antelope (*Boocercus euryceros*). The *ɔtrommo* was a mainly nocturnal animal, with very elusive habits, a cry like a human being, and a dramatically distinctive, and obviously significant, red or chestnut hide barred with clearly demarcated white stripes and giving way to black underparts. Apart from being a kaleidoscopic embodiment of the three primary colour signifiers in Asante thought, the *ɔtrommo* had a further striking characteristic. It possessed very enlarged and diffused sebaceous glands, and these generated pigment such that, when it rained, the *ɔtrommo* appeared to bleed. Thus, the *ɔtrommo* – phenomenologically an inoffensive antelope – was ontologically understood by the Asante to be possessed of the most powerfully dangerous *sasa* ('spirit') of any creature in the wild. Tradition drew parallels between the *Asantehene* and the *ɔtrommo* in terms of their styles – unheeding, detached, lordly, potent, dangerous – of authority and power. Above all, the two proposed a comparable certainty of stillness and authoritative presence. In the 1920s, Cardinall inadvertently caught something of the Asante reading of the matter in a simple hunting account.

All the natives laugh when one tells them that white men have never killed one of these animals [*ɔtrommo*]. They say that it is the easiest animal of all to hunt. They are usually in groups of four or five, and even as many as twelve ... They are not shy and will not make off even after a shot has been fired ... It is only because of their 'magic' [*sasa*], which inspires respect, that they have not been exterminated, for very few men will dare to kill more than three, and few dare kill any.[274]

The *Asantehene*, smeared red and clad in *kyɛŋkyɛŋ* (barkcloth: *Antiaris spp.*), now placed new-season yams on the *odwira suman*. The use of barkcloth was yet another archaism that made reference to the Asante past. In its nineteenth-century employment by the *Asantehene* it connoted not merely a contrived poverty, but also a sense of humility with regard to the successful negotiation of past time (history).[275] In the guise and attitude of a supplicant, the reigning *Asantehene* then requested the mediation of the *odwira suman* in securing assistance from the ancestors and the *abosom* in overcoming the state's enemies and all other troubling or challenging contingencies. The enemy skulls from Bantama were now carried in and set before the *Asantehene*. They were painted in bands of red, and garlanded with strongly smelling herbs (*εme, ɔnunum*: Bowdich said that these resembled thyme) in order to ward off any residue of evil intent on the part of the *asamanfoɔ*, and to placate them.[276] In token of *historical* triumph, the reigning *Asantehene*, representing here the collective individuation of all *Asantehenes*, placed his left foot on each of the skulls in turn.[277] He addressed each one individually, reminding it of the particular, individual *Asantehene* who had consigned it to a permanent residence at Bantama, offering a portion of new yam to its 'ghost', and all the while repeating his imprecation that future foes might expect to be reduced to the same abject condition.

The ritual observance that closed the *odwira nwonakwasie* took place in the night, in circumstances of prohibitive secrecy, and it is consequently difficult to reconstruct in any great historical, rather than ethnographic, detail. It would appear that the *Asantehene* proceeded to that point (*ŋkwantanaŋ*) where the road to Cape Coast crossed the marshy ground formed by the Nsuben river on the southern edge of Kumase. Some accounts imply alternative venues. But, always and of necessity, all such locations were sited on the outskirts of the capital.[278] Reports of *odwira nwonakwasie* 17 December 1871 and *odwira nwonakwasie* 25 August 1872 suggest, somewhat circumstantially, that the enemy skulls were borne in procession to the Nsuben. This would appear to have been the case, although traditional accounts (and Asante informants) are, most understandably, reticent on the precise structuration and details of this crucial ritual passage.[279] Certainly, the *Asantehene* went to the Nsuben, or any alternatively chosen location, accompanied by *adumfoɔ* bearing new yams smeared red and black, and by a guard of seven selected *atumtufoɔ* (gun-bearers).

At the designated place, a royal *ɔkyeame* directly addressed and summoned a personage called *awo*. Informants recounted to Rattray and to Fortes that *awo* was a hermaphrodite, and that she/he was the first sacrificial oblation ever made to the earth (*asase yaa*) to make 'her' fruitful and productive.[280] This is a complex and obscure matter, and it is particularly resistant to definitive explication. The following possibilities may be adduced. The noun *awo* means birth, and by extension it embraces ideas of descent, genealogy and common associative kinship. In this last formulation, it is sometimes rendered and understood in terms of 'race', i.e. in direct relation to belonging in the *Asantemaŋ* (or, colloquially, to the description of the concept of 'Asante-ness'). In some traditions and accounts the *odwira* in general is synonymously termed *apafram*. No satisfactory etymology of this word exists, and none has been produced by persistent questioning. However, the word *apafram* is *conceptually* understood as making reference to the *nature* of being Asante (collective *sunsum* in the understanding of the *Asantemaŋ*).[281] Thus, the invocation of *awo* (significantly, embodying both genders) may have been a focused meditation on and mnemonic of the spiritual quiddity and inclusiveness, proposing an equivalent exclusiveness, of actually *being* Asante. However, a linguistic affinity is also postulated as existing between the nouns *awo* and *owu* (death), whatever the opacity of the actual grammatical link between them.[282] In terms of thought, as has been severally demonstrated, a contrast was made between the agency of accumulation in all of its forms (i.e. 'birth') and the entropic idea of societal collapse (i.e. 'death'); 'the true contrast of death', as Danquah acutely remarked of the Akan, 'is birth, not life'.[283] We can take this no further than to note that at this most quintessential and critical juncture in time (agricultural, calendrical), the polarity of birth/death was rendered in starkly explicit expression.

The entity summoned as *awo* 'replied' or affirmed its presence, and the *ɔkyeame* then addressed the *asamaŋfoɔ* of all of the deceased foes (foreign and indigenous) of Asante. He announced the celebration of the *odwira*, asked the *asamaŋfoɔ* to reconcile themselves to their assigned status, requested them to come and eat of the offering of new yam, and asked that all future enemies might suffer the same fate as themselves in the interests of the preservation and progress of Asante. The new yams were then thrown towards the *asamaŋfoɔ* – that is, ejected from the discourse of culture across the boundary (*kurotia*) into the discourse of the (super)natural – while the gun-bearers fired a volley (*odwira tuo*), at once celebratory and valedictory, into the air. Ethnographic accounts record that everyone concerned now ran homeward in total silence, and that anyone who stumbled or fell was killed by the *adumfoɔ* on the spot. In fact, the prohibition seems to have been even more extensive; reports from the 1870s assert that complete silence was maintained throughout the entire ritual, and that death was the automatic penalty for any form of coughing, yawning, spitting, sneezing, and any and all other kinds of involuntary noises.[284] This was a heightened but recognizable version of the identification of the *Asantehene* with the awesome powers of death and night. When the

Asantehene went abroad in Kumase at night, as often happened, his progress signalled his unique status.[285] He proclaimed thereby his sovereign ability to traffic with death, to make an ally of it, and so to underline both his proprietary and protective roles in the definition and defence of culture. Kumase, it was averred, 'belonged' to the *Asantehene* by right, and this was most pointedly the case at night. In the hazardous hours between sunset and sunrise, the *Asantehene* took full and sole (human) possession of his domain.

The king seldom went out in the afternoon except when attending the funeral of a prominent person, or when performing the annual purification ceremony of *odwira*. He normally went out in the dead of night to oversee his city. He was then accompanied by a host of people, but all [of these] were forbidden to speak or even to cough. There was a deadly silence. The only noise to be heard was that of the king's sandals, which he moved very gently. He was announced by a torch, but while he was still a long distance off the rapacious, towering, brawny *asomfo* [servants] preceding him pounced on anyone who tried to flee when they saw the light. If such persons were unable to give a reasonable explanation for being abroad, they ceased to be counted among the living that very night. It was then said the following morning that such and such a person was missing. Thus, in the days of the supremacy of the state, it was rare for anyone to venture out at night in Kumase. If one was found [by the king] wandering at night, investigations took place. The onus of explaining [where one had been] was always on the wanderer. Even if the explanation was found reasonable, the wanderer was spared but fined. Thus many people were afraid of living in Kumase.[286]

The rite just described was the culminating event on the climactic day in *odwira*. However we construe the resistant obscurities – in, for example, the symbolism of *awo* and *owu* – there can be no doubt at all that, in Asante thought, this was the irreducible moment in time at which the past and the future faced one another. Let us reflect upon the following points. The performative and representational structure that framed this nocturnal encounter was entirely consonant with perceptions and ideas that have been discussed throughout. The 'meeting' took place in silence and at night. It was immensely dangerous by definition and so it precluded the presence of all but the *Asantehene* and a select retinue of attendants. It always occurred at some point on the outskirts of the Asante capital; that is, in the boundary zone of *kurotia*. The *asamanfoɔ* and *awo*, and beyond them, in shadowy presence, the ancestors and the *abosom*, were somewhere 'out there' in nature. They were coaxed, besought and summoned to direct intercourse or dialogue with the presently living embodiment(s) of culture. And at the end, new season yam was thrown to and at them – literally ejected from one realm into the other. It is notable that even with the preparation for the encounter with these powers that had been engendered in a chaotic liminality (that eerily resembled their own unpredictable modes of being), and with the added surety guaranteed by the mediation of the *odwira sumaŋ*, this 'meeting' was not prolonged one instant beyond absolute necessity. Then, the human participants quite literally ran away from it, leaving nothing of their selfhood – accoutrements, discharges, even utterances – behind. With the solitary exception of the *Asantehene*, those who fell down or otherwise transgressed were immediately killed, as if in tacit acknowledgement of the fact that they had in some way been claimed by that other realm that lay beyond the boundary.[287]

The nocturnal ritual was the quintessential moment, but motifs and componential elements of belief played a significant role during all of the *odwira nwonakwasie*. These fluctuated in their explicit centrality or implicit contingency across the transactional sequence, but they were ubiquitous throughout. It is notable, and should be emphasized, that these features were hardly articulated, if at all, through the medium of *akɔmfoɔ*. That is, they were not the representational and/or expressive properties of an autonomous structuration of belief. They were marked by and compromised in knowledge, and were thoroughly mired in ideology and historicism. Indeed, in their mode of articulation they are arguably to be identified most closely with that particular construction of belief that is a historically grounded affirmation or intellectual assent to an idea or ideas. In this sense, Asante practice can be seen as having much in common with that category of postulates that frame sense statements as being (*A*) accepted as true without themselves having proofs given for them, and (*B*) then used to derive other statements that form a coherent system of analysis.[288] This neither calls into question any alternate conceptualizations of belief, nor does it seek to impugn the motivation of the individual by levelling charges of false consciousness.

In point of fact, the interrogation of individual consciences or sensibilities is not at issue here. It is quite beside the point. Any given *Asantehene*, to take the leading example, may have invested degrees of personal belief – in the commonsensical use of the term – in what he was centrally engaged in practising. Equally, any given *Asantehene* may have subscribed to degrees of personal unbelief in ritual action: the case of the *Asantehene* Mensa Bonsu has already been discussed in terms of these parameters. These are interesting issues without doubt, but in truth they frame questions of the second order. As missionaries found to their discomfiture, the ideological articulation of postulates (always and unremittingly referenced to a historical framework) took an absolute priority and precedence over degrees of individual belief or unbelief. In the framing of the text of ideological discourse during the pivotal day of *nwonakwasie*, and throughout all of *odwira*, *A* (above) was of a clear and undoubted significance (and, in all probability, it was very generally subscribed to), but *B* was intentionally privileged over it.

A itself, whatever its resonance for the individual in the idiomatic rhetoric usually called religious belief, was simply assumed and was thereby assigned to and characterized by latency. In terms of an individual Asante participant, belief statements might possess veracity on their own terms, but only at the atomized and reductionist level of the isolated self. Sensibility did not translate to social efficacy, for belief statements *qua* themselves sustained no expressive force beyond the hermetic circularity of conscience. That is, the assertion that in Asante beliefs were *believed* is both unquestionably, if variably, valid, and a null explanation. Any mobilization from inertness to dynamism – a necessary translation *into* ideology – had to be articulated by external agency. But in Asante, as has been seen, there existed no appropriately evolved theological framework that might essay this task; and any effort at postulating a transcendental reading of history in terms alternative to material perception foundered on the lack of any distinction of kind between lived existence and the afterlife. Even the *abonsamkɔmfoɔ*, it should be recalled, were constrained in their critical role to structure belief in terms of a simulation or mimicry of the tenets of the state's construction of ideology and reading of history. Articulation was the property of the state, and in its hermeneutics it dissolved all of the possible qualifying distinctions between belief and knowledge, and moved them from the realm of the individual to that of the social by dint of unchallenged arrogation. The resulting structuration was a formulation of ideological reading that precluded any systemic interrogation, and that promulgated a sovereign master text that described all historical experience by circumscribing it. Anyone on the margin of this was simply bereft of usable weapons, while the state's monopoly over such armaments was endlessly displayed, affirmed and refurbished – quintessentially in the course of such recurrent calendrical periodicities as the *odwira nwonakwasie*.[289]

Throughout the *odwira nwonakwasie* the *Asantehene* evidently and without respite assumed the crucial enabling and mediating roles. He was the centre and focus of the action, the performative trope through whom the sequence of events unfolded as coherent narrative. He was the device of an emplotment that sustained an explicative pedagogy in which he was also (and simultaneously) the main character.[290] Prominent among the most significant elements of belief and knowledge that he engaged with in the course of the day were emblematic representations from, and also metaphors for, the state's historic past. Note that the *asamaɲfoɔ* who were implicated in articulation were not *simply* a category or class of statements in belief. Whatever the specificity of their otherworldly projection in belief, they were precisely identified as figurations in and of a historical time, tangibly evidenced by their skulls, and thus very clearly derived as properties from the structuration of knowledge. The *asamaɲfoɔ* involved were historical personifications, either of the Asante state (deceased

Asantehenes), or of subversion of the state's project in time (political, social and spiritual enemies). The ritual observances practised on *odwira nwonakwasie* paved the way for and 'authored' the rehearsal of a textual discourse that united the two groups in a public recitation of historical narrativity. At the level of ideology – of the projection of rectitude – the category of enemies only existed dialectically as binary, dependent 'creations' of the category of *Asantehenes*.[291]

The single most important symbolic artefact deployed on *odwira nwonakwasie* was the *odwira suman*. This too can be interpreted as a most potent determination of belief by ideological articulation. To take the leading instance, the power and dissemination of the very concept of *sasa* (as in *ɔtrommo*) surely derived as a sub-text from the master reading of the historical experience of culture in nature. At this level of belief, *sasa* existed as an ontological resolution to areas of anxious unknowing in culture (including religion and psychology, but again this is beside the point). The *odwira suman* was a discrete mobilization of description, in historical time and for historical ends. After all, it could only be articulated by the *Asantehene*, and this was done on behalf of the state's ideological project. That this articulation encompassed a protective superordination in relation to society, together with the annual renewal and reinforcement of affective subscription to a particular descriptive item, is an important variable – but only a dependent one. Other dependent variables are more easily stated. Thus, the *asamanfoɔ* of ordinary Asante citizens might only be commemorated once the *Asantehene* had taken the initiative, and had started to enact the indispensable part of primary interlocutor. The temporal boundaries that framed appropriate commemoration (that is, since the celebration of the preceding *odwira*) were defined by the state, and the conditions that guaranteed access to departed kin and to public remembrance of them were similarly circumscribed.[292]

Much of the *odwira nwonakwasie* was devoted to situating present reality in past perspective and in future projection. Unremitting attention was paid to explicating and reinforcing the essential rectitude of the present, and to validating that dispensation within an organic continuum that seamlessly united it with the past and the future. The Asante experience of history was celebrated and affirmed in relation to the ascendant trajectory of the state and its works. Most explicitly, these works were about military power and expansion; and we have seen how the emotions were recruited to an identification with this theme. If the resulting mix was 'nationalism', then the term requires very specific qualification, and in the Gramscian sense. It was not in the slightest sense a given, but a unilateral structuration of consent and coercion. Identification with the *Asanteman* or 'nation', like identification with a self-sustaining autonomy of belief, was not exactly false consciousness. Rather, it was a form of displaced consciousness. Both objects of identification were enjoined. But both were fully accessible only via the channels of structuration and mediation interposed by the state. These channels were ideological prisms, by means of which epistemological distinctions were severely refracted. Structured and mediated experience enclosed speculation in consent and coercion, and all were made to serve one another in an encompassing hermeneutical design.

The effectiveness of all of this cannot be in doubt. Its structuration was such that the entire spectrum of possible dysfunctions, from public disorder to private conscience, was collapsed in on itself. As previously noted, Asante experienced neither disruptive social insurrection nor its chiliastic counterpart. Yet the eighteenth and nineteenth centuries were marked by highly explicit economic and political inequities, or by the existence of objectively situated Classes *in* Themselves. Simply, appeals to national identity or to communal belief would not have met this case. It necessitated a highly coherent structuration of the most intense and subtle kind. The overall success of this project may be gauged by a basic consideration. On *nwonakwasie*, and throughout all of *odwira*, the fundamental human need to eat was ideologically formulated as being instituted, guaranteed, controlled and renewed by the state. That is, the place of food itself in the history of Asante consciousness was subjected to articulation by the state.

Transacting *odwira* 3: *nkyidwo* to *afe*

nkyidwo *(20: Monday) to* monoyawo *(23: Thursday)*

On *odwira nkyidwo* relative calm returned to the streets of Kumase. A start was now made on the agenda of state business; thus, the *odwira nkyidwo* 8 September 1817 was entirely and fully 'occupied in state palavers'.[293] The *Asantemaŋhyiamu* met together, assented to decisions, deliberated on the future, and heard office holders 'report the events of the year in the parts under their jurisdiction'.[294]

By far the greater part of this busy and condensed schedule was taken up with implementation of the juridical machinery of political control. Indeed, this occupied much time throughout the remaining days of the *odwira*. Constituted as the supreme court of sentencing and appeal, the state arbitrated power, and made adjustments in the promotion and demotion of its own personnel. These procedures were the culmination of long deliberations, and of instrumental policy decisions that had been arrived at in the period since the closure of the previous *odwira*. As Bowdich observed,

If an Ashantee chief has offended or if his fidelity be suspected, he is seldom accused or punished until the Yam Custom, which they are all compelled to attend, even from the most remote provinces, frequently unconscious and always uncertain of what may be laid to their charge.[295]

Dossiers of charges were sedulously amassed or otherwise contrived. Freeman noted,

It often happens that from the system of Espionage which extends from the Palace to all parts of the country, and from complaints made to the supreme court of appeal, that some of the secondary and other subordinate Chiefs, who have come up from the Provinces [for *odwira*] fall into disgrace and never return to their homes.[296]

From *nkyidwo* onwards, such office holders were arraigned and tried. Thus, immediately prior to the *odwira* of 1845, the *Mamponhene* Abonyawa Kwadwo was murdered by his own subjects. Those suspected absented themselves from the Kumase *odwira* of that year, despite the *Asantehene* Kwaku Dua Panin's 'desire and expectation' that they attend. In the following year, they were again summoned to *odwira*, and this time Kwaku Dua Panin disarmed them by offering reassurances and unspecified inducements through an *ɔkyeame*. Once in Kumase, they were immediately arrested and charged. In a hearing lasting several hours, they pleaded mitigating circumstances in that the assassinated Abonyawa Kwadwo had been an adulterer, and generally *nɛ subaŋ nye* ('a bad character'). This defence failed. Twelve Mampon office holders and *akyeame* were found guilty of murdering their superior as charged, and were executed. In addition to these ringleaders, numbers of other *Mamponfoɔ* were beaten and imprisoned, and those not implicated were released.[297] Similarly, during the *odwira* of 1872, in the days prior to *kurufie* (3: Friday) 20 September, no less than six provincial office holders from Asante Akyem were convicted *en masse* of an unspecified crime, and summarily executed together.[298]

Charges of incompetence or dereliction in the service of the state were also heard during *odwira*. An instructive if complex instance of this occurred during the reign of the *Asantehene* Osei Tutu Kwame. In 1815, the *Anantahene* Apea Dankwa was in overall command of the field army that had been charged with the military reoccupation of Fante. His second in command was the *ɔheneba* Bariki, an elderly son of the *Asantehene* Opoku Ware, and possibly the *Akyinakuromhene*. Attached contingents were commanded by the *Nkonŋwasoafoɔhene* Yaw Kokroko (Dabanka), and by Amankwa Abinowa of the Kumase Ankobea *fekuo*.[299] In late 1815 or early 1816, Apea Dankwa died while still in the field, and he was immediately succeeded in his office and command by his brother Apea Nyanyo (whose accumulated wealth has already been discussed). Disputes over precedence and spoils broke out among the generals, and partisan quarrelling demoralized their troops.[300] Yaw Kokroko disengaged and returned to Kumase on 14 August 1816; the *ɔheneba* Bariki similarly broke camp and re-entered the capital, but evidently 'without leave' of the *Asantehene*.[301] During the *odwira* of 1816, for the space of nine hours on *nkyikwasie* (26: Sunday) 1 September, the *ɔheneba* Bariki was prosecuted for desertion and aggravated disobedience. At least six witnesses were called, and he was 'execrated on all sides'.[302] He was additionally charged with having publicly complained to witnesses of the 'procrastinations and labours' of the campaign in Fante, and of having stated that,

as the King had declared when he invaded Fantee in person [in 1807], that he would have the head of every Fantee caboceer, and yet returned with a part only; so he [Bariki] could not be expected to forego the enjoyment of the riches and luxuries of his home, until every revolter was killed.[303]

This, trumped up or not, was *lèse-majesté*. On *kurudwo* (27: Monday) 2 September, the *ɔheneba* Bariki was found guilty as charged, and was stripped of his office, slaves and property. After the end of *odwira*, on *monodwo* (41: Monday) 28 October, he was appointed 'the overseer of a small river', but subsequently committed suicide.[304] The acting *Anantahene* Apea Nyanyo, who re-entered Kumase with Amankwa Abinowa on 3 March 1817, was also tried for dereliction and cowardice in the face of the enemy, and was convicted and disgraced.[305]

The hearings that took place during *odwira* clearly served as a barometer of intra-elite power and status. Individuals rose and fell. The very act of arraignment signified that a given office holder had become politically isolated, or had antagonized a group of his peers to the point where, at the very least, they were prepared to testify against him. Forensic arguments over guilt or innocence, and the nature of the sentence imposed in cases that ended in conviction, revealed much to participants about shifts in enmities and loyalties, changes in alignment in the membership of elite cohorts, and adjustments in the relative authority of the *Asantehene*. It needs to be emphasized, however, that all of this took place *within* the state itself.

The role of the *Asantehene* evidences the distinction being made between intra-elite conflict *within* the state, and the presentation of the state itself to those *without* membership in it. An *Asantehene*, as has been seen, was the unchallenged embodiment of the state in its externalized public (re)presentation of itself. But *within* the state apparatus, he was subject to a number of the constraints imposed upon all political actors. An *Asantehene* – and particularly one who was isolated, or who had a fragile personal constituency – could by no means always carry the opinion of the court. For example, during the *odwira* of 1871, in the days prior to *nwonafie* (31: Friday) 29 December, two major cases were heard and judged before the court. The first, which involved grave but unspecified charges, had as its protagonists the *Asantehene* Kofi Kakari himself and an unnamed office holder. Kofi Kakari was awarded judgement by the court, and was smeared in white clay (*hyire*) in token of his acquittal and innocence. The second was a case in which the *ɔheneba* Owusu Ntobi, a son of the *Asantehene* Osei Tutu Kwame, had been charged with the capital offence of committing incest with two of his uterine sisters. Judgement was given against him. The *Asantehene* Kofi Kakari argued for a sentence of internal exile rather than death (in some ways a more severe condemnation). Although the final outcome is unrecorded, it is known that the court adamantly opposed the *Asantehene*, refused to countenance his recommendation, and urged execution on the grounds that it was the penalty stringently mandated and prescribed in law for such cases.[306] Of course, all such proceedings took place *in camera*, and were an intra-elite affair. The external (re)presentation of the ideology of state unity ordained that only final judgements were promulgated in public.[307]

On *odwira kurubena* (21: Tuesday) or *odwira kwawukuo* (22: Wednesday), there took place the culmination of a key ritual connected with the reigning *Asantehene's ntɔrɔ*. Temporal variation was determined by the *ntɔrɔ* affiliation of the incumbent *Asantehene*. That is, *kurubena* (and arithmetically every Tuesday) was the observance day of the *Bosommuru ntɔrɔ*, and *kwawukuo* (and arithmetically every Wednesday) was the equivalent for the *Bosompra ntɔrɔ*. On *odwira nwonakwasie* (19: Sunday) or *odwira nkyidwo* (20: Monday), the reigning *Asantehene* ritually defiled his *ntɔrɔ* by participating in the killing of an *akyiwadeɛ* animal, just as he had done on *kwayawo*. He struck the beast thrice with the appropriate sword (*afena*) – *Bosommuru* or *Bosompra* – and the attendant *adumfoɔ* then butchered it. Then, on *odwira kurubena* (after *nwonakwasie*) or on *odwira kwawukuo* (after *nkyidwo*), defilement was ritually reversed by acts of propitiation and restorative purification. The appropriate *afena* was dipped in sheep's blood, and a ritualistic cleansing took place using white clay (*hyire*), herbs, and water from the riverain *atano* (and usually from the river Tano itself). The *Asantehene* completed the circle of these private rituals of defilement and purification by directly addressing the *afena* of his *ntɔrɔ*. He freely confessed to injuring it by defilement, offered it appropriate amends, and invoked the support of its restored and renewed power, as in the past, against all of the enemies of Asante. Throughout the three-day period of observance of this culminating liminal episode, which encompassed the transit through pollution back to purity, strict fasting remained obligatory upon everyone.[308]

fofie *(24: Friday)*

The transactions that dominated the *odwira fofie* were the wholesale ritualistic purification of people and significant objects, and the sanctioned eating of new-season yam. The day marked a decisive egress from the preceding period of chaotic liminality, and it witnessed the first clear steps in the integrative reconstitution of the cultural master text. From this day onward, the progress of *odwira* shifted from incline to anticline, as Asante moved purposefully towards the future that was represented by the next nine *adaduanan* cycles.

Before sunrise on the *odwira fofie*, office holders belonging to the *Oyoko Kɔkɔɔ abusua* and *Oyoko ne Dako abusua kɛsɛɛ* – 'more closely connected with the royal family than others, by a kind of tribal relationship' – proceeded to the Nsuben river to commence the purificatory rite. This was done piecemeal, and not in any state or formal procession. Office holders went,

accompanied by their respective families, and taking with them all their most valuable moveable household furniture, the family stool in particular, and a sheep, and a few Yams intended for the family New Yam feast of that day. Arrived at the rivulet, the head of the family sprinkles himself, and all the members of the family, and all he has brought with him with the sacred waters to cleanse and purify them from all evil taints which may have been contracted during the year.[309]

Sustained volleys of celebratory gunfire accompanied progress to and from the water.[310] Once these ablutions were concluded, the principal rite of purification was set in motion. The *Asantehene* and his household, and the great mass of office holders and their retinues, processed in state to the Nsuben.

This was a great public occasion. Thousands of cheering spectators lined the streets of Kumase, firing muskets and invoking 'long life and blessings on the head of their Sovereign'; on *odwira fofie* 22 December 1871, this progress took nearly three hours to pass one point, and some 50,000 people watched or followed it.[311] Everyone, the *Asantehene* included, was dressed in white to signify joy and purity of intent. Large numbers of sheep were carried in the procession; twenty of them on *odwira fofie* in 1817; 'about seventy' on *odwira fofie* 22 December 1871; and on *odwira fofie* 8 September 1843, no less than 176 were 'carried on the shoulders of the King's slaves'.[312] Prominently displayed on this occasion was 'fetish water, brought in bottles from distant springs'; on *odwira fofie* 20 September 1844, a number of 'bottles filled with water from the sacred "river Tandoe" [Tano] was carried by several boys'.[313] The river Tano, to reiterate, gave its name to, and was senior among, that category of *abosom* that was associated with water (*atano*).

The royal wives also took part in this procession. Some 250 of them were present on *odwira fofie* 22 December 1871, but 'the prohibition to look at them was again in force, for the men retired'; and on *odwira fofie* 8 September 1843, as the royal wives 'passed along the street, they were preceded by a company of armed eunuchs, who with naked swords drove away all the men'.[314] This was a clear indication of the restoration of customary norms. The *sika dwa kofi*, the blackened *Oyoko Kɔkɔɔ* ancestral stools, the *odwira sumaŋ*, the *Bosommuru* (or *Bosompra*) *afena*, numerous shrines, much regalia and all of the *Asantehene's* household effects were carried down to the Nsuben. Some of the paraphernalia – 'such as pictures, mirrors, dressing cases and other fancy boxes' – seemed exotically incongruous to European eyes. Thus, on *odwira fofie* 22 December 1871, the *Asantehene* Kofi Kakari's 'looking-glass, which is always carried with him, was on this occasion so large that two men could barely stand upright under it'. Another mirror on a stand was borne in this same procession, together with large numbers of objects in silver, including several magnificent silver teapots, 'crew stands' and a variety of champagne goblets.[315] A major purpose of this display was to impress onlookers with the wealth and power of the state. On this occasion, for instance, all of the gold ornaments that had been recast in preparation for the *odwira* were publicly displayed.

At the Nsuben, the *sika dwa kofi* was set upon the *hwedom tia* war chair ('drive back the enemy'). The *Asantehene* then sprinkled water over it in purification. All the while that the *Asantehene* was engaged in this, he uttered a formalized litany. This recitative passage was understood as a conversational dialogue or binary interaction between the living embodiment of the state's present and future (the *Asantehene*) and the *ur* symbolic embodiment of the history, authority and rectitude of the state's past (the *sika dwa kofi*). This interaction was framed with reference to issues of belief and identity, but these were subordinated to the primary intent and drive of the discourse. The unfolding of the text, supplicatory although not hieratic in origin, was an essential catechism. The *Asantehene* uttered, and the *sika dwa kofi* silently confirmed. The text itself linked past, present and future in an ideological charter. It rehearsed fundamentals in a sequence of voiced interrogations, and affirmed, non-verbal responses. It was a supreme instance of the structuration of latency, and of the enfolding of all concerns – as contingencies – within the state's historical project. The relevant sequence is recorded in a number of authoritative traditions, and it unfolded as follows:

1 an invocation that, through purification, the powers inhering symbolically in the *sika dwa kofi* be confirmed and renewed (*that is, that the rectitude of received historical order be affirmed and continued*);

2 a request that in any future military conflict the outcome should be the same as when Osei Tutu overcame the *Denkyirahene* Ntim Gyakari at Feyiase, and – in a recited sequence of names – as when he and subsequent *Asantehenes* overcame all of those whose skulls were preserved in the Bantama *baamu* (*that is, that the historic integrity and power of the state be affirmed and continued*);

3 an announcement that it is now *odwira*, and that 'the edges of the year have

come together', accompanied by a request for the survival and the prosperity of the *Asanteman* (*that is, a grateful acknowledgement for the past, and a plea for continuance*);

4 a request that women bear children (*that is, for the continuity of the* mmusua *and of Asante society through the birth and 'accumulation' of children*);

5 a request for abundant crop harvests (*that is, for the continuity of the social order through the 'accumulation' of food*);

6 a request that the forest might continue to yield game (*that is, for the maintenance of a symbiosis between culture and nature*);

7 a request that an abundance of gold be mined, and that 'I get some for the upkeep of my Kingship' (*that is, a recognition of the primacy of the accumulation of wealth in gold, and an affirmation that* sika *flows upwards as a property of received hierarchy, and that its possession by right is fundamental to state power*).[316]

All of the other objects and people present were then laved in ritual purification. The sheep too were dipped in the water, although very few were actually sacrificed at the Nsuben.[317] The ritual was completed by the offering of new yams, and the procession then returned to Kumase.

The King's fetish men walk first, with attendants holding basins of sacred water, which they sprinkle plentifully over the chiefs with branches, the more superstitious running to have a little poured on their heads, or even on their tongues... Three white lambs are led before him [the *Asantehene*], intended for sacrifice at his bed chamber.[318]

Bowdich, whose account is chronologically confused at this point, reported that on the day before the procession to the Nsuben – deductively, *monoyawo* (23: Thursday) – the *Asantehene* performed his 'annual ablutions' in the river Oda at 'Sarrasou' (Esereso).[319] The *Eseresohene* was himself *Oyoko*, and his village was 'blessed with a plentiful supply of excellent water'.[320] However, there is no other extant account of this (possibly) additional ceremony, although there is some evidence to suggest that the *odwira fofie* ritual might itself on occasion have taken place at Esereso, rather than at the point where the *akyeremade* ward abutted upon the Nsuben.[321]

When the procession had returned to the palace, 'contrary to usual custom, none but those [office holders] of the first rank are allowed to enter'; the *sika dwa kofi* and all of the other items were placed in the *patokromu* courtyard, and the palace doors were locked and guarded.[322] The entire palace precinct was itself then purified, using the blood of the sheep sanctified at the Nsuben. This was 'poured on the stools and door posts. All the doors, windows, and arcades of the palace, are plentifully besmeared with a mixture of eggs, and palm oil; as also the stools of the different tribes and families.'[323] New-season yams were again offered, and the *Asantehene* now finally broke his fast and ate some of the crop.

The eating of yams by the *Asantehene* was the signal for a generalized consumption. A drinking party (*sadwa*) was held throughout Kumase. At this time, observed Ramseyer in 1870, 'the street was ornamented with hundreds of vessels, and the mirth knew no bounds'.[324] The *Asantehene* personally bestowed gifts of cloth and trinkets, and a general exchange of presents, including yams, took place in token of the passing of *odwira* and the imminence of the 'new year'.[325] 'As far as heathens can be joyous', noted Chapman on *odwira fofie* 20 September 1844, 'the people are so this evening. It is no small relief to them, after being for a long time not more than half fed, to be able to "eat to the full". Provisions of every kind, have for two months past been very scarce in and about the Town.'[326]

To Bowdich, the excesses of the *odwira nwonakwasie* had been 'like the Saturnalia'.[327] By contrast, Bonnat likened the eating, drinking and gift giving of the *odwira fofie* to the joyous celebration of Christmas in England or New Year in France.[328] These derived comparisons were reasonably apt. The contrasting general atmosphere and emotional *ambiance* of each of the two days reflected quite distinct and very different evolutionary moments in the transit through *odwira*.

On the *odwira fofie*, however, amidst the euphoric release afforded by sudden abundance and plenty, there was another reason for relieved gratitude. Rattray, citing an 'important actor' in *odwira*, put the matter succinctly: 'There was little real rejoicing at the coming in of the New Year. My Ashanti friend remarked, "*Eyee me de na menya me'ti*" ("I was glad I still had my head").'[329] The burden of the meaning expressed here is that the power of the state was understood to be analogous to those inexplicable but irresistible interventions, natural and supernatural, that determined the issues of life and death for the individual between one *odwira* and the next.

The performance of the *odwira* ceased in 1896. Interestingly, a number of its features found recognizable if distorted expression in the celebration of Christmas and New Year in the alien dispensation of the early colonial period. There are echoes of both *odwira nwonakwasie* and *odwira fofie* in the following Basel Mission accounts from Kumase.

The foolish idea by which they behave so rudely is this: A year has come round and we are still alive, we ought to therefore rejoice, eat, drink, dance or do what ever we are able to do. The same act is repeated at New Year's Day.
(*Christmas, 1904*: compare n. 329 above)
At Xmas day, only few people use to chop [eat], they all drink to excess, and were drunk and here and there you meet people playing, dancing, making noise to the top of their voices...
(*Christmas, 1906*)
The motto of these people is: Christmas time is a time of confusion and every body can move about according to his own disorientation because no punishment is to be inflicted on any crime whatever.
(*Christmas, 1910*: compare n. 245 above)[330]

There were novel or aggravated features as well. Widespread armed robbery, beatings, rape and even murder were characteristic of Christmas and New Year in early colonial Kumase.[331] Under the *Asantehene* Osei Tutu Kwame, a century before, 'theft, intrigue or assault' and sexual licence had all been expressive features of the liminal stage of *odwira*.[332] But then the Asante state had prescribed their temporal duration, and defined their behavioural limits. It was to be some time before the British could enforce a degree of control that began to approximate to the authority exercised by the precolonial state.

nwonamemene (25: Saturday) to kwadwo (34: Monday)

On the *odwira kurudwo* (27: Monday), three days after *fofie*, the *Asantehene* secluded himself in the palace in order to prepare for the *akwasidae* on *kurukwasie* (33: Sunday). As previously noted, this withdrawal was a feature of each and every *adaduanan* cycle. Europeans, however, sometimes thought that it was a practice that was specific to the celebration of the *odwira*. On *foyawo* (30: Thursday) 14 September 1843, for example, it was observed that it was 'contrary to rule for His Majesty [Kwaku Dua Panin] to leave his house before Sunday [*kurukwasie*]', because of 'a ceremony connected with the Yam Custom'.[333] Because of the intense pressure of business during the course of *odwira*, however, court hearings and discussions apparently continued unabated within the palace walls throughout this particular period of seclusion.[334]

Some office holders had not yet eaten new-season yam, for the day prescribed for ritual consumption varied from stool to stool; individual office holders had 'each a particular day on which they attend to this, to them, important business'.[335] Of course, every single one of these variations fell on a day *after* the *Asantehene* had eaten new-season yam on the *odwira fofie*. The Kumase *Bantamahene* and *Krontihene*, for example, ate new-season yam seven days after the *odwira fofie*, on *nwonafie* (31: Friday).[336] Thus, the *Bantamahene* and *Krontihene* Adu Gyawu performed this ritual and distributed gifts on *nwonafie* 27 September 1844.[337] This was a public occasion – the *Bantamahene* and *Krontihene* being a very important office holder – but the *Asantehene* was disbarred from attending because of his seclusion. On *nwonafie* 15 September 1843,

all the principal Chiefs have visited Bantama. The King watched the procession, from the top of his house [the stone *aban*], but is forbidden to join in it. The Chief of Bantama is obliged to present every Chieftain, who may visit him, on this occasion, with a sheep, rather an expensive custom, when the number of visitants is so great.[338]

The celebration of the *odwira akwasidae*, which took place on the *odwira kurukwasie* (33: Sunday) at *dwaberem*, was attended by the very large number of visitors then present in Kumase. This was 'the most riotous Adai [adae] in the year', during the course of which much drinking occurred.[339] Public dancing also took place to the musical accompaniment of the ɔsekye (atɛntɛ) and the kete ensembles.[340] In addition to the customary reciprocities of the adae, particular felicitations were offered to the Asantehene for this 'happy occasion' that marked the successful celebration of the odwira.[341] A second drinking party (sadwa) was held in the evening of the odwira kurukwasie at dwaberem or in the dadeɛsoaba ward. Again, this was a celebratory occasion. The Asantehene ritually smoked both his gold and silver pipes, the shield-bearers (akyamfoɔ) displayed their dexterity and skills at manipulation, and palm wine was liberally distributed.[342]

On the odwira kwadwo (34: Monday), as was customary on the day following an adae, the Asantehene visited the Bantama baamu. On the odwira kwadwo 18 September 1843, the Asantehene Kwaku Dua Panin rode to Bantama in great state in the carriage that had been presented to him in 1841 by the Wesleyan-Methodist mission. On this particular occasion, Kwaku Dua Panin wore the uniform of a Dutch officer, the heir apparent Osei Kwadwo was attired in 'a French Lancer's dress', and many of the royal attendants 'also wore [European] clothes'.[343] Such garments – strikingly visible indicators of accumulated wealth, and of the state's range of commercial and political contacts – were also favoured in the public ceremony in which the Asantehene bade farewell to the great provincial office holders.

This is done by presenting them with swords, tent umbrellas etc., and by entertaining them with a farewell banquet at the palace. This banquet is termed by the King, 'European Feast', and is distinguished by himself and many of his guests being curiously dressed in European costume.[344]

These embellishments may have been unique to the reign of the Asantehene Kwaku Dua Panin, for they are reported from no other period in the specific context of the odwira. During his tenure of office (1834–67), the legitimate trade in European goods and manufactures was at its height, and most notably in the late 1830s and 1840s; European clothing was a sign of wealth, and it was greatly in demand in Kumase among the mid-nineteenth-century office-holding elite.[345]

monobena (35: Tuesday) to nwonawukuo (1: Wednesday)

Only one major ceremony strictly connected with the odwira remained to be performed. This was the rite of purification of the shrine that contained the manifestation of Bosommuru (or Bosompra), as distinct from the afena belonging to the ntɔrɔ, which had been cleansed on the odwira fofie. This took place on the odwira fobena (42: Tuesday) for Bosommuru, or *nwonawukuo* (1: Wednesday) for *Bosompra*. The externals of the ceremony, involving a procession to the Nsuben and ritual lustrations with water, were similar to those of the *odwira fofie* rite. Thus, on *nwonawukuo* 27 September 1843, the *Asantehene* Kwaku Dua Panin of the *Bosompra ntɔrɔ*

and his Chiefs have walked in public procession from the royal residence to the stream of water, by which the Town is surrounded. The same ceremony was repeated today, as mentioned in a preceding page [entry for *odwira fofie* 8 September]. It being the last procession connected with the present custom, we went to see them pass. The order of the day seemed in every respect the same, as when we on a former occasion were spectators of this ceremony.[346]

Similarly, on *fobena* 30 September 1817, the Acting British Consul Hutchison accompanied the *Gyaasewahene* Opoku Frɛfrɛ to observe the *Asantehene* Osei Tutu Kwame of the *Bosommuru ntɔrɔ* 'finish his ablutions'.

We walked along through an immense crowd; the streets were lined with the chiefs and their respective suites. We went down to the place where the King washes; a low platform was erected where the stools were laid on their side... The King performed the ceremony of laving the water over himself, sprinkling the various articles.[347]

This was, as Freeman observed, the official public 'procession to close the Yam Custom'.[348]

This was the sole occasion upon which the shrine (*ayowa*) connected with the *Asantehene's ntɔrɔ* was removed from the palace and displayed in public. That connected with the *Bosommuru ntɔrɔ* was observed on *fobena* 9 January 1872. It was contained in a red wooden chest (*adaka*) that measured about $35 \times 20 \times 20$ cm. This was ornamented with silver clasps and brass nails, and surmounted by a leather lid 'in the form of a bellows'. On this occasion, the shrine was followed in procession by men bearing some 20 to 25 brass basins covered in white cloth, containing the shrines and *asuman* of the *Asantehene*. Gold ornaments were displayed on the top of these vessels. The shrine of the *Bosommuru ntɔrɔ* itself was borne on the head of an *akradwareni* (pl. *ŋkradwarefoɔ*: an 'okra': an individual who had been dedicated to the service of the *kra* of the *Asantehene*). Hundreds of other *ŋkradwarefoɔ* followed the procession, all clad in white cloth, and all wearing their insignia of a circular gold breastplate (*akrafoɔ kommu*). The shrine also had its own umbrella carriers, and its own 'personal' wealth was carried behind it.[349]

The *ŋkradwarefoɔ* were confidential servants and privileged persons, selected because they shared their day of birth with the *Asantehene* whom they served, or because they were personal intimates of their ruler.[350] However, they were ultimately differentiated from each other by considerations of social or political status:

many of them are favourite slaves, many, commoners who have distinguished themselves, and who are glad to stake their lives on the King's, to be kept free from palavers and supported by his bounty, which they are entirely; some few are relatives and men of rank. All of the two former classes, excepting only the two or three individuals known to have been entrusted with the King's state secrets, are sacrificed on his tomb.[351]

Thus, for example, the ɔheneba Kwaku Bosommuru Dwira (and note the name), an akradwareni of elite origin, played a prominent part on fobena 9 January 1872. He was promoted Akomfodehene by the Asantehene Kofi Kakari, and he went on to play a significant role in diplomacy under the Asantehene Mensa Bonsu.[352] Less well-connected ŋkradwarefoɔ paid for their privileges with their lives. They were summarily killed to form part of the retinue deemed to be indispensable to an Asantehene in the afterlife.[353]

odwira to afe

The fobena (or nwonawukuo) ceremony concluded the odwira. This was followed by the beginning of a new cycle of nine adaduanan cycles, collectively known as afe. Thus, on fobena (42: Tuesday) 30 September 1817, Hutchison visited the Kumase Adumhene Adum Ata immediately after he had observed the 'washing' of the Bosommuru ntɔrɔ. 'This he [Adum Ata] told me is the last day of the year, according to their calculation, but from what reason I do not know.'[354] Bowdich, who had access to Hutchison's diary, had some inkling that there were annual variations in the timing of the end of the odwira and the beginning of a new afe cycle. He was puzzled and unfortunately misled, however, by the coincidence that the beginning of the new afe cycle that fell in 1817 happened to be on the first day (1 October) of a Gregorian month. 'I have stated the Ashantee year to begin on the first of October, on the authority of Mr. Hutchison, my own memorandum referring it to the beginning of September.'[355]

Bonnat erred in an equally understandable but different way. He dated the closing of the odwira and the advent of the 'New Year' to kurufie (3: Friday) 12 January 1872 – three days after the end of the adaduanan cycle in which odwira had been celebrated. This was because on kurufie he happened to witness the annual performance of the asumaŋ nnɔrɔ (a ritual ceremony with dancing). This was customarily held shortly after the ending of the odwira, but in the new afe cycle. Bonnat simply assimilated the events of kurufie 12 January 1872 to the recently concluded odwira of that year. He was also confused by the fact that kurufie was a name day of the then reigning Asantehene Kofi Kakari, Kofi signifying being born on a 'Friday', and so it was one of the regular days devoted to the 'washing' of that ruler's kra.[356]

The *asuman nnɔrɔ* was not part of the *odwira*. It was an annual festival day dedicated to all of the *Asantehene's asuman*. It was marked and characterized by deranged behaviour, by acts of self-mutilation and by human sacrifices. These features may also have led Bonnat to identify it too readily with some aspects of the *odwira*. Hutchison gave a very partial and oblique account of the *asuman nnɔrɔ*, which in 1817 was celebrated on *kurufie* 3 October.

As I was going home I met a man white-washed, carrying a vessel covered over with a white cloth: this I have been often told is Tando fetish [a *suman* that derived its power(s) from the river Tano, or one of the other *atano* group of *abosom*], but can learn nothing more. Music and a great crowd went with it to Adoo Quamina's [*Atene Akotenhene ɔheneba* Adu Kwame's] house, at the front of which they put it down, and sacrificed a child of Cudjoo Cooma's, the Akim revolter [the usurpatory *Akyem Kotokuhene* Kwadwo Kuma] over it, as an annual sacrifice of the King's.[357]

As already noted, on *kurufie* 12 January 1872, this annual ceremony took place simultaneously with the observance of the *Asantehene* Kofi Kakari's name day. Then,

whoever wished to honour him [Kofi Kakari] appeared on that day with white garments, and painted white on the breast, shoulders, and forehead. We saw hundreds of these 'servants' of the 'King's souls' [*sic*], who enjoyed the prerogative of not being beaten or insulted by anyone.[358]

The 'King's souls' that were observed being carried through the streets of Kumase on this occasion were, in fact, the *asuman* containers from the royal palace.[359]

By this time, nearly all of the visiting office holders and their retinues had left Kumase for home. Thus, Kumase was 'all quiet' on *nkyiyawo* (2: Thursday) 19 September 1816, two days after the *odwira fobena*, as 'most of the Kings and caboceers [office holders] have returned to their villages'.[360] In fact, for some the exodus began while the last stages of the *odwira* were still taking place. In 1843, the *Dwabenhemaa* Amma Sewaa quit Kumase for Dwaben on *monobena* (35: Tuesday) 19 September, the day after the *odwira kwadwo*.[361] The great *amanhene* and the provincial office holders, and their subjects, returned to their own towns and villages to 'celebrate the great annual festival in their own capitals after they have assisted in that of Coomassie'.[362] That is, the state only permitted local celebrations of what one observer called 'the Chiefs' petty Yam Customs' after the ending of the Kumase *odwira*.[363]

Immediately after *kurufie*, the *Kumasefoɔ* too began leaving the capital in large numbers. They returned to their natal villages, for as the centre of the state and of government, as has been noted, Kumase counted numerous citizens who had been born elsewhere. They travelled to observe the first *fodwo* (6: Monday) of the new *afe* cycle in their birthplaces. This day was a very notable *dabɔne*, upon which prohibitions against travelling and work were in force. Thus, for example, *fodwo* 15 January 1872 was devoted to ritual observances, to reflection and to 'playing'.[364] In the villages throughout Asante, *fodwo* marked the fact that another series of *adaduanan* cycles had begun.

Reflections

Ethnographers, cultural critics, and those interested in the aesthetics of performance have all justly remarked that the (con)textual narrativity of the Asante *odwira* – the unfolding shape of its events in and through time – was such as to obscure its overall meaning or sense, not only from observers, but also from the great mass of those actively participating in it.[365]

This is a problem as old as our eyewitness sources. The effort to make sense of the Asante *odwira* – to distil, to pin, and somehow to fix an essential meaning – was the reason why, in 1817, T.E. Bowdich resorted to an abstraction of his sensory experiences in the form of a pictorial representation. His crowded, swarming, intensely busy summary is an engraving, simply entitled *The First Day of the Yam Custom* – but it is all at once both less and more than that.[366] (See Appendix I.) In reality, it is an attempt (and a valiant one at that) to secure and to convey narrative sense by divorcing action from temporal sequence. The depiction of the momentary in a static situation bows, appositely, to history. It implies what went before, and predicts, forgivably if a little knowingly, what will come afterwards. It strains for the closure and sense of completion that will guarantee narrative meaning. It is the pursuit of quietus. Bowdich was not much of an artist (as he very freely confessed), but his technique is an intellectual commonplace of Western painterly essays in deriving sense and assigning meaning. It has been very extensively deployed in the European tradition to recast all alien worlds, mythological and actual, into a bounded narrativity. Thus, it might be said that Bowdich's clumsy engraving shares an objective with more artistically exalted examples of the genre; with, for example, Jan van Kessel's *America*, Jacopo del Sellaio's *The Story of Psyche* or Piero di Cosimo's *The Discovery of Honey*.[367] Bowdich's effort may also be seen as a version of 'orientalism'; that is, it simultaneously offers a thrilling celebration of the 'barbaric' and seeks to familiarize it to a set of categories that render it, satisfyingly, both domesticated (in reception) and alien (in representation).[368]

In addition, in resorting to – in fleeing into – an image, Bowdich was trying both to breach and to escape from the limitations of language. If, as he admitted, he found it difficult to make (con)textual sense of the pyrotechnic unfolding of events over time, then he found it equally hard to reduce to verbal description (his adjectives especially fail him) the sheer vertiginous sensory impact of the whole, let alone the kaleidoscopic flux of nuance and detail contained within it. As a subject, the Asante *odwira* overflows, spills or slides away from all of Bowdich's best efforts to contain it in language. Bowdich very clearly *thought* that he recognized a *fasces* of multiple, discordant (con)textual 'voices' propounding ambiguity, incompleteness and even contradiction, but he *sensed* (or was intellectually predisposed so to do as a European) an overall unity of meaning. And he believed that if that essential(ist) meaning could somehow be captured and represented, then the perplexing and hugely confusing edifice of ancillary detail would immediately offer itself up to appropriate resolution, and surrender to calm explanation. His own cultural solution to this – very real – problem was to enlist his drawing skills in aid of his pen.

The purpose of all bounded (con)textual narrativity is to reward interrogation with disclosure. This presupposes detachment and/or reflection in the construction of the necessary narrative order. This is an appropriate procedural method for the historian, or for someone in Bowdich's position, or indeed, for anyone striving to practise a form of disinterested analysis. But even from such perspectives, as we have seen in the case of Bowdich, the necessary distancing is extraordinarily difficult to attain. How much more so then for the Asante, for neither the Asante state nor those huge numbers of Asante who participated in the annual *odwira* were engaged in this sort of exercise. In summary, the Asante state's ideological structuration of the *odwira* was *not* dedicated to, or calculated in relation to, any such disclosure of explanation, or objective intent(ion), or meaning.

In the mechanics of the Asante state's ideological reading and structuration of the *odwira*, dismemberment into finite episodes, the sedulous isolation of discrete elements, and, above all, the provision of any occasion for analytic reflection were *all* firmly subordinated to a trajectory of continuous increment, to the multiplicity of overlapping elements, and to the ruthless promulgation of sustained flow. The intent of the state's pedagogic narrativity was not explanation (and certainly not resolution), but the creation of what Goodman has termed, in a most felicitous usage, 'world structure' – a discourse through power that was dependent upon the discretionary ordering of elements and the imposition of comparative weights of kinds within itself. Reordering and intensive weight shifting, the defining actions of the *hermeneus*, are the most potent narrative instruments that can be brought to bear in making (and endlessly remaking) facts and worlds.[369] The object of this exercise was that the master text that proposed the resulting 'world structure' served hermetically as its *own* explanation and meaning.

That is to say, the Asante state authored and constructed the narrativity of the *odwira* as meaning *qua* meaning, and not as a series of episodic disclosures of, or seductions to, meaning. The distinction can be framed in the language terms that have been used elsewhere in our argument. The 'world structure' constructed, presided over and dispensed by the Asante state *as* the *odwira* was a seamless accounting of narrative that was intended to give *argument* the unarguable authority of confirmed and ineluctable *statement*. The text unfolded ruthlessly to this end. It was confessedly linear in (re)presentation: from the preliminaries to the procession and defilement of *kwayawo*; through the public formulation of state and social order on *monofie* and *fomemene*; across the transit of liminality of *nwonakwasie*, and into the relative shift of *nkyidwo*; and so to the cleansing renewal of *fofie*, and the passage to a new (another) *afe*. However, although it was linear in presentation, being an item of inscription in historical time, it was indivisible or already complete as ideology. That is, the (con)textual narrativity of the Asante *odwira* held within its own completedness the prediction of closure and of the self-conscious circularity of fulfilment.

The immense plethora of sub-texts within the Asante *odwira*, its staggering heteroglossia, should not be allowed to distract from the driven single-mindedness (the singularity) of its intention. It drew all of the principal constituents of belief and knowledge into the still centre of a highly purposeful ideological structuration. The efficacy of this, its capacity to work in and across historical time, relied in the first place upon a consensual understanding, albeit one shadowed by the state's coercive potential. In this structuration, past, present and future were unified in a reading of the Asante cultural experience that was conducted under the presiding aegis of the state and orchestrated by it. The overarching intention of this reading was hegemony. In this, the Asante *odwira* was both the most directed and the most highly elaborated of all of the ideological structurations that determined the history of eighteenth- and nineteenth-century Asante. It was continuous with – and parsed, framed and contained – all of the other structurations that have been discussed throughout this book.

5 The Asante past considered

Eduabin, 1862

Consider the following narrative. On 5 March 1862 the Wesleyan-Methodist missionary W. West, in the company of the Winneba merchant R.J. Ghartey and the English-educated *ɔheneba* Owusu Ansa, left Cape Coast to travel north to Kumase to evaluate Christian prospects there. Having crossed the virtually dry Bosompra river and negotiated the barrier of the Adanse hills, these principals and their retinue of carriers arrived in Fomena on 11 March. There they were formally welcomed to Asante by a delegation of royal *nhenkwaa*, comprising *afenasoafoɔ* (sword-bearers) and *nsenieɛfoɔ* (court criers). These 'messengers' had been dispatched by order of the *Asantehene* Kwaku Dua Panin, with instructions to conduct West and his party to Kumase, and to ensure, as was mandatorily required, that the foreign visitors should enter the Asante capital on a set day that was deemed to be appropriately auspicious. The day appointed for West's official entry into Kumase was *kurudwo* (27: Monday) 17 March.[1] As a direct consequence of this timetable, and in spite of West's repeated protests, procrastination and delay ensued in the journey north from Fomena. The escorting royal *nhenkwaa* constrained West's party to halt in the village of Eduabin, only some 10 miles south of Kumase, from Thursday 13 March until its sanctioned departure for the Asante capital early on the morning of Monday the 17th.

West (who had never previously visited Asante) chafed at the delay, and not least because Eduabin proved to be 'a miserable, little' and generally 'wretched' settlement. In fact, Eduabin was a village that had been more or less in decline since *c.* 1765, when the then incumbent Kumase *Adontenhene* Amankwaa Osei had chosen to commit suicide after having been arraigned on the charge of impregnating one of the widows of the *Asantehene* Kusi Obodom. In the aftermath of this shameful episode, the *Asantehene* Osei Kwadwo cancelled (*paɛ din*) the rights of succession in the Adonten stool of the *Aseneɛ abusua* of Agyeiwaa Badu of Eduabin (to which Amankwaa Osei belonged), and transferred the office to the *Aseneɛ abusua* of

243

Aberewaa Kwanti of the village of Baaman (in the person of Kwaaten Pɛtɛ and his heirs). Eduabin had then ceased to enjoy the status and prestige of being the natal village and seat of the powerful and influential Kumase *Adontenhene*, and had duly lost much of its erstwhile importance. In 1832 Eduabin only counted some eighty to one hundred dwellings; in 1839 it was 'in a very dilapidated state, many of the houses being tenantless and tumbling down'; in 1841 it had improved somewhat, and had some 700 to 800 people in it (presumably many of these being transients involved in the booming coastal trade); in 1843 it was again said to be 'dilapidated'; and by 1846 one traveller was reduced to lodging there 'in a hut in a very ruinated state'.[2]

In March 1862, however, a sequence of events did transpire in the 'wretched, impoverished' village of Eduabin that forcibly impressed themselves upon West during his brief, enforced sojourn there. To the missionary observing and recording in his journal, these happenings were simply a vividly exemplary instance of that arbitrary violence that was to be expected among a people enslaved to superstition and bereft of the blessings and saving grace of the Christian revelation. Be all that as it may, the occurrences detailed by West were in truth relatively banal and mundane in and of themselves – at least in as much as they involved no person in Eduabin of any great consequence, power or historic import. But it is the quotidian or commonplace in these events, their momentary and almost laconic textural encapsulation of the essential in the contingent, that engenders an implicative density (and an explicative potential) far beyond the fleetingly circumstantial, the anecdotal or the everyday. Appropriately contextualized, these events (as we shall see presently) have a resonant suggestiveness and a distilled veracity of the most revealing kind.

'A circumstance occurred, while we were resident in Eduabin', observed West, that centred on the personal behaviour of 'an old man in the town.' The old man's name is unrecorded, but West and his companions were informed by the townspeople of Eduabin that this individual had 'once been in good circumstances' and relatively wealthy (perhaps from trading to the coast?), but that over the intervening years he had become more and more impoverished 'by paying various fines, which had been imposed on members of his family, for their misconduct at different times'. Early on the morning of the *dabɔne* of *fofie* (24: Friday) 14 March 1862, this old man had asked his daughter – again no name is supplied – to give him some of her 'coco' (generically a maize or millet gruel: cf. *kukuradabi*: maize stored from last season's harvest) to eat. The daughter refused. The old man then intimated that he was exceedingly hungry, and he 'begged her' (and more than once) for a portion of the food. She adamantly declined to listen to his repeated importuning, at last angrily telling him that he might not have any of her food, and informing him that she intended to finish cooking the 'coco' (in his presence) and then to offer it for sale in Eduabin market. Her father now became 'enraged at her refusal', and in this state of excitability and greatly heightened passion he suddenly

determined to revenge himself by putting the whole family to expense and inconvenience, though at the risk of his own life. He therefore as the natives express it, 'cursed the King'. He swore, for instance, that the King would be killed by the fetish, if they did not, at once, bring him an anker of rum. This they were obliged to procure at any cost, for, had they refused to do so, their own lives, as well as that of the old man, would have been forfeited on the plea, that they wished the King to be killed, or they would have procured the rum to prevent it. He next swore that the King would be killed, if they did not get him six sheep; these also had to be procured, and the little town was ransacked in order to obtain them: and in a similar way he demanded a number of fowls. By this time the whole town was in a state of alarm, for no one could see where it would end.[3]

While all of this commotion that he had occasioned was going on, the old man busied himself in steadily drinking up the alcohol provided by the townspeople, to the point where he was visibly 'becoming insensible'. In the midst of this drinking bout, the old man ordered that four of the six sheep that he had demanded be slaughtered, and this command was promptly executed. At this point – with everyone in Eduabin reduced to 'a state of alarm' – West's escort of royal *nhenkwaa* intervened. They gathered together and 'packed up' the jointed sheep and the (now dead) fowls 'in baskets', and one of their number ('one of the King's messengers'), conveying the meat as evidence, then set out from Eduabin to Kumase, 10 miles away, to tell the *Asantehene* Kwaku Dua Panin 'what had happened'. Meanwhile, the old man became 'so ill' from prolonged imbibing that the Eduabin townspeople all

feared he would die before the messenger returned, in which case, they would all be in danger, as it would be said, they had killed him in order that he might escape the King's vengeance. I shall not soon forget the appearance of the poor people, as they, with anxiety written on their countenances, collected in small groups, and, seating themselves on the ground, talked in a low tone of what had occurred.[4]

The denouement swiftly followed. About midnight on 14 March, West was suddenly awoken from his sleep 'by the discharge of musketry'. He heard no less than 'three distinct reports'. Seeking enlightenment, he and his companions were informed by the townspeople that 'the King's men' from Kumase had just arrived in Eduabin. West was then further 'informed that after discharging their muskets' at the inebriated old man and killing him, the royal *nhenkwaa* had immediately 'cut off' the head from the dead body.

The bald recorded facts of this narrative may be submitted to the following initial reading. The clear implication of the evidence is that, for a long but unspecified number of years, the anonymous old man had met and satisfied all of the customary obligations incurred by those other persons over whom he exercised jural authority, and for whom, as a result, he held reciprocal responsibility. In different degrees and in a variety of situational contexts these personages included his wife (or, more likely, wives) and child (or, again more likely, children). There is a clear suggestion too that, by 1862, the old man was the senior male (*wɔfa*) within his lineage stirp or group (*ɔyafunu koro*) resident in Eduabin, with authority over and responsibility for his close uterine kin ('the whole family'), and hence burdened with an ultimate, onerous accountability in discharging the monetary costs of their assorted transgressions and derelictions. The specific history of the interpersonal dynamics in all of this is unrecorded, but the evidence indicates that the repeated, or aggravated, offences committed by some or all of his relatives had systematically reduced the old man from a condition of material comfort and even comparative wealth to one of near penury, and that he increasingly resented all of those whom he perceived as having brought him to this pass in old age. The intemperate exchange with his daughter on the morning of 14 March 1862 has much of the last straw about it; his hungry importuning and her steadfast denial of his insistent expressions of need were evidently a litany, a long-familiar rehashing of the stock exchanges of a mutual resentment. But this time – and who knows why then and there – the old man's frustrated anger broke forth and erupted. In the momentary grip of a seemingly heedless passion, the old man took immoderately drastic and irrevocable steps to gain revengeful redress for the persistent, uncaring, cynical neglect and exploitation that he felt himself to have suffered at the hands of his 'family'. But was his action entirely innocent of calculation?

An exact recovery of the old man's reasoning is not possible, but the question is posed because – outlandish though it all may have seemed to West and his companions – the particular situation described is *structurally* and *conjuncturally* familiar, and it is attested to in Asante tradition and ethnography. That is, there is a documented rationale for the leading features of this case within the known parameters of Asante social thought and historical practice. It is very well understood, and is a motif of folklore, that elderly Asante men were sometimes marginalized by kin and even children, and most especially if their financial and other material resources had been 'eaten' or used up; equally, it is widely known and recounted that old men were sometimes reduced to a galling, frustrated condition of economic dependence upon others, even for their basic daily sustenance; and it is generally held that some old men – confined to this bleak existence, and aware that death was not far off – might elect to seek revenge for the ills, real or imagined, visited upon them by their relatives by resort to an extreme personal act that was calculated to encompass the ruin of the many in the downfall of the one.[5]

For whatever personal motives, this last was the course of action followed by the old man in Eduabin in March 1862. His choice of method was in fact predictable, but it requires contextualization. His quarrel with his daughter was a domestic matter (an item of *afisɛm*) that was properly subject in law to acts of arbitration and to resolution within the jurisdictional arenas of the *ɔyafunu koro* and the *abusua*. But on this particular occasion, the old man wilfully elected to remove the matter at issue from the jural competence of the kinship structures of society, and instead to involve the legal machinery of the Asante state. He did this by the deliberate and public commission of a grave offence against duly constituted order, in the person of the *Asantehene*. The old man perpetrated the verbal crime of *ohyira ɔhene* (lit., 'blessing the *Asantehene*'), an idiomatic and formulaic euphemism for its unmentionable opposite – simultaneously cursing the name and life of the *Asantehene*, and, by extension, referencing and deploying items in belief (*abosom*, *asumaŋ* and/or *bayi*) to invoke and conduce his untimely death. Such a procedure connoted a generalized repudiation of and curse upon historic norms and received order. Indeed, this heinous utterance was held to be so criminally maleficent that it was customarily referred to by third parties and witnesses by use of the circumlocutory phrase, *wa sɛ biribi* ('he has said something').[6]

By resorting to and practising *ohyira ɔhene*, the old man had knowingly committed suicide – as certainly as if he had done away with himself – for the offence carried a mandatory death sentence. However, by employing the verbal flexibilities that were inherent in *ohyira ɔhene* for attaching the actions of others, like so many dependent, conditional clauses, to his own initiatory statement of intent, the old man had very roundly implicated his own relatives and all of the people of Eduabin in his crime by making the non-fulfilment of his invocation dependent upon *their* behaviour in meeting his demands. In law, the old man had placed himself in the status of a self-confessed regicide and enemy of received order, and he had accomplished this in a way such as to make his family, kin and fellow Eduabin citizens co-regicides and heinous criminals if they failed in the injunction to negate his sweeping inclusion of them in his curse by satisfying the conditions that he had imposed. That is, it was only by cooperating in the provision of the alcohol, the sheep and the fowls that any individual in Eduabin could attest to an absence of complicity in the malevolent ill will directed at the life of the *Asantehene* Kwaku Dua Panin, and all that that implied.[7]

The old man's choice of behaviour had the effect of recruiting a reluctant and fearful constituency. That is, it was the terrifying potential of his strategy that generated the escalating despondency and alarm noted by West, and that elicited the frightened and unconditional provision – in, recall, a poor and disadvantaged village – of the stated requirements of drink and food. As word spread throughout Eduabin, so we may imagine, generic unease turned to collective anxiety, and then to near panic, when it was rumoured that the old man might well expire in a drunken fit. Had he done so, then the entire village, as everyone in it knew, in its foreknowledge and/or in its presumed complicity, would have been held corporately responsible for conspiring against the state in the personage of the *Asantehene* (the old man now being unable to testify under oath that this was *not* the case), and/or of having done away with the miscreant to cover up its wholesale participation in his crime.

Fortuitously or not (but certainly so for the historian), the old man had picked his occasion to practise *ohyira ɔhene* with a most apt acuity. Because of West's reluctant presence in Eduabin, there were numbers of royal *nhenkwaa* temporarily billeted there. When word of the old man's actions reached them, these *nhenkwaa* took swift possession of all of the relevant material evidence, and promptly forwarded this on to Kumase together with an account of all that had transpired. The sheer gravity of the offence meant that, upon receipt of the details, the *Asantehene* Kwaku Dua Panin immediately ordered *adumfoɔ* to Eduabin to carry out the death sentence on the spot. The old man was duly executed on the very same day – *fofie* (24: Friday) 14 March 1862 – that he had quarrelled with his daughter, and then cursed the name and life of the *Asantehene*. The fact that the old man was still alive when the *adumfoɔ* reached Eduabin, and so was able to pay for his crime with his own life, must have come as a considerable relief to all of his relatives and fellow townspeople.

By way of conclusion I: horizons of interpretation

The simple personalized dyad of the *Asantehene* Kwaku Dua Panin and the anonymous old man of Eduabin is emblematic of the ideology and structure of relations between state and society. The diegetic level of the narrative that has been recounted is at once a historical event (of one day's duration), and, at least from the exclusive perspective of the old man, a record of a momentary 'entitlement' in the emotion and affect of a defined personhood in historical time. The narrative has a predictably aporetic dimension, in that the nameless old man's *personal* sequence of thought (his cognitive rehearsal of motives) is strictly undecidable, and/or lies beyond the reach of historical appropriation. This is, as ever in such cases, unfortunate, but our principal concern here is with the extradiegetic level of the narrative. Its emblematic quality suggests much else beyond its epiphenomenal status as event. But what, precisely? That is, can the conceptual economy of such relations in and across Asante history be refined in ways that build upon our argument? Can the (inter)personal 'foreground' of the Asante past be itself foregrounded?[8]

Let us begin with the most obviously pressing question. Are there identifiable (and recoverable) protocols that have served to inscribe Asante reasoning in Asante ideology, and in what ways, if at all, is the resulting historical palimpsest 'legible'? How, in sum, did Asante actors, and actresses, act? There is, of course, a formidable and complex philosophical discourse that seeks to construe reasoning, and that attempts to address the resistant problems of contextualizing rationality in relation to interpretation and understanding. A highly economic – but scrupulously argued and refreshingly lucid – summation of the principal difficulties of interpretation is given by Hollis. As an abstract framework and anatomy of the *problem*, this is applicable to the Asante, as to other human societies, and may serve as a usable point of departure. '*Verstehen*', Hollis has pointedly observed, 'calls for a fourfold apparatus for adequacy at the level of meaning.' This he writes as follows:

	ACTION'S MEANING	ACTOR'S MEANING
WHAT?	*conventions*	*intentions*
WHY?	*legitimating reasons*	*real reasons*[9]

This is admirably elegant, but it is immediately qualified by its author with the honest if disheartening disclaimer that the 'epistemological problems of knowing that an interpretation is correct on all four counts are formidable', in as much as the 'answers to the two "What?" questions often need justifying by reference to the two "Why?"'s'. (Witness here the knotty difficulties that inhibit *Verstehen* in our own very 'simple' exemplary narrative recounting; the recovery of 'meaning' – in the acts of/for the persons of the *Asantehene* Kwaku Dua Panin and the old man of Eduabin – proves elusive, even in relation to the basic grid.)[10]

These are complex problems, but they are ones common to the issue of a historical understanding of any and all human societies. It has been our argument throughout that numbers of historians (of Asante, Africa, and elsewhere) have evaded or otherwise subsumed the most basic, and most basically significant, indigenous structurations of knowing and believing. Instead, they have practised a form of narrative sleight of hand. This has customarily involved the reworking into narrative of a tumultuous register of adventitiously preserved descriptions. The key to this enterprise is to define the 'facts' as being intellectually and/or ideologically unproblematic in their own right, and then to permit them 'to speak for themselves' (as being prior to and as a substitute for *Verstehen*). At best this is unacceptable innocence; at worst it is an arid positivism, a species of teleological history in bad faith. We can clearly illustrate this by returning to a consideration of Weber, and to the (ab)uses severally visited upon his intellectual project by those who have recruited the authority of his name (but not the complexity and density of his insights) to buttress and to construe the 'facts' of the Asante past.

In existing Asante historiography, Weber is substantively the *only* theoretical touchstone. It should be recalled that a rudimentary *explanandum* of the political history of Asante has been constructed by Wilks, ostensibly on the basis of Weber's construction of 'bureaucracy'. This is a history in bad faith, and it has been criticized as such – *inter alia* on the strictly contextual and mechanical grounds that the application of the concept is misconceived, its crude deployment being rooted in a highly incautious, incomplete, facile and extremely 'thin' (mis)reading of usable selections (bits and pieces, or gobbets) from Weber's work.[11] Wilks does not theorize *from* Weber, and neither does he argue back and forth between Weber's findings and his own. Rather, he presents a positivist narrative – as previously noted, a tautological *wie es eigentlich gewesen ist* – and appends Weber to his '(hi)story' in the manner of an ornamental embellishment on a rather plain, but already completed, building. This is *bricolage* rather than understanding, and Yarak, from a perspective different from my own, has correctly called attention to Wilks' abject failure to theorize what he is doing, or to make explicit the premises that underpin, and the choices that inform, his seamless catalogue of 'facts'.[12] Wilks' response to criticism of this sort shows the *bricoleur* at his magpie work. In 1989 he wrote of his findings in 1975 (emphases added):

I have supplemented my treatment of recruitment and promotion within the administration and of 'the bureaucratic process' generally (pp. 465–76), by a more systematic study of the subject published in 1987. My starting point was Yarak's comment that, in Weberian terms, I had treated what was essentially a patrimonial system as a formal one in *ASNC* [i.e. *Asante in the Nineteenth Century: The Structure and Evolution of a Political Order*, 1975]. **In an attempt to circumvent that particular problem, I redefined the issue as one of class**, notwithstanding Arhin's reservations – also made from a Weberian perspective – about the dangers of using that concept in the analysis of Asante society.[13]

The proposal that arises from the work of Arhin and Yarak is that Asante political history approximates to another Weberian typology: the 'patrimonial' rather than the 'bureaucratic'. Let it be admitted immediately and with all forceful conviction that if the analytic frame of reference is artificially confined to this either/or, then even the most cursory reading of the historical evidence will end by assigning Asante to the 'patrimonial' rather than to the 'bureaucratic' Weberian model.[14] But the foregoing – in reality a spurious dispute rooted in the wilful falsity of winnowing out something called political history and conferring an almost hermetic autonomy upon it – is not the crucial point at issue.

Historians of Asante who have deployed Weber in this highly mechanical, ungrounded or non-reflexive manner are guilty of overlooking the fact (and leaving aside his own problematic *historical* status as a radical pessimist, with shifting priorities and views, of a discretely European modernism) that he himself was self-consciously engaged in the modelling of *ideal types*. In consequence, Weber was acutely aware of the profound difficulties that lay in the path of interpretative efficacy or *Verstehen* in applying any such models ('bureaucracy', 'patrimonialism' and the rest) to historical action. 'Nothing, however, is more dangerous than the *confusion* of theory and history stemming from naturalistic presuppositions', he urged (in criticizing the tradition of 'naturalism' from Plato to Hegel and Marx),

whether in the form of a belief that one has recorded the 'actual' content, the 'essence' of historical reality in such conceptual images [*Begriffsbilder*]; or that one uses them as a procrustean bed into which history must be forced; or even that one hypostatizes the 'ideas' as a 'true' reality, as real 'forces' standing behind the play of appearances and working themselves out in history.[15]

'The science of society', Weber famously, and succinctly, postulated, '*attempts the interpretative understanding* of social action' (emphases added).[16]

For Weber's own project, the retrieval and reconstruction of any such understanding came to reside most explicitly in the heuristic device of (historical, evolutionary) rationality. But here, again, using his preferred terms, in relation to ideal types, he was relentlessly constrained to an honest bafflement and grappling with the illegibility of certain types of action. The Weberian classification of action, as is well known, was originally formulated in the course of his investigation into certain historical aspects and materialist problems of political economy, and it posited two typological categories – the rational and the residual; on the one hand, the instrumental- or purposive-rational (*zweckrational*) and the expressive-rational (*wertrational*); on the other hand, and it is an extremely large and capacious other hand, the 'pre-rational', residual types of tradition and affect. In light of this, the perplexed honesty of Weber, his unswerving recognition that his ideal types were just that – *ideal*, no more than yardsticks, modelled attempts to give hermeneutics teeth – is wholly estimable. Equally admirable in this context is Weber's recognition of the power of that force in human action that resides in a totalizing ideology, however defined, in the making of which the 'pre-rational', the subjective and the ubiquitous impress of 'tradition' and 'affect' (his terms, not mine) cast a looming shadow over any historical landscape. Weber's own project is notoriously replete with contradictory impulses. It is *not* a finished building. It is, rather, a building site. Randomly to isolate and to lift from that site one brick labelled 'bureaucracy' or another marked 'patrimonialism' flies in the face of Weber's own understanding of the complexities of history.[17]

Weber struggled throughout his life with densely elaborated, historicist variants of our 'What?/Why?' figuration of meaning, but always with an acknowledgement of the extent of the difficulties of recovery. Certainly, he never practised the bad faith of abandoning to silence crucial areas of recalcitrant puzzlement that somehow eluded the explicative capacities of his models. In what follows, let us bear in mind the intellectual thrust of Weber's project, rather than the limited applicability (the 'orienting function') of his ideal types, which 'are never to be confused with the data of "history"'.[18]

Even if we restrict ourselves to the skeletal simplicity of form of our model of a conceptual economy, very severe difficulties, well known to Weber, immediately flood in when we try to anchor Asante historical reality within this (or any analogous) construct. But it is absolutely vital to confront this issue, as we have done throughout, for it embraces and circumscribes crucial arenas of understanding. To admit difficulty neither absolves us from the historian's responsibility for interpretation, nor implies that nothing can be said. In point of fact, a great deal can be said by way of appropriating and reflecting upon key (residual?) dimensions of the lived realities of the Asante past. Let us address ourselves here to two such areas of concern, both of which are insistently inscribed as being significant in language, in discourse and in Asante historical practice. It need hardly be stated that our two areas of concern are importantly exemplary, and not at all exhaustive. They may be formulated and summarized under the rubrics of *TRUTH* and *THE BODY*. Everyone – from an *Asantehene* in Kumase to a drunk, enraged old man in Eduabin – was qualified in and through both of these categories (of 'tradition', of 'affect'). How, then, can these rubrics be fed into the 'What?/Why?' model? Where do they attach and fit? Where are they to be 'spatially' (that is, cognitively) located in relation to the flux of indeterminacy at the core of the 'What?/Why?' grid? In the first place, what can be said about them?

A. TRUTH
Here I defer (with due gratitude) to the findings of native Twi speakers who are trained in philosophical method. Wiredu has made the crucial point that in Akan (Asante) Twi the idea of truth as a *cognitive* concept is not expressed as a single term. He has drawn attention to the word *nokware* (which is given by Christaller, and significantly, as truthfulness, but in the transitive sense of *acting* honestly, truthfully, or with probity). Therefore, to translate *nokware* as truth, as Wiredu has noted, is 'acceptable only as a translation of the moral rather than the cognitive'; *sensu stricto*, that is, *nokware* 'conveys the notion of truthfulness or veracity'.

So where in language and in Asante thinking does the concept of cognitive truth reside? Wiredu has argued that it has to be rendered by a coinage, a phrase, an approximate construct – as in, *nea ate saa* ('that which is so'). Most importantly, as he has pointed out, 'when doing epistemology' a linguistic invention would again have to be made. Wiredu has addressed possible/plausible resolutions, and has concluded by saying that 'it is obvious that such a language [Twi] gives little encouragement to the suggestion that a claim to the effect that something is so ['*asem no te saa'*] should be proffered as itself being so ['*te saa'*]'.[19]

We are not very far here from the Quinean problematic of 'radical translation', and his notions that mind can never be totally self-effacing and that there is no such item as 'unvarnished news'.[20] Be that as it may, however, where does this leave the *Asantehene* Kwaku Dua Panin and the old man of Eduabin (and Asante historical actors/actresses generically)? The answer to that – with clear and obvious implications for the 'What?/Why?' model (or other constructs of understanding) – is that situational resolutions in Asante morality (ethics) are not at all necessarily equivalent resolutions in cognition. If Asante 'truth', as evidenced by language, is mired in an ethics of presentation rather than being rooted in any parsimonious drive for epistemological definition and clarity, then the *Asantehene* and the old man are locked in a battle defined in and through the ideologies of power; we might say that both are constrained to subscribe to the 'ethics' of 14 March 1862, but completely without the prior establishment of protocols in cognition.

This persuasion effectively prevents 'truth' from (*a*) grounding opposition to the shaping grasp of ideology, and (*b*) referencing action to an agreed criterion beyond any given historical situation. Since morality/ethics has an interpretative elasticity of a negotiable kind unavailable to a cognitive definition of truth, so the ideology of the Asante state is the consequent beneficiary of a potent instrument of appropriateness and instrumental use in the realm of interpersonal power. That is, (*a*) there is no intellectual point of insertion available in this case (or others) where the *Asantehene* Kwaku Dua Panin might submit his decision (to kill the old man) to any presumption of error, and (*b*) the old man of Eduabin dies in a matrix of ideological complicity, for there is no counter-argument or appeal that lies beyond or outside the contingency of historically 'lived' (moral) truth.

This has immensely important implications for our understanding. Not the least of these is that it suggests – beyond considerations of literacy, and other matters already reviewed – a powerful intuition towards explaining the absence of any category of dissident 'intellectuals' in eighteenth- and nineteenth-century Asante. As both Gramsci and Weber knew, to 'stand outside' requires *inter alia* an identifiable (and a more or less rigorously defined) channel for appealing over the head of ideological constructs to the 'objective' truth. But, in turn, such a procedure needs a category in *cognition*. This was simply absent from the Asante experience (as is reflected in Twi).

Thus, 'truth' in our 'What?/Why?' model breaks down somewhere on the spectrum between 'conventions' and 'intentions' (with the former guiding but certainly not defining the latter), and analogously in the gap between legitimation and reality. It was not a null category historically, but its ethical rather than cognitive weighting meant that it was not equipped to develop the momentum or 'escape velocity' to break away from ideological structuration. Thus, a movement such as *ɔdomaŋkama* was really about the restitution of an 'ethical' truth abandoned, betrayed or otherwise disfigured by the state; it proposed no 'revolutionary' agenda grounded in cognition. In Asante history power fills truth, endlessly works it over, and generates subscription in it.[21]

B. THE BODY

In our illustrative narrative, the old man of Eduabin 'pays' for his behaviour with his body (the vessel of his corporeal existence). Gyekye (again, a native Twi speaker trained in philosophical method) has noted that 'the Akan belief in disembodied survival in the form of spirit or soul presupposes a nonmaterial conception of a human being'; he then proceeds to argue that the 'ontological pull of the Akan language towards materialism is consequently enfeebled'.[22] This, as we have argued throughout, establishes the correct order of priority in Asante belief, and it does so with admirable economy (again, working outward from linguistic usage).

But the foregoing is not to say (and Gyekye, I think, is not saying) that the corporeal body is bereft of its own specificity and its own discrete significance(s). The thrust of the historical record and of all ethnography indicates that in Asante thinking the body, albeit a secondary item in belief, served as a paradigm for key instrumentations in cognitive mapping – notably references to appropriate wholeness, and to rituals of enclosure/disclosure in death.[23] How one died was very important. But so too was the issue of what happened to the body at and in death. Relatively straightforward versions of this have already been discussed; they are the ethnographic staples of whether and where one was buried (and, of course, by whom).

But the issue is of much greater complexity. The prelude to an understanding is the centrality of the idea of corporeal integrity. Apposite wholeness was the mark of the body's 'success' – in death no less than in life.[24] The 1862 narrative furnishes a clue. The old man of Eduabin was shot to death (the killing) and *then* he suffered beheading (the punishment – compare the case discussed above of the rebel *Gyamanhene* Kwadwo Adinkra). Clarification is provided by the extreme case. For the most heinous crimes (including murder and adultery with the wives of the *Asantehene*), the convicted party was liable to be subjected to death by *atɔperɛ* (cf. *ɔperɛ*: death agonies, with the sense of a struggling). Details of the practice of *atɔperɛ* are given in the ethnographic literature, and there are a number of graphic accounts of specific nineteenth-century cases of it.[25]

The term *atɔperɛ* is often rendered as the 'dance' or the 'theatre' of death in an attempt to capture not only the physical horrors of its mediated actualization, but also its overwhelming sense of *performative structuration*. In *atɔperɛ*, to put the matter in brief, the following occurred: (*a*) the person suffering it was killed over the space of an entire day (and was intermittently revived throughout to enable the performative ritual to continue); (*b*) the process of killing was itself a highly structured and progressive dismemberment – sequentially, piercing the cheeks with *sɛpɔ* knives (to prevent the victim from uttering curses), cutting the nasal septum (so that the victim might be led around by a thorn or rope passed through the incision), scraping the legs to the bone, cutting off the ears, removing the arms below the elbows, severing the legs below the knees, removing the eyelids, amputating the buttocks, flaying the back (and then showing the results of this procedure to the victim, with ironical comments on how the person undergoing *atɔperɛ* had never seen this part of their body before), cutting pieces of flesh from the torso, reviving the broken body (with astringents like lime juice, gunpowder burns and taunts) and ordering it to 'dance', and lastly – on the command of the *Asantehene* – severing the head; (*c*) the *disjecta membra* of the ruined corpse were not buried but were thrown away (into the bush).

In effect, *atɔperɛ* was a punishment that *included* death, but that accorded priority as a first principle to the systematic dissolution of the corporeal body. This represented the invasive ideological power of the state at an absolute level – the body (its wholeness, its integrity) simply disappeared, and literally vanished from history. Nor was this all. The dismemberment of the body in the course of $at\jmath per\varepsilon$ was accomplished as a morphological analogue of the 'shape' of the state itself. That is to say, the person undergoing $at\jmath per\varepsilon$ was conducted over a prescribed route in Kumase; and – at fixed venues in this itinerary – given office holders appropriated items from the part of the body that was the equivalent of their cognitive identity ('position') within the state. This was also an incremental process that was transacted in relation to rank and status. Thus, the *Asantehene* 'took' the head – and did so last of all; the Kumase *Akwamuhene/Asafohene* (general of the *beŋkum* or 'left') 'took' the left ear, and part of the left leg; the Kumase *Bantamahene/Krontihene* (general of the *nifa* or 'right') 'took' the right ear, and part of the right leg; and so on. (As Chapman noted in 1844, the 'victim' that he observed was taken to the dwelling of every major office holder in Kumase for the same purpose.)[26] In sum, in $at\jmath per\varepsilon$ the very existence of the body was appropriated by and liquidated within the framework of the state's morphological representation of itself.

Here, in terms of the destiny of the corporeal body, the state as actor in 'intentions' reserved to itself the right of overriding 'conventions'. It could 'reason' the destiny of physical remains beyond any autonomy of referencing to selfhood. In short, it could inflict itself – via $at\jmath per\varepsilon$ and through the ideological power it connoted – on a discretionary construct of even the most intimate/private kind. It posited invasiveness as pervasiveness, thereby effectively framing the argument (as statement) to say that *you* (anyone) might practise and reason 'legitimation' *in situ*, but *we* (the state) reserve the right to qualify any such definition into (a quite literal) non-existence. The performative structuration of that qualification might vary. Thus, the old man of Eduabin and the victims of $at\jmath per\varepsilon$ were consigned to oblivion by differently marked and signposted routes. But all led to the same destination – an expulsion and a vanishing from history in the shattering of the body.

As is clearly evident from these two exemplary instances, the elegant simplicity of our 'What?/Why?' model of understanding becomes – and very rapidly so – cluttered and occluded, and finally opaque. The capacity to 'take things on', to attach and situate them unequivocally (if never neutrally), suffers overload, and the presumptive role of an objective rationality, as an obvious organizing principle, is overtaken and then swamped by the inputs of a specifically Asante historical ideology. But what kind of ideology? As has been argued throughout, it is an ideology encompassed by and dedicated to hegemonic intent. This is why Gramsci's adversarial framework of interpretation – the situating of hegemony in consent/coercion, and the distinction, in his terms, between Classes *in/for* Themselves – is relevant to the Asante case. The concept of hegemony is, above all, *historical*, and its implementation moves the reading of ideology from a static system of ideas (as promulgated by a vulgar Marxism) to the conceptualization of a ubiquitous practice that saturates and fills the horizon of lived existence. Hegemony, we might say, necessarily furnishes ideology with a dynamic, and that dynamic in turn is rooted in the relational imperative characteristic of hegemony. The Gramscian agenda,

10 'The *gyabom suman* is Placed upon his Lap'

Two of a number of Asante carvings commissioned by Rattray and displayed at the Wembley Exhibition (London, 1924). Both tableaux portray passages – preliminary moments – from the prescribed performance of *atɔperɛ*. Plate 10 shows (from the left) a court crier, an executioner, and a man condemned to death by ritual dismemberment. The condemned has a *sɛpɔ* knife thrust through his cheeks to prevent speech (thereby stopping him from swearing an oath 'on the life of the *Asantehene*'). On his lap is seen the *gyabom sumaŋ* – the property of the *Asantehene* – which was dedicated to driving away evilly disposed 'ghosts'. The fish eagle feathers

11 'The Nasal Septum is Pierced'.

(and porcupine quills) chiefly composing the material component of *gyabom* are visible in the carving. Plate 11 shows (from the left) an executioner leading the condemned by a rope or a thorny creeper inserted through the nasal septum. It was by this means that the person undergoing *atɔpereɛ* was ritually 'led forth' to a succession of sites – and before a series of office holders – throughout Kumase. Rattray himself made published use of these carved representations of a practice that was last transacted, so it is said, in the 1880s. See R.S. Rattray, *Religion and Art in Ashanti* (Oxford, 1927), Figs. 41 and 42.

as we have tried to show, is evident in the historical practice of the Asante state. That is, in sum:

To win hegemony, in Gramsci's view, is to establish moral, political and intellectual leadership in social life by diffusing one's own 'world view' throughout the fabric of society as a whole, thus equating one's own interests with the interests of society at large. Such consensual rule is not, of course, peculiar to capitalism; indeed one might claim that *any* form of political power, to be durable and well-grounded, must evoke a degree of consent from its underlings.[27]

A more precise, general specification of the figuration of hegemony/ideology in the Asante case arises from our argument. That is, all of the evidence points to the ineluctable conclusion that the Asante state, in its historical construction of knowledge and belief, lacked a *transcendent* grasp on history, but that it built, tended, embedded and systematically renewed a very complex and pervasive *transvaluation* of the text(s) of experience. The context(s) of this transvaluation have been discussed throughout. That is, when the persons composing Asante society – when the old man of Eduabin – addressed transvaluation in the everyday, they/he simply and directly engaged in practical resolutions to impinging aspects of the text(s) of Asante historical experience. In the eighteenth and nineteenth centuries, Asante people were primarily and overwhelmingly concerned with the immovable givens of survival and 'the facts of life' (a nexus that foregrounded birth, death, food, kin, reproduction, disease, finitude and the rest, and that correspondingly underprivileged a liberating distancing in the direction of larger and more 'driven' speculations). Their orientation towards and capacity for an ontological understanding were alike sublimated in a quotidian agenda and endlessly subverted by the demands of immediate, fragmented and very 'localized' issues. In short, the horizon of existence was close, and it was often difficult to perceive. As a result, Asante people were fixed in and devoted to rehearsing the limits of a finite comprehensive sense (as is seen most clearly in the constructions placed upon belief), and were persuaded to living the 'facts' of life within these parameters.

The state, however, situated itself above all this, and it was correspondingly free to speculate and direct from a uniquely privileged vantage point. Thus, the cornerstone of its hegemonic practice was this capacity to implement a singular, overall transvaluation of the text(s) of experience. The state alone was (self-)liberated into the 'knowledge' that the 'text-in-itself' of history inertly awaited articulation, and the conferral of meaning(s), through interpretative understanding. Thus, as we have seen, the Asante state stood ever ready in its hermeneutical promulgation of responses and answers to questions of 'what is . . . ?'. Its membership was admitted to the understanding, by very definition of its self-referencing privilege of belonging, that Asante history – as in the performance of *odwira* – was not an 'object' in independent existence or status, but rather a heuristic and pedagogic aggregate of all of the possible hermeneutic acts that might (come to) be performed upon it. In effect, the Asante state may be construed as *the* instrument by means of which the text(s) of experience was/were transvalued. The Asante state, by dint of relentless application, worked to forge apprehension of, and to monopolize implementation of, the constructed truism that history and its interpretations/interpreters only existed within a closed circle of reciprocal creation. In this transvaluation, the 'facts' of history were ideological determinations, inserted and 'managed' by the state in its own hegemonic interest.

The major problem faced by the Asante state, as we have seen in its efforts to translate argument to statement, is that any process of transvaluation dependent upon hermeneutic interventions requires the most careful monitoring and the most unremitting attention. In addition, hegemony cannot *be* done; it must constantly *be seen to be* done. In light of these considerations, the 'facts' of history take on a very specific colouration. The Asante state was aware that the 'facts' of history were constantly in danger of becoming markedly unstable in the sense that the authorized meaning of any component of the text – any moment of the past – might come to betray tendencies to exceed that intended by an original author or a present custodian. There can be no doubt that this situation was exacerbated by the pre-literate status of Asante society. The Asante state acted, and acted again and again, to prevent its own construction of history from dissolving in a congeries of possible genealogies. With the passage of time key 'facts' – like, for example, the *sika dwa kofi* – might well become the site of a sedimentation of accreted significations and traditions. Hegemony was the vigilant censor that worked to prune away any such luxuriant speculation, and to eliminate any possibility of the emergence of alternative genealogies of the past. Indeed, as we have seen, it worked counter to speculation *per se*, assiduously recalling its audience to the singular veracity of authorized meaning.[28]

Articulation, of necessity, requires to be articulated. Thus, it will be readily apparent that the *Asantehene* – as personage(s), as role(s) – has occupied a central position in our account. But how are we to conceptualize this? Evidently, much of Asante historical practice, ritually and otherwise, revolved around the person of the *Asantehene*. But when we look more closely we can see that this individuation (often and misleadingly interpreted in relation to the descriptive category of 'divine kingship') fragments into innumerable ideological splinters. A ruler was most certainly a ruler, but in differentiated, discrete ways that were orientated towards and conformed with key ideological passages in transvaluation.

That is, the *Asantehene* as person was both a living, three-dimensional embodiment (a presence *in* history), and an arena in which the teeming representations/metaphors of ideology were accorded focus, distillation and rehearsal (a presence *of* history). The person of the *Asantehene*, moving through his life, was the forum in which his *aspectual* capacity for articulating understanding literally took place.

Any *Asantehene* was a congeries of ideological clues, directives and statements. And, in consequence of his unique status as representation, literally everything about him was weighted with overt significances. It is in this context that we might locate the Asante understanding that an *Asantehene* lived out his public existence within a framework of commentary and explication; that is, for example, when an *Asantehene* took the lead on a ritual occasion, his movements and actions were described, as they were taking place, by designated *nhenkwaa*. In this way (and supremely so at *odwira*) an essential pedagogy was visually displayed and, at the same time, verbally reinforced.[29] Rectitude and power were distilled in an *Asantehene*, and then refracted through him. A leading illustration of this is the concept and practice of *anibɔne* – gazing, staring at – often glossed as the 'evil eye', but understood in the case of an *Asantehene's* look as being something that was capable of modifying or altering reality. This constituted a very basic reification in a society that, as we have seen, invested a great deal in, and placed a high premium on, visual (re)presentations of all kinds. Across Asante society the practice of *anibɔne* worked as a form of non-verbal duelling (or wordless *mpoatwa*), an endlessly repeated contest either to assert or to deny the individually presumed specifics of relational 'positioning' between people. The gaze of an *Asantehene* was the expressive masterpiece of this form of behaviour, for it, and it alone, carried with it the full burden of ideological address, and the unequivocal understanding of what lay behind it. Thus, we can know about, and must be aware of, even if we cannot *see*, the eyes endlessly addressing one another, in crucial if transient ideological figurations of power, whenever our historical sources report an *Asantehene* presiding over a court case or a discussion of policy.[30]

Implicitly (and often explicitly) throughout our account it can be seen that in pre-literate Asante culture the human body and the conceptualization of the person furnished, unsurprisingly enough, an essential dictionary of references and tropes that framed and described Asante understanding. In effect, there existed a powerful imperative to situate understanding by reducing its complexities to the economies of this readily comprehensible fixity. The state itself was morphologically constructed and read, in one pervasive version, as a 'body'. Equally, it was the state as guarantor that presided over the individuated 'personhood' named Asante (embodied in the collective *sunsum* inhering in the *sika dwa kofi*). Thus, the actual bodies and persons of Asante office holders – those who articulated the state in history – possessed and displayed the most dense repertoire of meanings. This understanding is paralleled in Asante tradition, which is devoted to and focused upon the foregrounding of individual office holders. As ideology, the issue can be seen, as was intended, in the simplest, most direct terms; office holders' bodies, exuviae, spatial (re)presentations, boundaries, speech, dress, ornamentation, situational norms of behaviour (in their movement, decorum, eating, dancing, celebrating, mourning, etc.), and all of the myriad constituents of a visible, social personhood of belonging in and to the state, taken together, constituted an ideological site of the highest definition and impact.

The most prominent landmark on this site – the *ur* embodiment of all of the mnemonics, traces and residues of ideology and history – was, of course, the *Asantehene* himself. As we have seen, he was all at once an expressive metaphor *for* the state's hegemonic project, and an aspectual personification *of* that project. A crucial implementation – a tool, a blunt instrument – flowed from this. That is, the commemoration and recounting of the state's hegemonic construction of the past (and the present and the future), as in the *odwira*, could be distilled to the focus of a single person and body, and pedagogically explicated in the barest and most direct terms via the medium of that agency. As has been indicated, the impress of this was the distinguishing hallmark of Asante tradition, and the key to its formulated content and expression. That is, to reiterate, Asante tradition was relentlessly *personalized* in and through the being and identity of those individuals, up to and including the *Asantehene*, who had occupied the office-holding apparatus of the state. In hegemonic intention (and as ideological statement) such a determination of historical narrative constituted a seamless evolution that was simply imparted. It both preserved the past and proclaimed the future in a single register. Tradition, it might be said, employed this device to authorize the 'continuous present' of the Asante experience. Thus, in 1817, in a momentous aside, a highly bemused Bowdich noted that in speech (via an *ɔkyeame*) the *Asantehene* Osei Tutu Kwame 'always spoke of the acts of all of his ancestors as his own'.[31]

The *Asantehene* personified the state's project. The framing of warfare in Asante tradition is a succinct, exemplary illustration. That is, whatever the complex shadings of cause and effect, the understanding of war in tradition – informed and shaped by the ideological agenda that has been reviewed – was cast overwhelmingly as a *personalized* encounter between rectitude (the *Asantehene* as the state) and varieties of deviant error (the enemy chief, general or leader as negation of the project of the Asante state). As one typical traditional accounting confesses,

The causes of wars are numerous and varied but most wars originated from the insults inflicted on the *Asantehene's* personal servants [*nhenkwaa*] by the subjects of another chief. If the King's servant has been maltreated he sends a message to the other chief demanding the punishment or surrender of the culprit. It is an act of great disrespect [to the person of the *Asantehene*] if the chief of the offending subject refuses to deal with the case personally or to hand it over to the King, who, if he decides to fight calls a meeting of his elders, puts the matter before them and urges them to uphold the dignity of their King. Wars are not declared when any commoner is treated harshly, or even killed. If this is done the offence is treated as a civil case. But if the King's servants, for example 'esen, kradwarefo, baamufo' [all types of *nhenkwaa*] are maltreated the case, unless it is well handled, is likely to bring about a war.[32]

In the foregoing, other persons (*nhenkwaa*) are construed as being attached to the *Asantehene*, in the direct sense of being viewed as extensions of his own personage. This sovereign metaphor of the person of the *Asantehene* was variously employed throughout tradition. Thus, the reported (constructed) utterances of an *Asantehene* – commonly rendered in tradition in systematized, formulaic ways – were themselves directed towards situating and then explicating the ideology of which he was the embodied expression. In tropes of this kind the *Asantehene's* speech (in discourse with an interlocutor) was vividly instructive; his utterances were constructed to form an instrumental prism through which the shadow of ideology could be seen with great and pointed clarity. But the effect was achieved in a particular way. Just as the *nhenkwaa*, as 'part' of the *Asantehene*, served to mobilize assertive declamation by that which they represented, so tradition customarily cast the *Asantehene's* interlocutor in the role of catalyst. Thus, in many traditions the *conditions* of the ideological statement being conveyed are actually put into the mouth of the interlocutor(s). The *Asantehene* then – by utterance, or in numerous other gestural ways – gives definitive *assent* to them. His role is that of affirming an unequivocal veracity.

In the following example, attention should be paid to the way in which metaphors of apposite power are accreted and piled up; in this exchange, ostensibly about the *Gyamanhene* Kwadwo Adinkra, the pattern of the wording is also employed to confirm the nature of other ideological relationships. The right order of husband/wife, male/female is a knowing mirror – not only of *Asantehene* (Asante)/*Gyamanhene* (Gyaman), but also of Asante state/Asante society. It might also be observed that the very structure of the discourse – characteristically, it is not driven by the *Asantehene*, but by his interlocutor – liberates the *Asantehene* into that realm that transcends contingency. He is meditated power, and as such he is simply encouraged by another to the appropriate ideological stance or manifestation of his leadership of the state. Because tradition is *ex post facto*, and because the state cannot be in error, the interlocutor functions as an enabling mechanism for the ongoing realization of a historic destiny. The tradition purports to recount how and why the *Asantehene* Osei Tutu Kwame came to declare war upon the *Gyamanhene* Kwadwo Adinkra in 1818. The interlocutor is one Sampanne (whom we have already encountered), the son of an Asante father and a Gyaman mother, an *ahenkwaa* in service to Osei Tutu Kwame, and subsequently, perhaps, Kumase *Adumhene*.

On his return [from visiting his relatives in Gyaman] Sampanne intimated as follows to the warrior *Asantehene* Osei Bonsu [Osei Tutu Kwame]: 'Nana, the Gyaman state has not only developed, but it has also become wealthy; you had best bestir yourself and rise up and go there to seek riches and captives for the development of your [own] state.' The King replied as follows: 'I refer to the *Gyamanhene* [Kwadwo Adinkra] as my wife; if a wife renders good service to her husband without any malice, he should not pick any quarrel with her. I have no good motive for invading Gyaman. As you are well aware, I am a warrior but I do not like or want to go to war without cause.' The roguish Sampanne replied to the King as follows: 'Nana, all that you are saying is true enough, but a man who intends to beat his wife can always find a pretext. If you intend beating her, you can complain about why she has given you such cold water to wash with when it is not hot enough; when it is too warm, you can complain it is too hot and does she therefore intend to burn you? If your food is under or over salted, that could be a pretext for beating her. In a nutshell, I know how to "stir the war". With your permission, I can travel there [to Gyaman] and provoke the King and his subjects to furnish you with the necessary pretext; so permit me to spend a few days there.'

No King hates to amass wealth, so eventually he [Osei Bonsu] gave Sampanne permission to travel to Gyaman. [emphases added][33]

By way of conclusion II: ideology and inscription

If we look for the self-sustaining qualities in, or the 'shape' of, the ideological matrix of power that structured the Asante experience in the eighteenth and nineteenth centuries, what do we find? Here, finally, I think that the Gramscian perspective (or any reading ultimately grounded in Marx) can be enlarged and refined, at least in that crucial area in which transvaluation takes clear precedence over transcendence. A history constructed in this manner, and as promulgated by the Asante state, is an ongoing essay in the textual reconciliation of discrete, putatively divergent genealogies. Consequences, and great difficulties, necessarily arise from this way of 'doing epistemology', and, as has been seen, it is precisely the hermeneutic debris of this focus that litters the explicative transit through *odwira*. In relation to managing its own project, the Asante state is cast in the part of *bricoleur* – at least in the very significant sense of its commitment to the unremitting process of (re)evaluating, (re)assembling and then (re)directing relevant genealogical items. But, of course, the object of this ceaseless exercise in 'making and mending' is to capture history – that is, to dissolve argument in statement, and thereby to embed the rectitude of state power.[34]

Many commentators – Weber, very notably – have emphasized the abiding gap that inevitably exists between power and legitimation in the (re)presentation of political institutions, and have then pointedly and accurately identified ideology (of whatever construction) as being *the* crucial technique of closure between the two. Hegemonic intention both foregrounds the significance and exacerbates the urgency of constructing resolutions to this problem. Thus, in terms of its implementation in the Asante context, ideology evinces an identifiable dissimulation. That is, the Asante social formation that hegemonic intention penetrates, shapes and saturates is conditioned by this very process not to *desire* ideology *per se*, but rather to *desire within* it. A conceptual web (rooted in both knowledge and belief, and expressed in reference and symbol), dedicated to the task at hand, defines and polices the parameters of that *within*. The propulsive dynamic that drives Asante ideological structuration (the indispensable instrument that persuades to desire within) is, as we have documented, a mnemonic capacity endlessly to recall and to rehearse history as a series of authorized epiphanies, directly traceable to and emanating from the sense of a continuity from a beginning in time.

This understanding (*Verstehen*) of a beginning is nuanced to furnish an arsenal of weapons appropriate to a plethora of situational interventions. Thus, and summarily, the Asante state availed itself of and deployed a kaleidoscopic, but intertwined, battery of commentaries on beginnings: the fundamentals of knowledge and belief; the insertion of the agrarian order (a heroic episode, buttressed by commemoration of its hunting and gathering predecessor); the 'invention' of kinship and society, of political authority and the state; the determination of the conditions of accumulation and wealth, and all that that implied; and, most pointedly, the coming of the key mnemonic device of the *sika dwa kofi*, together with the initiatory, and 'absolutist', codification and valorization of the fundamental, ubiquitous determinations of the power of the Asante state (the diagram of desiring within) authored by the first *Asantehene* Osei Tutu and the eponymous Komfo Anokye. In hegemonic intention, Asante ideology served as the means – in Ricoeur's apposite phrasing – recurrently 'to prolong the shock wave of the founding act', and thereby to induce and to reinforce a consent in which people 'think *from* it [ideology] rather than *about* it' (emphases added).[35] In our most fully detailed instance – the recurrent performance of the *odwira* – individual reflection (the project of the person) could be subsumed in a construct that affirmed a desiring within history (the project of the state).

Throughout the eighteenth and nineteenth centuries, therefore, the articulation of the Asante past in the Asante present was crucial to the structuring of the conditions of temporal evolution. Although it is extremely difficult to describe with any very apt economy, it is perhaps a just summary to characterize the realization (the working out) of this trajectory in terms of the superimposition of discourse on language, and the subordination of both to a conscious historical sense. Obviously and clearly, Asante Twi furnished the linguistic structure of signification as such. But equally patently, this bedrock structure was activated in and through a discourse that was itself subjected to determination(s) by a historical ideology. Indeed, the ideological production over time of myriad discursive effects denotes or punctuates those seemingly endless, and endlessly repeated, points where the Asante state impacted upon society and/or the individual, and inscribed its own version(s) of the historical within them. In these terms, it was precisely inscription of this kind that constituted and determined the 'event' called *odwira*. It was also, however, inscription of this kind that killed the old man of Eduabin.[36]

Ideological inscription rests upon and resides in historical inequities in power. That is manifestly obvious. But simply to enumerate such features as a 'political history' – or, by extension, to associate them with circumspectly derived (and crude) generalizations about class and class fractions in relation to base, superstructure and the rest – is to substitute narrative mechanics for analysis. This error is a form of solipsism, in effect a blind flight into Marxian idealism (or one of its many *marxisant* variants). As has been observed, such procedures are common throughout the corpus of Asante and a deal of other Africanist historiography, and, to reiterate, they are teleological in at least two ways. First, they constitute (to return to Peel's felicitous phrasing) a type of 'left functionalism': a circular, self-validating *description* that eliminates the requirement to analyse *how* and *in what ways* Asante ideology was constructed and maintained. Second (and in the bleakest of ironies), the naive descriptive technique employed serves to impose a redundancy notice on the laborious, narrative reconstruction of 'facts' that is its own substance. That is, the Asante historical experience is construed and represented as being an elaborately footnoted pendant to a mechanical, descriptive model that is prior to it intellectually (at least in the mind of the practitioner). This can hardly be dignified as *theorizing*, either *from* Asante history, or *between* that history and any cogent level of analysis. Such procedures, it might also be remarked, carry within themselves discomforting echoes of older modes of writing in which cultures such as that of Asante were denied any specificity or autonomy of thought or action.

As has been argued throughout, it is essential that the ideological dimension of Asante history be understood both in relation to its structurations (its recoverable 'given-ness'), and in terms of its active voice. With regard to this second area of focus, it is clear that the determination of the conditions of Asante intersubjectivity (as is revealed, for a fleeting, documented moment in 1862, in an encounter between an *Asantehene* and an old man) was contextualized within a highly complex reciprocity – an interactive site in which ideology 'made' people, and people 'made' ideology. This conclusion is unexceptionally commonsensical, in cultural criticism, if not in Africanist history. A usable, now very famous analogy is provided by the example of the 'game of cards', as formulated by Elias. First, the 'game' itself (ideology) has no existence of its own outside of the players involved in it. But second, and in an equivalent way, the actual 'card playing' (the acting out of historical identity) of each and all individual 'players' (actors and actresses in history) is conditioned and indeed governed by rules of interdependence implied in the very formation/figuration of the 'game' itself. Hence:

The 'game' is no more an abstraction than the 'players'. The same applies to the figuration formed by the four players sitting around the table. If the term 'concrete' means anything at all, we can say that the figuration formed by the players is as concrete as the players themselves. By figuration we mean the changing pattern created by the players as a whole – not only by their intellects but by their whole selves, the totality of their dealings in their relationships with each other.[37]

Let us briefly pursue this analogy. Elsewhere I have argued that in terms of 'a coherent world view and an integrated belief system, the nineteenth century – together with all antecedent Asante history – effectively ended in the 1880s'.[38] That is to say, the 'rules of the game' underwent drastic modification and change. The instruments of this transformation included unprecedented levels of external pressure (that culminated in British colonial overrule); incremental exposure to a vast range of novel ideas and alien influences (that prompted – to summarize work done on the matter – partial, unevenly deep, but significant shifts in perceptions of individual selfhood and of the historic bases of power and the liens of authority); and – enabling, exacerbating, and in no way successfully mediating or controlling the foregoing – an increasing loss of direction within the Asante polity. There can be no doubt at all that the inexorable momentum of European imperialism accelerated this loss of direction. But the crucial mechanics of this process took place in the 1880s. Then, a bewildering succession of individual dynasts, Kumase factions, disaffected provincials and alienated subjects resorted to a prolonged, murderous series of civil wars in a forlorn attempt, not merely to arrogate power, but, more importantly, to restore the coherent *status quo ante* of the eighteenth- and nineteenth-century past. Thus, the object of all contesting factions, it should be noted, was to dispose of the received continuity of ideological authority. In the most literal of senses, as the sources document, the wars of the 1880s were about the actual, physical *possession* of the *sika dwa kofi*. But the 'rules of the game' were in the process of drastic change, and it proved impossible to sustain, let alone 're-invent', a dissolving certainty. In the event, in the desperate attempt at recovery, political authority became cynically predatory upon Asante society, and the legitimacy of the Asante state, already under severe external threat, was systematically fractured and undermined from within.

If all sovereign ideologies of authority and legitimacy carry within themselves, as is commonly conceded, the seeds of contradiction and conflict which their effective articulation is calculated to mask or otherwise to suppress, then they also – when the conditions of their being (the 'rules of the game') are altered by historical developments – never make themselves over absolutely *de novo*. There is no such thing as a historical clean sheet or *tabula rasa*. Thus, the ideological formation of Asante in the eighteenth and nineteenth centuries may be construed as composing, in the circumstances of the twentieth century, an enormous quarry of residues, traces, echoes, hints, ambiguities, and all of the rest. Throughout the British and Ghanaian periods of overrule Asante has 'trailed' the past that has been examined here. But it has done so under the aegis of another dispensation, and within the very real constraints of a radically curtailed autonomy. The continuing history of the Asante in the twentieth century requires another interpreter, or, at the least, another book.

APPENDIX I
Bowdich's *The First Day of the Yam Custom*

(18: *odwira fomemene*; Saturday, 6 September 1817)

The *odwira fomemene* has been discussed above (pp. 203–12). Bowdich's engraving of *The First Day of the Yam Custom* has likewise been contextualized and interpreted (pp. 240–2). The full text of Bowdich's description of the *odwira fomemene* of Saturday, 6 September 1817 is reproduced below. It is taken from T.E. Bowdich, *Mission from Cape Coast Castle to Ashantee, with a Statistical Account of that Kingdom, and Geographical Notices of Other Parts of the Interior of Africa* (John Murray, London, 1819), 274–8. I have identified the individuals named in Bowdich's text; I have also given notes on items of especial interest. Otherwise, I have added nothing to Bowdich's words.

/274/ In the afternoon of Saturday, the King [the *Asantehene* Osei Tutu Kwame, reigned 1804–23] received all the caboceers and captains in the large area, where the Dankara canons are /275/ placed.[1] The scene was marked with all the splendor of our own entre, and many additional novelties. The crush in the distance was awful and distressing. All the heads of the kings and caboceers whose kingdoms had been conquered, from Sai Tootoo [the first *Asantehene* Osei Tutu, died 1712 or 1717] to the present reign, with those of the chiefs who had been executed for subsequent revolts, were displayed by two parties of executioners, each upwards of a hundred, who passed in an impassioned dance, some with the most irresistible grimace, some with the most frightful gesture: they clashed their knives on the skulls, in which sprigs of thyme were inserted, to keep the spirits from troubling the King. I never felt so grateful for being born in a civilized country. Firing and drinking palm wine were the only divertissemens to the ceremony of the caboceers presenting themselves to the King; they were announced, and passed all round the circle saluting every umbrella: their bands preceded; we reckoned above forty drums in that of the King of-Dwabin [the *Dwabenhene* Kwasi Boaten, fled into exile 1832, and died there 1839].[2] The effect of the splendor, the tumult, and the musquetry, was afterwards heightened by torch light. We left the ground at 10 o'clock; the umbrellas were crowded even in the distant streets, the town was covered like a large fair, the broken sounds of distant horns and drums filled up the momentary pauses of the firing which encircled us: the uproar continued until four in the morning, just before which the King retired.[3] I have attempted a drawing, (No. 2.) it is by no means adequate, yet more so than description could be.

On the left side of the drawing is a group of captains dancing and firing, as

12 *The First Day of the Yam Custom*, from T.E. Bowdich, *Mission from Cape Coast Castle to Ashantee* (London, 1819). Bowdich's drawing records events during the *odwira fomemene* in Kumase on Saturday, 6 September 1817. The original is in colour, and is one single continuous panorama measuring 28×8.25 inches. This reproduction should be read from left to right and from top to bottom. In the bottom picture the *Asantehene* Osei Tutu Kwame is shown seated under the large umbrella surmounted by a finial in the form of an elephant. The remaining officers of the British mission to Asante – Hutchison, Bowdich and Tedlie (James having already left Kumase on 12 July) – are to be seen in full dress uniform on Osei Tutu Kwame's left (in the centre of the bottom picture).

described in our entre.[4] Immediately above the encircling soldiery, is a young caboceer under his umbrella, borne on the shoulders of his chief slave; he salutes as he passes along, and is preceded and surrounded by boys (with elephant tails, feathers, &c.) and his captains, who, lifting their swords in the air, halloo out the deeds of his fore-fathers; his stool is borne close to /276/ him, ornamented with a large brass bell.[5] Above is the fanciful standard of a chief, who is preceded and followed by numerous attendants; he is supported round the waist by a confidential slave, and one wrist is so heavily laden with gold, that it is supported on the head of a small boy; with the other hand he is saluting a seated caboceer, sawing the air by a motion from the wrist. His umbrella is sprung up and down to increase the breeze, and large grass fans are also playing; his handsomest slave girl follows, bearing on her head a small red leather trunk, full of gold ornaments, and rich cloths; behind are soldiers and drummers, who throw their white-washed drums in the air, and catch them again, with much agility and grimace, as they walk along. Boys are in the front, bearing elephants tails, fly flappers, &c. and his captains with uplifted swords, are hastening forward the musicians and soldiers. Amongst the latter is the stool, so stained with blood that it is thought decent to cover it with red silk. Behind the musicians is Odumata [the Kumase *Adumhene* Adum Ata, born *c.* 1752, appointed *Adumhene c.* 1785, died *c.* 1822],[6] coming round to join the procession in his state hammock lined with red taffeta, and smoking under his umbrella, at the top of which is a stuffed leopard.[7] In the area below is an unfortunate victim, tortured in the manner described in the entre, and two of the King's messengers clearing the way for him.[8] The King's four linguists are seen next; two, Otee [Kumase *Boakye Yam Panin ɔkyeame* Oti Panin, enstooled 1814, murdered in Akwamu 1826] and Quancum [Kumase *Akankade ɔkyeame* Kwasi Kankam, killed at Katamanso 1826],[9] are seated in conversation under an umbrella; the chief, Adoosey [Kumase *Gyakye ɔkyeame* Kwadwo Adusei 'Kyakya', i.e. 'hunchback', enstooled *c.* 1807, executed by the *Asantehene* Osei Yaw Akoto *c.* 1829],[10] is swearing a royal messenger, (to fetch an absent caboceer,) by putting a gold handled sword between his teeth, whilst Agay [Kumase *Ankobea ɔkyeame* Asante Agyei, enstooled 1814, died *c.* 1823][11] delivers the charge, and exhorts him to be resolute. The criers, all deformed and with monkey skin caps, are seated in the front.[12] Under the next umbrella is the royal stool, thickly cased in gold. Gold pipes, fans of ostrich wing feathers, captains seated with gold swords, wolves heads and snakes as large as life of the same metal, depending from the handles, girls bearing silver bowls, body /277/ guards, &c. &c. are mingled together till we come to the King, seated in a chair of ebony and gold, and dressed much in the same way as described at the first interview.[13] He is holding up his two fingers to receive the oath of the captain to the right, who, pointing to a distant country, vows to conquer it. On the right and left of the state umbrellas are the flags of Great Britain, Holland, and Denmark.[14] A group of painted figures are dancing up to the King, in the most extravagant attitudes, beating time with their long knives on the skulls stuck full of thyme.[15] On the right of the King is the eunuch, who superintends the group of small boys, the children of the nobility, waving elephants tails, (spangled with gold,) feathers &c.:[16] behind him is the above mentioned captain and other chiefs dressed as in the left end of the drawing. Musicians, seated and standing, are playing on instruments cased or plated with gold.[17] The officers of the Mission are next seen [Messrs Hutchison,

Bowdich, Tedlie][18], their linguists in front, their soldiers, servants, and flag behind, at the back of whom is placed the King's state hammock, under its own umbrella. Adjoining the officers is old Quatchie Quofie [Kumase *Akwamuhene/Asafohene* Kwaakye Kofi, enstooled in the 1770s, died early 1820s][19] and his followers; at the top of his umbrella is stuck a small black wooden image, with a bunch of rusty hair on the head, intending to represent the famous Akim caboceer who was killed by him [the rebel Akyem ɔhene Ofosu, killed late 1770s/early 1780s?][20]; vain of the action, he is seen according to his usual custom, dancing before and deriding his fallen enemy, whilst his captains bawl out the deed, and halloo their acclamations. The manner of drinking palm wine is exhibited in the next group, a boy kneels beneath with a second bowl to catch the droppings, (it being a great luxury to suffer the liquor to run over the beard,)[21] whilst the horns flourish, and the captains halloo the strong names. The Moors [Muslims] are easily distinguished by their caps, and preposterous turbans. One is blessing a Dagwumba [Dagomba] caboceer, who is passing on horseback, (the animal covered with fetishes and bells,) escorted by his men /278/ in tunics, bearing lances, and his musicians with rude violins, distinct from the sanko.[22] The back of the whole assembly is lined with royal soldiers, and the commoner ones are ranged in front, with here and there a captain and a group of musicians, who, some with an old cocked hat, some with a soldier's jacket, &c. &c. afford a ludicrous appearance. This description will be rendered more illustrative of the drawing, by referring to that of our entre.[23]

APPENDIX II
A glossary of some Asante Twi terms

Included here are some of the principal words, terms, compounds or phrases that have been used throughout the text. The chief purpose of this glossary is to provide cultural and historical context, rather than any detailed or formal linguistic analysis. Each entry has the page number in the main text at which it (commonly first) appears, and where its contextual usage is most fully discussed and defined. The following abbreviations have been used throughout:

sing.   singular
pl.   plural
der.   derivation, derived from
der(?).   possibly and/or probably but not certainly derived from
lit.   literally
syn.   synonym
ant.   antonym
cf.   compare
impl.   implying, by implication, carrying the sense of
alt.   alternative or variant spelling

The grammatical identification or naming of each part of speech (verb, noun and pronoun – the core lexical items in Twi – and derived forms such as infinitives, gerunds, etc.) has been generally eschewed, for it is normally self-evident. However, the matter of context is of the highest importance in another, but allied, sphere. That is, many words or terms can only be understood in contexts of use, and must be translated accordingly. I have followed an Occamist principle of first stating the meaning(s) as used in the text, and then giving explanation of additional meaning(s) – not exhaustively, but as these bear upon or have relevance to the issues at hand. All entries have been checked, as far as is possible, against existing Twi dictionaries, wordlists and grammars, and over the years with numerous interlocutors in Asante. One or two other preliminaries need to be addressed. First, there are abiding uncertainties in current Twi orthography. Thus far, Twi has not been subjected to the rigorous orthographical treatment accorded to, for example, Yoruba. Moreover, Asante Twi is but one among a number of

272

dialect forms of the language. One result of all this is that, for some words, alternative spellings are used and are acceptable; equally, for some words, no agreed standardized form of spelling is universally subscribed to, and variants occur. I provide the spelling as used in the text, but I also give such common alternatives or variants as are known to me. Second, and obviously related to the foregoing, problems inhere in the structuration and very nature of Twi. As is well known, relative and/or positional intonation (low, high, middle) applies to each and every syllable in Twi. No systematic attempt has been made in this glossary to render this feature – except in one vital particular, which is of the highest cultural and historical import. Intonation relative to meaning and/or expressive use is among the glories of Twi utterance, permitting as it does to Asante speech a variety of punning, word play, suggestion, ambiguity and weighted misdirection. Thus, *kakra*, with the tone rising on the second syllable, and a long final *a*, means huge; but the same word *kakra*, with an even intonation throughout, means small or little, the exact opposite.

This feature of the language finds its most formalized, and formulaic, expression in the proverbial form known as *ɛbɛ* (pl. *mbɛ*: see below). Thus, by way of brief example, the word *guaŋ* – differently stressed (*guaŋ*; *(o)guaŋ*) – can mean either trouble/to be troubled *or* a sheep. Hence, the punning *ɛbɛ*: *akoa di guaŋ a, ne ho guaŋ no* ('When a subject or a slave eats a sheep, he is in/has trouble'). A simple play on words here, moreover, very typically opens into broader areas of cultural understanding. Thus, and literally, it was inappropriate for someone in the status of *akoa* to eat a sheep, and any such action would get him/her into trouble. But 'eats a sheep' also connotes an act of oblation or sacrificial offering, and so the embedded understanding is that any *akoa* who had resort to such a measure must be (*a*) already in trouble or troubled; (*b*) guilty of committing some crime unknown to his/her overlord or master; and (*c*) making a promissory offering in (clandestine) expiation. The master of an *akoa* would want to be informed of *a*, *b* and *c*, and so the offending subject or slave was in trouble/troubled in yet another way. I have tried to suggest and to flesh out something of this kind of density (intonation, meaning, cultural resonance) in various places in this glossary.

In 1916, Rattray – an assiduous, gifted student of Asante Twi – noted correctly that the language embraced a 'variety of vowel sounds which (in words otherwise spelt the same) alters the entire meaning'; his own examples of this (in his preferred orthography) were: *(e)sen*; a court herald (*(e)* as in English 'fed'); *(o)sen*; a pot (*(o)* as in broad e in English); *(o)sen*; from *sen*, to surpass (*(o)* as in nasal e in English); and *(a)sen*; the waist (*(a)* between English i and e). This feature, he continued, 'makes the Twi language one of exceptional difficulty for the European to master'. This point is well taken. Accordingly, in this glossary I have simply dropped the initial vowel in the interests of clarity. Similarly, I have ignored medial vowel duplication (hence, for instance, the word *baamu* appears in order as *bam* not *baa*). Finally, I have dropped the nasalized consonants '*m*' and '*n*' (such that, for example, *mfufuwa* appears under '*f*' and *nhenkwaa* appears under '*h*'). For the rest, I have followed that set of orthographical conventions first set out by the Rev. J.G. Christaller in 1881.

b

bakoma   (p. 79) pl. *mmakoma*: der. *ɔba* (child) + *koma* (heart): lit. 'a beloved child': used of someone to indicate that they were noble and genteel: impl. respectable, well-born; sometimes honorifically applied to those of noble birth, high-born 'aristocrats': however, by impl., the verbal phrase *di bakoma* (syn. *di ɔdehyeɛsɛm/di adehyeɛsɛm*) connoted wilful, imperious and arbitrary behaviour; it suggested the concept of 'lording it over' someone, often in a rude, aggressive or 'aristocratic' manner.

baamu   (p. 159) der. *baŋ* (fence, enclosure) + *mu*: lit. 'a fenced/enclosed place': used of a mausoleum: syn. *barim, barem, banem*: in the sense of a fenced-in place where kings were buried, it was applied to the *Oyoko Kɔkɔɔ* mausoleum in the Kumase ward of *bantama* where those *Asantehenes* who had died in office were buried: deposed *Asantehenes* and other members of the *Oyoko Kɔkɔɔ abusua* were interred in the royal Kumase graveyards of *akyeremade* or *ahemaho*, or in the village of Breman.

barimfoɔ   (p. 214) lit. 'people of the *barim*' (syn. *baamu*): mausoleum caretakers and attendants.

bayi   (p. 133) witchcraft: der(?). *ɔba* (child) + *yi* (to remove, take away): lit. 'to take away a child', encapsulating the belief that witchcraft operated most potently within the *abusua*: cf. *bayi yɛ abusuade*, 'witchcraft is inborn among or hereditary between [members of] an *abusua*': syn. *abayisɛm, abayigoru, abayide*: cf. *ɔbayifo* (pl. *abayifoɔ*, a witch or wizard): syn. *ayɛn, kaberɛ, ɔbonsam*: the word *ayɛn* (cf. *yɛŋŋ*, a fiery red; *yɛŋ*, to foster, to breed; *ye*, to have the condition of, to manifest or display) gives some insight into the conceptualization of witchcraft: cf. also that *ɔbayifo* might mean an old woman (a hag), and that *mberewa* (old women) were widely regarded as adepts of witchcraft (being ideally placed in *abusua* terms, and 'jealous' of those who could still bear children): the Asante distinguished between the practices of *bayi boro* ('hot' or maleficent witchcraft: cf. *aboro*, injury, hurt, malevolence) and *bayi papaa* ('cool' or beneficent witchcraft: cf. *papa*, moral good, benefit, welfare: impl. prosperity).

$\varepsilon b\varepsilon$ (p. 81) pl. $mb\varepsilon$: a proverb or aphorism: der. $b\varepsilon$ (to recite, to declaim, to pronounce in a fixed or rhetorical manner): cf. *abebu*, 'speaking in proverbs'; *abebu de*, a symbol or a kind of mnemonics, using *burohono* (maize husks), cowries, feathers, etc. strung together to assist in recalling and repeating proverbs.

$b\varepsilon y\varepsilon\varepsilon\ d\varepsilon n$ (p. 131) a praise poem of the *Asantehenes*: der. $b\varepsilon$ (to emit or enunciate a sound) + *edi* (a name; impl. renowned): cf. *abodiŋ*; *abodɛn*, praise, naming with praise, the appellations of an office holder: the recital of *abodiŋ* (see $\jmath boadeni$) is a characteristic feature of the opening stanza(s) of *apaeɛ* (der. *pae*, in the sense of to cry out the titles of someone), poetry that celebrated the personality of an office holder, and that was recited in his presence.

obirebire   (p. 179) unseemly loquacity, loose talk, prattling: impl. noisy quarrelling, rowing, brawling: syn. *berɛberɛ* (also voluble, glib), *kurokuro*, *bɛtebɛte*: der(?). *berɛ*, with the sense of to weary, to wear down or to harass: cf. *obirebirefo* (pl. *abirebirefoɔ*), a prattler, idle talker: cf. the syn. *kurokuro* which impl. grumbling, garrulousness, meddling.

$\jmath bir\varepsilon mp\jmath n$ (p. 42) pl. *abirɛmpɔn*. lit. 'big man'. der. $\jmath barima$ (a man, a male person; a valiant man; manhood) + $p\jmath n/p\jmath\eta$ (great, large): impl. rule, power, wealth: a hereditary title held by the heads of territorial chiefdoms, and also conferred upon the very wealthiest accumulators: the title was symbolized by the possession of the *mena/mmra* (the elephant tail), the heraldic badge of the $\jmath bir\varepsilon mp\jmath n$: ant. (perhaps) $\jmath ber\varepsilon\varepsilon fo$ (syn. *ohiani*), a poor, needy, destitute man.

$\jmath bo$ (p. 108) lit. a stone or rock: pl. *abo*: one of the three major categories of *abosom*: powers that derived from the forest, in the broadest sense of whatever grew wild: a stone or rock was a common locus for this class of manifestation: the $\jmath bo$ was held to have a special relationship with *mmoatia*, and was associated with healing: syn. *ŋkwatia ŋkwatia wuram*: der(?). $(\eta)kwati(\varepsilon)$, impl. avoidance + *wuram* (syn. *wura*), weeds, grass, bush, whatever grows wild.

$\jmath boadeni$ (p. 172) pl. *aboadenfoɔ*: lit. a famous person (*onipa a wagye di*): used of the 'great names' of a patrilineal *ntɔrɔ*: cf. *boa*, to help, to assist; cf. also *aboade* (*ɔboa ade*), a thank-offering.

bogya   See *mogya*.

$b\jmath k\jmath\jmath$ (p. 179) soft, gentle: impl. quietness: used to describe the modulated softness of an *Asantehene's* speech: der. $b\jmath$ (to utter, to address) + $k\jmath$ (in the sense of setting about something in one particular way): syn. *bɔkɔbɔkɔ*: cf. *bɔtɔ, bɔtɔbɔtɔ*, soft, mild, impl. lenient: but cf. also *bɔtebɔte*, loquacious, but in the sense of voluble, glib: there is a punning component here, for $b\jmath$ (to utter) + $k\jmath k\jmath$ (to threaten) means to warn or to menace: i.e. the speech of an *Asantehene* carries the passive meaning of 'warning' (it is to be listened to carefully) and the active meaning (it is or can be a warning or threat).

abonsamkɔm   (p. 133) a cultic movement that arose in Asante in 1879–80: der. *abonsam* (wizard, sorcerer, witch) + *akɔm* (a possession dance): the *abonsamkɔm* movement was also known as *ɔdomaŋkama* (see *ɔdomaŋkama*).

borɔŋ   (p. 78) pl. *mborɔŋ*. lit. a street, a lane: used of the 'wards' of an Akan town: Kumase was described as the city of 77 such 'wards' or quarters, each under the authority of a designated office holder: syn. *abɔnteŋ* (pl. *mbɔnteŋ*): der. *b(o)ɔ + te (teŋ)*, long; impl. straight, regular: thus, *abɔnteŋ* also described the long, straight, main street that generally ran through the middle of an Asante settlement.

ɔbosom   (p. 108) pl. *abosom*; the ultimate der. of this basic word remains unclear: cf. *ɔbo*, a stone, a rock/*bɔ*, generically a verb of action or movement, specifically (in one aspect) impl. originating or creating + *som*, to serve, to be a servant of (a master, including *onyame*): but cf. also *so*, in the sense of attaining to, being able to: *ɛso*, over, above, up on high: *soa*, to thrive, to flourish: *som*, suggesting a continuance: the *abosom* have been variously rendered as gods, tutelary spirits and 'fetishes': they were in fact powers of supernatural origin, anthropomorphized as the 'children' or as the 'servants' of *onyame*: the essence of an *ɔbosom* was *tumi* (power) that emanated from *onyame*: many classifications of *abosom* assign them an identity by dedicated use – i.e. state, town, lineage, family or a particular *ɔkɔmfɔ*: but underlying this is the classification, used here, that orders the *abosom* by the '(super)natural' point of origin of their powers. See *atano*, *ewim*, *ɔbo*.

ɔbosom diakɔmfoɔ   (p. 132) 'the eater of priests': der. *ɔbosom* (see entry) + *di*, to eat, consume, devour + *akɔmfoɔ*, 'priests': the *ɔbosom diakɔmfoɔ* was a shrine in Kumase belonging to the *Asantehene*: it was the place where condemned *akɔmfoɔ* were 'consumed' or killed: it was located in the *adum* 'ward' of Kumase, and was marked by a large silk-cotton tree (*onyaa: Ceiba pentandra*).

bosommuru   (p. 170–2) one of the patrilineal (and patrifilial) Asante *ntɔrɔ* groups, dedicated to the purification and 'washing' of the *kra*: as has been discussed in the text, a number of *Asantehenes* belonged to the *Bosommuru* sub-divisions of *Adufudeɛ* (which used the names Osei and Owusu in alternate generations) or *Asafodeɛ* (which used the names Opoku and Adu in alternate generations): der. *ɔbosom* (see entry) + ? *mmoro/mmuru*, in the sense of a common stalk, and/or *mu*, in the sense of wholeness, completeness, impl. perfection: central to the rite of purification with regard to the *Asantehenes* of this *ntɔrɔ* was the *Bosommuru afena* (sword), which was kept in the room called *akrafiesɔɔ* in the palace in Kumase: this chamber was in the charge of the *Akrafoɔhene*, while the sword was 'manipulated' by the *Bosommuruhene*.

bosompra

(p. 170–1) one of the patrilineal (and patrifilial) Asante *ntɔrɔ* groups, dedicated to the purification and 'washing' of the *kra*: as has been discussed in the text, a number of *Asantehenes* belonged to the *Bosompra* sub-division of *Aboadeɛ* (which used, *inter alia*, the names Boakye and Akyampon in alternate generations): der. *bosompra*, the *ɔbosom* and river of that name (cf. ? *pra*, in the sense of a gathering together): the *Bosompra afena* was kept and used in the same way as its *Bosommuru* counterpart (see *bosommuru*): it was 'manipulated' by the *Bosomprahene*.

abrabɔ

(p. 168) syn. *ɔbra*: the realization on earth of the individual's *ŋkrabea* borne by the *kra*: lit. life in the world, impl. behaviour, conduct: der. *bra*, to come into the world + *bɔ*, with the sense of something ordained.

abrafoɔ

(p. 108) sing. *ɔbrafo*: 'executioners': but, more precisely, those who saw that laws were carried out (the 'constabulary'): der. *bra* (syn. *bara*), to make or enact a law, to lay an injunction upon, to command; impl. to prohibit: the *abrafoɔ* were also charged with the reciting of history and panegyrics, notably in the form of the *apaeɛ* of the *Asantehene*: it is said that the *abrafoɔ* and *adumfoɔ* were once one group, but were divided: the *Abrafoɔhene* and *Adumhene* are both in Kumase *Akwamu*, but the alleged seniority of the *Adumhene* has been often a matter of constitutional dispute: certain *abosom* were most commonly anthropomorphized as *abrafoɔ* (and cf. in Fante, *ɔbrafo* is also the name for an assistant of an *ɔkɔmfɔ*).

abusua

(p. 77) pl. *mmusua*: matrilineage, descent and kinship reckoned by matrifiliation: maximal matrilineage: family, kin, relatives on the mother's side: the der. of this fundamental word is obscure: the most common traditional explanation is that it means lit. 'imitating Abu', i.e. *Abu*, a proper name + *sua*, to imitate, to learn: cf. *osua*, the act of learning by imitation: i.e. an *Adansehene* (a ruler of the pre-Asante Akan polity of Adanse) had an *ɔkyeame* called Abu: he offended the *Adansehene*, and was heavily fined: at that time a child inherited from his/her father: Abu asked his children (his heirs) to help to pay his fine, but they refused and went to live with their mothers' relatives: but Abu's sister's children helped him to pay his debt: so, when Abu died he left all of his property to his sister's children: other people began to imitate him, hence *abusua*. This account is clearly aetiological. But it shows (*a*) the bedrock antiquity of the institution, (*b*) the Asante understanding that other peoples trace descent in the paternal line, and (*c*) awareness of the abiding tensions in

Asante social structure between the claims of matriliny and patriliny: cf. *obusuani*: syn. *oni*: pl. *abusuafoɔ*, a kinsman, a relative: *abusua panin*: pl. *abusua mpaninfoɔ*, the senior member(s) of a matrilineage: *ɔbaa panin*, the senior female in an *abusua*, the holder of the 'royal' stool.

abusua kɛsɛɛ (p. 77) pl. *mmusua kɛsɛɛ*: lit. 'big' *abusua*: der. *abusua + kɛsɛɛ*, big, large: a territorially dispersed matriclan.

d

dabɔne (p. 153) pl. *nnabɔne*: a 'bad' or 'unlucky' day: i.e. a day that was ritually important and devoted to some ritual observance: der. *ɛda* (pl. *nna*), a day *+ bɔne*, bad, evil, wicked: impl. powerful, fraught, demanding due attention: sometimes used of those days upon which no farm work might be done, but only domestic or household tasks: in this sense syn. *fo fida*; der. *afo fi*, refraining from farm work, staying at home resting or doing domestic chores: cf. *ɔbɔne*, a bad man: ant. *dapaa*.

adaduanan (p. 152) the forty-two (named) day cycle of the Asante calendar, combining the *nanson* cycle (six days) with the *nawotwe* cycle (seven days): alt. *adaduana*: der. *ɛda*, a day *+ aduanan/aduanaŋ*, forty: cf. the common – but erroneous – rendering 'forty days': in Asante oral tradition, the phrase 'forty days' is used to connote a short, finite period of time (as in, a given office holder died 'after forty days' in office): the colloquial usage underlines the basic centrality of this calendrical unit.

adae (p. 152) lit. a lying down, resting or burial place: der. *da*, to lie down, to sleep, to remain, to rest: cf. also *ɛda*, a day: *ɔda*, a tomb, a grave: *adae* were festival days upon which offerings were made to the ancestors: there were two *adae* in every *adaduanan* cycle: these were *awukudae* (the 'small' or Wednesday *adae*) which took place on day 15: *kurudapaawukuo*, and *akwasidae* (the 'big' or Sunday *adae*) which took place on day 33: *kurukwasie*: it is sometimes said that the distinction between *awukudae* and *akwasidae* is that it is only on the latter that the ancestral stools are actually taken out of the stool house and carried in procession to the burial ground (see *baamu*): certainly, people 'petitioned' the ancestral stools on the *akwasidae*, on the grounds that they were temporarily 'occupied': on both of the *adae*, the reigning *Asantehene* made offerings to his ancestors, processed to the *bantama baamu*, and held a public reception in the afternoon.

ɔdampaŋ (p. 15) pl. *adampaŋ*: a house with an open front: a house containing a room with an open front: a room with an open front: der. *ɔdaŋ* (pl. *adaŋ*), a house, a room *+ pa*, empty, void (used in compounds like the present word): cf. *hunu*, empty, void, but with moral implications: cf. *abɔnteŋ dampaŋ*, a house with an open front towards the street. This was one of the commonest forms of Asante vernacular architecture, and was even repeated in death: i.e. common burial (*ayi*) took place in a grave (*ɔda*) that was customarily a trench some 6 to 8 feet deep, in one side of which a further cavity was excavated: this formed, as it were, a room with three walls (*ɔdampaŋ*): the corpse was placed in this cavity and a symbolic screen was erected before it.

dapaa   (p. 153) pl. *nnapaa*: a 'good' or 'lucky' day: i.e. a day that was deemed to be particularly auspicious (in the sense of being free from ritual demands): (for Asante reasoning on *dapaa/dabɔne* see p. 154): der. *ɛda* (pl. *nna*), a day + *pa/paa/papa*, good, impl. proper, true, real, genuine: syn. *dapɔnna* (pl. *nnapɔna*), a 'holiday': Asante situational use of *dapaa/dabɔne* has been further confused in this century by the spread of Christianity: I have been told that the day preceding an *adae* and Christmas Eve are now regarded as *nnapaa*.

ɔdehyeɛ   (p. 64) alt. *odehyeɛ*. pl. *adehyeɛ*: der(?). *de*, to hold, to have, to possess (something) + *hyɛ*, to be fixed in or appointed to (the status of): cf. *ɔdede*, owner, possessor: *ɔdedifo*, heir: at its most general the word *ɔdehyeɛ* means a free-born person; but it is used more narrowly to describe the status of 'nobility', and even more precisely to describe the matrilineally descended 'royals' of a stool or office.

adehyeɛ kasa   (p. 179) lit. 'royal speech': used here to characterize the manner of speaking used by an *Asantehene*: der. *adehyeɛ* (see *ɔdehyeɛ*) + *ɔkasa*, speech (see *ɔkasa*): *adehyeɛ kasa* was formally transmitted via a third party (see *ɔkyeame*): *adehyeɛ kasa* was low, measured, marked by a whistling nasality, characterized (sometimes) by a stuttering inflection, and always soft.

odekuro   (p. 30) alt. *ɔdekuro*. pl. *adekurofoɔ*: the head of a village, answerable to higher authority for the management of its affairs: der. *de*, to hold (in the sense of possession) + *akuraa* (pl. *ŋkuraa*), a village.

ɔdomaŋkama   (p. 104) alt. *ɔdomaŋkoma*: eternally abundant, fecund creator of all, infinite, absolute, boundless, limitless: a byname of *onyame*: der. *domaŋkama*, manifold, plentiful, abundant: as Danquah (1944) pointed out, the ultimate der. of this word, and the range of meanings that it implies, are open to analysis at multiple levels. Here I can do no more than direct the reader to Danquah's discussion: *ɔdomaŋkama* was one name for the cultic movement that sprang up in Asante in 1879–80.

adommere   (p. 145) the second rains (about August, September, October):

der. *adom*, a favouring; *ɔdom*, grace, favour: syn. *adom, adonsu*.

ɔdɔnkɔ (p. 95) pl. *nnɔnkɔfoɔ*: a foreign-born slave, generally marked by cicatrization: also generically applied to the peoples of Asante's northern hinterland (who provided many of the foreign-born slaves in Asante): der. is unclear: cf. *dɔ*, to love + *kɔ*, to go off, to run away, i.e. 'some one whom you love but who may run away': but cf. also *dɔ*, in the root sense of multiplying, becoming numerous, and *adɔn(a)*, a difficulty in loving, a disaffection, an alienation: and cf. *dɔ*, to move slowly, stealthily; *dɔŋko*, military concerns: some sources give the alt. word *nnɔŋko* for the peoples (in a geographical sense) of the northern hinterland: *nnɔŋko* is syn. *ntamaŋ mu*: cf. *nta*, the Asante word for Gonja: cf. *taa*, to pursue, persecute. Much persistent questioning in Asante has failed to supply me with any conclusive etymology for this word: *ko*, abbreviated from *ɔdɔnkɔ*, was commonly prefixed to the proper names of slaves of this type (e.g. Kobuobi).

ɔdɔsɔ (p. 121) a fringed, skirt-like raffia girdle worn by *akɔmfoɔ*: it was commonly made from the fibres of the *adɔbɛ* (bamboo palm).

adumfoɔ (p. 202) sing. *odumfo*: executioners: properly speaking, only the *Asantehene* had *adumfoɔ*: the name is said to be a corruption of the proper name Anum, belonging to Anum Asamoa: Anum Asamoa was one of those faithful retainers who accompanied Osei Tutu on his journey home from Akwamu to Kumase to become the first *Asantehene*: Anum Asamoa and his people (*anumfoɔ*) were settled in Kumase by Osei Tutu and the name *anumfoɔ* became corrupted to *adumfoɔ*: Anum Asamoa was the first Kumase *Adumhene* (under the Kumase *Akwamuhene/Asafohene*), and he and his people resided in the *adum* 'ward' of Kumase: some sources propose that *adumfoɔ* is der. *dum*, to extinguish: *adumfoɔ* were charged with *twa ti*, 'cutting off the head', beheading.

dutu (p. 61) charcoal, brass filings, other dross, impl. false gold: der(?) *adutu*, poison, something that spoils: syn. *mporoporowa*, filings, fragments, splinters.

dwa See *sika dwa kofi*.

dwaberem (pp. 35, 162) lit. 'a place for assembling': *dwaberem* in Kumase was a site where the *Asantehene* sat in public assembly: it was also the site of the largest Kumase market: der. *dwa*, to state, report, propose + *(ɛ)bere*, a place (in compounds): hence, *dwabere*, a place of assembling together (for talking).

dwamu (p. 16) airing or talking over household matters in public: der. *dwa*, to state, report + *mu*, used in the sense of amongst, in that manner: *dwa* also means to stand out, to be prominent: cf. *ɔde asɛm no abedwa hɔ* ('he told the matter publicly, in the public place').

odwareɛ nɔ kra (p. 170) 'washing', cleansing or purification of the *kra*: alt.

ɔdware, guare: der. dware, to wash, to bathe (the whole body): syn. asumguare: cf. hoho, to wash (the hands, face); horo, to wash (utensils, clothes): an ordinary Asante citizen might perform this only once a year: on the appointed day, offerings of white fowls (asumguare de) were taken to a nearby stream in brass bowls (ŋwowa): herbal leaves (adwira, nsome) were dipped, and the fowls sprinkled with them: the supplicant then addressed his/her kra, asking for prosperity and long life: the blood of the offerings was then sprinkled about the supplicant's dwelling and compound: relatives and friends ate the fowls, generally with mashed yams (to which no oil had been added – the mixture being required to be white rather than yellow): on this day the supplicant was free from incurring a debt, and was exempt from being involved in the swearing of oaths: a helpful kra was said to be white, while kra biŋ – an 'unhelpful' kra – was said to be black: these states were autonomous to the kra, and had no connection with the moral actions of the individual supplicant.

odwira   (p. 144 et seq.) the name of the festival is der. dwira, to cleanse, to purify.

dwo   (p. 207) 'coolness', a metaphorical and physical property of the space of culture; impl. harmony, peace, order, protection: der. dwo, (a) to cool, (b) to be appeased, to be calmed, (c) to abate, to relax, to subside, (d) to quieten, to make quiet, (e) to feel comfortable, to come to rest.

f
afe   (p. 157) pl. mfe. syn. afrihyia/afirihyia: often translated in the twentieth century as a 'year', but lit. a unit of time composed of nine successive adaduanan cycles, at the conclusion of which a new afe began: der. fe (firi), with the sense of proceeding, going forth: cf. hyia, with the sense of to meet (again) by returning in a circuit to a starting point.

afedaŋ   (p. 157) the conclusion of an afe: lit. the turning (renewing) of the 'year', i.e. the end of the 'year': der. afe + daŋ, to turn, to change, to alter.

afefoforo   (p. 157) the beginning of an afe: syn. afeforo: der. afe + foforo/ foro, new, fresh, young, impl. another: cf. afefoforo da, the day of a new afe, 'New Year's day'.

fekuo   (p. 40) lit. 'a group of persons': syn. fekuw: der. afɛ, a person (generally of the same age, rank), a comrade + (e)kuw, a body of persons, a group, a collectivity: in Kumase the word fekuo was employed to describe those ten discrete units (administrative and/or military) throughout which office holders were distributed: these were Kronti, Akwamu, Nifa, Beŋkum, Adonten, Kyidom, Oyoko, Gyaase, Ankobea, and Manwere: the word was also used to describe discrete categories of nhenkwaa – e.g. the afenasoafoɔ or sword-bearers constituted an identifiable group or fekuo.

afenasoafoɔ   (p. 62) sword-bearers: der. *afena*, a sword: pl. *mfena*: syn. *afoa*: hence *mfoafoɔ*, sword-bearers: the swords in question were insignia of the authority of the *Asantehene*, and were paraded before him by the *afenasoafoɔ* on public or state occasions: the *afenasoafoɔ* were used as state messengers, the swords that they carried serving as badges or emblems of the authority of their commission from the *Asantehene*: their head was the *Afenasoafoɔhene/Asomfoɔhene*, who served in the *Kronko* sub-division of the Kumase *Gyaase fekuo*.

(ɔ)fie   (p. 188) a house. pl. *afi*: syn. *ofi*, *ofie*: der(?). *fi*, to come out (from), to issue forth (from), to appear, to come and go (from): cf. *pue*, to come forth: *(ɔ)fie* is a house in the sense of one's own house (home), or the family dwelling or compound in which one grew up and/or lived: as such, it is distinct from the houses of other persons or groups: unlike *ɔdaŋ*, *abaŋ*, etc., it does not designate a type of building: in kinship terminology, *(ɔ)fie* is sometimes used to describe the uterine group or stirp.

(ɔ)fie panin   (p. 188) lit. 'head of the house': der. *(ɔ)fie + panin/panyiŋ*, in the senses of aged, elder, adult, chief, senior (ant. *abofra*, a child, minor, juvenile): Christaller identifies the function of the *(ɔ)fie panin* with 'stewardship', and this is acceptable in a broad sense: it is used here specifically as the title and honorific of the senior male or mother's brother (*wɔfa*) in his capacity as 'head of the house' formed by the uterine group or stirp [*ɔyafunu koro*].

afisɛm   (p. 179) household matters, 'things within the house(hold)'; i.e. kinship, domestic or family matters of a private nature; 'secrets': der. *(ɔ)fie*, house(hold) + *asɛm*, matters, affairs, impl. for talking over, discussing.

fotosanfoɔ   (p. 62) sing. *fotosanaani*: syn. *ɔfotosanfo*; pl. *afotosanfoɔ*: the group of *nhenkwaa* who worked as weighers and counters of gold in the service of the *Asantehene*: der. *foto*, a leather bag: *foto* was also the name used for the place where the *fotosanfoɔ* worked weighing and counting gold (the 'treasury'): the head of this group was the *Fotosanfoɔhene* (now called *Nnibihene*) under the *Sanaahene* in the sub-division of the *gyaase fekuo* headed by the *Gyaasewahene*.

mframa   (p. 120) the wind. der(?). *fra*, to be stirred up, mixed together, mingled; impl. evanescence, 'uncapturability': *mframa* was a characteristic (albeit not universal) feature of the manifestation of the *abosom*: the power(s) of the *abosom* – evident, ubiquitous, unbiddable, evanescent – were likened to *mframa*.

fufu   (p. 203) white: with red (*kɔkɔɔ*) and black (*tuntum*) one of the three primary colour classifications in Asante thought: held to be auspicious, and linked to spiritual purity, victory, and joy.

fufuu   (p. 83) alt. *fufu*: the staple food of the Asante: yam, plantain or cassava boiled, pounded in a wooden mortar ($\jmath w \jmath a d u r u$) and rolled into balls, and eaten with a relish or 'soup' ($\eta k w a \eta$) of meat or fish: der(?). *fufu*, white.

mfufuwa (p. 29) 'non-farm' or land currently under fallow: der. *afuo*, a farm+*fuo/fuw*, in the sense of to overgrow: alt. *mfuwa mfuwa*: the *mfufuwa* was overgrown with bush, but kept clear of trees.

mfufuwa nini (p. 31) 'barren fallow': syn, *mfuwa nini*: der. *afuo + nini*, barren or unproductive: this was land that had once been cultivated as part of an *afuo* (farm), but that had lain uncultivated – for whatever reason – for some time: Christaller seems to suggest that the elapse of eight years (until the bush had reached a man's height) turned formerly cultivated land into *mfufuwa nini*.

afuo (p. 29) pl. *mfuo*: alt. *afuw*: syn. *kua*: a farm: impl. planting, cultivated ground: der. *fuo/fuw*, to shoot up, to come forth, to grow abundantly, to produce plentifully: cf. also *fi*, to come forth, to grow above the ground, to be usable, impl. prosperity: the *afuo* was started as an *afuo dɔ(w)*, 'cutting of the bush for farming'; der. *dɔ(w)*, to cut the bush, to weed, to hoe.

afuwa (p. 29) diminutive of *afuo*: pl. *mfuwa*: that part of an *afuo* currently under crops: lit. a 'little' farm.

g

oguaŋ (p. 160) pl. *ŋgwaŋ*. syn. *odwan(e)*: a sheep: the word was used generically of the goat as well as the sheep: but the precise term for a goat was *aberekyi*, so that when the word *oguaŋ* was used in general conversation it most commonly referred to a sheep: in speech where a sheep was actually distinguished from a goat, the term used for the former was *oguaŋteŋ* (der. *teŋ(teŋ)*, long, here meaning long legged; i.e. 'the long-legged one' as distinct from the goat): the sheep was symbolic of peace, innocence and spiritual 'coolness' (see *dwo*), and was the preferred oblation in many ritual sacrifices.

agya ba (p. 195) lit. 'father's child': der. *agya* (pl. *agyanom*), father, genitor, male parent + *ɔba* (pl. *mma*), child, offspring: in Asante kinship, the term *agya ba* was used of a patri-sibling, i.e. a child of one's own father by a woman other than one's own mother: thus, it was distinct from the term *onua*, brother/sister in the sense of a matri-sibling (der. *ɛna/oni*, mother + *ɔba*, child).

gyadua (p. 207) pl. *gyannua*: a large tree offering shade: der. *gye*, to receive, shelter, harbour, take in + *(e)dua*, a tree: such trees, of different species, were planted in settlements to symbolize the act of foundation, and to betoken stability and permanence: *gyannua* were givers of shade, literally and metaphorically (impl. 'protection' and 'coolness'; cf. *dwo*): in the senses of receiving, sheltering, 'protecting' and 'cooling' the *gyadua* was symbolic of (and a metaphor for) the *Asantehene* as the guarantor and 'protector' of culture: hence *(ɔ)tew gyadua ahabaŋ* ('he tears the leaves of *gyadua*') was used of someone who had cursed (*ohyira ɔhene*) or otherwise acted against the life of the *Asantehene*: *gyadua* was also sometimes used to signify the shaft of an umbrella to which the radial ribs were fastened (and here, again, impl. shade, 'protection' and 'coolness').

agyapadeɛ   (p. 159) lit. a heritage, inheritance ('things from ancestors'), 'treasures': mnemonic 'heirlooms' (of various sorts): der. *agya*, father, impl. ancestor + *apadeɛ/apɛde*, things acquired, impl. of value.

gyaasefoɔ   (p. 205) sing. *gyaaseni*. lit. the domestics, household attendants of an *ɔhene*: der. *ogya*, fire, hearth + *ase*, in the sense of under or beneath: *gyaase*, lit. 'under the fire', i.e. the place where the hearth stands, the cooking area (kitchen), impl. house(hold): hence *gyaasefoɔ*, lit. 'those who sit under (by) the hearth': this der. is indicative of the antiquity of the concept of this category of persons: clearly, it originally meant those dependent upon and in service to the master of a house *((ɔ)fi(ɛ)wura)*: it was presumably then extended to mean those who stood in the same relationship to the earliest Asante *abirɛmpɔn*: finally, it came to mean the household servants of an office holder (*ɔhene*), and is employed in this text to describe the *gyaasefoɔ* of the *Asantehene*: in practice, these very many royal *gyaasefoɔ* were differentiated by function, and organized into a variety of discrete service groups (*fekuo*) (see e.g. *abrafoɔ, afenasoafoɔ, ahoprafoɔ*, etc.): in Kumase the *gyaase fekuo* (one of the ten administrative and/or military divisions: see *fekuo*) was under the titular/ constitutional headship of the *Gyaasehene* (who was also the *Saamanhene*, with his seat at Saawua).

ogye   (p. 48) 'the highest level at which wealth could be appropriated', symbolized by the *sika mena*, and personified in the *Asantehene*: der. *gye*, to take, to appropriate (sometimes impl. against the will of the possessor; to exact), to require (impl. to be entitled to, have a right to); but also, to accept (with the sense of receiving with graciousness that which is freely offered or pressed upon one): *gye* is a simple word, but its shades of contextual meaning are manifold and subtle: in the sense in which *ogye* is used here the word can be taken to connote both the *Asantehene's* right to take and his royal graciousness in accepting that which was 'offered' to him: *ogye* is an act – of taking/receiving.

agyeman   (*passim*) alt. *agyemaŋ*: lit. *nea ogye ɔman*: byname/praise name of the *Asantehene* Kwaku Dua Panin: a defender, upholder, saviour of the 'nation' (*Asantemaŋ*): der. *ogye*, in the sense of salvation, deliverance/*gye*, in the sense of to protect, save, defend, preserve + *ɔman*/*ɔmaŋ*, in the sense of a people, a 'nation' (*Asantemaŋ*).

h

ɔhene   (*passim*) pl. *ahene*. king, chief, ruler, head, office holder (a term of broad application): e.g. *Asantehene*, 'king' of Asante: *Dwabenhene*, 'ruler' or 'chief' of Dwaben: *Abrafoɔhene*, 'head' of the *abrafoɔ*.

ɔheneba   (p. 64) pl. *ahenemma*: der. *ɔhene* + *ɔba*, a child: lit. 'the child of an *ɔhene*': the male and female children of an *Asantehene* were the corporate *ahenemma* of the *sika dwa kofi* ('the children of the Golden Stool'): in conventional understanding the word is given as 'prince' or 'princess' in contradistinction to 'royal' (see *ɔdehyeε*), the latter status being defined by matrilineal descent.

ahenfie   (*passim*) syn. *ahemfi*. der *ɔhene* + *(ɔ)fie*, a house: lit. 'the house of an *ɔhene*': used here of the palace of the *Asantehene* in Kumase.

ahenkwaa   (p. 35) pl. *nhenkwaa*. der. *ɔhene* + *akoa*, in the senses of servant and subject: lit. 'the servant of an *ɔhene*': used here of those who served in the status of *nhenkwaa* to the *Asantehene*: syn(?). *ɔsomfo*; pl. *asomfoɔ*: der. *ɔsom*, to serve a master (human or supernatural): Christaller gives three glosses: (*a*) the servant of a king; (*b*) a courtier (which is a good, very suggestive reading); (*c*) (in another context), a type of performance with singing and dancing: recruitment to the status of *ahenkwaa* to the *Asantehene* was a somewhat haphazard business that might involve a number of factors – residence in Kumase, the chance to be noticed and/or to demonstrate talent, personal liking on the part of the *Asantehene* and/or a senior office holder, finding oneself delivered up to the *Asantehene* in settlement of a debt or fine, etc.: numbers of Asante informants emphasize the *personal* link in this pattern of recruitment: by contrast, a minority of the royal *nhenkwaa* were recruited on a hereditary basis (but the son appears only to have succeeded the father as *ahenkwaa* if the mother herself was an *akoa* in direct service to the Golden Stool): the nature of the relationship between the two categories of *nhenkwaa* remains uncertain: *nhenkwaa* formed the base or bottom tier of officialdom, but, crucially, this status bespoke *inclusion* within the state: a variety of factors, analogous to those that governed selection, was operable in determining whether or not someone who achieved or inherited the rank of *ahenkwaa* might rise to any higher office: the central idea of *personal* service is also evidenced in the case of those *nhenkwaa* who served an *ɔbosom* in the status of *ɔbosomkwaa*, 'a servant of an *ɔbosom*': both the *abosom* and the *Asantehene* were the legal heirs to the property left by their respective *nhenkwaa*.

hiaa   (p. 216) syn. *hiawa*: alt. *hyiaa*. the women's/wives' quarters: used here of that secluded part of the palace in Kumase where the wives of the *Asantehene* were kept: der(?). *hyia*, to meet together, to assemble/*ahi*, with the sense of frightening, a warning/*ɔhia*, in the sense of being required: syn. *mmammu*, 'a place of women', der. *mmaa*, sing. *ɔbaa*, women: syn. *adafae*, der. *adafa*, to allure, to entice, to seduce.

ahohuru   (p. 207) 'heat', a metaphorical and physical property of the wild or space of nature; impl. disruption, threat, disorder: der. *huru*: (*a*) to effervesce, to boil, impl. to be violently agitated, to rage; (*b*) to excite, to provoke, to incense; (*c*) *ho huru*, to be hot, to be heated; (*d*) to fret, shout, roar (in compounds): ant. *dwo*.

ahomaso   (p. 80) an exaltation of self, excessive or undue pride: used here to characterize the persistent, strident or unacceptable exercise of *mpoatwa*: (see *mpoatwa*): der. *ahom*, to be haughtily proud, impl. overweening or 'despotic' behaviour: cf. *ahupoo*, imperiousness, arrogance, insolence, 'bullying', impl. boasting: hence *ahupoofoɔ*, sing. *ahupooni*, persons behaving with *ahupoo*, overbearing 'bullies': the word *ahupoofoɔ* was often used of those Asante who behaved in an arrogant, extra-legal way, impl. illicitly throwing their weight around: hence, those individuals who collaborated with the British after the removal of the *Asantehene* Agyeman Prempe in 1896 were collectively known as *ahupoofoɔ*, impl. illegal oppressors: the word *ahomaso* is sometimes used in describing the character and personality of some of these *ahupoofoɔ*, such as the British-appointed client and usurpatory Kumase *Gyaasewahene* Kwame Tua (1901–6).

ahoprafoɔ   (p. 53) sing. *ɔhoprafo/ahoprani*. elephant tail (*mena/mmra*) bearers; those who 'swept away flies', impl. removing nuisances or 'insignificances' with the elephant tail: der. *pra/para*, to sweep, to perform a sweeping motion: cf. *apra*, sweeping: the actions of those *nhenkwaa* who were royal *ahoprafoɔ* symbolized the wealth, power and remote majesty of the *Asantehene*, impl. the removal of minor irritations (mere contingencies) from the awesome royal presence.

ɔhwɛfo   (p. 176) pl. *ahwɛfoɔ*. caretaker, trustee, overseer, guardian (of lands or an office): the *ɔhwɛfo* of an office was entrusted with the exercise of a temporary oversight, pending the installation of an appropriate incumbent (not surprisingly, frequent disputes were the consequence of this arrangement): the word was also used to describe the exercise of an absentee caretakership by Kumase office holders over distant villages, e.g. in Ahafo: in this case $\jmath hw\varepsilon fo$ might also impl. guarding or watching over (as of a 'frontier'): der. $hw\varepsilon$, to look after, to watch, to oversee, to guard: some sources give syn. $\jmath hw\varepsilon sofo$, pl. $nhw\varepsilon sofo\jmath$.

hyɛbea   (p. 107) an ordered destiny, in the sense of an *nkrabea* (fate) that was directly assigned to an individual by *onyame*: sometimes rendered as predestination: der. $hy\varepsilon$, to set, to fix + *bea*, a manner, a way of doing something.

hye mara   (p. 87) alt. $hy\varepsilon$ *mara*/*mmara*. the practice of legislation, the act of making and giving law, legislation *per se*: syn. *di mara*: der. $hye/hy\varepsilon$: (*a*) to impart, to establish; (*b*) to order, to commission; (*c*) to appoint, to prescribe; (*d*) to institute; (*e*) to command, to charge + *mara*/*mmara*, legal enactments and rules, edicts, commandments, orders, statutes, laws: *bara*/*bra*: (*a*) to make or enact a law; (*b*) to order with authority; (*c*) to lay an injunction upon; (*d*) to command, impl. forbid, prohibit: the practice of *hye mara*, at the level of legal philosophy, was chiefly dedicated to the ordering of Asante society, and directed at *Asante* people; hence, $\jmath h\jmath ho$ $nt\jmath mara$, 'a foreign person [impl. guest or stranger] does not break laws'.

ahyiamu   (p. 72) 'a place of meeting': this was customarily a (neutral?) venue that was agreed by participants for the swearing of an oath, for the solemnizing of a contract or agreement, or generally for the holding of an assembly, conference or parley: syn. *ahyiae*: der. *hyia*: (*a*) to meet, come together, assemble; (*b*) to agree, to reach accord; (*c*) to meet, encounter in hostility.

ohyira ɔhene   (p. 247) lit. 'blessing the *Asantehene*', a euphemism for exactly the (unmentionable) opposite, i.e. 'cursing the *Asantehene*': der. *hyira*: (*a*) to bless; (*b*) to invoke, impl. (euphemistically), to blaspheme or curse.

ohyira nɔ ano   (p. 170) 'blessing the mouth' (with water): der. *hyira*, to bless, to invoke + *ano*, the mouth: a generic ritual of cleansing, performed most particularly by an Asante on the specific observance day (*kra da*) of that person's $nt\jmath r\jmath$: the core of the ritual was the ejection of water from the mouth in a spray: cf. *hinam*, to squirt or spurt water: some sources differentiate as follows: (*a*) ejecting water into a calabash signified a petition for wealth, longevity, etc.; (*b*) ejecting water onto the ground signified the invoking of a blessing or a curse upon others; (*c*) ejecting water mixed with 'medicine' signified the desire to have something 'accursed' removed from one's own life.

hyire   (p. 230) alt. *hyirew*. white clay. der(?). *hyira*, to bless: *hyire* connoted innocence or celebration: it was smeared on people *inter alia* to signify: (*a*) acquittal in a court case; (*b*) the dedication or freeing of a slave; (*c*) the freeing of a woman to marry again.

k

ɔkanniba — (p. 147) alt. *okaniba*. der. *ɔkanni*, pl. *akanfoɔ*, a person speaking Twi, a person of true Asante descent + *ɔba*, offspring: used to denote the good breeding, manners and morals of a 'true' Asante: in terms of inclusion/exclusion, a 'citizen' as opposed to a 'non-citizen' of Asante: used to characterize the 'good citizen', i.e. someone embodying an Asante ideal: hence used (as in the text) as a title or praise name of the *Asantehene* to mark his status as 'first citizen' (*ur* embodiment) of the *Asantemaŋ*.

ɔkasa — (p. 178) speech actions: (*a*) speaking, speech, way of speaking, the sound uttered; (*b*) language, dialect; (*c*) word, expression (syn. *asɛm*, word, talk, saying, tale, speech): der. *ka*, to emit a sound + *asɛm*, impl. utterance: cf. *kasa*, to speak, to talk, but also used of active noises in general (e.g. the sound of birds, of fires, of winds, etc.): in one discrete sense *kasa* can mean to admonish, to censure, impl. to abuse: cf. *diɔkasa*, to fine: the understanding of *ɔkasa* by the Asante is complex, situational, and needs extended analysis in its own right.

kasae — (p. 179) syn. *ŋkasae*. common talk, public discourse, 'sayings', rumour, impl. reportage, gossip (see *ɔkasa*).

ɔkasafo — (p. 179) pl. *akasafoɔ*. a gossiper, a gossip, impl. chattering, prattling, babbling: syn. *obireku/obereku*, a common bird that calls out – endlessly, by day and night – *'ku, ku'*, impl. endless 'busy' talk (see *ɔkasa*).

ɔkasa guaa — (p. 179) backbiting, impl. slander, calumny: der(?). *kasa* + *egua*, to trade in, to traffic in: sometimes syn. *ntwiri*, muttering, grumbling (see *ɔkasa*).

ɔkasa ho — (p. 179) a subject of conversation. der. *kasa*, to speak, to talk + *ho*, suffix used of localized relations, impl. about (something or someone): syn. *ŋkasahosɛm*, impl. a topic of conversation, a subject of discourse.

kasakoa — (p. 81) lit. the aim, object, end of a speech act, impl. design, purport, tendency (in meaning): der. *kasa*, to speak + *(ŋ)koa*, an end, impl. object(ive): cf. also *koa*, to bend, to shape, to curve: hence (a particular) idiom, directed or 'bent' speech, idiomatic metaphor.

katamanso — (p. 165) lit. 'covering the whole nation': der. *kataman/katamaŋ*, i.e. *nea ɔkata omaŋ*, 'one that covers the whole nation': cf. *kata*, to spread over, to cover, to envelop, to enfold + *omaŋ*, people and 'nation': used as an appellation of the *Asantehene* as a 'mighty ruler', impl. one who 'covers', impl. shades, 'cools', protects the *Asantemaŋ* (see *dwo, gyadua*): also used (with the same sense) as a name for one of the *Asantehene's* very large state umbrellas.

kete

(p. 194) (*a*) a riverain reed, used to make e.g. walking sticks or musical instruments; (*b*) a flute, a pipe; (*c*) a band, an 'orchestra' of flutes and pipes, accompanied by drums, bells, etc., and played before the *Asantehene* (and those other senior office holders who were entitled to keep a *kete* band): some authorities associate *kete* playing with good humour in an *Asantehene* (or an office holder), but nineteenth-century reports link the *kete* with night and executions: this (characteristically deliberate?) ambiguity seems to have depended upon which piece the *kete* was playing: thus, the *Asantehene's kete* played at least eight set pieces: some, e.g. *yɛtu mpɔ* ('we are digging gold'), were used in public celebrations: others, e.g. *atɔperɛ*, were used to accompany executions.

akitawonsa

(p. 159) a period or season of the year, a 'month': generally about July (preceding *ɔsanaa*): der. *kita*, to have, to hold + *wo*, a linking adjunct of place + *nsa*, a hand, i.e. 'to hold or have in the hand', impl(?). to eat what is available (to hand), a time of shortage, in anticipation of the (yam) harvest.

akoa

(p. 38 and *passim*) pl. *nkoa*. alt. *ɔkoa*: this term was ubiquitous and was clearly of remote origin: it had very wide application, but was most commonly used to denote a 'subject': der(?). and highly speculative, *ko*, to go (away), with the sense of into (or fleeing from) an obligation, a debt, a court case, impl. to be in a state of + *ba*, to come, to attend (upon) or *ɔba*, offspring, child, impl. a sense of dependence: in the sense of a 'subject', an *akoa* might be of slave or free status: i.e. a slave was an *akoa* of his or her master, but equally every free Asante was an *akoa* of one or another office holder, and ultimately all were *nkoa* of the *Asantehene*: the complex ambiguity of the matter was encapsulated in the categorical term *akoa ɔdehyeɛ*, a person who was freeborn (*ɔdehyeɛ*, and so *akoa* as a free 'subject'), but who had then fallen into some category of dependence, servitude or outright slavery (*akoa*, in the sense of a dependent, servile or slave 'subject', but formerly of freeborn or *ɔdehyeɛ* status): the pervasiveness of jural intervention massively complicated the issue: thus, numerous freeborn Asante – under the impact of debt, pawning, pledging, crime, etc. – found themselves reassigned by (and in) law to one or another reduced-status niche (defined by differentiated levels/degrees of servitude): any such change was always reversible in principle, and very often in fact, but for that small minority of freeborn Asante who fell all the way out of jural corporateness into being *akoa pa*, 'in bondage', impl. slavery, redemption was virtually impossible: such unfortunates – abandoned by kin and/or prosecuted to the utmost by the state – had traversed the spectrum from free to slave 'subject' (they remained *nkoa*, but at the furthest jural extreme from their ascriptive point of origin): of course, anyone who became *akoa pa* – being an Asante – was quite distinct from an *ɔdɔnkɔ*.

kɔkɔɔ (p. 203) alt. *kɔbene, memene*. red: with white (*fufu*) and black (*tuntum*) one of the three primary colour classifications in Asante thought: held to embrace that part of the spectrum ranging from red through purple and orange to violet and pink: unlike either white or black, red was ambiguous and full of equivocal meanings: it was symbolic of blood (*mogya*) in both its life and death aspects: it signified heightened (and confused) emotional states – combinations of danger, sorrow, impurity, anger, defiance: when an Asante donned a red cloth and smeared himself with red ochre (*ntwoma*), it denoted angry defiance (*ogyina kɔdom ano*): *kɔbene*, syn. *kɔbe*, could mean red itself or a cloth dyed red, which was worn at funeral customs and in warfare.

akɔm (p. 113) a possession dance, in which an individual – generally a trainee or adept *ɔkɔmfɔ* – was unilaterally seized, possessed or otherwise 'mounted' by the power(s) of an *ɔbosom*: the practice of *akɔm* conduced rather than commanded the manifestation of an *ɔbosom*, and true mastery of the dance was a defining characteristic of the *akɔmfoɔ*: der. *kɔm*, to dance wildly, impl. frenzy and a trance-like ecstasy: in dancing *akɔm*, the adept might be assisted by *akɔm nwontofoɔ* ('singers for calling up the spirits'): cf. *kɔm bosom*, to prophesy, to soothsay, to foretell, impl. the *ɔbosom* 'speaking through' the person dancing *akɔm*: cf. *ŋkɔm*, an oracle, a prophecy, a revelation, communicated by the *ɔbosom* via the person dancing *akɔm*.

ɔkɔmfɔ (p. 113 and *passim*) alt. *ɔkɔmfo*. pl. *akɔmfoɔ*: lit. 'one (who is) possessed', as in *akɔm*: conventionally but misleadingly rendered as a 'priest' or a 'fetish man': in *akɔm* the *ɔkɔmfɔ* was possessed or 'mounted' by the *ɔbosom* that he served, and the *ɔbosom* communicated with the Asante – in words and/or signs – using the *ɔkɔmfɔ* as its mouthpiece: cf. *akɔmfoɔsɛm*, the speech, manner and behaviour of *akɔmfoɔ* (often given as 'magic arts', especially by Christians): there were numbers of female *akɔmfoɔ mma* (sing. *ɔkɔmfɔ ba*), but the majority of these 'tended' the shrines of the *abosom*, rather than being directly involved in *akɔm*: in practising the rites of an *ɔbosom*, or in carrying out 'service' to it, an *ɔkɔmfɔ* was also *ɔsɔfo*, der. *sɔre*, to perform rites, now Christianized as to 'worship': an *ɔkɔmfɔ* was also syn. *bu(w)frɔfo*, der. *bu*, to go beyond, to surpass+*frɔ*, to call, to summon: this encapsulates an important point – by dint of dedicated application to *akɔm*, an *ɔkɔmfɔ* might conduce the manifestation of an *ɔbosom*, but he could not command it.

ŋkɔmmɔ(bɔ)   (p. 179) familiar conversation or discourse. der(?). *kɔ*, to prattle (significantly, also used of the gurgling noise made by liquid pouring out of its container) + *bɔ*, in the sense of to practise: the suggestion is one of lack of control or of social inappropriateness e.g. undue familiarity.

akonkofoɔ   (p. 71) syn. *akoŋkofoɔ*. der. *koŋko*, to retail, to broker: cf. *koŋkosifo*, a retailer, pl. the same: this term was used to describe the prominent Asante 'businessmen' of the early colonial era: no exact translation is adequate, but the term carried clear implications of wealth (initially rooted in retailing goods between the Gold Coast and Asante), of capitalist 'individualism', and of 'modernity' in consumption patterns and attitudes: *akonkofoɔ* were themselves often illiterate, but they commonly funded the education of junior relatives and/or dependants: the origins of this group lay in those *nhenkwaa* and others who rebelled against the fiscal policies of the Asante state in the 1880s/90s, who fled into the Gold Coast Colony and prospered there, and who returned to Kumase after the deportation of the *Asantehene* Agyeman Prempe (1896) and the annexation of Asante by the British Crown (1901): the *akonkofoɔ* were *arrivistes*, and something of this is suggested by the (twentieth-century?) meaning of *koŋkɔm* (der. *koŋko*), to flaunt oneself, to be haughty, to strut, to 'look big'.

nkɔntwima   (p. 125) an instrument made of leather strips, used by an *ɔkɔmfɔ* to supply resolutions to certain specific problems, e.g. detecting and identifying a thief: der(?). *nkɔn*, syn. *akɔm* in some compounds + *(ŋ)wima/(ŋ)woma*, syn. *(ŋ)homa*, animal skin, leather: but see too *twom/twim*, to snatch away quickly (as in the agitated motion of the *nkɔntwima*).

konnurokusɛm   (p. 193 and *passim*) used as a euphemism, metaphor or idiomatic indirection (see *kasakoa*) to refer to the crisis that took place in the 1850s between the *Asantehene* Kwaku Dua Panin and his closest matrilineal kin: der. *konnuroku*: (*a*) mean, vile or despicable, impl. worthlessness, paltriness, impl. shamefulness, a shameful thing; (*b*) a very inferior cloth. syn. *burohono* which also means maize husks (der. *aburo*, maize + *hono/hunu*, merely, only, for nothing, impl. useless), a residual or worthless part of that crop: cf. also the root senses of *ko*, to fight (with), to oppose + *nuru/nunu*, to blame another, to blame oneself (i.e. to repent).

nkonnwasoafoɔ   (p. 176) stool carriers of an office holder; the bearers of his white stool of office, and the bearers of and attendants upon the blackened stools of his ancestors/predecessors in office: der. *dwa*, a stool. syn. *akoŋŋua*: the *sika dwa kofi* (the Golden Stool) was in the care of those royal *nhenkwaa* who were *nkonnwasoafoɔ*, headed by the *Nkonnwasoafoɔhene* who served the *Asantehene* in the *ananta* sub-division of the Kumase *gyaase fekuo*.

kra (p. 167) syn. *ɔkra*. pl. *akra*. the essence or 'soul' of a human being, given directly to each person by *onyame*: the understanding of the *onyame–kra* relationship is distilled in the meanings of the verb *kra/kara*: (*a*) to say farewell to, to take leave of; (*b*) to go away, to depart (from); (*c*) to dismiss, to send on an errand; (*d*) to send word, to send a message; (*e*) to appoint, to ordain beforehand, to predestine (see *nkrabea*): the *kra* was understood to exist prior to the birth of an individual, and it survived physical death: the *kra* quit a dying person gradually (*twe kara*, with a sense of being called back), but when it finally left the person was dead: *onyame* might confer upon a person about to be born the *kra* of a deceased close relative (see *kra pa*) or of another.

nkrabea (p. 107) alt. *ŋkrabea*. a component of a human individual that is best understood in terms of fate, destiny: der. *kra/kara*, to take leave of, etc. (see *kra*)+*bea*, a manner, a way of doing something: *nkrabea* was borne by the *kra*, and both emanated from *onyame*: the fate, destiny, appointed or allotted life of a person inscribed in *nkrabea* was realized in lived existence as *abrabɔ/ɔbra*: *abrabɔ/ɔbra* was literally life in this world, encompassing a state of existence defined by conduct, manner, etc.: der. *bra/bara*, to be born (again) into this world, to come (again), the impl. of recurrence being an acknowledgement that the *kra* – the bearer of *nkrabea*, the 'author' of *abrabɔ/ɔbra* – was an indestructible property of *onyame*, and went back to *onyame* at physical death: the relationship between *nkrabea* and the *kra* is resistant to clarification beyond that offered in the text: i.e. Asante informants construe *nkrabea* as fate (with an implication of unalterability), but also assign to the *kra* the situational capacity to give 'good' or 'bad' advice.

akraboa (p. 170) pl. *akrammoa*. an animal that was sacred to the members of an *ntɔrɔ* group: der. *kra*+*aboa* (pl. *mmoa*), an animal: animals in this category were avoidances (*akyiwadeɛ*) of the members of the *ntɔrɔ*.

kra da (p. 170) the observance day of an *ntɔrɔ*: der. *kra*+*da/ɛda*, pl. *nna*, a day: on such a day an Asante performed the prescribed rites and rituals associated with membership in an *ntɔrɔ*.

kradin (p. 168) a 'day name': der. *kra*+*edin/ediŋ*, a name: such a name was a derived characterization of a *kra* 'born' on a particular day: i.e. each birth day was governed by a *kra* 'spirit': hence, a child born on (compound) – *yawo* ('Thursday's child') was predisposed to war and heroic behaviour: thus, male names such as Yaw Barima (*ɔbarima*, a hero, a valiant man).

ŋkradwarefoɔ (p. 209) 'soul', i.e. *kra* 'washers'. sing. *akradwareni*. syn. *ɔkra*, pl. *akrafoɔ*: used here of that group of *nhenkwaa* who were dedicated to the service ('washing') of the *kra* of the reigning *Asantehene*: der. *kra + (o)dware*, to wash, to bathe: the *ŋkradwarefoɔ* were recruited from various sources – favourite slaves or servants of an *Asantehene*, childhood friends, ordinary citizens (distinguished by some personal deed), relatives, office holders: *ŋkradwarefoɔ* were entirely supported by the *Asantehene*, and had a range of legal exemptions and privileges: when an *Asantehene* died large numbers of his *ŋkradwarefoɔ* were killed (or volunteered to be killed) to accompany him: two categories appear to have been spared: (*a*) those intimates of the deceased *Asantehene* who had been entrusted with his dying wishes and/or 'secrets' e.g. concerning buried or hoarded gold; (*b*) those few of the highest ascriptive or achieved rank: precise, detailed information concerning this group of *nhenkwaa* is difficult to obtain from oral sources.

akrakoŋmu (p. 209) syn. *ɛkyerɛ*. syn./pl. *akrafoɔ koŋmu/kommu*. a round, gold disc or plate suspended from the neck and worn on the breast of the *ŋkradwarefoɔ* of the *Asantehene*: der. *kra + koŋmu*, around or about the neck.

ŋkramo (p. 140) sing. *kramo*. anglicized as 'Cramos': Muslims: this is an adaptation of a loan word: der. from Malinke *karamoko*, 'one who can read': cf. Arabic *qarā'a*, to read: to the Asante, literacy and/or physical possession of the *Qurʻān* were the basic distinguishing features of Muslims (cf. the Islamic self-identification 'people of the book').

kra pa (p. 173) an 'ideal (re)incarnation' of a famous ancestor, held to be induced most propitiously via fatherhood in a cross-cousin marriage: der. *kra + pa*, true, genuine, real, impl. good, desirable, ideal.

kuduo (p. 159) a cast-brass vessel, box or bowl: *kuduo* were used to store an owner's personal 'treasures' – gold, valuables, ornaments, jewellery, precious beads, small items of an intimate kind: vessels of this sort were linked to the purification of the *kra* and to the rites of the *ntɔrɔ*: *kuduo* were placed before blackened ancestral stools: they were also commonly filled with gold and buried with important individuals (but *kuduo* might sometimes be dug up and the contents used, with due propitiatory apology, in circumstances of dire need; the principle was that any such 'borrowing' was a loan that would eventually have to be repaid): because of their ritual, material and personal significances, *kuduo* were regarded as being mnemonic 'heirlooms' (*agyapadeɛ*): the *kuduo* of the *Asantehenes* – stored before the coffins in the Bantama *baɔmu* – contained reserves of gold dust that the reigning *Asantehene* might 'borrow' for the celebration of *odwira*, or to meet an emergency need, e.g. warfare: but – in principle at least – any such 'borrowing' eventually had to be made good.

kumase   (*passim*) the Asante capital. der. *(o)kum*, inflected to produce a pair of linked meanings: (*a*) the name of a type of tree; (*b*) to kill, to execute, the act of killing + *ase*, under, underneath: i.e. the place under the *(o)kum* tree/the place where executions took place.

akuraa   (p. 34) a village. pl. *nkuraa/ŋkuraa*: differentiated by size, importance and/or history from the larger *kuro*, pl. *nkuro/ŋkuro*, a town: cf. the syn. *akurowa*, der. *kuro + wa*, a diminutive, i.e. *akuraa* = a smaller *kuro*: by minimum definition, an Asante *akuraa* might be no more than a tiny farm settlement, inhabited by a few family members and *nkoa*, and named for the head and/or master of the incumbents (gazetteers of modern Asante contain innumerable tiny *nkuraa* of this type, named for specific individuals): a farm settlement of this sort that became established, and attracted a range of people to it, became an *akuraa* in the jural sense, i.e. its original head (or his senior lineal descendant) was recognized as *odekuro*, pl. *adekurofoɔ* (see *odekuro*): but *adekurofoɔ* were all answerable to more senior office holders, and in time these latter might select or otherwise impose *adekurofoɔ* of their own choosing: again, in jural-political terms, the distinction between an *akuraa* and a *kuro* resided in the fact that *nkuro* were headed by a range of titled office holders (up to and including *ahene*) and never by an *odekuro*: a system of ranking is implicit here, but any simplistic abstraction is undercut by Asante historical experience: i.e. while the poles (smallest *akuraa*, largest *kuro*) are readily identifiable, the crowded middle ground saw many historically conditioned upward or downward shifts in *actual* as opposed to *jural* status: thus a 'booming' *akuraa* might come to overshadow a 'declining' *kuro*, while still remaining its jural-political subordinate: shifts of fortune of this sort require detailed research attention in their own right: an important, but neglected, feature (addressed in the text) was (and is) the identification of the *akuraa* with an unsophisticated or 'rustic' culture (see *nkuraasefoɔ*).

nkuraasefoɔ   (p. 84) villagers, *nkuraa* dwellers: (*a*) villagers; (*b*) 'country' or rural people, people living on rural farms and never coming to a town (*kuro*); (*c*) rustics, 'peasants', uncouth or 'uncivilized' people: sing. *akuraaseni/okuraaseni*. alt. *ŋkuraasefoɔ*: syn. *afumfoɔ/mfumfoɔ*. sing. *ofumni*. der. *afuo mu ni*, impl. 'country', 'farm' or 'bush' people: Christaller summarized the matter well (if in High Victorian phrasing), noting that *nkuraasefoɔ* led 'a secluded life' on farms, and so were '*ignorant* [his emphasis] of the rules and manners of the more extended spheres of social life': a further syn. was *kɔdaafuom*, lit. 'goes to sleep in the farm', impl. crude, boorish, 'uncivilized': the *Kumasefoɔ* looked down on and were very dismissive of anyone who was not a resident of the Asante capital, qualifying degrees of inferiority by reference to such items as geographical distance from Kumase, speech patterns, dress codes, hairstyles, manners, etc.: i.e. to the *Kumasefoɔ*, everybody else in Asante was a 'villager' of one sort or another (including, most especially, the actual *nkuraasefoɔ* themselves): unsurprisingly, this metropolitan attitude still persists, and current folklore in Kumase is replete with tales ('tall' and otherwise) concerning the abiding characteristics of the 'bumpkin': reports from the early colonial period – when Kumase first became a fully 'open' city – are full of accounts of unsuspecting, gullible *nkuraasefoɔ* being duped of money by wily, 'street-wise' *Kumasefoɔ*: this is another subject that needs extended treatment in its own right.

kurotia   (p. 119) a boundary at the edge of an Asante settlement (a zone of interaction between the space of human culture and that of the wild): der. *kuro*, a town, a settlement + *tia*, boundary, border: cf. *eti/tiri*, head, impl. furthest point: the liminal status of *kurotia* as a 'fringe' area may be seen in the fact that here were located the huts used by menstruating (polluting) women, middens, latrines and (some) *abosomfie*: at the furthermost edge of *kurotia* were situated burial grounds and 'the grove of the ghosts': every item that was anomalous, ambiguous or alien in human culture was 'managed' into *kurotia*: dirt (*efi*) – including broken and useless objects – was sometimes (literally) 'swept' out of a village into *kurotia* during the ritual named *mmusuyiedeɛ*, der. *mmusu*, a thing causing evil mischief, a disaster, a calamity: this was undertaken in order to avert any general threat of danger and anarchy, or for a specific purpose, e.g. to exclude a particular disease: *kurotia* was the site preferred by the *abosom* for manifesting themselves, and it was the place where witches met together and conversed with one another: the limits of *kurotia* were marked by *pampim*, symbolic fences against ingress by unwelcome (super)natural powers, der. *pam*, to join together (pieces of wood) + *pim*, with the sense of being sturdy.

akutia   (p. 81) innuendo. der(?). *ku(w)*, with the sense of cutting (down) or clipping + *tia*, with the sense of kicking against (cf. *ɔkasa tia me*, 'he speaks against me'): commonly rendered as to traduce, to chide, to slander someone publicly, but without directly mentioning his or her name: syn(?). *ɔkasa guaa*, backbiting: cf. *ntwiri*, muttering, grumbling, impl. against someone, but not in his or her hearing: *akutia* was not simply gossip, but impl. sustained innuendo, maliciously aimed at another person.

ŋkwaŋtanaŋ   (p. 164) a crossroads. der. *ɔkwaŋ*, pl. *ŋkwaŋ/akwaŋ*, a path, way or road + *anaŋ*, four: impl. the start of the paths leading out of a settlement, a town or village from which four roads proceeded: *ŋkwaŋtanaŋ* were regarded as being nodes of great spiritual power, at which protective 'medicine' was often buried, and where rituals to defend and affirm cultural space were enacted.

ŋkwantempɔŋ   (p. 26) 'great roads', a designation of the main commercial and military arteries of Asante: syn. *ŋkwaŋtempɔŋ*: der. *ɔkwaŋ*, pl. *ŋkwaŋ/akwaŋ*, a path, way or road + *ɔtempɔŋ*, pl. *atempɔŋ*, a highway, a main road: the literal understanding seems to have been to do with the number of persons constantly moving along such a road, i.e. a road where one constantly encountered travellers.

akwasidae   (*passim*) the 'big' or 'Sunday' *adae*: celebrated on 33: *kurukwasie* in each successive *adaduanan* cycle.

akyamfoɔ   (p. 236) shield-bearers. sing. *okyamfo*: alt. *akyɛmfoɔ*. sing. *ɔkyɛmfo*: der. *ɔkyɛm*, pl. *akyɛm*, a shield: in the eighteenth and nineteenth centuries, shields were no longer used in war, but this group of royal *nhenkwaa* 'manipulated' shields – as a mnemonic – on a variety of ritual and celebratory occasions.

akyamfoɔ dumienu   (p. 165) 'the twelve shield-bearers'. der. *akyamfoɔ*, shield bearers + *dumienu/ɛdumieŋ*, twelve: *akyamfoɔ dumienu* is a reference to the reorganization of the *akyamfoɔ* by the *Asantehene* Opoku Ware: he first created three offices and then nine more for the *akyamfoɔ* within the *gyaasewa* sub-division of the Kumase *gyaase fekuo*: the *Asantehene* Osei Kwadwo added one further office, but the group was still referred to as 'the twelve shield-bearers'.

ɔkyeame   (p. 55 and *passim*) pl. *akyeame*. often translated as 'linguist' or 'spokesman': sometimes given as speaker, interpreter, reporter: the royal *akyeame* acted as the conduit of speech between the *Asantehene* and his interlocutors, i.e. the *Asantehene* neither spoke directly to his subjects, nor did they speak directly to him: the *ɔkyeame* was a 'linguist' in the sense that his speech was required to be accurate, fluent, conditioned by appropriate rhetorical devices and etiquette, and informed by a knowledge of history, social custom, and legal precedent: *akyeame* counselled the *Asantehene* on a range of issues to do with his role, and served as expert counsel in all court cases: the root der. is *kye(re)*: (*a*) to exhibit, to show forth; (*b*) to guide, to lead; (*c*) to speak, to explain, to interpret; (*d*) to teach, to instruct; (*e*) to advise, to counsel, to exhort: but informants sometimes make punning references to *akyeame*: cf. *kyɛ*, to continue, impl. a long time: *kyɛ*, to share out, to divide up, to distribute: *kye*, with elegance: *kyea*, to strut about.

akyɛmpɔ (p. 68) a liberal, benevolent person: a beneficent distributor of gold and largess: the term connotes buying popularity as well as practising philanthropy: der. *nea ɔkyɛ mpɔw*, 'a distributor of gold nuggets'; *kye*, to distribute, to give away; *pɔw*, pl. *mpɔw*, a lump, i.e. (of gold), a nugget, an ingot, or rock gold *per se*: *akyɛmpɔ* was a byname or epithet applied to the *Asantehene* Kofi Kakari.

akyere (p. 98) 'one destined to be sacrificed': pl. *ŋkyere*: der. *kyere*, with the sense of to seize, detain, bind up: cf. *ɔkyere*, catching, impl. tying up: cf. *akyerekuraa*, a village of *ŋkyere*, i.e. a place where such people (and their descendants) were kept until such time as they were required for ritual sacrifice: *ŋkyere* were sometimes criminals, but more generally they were (troublesome or useless?) slaves placed in this terminal status by their masters: Christaller catches this severance of the *akyere* from the networks of societal belonging, and from all but the most tenuous, threadbare level of jural identity – 'a wretch worthy or destined to be killed'.

kyiɛafaseɛ (p. 202) the name given to those knives used by the royal *adumfoɔ* 'for cutting heads': der. *kyi*, to avoid, to abhor, to abstain from (see *akyiwadeɛ*) + *afasie/afaseɛ*, a type of yam (the 'water' yam: *Dioscorea alata*?): i.e. 'I avoid or abhor *afaseɛ* yams', impl. the knives in question were not for cutting yams (or anything else), but only for severing heads.

kyiɲiɛ (p. 207) a large, state umbrella. pl. *ŋkyiɲiɛ*: der. *kyiɲi/kyim/ kyini*, to turn or twist (about), to whirl, to wheel, to revolve, to circulate: cf. *kyinhyia*, lit. a turning around and meeting again, i.e. a revolution: the state umbrellas of the *Asantehene* were in the charge of that group of *nhenkwaa* called *akyiɲiyekyimfoɔ*: the *Akyiɲiyekyimfoɔhene* served in the *gyaasewa* sub-division of the Kumase *gyaase fekuo*: the *Asantehene's* state umbrellas represented actual and metaphorical 'coolness' and protection.

kyiɲiɛhyiamu (p. 160) the place of the 'whirling' or 'turning around', the name of a courtyard in the *Asantehene's* palace: der. *kyiɲi/kyini/kyim*, to whirl, to turn around, etc. + *(a)hyiamu*, 'a place of meeting'.

akyiwadeɛ (p. 170) a forbidden thing, an avoidance, a taboo: syn. *akyideɛ*: der. *kyi*, to avoid, to abhor, to abstain from, to abominate (lit. turn the back to; cf. *akyi*, the back) + *ade*, a thing, an object.

m

mmagyegyeni

(p. 53) a personal servant, a 'nanny', appointed to look after a child/young person (usually an ɔdehyeɛ), and often becoming a close intimate of the latter: pl. *mmagyegyefoɔ.* der(?). *mma*, children + *gye*, in the sense of to look after, to shelter + *gyina*, to sustain to support.

mmamma

(p. 61) children, grandchildren, progeny in the male line from a father (and his paternal ancestors): der. *ɔba*, a child, offspring, pl. *mma* (and duplicated/emphasized as *mmamma*): more narrowly, the term was used of certain corporate groups: thus, the *ahenemma* and *ahenenana* of the *Asantehenes* might be referred to as the *mmamma* of the *sika dwa kofi*: even more narrowly, *mmamma* referred to the sons and paternal grandsons of those persons who occupied an office that was in the *Asantehene's* gift (*mmamma dwa*), i.e. an office that was or might be filled other than by matrifiliation: the head of such a group was *Mmammahene*: the corporate unity of *mmamma* was ambivalent: numerous court cases attest to profound *disunity* among them over succession to office; but sources also suggest a 'banding together' among them when their corporate access to office was threatened by contesting outsiders: any principle of hereditary succession by or of right was vitiated by severe constraints: (*a*) the final right to disposition of any such office was retained by the *Asantehene*; the *mmamma* might only expect *preferred* consideration at best, rather than any *guaranteed* access to the succession; (*b*) as noted, there was a tendency to produce exponentially ever larger numbers of (competitive, quarrelsome and antagonistic) *mmamma* in descendent generations.

ɔman/ɔmaŋ

(*passim*) pl. *aman/amaŋ.* a term of broad connotation: its original meaning (with reference to the earliest period of Asante history) may simply have been a settlement and its inhabitants: it came to mean 'nation' or 'people' (as in *Asantemaŋ*), and also constituent 'territorial divisions' within the *Asantemaŋ* (Mampon, Dwaben, Nsuta, Asumagya, etc.): the largest and historically most senior *aman* or 'territorial divisions' within the *Asantemaŋ* were termed *amantoɔ*: the five 'core' (oldest, largest) 'territorial divisions' among the *amantoɔ* were termed the *akan (Asante) aman nnum* ('the five *aman* of the first rank'): these five are normally named as Dwaben, Mampon, Bekwae, Kokofu and Nsuta, but this list has been contested by other *aman* at various times, and quarrels over precedence have taken place between the five customarily 'agreed' members: *ɔman* was also sometimes used to mean (the mass of the) 'people', as distinct from those holding office: the ruler of an *ɔman* was an *ɔmanhene*, pl. *amanhene* (in eighteenth- and nineteenth-century practice this title was reserved to the heads of 'territorial divisions' – most notably the *amantoɔ* – and to the heads of a few larger districts centred on an important settlement): thus, e.g., the *Mamponhene* was *ɔmanhene* of the *ɔman* of Mampon.

amaŋ bre   (p. 87) jural custom that might be changed or adjusted by acts of legislation. der. *ɔmaŋ*, 'people', 'nation', impl. community and polity + *bra/bara*, to make or enact a law, to order with authority: the term embraces the senses of submission to and habituation to a legislative framework governing behaviour: cf. *ɔbra*, behaviour, conduct, impl. guidance in (an appropriate) manner of living.

amaneɛboɔ   (p. 16) talk, discussion, 'news of the day'. der. *aman*, in the sense of the 'people', the community + *bɔ*, to converse, to relate, to report, to discourse.

amaŋ mmu   (p. 87) immemorial custom that ordered a community (and so not subject to fundamental change by legislative enactment). der. *ɔmaŋ*, 'people', 'nation', impl. community and polity + *mmu/mu*: (*a*) whole, entire, complete; (*b*) true, real, genuine; (*c*) perfect, accomplished, finished: cf. *amammusɛm*, customs, conventions, traditions, regulations governing the community (as opposed to legislative acts).

mara/mmara   (p. 87) legal enactments, rules, law(s), impl. decrees, edicts, statutes, orders, regulations, commandments. der. *bra/bara*, to make or enact a law, impl. to order with authority, to establish as the norm: cf. *mara yɛ*, keeping a law/*mara to*, breaking a law: legal enactments might be classified by their object, or their realm of competence (although these categories had areas of overlap): thus, *ɔbra ho mara*, laws concerning moral behaviour; *asɔre ho mara*, laws concerning ceremonial; *ɔmaŋ ho mara*, laws relating to 'politics', etc.: the term *mara asɛm* was sometimes used of a decree.

mena/mmra   (p. 42 and *passim*) alt. *mmara, mmana.* the elephant tail: (*a*) the 'heraldic badge' of the *ɔbirɛmpɔn*; (*b*) the whisk (Christaller gives 'broom, fan') used by the *ahoprafoɔ* in a sweeping or fanning motion around the person of the *Asantehene*: the root der. is *pra/para*, to sweep, impl. to sweep away, to disperse (enemies, annoyances, etc.): the basic symbolism is of the *Asantehene* or the *ɔbirɛmpɔn* – in the manner of the huge, lordly elephant – 'sweeping away' all irritants and distractions (these being defined, like flies around elephants, as petty, minor and inconsequential): implicated in this are ideas about volume, mutable substances (gold, excrement), and of a status of loftily 'presiding' over affairs: there is a clearly calculated signal in all of this pertaining to social 'distancing': i.e. the possession of the *mena/mmra* is a mark of those (the *Asantehene* and the *abirɛmpɔn*) who are 'above and beyond' concern with the mundane traffic of life: thus, the *mena/mmra* is a symbol of 'completion' – by definition in the case of the *Asantehene*, by accumulation and manifest achievement at the highest notional level in the case of the *abirɛmpɔn*: it should be noted that the word *mena/mmra* is one that describes action, impl. function, purpose: i.e. the standard term for any quadruped's tail is *dua/edua* (der(?). *edua*, a stick or stalk), hence *bodua* (*aboa*, animal + *dua*), an animal's tail; thus, *nantwi dua*, a cow's tail; *pɔnkɔ dua*, a horse's tail; *ɛsono dua*, an elephant's tail: only the elephant's tail has a syn. (*mena/mmra*) of function, purpose, impl. symbolic value: that said, other (lesser) animals' tails were used as signs of rank and/or were held to have 'powers': thus, *pɔnkɔ dua* was the insignia of generals and warriors (and, clearly, ranked below the *mena/mmra*); it was also regarded as a potent 'war charm', and military casualties were 'fanned' with a horse's tail to effect their recovery.

mmoatia   (p. 119) sing. *aboatia*. often translated as 'fairies', 'goblins' or 'little people': some informants describe them as being 'half man, half monkey', impl. both physically and categorically: it is this construction that confused Christaller, who thought *aboatia* was 'a kind of ape, which never climbs trees; the gorilla?' [*sic*], and reported that it was alleged to be able 'to kill twenty men at once': the *mmoatia* were 'messengers' or intermediaries between the realm of the (super)natural and human culture: der(?). *aboa*, pl. *mmoa*, an animal, beast, creature + *tia*, (of the) boundary, border.

mogya   (p. 168) syn. *bogya*. blood, the blood (both physiologically as substance and philosophically as concept): most importantly, *mogya* was synonymous with *abusua*, being transmitted via the mother as an exclusive property of uterine descent: as such, *mogya* was one of the four essential elements composing a human being: the importance of *mogya* in descent (in defining matrifiliation, identity, exogamy, social structure, etc.) was reflected in the complex of attitudes towards blood as substance: the shedding of blood (*mogya gu*) – by execution, accident, menstruation, etc. – was in all circumstances hedged about with rituals (of performance, avoidance, management, atonement, etc.): the *deliberate* shedding of blood was at once an *attribute* of power and an *involvement in* or *dialogue with* another, larger autonomous power that was a property in belief: thus, the right to kill (to 'take' blood *in extremis*, 'to hold the knife' as the Asante said) was a prerogative of the *Asantehene*: the root der. is (ultimately) *bo*, in the sense of creation.

n
nanson   (p. 151) the six-day cycle of the Asante calendar: der. *(n)na*,

days + *ason/asoŋ*, seven: this anomaly (six/seven) is explicable as follows – when the Asante talked of the six-day *nanson* as a unit they counted inclusively, i.e. as if the European week of seven named days was counted inclusively (Sunday–Sunday, every Sunday being counted in two successive weeks), giving eight days in a seven-day week.

nawotwe   (p. 151) the seven-day cycle of the Asante calendar: der. *(n)na*, days + *awotwe/ɔwɔtwe*, eight: this anomaly (seven/eight) is explicable on the same principle as the six/seven of *nanson* (see *nanson*): syn. *dapɛŋ*, 'a series of days'; der. *ɔda*, a day + *pɛŋ*: in compound use *pɛŋ* denotes a series, a number or a succession (of things).

nɔ ano awo   (p. 81) 'his lips are dry', 'dry speech', impl. controlled or measured eloquence; admired, and associated with truth telling and mastery over a situation (in discourse): der. *ano*, the outward mouth, the lips + *wo*, to dry, to grow dry, to become free from moisture: syn. *nɔ ano tew*, 'he is eloquent', 'he speaks fluently': der. *ano* + *tew*, to be 'open', clear, distinct, intelligible.

nɔ ano nwoo   (p. 81) 'his lips are wet', 'wet speech', impl. uncontrolled or immoderate talk (prattling, babbling in the manner of a child or a mentally infirm person); distrusted, and associated with duplicity and evasion in discourse: lit. 'his lips are not dried up': der. *ano*, the outward mouth, the lips + *wo* (negated), not dry, not free from moisture: the impl. is of someone (a child, etc.) who cannot control the flow of saliva, and so cannot speak properly: cf. the installation oath taken by office holders before the *Asantehene* included the phrase, 'I will never come and address you with water in my mouth' (i.e. an undertaking neither to lie nor to talk in an inappropriately disrespectful manner): cf. *nɔ ano toto*, 'he speaks confusedly': der. *ano* + *toto*, tangled up, entangled, confused.

anibɔne   (p. 260) conventionally 'the evil eye', but conceptualized as a stare, gaze or (particular) fixed look – centred on the eyes, but embracing the entire face – expressive of the emotional and moral dimensions of the person, and sometimes capable (most potently in the case of the *Asantehene*) of modifying reality: der. *ani*, pl. the same: (*a*) the eye, eyes; (*b*) the countenance, the visage; (*c*) the plane surfaces of the face + *bɔne*, 'bad', but impl. here dangerous or hazardous: *ani* was held to reflect *dweŋ*, the process of thinking (of), meditating or reflecting (upon), or considering (something or someone): the range of constructs combining *ani/ani so* + a verbal phrase is very large, and this demonstrates the centrality of *ani* as a crucial expressive indicator of personhood and its emotional and moral shifts; cf. for example, *nɔ ani abere*, 'he is in a state of (heightened) passion' (grief, anger, rage, melancholy, sorrow, etc.): cf. *wanya me ho anibɔne*, the recognition that someone has 'bad' intentions towards one's person, expressed via *ani* (eyes *and* facial demeanour): cf. *gyeŋ*: (*a*) to be pure, clear, still (as in water); (*b*) to be sincere, impl. 'harmless'; (*c*) to gaze (to 'clear' the eye, to look sharply): *anibɔne* encompasses two intentions: (*a*) the direct apprehension of someone's malevolent intent; (*b*) a larger sense (embracing *a*) of the engaged challenge of another (a duel of power between *ani* in which the 'dominating' gaze imprints itself as a modifier on another personhood): informants often frame *anibɔne* in terms of 'challenge' and 'response'.

nipa koro (p. 187) full matri-siblings, conceptually 'one person, of a single womb' (a corporate unit in the very narrowest matrilineal sense): der. *(o)nipa*, a person, a human being + *koro*, one, single (but or only one), the same, impl. unique.

nokware (p. 252) the notion of truthfulness or veracity (ethical or moral rather than cognitive 'truth'): der(?). *ano*, the mouth, impl. speech + *koro*, one, single, impl. unique (lit. 'one mouth'?) or *(ko)kware*, to evade a difficulty (cf. *ŋkokware me asɛm misa ho*, 'he goes by or around the question', i.e. he does not give a straight answer): cf. *twa ŋkontompo*, to tell lies (lit. 'to cut something from the truth'). der. *twa*, to cut + *konto*, to bend, to curve, impl. to be perverse: cf. *atoro*, an untruth, a lie. der. *toro(toro)*: (*a*) glib, smooth, slippery, oily tongued; (*b*) false, spurious: clearly, there is a link between telling truths/untruths and the construction put upon 'ways of speaking'. (see *nɔ ano awo, nɔ ano nwoo*): relations between the ethical dimension of personal 'truth telling' and the ideological dimension of state power are cogently summarized in the proverbial locution *wutwa ŋkontompo a, wusuro kumase* (lit. 'When you tell a lie, you will fear Kumase').

nnuabɔ (p. 194) cursing, a curse. der(?). *edua*, pl. *nnua*, a piece of wood + *bɔ*, to speak out, to utter (Christaller cites the original practice as being the 'cursing' of someone by invocation, while simultaneously driving a piece of wood into the ground; some Asante informants concur, and this seems the most plausible der.): syn. *nnome*, execration, der. *dome*, to execrate (someone).

nnuraho (p. 48) 'enfolding', 'being wrapped around': lit. understood as (*a*) the act of covering, wrapping, decking or garlanding; (*b*) a cover or covering, a wrapper, a coat, impl. embellishment, 'finishing' in the sense of adding to (in support): der. *dura*, to cover over, to coat, to overlay, to wrap + *ɛho*, around (the outside of things): used here of the metaphysical understanding of the way in which the *sika mena* was 'wrapped around' or 'enfolded' the *sika dwa kofi*, impl. help, assistance, support.

onyame   (p. 104 and *passim*) the ('withdrawn') sole creator of the world: conventionally rendered as 'God': der. *onya*, to get, to achieve + *mee*, to be full up; or complete, impl. plenitude, a fulfilled state: bynames commemorated discrete aspects or specific determinations of the omniscience of *onyame*.

nyame dua   (p. 107) lit. 'God's tree': der. *onyame + dua/edua*, a tree: a simple household shrine dedicated to *onyame*, and made from a forked branch of the actual tree called *(o)nyame dua* (*Alstonia congensis*): the branches of this tree are produced in fours from the apex, forming a natural crock-like receptacle in the *nyame dua* shrine into which a bowl was placed: ritual offerings (food, etc.) were left in this bowl: the shrine itself was a mnemonic of the 'withdrawn' *onyame*.

p

pae/pae abusua   (p. 87) expulsion from the *abusua* (matrilineage) by corporate agreement: der. *pae/pae*: (*a*) to part, to divide, to rend, to split (up), to break (apart); (*b*) to proclaim, to exclaim + *abusua*: *pae/pae* encompasses both the juridical act of separation and the mandatory public promulgation of that decision.

pae/pae din   (p. 181) 'cancellation' (e.g. of individual or corporate rights to the occupancy of a stool or office): der. *pae/pae*, to part, to divide, etc. + *edin/edin*, a name: the underlying general conception is *pae ne din* – 'to forbid someone's name (and give them another one)': a well-remembered instance of this general application took place when the *Asantehene* Opoku Ware 'cancelled the name' of those of *Tana/Tena* descent in Asante – because one of them perpetrated a heinous offence against his person – and 'gave them another name' by amalgamating them with those of *Bretuo* descent.

apafram   (*passim*) used as a syn. for *odwira*: the most authoritative Asante sources (including the *Asantehene* Osei Agyeman Prempeh II) give the word *apafram* as, strictly speaking, a name for the *odwira suman*, rather than for *odwira* itself: following this lead, and considering the origin of the *odwira suman*, the der. is (very tentatively) *apa*, a frontier, a border region + *fram*, to be on fire, to burn up, to blaze or/and *mframa*, the wind (i.e. something from 'beyond' that is associated with an expression of great, (super)natural power): that said, it must be admitted that the der. of *apafram* has puzzled many knowledgeable commentators, and it continues to be opaque and to be disputed among informants: as a concept it is sometimes associated with *asase yaa*, or with the idea of an Asante 'race god': everything points to the (pre-Asante?) antiquity of the term, but etymological clarification remains elusive.

papa   (p. 78) the concept of moral goodness; lit. goodness, kindness, wellbeing, impl. consensus, communality, concern for the welfare of others: der. *pa*, good: cf. *papani*, a good, caring or righteous person: the underlying concept is of humility and selflessness: *papa* was much admired, and it was favourably contrasted with undue self-seeking and hubris.

apeatɔɔ   (p. 59) a special levy to raise revenue for military purposes, imposed on office holders by prerogative of the *Asantehene*: it is said that the concept of *apeatɔɔ* was introduced (by Apea?) from Takyiman when that place was conquered by Asante in the 1720s: der. *apea*, a proper name + *ɛtoɔ*, a tax, tribute, toll.

pɛmɛ   (p. 42) pl. *mpɛmɛ*: a spear, a lance: a symbolic accoutrement of the earliest *abirɛmpɔn*: der(?). *pem*, to strike, to thrust, to hit.

ɔpɛnimma   (p. 157) the 'small' dry season (in December/January immediately prior to the 'big' dry season, *ɔpɛpɔŋ*): der. *ɔpɛ*: (*a*) the dry, cool northeasterly wind from the interior, the *harmattan*; (*b*) the season of dryness + *nimma*, in the sense of small.

ɔpɛpɛɛfo   (p. 61) pl. *apɛpɛɛfoɔ*. a person given to avarice, but often used admiringly of the thrifty (those careful in amassing wealth): der. *pɛ*, to try to get, to seek, to desire: cf. *pɛpɛɛ*: covetousness of things, avarice, dedicated desire: *pɛpɛɛ* is one among a cluster of closely related words: cf. *anibere*, desire, impl. cupidity, in a sexual and other senses: cf. *ŋkyekye*, avarice (but in an entirely negative sense?), hence *ɔkyekyefo*, a miser: cf. *ayamɔŋwene*, to be stingy, stinginess: the various shades of meaning reflect a basic ambivalence in social thinking and practice – accumulation versus expenditure on/generosity towards others (with personal, emotional and moral dimensions, as well as structural resonances in kinship and relations of power).

ɔpɛpɔŋ   (p. 157) the 'big' dry season (in December/January immediately following the 'small' dry season, *ɔpɛnimma*): der. *ɔpɛ*: (*a*) the dry, cool northeasterly wind from the interior, the *harmattan*; (*b*) the season of dryness + *pɔŋ*, great, large, big.

mperedwan   (*passim*) sing. *peredwan*. an Asante gold weight equivalent to $2\frac{1}{4}$ Troy ounces, and conventionally valued throughout the nineteenth century at £8 sterling.

mpɛsɛmpɛsɛ   (p. 121) lit. 'I do not like it at all' (the repetition shows the emphatic nature of the sentiment): *mpɛsɛmpɛsɛ* was used of the long, matted, unkempt hairstyle with greased plaits favoured by *akɔmfoɔ, abrafoɔ, adumfoɔ* (and, unselfconsciously, by madmen): the style was contrived, deliberately odd and 'anti-social': i.e. it was meant to signify challenge, aggression, unpredictable behaviour, distancing, and a degree of derangement: der. *pɛsɛ*, to tug, to worry, to pull apart, to rend into pieces, impl. dishevelled, disordered, lack of care.

apetesɛŋɛɛ   (p. 202) a location on the edge of Kumase south of *dwaberem* where criminals were killed: der. *pete*, to scatter, strew, throw about + *asɛneɛ*, any place where criminals (or others) were killed: cf. *seṇ*: (*a*) to suspend, to hang; (*b*) to cut; (*c*) to pass away, to perish.

mpoatwa   (p. 79 and *passim*) pl. *mpoatwitwa*. lit. a challenge, a setting at defiance, an act of defamation: root der. *poa*, to challenge or defy with vilification or debasing words, gestures or other understood forms of expression + *twa*, to cut into small pieces, to cut down: as widespread social practice, *mpoatwa* was a form of 'distancing' and 'positioning', i.e. it connoted defiance and defamation of some other person, primarily by means of an assertion or display (verbal, gestural, behavioural) of superior social position by the person practising it: syn. *mpoatwerɛ*, der. *poa* + *twerɛ*, to grate upon, to grind, to chew up, to abrade: although some proverbial sayings make direct reference to *mpoatwa*, the most indicative illustrations of the network of understanding surrounding the practice are indirect: e.g. (*a*) of the claims of high birth – *ɔdehyeɛ mu nni abofra*, 'Among royalty no one is a child'; i.e. no *ɔdehyeɛ* is a jural minor (and *abofra* can also mean servant as well as child); (*b*) of the claims of (connection with) power – *ade hia ɔhenenana a, okita tuo na ɔnsoa akɛtɛ*, 'When a chief's grandson is poor, he [still] holds a gun but he does not carry a sleeping mat'; i.e. an office holder's grandson is fitted by status for war, but, however poor, would never carry his own sleeping mat (*akɛtɛ*); the carrying of one's own sleeping mat was held to be very degrading; (*c*) of the claims of wealth over birth – *ɔdehyeɛ wɔnnoa wonni na sika ne asɛm*, 'Royalty [an ancient name] cannot be cooked and eaten; after all, money is the thing': a full study of *mpoatwa* (paying due attention to its shifting modes of expression, notably in the twentieth century) would require a book in its own right.

pɔw   (p. 79) (*a*) selfless values, refinement, cultivation; (*b*) pride, arrogance, self-seeking: *pɔw* is another term (see *ɔpɛpɛɛfo*) that is illustrative of the ambiguous boundary between selfless advancement (to serve others) and self-seeking advancement (to serve oneself): thus *pɔw* has an 'evolutionary' series of meanings: (*a*) to rub, scrape, clean; (*b*) to polish, burnish, refine; (*c*) to become polite, refined, civilized; (*d*) to grow rich, to rise in the world; (*e*) to become puffed up, arrogant: cf. *ɔpɔw*: (*a*) politeness, civilization; (*b*) haughtiness, arrogance: cf. also *pɔwampɔw*, a lack of culture, to be rude, uncivilized.

pramakɛsɛɛsɔ   (p. 219) alt. *bampanase*. 'the great court' of the *Asantehene's* palace in Kumase: der. *prama/pramma*, a large courtyard, enclosed by dwellings, and not fronting on a street + *kɛsɛɛ*, big, large + *ɛsɔ*, at (a place): cf. from the same root der. *pra*, to sweep, to clear, *mprae(so)*, an open, swept space for trading etc.: alt. *bampanase* is der(?). *bam(ma)/baŋ*, a seat (the projecting wall of a dwelling) + *mpeneso*, assent, agreement, concurrence: the *pato* around the *pramakɛsɛɛsɔ* were used to store umbrellas, palanquins and drums: the *Asantehene* often sat in state in the *pramakɛsɛɛsɔ* – for court cases, policy discussions, oath swearings, and to observe parts of the *adae* (thus, the *pato* holding palanquins and drums was named *Kronti ne Akwamu*, because on state occasions the *Krontihene/Bantamahene* and *Akwamuhene/Asafohene* sat there with their assembled office holders).

apremoso   (p. 205) 'the place of the cannons', an open space (and a ward or quarter) close by the *Asantehene's* palace in Kumase: der. *ɔprɛm*, pl. *aprɛm*, a cannon: *apremoso* was named for the European cannons preserved on an elevation on the site (it was said that these guns had been captured from the Denkyira at Feyiase (1701), the decisive military victory that led to the 'creation' of the Asante state).

puruw   (p. 209) (*a*) round, circular, globular, spherical, cylindrical; (*b*) a completed circle, a disc, a globe, a cylinder: syn. *puruo*: der(?). *pu*, completely, perfectly (from *pɛ*, to be complete, perfect): the completed circle (in its many forms) connoted an aesthetic and morally integrated unity or perfection.

s

nsa   (p. 42) syn. *nsaa*. a coarse covering, a blanket (generally of non-Asante origin, but from Gonja, Dagomba, etc. to the north, and, so it is said, made from a camel hair and wool mix): used in a range of ritual contexts, and most especially to prevent a 'forbidden' contact between an object or person and the earth: root der(?). *saa*, to weave (in different colours): on public occasions the *sika dwa kofi* 'rested' on either *nsa* or *banwoma* (made from the membrane of an elephant's ear).

sadwa   (p. 233) a drinking party (a reception in a public place at which the *Asantehene* distributed alcohol and gifts): der. *nsa*, alcohol, liquor, palm wine + *dwa/egua*, a public place of assembly: cf. *sadwaasefoɔ*, drinkers, revellers.

asafo   (p. 56) pl. the same. a company, a band (of *nkoa*) organized for war, or for some other communal purpose: der. *ɔsa*, war + *fo(ɔ)*, people: cf. *asafohene*, a captain, a military officer: but cf. *ɔsahene*, a general: the Kumase *Akwamuhene* was *Asafohene* in the sense of presiding over the *asafo* quarter of the Asante capital.

ɔsako   (p. 210) pl. *asako*. a palanquin. der(?). from warfare, *ɔsa*, war + *ko*, to fight: alt. *deŋkyedeŋkye*, lit. shaking about, oscillating: hence, *ehim deŋkyedeŋkye*. lit. 'to shake to and fro', i.e. the agitated action of 'dancing in the palanquin' by office holders being borne along in public procession.

asamaŋfoɔ   (p. 160) syn. *asamaŋ*. sing. *ɔsamaŋ*: ancestral spirits of the dead or departed, 'ghosts': der(?). *sa*, to end, to pass away, to die out, to be gone, to depart, to be past + *ɔman*, community, etc. + suffix *foɔ*, people: ancestral spirits were conceptualized as having senses (hunger, thirst, feelings, etc.), rather than as being disembodied (in the sense of a 'soul'): thus *ɔsamaŋ* was sometimes used to mean a skeleton: 'the land of ghosts' (*asamaŋdow*) was variously said to be in the heavens or under the ground: thus, some informants give the ultimate root der. as *ase*: (*a*) the lower or nether part; (*b*) an end or beginning; (*c*) down, beneath, below; (*d*) a place or time of; (*e*) the ground; (*f*) issue, progeny, etc.: be that as it may, *asamaŋfoɔ* sometimes behaved in recognizably 'human' ways: thus, the *ɔsamaŋ twɛŋ twɛŋ* (der. *twɛŋ*, to wait about, to linger) appeared to those still alive, dressed in white cloth and white clay: it was held to 'linger' because of some dissatisfaction or unfinished business in life: most *asamaŋfoɔ* of this category were diffident: but the *ɔtɔfo* was a type of 'lingering ghost' of someone who had been killed and/or had been improperly buried, and was 'dangerous' (appearing in dreams and as a threatening apparition): the *ɔsamaŋ pa*, 'the good spirit' was one that had departed for *asamaŋdow*, and that avoided human contact: ritual connection with the *asamaŋfoɔ* involved giving them food and drink, and their intercession was sought to ensure communal prosperity and growth.

asamaŋpomu   (p. 202) 'the bush of the ghosts': i.e. the grove of the departed *asamaŋfoɔ*: in Kumase this was located on the edge of town, south of *dwaberem*: der. *asamaŋ + pɔw*, a grove, a thicket, a small stand of trees.

ɔsanaa   (p. 145) a period or season of the year, a 'month': generally about August (following *akitawonsa*): der. *sanaa*, a store, a hoard; cf. *ɔsaŋ*, a shed to store food.

asantemaŋhyiamu   (p. 146) 'the assembly of the Asante nation': a 'national' assembly of office holders, presided over by the *Asantehene* and constituted as the supreme deliberative body: by the nineteenth century, it met – only? – at *odwira*, the day-to-day executive running of government having been taken over by the *Asantehene* with a council of Kumase office holders: the *asantemaŋhyiamu* continued as a 'supreme court' of law, but its powers to initiate (in policy, in legislation) were eroded, *de facto* if not *de jure*: der. *asante*, Asante + *ɔman*, state, people, 'nation' + *hyiamu*, a meeting together, a place of assembly.

ɔsape   (p. 69) pl. *asape*. a spendthrift, a prodigal, a swindler: the term connotes generosity to others, but in an irresponsible or even duplicitous way: der. *sa(w)*, to gather (up) + *pe/pɛ*, to scatter, to strew about: *ɔsape* was a byname of the *Asantehene* Kofi Kakari.

sasabonsam   (p. 118) a hybrid (human/non-human), predatory 'creature' of the deep forest, servant of the *abosom*, and hostile to human order: it expressed antipathy by preying directly upon individuals and/or by fostering witchcraft: der. *sasa*, used here of someone 'possessed' + *abonsam*, wizard, sorcerer, witch.

asase yaa   (p. 154) the 'spirit' of the earth: der. *(as)ase*, that beneath or below, the ground, the soil, the earth + *yaa*, name day of a female born on 'Thursday' (cf. *yawo* in the *nawotwe* cycle): the earth was anthropomorphized and personalized as female, and no 'disturbance' (i.e. agricultural work) of 'her' was permitted on her 'name day', i.e. every recurrent 'Thursday' in the *adaduanan* cycle.

aseda   (p. 62) thanks, gratitude, thanksgiving. der. *ase*, down + *da*, to lie, lit. 'to lie down', impl. to thank: *aseda* was the term used for the customary thank-offering (monetary or otherwise) paid over to a court or tribunal by a successful plaintiff or petitioner.

ɔsekaŋ   (p. 201) pl. *asekaŋ*. a knife. der(?).: (*a*) Portuguese, *secare* (from the earliest period of European trade with the coastal Akan); (*b*) *ɔse*, a father + *kaŋ*, with the sense of first in place or rank: the latter gains some credence from the fact that the knives carried by the *adumfoɔ/abrafoɔ* (see *kyiɛafaseɛ*), and used in executions, were generically *asekaŋ*: as such, these knives embodied the precept that the *Asantehene* alone ('father', 'of first rank') 'held the knife' (*ɔsekaŋ*), i.e. possessed an ultimate power of discretion to order or to commute the death sentence.

nseku   (p. 179) a voicing of calumny, innuendo, defamatory insinuation. der(?). *asɛm*, matters, things + *ku(w)*, to cut (off, down), to clip: cf. *nseku di*, slander, aspersion, detraction (verbally, *di nseku*, to slander, backbite, disparage, defame, etc.): syn. *nsekubɔ*, der. *nseku* + *bɔ*, with the sense of practising something: hence *osekufo*, pl. *asekufoɔ*, a detractor, an insinuator.

ɔsekye/atɛntɛ   (p. 236) an 'orchestra'/musical ensemble of the *Asantehene*, using double-headed drums and bamboo pipes: *atɛn* was a distinctive style of vigorous drumming and dancing, and it was employed on a variety of public and ceremonial occasions, most notably to accompany the *Asantehene*-in-procession.

nsenieɛfoɔ   (p. 55 and *passim*) sing. *nsenieni*, *ɔsɔn/ɛsɛŋ*. 'court criers' or 'court heralds': i.e. that group of *nhenkwaa* who commanded silence when the *Asantehene* spoke in court (by repeatedly declaiming *tie!*, *tie!*, 'listen!, listen!'), and who called the assembly's attention to any other speaker's address: *nsenieɛfoɔ* wore a distinctive cap called *adomasa*, made from the skin of the black colobus monkey (*Colobus polykomos*); a male child born a hunchback (*akyakya*) was given to the *Asantehene* for training as an *ɛsɛŋ*, although only a minority of the *nsenieɛfoɔ* were deformed; in addition to duties at court, *nsenieɛfoɔ* were extensively used as messengers (flogging or maiming them being formulaic rejections of the *Asantehene's* power, and so tantamount to a declaration of war): *nsenieɛfoɔ* had a deal of license, and were the *Asantehene's* 'jesters' and 'spies' (their taste for 'gossip' being legendary, even in modern Asante): they were headed by the *Nsenieɛhene*, who served in the *gyaasewa* sub-division of the Kumase *gyaase fekuo*.

asetena kɛsɛɛ (p. 41) 'the great sitting down together', a term used for the supreme court of law, as presided over by the *Asantehene*: der (?). *ɔsete*, submission to authority, obedience (cf. *se*, to tell, to command; *ose*, the outcry of a multitude; *asete*, an understanding, an agreed comprehension) + *kesɛɛ/kɛsɛɛ*, big, large, huge, impl. significance.

sika (p. 38 and *passim*) (*a*) gold; (*b*) 'money' in general. the concept of *sika* (fully discussed in the text) was of central importance: *sika* itself as substance might be: (*a*) *sika futuro/futuru*, gold dust, i.e. ready or negotiable currency; der. *futuro/futuru*, raw, unwrought, composed of small particles; (*b*) *sika pɔw*, a rock, lump, nugget, or ingot of gold; der. *ɛpɔw*, a lump, syn. *pɔkɔwa*, a lump; (*c*) *sika amapa*, unmixed, pure, 'solid' gold; der. *ma*, very (much so) + *pa*, good, proper, genuine.

sika dwa kofi (p. 48 and *passim*) lit. 'Friday's Golden Stool'. der. *sika*, gold, golden + *dwa*, a stool + *kofi*, the day name of a male person born on a 'Friday' (i.e. *fie* in the *nawotwe* cycle): it is said that, with the enabling mediation of Komfo Anokye, the *sika dwa* descended from the skies and settled on the knees of the seated Osei Tutu on a particular *fie* ('Friday'): an incumbent *Asantehene* was the living custodian of the *sika dwa kofi*, and was responsible for exercising and discharging that political authority at the highest level that was embodied in it: the *sika dwa kofi* was held to contain within it the collective *sunsum* of the *Asantemaŋ* (as ordained and reinforced by prescriptive ritual measures 'dictated' by Komfo Anokye).

sika mena/mmra (p. 47 and *passim*) lit. 'The Golden Elephant Tail'. der. *sika* + *mena/mmra*, an elephant's tail (see *mena/mmra*): the *sika mena* was a crucial item of regalia of the *Asantehenes*: it symbolized the very highest level at which wealth was appropriated, and as such it was conceptualized as being the indispensable 'helper' or 'supporter' of the very highest level of political authority (embodied in the *sika dwa kofi*): in metaphorical recognition of this relationship, the *sika mena* was understood: (*a*) to 'enfold' (*nnuraho*) the *sika dwa kofi* (with the sense of 'assisting' it), and (*b*) to 'preside' as the most senior (as a 'parent') over the lesser elephant tails of the *abirɛmpɔn*: each *Asantehene* 'made' his own *sika mena*, but detailed information concerning this most potent ritual object is difficult to recover: in part this is because the *sika mena* was a property of the reticent 'mystery' that surrounded power at its highest levels (i.e. its ideological articulation was pervasive, but by corollary its ritual quiddity – its 'being' – was opaque): it is also because the *sika mena* 'vanished' with the *Asantehene* from Asante life from 1896 to 1935, and when the *Asantehene* Osei Agyeman Prempeh II had one 'made' for himself (to commemorate the British 'restoration' of the 'Ashanti Confederacy') the precolonial systems of accumulation and appropriation of wealth had eroded and effectively vanished: it would appear that the appointed head of the *ahoprafoɔ* was charged with responsibility for the *sika mena* of the first *Asantehene* Osei Tutu (and that this was kept in the *bantama baamu*): each successive ruler consigned his *sika mena* to the care of a trusted and greatly honoured individual (Kwasi Brantuo in the case of the *Asantehene* Kwaku Dua Panin), but the person thereby selected was not always or necessarily the *Ahoprafoɔhene* (that office itself undergoing a formal 'revival' after 1935, when it was (re)assigned to the mid-nineteenth century created *Manwere fekuo*): current readings of the 'passing' of the *sika mena* in its original formulation/meaning are associated, significantly enough, with the avaricious *Asantehene* Mensa Bonsu (1874–83): it is variously said that Mensa Bonsu's *sika mena*: (*a*) 'disintegrated' and 'vanished' because it was the product of non-licit accumulation; (*b*) was appropriated by the people of Saawua; (*c*) drove its custodians 'mad' and then 'vanished'; (*d*) was interred with its creator's bones in Kumase, or otherwise 'became lost' during the funeral obsequies.

sikani　(p. 56) pl. *asikafoɔ*. lit. 'a man of wealth'. der. *sika*, gold: alt. *ɔdefo*, pl. *adefoɔ*, der. *ɔde*, property, possession; *ɔhonyafo*, pl. *nhonyafoɔ*, der. *ahonya* (*nya ne ho*), lit. the condition or state of 'having obtained one's own self', i.e. of gaining gold, wealth: a *sikani* was a person of acknowledged substance, whether in a local community or on a broader scale (thus, it is sometimes averred that Atwoma and Manso-Nkwanta were 'famous' for their *asikafoɔ*, but that Kwabre and Mponua were not): *asikafoɔ* – who might acquire riches from trading, from lending and/or hoarding gold dust, or, as seems often to have been the case, from illegally secreting finds of rock or nugget gold – had a somewhat ambiguous folk reputation: on the one hand, they were 'model' citizens (at one level, the *abirɛmpɔn* were simply accumulative *asikafoɔ*, but on a maximal scale): but on the other hand, neighbours often saw opulence as ostentation, or resentfully accused *asikafoɔ* of being self-seeking usurers, driven by a selfish 'thirst for gold' (*sika nibere*): the difficulties of *asikafoɔ*, and notably those of non-Kumase or provincial origins, were compounded by the fact that many of them were marginal to, or even outside of, the office holding structures of the state: thus, and despite a range of legal guarantees, *asikafoɔ* lived in uneasy awareness of the state's command over the law and of its predatory potential regarding wealth (for many, this unease was compounded by the jealousies of their fellow citizens, who might be motivated to report or even to invent the 'criminal' sources of someone's wealth in gold).

asokwafoɔ   (p. 216) sing. *asokwani*. the hornblowers of the *Asantehene*: der (?). *ɛsono*, an elephant (elephant tusks were used for making horns) + *kwa*, an abbreviated form of *akoa*: *asokwafoɔ* also drummed, acted as 'sextons' of the royal graves, and traded on behalf of the *Asantehene*: this group of *nhenkwaa* was headed by the *Asokwahene/Batahene*, who now serves with the *Akyeremadefoɔhene*, the head of a group of drummers, in the *gyaasewa* sub-division of the Kumase *gyaase fekuo*.

asomfoɔ   (p. 14) sing. *ɔsomfo*. those charged by authority with a duty or responsibility (and so applied to include all those appointed to such a status – non-hereditary office holders, *nhenkwaa*, household or palace servants, etc.): der. *som*, to serve a master, to be in a position of servant or subject to someone/something (thus, *abosom*, for example, had *asomfoɔ* just as the *Asantehene* had): cf. *ɔsom/ɛsom*, (the concept of) service, servitude: generically, *asomfoɔ* was applied to attendants and servants of all kinds: thus, all *nhenkwaa* were *asomfoɔ*, but only some *asomfoɔ* were *nhenkwaa*: someone in this category charged with a specifically designated function, service, office, duty or trust conferred by authority was given *ɛsom adwuma* to perform: der. *dwuma*, an employment, business, duty, function or office.

ɛsono   (p. 42 and *passim*). the elephant. lit. 'the big one': der. *so*, to be big, large, great, impl. attainment, supremacy + *no*, the (pronoun, impl. self): cf. *susono*, the hippopotamus, lit. 'the big one of the water', der. *(n)su*, water + *so* + *no*: *ɛsono* was an animal with a 'dangerous' *sasa*, and dense folklore reflects this status in Asante ritual and belief: cf. *ɛsono dua*, syn. *mena/mmra*, the tail of the elephant ('used to fan Kings'): cf. *ɛsontɔ*, the ear of the elephant (used to make the membrane of certain drums): wordplay is implicit in *sono*, to differ from, to be different from (all else): cf. too *nsono*, bowels, intestines.

nsɔre   (p. 202) a place outside of a settlement where corpses were thrown or buried: der. *sɔre*: (*a*) to part, leave, go away, cease; (*b*) to rise up, impl. rise from the dead: cf. *sɔre* (a different verb?): (*a*) to worship; (*b*) to perform religious rites: hence *nsɔre*, (by metonymy?) the offering placed on a grave: syn. *nsɔrem, asɔreso*.

subaŋ   (p. 168) lit. a figure, form, shape, impl. character, nature: an individual's *subaŋ* was determined by the *sunsum*: the *sunsum* itself could be altered by training and application from *hare* ('light') to *duru* ('heavy'), with an effect on the formation of the *suban* (to make one braver, more responsible, etc.): der. *(e)su*, a property, a kind, a manner + *ba*, form or shape (of).

asuman (p. 111 and *passim*). sing. *suman*. charms, amulets, talismans (all dedicated to prescribed, circumscribed functions: all aspects or derivations of a much larger embodiment of power: all – unlike the *abosom* – man-made): *asuman* were the most evident/apparent feature of Asante belief practices, and so Europeans erroneously accorded these 'fetishes'/'saphies' a central (sometimes an exclusive) role as 'Asante religion': der. *suma*, to hide, to be hidden: *osumanni* was a maker, owner and/or a wearer of *asuman* (cf. *bɔ suman*, to make or wear a *suman*; *tu suman*, to make or introduce a *suman*; *gye suman*, to procure or buy a *suman*): *asuman* were commonly worn round the neck or limbs, and might be composed of virtually anything that 'held' an efficacious aspect of power(s) (e.g. hair, beads, teeth, feathers, leather, scraps of paper with Koranic writing/Islamic cabalistic formulae, etc.): *asuman* were owned by individuals, and might be protective (against malice, witchcraft, disease, etc.), or aggressively intended (to 'poison' others): some purpose-specific *asuman* seem to have been known by generic names; e.g. *gyabom*, the 'helpers', der. *gya*, to help, assist, save: *dwenfa*, worn to assist in acquiring property, lit. 'a thing or person found or seized': *ayera*, 'making someone vanish', der. *yera*, to vanish, to be killed, syn. *otuo suman*, 'the gun *suman*'.

asuman nnɔrɔ (p. 238) a 'yearly' ritual ceremony with dancing, devoted to the *asuman* of the *Asantehene*: der. *asuman* + *nnɔrɔ/noru*, verbal noun of *goru*, to play, to celebrate.

sumpene (p. 161) sing(?). *sumpi*: elevated mounds of sun-baked clay, from where the *Asantehene*, seated in state, presided over many of the public rituals of life in Kumase: there were many of these, but the most important were at *dwaberem* and *apremoso/bogyawe*: der(?). *sum*, to stand (up), impl. things heaped up together + *pi*, in the sense of many.

sunsum (p. 168) pl. *asunsum*. an intangible constituent of the person: non-human in origin, the *sunsum* determined an individual character (see *suban*), but might also be construed as a collective or group 'essence' (e.g. the *sunsum* of the *Asanteman* was contained within the *sika dwa kofi*): the *sunsum* could be 'cultivated' in a variety of ways, chiefly dedicated to defending its host against hostility and 'illness' (witchcraft, etc.): der(?). *(e)sum(a)*, shadow, dark, shade, impl. mysteriousness, hiding: cf. *sunsuma*, a shade, a shadow (sometimes used as syn. *sunsum*).

asusow (*passim*) the 'first' or 'great' rains (about April–July): der.

osu, rain (*nsu*, water) + *so/sɔ/sɔsɔ*, to fall in drops, to run down.

t

ntamkɛsɛɛ

(p. 70) lit. 'the great oath', der. *ntam*, an oath + *kɛsɛɛ*, big or great: i.e. 'the Asante great oath(s)', the oath(s) belonging to the *Asantehene*: the *ntamkɛsɛɛ* embodied and made formulaic reference to the unmentionable, i.e. to historical calamities or catastrophes that had befallen Asante, the *Asantehenes*, or the Kumase *Oyoko Kɔkɔɔ abusua*: these formulae included swearing by: *(a) memene(da) koromante* ('Saturday' and the coastal Fante town of Kormantin); this referred to the deaths (*mekɔeɛ deɛ nanso mante*, 'I went, but did not hear') by illness (smallpox, dysentery) of the royals Osei Badu and Akua Akrukruwaa (some sources add Osei Kofi and Yaa Dufi) in 1807 during the *Asantehene* Osei Tutu Kwame's campaign in Fante; (*b*) *katamanso*; this referred to the battle in 1826 where the *Asantehene* Osei Yaw was routed by the British and their coastal allies; (*c*) *wuku(o)da* ('Wednesday'); this, the oldest of the three, referred to the day upon which the *Asantehene* Osei Tutu either lost his life fighting the Akyem, or the Asante army temporarily lost his body/coffin to the Akyem (1712, 1717?): these three were *ntamkɛsɛmmiensa*, 'the three great oaths': *abaŋakyi* ('behind the castle'), a reference to the unsuccessful Asante siege of the British fort in Kumase in the *Yaa Asantewaakoɔ* (1900–1), is added by some present informants: to use *ntamkɛsɛɛ* (*me ka ntam . . .*, 'I swear the oath of . . .') was a grave matter, for the party sworn upon was legally bound to respond (*bo ntam so*, lit. 'to beat upon the oath', i.e. to swear the same oath to assert the opposite case), and once these exchanges had occurred the *Asantehene* was himself obliged to investigate the matter that had led to the use of his oath, in a court of law: the unsuccessful litigant in a case involving *ntamkɛsɛɛ* was liable to be fined very heavily, sometimes bankrupted or simply put to death: those already sentenced to death had *sɛpɔ* knives pushed through their cheeks to prevent direct 'cursing' of the *Asantehene*, but also to stop them uttering/invoking *ntamkɛsɛɛ* (any such utterance would have halted the due process of execution, for *ntamkɛsɛɛ* proposed a mandatory hearing or investigation before the *Asantehene*).

atano

(p. 108) der. River Tano in northwestern Asante: one of the three major categories of *abosom*: powers that derived from water: I have used an Occamist principle (but based on Asante understanding) in defining *atano*: i.e. some informants (partisan or otherwise) talk of e.g. River Bosompra, Lake Bosomtwe as being *abosom* every iota as 'powerful' as River Tano: this conceded, it is then said that Tano has most 'children' (*taa*) among such powers, and so – whatever the specificity and authority of other rivers, lakes, etc. – the word *atano* is used generically to describe this category of *abosom*: thus, *atano* is used here, in the Asante manner, to classify those *abosom* united together by their 'point of origin' in water: by this particular reading Lake Bosomtwe is *atano*, but it is not at all a 'child' of Tano *per se*.

atitɔdeɛ (p. 41) lit. 'buying one's head', sometimes imposed in lieu of the death sentence (as a prerogative of the *Asantehene*): der. *ti/tiri*, a head + *tɔ*, to buy, to purchase.

atɔperɛ (p. 254) often translated as the 'dance (or theatre) of death': a day-long process of execution by progressive ritual dismemberment, reserved to those convicted of the most heinous offences: root der. *perɛ*, to struggle, contend, use great effort, impl. contorting the body; hence *ɔperɛ*, a (life and) death struggle, death agonies.

ntɔrɔ (p. 168) pl. the same. syn. *ntoro*, *ntɔŋ* (although *ntɔŋ*, in the generic sense of 'counting descent', is sometimes loosely used in relation to matrilineality as well as patrilineality): an essential element of a human being that defined consanguinity in patrilineal terms, i.e. descent from a father, descent in the male line: Asante *ntɔrɔ* groups are extensively discussed in the text: *inter alia* they were 'cultic' organizations, whose members participated in rituals in common (e.g. the 'washing' of the *kra*): the root der(?). seems to be *tɔ/to*, with a sense of belonging, counting together (cf. also *ana*, 'mothers', but more broadly 'ancestry', a genealogy).

ɔtrommo (p. 220) the Bongo antelope (*Boocercus euryceros*): alt. *saakwa*, *tenkwa*, bynames which simply connoted an entity with a reputation (for something): by common consent, *ɔtrommo* was held to be the most 'dangerous' of all *sasammoa*: i.e. it possessed the most powerful *sasa* 'spirit' of all animals.

otumi (p. 48) 'the highest level at which political authority could be exercised', symbolized by the *sika dwa kofi*, and personified in its custodian the *Asantehene*: der. *tumi*, to be able (to do something), impl. ability, influence, power: cf. *atumisɛm*, 'things of power', i.e. the externalized display of strength, authority: cf. *otumfo*, *otumfoɔ*, 'one who has great power', i.e. the *Asantehene*.

atumtufoɔ (p. 221) sing. *otumtufo*. gun-bearers, the *Asantehene's* bodyguard: der. *tumi*, to be able, impl. power + *otuo*, a gun/*tɔw*, to shoot (a gun): the *atumtufoɔ* were under the authority of the *Ankobeahene* in the Kumase *ankobea fekuo*.

tuntum (p. 203) black: with white (*fufu*) and red (*kɔkɔɔ*), one of the three primary colour classifications in Asante thought: *tuntum* was held to embrace that part of the spectrum ranging from black to blue/indigo, and including the dark browns: it connoted death and loss, ill luck (it was never used to denote victory), and darkness (but not necessarily defilement: cf. the 'blackening' of ancestral stools): in some contexts *tuntum* impl. spirituality attaching to age (expressed in the 'blackening' of heirlooms, regalia): cf. *tuntu(u)ntum*, very black: the word is related to the root *tum(i)*, impl. power.

ntwiri (p. 179) talking slanderous lies, splenetic grumbling: der. *twiri*, to rail against, to slander: cf. *otwirifo*, pl. *atwirifoɔ/ntwirifoɔ*, a false accuser, a slanderer, impl. a grudge, muttering against, calumniating.

ntwoma (p. 203) red clay, earth, ochre: the smearing of *ntwoma* (on limbs, face and dress) betokened a person in hazardous contact with and/or exposure to ambiguous (super)natural power(s): thus, *ntwoma* meant a state of grieving/grief: in non-ritual contexts, *ntwoma* was used to stain (*kwaw*) floors and (parts of) buildings: cf. *twa*, to streak, smear, make lines; root der(?). *ntwo*, to suffer a defeat, impl. grief, desolation, mourning.

w
ewim (p. 108) one of the three major categories of *abosom*: powers that derived from the sky: *ewim* was: (*a*) the air, atmosphere, sky, heaven; (*b*) weather; (*c*) the course of things, impl. one's situation in the world (see *abrabɔ*): syn. *(e)wi*; alt. *ahunum*, der. *hunu*, emptiness, void: cf. *(o)wia*, the sun: *ewim* were reputed to be merciless, and were often anthropomorphized as executioners.

awo (p. 222) lit.: (*a*) birth, impl. labour, child; (*b*) nativity, impl. extraction, descent: *awo* was a hermaphrodite, the first ever oblation made to the earth (*asase yaa*) to make 'her' fruitful: *awo* had connotations of 'being born in/belonging in "Asante-ness"' (see *apafram*): the part 'played' by *awo* in *odwira* is discussed in the text: the matter of *awo* is obscure (some informants stating that it is pre-Asante, and that the word itself impl. an objectification – 'you', another, the other): it is sometimes said that *awo* was the first 'person' killed by the first 'executioner', and the name is thereby linked to the origins of power (differentiation, hierarchy and law).

wɔfa (p. 182 and *passim*) pl. *wɔfanom*. lit. mother's brother, maternal uncle (in the *abusua*): (*a*) a title of (respectful) address; (*b*) the title (and/or honorific) of the senior male in a maximal lineage segment (*ɔyafunu koro*).

wɔfase (p. 188) pl. *wɔfasenom*. lit. the sister's male child, mother's brother's nephew (in the *abusua*): a title of address: cf. *wɔfasewa*, the sister's female child, mother's brother's niece.

wonni mu (p. 172) lit. 'lacking a whole body', i.e. lacking a known or acknowledged genitor, *ergo* lacking identified *ntɔrɔ* affiliation: der. *wonni*, negative of *di*, with the sense of possessing, having, inheriting, owning + *mu*: (*a*) whole, entire, complete; (*b*) true, real; (*c*) perfect, excellent.

awowa   (p. 40) pl. *ŋwowa*. surety, pawning, pledging, impl. 'mortgaging' as security on a loan: as has been discussed in the text, virtually any asset (human or non-human) might be placed in *awowa*: the root der(?). seems to be the cluster of impl. meanings of *wa(w)*: (*a*) to sustain, maintain, prop up; (*b*) to assist, to further: cf. *ɔwowani*, pl. *awowanifoɔ*, a person pledged for a debt: *awowa si*, (the act of) 'mortgaging': *awowa gye*, taking something in pledge: interestingly, Christaller gives syn. *(di) afurum*, to be in pawn, and to labour or work for the lender, creditor; der. *afurum*, an ass, a donkey.

owu   (p. 222) death. der. *wu(wu)*: (*a*) to die, expire, decease, perish; (*b*) to be/become lost, to be/become extinct: the root verb is very widely used; e.g. *di awu*, lit. 'to do a death', i.e. to commit a murder, but *sika wu*, 'to die in money', i.e. to pay out money well beyond one's ability or resources: cf. *owufo*, pl. *awufoɔ*, a dead person, (the) deceased: *owu* is variously personified by the Asante (as a skeleton, with empty eye sockets, but having ears: sometimes with 'smoke' surrounding it like a nimbus: sometimes with a dry or scratching 'rustle' when in motion): 'death' as an agency of state power is revealed in *awude*, lit. things pertaining to death *or* to execution.

awukudae   (*passim*) the 'small' or 'Wednesday' *adae*: celebrated on 15: *kurudapaawukuo* in each successive *adaduanan* cycle.

awunnyadeɛ   (p. 48) death duties levied by the state on an individual's self-acquired movable property: root der(?). *wu*, to die + *nnya*, with the sense of leaving, loosening one's grip (impl. of something) + *ade*, things, possessions, movable property: hence, 'heritage' (*ade a obi awu de agyaa wo*), the things left behind: cf. *owunnyafo*, pl. *awunnyafoɔ*, a survivor, an heir ('someone left behind'): ant. *anikanne*, property given (to a son?) in a father's lifetime.

wuram   (*passim*) i.e. *wura mu*, lit. 'in the bush', i.e. out there, away from human settlement: der. *wura*: (*a*) bush, weeds, grass, forest: (*b*) overgrown land outside of inhabited places: cf. *kwaem*, i.e. *ɛkwae mu*, lit. 'in the dense forest': der. *ɛkwae*, dense forest, thicket, wood: cf. *kwae*, to go round about, to follow a circuitous route; *ɔkwa*, unused, unemployed, idle (of things): *ɛkwae* impl. inland, the forest country (ant. *ɛpom*, seaward, by the sea): cf. also *ɛha*: (*a*) bush, forest; (*b*) hunting, the chase: *yɛ ha*, to go hunting; *ahayɔ*, the chase: in all these usages 'nature' is cast as being something 'out there', the opposite of human settlement – dense, entangled, and threateningly alien in its scale and inert 'uselessness'.

y
ɔyafunu koro

(p. 77 and *passim*) syn. *(ɔ)fie*: the 'family', the uterine group or stirp, the maximal lineage segment (within an *abusua*): lit. 'the offspring of a single womb': der. *ɔyafunu*: (*a*) belly, abdomen, area between breast and thighs; (*b*) the womb + *koro*, one, single, alone, the same: the Asante *ɔyafunu koro* typically comprised the uterine descendants of an identified common ancestress, and was usually no more than three/four (and rarely as much as six) generations deep: the *ɔyafunu koro* was a key locus of interpersonal affect, intimacy and interaction, buttressed by shared life experiences or memories: Asante thinking cast a woman, her maternal brother, and her offspring of both sexes as the irreducible building blocks of the *ɔyafunu koro*: implicit in these elementary relationships were all of the fundamentals that (in expansion and combination) were understood to characterize the dynamics of the *ɔyafunu koro* itself and the even larger *abusua* (matrifiliation, siblingship, fraternal and avuncular authority, and generational succession): the senior male member of the *ɔyafunu koro* – vested with jural authority over its members – was not defined as a lineage head (*abusua panin*), but as a mother's brother (*wɔfa*) who was 'head of the house' (*(ɔ)fie panin*): this was normally but not necessarily the senior brother (*ɔnua panin*): the *wɔfa* upheld the claims of matrilineality in the face of potentially conflicting ties, and notably those of marriage and paternity.

ɔyere

(p. 146) pl. *ayere(nom)*. a wife, spouse, consort: cf. *ayere aware*, polygamy: used here to characterize those subordinate male office holders (Asante or otherwise) who were 'married' by the *Asantehene* to signify their inferior status to him: as a rhetorical item, such 'marriages' were often elaborated along the (idealized) lines of an actual husband/wife relationship – prestation, exchanging favours, a language of affect (and corresponding betrayal), etc.

ayibuadeɛ

(p. 48) inheritance taxes levied by the state on the immovable part of a deceased person's property (and notably land) before the residue was restored to the legitimate heirs or successors: der. *ade a wɔde boa (bua ayi)*, lit. the 'contributions made to the costs of a funeral': cf. *ayi/yi*, 'removal', with reference to a corpse (i.e. a funeral custom or ceremony) + *boa*, to help, assist + *ade*, things: cf. *aboade*, a promised payment, a thank-offering: cf. *ɔpɛgyafo*, an heir, a successor (*pɛ nea gyaw fo*, 'someone to leave to?'): cf. *pɛ*, to seek, impl. to look for/to be going to; *gyaw*, to leave behind, impl. to entrust: *ayibuadeɛ* and *awunnyadeɛ* are sometimes used synonymously, in the sense of being 'taxes at death', but they were distinct practices and procedures.

yi adow   (p. 87) the seizure (by a creditor) of an individual as a substitute for a defaulting debtor from the same *abusua*: der. *yi*, to take (to one's self) + *ad(w)ow*, appropriation, here with the sense of seizing, kidnapping ('panyarring a relative' to hold in pawn against the settlement of an outstanding debt by his/her kin).

ayowa   (p. 117) shrines. sing. the same: syn. *ayawa*: lit. an earthen dish or clay vessel (the original 'shrine'?): syn. *awowa*, pl. *ŋwowa*, a brass bowl or basin (also used as a 'shrine'): shrines were conceptualized as being 'containers' in which the power(s) of an *ɔbosom* might elect to take up residence.

Abbreviations used in the notes

AA	*African Affairs*
ACBP	Asante Collective Biography Project
AESC	*Annales: Economies, Sociétés, Civilisations*
AfAr	*African Arts*
AHR	*American Historical Review*
AJS	*American Journal of Sociology*
AK	MRO, Kumase, MS, 'The History of Ashanti Kings and the Whole Country Itself, Written by me, F.A. Prempeh, and was Dictated by E. Prempeh. Commence [*sic*] on 6th August 1907' (Prempe I)
ARA	Algemeen Rijksarchief, The Hague, Netherlands
ARA	*Annual Review of Anthropology*
ARIIA	*Africa: Rivista trimestrale di studi e documentazione dell'Istituto Italo-Africano*
ASC	African Studies Centre, Cambridge, UK
ASR	*African Studies Review*
ASSM	Ashanti Social Survey Manuscripts, Notes, etc.
BJS	*British Journal of Sociology*
BM	*Blackwood's Magazine*
BMA	Basel Mission Archives, Basel, Switzerland
BSNG	*Bulletin de la Société Neuchâteloise de Géographie*
CA	*Current Anthropology*
CEA	*Cahiers d'Etudes Africaines*
CI	*Critical Inquiry*
CSSH	*Comparative Studies in Society and History*
GJ	*Geographical Journal*
GJS	*Ghana Journal of Sociology*
GNQ	*Ghana Notes and Queries*
GPRL	George Padmore Research Library, Accra, Ghana
HA	*History in Africa: A Journal of Method*
HA	MRO, Kumase, 'The History of Ashanti', MS prepared by a Committee of Traditional Authorities under the Chairmanship of *Ashantihene* Osei Agyeman Prempeh II, n.d.

HT	*History and Theory*
IAS	Institute of African Studies, Legon, Ghana
IAS/AS	Institute of African Studies/Asante Stool Histories
IAS/CR	Institute of African Studies/Asante Court Records
IASRR	*Institute of African Studies Research Review*
IJAHS	*International Journal of African Historical Studies*
JAH	*Journal of African History*
JAS	*Journal of African Studies*
JCI	*Journal of Communication Inquiries*
JHI	*Journal of the History of Ideas*
JHP	*Journal of the History of Philosophy*
JPhil	*Journal of Philosophy*
JRAS	*Journal of the Royal African Society*
KITLV	Koninklijk Instituut voor Taal-, Land-, en Volkenkunde, Leiden, Netherlands
KTC	Kumase Town Council, Kumase, Ghana
LO	Lands Office, Kumase, Ghana
MFU	Meyer Fortes: Unaccessioned Manuscripts, Notes, etc.
MLC	Mampon Literary Club
MRO	Manhyia Record Office, Kumase, Ghana
NAG	National Archives of Ghana (Accra: Koforidua: Kumase: Sunyani)
NAS	National Archives of the Seychelles, Victoria, Mahé
NLR	*New Left Review*
OMP	Old Manhyia Palace, Kumase, Ghana
PD	Private Deposit (Bonnat Manuscripts)
PI	*Praxis International*
PRM	Pitt-Rivers Museum, Oxford
PRO	Public Record Office, London
QS	*Quaderni Storici*
RAI	Royal Anthropological Institute, London
RAL	*Research in African Literatures*
RH	Rhodes House, Oxford
RLJ	*Rhodes-Livingstone Journal*
RP	*Radical Philosophy*
RU	Rhodes University, Grahamstown, South Africa
THSG	*Transactions of the Historical Society of Ghana*
TOR	William Tordoff: Unaccessioned Manuscripts, Notes, etc.
WMMS	Wesleyan-Methodist Missionary Society, London

Notes

1 VARIETIES OF THE ASANTE PAST

1 J. Lonsdale, 'States and Social Processes in Africa: A Historiographical Survey', *ASR*, 24, 2/3 (1981), 139.

2 On the 'ancient economy' M.I. Finley, *The Ancient Economy* (2nd edn, London, 1985) and *Ancient History: Evidence and Models* (London, 1985); P.D.A. Garnsey, *Famine and Food Supply in the Graeco-Roman World: Responses to Risk and Crisis* (Cambridge, 1988); P.D.A. Garnsey and R.P. Saller, *The Roman Empire: Economy, Society and Culture* (London, 1987); C.R. Whittaker (ed.), *Pastoral Economies in Classical Antiquity* (Cambridge, 1988). G.E.M. de ste Croix, *The Class Struggle in the Ancient Greek World* (London, 1981) is a Marxist reading of political economy, but his analysis in *The Origins of the Peloponnesian War* (London, 1972) shows an unavoidable indebtedness to a very few sources (Thucydides *et al.*). Lacunae in certain categories of evidence are apparent in such disparate treatments as the resolutely empiricist A.W. Lintott, *Violence, Revolution and Civil Strife in the Classical City* (London, 1982) and the philosophic-economic reading of the 'euergetic tradition' in P. Veyne, *Le Pain et le cirque* (Paris, 1976). From a huge literature on popular ideas and attitudes in medieval and early modern Europe see, most recently, J. Le Goff, *L'Imaginaire médiéval: essais* (Paris, 1990); N. Zemon Davis, *Fiction in the Archives: Pardon Tales and their Tellers in Sixteenth-Century France* (Stanford, 1987); P. Burke, *The Historical Anthropology of Early Modern Italy: Essays on Perception and Communication* (Cambridge, 1987). Much-lauded studies have been geographically highly localized, temporally very restricted, and correspondingly difficult to generalize from; see E. Le Roy Ladurie, *Montaillou: village occitan de 1294 à 1324* (Paris, 1975) and *Le Carnaval de Romans: de la chandeleur au mercredi des cendres, 1579–1580* (Paris, 1979); N. Zemon Davis, *The Return of Martin Guerre* (Cambridge, 1983); C. Ginzburg, *Il formaggio e i vermi: il cosmo di un mugnaio del 1500* (Turin, 1976); and for the *microstoria* of Ginzburg and other historians associated with *Quaderni Storici*, E. Muir and G. Ruggiero (eds.), *Microhistory and the Lost Peoples of Europe* (Baltimore, 1992).

3 On the contested politics of Asante identity during decolonization see, most recently, A.S.Y. Andoh, 'The Asante National Liberation Movement of the 1950s in Retrospect', in E. Schildkrout (ed.), *The Golden Stool: Studies of the Asante Center and Periphery* (New York, 1987), 173–83; J.M. Allman, 'The National Liberation Movement and the Asante Struggle for Self-Determination, 1954–1957', Ph.D. (Northwestern, 1987) and 'The Youngmen and the Porcupine: Class, Nationalism and Asante's Struggle for Self-Determination, 1954–57', *JAH*, 31 (1990), 263–79; R. Rathbone and J.M. Allman, 'Discussion:

The Youngmen and the Porcupine', *JAH*, 32 (1991), 333–8. An intriguing personal insight into current relations (1990) between Asante and Ghanaian authorities is in K.A. Appiah, 'Epilogue: In My Father's House', in his *In My Father's House: Africa in the Philosophy of Culture* (London, 1992), 294–313; see too J. Appiah, *Joe Appiah: The Autobiography of an African Patriot* (Westport, 1990). In conversation many Asante continue to privilege an identity within the *Asantemaŋ* over its Ghanaian counterpart, and regard the Ghanaian government in Accra as being 'foreign' (and presently 'dominated' by the southeastern Ewe). By corollary, in conversations in the Volta Region (1988: Ho, Amedzofe, Gbadzeme, Vane, etc.) I was impressed by the abiding folk-perception of the Asante as historic oppressors bent upon resurrecting their hegemony. For similar views among the Bron see J. Dunn and A.F. Robertson, *Dependence and Opportunity: Political Change in Ahafo* (Cambridge, 1973) and F.K. Drah, 'The Brong Political Movement', in K. Arhin (ed.), *Brong Kyempim: Essays on the Society, History and Politics of the Brong People* (Accra, 1979), 119–62.

4 K. Hart, 'The Social Anthropology of West Africa', *ARA*, 14 (1985), 257.

5 J. Le Goff, 'Is Politics Still the Backbone of History?', *Daedalus*, 100, 1 (1971), 1–19. See further J. Le Goff and P. Nora (eds.), *Faire de l'histoire*, 3 vols. (Paris, 1974). Two overviews that situate the *annales* in relation to political history are the useful if dated T. Stoianovich, *French Historical Method: The* Annales *Paradigm* (Ithaca, 1976) and the acute H. Couteau-Begarie, *Le Phénomène 'nouvelle histoire': stratégie et idéologie des nouveaux historiens* (Paris, 1983). On the 'founding fathers' of the *annales* H.-D. Mann, *Lucien Febvre: la pensée vivante d'un historien* (Paris, 1971) and C. Fink, *Marc Bloch: A Life in History* (Cambridge, 1989). Whether or not the *annalistes* lived up to their programme is another matter. See R.H. Brown, *Social Science as Civic Discourse: Essays on the Invention, Legitimation, and Uses of Social Theory* (Chicago, 1989), 79–122 for a critical account of 'the *annales* paradigm' as historical discourse.

6 On the contested problem of (re)presenting the history of cultural practice (in terms of concrete historical analyses rather than discursive strategies or textual figurations) see P. Veyne, *Comment on écrit l'histoire: suivi de Foucault révolutionne l'histoire* (Paris, 1978): M. de Certeau, *L'Ecriture de l'histoire* (Paris, 1975), *L'Invention du quotidien: I. Arts de faire* (Paris, 1980), *La Fable mystique, XVIᵉ-XVIIᵉ siècle* (Paris, 1982), *Heterologies: The Discourse of the Other* (Minneapolis, 1986); R. Chartier, *Cultural History: Between Practices and Representations* (Oxford, 1988) and *Les Origines culturelles de la révolution française* (Paris, 1990). On (re)presenting 'memory' see, most recently, P. Connerton, *How Societies Remember* (Cambridge, 1989); M. Carruthers, *The Book of Memory: A Study of Memory in Medieval Culture* (Cambridge, 1990); and J. Fentress and C. Wickham, *Social Memory* (Oxford, 1992). Epistemological difficulties are explored, most recently, in F.R. Ankersmit, 'Historical Representation', *HT*, 27 (1988), 205–28, 'Historiography and Postmodernism', *HT*, 28 (1989), 137–53, 'Reply to Professor Zagorin', *HT*, 29 (1990), 275–96; P. Zagorin, 'Historiography and Postmodernism: A Reconsideration', *HT*, 29 (1990), 263–74; and H. Kellner, *Narrativity in History: Post-Structuralism and Since, HT Beiheft* 26 (1987). Recent Africanist work that foregrounds or

otherwise takes account of the problem of (re)presenting and articulating cultural specificity (but not always with an adequate grounding in the historical dimension) includes J.D.Y. Peel, *Ijeshas and Nigerians: The Incorporation of a Yoruba Kingdom, 1890s–1970s* (Cambridge, 1983); W. MacGaffey, *Religion and Society in Central Africa: The BaKongo of Lower Zaire* (Chicago, 1986); D.W. Cohen and E.S. Atieno Odhiambo, *Siaya: The Historical Anthropology of an African Landscape* (London, 1988); K. Barber, *I Could Speak Until Tomorrow: Oriki, Women and the Past in a Yoruba Town* (Edinburgh, 1991); and J. and J. Comaroff, *Of Revelation and Revolution: Christianity, Colonialism and Consciousness in South Africa*, I (of 2) (Chicago, 1991). Note that I urge the *integration* of the material and the cultural, and make no case in endorsement of the discursive and/or the signifying autonomy of the latter (in the manner of much 'new' literary historicism and 'reflexive' anthropology); such literary or anthropological accounts tend to disseminate and to displace the conjunctural mediation of historical culture by the structures of material power onto a symbolic palimpsest or into a tropological figuration. See, from an ever growing literature, S.J. Greenblatt, *Shakespearean Negotiations: The Circulation of Social Energy in Renaissance England* (Berkeley, 1988), and M. Taussig, *Shamanism, Colonialism, and the Wild Man: A Study in Terror and Healing* (Chicago, 1987). For some preliminary discussion of the issues involved in an Asante context see T.C. McCaskie, '*Asantesɛm*: Reflections on Discourse and Text in Africa', in K. Barber and P.F. de Moraes Farias (eds.), *Discourse and Its Disguises: The Interpretation of African Oral Texts* (Birmingham, 1989), 70–86; *ibid.*, 'Armah's *The Healers* and Asante History', in M. Gray and R. Law (eds.), *Images of Africa: The Depiction of Pre-Colonial Africa in Creative Literature* (Stirling, 1990), 42–60; and *ibid.*, 'Inventing Asante', in K. Barber and P.F. de Moraes Farias (eds.), *Self-Assertion and Brokerage: Early Cultural Nationalism in West Africa* (Birmingham, 1990), 55–67.

7 Gramsci was an engaged and persecuted activist, and a prolific but unsystematic writer, much given to reiteration, revision and expansion. Therefore, whatever one's specific interest in his work, reading in it should aim to be as comprehensive as possible. The fullest edition of Gramsci's writings is *Opere di Antonio Gramsci* (Turin, 1947–72), 12 vols., of which II–VII (1949–51), ed. F. Platone *et al.*, comprise the *Quaderni del Carcere* (Prison Notebooks). Materials relevant to the present study are to be found in numerous passages of the *Opere*, but notably germane are the *Quaderni del Carcere* volumes: IV. *Il Risorgimento* (1949); V. *Note sul Machiavelli, sulla politica, e sullo stato moderno* (1949); and VII. *Passato e presente* (1951). The *Quaderni del Carcere* (Turin, 1975), 4 vols., ed. V. Gerratana for the *Istituto Antonio Gramsci* reproduces the notes in chronological order of writing rather than under topic headings, and the fourth vol. has an excellent *apparatus criticus*. *Scritti politici* (Rome, 1973), 3 vols., ed. P. Spriano, is the fullest collection of Gramsci's pre-prison writings, and should also be consulted. An English translation of passages from the *Opere* edn of the *Quaderni del Carcere* (but cross-checked against a copy of Gramsci's MSS) is Q. Hoare and G. Nowell Smith (eds.), *Selections from the Prison Notebooks of Antonio Gramsci* (London, 1971). See

too D. Forgacs and G. Nowell Smith (eds.), *Antonio Gramsci: Selections from Cultural Writings* (London, 1985); D. Forgacs (ed.), *A Gramsci Reader, 1916–1935* (London, 1988); and H. Henderson (trans. and ed.), *Antonio Gramsci: Gramsci's Prison Letters* (Edinburgh, 1988).

8 For conceptual analyses see W.L. Adamson, *Hegemony and Revolution: A study of Antonio Gramsci's Political and Cultural Theory* (Berkeley, 1980); M.A. Finnochiaro, *Gramsci and the History of Dialectical Thought* (Cambridge, 1988); and C. Buci-Glucksmann, *Gramsci et l'état* (Paris, 1975). A most useful overview is J.V. Femia, *Gramsci's Political Thought: Hegemony, Consciousness, and the Revolutionary Process* (Oxford, 1981); insightful but contentious is E. Morera, *Gramsci's Historicism: A Realist Interpretation* (London, 1990); Gramsci's continuing relevance to current debates in critical theory is discussed in R. Holub, *Antonio Gramsci: Beyond Marxism and Postmodernism* (London, 1992). A seminal critical essay is P. Anderson, 'The Antinomies of Antonio Gramsci', *NLR*, 100 (1976–7), 5–78. For Gramsci's reading of 'consciousness' in relation to his critical adumbration of the philosophical tradition see L. Salamini, *The Sociology of Political Praxis: An Introduction to Gramsci's Theory* (London, 1981). In the context of the discussion developed here an interesting perspective is G. Shafir, 'Interpretative Sociology and the Philosophy of Praxis: Comparing Max Weber and Antonio Gramsci', *PI* (April 1985), 63–74.

9 See D. Hume, 'Of the Origins of Government', 'Of the First Principles of Government', and 'Of Civil Liberty', essays IV, V and XII in *Essays: Moral, Political, Literary*, ed. E.F. Miller (Indianapolis, 1985). On the Crocean background E.E. Jacobitti, 'Hegemony before Gramsci: The Case of Benedetto Croce', *Journal of Modern History*, 52 (March 1980), 66–84. In addition to items cited, for Gramsci and *egemonia* see C. Mouffe, 'Hegemony and Ideology in Gramsci', in *ibid.* (ed.), *Gramsci and Marxist Theory* (London, 1979), 168–204; T.R. Bates, 'Gramsci and the Theory of Hegemony', *JHI*, 36(1975), 351–66; L. Gruppi, 'Le Concept d'égemonie chez Antonio Gramsci', *Dialectiques*, 4/5 (1974), 4–54 and his analysis in *Il concetto di egemonia in Gramsci* (Rome, 1977). A suggestive historical overview is T.J.J. Lears, 'The Concept of Cultural Hegemony: Problems and Possibilities', *AHR*, 90 (June 1985), 567–93. A short treatment of an important aspect is D.J. Cheal, 'Hegemony, Ideology and Contradictory Consciousness', *Sociological Quarterly*, 20 (Winter 1979), 109–18.

10 This formulation of Gramsci's conceptualization of civil society is generally agreed. I remain aware, however, of those equivocations in Gramsci's writings where he discusses this key dimension of his own project in relation to the arguments advanced by the Hegel of the *Philosophie des Rechts* (1821). Specific analyses include W.L. Adamson, 'Gramsci and the Politics of Civil Society', *PI* (Oct. 1987/Jan. 1988), 320–39; N. Bobbio, 'Gramsci and the Conception of Civil Society', in Mouffe (ed.), *Gramsci*, 21–47; J. Hofmann, *The Gramscian Challenge: Coercion and Consent in Marxist Political Theory* (New York, 1984). For comparative analysis F. Ferrarotti, 'Civil Society and State Structures in Creative Tension: Ferguson, Hegel, Gramsci', *State, Culture and Society*, 1 (1984), 3–25.

11 An exception to this, but in a limited sense, is M.D. McLeod, *The Asante* (London, 1981). McLeod shows an awareness of the temporal dimension, but he tends to deploy historical data as unproblematic illustrative embellishment in support of an ethnographic portrait in the Fortesian manner.

12 Much recent scholarship on race, ethnicity, identity, gender, 'otherness' and relations between dominant and subordinate discourses of power makes explicit or inexplicit use of Gramsci. Seminal and much debated is E.W. Said, *Orientalism* (London, 1978). See too S. Hall, 'Gramsci's Relevance for the Study of Race and Ethnicity', *JCI*, 10 (1986), 5–27. An active debate (influenced by Said and Foucault) derives from Gramsci's conceptualization of 'subaltern groups' in relation to hegemony (see 'Ai margini della storia (Storia dei gruppi sociali subalterni)', *Quaderni del Carcere*, ed. Gerratana, III, 2277 ff.). See G. Chakravorty Spivak, *In Other Worlds: Essays in Cultural Politics* (New York, 1987); the work published in R. Guha (ed.), *Subaltern Studies*, I-VI (Delhi, 1982–9); and R. Guha and G. Chakravorty Spivak (eds.), with a Foreword by E.W. Said, *Selected Subaltern Studies* (New York, 1988). Debates over hegemony and the constitution of the historical subject are leading features of current Indianist rather than Africanist historiography, for which see G. Prakash, 'Writing Post-Orientalist Histories of the Third World: Perspectives from Indian Historiography', *CSSH*, 32, 2 (1990), 383–408; R. O'Hanlon and D. Washbrook, 'After Orientalism: Culture, Criticism and Politics in the Third World' and G. Prakash, 'Can the "Subaltern" Ride?: A Reply to O'Hanlon and Washbrook', *CSSH*, 34, 1 (1992), 141–67 and 168–84. Those who deploy Foucauldian and/or Lacanian perspectives in work on 'the production of knowledge' are still engaged in addressing the Gramscian problematic of hegemony, even if the debt to Gramsci is attenuated or masked; see H.K. Bhabha, 'Signs Taken for Wonders: Questions of Ambivalence and Authority under a Tree outside Delhi, May 1817', *CI*, 12, 1 (1985), 144–65; *ibid.*, 'Foreword: Remembering Fanon: Self, Psyche and the Colonial Condition', in F. Fanon, *Black Skin, White Masks*, trans. C. Lam Markmann (London, 1986); *ibid.* (ed.), *Nation and Narration* (London, 1990). A sympathetic overview is R. Young, *White Mythologies: Writing History and the West* (London, 1990). Critical of Spivak, Guha and the 'deconstructionist' veneer on the historical analysis of hegemony is R.A. Berman, 'Troping to Pretoria: The Rise and Fall of Deconstruction', *Telos*, 85 (Fall 1990), 4–16.

13 J. and J. Comaroff, *Of Revelation*, 17, electing 'to intervene in the name of a [South African] historical anthropology' – in clarification of Gramsci's project and *contra* the ahistorical excesses of post-modernism – point out (317, fn. 14) that many conventional glosses on 'hegemony' largely derive from R. Williams, *Marxism and Literature* (London, 1977), an influential book that appears puzzlingly innocent of any direct contact and engagement with the *Quaderni del Carcere. Of Revelation*, 13–39, makes a sustained effort to evaluate the heuristic significance of Gramsci's thought in relation to the encounter between the Tswana and British missionaries in nineteenth-century South Africa. This is a clear-headed reading of Gramsci, the most sophisticated in Africanist discourse, but its impact is lessened by a questing tendency towards essentialist definition (a very un-Gramscian over-determination).

However, *Of Revelation* is to be preferred to less precise invocations of Gramsci in Africanist discourse; compare D. Laitin, *Hegemony and Culture: Politics and Religious Change among the Yoruba* (Chicago, 1986), and the oddly arbitrary Gramscian gloss that is placed upon the 'conceptual framework of African thinking [*sic*]' in V.Y. Mudimbe, *The Invention of Africa: Gnosis, Philosophy and the Order of Knowledge* (Bloomington, 1988), 185. Of course, and predictably, Gramsci is notable by his absence from certain 'sectarian' Marxist and *marxisant* contributions; see the Althusserian H. Bernstein and J. Depelchin, 'The Object of African History: A Materialist Perspective', 1 and 2, *HA*, 5 (1978), 1–19 and 6 (1979), 17–43, and the riposte by R. Law, 'For Marx, But With Reservations about Althusser: A Comment on Bernstein and Depelchin', *HA*, 8 (1981), 247–51; see too the *marxisant* A. Temu and B. Swai, *Historians and Africanist History: A Critique. Post-Colonial Historiography Examined* (London, 1981). Some reject the insights and heuristic value of the Marxist tradition (Gramsci included) *tout court*, seemingly on account of the simplistic platitude that Marx, Gramsci *et al.* were themselves (like all authors) 'deluded captives' of their own historical situation; for example, T. Sereque Berhan, 'Karl Marx and African Emancipatory Thought: A Critique of Marx's Euro-Centric Metaphysics', *PI*, 10, 1–2 (1990), 161–81.

14 Abiding tensions between a cultural phenomenology and a cultural history are evident in numbers of recent assessments of the field. For example, D. Lindenfeld, 'On Systems and Embodiments as Categories for Intellectual History', *HT*, 27 (1988), 30–50; J.R. Censer, 'Review Article: Revitalizing the Intellectual History of the French Revolution', *JHI*, 50, 4 (1989), 652–66; and the synoptic D.R. Kelley, 'What is Happening to the History of Ideas?' *JHI*, 51, 1 (1990), 3–26. A symbology which ostensibly commences with the 'deep' structures of power, but which all too often ends with an implicative reaffirmation of the autonomy of cultural practice is a feature common to much of what is termed the 'new history'; see D. LaCapra, *Rethinking Intellectual History: Texts, Contexts, Language* (Ithaca, 1983) and *History and Criticism* (Ithaca, 1985); D. Boucher, *Texts in Context* (Dordrecht, 1985). A congeries of approaches to situating the text-in-context remains ultimately rooted in a literary tradition; compare the magisterial J.G.A. Pocock, *The Machiavellian Moment: Florentine Political Thought and the Atlantic Republican Tradition* (Princeton, 1975), and the discourse-orientated A. Pagden (ed.), *The Languages of Political Theory in Early Modern Europe* (Cambridge, 1987). Similarly, intellectual history has consistently used the figure of the *maître à penser* as a template for the exploration of the literary tradition; see for example the work of the 'Geneva School' from the 1940s onwards, and its mature apotheosis in the writings of Richard, Rousset, and above all in J. Starobinski, *Jean-Jacques Rousseau: la transparence et l'obstacle* (Paris, 1971). By contrast, Africanist intellectual history – lacking a literary tradition, and contested foci (Machiavelli, Rousseau) central to such a tradition – has often tended to subsume thought in belief; see the (otherwise meticulous) reconstructions in for example J.D.Y. Peel, *Aladura: A Religious Movement among the Yoruba* (London, 1968) or J.W. Fernandez, *Bwiti: An Ethnography of the Religious Imagination in Africa* (Princeton, 1982). Whatever their

shortcomings, however, such analyses are to be preferred to the phenomenological cataloguing ('literary eventism') characteristic of many accounts of twentieth-century African intellectual history (where, of course, there is a literary tradition); see R.W. July, *The Origins of Modern African Thought* (London, 1968), and his similarly grounded *An African Voice: The Role of the Humanities in African Independence* (Durham, 1987). In a narrower focus, twentieth-century Africanist intellectual history is often mired in an idealist 'life and times' accounting; contrast Starobinski on Rousseau with, randomly, I. Geiss, *The Pan-African Movement* (London, 1974) or A.J.G. Wyse, *H.C. Bankole-Bright and Politics in Colonial Sierra Leone, 1919–1958* (Cambridge, 1990).

15 For the development of debate in Britain see H.J. Kaye, *The British Marxist Historians* (Oxford, 1984) and H.J. Kaye and K. McClelland (eds.), *E.P. Thompson: Critical Perspectives* (Oxford, 1990). Useful overviews of the historiography of *mentalités* are R. Chartier, 'Intellectual History and the History of *Mentalités*: A Dual Re-Evaluation', in his *Cultural History*, 19–52 (and see the references at 49–50, fn. 15), and the synoptic J. Revel, 'Mentalités', in A. Burguière (ed.), *Dictionnaire des sciences historiques* (Paris, 1985), 449–56; two recent considerations are A. Boureau, 'Propositions pour une histoire restreinte des mentalités' and R. Chartier, 'Le Monde comme réprésentation', both in *AESC*, 44, 6 (1989), 1491–1504 and 1505–20. N. Elias was a seminal thinker and a prolific writer, but his contribution is still relatively undervalued. See N. Elias, *Über den Prozess der Zivilisation: Soziogenetische und psychogenetische Untersuchungen*, 2 vols. (Basel, 1939), trans. E. Jephcott with Elias' own revisions as *The Civilizing Process: Sociogenetic and Psychogenetic Investigations*: I. *The History of Manners* (Oxford, 1978) and II. *State Formation and Civilization* (Oxford, 1984); and *Die höfische Gesellschaft, Untersuchungen zur Soziologie des Königtums und der höfischen Aristokratie mit einer Einleitung: Soziologie und Geschichtswissenschaft* (Berlin, 1969; author's revised edns, 1975, 1983), trans. E. Jephcott with Elias' own revisions as *The Court Society* (Oxford, 1985). Elias' work was long neglected, in part because he exiled himself from Germany when the National Socialists assumed power in 1933; he submitted the earliest version of *Die höfische Gesellschaft* as a *Habilitationschrift* in Sociology in that year (under Karl Mannheim at Frankfurt), but he left before defending it. See S. Mennell, *Norbert Elias: Civilization and the Human Self-Image* (Oxford, 1989). Arguably, it was Elias who began a sociological 'naturalization' of intellectual history, bridging the gap between ideas *per se* and the 'deep structures' of *historically* – as opposed to anthropologically – recoverable norms of speech, gestures, body language, affect, distance, positioning and so on; thus, for example, his reflections on historically conditioned 'thresholds of embarrassment' have informed my reading of the Asante concept of *mpoatwa*. See further N. Elias, *Involvement and Detachment* (Oxford, 1987, trans. from the German edn of 1956), and *The Society of Individuals* (Oxford, 1991, essays from the German 1939–87). It has been said, with some justice, that Elias is the 'sociological' counterpart of Marc Bloch.

16 For the extreme case of *mentalités* as the 'history' of the emotions and senses see J. Delumeau, *L'Histoire de la peur* (Paris, 1979) and A. Corbin, *Le Miasme*

et la jonquille (Paris, 1983). Interiorization and the subjective in Corbin's 'history' of odour in France are carried to one of their implicative conclusions in P. Suskind, *Das Parfüm* (Zurich, 1985), a fiction about an eighteenth-century *parfumeur*. Historians have adopted a number of strategies to close the gap between *mentalités* and the subjective 'history' of the individual; see R. Darnton, *The Great Cat Massacre and Other Episodes in French Cultural History* (New York, 1984), *The Kiss of Lamourette: Reflections on Cultural History* (London, 1990), and the comments in P. Benedict and G. Levi, 'Robert Darnton e il massacro dei gatti', *QS*, 58 (1985), 257–77; J.D. Spence, *The Memory Palace of Matteo Ricci* (London, 1985); and S. Schama, 'The Many Deaths of General Wolfe', *Granta*, 32 (1990), 15–56, and his *Dead Certainties (Unwarranted Speculations)* (London, 1991). I remain unconvinced, however, by current impulses to articulate cultural representations as 'episodes' in the narrative imagining of an individual sensibility, whatever the innovatory accomplishment or power of the author's synthetic technique(s) of writing. Elias, most succinctly in *The Society of Individuals*, sustained a nexus of argument between the history of collective and individual identities that, admittedly precarious in parts, has rarely been bettered by other writers; but compare W. Benjamin, *Parigi: capitale del XIX secolo* (Turin, 1986). By contrast, the problems of British 'Marxist' historiography are not those of (very largely unconsidered) modes of inscribing the subjective experience of the individual, but rather of an unresolved tension between class analysis and the history of cultural practice. 'Culture' is often appended 'commonsensically' rather than theorized; see the now 'classic' E.P. Thompson, *The Making of the English Working Class* (London, 1963), and his *The Poverty of Theory and Other Essays* (London, 1978), in which a just repudiation of Althusser is clothed in the characteristic language of British 'suspicion' towards cultural theory.

17 See P. Chaunu, 'Un Nouveau Champ pour l'histoire sérielle: le quantitatif au troisième niveau', in his *Histoire quantitative, histoire sérielle* (Paris, 1978), 216–30. See too the methodology in the influential M. Vovelle, *Piété baroque et déchristianisation en Provençe au XVIIIe siècle* (Paris, 1973).

18 L. Febvre, *Le Problème de l'incroyance au XVIe siècle: la religion de Rabelais* (Paris, 1942; reprinted 1968), *Amour sacré, amour profane: autour de l'Heptaméron* (Paris, 1944; reprinted 1971), and *Combats pour l'histoire* (Paris, 1953); M. Bloch, *Apologie pour l'histoire, ou Métier d'historien* (Paris, 1949), and *Les Rois thaumaturges: études sur la caractère surnaturel attribué à la puissance royale, particulièrement en France et Angleterre* (Strasbourg, 1924; new edn, Paris, 1983). As is well known, Febvre and Bloch were influenced by Berr and by those (Mauss, Halbwachs) associated with Durkheim's very influential journal *L'Année Sociologique*. A fascinating commentary on Febvre's *Le Problème* is M. Bakhtin, *Tvorchestvo Fransua Rable* (Moscow, 1965), trans. H. Iswolsky as *Rabelais and His World* (Bloomington, 1984), especially 131 ff.

19 In the African context see for example V. Turner, *The Forest of Symbols: Aspects of Ndembu Ritual* (Ithaca, 1967), *Revelation and Divination in Ndembu Ritual* (Ithaca, 1975), and *On the Edge of the Bush: Anthropology as Experience* (Tucson, 1985). Belated shock at the failure of much anthropology to situate

itself *historically* is surely one of the imperatives that has led to self-questioning in that discipline; see J. Clifford and G. Marcus (eds.), *Writing Culture: The Poetics and Politics of Ethnography* (Berkeley, 1986) and J. Clifford, *The Predicament of Culture: Twentieth-Century Ethnography, Literature, and Art* (Cambridge, 1988). Unfortunately, this anthropological engagement with history is all too often leached away into a self-absorption with authorial role or subjective practice; see S.A. Tyler, *The Unspeakable: Discourse, Dialogue and Rhetoric in the Postmodern World* (Madison, 1987) and V. Crapanzano, *Hermes' Dilemma and Hamlet's Desire: On the Epistemology of Interpretation* (Cambridge, 1992). More germane and insightful is M. Jackson, *Paths Towards a Clearing: Radical Empiricism and Ethnographic Inquiry* (Bloomington, 1989), which reflects upon the author's fieldwork experience among the Kuranko of Sierra Leone. But abiding problems in the recovery of the African past, already noted, may be instanced here by the contrasting density of specifically historical materials pertaining to the Ndembu, Kuranko and Asante.

20 C. Geertz, *Negara: The Theatre State in Nineteenth-Century Bali* (Princeton, 1980). A radical comment on the Geertzian Negara is M. Hobart, 'Summer's Days and Salad Days: The Coming of Age of Anthropology?', in L. Holy (ed.), *Comparative Anthropology* (Oxford, 1987), 22–51, especially 36; see further M. Hobart, *Ideas of Identity: the Interpretation of Kinship in Bali* (Denpasar, 1980); A. Vickers, *Bali: A Paradise Created* (Victoria, 1989) and 'Balinese Texts and Historiography', *HT*, 29 (1990), 158–78. For the place of *Negara* in the evolution of Geertz's ideas (from 'thick description' to 'reflexivity') compare his *The Interpretation of Cultures* (New York, 1973) and his *Works and Lives: The Anthropologist as Author* (Stanford, 1988). The recovery of the past has consistently served Geertz as an essentially synchronic mechanism, dedicated to illustrating the precept that symbols (temporally as well as cognitively) 'go all the way down'.

21 M. Sahlins, 'Supplement to the Voyage of Cook; or *le calcul sauvage*', in his *Islands of History* (Chicago, 1985), 1–31, quotations at 19. Sahlins invokes Bloch throughout, but at 31 he reveals his hand: 'In the end, we must return to dialectics. I did not really mean to ignore the interplay of structure and *praxis*, only to reserve for it a proper theoretical place, viz., as a symbolic process.' A trenchant review that makes one kind of historical case against *Islands of History* is by J. Friedman in *HT*, 26, 1 (1987), 72–99; also J. Friedman, 'Beyond Otherness or: The Spectacularization of Anthropology', *Telos*, 71 (Spring 1987), 161–70, especially 169. Sahlins on Hawaii should be read in conjunction with the impressive V. Valeri, *Kingship and Sacrifice: Ritual and Society in Ancient Hawaii* (Chicago, 1985). For Sahlins' view of history see further his *Historical Metaphors and Mythical Realities: Structure in the Early History of the Sandwich Islands Kingdom* (Ann Arbor, 1981).

22 See for instance the various uses made of Bakhtin by those influenced by Foucault, but committed to writing 'history' *mutatis mutandis* under the shadow of the 'closure' proposed by Foucauldian historical theory; M. Bristol, *Carnival and Theater: Plebeian Culture and the Structure of Authority in Renaissance England* (New York, 1985) and J. Dollimore and A. Sinfield (eds.), *Political Shakespeare: New Essays in Cultural Materialism* (Manchester,

1985). For context see R. Schurmann, 'On Constituting Oneself an Anarchic Subject', *PI*, 6 (1986), 294–310. Intelligent – but still beset by the sheer difficulty of recuperating the symbolic referent and situating it within historical action – is J.J. Winkler, *The Constraints of Desire: The Anthropology of Sex and Gender in Ancient Greece* (New York, 1990). A Cameron (ed.), *History as Text: The Writing of Ancient History* (London, 1989) is an instance of the mixed results that typify the current application of novel theories to established (sedimented?) fields of historical inquiry.

23 The centrality of a disembodied sense of *enactment* is common both to Geertz's Negara and Sahlins' Hawaii. It is also apparent in those Africanist works in which self-consciously sophisticated anthropological modelling structures, subsumes or simply overwhelms a very parsimonious historical record; see the ordering of the data and the argument in the substantial M. Izard, *Gens du pouvoir, Gens de la terre: les institutions politiques de l'ancien royaume du Yatenga (Bassin de la Volta Blanche)* (Cambridge and Paris, 1985).

24 J. Joll, *Gramsci* (London, 1977) and Hoare and Nowell Smith, *Prison Notebooks*, xvii–xcvi for summaries of the intellectual biography in the light of Italian politics.

25 See T.E. Bowdich, *Mission from Cape Coast Castle to Ashantee* (London, 1819), 95, 120, 250; RU, Grahamstown, Cory MS 15, 104, 'Journal of the Rev. George Chapman, 1843–1857', entries dd. Kumase, 6 August and 29 September 1844; WMMS, London, GCC, 'Journals of the Rev. Thomas B. Freeman', entry dd. Kumase, 17 January 1841; *ibid.*, GCC, Hillard to Beecham, dd. Kumase, 16 January 1849 and Picot to Boyce, dd. Cape Coast, 3 May 1876; compare W. Hutton, *A Voyage to Africa* (London, 1821), 317 and B. Cruickshank, *Eighteen Years on the Gold Coast of Africa*, 2 vols. (London, 1853), I, 80. For context and discussion T.C. McCaskie, 'The Paramountcy of the *Asantehene* Kwaku Dua (1834–67): A Study in Asante Political Culture', Ph.D. (Cambridge, 1974), 183 ff.

26 WMMS, London, GCC, T.B. Freeman, 'Life and Travels: Gold Coast, Ashantee, Dahomey', MS, n.d. (but c. 1860), ch. xiv 'Introductory Chapter on Dahomey', 154–61. A version of parts of this MS was serialized as 'Life and Travels on the Gold Coast' in *Supplements* to the newspaper *The Western Echo*, Cape Coast, 17 March to 30 June 1886; the extract quoted appeared in the issue for 30 June as part of Freeman's (eyewitness) meditative comparison between Asante and Dahomey, 'the two great rival despotisms of the Gold and Slave Coasts'. This MS is presumably to be identified with the proposed work, *The Gold and Slave Coasts* by T.B. Freeman, which was advertised in *The African Times*, London, 23 July 1863 as being shortly due for publication (by Trubner, in 3 vols.). This book was never published. Freeman's MS journals of his visits to Kumase – 1839, 1841, 1843, 1848 – are in WMMS, London, GCC. Extracts from this material were first published in *Wesleyan Missionary Notices*, London, January 1840, November 1842 and October 1843. Versions of the 1839 and 1841 journals were published in T.B. Freeman, *Journal of Two Visits to the Kingdom of Ashanti* (London, 1843), and reprinted in T.B. Freeman, *Journal of Various Visits to the Kingdoms of Ashanti, Aku, and Dahomi in Western Africa* (London, 1844). A version of the 1848 journal is in

GPRL, Accra, Missionary Papers. This should be compared with NAG, Accra, ADM 1/2/4, Governor's Despatches to Secretary of State, Book 3, 13/1/1848–20/6/1849, 'Journal of Governor Sir William Winniet's Visit to Kumasi in 1848', MS. Freeman served as Winniet's adviser and secretary on the latter's official visit to Kumase; see too WMMS, London, GCC, Freeman to General Secretaries, dd. Mansu, Kumase and Cape Coast, 2 and 19 October and 4 November 1848.

27 Freeman, 'Life and Travels', xiv, 154–61; *The Western Echo, Supplement*, 30 June 1886. For another perspective compare PD, Manuscrits de M.-J. Bonnat (copié par M. L'Abbé Bonnat), Cahier 15, *Mœurs et coutumes de l'Achanty*, dd. Kumase, 19 September 1871. Illustrative instances of the discourse of power in an intimate speech setting ('The king ... surrounded by a few favourites') – formulation, gesture, expressive modes, relational positioning *et al.* – are given in the words and actions attributed to the *Asantehene* Osei Tutu Kwame, the *Gyakye ɔkyeame* Kwadwo Adusei Kyakya, the *Akankade ɔkyeame* Kwasi Kankam, the *Gyaasewahene* Opoku Frɛfrɛ, and the *Adumhene* Adum Ata on 1 March 1820, and reported with some bemusement in J. Dupuis, *Journal of a Residence in Ashantee* (London, 1824), 89–93. Contrasting examples of the formalized rhetoric of power are given in J.H. Kwabena Nketia, compiler, IAS 01/A2, *Kwadwom* (Legon, 1962), IAS 01/A3, *Apaeɛ*: Poems recited by the *Abrafoɔ* of the *Asantehene* on State Occasions (Legon, 1966), and IAS 01/A4, *Ayan*: Poetry of the *atumpan* drums of the *Asantehene*, I (Legon, 1966). For the 'verbal wit and high energy drama' in one formal performative situation – the recitation of *apaeɛ* – see K. Yankah, 'To Praise or Not to Praise the King: The Akan *Apae* in the Context of Referential Poetry', *RAL*, 14, 3 (1983), 381–400, quotation at 397; see further K. Arhin, 'The Asante Praise Poems: The Ideology of Patrimonialism', *Paideuma*, 32 (1986), 163–97, and especially the remarks at 167. Though ignorant of Twi, many early nineteenth-century Europeans were conscious of *situational* shifts and complexities (attitudinal, verbal, gestural, behavioural) in Asante interaction. As with Freeman, this resulted from a puzzled engagement with observable nuances and inexplicable contradictions. All such engagement vanished in the Anglo-Asante war of 1873–4, and the literature of high imperialism reduced Asante to a barbaric stereotype that functioned in and through an autocratic militarism. Of course, the denial of a society's autonomous complexity – achieved via strategies of willed detachment – has customarily served as prelude to imperial Western constructions of the 'other'; thus, compare the attitudes displayed in H. Brackenbury, *The Ashanti War: A Narrative*, 2 vols. (London, 1874) or R.S.S. Baden-Powell, *The Downfall of Prempeh: A Diary of Life with the Native Levy in Ashanti, 1895–96* (London, 1896) with those discussed in I. Clendinnen, *Ambivalent Conquests: Maya and Spaniard in Yucatan, 1517–1570* (Cambridge, 1987) and M.L. Pratt, *Imperial Eyes: Travel Writing and Transculturation* (London, 1992). European discourse on precolonial Asante still awaits detailed analysis on its own terms.

28 See I. Wilks, *Asante in the Nineteenth Century: The Structure and Evolution of a Political Order* (Cambridge, 1975; reprinted with a new *Preamble*, 1989), 166–206, and especially 184; *ibid.*, 'What Manner of Persons were These? Some

Reflections on Asante Officialdom', in Schildkrout (ed.), *The Golden Stool*, 109–29, for Wilks' equivocally formulated second thoughts on 'bureaucratization' (see note 62 below), and a summary acknowledgement of newly recognized difficulties in analysing what he terms, at 129, the 'institutional development' (but no longer as a 'bureaucracy'?) of the Asante 'administrative class'. For the earlier Wilksian reading of Asante 'bureaucratization' in relation to diplomacy carried to an extreme, see J.K. Adjaye, 'Asante and Britain in the Nineteenth Century: A Study in Asante Diplomatic Practice', Ph.D. (Northwestern, 1981), since revised and published as *Diplomacy and Diplomats in Nineteenth Century Asante* (Lanham, 1984). For a revisionist corrective to Wilks' Asante 'bureaucracy' – specifically with regard to foreign relations and diplomatic practice – see L.W. Yarak, 'Asante and the Dutch: A Case Study in the History of Asante Administration, 1744–1873', Ph.D. (Northwestern, 1983), since revised and published as *Asante and the Dutch 1744–1873* (Oxford, 1990).

29 The Asante state – intermittently, discontinuously, and without developing any cadre of institutionalized specialists with routinized, transmissible skills – employed a tiny number of foreign 'letter writers' on an *ad hoc* basis. For literate Muslims in Kumase *temp.* the *Asantehene* Osei Tutu Kwame (a presence that was not systematically built upon, or even coherently sustained) see N. Levtzion, 'Early Nineteenth Century Arabic Manuscripts from Kumase', *THSG*, 8 (1965), 99–119; for background I. Wilks, *The Northern Factor in Ashanti History* (Legon, 1961) and I. Wilks, N. Levtzion and B.M. Haight, *Chronicles from Gonja: A Tradition of West African Muslim Historiography* (Cambridge, 1986); for overestimations of the 'bureaucratic' significance of Muslims – peripatetic or intermittently resident in Kumase – see I. Wilks, 'The Position of Muslims in Metropolitan Ashanti in the Early Nineteenth Century', in I.M. Lewis (ed.), *Islam in Tropical Africa* (London, 1966), 318–41 and *Asante*, 344–53 and 310 ff.; for the attenuated nature of the literate Muslim 'tradition' in the later nineteenth century see the fugitive instance discussed in I. Wilks, 'A Letter of 1888 from Abū Bakr b. 'Uthmān Kamaghatay to Asantehene Agyeman Prempe', *Asante Seminar*, 4 (1976), 42–4, Muslim literacy was most valued in Asante for its supernatural potency (as a cabalistic component of *unread* talismans); the most recent accounts are D. Owusu-Ansah, 'A Talismanic Tradition: Muslims in Early Nineteenth Century Kumase', Ph.D. (Northwestern, 1986), since revised and published as *Islamic Talismanic Tradition in Nineteenth-Century Asante* (Lewiston, 1991) (but see note 59 below); *ibid.*, 'Power or Prestige? Muslims in 19th Century Kumase', in Schildkrout (ed.), *The Golden Stool*, 80–92; *ibid.*, 'Islamization Reconsidered: An Examination of Asante Responses to Muslim Influence in the Nineteenth Century', *Asian and African Studies*, 21, 2 (1987), 145–163; more speculative is *ibid.*, 'The State and Islamization in 19th Century Africa: Buganda Absolutism *versus* Asante Constitutionalism' *Journal: Institute of Muslim Minority Affairs*, 8, 1 (1987), 132–43. European 'letter writers' were extremely few in number, and were generally reluctant individuals who had been detained in Kumase; see, for example, PRO, London, CO 267/95, the *Asantehene* Osei Yaw to Governor, Cape Coast, dd. Kumase, 12 April, 4 and 12 July 1828 (written by the detainees J. Carr and J. Buckman); WMMS, West

to Boyce, dd. Cape Coast, 7 February 1867 (with reference to the WMMS catechist J.S. Watts, already detained in Kumase for six years and acting periodically as English 'letter writer' to the *Asantehene* Kwaku Dua Panin); for the *Asantehene* Mensa Bonsu's employment of one or two literate European adventurers see Wilks, *Asante*, 606 ff. The history of very sporadic attempts by some *Asantehenes* to procure European education for selected Asante individuals, and the failure of such ventures to provide any cadre of literate functionaries in state service in Kumase is summarized in L.W. Yarak, 'Asante Interest in Europe in the Reign of Opoku Ware I', *Asantesɛm*, 9 (1978), 70–1; *ibid.*, 'Kwasi Boakye and Kwaku Poku: Dutch-Educated Asante"Princes"', in Schildkrout (ed.), *The Golden Stool*, 131–45; K. Owusu-Mensa, 'Prince Owusu Ansa and Asante-British Diplomacy, 1841–1884', Ph.D. (Wisconsin, 1974). A very general overview of Asante attitudes to literacy and to the outside world is T.C. McCaskie, 'Innovational Eclecticism: The Asante Empire and Europe in the Nineteenth Century', *CSSH*, 14, 1 (1972), 30–45. The specific issue of Christian schooling in Kumase is dealt with in the text at pp. 137ff., and in the accompanying notes.

30 Generally on the civil war(s) (1883–8) see A.A. Aidoo, 'Political Crisis and Social Change in the Asante Kingdom, 1867–1901', Ph.D. (UCLA, 1975); T.J. Lewin, 'The Structure of Political Conflict in Asante, 1875–1900', Ph.D., 2 vols. (Northwestern, 1974), since revised and published as *Asante Before the British: The Prempean Years, 1875–1900* (Lawrence, 1978); Wilks, *Asante*, 549ff. For some of the consequences see T.C. McCaskie, '*Ahyiamu* – "A Place of Meeting": An Essay on Process and Event in the History of the Asante State', *JAH*, 25, 2 (1984), 169–88; for a reading of the overall impact of the civil war era see *ibid.*, 'Accumulation, Wealth and Belief in Asante History. 1. To the Close of the Nineteenth Century', *Africa*, 53, 1 (1983), 23–43, especially 37–40; a misreading of my views is in the curious gloss provided by K. Arhin, 'Trade, Accumulation and the State in Asante in the Nineteenth Century', *Africa*, 60, 4 (1990), 524–37, at 534.

31 There is – astonishingly – no comprehensive account of the Dwaben defections. The authoritative Kumase view is in MRO, Kumase, 'The History of Ashanti', MS (with letters and accompanying notes) prepared by a Committee of Traditional Authorities under the Chairmanship of *Ashantihene* Osei Agyeman Prempeh II, n.d., but in the 1940s (henceforth HA). Dwaben accounts are recorded most fully in ASSM, *Asafo Agyei Ko*, MS compiled from interviews with 'elders of Juabin, Asokore, Konongo, etc.' by M. Fortes, 1946. Traditional materials are also contained in C.C. Reindorf, *History of the Gold Coast and Asante, based on Traditions, and Historical Facts ... from about 1500 to 1860* (Basel, 1895), 285–304; R.S. Rattray, *Ashanti Law and Constitution* (Oxford, 1929), 169–97; IAS/AS 16: Juaben Paramount Stool History, recorded by J. Agyeman-Duah, 29 January 1963; T.C. McCaskie, Interviews with Nana Akrasi, ex-*Omanhene* of New Juaben, dd, Koforidua, 24 to 27 September 1968, and with I.K. Agyeman, dd. Kumase, 5 to 9 January 1976; NAG, Accra, ADM 11/1/1122, 'Notes on the History of the New Juaben Settlements'. IAS/CLS 5: Dwaben *Ntahera*, compiled by K. Ampom-Darkwa and K. Asante Darkwa, 1973, contains oral evidence (and provides an instance

of the disruptions caused by the Kumase–Dwaben conflicts). For a sense of the underused materials in the Copenhagen *Rigsarkivet* see R.A. Kea, 'The Danes and the Gold Coast: Ten Danish Documents of the Early 1830s', *Asantesɛm*, 10 (1979), 64–70. For Kumase, Dwaben and the British in the 1830s see G.E. Metcalfe, *Maclean of the Gold Coast: The Life and Times of George Maclean, 1801–1847* (Oxford, 1962), 124–44. Very useful materials on the 1870s are in K.A. Okai, 'The Juaben Revolt and the Founding of New Juaben in Akim Abuakwa', B.A. dissertation (Legon, 1972). For events after the 1870s see R. Addo-Fening, 'Asante Refugees in Akyem Abuakwa, 1875–1912', *THSG*, 14, 1 (1973), 39–64 and his 'The Background to the Deportation of King Asafo Agyei and the Foundation of New Juaben', *THSG*, 14, 2 (1973), 213–28. The two Kumase military assaults on Dwaben took place on the *awukudae* of 23 May or 4 July 1832, and from 31 October to 3 November 1875; see ACBP/42: Adu Borade and ACBP/47: Kwabena Awua, *Asantesɛm*, 10 (1979), 16–20 and 21–30. In general (but in need of much revision and enlargement), see McCaskie, 'Paramountcy', 116–32 and Wilks, *Asante*, 117–19 and 511–16.

32 See generally K. Arhin, 'Peasants in Nineteenth Century Asante', *CA*, 24, 4 (1983), 471–80; J.R. LaTorre, 'Wealth Surpasses Everything: An Economic History of Asante, 1750–1874', Ph.D. (Berkeley, 1978); A.N. Klein, 'Inequality in Asante: A Study of the Forms and Meanings of Slavery and Social Servitude in Pre- and Early Colonial Akan-Asante Society and Culture', Ph.D., 2 vols. (Michigan, 1981); ASSM, Juaso (File 2), Farming Records (File 37), Social Relations (File 51); MFU, 'A Schedule of Interviews and Conversations in the Lake Bosomtwe Villages and Mponua Towns', 1946. Short and incisive on social control is K. Poku, 'Traditional Roles and People of Slave Origin in Modern Ashanti – A Few Impressions', *GJS*, 5, 1 (1969), 34–8. Contrast the Asante experience with events described in R.A. Kea, '"I am here to plunder on the general road": Bandits and Banditry in the Pre-Nineteenth Century Gold Coast', in D. Crummey (ed.), *Banditry, Rebellion and Social Protest in Africa* (London, 1986), 109–32.

33 Wilks, *Asante*, 1–79 offers an optimally positive assessment of the 'great roads', choosing to emphasize their relative merits as against the obdurate limiting factors (technology, environment) upon maintaining – let alone upgrading – the network; at 39, however, he admits that between 1820–70 'no real revolution in communications was achieved'. In the Anglo-Asante war of 1873–4, road making in the Asante forest taxed European engineering technology to the full, and often defeated it; a professional engineering assessment is R. Home, *On the Engineering Operations in the Gold Coast during the Recent Expedition*, R.E. Papers (Chatham, 1876). For a ground-level view of the problems of road making (involving the projected realignment and upgrading of the Kumase to Elmina road) see W. Huydecoper, *Huydecoper's Diary: Journal from Elmina to Kumasi 28 April 1816 to 18 May 1817*, trans. G. Irwin (Legon, 1962), from the original in ARA, The Hague, NBKG 349, entries dd. Kumase, 2, 4, 7, 9, 18, 30 December 1816 and 4, 5, 6, 10 January 1817; entries (all 1817, describing Huydecoper's journey south from Kumase to Elmina) dd. Kaase, 22 April; Eduabin, 23 April; Asanso, 24 April; Asikaso, 25 April; 'Agyankromu' (?), 26 April; Betinase, 27 April; Nsodweso, 29 April;

Mbem, 10 May; Bepowkoko, 11 May; Kaireku (on the Asante–Wasa frontier), 12 May. For an overall sense of the precolonial Asante road network see BMA, Basel, D-31, 1, 25, Maps and Notes (Asante) by A.P.Bauer, dd. Kumase, 10 May 1907, and NAG, Kumase, encl. in 2509 (Reports of the Census of 1931), War Office Surveys and Maps of Asante, dd. 1906–7. The broader context of road and transport development is surveyed in K.B. Dickson, *A Historical Geography of Ghana* (Cambridge, 1971).

34 Bowdich, *Mission*, 29, 30, 152 and 150–5 for the fraught journey from Kumase south to the Bosompra river. Compare Dupuis, *Journal*, 59–61 and 181–2. Immediately upon setting out from Kumase along the 'great road' to Cape Coast (where he arrived on 5 April 1820), Dupuis was 'deluged with torrents of rain for five ensuing days; the forest was a continued sheet of water in many districts, through which we waded with the greatest difficulty and bodily exertion; for our feet sunk at every pace into an adhesive soil . . . The march was indeed most harassing . . .'.

35 WMMS, W. Terry Coppin, 'Journal (including a Visit to Ashanti)', MS dd. 1885, Notebooks 6 and 7. Condensed fragments from this journal supplied the material for its author's various published reminiscences; see for instance *Work and Workers in the Mission Field* (London, December 1901), 518–19. See also R.A. Freeman, *Travels and Life in Ashanti and Jaman* (London, 1898), 35–88.

36 On forest clearing technology see ASSM, Unnumbered Files on 'Land Use', 1945–6, and T.[E.] K[yei]?, 'Notes on Farming in Ashanti', n.d. but 1946; NAG, Sunyani, District Files (Goaso), C107/9, 'Notes on Land Clearing and Food Farming', 1931–40; technical inputs and labour costs are reviewed historically in MRO, Kumase, Letter Book (Asante Akyem), 37, *Wiosohene, Dwansahene et al.* to *Asantehene*, dd. Dwansa, 11 November 1949, 6 February and 23 March 1950. The farming cycle is generally discussed in E. Perregaux, 'Chez les Achanti', *BSNG*, 17 (1906), 7–312, and an historical model of agricultural development is outlined in I. Wilks, 'Land, Labour, Capital and the Forest Kingdom of Asante: A Model of Early Change', in J. Friedman and M.J. Rowlands (eds.), *The Evolution of Social Systems* (London, 1977), 487–534. Best on the transition to the cocoa economy is G. Austin, 'Rural Capitalism and the Growth of Cocoa-Farming in South Ashanti, to 1914', Ph.D. (Birmingham, 1984). Synoptic but stimulating on the broadest technological themes is J.R. Goody, *Technology, Tradition and the State in Africa* (Oxford and London, 1971). A very few horses – short-lived, prestige items – were imported into Asante from the northern savanna. See indicatively Bowdich, *Mission*, 67–8, 325; Chapman's 'Journal', entries dd. Kumase, 6 August and 5 November 1844; Dupuis, *Journal*, plate opp. 223; Hutton, *Voyage*, frontispiece, 62, 210 (the horseman described being the Kumase *Atene Akotenhene* Adu Kwame); Bonnat MSS, Cahier 7, entry dd. Kumase, 2 September 1871 for the 'deux chevaux arabes, un noir et l'autre blanc' that belonged to the *Mamponhene* Kwabena Dwumo (Mampon abutted on the savanna to the north). There is some general discussion in R. Law, *The Horse in African History* (London, 1980). Cattle were kept in Asante, but were relatively scarce and correspondingly valuable. See Bowdich, *Mission*, 325 and Dupuis, *Journal*, 180 and fn. Horses and cattle were both subject to debilitating

or fatal enzootic occurrences of trypanosomiasis caused by tsetse flies; see R.A. Hutchinson, 'Diseases and Pests of Stock' and F.A. Squire, 'Tsetse Flies', both in the generally very useful J.B. Wills (ed.), *Agriculture and Land Use in Ghana* (Accra, 1962), 437–40 and 441–4. For the wheeled carriage – a 'beautiful little phaeton' – brought to Kumase with great difficulty by the Wesleyan-Methodists for presentation to the *Asantehene* Kwaku Dua Panin on 13 December 1841, and for its restricted, ceremonial, man-drawn use, see McCaskie, 'Paramountcy', 175–6. In general see R. Law, 'Wheeled Transport in Pre-Colonial West Africa', *Africa*, 50, 3 (1980), 249–62.

37 See N.P.F. Machin, '"Understanding the Natives": The Life of R.S. Rattray, 1881–1938', unpublished MS, 1973, for the life and background. Relevant publications by Rattray include: *Ashanti Proverbs: The Primitive Ethics of a Savage People* (Oxford, 1916); *Ashanti* (Oxford, 1923); 'The Drum Language of West Africa', *JRAS*, 22 (1923), 226–36 and 302–16; *A Short Manual of the Gold Coast* (Accra, 1924); 'The Arts and Crafts of Ashanti', *JRAS*, 23 (1924), 265–70; with L.H.D. Buxton, 'Cross-Cousin Marriages', *JRAS*, 24 (1925), 83–91; 'A Wembley Idol', *BM*, 1325 (1926), 395–402; *Religion and Art in Ashanti* (Oxford, 1927); 'Some Aspects of West African Folklore', *JRAS*, 28 (1928), 1–11; 'The Mausoleum of Ampong Agyei', *BM*, n.s. 233 (June 1928), 842–53; *Ashanti Law and Constitution* (Oxford, 1929); *Akan-Ashanti Folk Tales* (Oxford, 1930); *Tribes of the Ashanti Hinterland* (Oxford, 1932); 'The African Child in Proverb, Folklore and Fact', *Africa*, 6 (1933), 456–71; *The Leopard Priestess*, a novel (Oxford, 1934); 'The Golden Stool of Ashanti', *The Illustrated London News* (2 March 1935), 333–5. RAI, London, MSS and Papers of R.S. Rattray, is an extensive series of MSS and notebooks containing a range of unpublished fieldwork items on Asante; PRM, Oxford, 1941.3.177–219, Rattray Collection, catalogues the deposit of 1,300 of Rattray's photographs, of which about 1,000 were taken in Asante. Rattray's celebrated memorandum on the *sika dwa kofi* is summarized in *Ashanti*, 287–93; see too RH, Oxford, CRP, MSS Brit. Emp. s.344, Papers of Sir Charles Henry Harper. MRO, Kumase, File on Seniagya and OMP, Kumase, Letter Book 5, Correspondence and Documents of the *Asantehenes* Agyeman Prempe and Osei Agyeman Prempeh II contain references to Rattray and his work. MFU, 'Notes and Documents by and on R.S. Rattray' contains materials and extensive comments on his work.

38 T.C. McCaskie, 'R.S. Rattray and the Construction of Asante History: An Appraisal', *HA*, 10 (1983), 187–206; see too T.H. Von Laue, 'Transubstantiation in the Study of African Reality', *AA*, 74 (1975), 401–19 and *ibid.*, 'Anthropology and Power: R.S. Rattray among the Ashanti', *AA*, 75 (1976), 33–54.

39 M. Fortes, 'Prologue: Family Studies in Ghana 1920–1970', in C. Oppong (ed.), *Domestic Rights and Duties in Southern Ghana*, Legon Family Research Papers 1 (Legon, 1974), 1–27, quotation at 2. At the same place Fortes wrote, 'I knew Rattray well, and it was owing to him that I chose the Gold Coast ... as the area in which I was to carry on my field research.'

40 *Ibid.*, 6. For extended treatments of his own career, approach and methodology see M. Fortes, 'Custom and Conscience in Anthropological Perspective',

International Review of Psycho-Analysis, 4 (1977), 127–54 (a reworking of the Ernest Jones Memorial Lecture of the British Psychoanalytical Society, London, 1973); *ibid.*, 'An Anthropologist's Apprenticeship', *ARA*, 7 (1978), 1–30. Useful perspectives on Fortes are in J.A. Barnes, *Three Styles in the Study of Kinship* (London, 1971) and A. Kuper, *Anthropology and Anthropologists: The Modern British School* (London, 1983); for general intellectual context see G.W. Stocking Jr (ed.), *Functionalism Historicized: Essays on British Social Anthropology*, History of Anthropology 2 (Madison, 1984). Fortes' main body of fieldwork concerned the Tallensi of northern Ghana, but relevant publications on his research in Asante include: 'The Ashanti Social Survey: A Preliminary Report', *RLJ*, 6 (1948), 1–36 (a longer – earlier? – draft of this was deposited in the Regional Office, Kumase, and is now in NAG, Kumase, D60/24, among papers pertaining to the Public Health Board; see too M. Fortes *et al.*, 'A Demographic Field Study in Ashanti', in F. Lorimer (ed.) *Culture and Human Fertility*, UNESCO Report (Paris, 1954)); 'Kinship and Marriage among the Ashanti', in A.R. Radcliffe-Brown and D. Forde (eds.), *African Systems of Kinship and Marriage* (London, 1950), 252–84; *Oedipus and Job in West African Religion* (Cambridge, 1959; reprinted 1983, with an essay by R. Horton, 'Social Psychologies: African and Western', 41–82); 'The "Submerged Descent Line" in Ashanti', in I. Schapera (ed.), *Studies in Kinship and Marriage* (London, 1963), 58–67; *Kinship and the Social Order: The Legacy of Lewis Henry Morgan* (London, 1969); *Time and Social Structure and Other Essays* (London, 1970). Fortes' contributions to general kinship theory also make use of Asante examples. See too the hugely influential M. Fortes and E.E. Evans-Pritchard (eds.), *African Political Systems* (London, 1940); also M. Fortes and G. Dieterlen (eds.), *African Systems of Thought* (London, 1965); and M. Fortes, R.W. Steel and P. Ady, 'Ashanti Survey, 1945–6: An Experiment in Social Research', *GJ*, 110 (1948), 149–79. The Ashanti Social Survey (1945–6) generated large amounts of data that have never been worked through and published (see Sources Consulted). Fortes' principal Asante assistant has produced two important MSS. See T.E. Kyei, *My Memoir*, 6 vols., n.d. and *ibid.*, *Marriage and Divorce among the Ashanti*, forthcoming from African Studies Centre, Cambridge.

41 The fullest exposition is Fortes, *Kinship and the Social Order*; see too *ibid.*, 'Kinship and the Social Order: The Legacy of L.H. Morgan', *CA*, 13, 2 (1972), 285–96.

42 T.R. Trautmann, *Lewis Henry Morgan and the Invention of Kinship* (Berkeley, 1987), 260.

43 Fortes was largely untroubled by questions of historical process, and certainly so by comparison with E.E. Evans-Pritchard, his peer and sometime collaborator. See E.E. Evans-Pritchard, *Anthropology and History* (Manchester, 1961); *The Azande: History and Political Institutions* (Oxford, 1971), and (posthumously) ed. by A. Singer, *A History of Anthropological Thought* (London, 1981). See too E. Gellner, 'Introduction' in Evans-Pritchard, *A History*, xiii–xxxvi, and M. Douglas, *Evans-Pritchard* (London, 1980).

44 M. Freedman, *Main Trends in Social and Cultural Anthropology* (New York, 1978), 73. In Geertz, *Works and Lives*, 16, Freedman's point is made very

bluntly indeed; there Geertz characterizes M. Fortes, *The Dynamics of Clanship among the Tallensi* (London, 1945; reprinted 1967) as being 'perhaps the most thoroughly objectivized of the great ethnographies – it reads like a law text written by a botanist'.

45 See for example N. Levtzion, *Ancient Ghana and Mali* (London, 1973), 3. The relevant passage from al-Fazāri is given in J.M. Cuoq, *Recueil des sources arabes concernant l'Afrique occidentale du VIIIᵉ siècle* (Paris, 1975). For Nkrumah's use and understanding of the term Ghana see his speech (moving adoption of the White Paper on Government's Revised Constitutional Proposals for Independence of the Gold Coast), G.C. Legislative Assembly, *Debates, 1951–7*, dd. 18 May 1956.

46 H.R. Trevor-Roper, *The Rise of Christian Europe* (London, 1965), 9.

47 Perspectives on the evolution of Africanist historiography since the 1950s are in C. Fyfe (ed.), *African Studies since 1945* (London, 1976); see too B. Jewsiewicki and D. Newbury (eds.), *African Historiographies* (Beverly Hills, 1985). It is instructive to compare – from a mass of possible instances – the *types* of questions asked of the evidence by two distinguished Africanists of successive academic 'generations' (and of different nationalities and genders); see the highly authoritative, empiricist narrative recounting of political history in the British J.D. Fage, *A History of Africa* (London, 1978), and compare the much more diverse, fragmented and self-conscious reading of the sources of power and authority in the French (and *annales* influenced?) C. Coquery-Vidrovitch, *Afrique noire: permanences et ruptures* (Paris, 1985). But differences in national styles apart, the loser in the pioneering Africanist enterprise of legitimating the past by 'getting the story straight' was the sustained, long-term or 'deep' analysis of specific African cultures, construed and comprehended *on their own historical terms*. Thus – and briefly – it is (still) the case, for example, that much more has been written on the *structures* of slavery (economic, commercial, institutional, demographic) as these affected African polities and peoples, than on the *meanings* of 'slavery' (cognitive, representational, relational, personal) as these were articulated within given historic African cultures. The distinction between these two types or strategies of discourse is one that much preoccupies African intellectuals (who often do not recognize their own cultural specificity or selfhood in the dominant exoteric thrust of Africanist historiography), and it should be a fundamental subject for explicit review in any future history of the Africanist historiographical enterprise.

48 Wilks, *Asante*, xiv. See too the muddled reiteration of this position in *Preamble* (1989), xlv–xlvi. Here Wilks bemoans the 'cult' or 'obsession of [anonymous] contemporary social scientists with definition'; but at *ibid.*, xxi–xxii he asserts his '*sneaking regard* [my emphasis] for logical positivism', and his ongoing 'commitment to the philosophy of "ordinary language"', as expounded by A.J. Ayer, J.L. Austin and G. Ryle. There is a paradox here, for it is axiomatic to the procedures of logical positivism and 'ordinary language' philosophy (and arguably analytic philosophy generally) that their practitioners famously (or notoriously) shared in an 'obsession' with every kind of 'definition' of terms; for the rise and decline of logical positivism and the fall into disrepute of Oxford 'ordinary language' philosophy see the judicious reviews by J.

Passmore, *A Hundred Years of Philosophy* (London, 1966) and his *Recent Philosophers* (London, 1985); some insight into the 'obsession' with 'definition' may be adduced by reading D. Pears, 'A Comparison between Ayer's Views about the Privileges of Sense-Datum Statements and the Views of Russell and Austin', and A.J. Ayer, 'Replies', in G.F. Macdonald (ed.), *Perception and Identity: Essays Presented to A.J. Ayer and his Replies to Them* (London, 1979), 61–83 and 277–333, especially 285–9; and for a sceptical and telling critique of truth-conditional semantics and of the claims of philosophy of language in general see G.P. Baker and P.M.S. Hacker, *Language, Sense and Nonsense* (Oxford, 1984). Wilks' lamentation at *Preamble* (1989), xlvi that 'definition' and its 'cult progressively constrains our use of everyday words (think of the fate of "tribe") and threatens to leave us without a language in which we can any longer enjoy fruitful discourse' is, all at once, an oddly obtuse reading of his acknowledged philosophical mentors, and a curt dismissal – clothed in 'commonsensical' (or 'ordinary language'?) terms – of the very real concerns of all those, excluded from the sovereign 'we' who 'enjoy fruitful discourse', for whom 'everyday words' (like 'tribe') are ideologically contested rather than descriptively neutral characterizations. Compare for example P.P. Ekeh, 'Social Anthropology and the Contrasting Uses of Tribalism in Africa', *CSSH*, 32 (1990), 660–700. Wilks' approach – oddly blinkered for a historian of Africa – should be read in the light of that large body of scholarship that has followed upon the arguments in, for example, Said's *Orientalism*.

49 Wilks, 'Land, Labour, Capital', 487. For the strained and adventitious attempt to draw parallels between the problems of 'nationalism' and 'nation building' in nineteenth-century Asante and in Nkrumah's Ghana see *ibid.*, *Asante*, 720–4, and 'Dissidence in Asante Politics: Two Tracts from the Late Nineteenth Century', in I. Abu-Lughod (ed.), *African Themes: Northwestern University Studies in Honor of Gwendolen M. Carter* (Evanston, 1975), 47–63, especially 63. For Wilks' concern with the 'heroic trope' of a failed 'nationalism' in quite another context see his *South Wales and the Rising of 1839* (London, 1984), and – with a (significant 'nationalist'?) shift in authorial signature – Ivor G. Hughes Wilks, 'Insurrections in Texas and Wales: The Careers of John Rees', *The Welsh History Review: Cylchgrawn Hanes Cymru*, 11, 1 (1982), 67–91. It is instructive to examine the rhetorical siting of the 'nationalist' theme in Wilks' work, *inter alia* in terms of the discussion of the tropological and stylistic underpinnings of historical narratives in, for example, H. White, *Tropics of Discourse: Essays in Cultural Criticism* (Baltimore, 1978).

50 Hart, 'The Social Anthropology of West Africa', 257.

51 I. Wilks, 'Aspects of Bureaucratization in Ashanti in the Nineteenth Century', *JAH*, 7, 2 (1966), 215–32 (see 216: 'I shall assume the value of a model of bureaucracy – thought of *more or less* [my emphases] in Weber's terms'); *ibid.*, 'Ashanti Government', in D. Forde and P.M. Kaberry (eds.), *West African Kingdoms in the Nineteenth Century* (London, 1967), 206–38, quotations at 207, 211. See the very influential G.R. Elton, *The Tudor Revolution in Government: Administrative Changes in the Reign of Henry VIII* (Cambridge, 1953); the comment in L. Yarak, 'State, Society, and Politics in Nineteenth

Century Asante', paper presented at the Symposium on the City of Kumase, Kumase, 13–16 December 1990, 13; and Wilks, *Preamble* (1989), xxxii.

52 I. Wilks, *Political Bi-Polarity in Nineteenth Century Asante*, Ninth M.J. Herskovits Memorial Lecture, Edinburgh University (Edinburgh, 1970), 1–22, quotations at 1; at the same place Wilks writes that for precolonial Asante 'the evidence is such as to indicate the presence of a bureaucracy characterized, *inter alia*, by a system of recruitment through achievement and skill, by the specialization of administrative role, by the existence of promotional hierarchies, and by the regular remuneration of service mainly through fixed commissions'. Wilks framed his 1970 argument concerning 'bureaucracy' in Asante with crucial reference to S.N. Eisenstadt, *The Political Systems of Empires: The Rise and Fall of the Historical Bureaucratic Societies*, 2nd edn (New York, 1969), a work that sought to qualify and to extend Weber's historical analyses. But oddly, by 1975 no reference to Eisenstadt was included in the comprehensive 'Guide to Sources Consulted' in *Asante*, 731–43.

53 Wilks, *Asante*, 468. There are a number of puzzles here. These are important and demand to be enumerated, not least because Wilks has systematically – if very inexplicitly – invoked Weber in postulating the existence of a historic Asante 'bureaucracy'. The footnote to the passage quoted from Wilks (468, fn. 227) cites Max Weber, *Wirtschaft und Gesellschaft* (1922), III, ch. 6, and H.H. Gerth and C.W. Mills, *From Max Weber: Essays in Sociology* (London, 1948). Gerth and Mills is referenced in Wilks' 'Guide to Sources Consulted', 734. However, there is no bibliographic citation whatsoever in Wilks' book to any edition of *Wirtschaft und Gesellschaft*; furthermore, there is no bibliographic reference to any other work by Weber; and – perhaps most surprisingly – 468 fn. 227 is the sole citation of Weber in a 724-page account in which 'the development of the civil administration is obviously central to the book' (*Preamble* (1989), 1), and in which the key passage in that process of 'development' – the alleged 'Kwadwoan revolution in government' – is characterized by Wilks as being 'bureaucratic' in the Weberian sense. This parsimonious reticence *vis-à-vis* Weber's voluminous writings is oddly incongruous, and doubly so as *Wirtschaft und Gesellschaft* is a notoriously problematic text. When Weber died (1920) he bequeathed only a draft of the text, which he had been working on since 1911. All of the 'complete' posthumous editions of this text were reworked by their respective editors: Marianne Weber in 1922 (the oldest, least authoritative edition, but the one cited – but unattributed – by Wilks?), 1925 and 1947; Johannes Winckelmann in 1956, 1972 and 1976. A sense of the complex difficulties involved in reading Weber's text (and in situating it in relation to the rest of his thought) is supplied by F.H. Tenbruck, 'Wie gut kennen wir Max Weber?' and 'Abschied von *Wirtschaft und Gesellschaft*', both in *Zeitschrift für die gesamte Staatswissenschaft*, 131 (1975), 719–42 and 133 (1977), 703–36 respectively (in English translation see *ibid.*, 'The Problem of Thematic Unity in the Work of Max Weber', *BJS*, 31 (1980), 316–51). For comment on the textual problems overall, and on the general understanding among scholars of Weber's work that *Wirtschaft und Gesellschaft* is simply 'not accessible without knowledge of what has gone before' (i.e. all of Weber's massive and disparate *œuvre*) see the authoritative D.

Käsler, *Max Weber: An Introduction to his Life and Work* (Oxford, 1988), 142–73 and 271. Finally – and most puzzling of all – Wilks makes no reference to G. Roth and C. Wittich (eds.), *Economy and Society: An Outline of Interpretive Sociology*, 3 vols. (New York, 1968). This is the standard English-language version of *Wirtschaft und Gesellschaft*, and is a translation of Winckelmann's German edition of 1956 (but with access to Winckelmann's draft revisions and notes for the – then forthcoming – 5th German edition of 1972). It is incomprehensible as to why Wilks used (apparently) the defective 1922 German edition of *Wirtschaft und Gesellschaft* in preference to the editions of 1956 or 1972, and favoured (apparently) the elderly, incomplete English translations of Gerth and Mills over the authoritative, complete and widely available critical English edition by Roth and Wittich. For some comment on Wilks' deficient use of Weber – but from a standpoint that insufficiently problematizes *Wirtschaft und Gesellschaft* – see Yarak, *Asante and the Dutch*, 1–28, and especially 20 fn. 74 and 26.

54 My views are summarized in T.C. McCaskie, 'Empire State: Asante and the Historians', *JAH*, 33, 3 (1992), 467–76.

55 Yarak, *Asante and the Dutch*, 22.

56 See 'bureau', 'bureaucracy' and 'burel' in *The Compact Edition of the Oxford English Dictionary: Complete Text [reproduced micrographically]* (Oxford, 1971), vol. 1, A-O, 296. A discussion is in R. Williams, *Keywords: A Vocabulary of Culture and Society* (Glasgow, 1976), 40–1.

57 Weber's key discussion is in Roth and Wittich (eds.) *Economy and Society*, III, 956–1005, 'Bureaucracy'. However – and in the first place – this needs to be read in conjunction with *ibid.*, 1006–69, 'Patriarchalism and Patrimonialism'; 1070–1110, 'Feudalism, *Standestaat* and Patrimonialism'; 1111–57, 'Charisma and Its Transformations'; 1158–1211, 'Political and Hierocratic Domination'; and 1212–1368, 'The City (Non-Legitimate Domination)'. But in addition to *Wirtschaft und Gesellschaft*, as is noted in R. Bendix, *Max Weber: An Intellectual Portrait* (London, 1966 edn), 423 fn. 15, there 'are many other passages in Weber's work where he deals with the problem of bureaucratization'. Useful in understanding Weber's conceptualization of bureaucracy, and in situating it in relation to his life and writings, are M. Albrow, *Bureaucracy* (London, 1970), and *Max Weber's Construction of Social Theory* (London, 1990); W.J. Mommsen, *The Political and Social Theory of Max Weber: Collected Essays* (Chicago, 1989) and *The Age of Bureaucracy: Perspectives on the Political Sociology of Max Weber* (Oxford, 1974); W.J. Mommsen and J. Osterhammel (eds.), *Max Weber and His Contemporaries* (London, 1987); W. Hennis, *Max Weber: Essays in Reconstruction* (London, 1988); and R. Collins, *Weberian Sociological Theory* (Cambridge, 1986). L.A. Scaff, *Fleeing the Iron Cage: Culture, Politics, and Modernity* (Berkeley, 1989) is an outstanding analytic reading of Weber's life and work.

58 Wilks, *Asante*, 726, and 381–3, 451, 466; at *ibid.*, Index, 769, 'dampans, *see under* bureaus'. Wilks' 'bureaucratic' terminology ('bureaus', 'offices') is misleading – and insupportably restrictive – when applied to the Asante understanding of *adampaŋ*. Informants testify and observation confirms that the *ɔdampaŋ* was an arena or theatre rather than an 'office'. That is, it was a

site in which a prolific sociability was enacted as a framing device for the display of status, wealth and power. Thus, and predictably, the right to use an *adampaŋ* in precolonial Kumase was a status prerogative accruing to membership in the state. Possession was authorized by the *Asantehene*, and appropriate upkeep – which had ritual as well as status dimensions – was monitored by him; see Bowdich, *Mission*, 305 and BMA, Basel, Jenkins (Ramseyer MS *et al.*), entries dd. Kumase, 12 and 14 December 1871. In this century, *adampaŋ* have been built in Kumase by office holders, wealthy businessmen, local and national politicians, and the *nouveaux riches* – in fact by all those who have sought public acknowledgement as 'big men' (and 'women') through the agency of this traditional means of asserting status; see ASSM, 'Notes on House D.B.477 Kumasi, built by Chief Kwasi Nuama in ca. 1907' and M. Fortes, 'Talks with Ashantihene on Landholding and Building in Kumasi', dd. Kumase, 16 December 1945; and for general context J.W. Brown, 'Kumasi, 1896–1923: Urban Africa during the Early Colonial Period', Ph.D. (Madison, 1972), and A.G. Tipple, *The Development of Housing Policy in Kumasi, Ghana, 1901 to 1981* (Newcastle, 1987). Dupuis, *Journal*, 83 observed that *adampaŋ* were 'designed for the dispatch of public business' – but this must be read in the broadest sense to embrace all of those myriad facets of the publicly enacted status of the 'big man'; decision making, no doubt, but also arguing, debating, adjudicating, bantering, gossiping, bargaining, exchanging news, entertaining, drinking, eating, playing, flirting, performing rituals, and – not least – displaying an aggrandized selfhood calibrated in dress, ornaments, hairstyles, etc. All of this occurred within a densely peopled, busy context, for a numerous retinue and a nimbus of activity were also status indicators. Importantly, for most of the time *adampaŋ* were not in the formal use just described. But they were virtually never deserted, for they served as a forum for the myriad exchanges of unstructured social intercourse between household dwellers and others; thus, for example, *adampaŋ* feature in folk accounts as venues for trysts between lovers. Certainly, in both formal and informal use *adampaŋ* were as far from evincing the transactional characteristics of a Weberian bureaucratic office as can be imagined! The matter was put with literal simplicity (but with an economy that might mislead a reader with a preconceived case to make) in NAG, Accra, ADM 1/2/4, Winniet's 'Journal', entry dd. Kumase, 9 October 1848; 'the houses looking into the streets [of Kumase] are all public rooms on the ground floor'. The 'verandahs' afforded by *adampaŋ* also provided a platform 'stage' for musical performances associated with the *abosom*; see M. Swithenbank, *Ashanti Fetish Houses* (Accra, 1969) and L. Prussin, 'Traditional Asante Architecture', *AfAr*, 13, 2 (1980), 57–65, 78–82 and 85–7.

59 *Preamble* (1989), xii is Wilks' latest, somewhat neutral notice of the Kumase Muslims. He writes that the Muslims have received 'much further attention' since 1975, and that the 'time for a synthesis of these materials is now approaching...'. Among this new work is presumably Owusu-Ansah, *Talismanic Tradition*, which at 134–7 produces a very odd defence of the Wilksian idea of an Asante 'bureaucracy' (Muslims included). Thus, at 137 Owusu-Ansah acknowledges the absence from Asante of Weber's bureaucratic criteria (while

only listing one or two of these desiderata), but adds the startling qualification that in nineteenth-century Asante 'rational and routinized procedures evolved *which served much the same purpose*' (my emphases).

60 Adjaye, *Diplomacy and Diplomats*, 152–218, quotation at 153; additionally, at *ibid.*, 152 the undocumented claim is made (but by what standard of measurement?) that 'Asante in the course of the nineteenth century poured forth an enormous volume of documents.' Be that as it may, the following statement at *ibid.*, 180 should be read bearing in mind the Weberian enumeration of bureaucratic criteria: 'The available evidence relating to the structure of the [Asante] chancery *does not suggest that it developed an efficient, integrated office that maintained an inventory of incoming and outgoing letters*' (my emphases).

61 See *Preamble* (1989), 1, for example, for Wilks' simplistic ideas about the precedence assumed by 'narrative' over 'broad generalizations of a historical-sociological kind'. This issue is more complex – and more contentious – than Wilks allows. For context and analysis see, most recently, E. Kiser and M. Hechter, 'The Role of General Theory in Comparative Historical Sociology', *AJS*, 97, 1 (1991), 1–30.

62 Wilks, 'What Manner of Persons Were These?', 111. As he acknowledges, Wilks is replying here to criticisms of his theorizing authored by Arhin and Yarak. See K. Arhin, 'Rank and Class among the Asante and Fante in the Nineteenth Century', *Africa*, 53, 1 (1983), 2–22, especially 3–4 where it is argued 'that the groups that Wilks calls "classes" should be called "status groups", and that Asante stratification should be seen as a system of "ranks" rather than as a system of "classes"'. Arhin is here engaging with the extremely abrupt introduction of the Marxist concepts of class and class consciousness towards the close of *Asante* (for which see note 64 below). Yarak, *Asante and the Dutch*, 4–27 sets forth a trenchant series of criticisms of what he terms – at 22, as noted – Wilks' 'peculiar use of Weber'. The core of Yarak's critique is given at *ibid.*, 20 fn. 74; Yarak situates Wilks' early (1966) adoption and subsequent application to Asante of Weber's formal-rational bureaucratic model – together with the construction derived from it of precolonial Asante as a 'modernizing' state – in a deficient reading, and *ergo* a fundamentally flawed understanding, of Weber. Specifically, Yarak suggests that Wilks' initial (and final?) comprehension of the Weberian problematic was formed by a perusal of the (very) selected passages from *Wirtschaft und Gesellschaft* translated in Gerth and Mills, *From Max Weber*. Missing *inter alia* from Gerth and Mills is Weber's discussion of patrimonialism (for which see note 57 above). Yarak and Arhin have both argued *contra* Wilks – and convincingly, at least in terms of their own postulated alternatives – that the precolonial Asante polity conformed much more closely by type to Weber's patrimonialism than to his formal-rational bureaucracy. Be that as it may, it remains the case that Wilks has sedulously pursued one line of reasoning – ostensibly inspired by Weber – without ever having given due attention to alternatives suggested by Weber himself, without ever having explicitly theorized the application of Weberian concepts to the Asante historical experience, and without ever having systematically explained his own reading of Weber in relation to any analysis

of the Weberian problematic. See further McCaskie, 'Empire State' (and note 63 below).

63 *Preamble* (1989), xx. See too chapter 5, note 13 below.

64 In *Asante* Marxist ideas of class and class consciousness are abruptly and sketchily introduced around page 700. A treatment of these matters, in any direct or serious analytical way, is markedly absent from the remainder of the book, and their anomalous interpolation towards the end of the text impresses itself upon the reader as an afterthought. Certainly, the highly compressed explication of these issues in the Asante context is most unsatisfactory, being poorly theorized and more *marxisant* than Marxist. And whereas Wilks' bibliographic referencing of Weber is inadequate, his citation of Marx, Engels or relevant Marxist literature is non-existent; yet again, very little attempt is made to argue a case between theory and the Asante data. As proof of his Marxist credentials Wilks cites – at *Preamble* (1989), xx – E. Terray's review of *Asante* in *AESC*, 32 (1977), 311–25. Terray himself writes from an avowedly Marxist perspective, and his claim – in Wilks' paraphrase – that *Asante* is 'a work of historical materialism in the Marxist tradition' is at once charitably imprecise and wholly to be anticipated. Wilks then undermines his own position by noting a further review of his book by the Marxist scholar J. Depelchin in *Africa Development*, 2, 4 (1977), 97–106. Depelchin identified *Asante* as being Weberian in inspiration, and castigated it for its inadequate attention to Marxist categories of analysis. That two Marxist scholars drew such contradictory impressions from Wilks' book *may* be due in part to Marxist sectarianism, but surely the underlying cause – once more – is Wilks' abject failure to provide any systemic account of his own theorizing, or otherwise to clarify his own intellectual position.

65 Bonnat MSS, Cahier 13, entry dd. Kumase, 21 January 1873 for a contemporary account of the disastrous loss of the war charm ('un fétiche célèbre') belonging to the *Anantahene* Asamoa Nkwanta ('Samöi-Canta, l'un des principeaux chefs de l'arrière'). Asamoa Nkwanta was the most skilful of all nineteenth-century Asante generals, and was popularly identified with a notable capacity to invoke supernatural protection for the troops under his command; see ACBP/7: Asamoa Nkwanta, *Asante Seminar*, 3 (1975), 7–9. He was *srafokra* ('the guardian spirit of the army'; lit. 'that which watched over soldiers in camp'), and his invincible war charm reputedly manifested itself in *bodua* (a cow tail switch, commonly carried by generals). This was understood to act as a 'sweep' that protectively surrounded his soldiers and 'cleared the path' ahead for them. Thus, it could 'disturb' the flow of a river to ensure a safe crossing (a supernatural attribute often ascribed to *bodua* in folklore; see the account in the story *Akokoa Kwasi Gyinamoa* in Rattray, *Folk Tales*, 220–1). In late January 1873, Asamoa Nkwanta planted his war charm on the north bank of the Bosompra to 'enable' the safe southward negotiation of that river by the Asante army sent to invade the Gold Coast. But the river inexplicably rose, the war charm was swept away and lost, and numbers of troops were drowned in the crossing; for a reference to the loss of life see F.A. Ramseyer and J. Kühne, *Four Years in Ashantee* (London, 1875), 209. The loss of the war charm portended military catastrophe. It is variously given in tradition as the 'cause'

of Asante defeat in 1873–4, and as the precipitating agent in Asamoa Nkwanta's military failure and death by suicide in the Dwaben war in 1875; see T.C. McCaskie, Interviews with Yaw Pepera, J.F. Opoku and others, dd. Abira and Kumase, 4, 5 and 9 April 1988; TOR, Kumasi District Record Book, 1916–18, no. 779, Opanin Kwame Ntem etc. *versus* Kwame Somo of Bare, commenced 13 August 1917. In A.K. Armah's *The Healers: An Historical Novel* (Nairobi, 1978), 292 ff., the omens of the Asante defeat in 1873–4 are treated in an imaginative – but historically grounded and recognizable – reworking. This is arguably closer to the specifically Asante understanding of the issues involved than are extant historical reconstructions; see McCaskie, 'Armah's *The Healers*'.

66 Wilks, *Preamble* (1989), xxii notes the author's 'respect' for 'R.G. Collingwood's stress on the importance of "getting into the minds" of people in the past'. This appears to be commonsensical, but Collingwood's famous dictum about the historian rethinking or re-enacting past thought is in fact suffused with idealist traces, contentiously ambiguous as to meaning, and problematic in relation to historical explanation. See L.O. Mink, *Mind, History, and Dialectics: The Philosophy of R.G. Collingwood* (Bloomington, 1969) and L.J. Goldstein, 'Collingwood on the Construction of the Historical Past', in M. Krausz (ed.), *Critical Essays on the Philosophy of R.G. Collingwood* (Oxford, 1972), 241–67. The impact of Crocean idealism on Collingwood's aesthetics is well known, but for its continuing influence on Collingwood during the actual writing of the *Idea of History* (Oxford, 1946) in 1936–9 see – pithily – S. Toulmin, 'Conceptual Change and the Problem of Relativity', in Krausz (ed.), *Critical Essays*, 201–21, especially 202. In recent years the interpretation of Collingwood's actual philosophical intentions has been made even more contentious by the ongoing analysis of his many unpublished MSS; see for example W.J. Van Der Dussen, *History as a Science: The Philosophy of R.G. Collingwood* (The Hague, 1981) and T. Modood, 'The Later Collingwood's Alleged Historicism and Relativism', *JHP*, 27, 1 (1989), 101–26.

67 R. Law, 'Human Sacrifice in Pre-Colonial West Africa', *AA*, 84 (1985), 53–87, especially 55–6. Law's point is developed in the detailed critique by C. Williams, 'Asante: Human Sacrifice or Capital Punishment? An Assessment of the Period 1807–1874', *IJAHS*, 21, 3 (1988), 433–41. I. Wilks, 'Asante: Human Sacrifice or Capital Punishment? A Rejoinder', *IJAHS*, 21, 3 (1988), 443–52 is a response to Williams. In this, at 452, it is suggested that the term human sacrifice is 'inappropriate', but that 'the killings at Asante "customs" ... were ... quite rational procedures *granted* [author's emphasis] the particular form that the belief in an afterlife took in Asante ...'. Thus, Wilks remains content to describe the form and structure of belief, rather than to essay any exploration of its quiddity or meanings.

68 J.D.Y. Peel, 'History, Culture and the Comparative Method: A West African Puzzle', in Holy (ed.), *Comparative Anthropology*, 88–118, quotation at 108.

69 Wilks, *Preamble* (1989), xxii.

70 *Ibid.*, xx–xxi.

71 Unfortunately, that which might be termed the 'royal household' in Asante – that is, the different groups of *nhenkwaa* and other functionaries intimately

involved with the person of the *Asantehene*, and with the day-to-day running of the Kumase *ahenfie* – is relatively understudied, and certainly so by comparison with the broader office-holding elite. Some insight into palace structure and personnel is provided by A.A.Y. Kyerematen, 'Ashanti Royal Regalia: Their History and Functions', D.Phil. (Oxford, 1966); *ibid., Kingship and Ceremony in Ashanti* (Kumase, n.d.); K. Arhin and K. Afari-Gyan (eds.), *The City of Kumasi Handbook: Past, Present and Future* (Legon, 1992), 5–11; ASSM, 'Sketch Plan of the *Ashantihene's* Palace, with Notes and Descriptions', n.d. (but mid-1940s); OMP, Kumase, Unaccessioned Drawings and Plans of Various Buildings, n.d.; T.C. McCaskie, Discussions with Kwasi Anane and Yaw Britwum, dd. Kumase, 3 and 4 January 1976, and with Kukua Nyame and Nana Ama Tiwaa, dd. Suame (Kumase), 27 March 1983. Compare RAI, Rattray MSS, 'Plan of the Chief's House at Juaben', n.d., encl. in MS bundle 107.

72 See Yarak, *Asante and the Dutch*; *ibid.*, 'State, Society and Politics'; *ibid.*, 'Elmina and Greater Asante in the Nineteenth Century', *Africa*, 56, 1 (1986), 33–52; K. Arhin, 'Rank and Class'; *ibid.*, 'Peasants'; *ibid.*, 'The Asante Praise Poems'; *ibid.*, 'A Note on the Asante *akonkofo*: A Non-literate Sub-elite', *Africa*, 56, 1 (1986), 25–31; *ibid.*, 'Trade, Accumulation and the State'.

73 Yarak, 'State, Society and Politics', 20, demonstrates some awareness of the issues that are involved. He observes that 'by focusing on the question of legitimate authority as Weber demands, one is also forced to investigate the question of the religious and other sanctions for authority, and how these are assembled and challenged. This is an area of investigation that cries out for further work.' The legitimation of Asante *imperial* authority, and the problem of the articulation of consent (via the export from Asante of ideologies and cultural models) among subordinate states and peoples, are distinct and resistant questions that require much more detailed work; for a range of approaches and insights see, for example, C.-H. Perrot, *Les Anyi-Ndenye et le pouvoir aux 18ᵉ et 19ᵉ siècles* (Paris, 1982); E. Terray, 'Une Histoire du Royaume Abron du Gyaman: des origines à la conquête coloniale', Doctorat d'Etat thesis, 5 vols. (Paris, 1984); T.C. Weiskel, 'Asante and the Akan Periphery: The Baule on the Western Akan Frontier', in Schildkrout (ed.), *The Golden Stool*, 260–71; P. Valsecchi, 'Lo Nzema fra Egemonia Asante ed Espansione Europea nella prima metà del XIX secolo', *ARIIA*, 41, 4 (1986), 507–44, and *ibid.*, 'Il Sanwi e l'Impero Asante: dati e ipotesi per una storia della relazioni politiche', *ARIIA*, 44, 2 (1989), 175–210; A.B. Stahl, 'Ethnic Style and Ethnic Boundaries: A Diachronic Case Study from West-Central Ghana', *Ethnohistory*, 38, 3 (1991), 250–75.

74 T.C. McCaskie, 'Komfo Anokye of Asante: Meaning, History and Philosophy in an African Society', *JAH*, 27, 2 (1986), 315–39; *ibid.*, 'Death and the *Asantehene*: A Historical Meditation', *JAH*, 30, 3 (1989), 417–44; *ibid.*, '*Asantesɛm*'; *ibid.*, 'Armah's *The Healers*'; *ibid.*, 'Inventing Asante'; *ibid.*, 'Empire State'; *ibid.*, 'People and Animals: Constru(ct)ing the Asante Experience', *Africa*, 62, 2 (1992), 221–47; *ibid.*, '*Konnurokusɛm*: An Essay on Kinship and Family in the History of the *Oyoko Kɔkɔɔ* Dynasty of Kumase', *JAH*,

forthcoming.
75 For a radical statement see M. Bloch, 'What Goes without Saying: The Conceptualization of Zafimaniry Society', in A. Kuper (ed.), *Conceptualizing Society* (London, 1992), 127–46.
76 See for example Clifford, *The Predicament of Culture*; and, from different perspectives, H.A. Baker Jr, *Afro-American Poetics: Revisions of Harlem and The Black Aesthetic* (Madison, 1988) and E. Said, 'Intellectuals in the Post-Colonial World', *Salmagundi*, 70–1 (1986), 44–81.
77 How cognition produces representations (through language or otherwise) is the subject of lively debate. See W. Lycan (ed.), *Mind and Cognition* (Oxford, 1990) and L. Nadel, P. Cooper, P. Culicover and R. Harnish (eds.), *Neural Connections, Mental Computations* (Cambridge, 1989). An incisively sceptical treatment of the problem of disengaging from historical representations (Foucault, Derrida, Nancy, Lacoue-Labarthe *et al.*), and of 'thinking' them *de novo* is N. Fraser, *Unruly Practices: Power, Discourse and Gender in Contemporary Social Theory* (Cambridge, 1989).
78 For an extreme case of the uninhibited, multiple reading of representations see N. Parker, *Portrayals of Revolution: Images, Debates and Patterns of Thought on the French Revolution* (London, 1990).
79 See T.C. McCaskie, '"You Must Dis/Miss/Mis/Re/Member This": Kwame Tua in Time, and Other Passages from Asante History', paper given at the Red Lion Seminar (Program of African Studies, Northwestern University/University of Chicago), Chicago, 1992.
80 History is littered with examples. A topical instance is the hybrid ideological 'text' constructed by Saddam Husain in Iraq. Here, the marriage of Babylonian, Muslim (Shi'ite – the martyrdom of Husain at Kerbala in 680 AD – as well as Sunni), 'heroic' modernist (the 'Victory Arch') and post-modernist (Venturi, Rauch and Scott Brown's plans for the Baghdad State Mosque) representations invites to – in an uncertain political climate – contradictory appropriations, and points to unforeseen consequences. See S. al-Khalil, *The Monument: Art, Vulgarity and Responsibility in Iraq* (London, 1991). Post-modernism, of course, celebrates these very uncertainties; see – and directly relevant to the Iraq case – the seminal R. Venturi, D. Scott Brown and S. Izenour, *Learning from Las Vegas: The Forgotten Symbolism of Architectural Form*, revised edn (Cambridge, 1977).
81 For example McCaskie, 'Komfo Anokye'; *ibid.*, '*Asantesɛm*'; *ibid.*, 'People and Animals'.
82 Current work on this problem – embracing discussion of the meaning(s) of 'modernity' and of the 'Enlightenment' – embraces many disciplines and is contentious. For one strand, of relevance to Africa and Africanists, see J. Habermas, *Der philosophische Diskurs der Moderne: Zwölf Vorlesungen* (Frankfurt-am-Main, 1985); R. Rorty, *Philosophy and the Mirror of Nature* (Oxford, 1980); *ibid.*, 'Introduction: Antirepresentationalism, Ethnocentrism, and Liberalism' and 'Unfamiliar Noises: Hesse and Davidson on Metaphor', in *Objectivity, Relativism and Truth: Philosophical Papers Vol. 1* (Cambridge, 1991), 1–20 and 162–74; *ibid.*, 'Philosophy as Science, as Metaphor, and as Politics' and 'Habermas and Lyotard on Postmodernity', in *Essays on*

Heidegger and Others: Philosophical Papers Vol. 2 (Cambridge, 1991), 9–26 and 164–76. For context see 'Rorty's Liberal Utopia', in R.J. Bernstein, *The New Constellation: The Ethical-Political Horizons of Modernity/Postmodernity* (Oxford, 1991), 258–92 and – on the revived interest in relativism, and the problem of *tertium non datur* – J. Margolis, *The Truth About Relativism* (Oxford, 1991), and especially 198 ff.

83 Unless I seriously misread him, this is a recurrent theme in the novels of Chinua Achebe.

84 A useful discussion by a Ghanaian philosopher is K. Wiredu, *Philosophy and an African Culture* (Cambridge, 1980), and especially 1–62.

85 See P.J. Hountondji, *Sur la philosophie africaine* (Paris, 1976); *ibid.*, 'Que peut la philosophie?', *Présence Africaine*, 119 (1981), 47–71; Mudimbe, *The Invention of Africa*.

86 See for example P. Ricoeur, *Temps et récit: I* (Paris, 1983), *II. La Configuration dans le récit* (Paris, 1984), *III. Le Temps raconte* (Paris, 1986); H.-G. Gadamer, *Wahrheit und Methode*, 4th edn (Tübingen, 1975), and *Truth and Method*, trans. G. Burden and J. Cumming from the 2nd German edn (London, 1975); R. Rorty, *Consequences of Pragmatism: Essays 1972–80* (Minneapolis, 1982). See too H.-G. Gadamer and P. Ricoeur, 'The Conflict of Interpretations' (with a discussion) in R. Bruzina and B. Wilshire (eds.), *Phenomenology: Dialogues and Bridges* (Albany, 1982), 299–320. For context see conveniently S.H. Clark, *Paul Ricoeur* (London, 1990) and G. Warnke, *Gadamer: Hermeneutics, Tradition and Reason* (Oxford, 1987).

87 My argument here is parsimonious, deliberately restricted to the historical matters at hand, although I am well aware of the burgeoning literature that addresses the vexed issues of 'modernity' and the (unfinished?) 'project of the Enlightenment' in relation to the history of the Western tradition itself. Two dissenting critical insights that treat contemporary Western concerns – but from radically different starting points from those of Rorty *et al.* – are R. Bhaskar, *Philosophy and the Idea of Freedom* (Oxford, 1991) and C. Norris, *Uncritical Theory: Postmodernism, Intellectuals and the Gulf War* (London, 1992).

88 Compare for example Bowdich, *Mission*, 274 ff. and Rattray, *Religion and Art*, 122 ff.

2 STATE AND SOCIETY IN ASANTE HISTORY

1 Authoritative Asante traditions are recounted in HA, and in MRO, Kumase, MS, 'The History of Ashanti Kings and the Whole Country Itself, Written by me, F.A. Prempeh, and was Dictated by E. Prempeh. Commence [*sic*] on 6th August 1907' (Prempe I) (henceforth AK). Compare the preliminary remarks on origins in many of the Asante stool histories collected in the series IAS/AS (Legon); and T.C. McCaskie, Discussions with the *Akyempemhene ɔheneba* Boakye Dankwa and Elders of the Akyempem Stool, dd. Kumase, December 1975–January 1976.

2 A recent, illuminating sketch of the argument is I. Wilks, 'Portuguese, Wangara and Akan in the Fifteenth and Sixteenth Centuries: The Matter of

Bitu' and 'The Struggle for Trade', *JAH*, 23 (1982), 333–49 and 463–72. For background see T.F. Garrard, *Akan Weights and the Gold Trade* (London, 1980).

3 See Wilks, 'Land, Labour, Capital' and McCaskie, 'Accumulation, Wealth and Belief . . . I'. See the seminal article by M. Douglas, 'Is Matriliny Doomed in Africa?', in M. Douglas and P.M. Kaberry (eds.), *Man in Africa* (London, 1969), 121–35 for an insightful perspective on kinship organization. Pioneering historical work is to be found in R.A. Kea, 'Trade, State Formation, and Warfare on the Gold Coast 1600–1826', Ph.D. (London, 1974), and an interesting reading is in R. Porter, 'European Activity on the Gold Coast, 1620–1667', D.Litt. (University of South Africa, 1975). A useful if general survey is G. Connah, *African Civilizations. Precolonial Cities and States in Tropical Africa: An Archaeological Perspective* (Cambridge, 1987).

4 For some illustration see the oral histories of Mpatuom, Denyase, Dadease, Adankrangya, Amoafo, Abodom, Asekyere, Wirempe-Mim, Atweri and Manso-Abodom in ASC, Cambridge, Fortes Papers, File 4, 'History Notes of Certain Towns in the Bekwai District – Ashanti', n.d. See too OMP, Kumase, 'The Chief and Chiefship in Ashanti', a memorandum prepared for the Ashanti Confederacy Council, dd. Kumase, 14 February 1941. Additionally, see *ibid.*, 'A Notebook on Office Holding', prepared for (and by?) the *Asantehene* Agyeman Prempe, dd. Kumase, 1927.

5 The fullest traditional account is in HA. See too the versions in Reindorf, *History*, 43 ff. and Sir Francis Fuller, *A Vanished Dynasty: Ashanti* (London, 1921), 8 ff. A detailed but undated and anonymous account of the battle of Feyiase (1701) is in LO, Kumase, 'Feyase Battle'. A (non-holograph) copy of parts of this is in GPRL, Accra, 'Papers on the History of the Gold Coast', assembled for (and by?) W.E.B. Du Bois. See too MRO, Kumase, 'A History of the Immigrants from Takyiman', MS (anon.), n.d., 61 ff.

6 For the crisis in the profitability of warfare in the first decades of the nineteenth century see the remarks on the *Nsutahene* Yaw Sekyere in McCaskie, 'Paramountcy', 40 ff. For a summary of the nineteenth-century northern trade see I. Wilks, 'Asante Policy towards the Hausa Trade in the 19th Century', in C. Meillassoux (ed.), *The Development of Indigenous Trade and Markets in West Africa* (London, 1971), 124–41 and K. Arhin, *West African Traders in Ghana in the Nineteenth and Twentieth Centuries* (London, 1979).

7 See G. Austin, 'Rural Capitalism' for Adanse and Amansie; ASSM, 'Mponua' and 'Towns and Markets in Asante Akyem' for the areas around Lake Bosomtwe and eastern Asante. There are recoverable – but unworked – data on late nineteenth-century Asante Akyem in BMA, Basel.

8 Bowdich, *Mission*, 325.

9 For example LO, Kumase, 'Farming Records, 1937–1940, District of Manso Nkwanta', and KTC, Kumase, 'The Hiring of Wage Labourers in Agriculture', n.d., but 1950s. See too, for comparison, NAG, Koforidua, A/114, 'Moshi and Grunshi Labourers in New Juaben', 1945–61.

10 On the typology of yams and on cocoyam see Perregaux, 'Chez les Achanti', 27 ff. See too J.G. Christaller, *A Dictionary of the Asante and Fante Language, Called Tschi* (Basel, 1881), entry for, *ɔde*, 69. For context see F.R. Irvine, *West*

African Crops (Oxford, 1969). For the increasing importance of cassava in this century see T.C. McCaskie, Interviews: A.K. (Osei) Nana Boateng, 'Chief Farmer', *et al.*, dd. Adwira Market, April 1988.

11 *Zea mays*, however, has made something of a comeback in Asante in recent years.

12 See A.B. Quarcoo, 'Cocoyam Cultivation in Asante: History and Prospects', B.A. dissertation (Institute of Administration, Greenhill, 1968). See too, for discussion of the perceived value of cocoyam, MRO, Kumase, 'Precis of Cases from the "A" and "B" Courts', 1945–52, Yaa Nkyiraa *versus* S.O. Oben and others, commenced 19 July 1950 (original not recovered). Revealingly, some Asante villagers persist in the idea that cocoyam is or can be potentially poisonous.

13 See T.C. McCaskie, Interviews: Nana Opoku, dd. Mampon, April 1988. It is interesting to note that M. Fortes, in the diary he kept of his tour around Lake Bosomtwe in the 1940s, as opposed to his fieldnotes, persistently referred to cassava as a 'hunger crop'. Certainly, Asante informants (and not least children) regard cassava as an 'undesirable' substitute for 'real' food; on priorities and market preferences see T.C. McCaskie, Interviews: Madame 'Kolo' and other foodstuff vendors, dd. Kejetia Market, Kumase, November–December 1990. See further E.V. Doku, *Cassava in Ghana* (Accra, 1969).

14 Freeman, 'Life and Travels' and *The Western Echo, Supplement*, 6 March 1886.

15 This is the case even now. See T.C. McCaskie, Conversations with the *Asantehene's* Protocol Secretary, dd. Kumase, 1990. See too NAG, Sunyani, C.1171, 'Livestock in Ashanti and among the Brong' by T. Fell, dd. Goaso, 1912. On the Asante calendar see T.C. McCaskie, 'Time and the Calendar in Nineteenth Century Asante: An Exploratory Essay', *HA*, 7 (1980), 179–200.

16 See GPRL, Accra, J.R. Wallis, 'The Kwahu Afram Plain or the Ancient Kingdom of Ataara Finam', n.d., but *c.* 1955; for elephant hunting in the 1840s see Chapman's 'Journal', entries dd. Fomena, 21 November 1844 and Ansa, 22 November 1844; for the hunting of game in northwest Asante in the 1920s see A.W. Cardinall, *In Ashanti and Beyond* (London and Philadelphia, 1927); some of Cardinall's unpublished 'Notes and Yarns on Hunting' are in Balme Library, Legon, Pamphlet and MS Box no. 112 (adjunct to the Furley MSS).

17 Freeman, 'Life and Travels', 117–18.

18 Cardinall, *In Ashanti*, 78–80.

19 See Bowdich, *Mission*, XI encl. H. Tedlie, '*Materia Medica* and Diseases', 370 ff.

20 MFU, 'Discussions with Persons in Konongo and Obo', 1946, records, in the words of the (then) old woman Abena Mfiri, a harrowing account of 'bush-living' and of survival by eating roots and insects in the (erstwhile) Kokofu villages south of Lake Bosomtwe in about 1887–8.

21 For a general picture see Wills (ed.), *Agriculture and Land Use*.

22 See T.C. McCaskie, Interviews: J.K. Agyeman, Agricultural Officer, dd. Kaase, April 1988. For context see Wilks, 'Land, Labour, Capital', especially 490 ff.

23 See M. Johnson, 'The Population of Asante, 1817–1921: A Reconsideration' and I. Wilks, 'The Population of Asante, 1817–1921: A Rejoinder', *Asantesɛm*,

13 (1978), 22–8 and 28–35.

24 This figure is Wilks' informed 'guesstimate'. My own 'guesstimate' would be that critical mass was only reached in terms of population – and only in certain areas immediately to the south of Kumase – in the 1940s. See NAG, Kumase, Files A.110, etc. on 'Production of Food and the War Effort', dd. Kumase, 1943 and 1944.

25 See MFU, 'Files on the Histories of Kuntanase, Kaase, Deduako et al.', 1946. The relative undercultivation of the Mponua area was reported, incidentally, in the 1920s–30s by geological surveyors and colonial road makers. See Geological Survey, Accra, Annual Reports on Eastern and Southern Ashanti, 1923–31.

26 For a summary see T.F. Chipp, The Forest Officers' Handbook of the Gold Coast, Ashanti and the Northern Territories (London, 1922); NAG, Sunyani, unaccessioned, 'The Forest Resources of Goaso-Mim', (?) 1920s; and, for some overview, see G. Mikell, 'Cocoa and Social Change in Ghana: A Study of Development in the Sunyani District', Ph.D. (Columbia, 1975).

27 Ghana: Policies and Program for Adjustment: A World Bank Country Study, The World Bank (Washington, 1984), 27 and 29.

28 ASC, Cambridge, Fortes Papers, 'Land Tenure: Talk with Goasohene', n.d. but 1946.

29 See MRO, Kumase, Notes by [E.E. Kurankyi-] Taylor (?) on Manwerehene Kwasi Brantuo IV versus A.P. Onim and Yaw Nkyem, dd. Kumase, 17 August 1949; see too LO, Kumase, Files and Correspondence on Usufruct and Land Alienation in Kwabre, 1935–50.

30 See MRO, Kumase, Papers of A.A.Y. Kyerematen, 'Notes on Ashanti Landholding'. See too the fascinating (but unpublished) essay compiled by Boakye Dankwa – when Atipinhene – on 'Land and Farming in Ashanti', Akyempem Stool Papers.

31 See – and indicatively – the lack of any detailed discussion of Asante material in J. Iliffe, The African Poor: A History (Cambridge, 1987). The most immiserated case known to me (but striking because of its exceptional nature) is in MRO, Kumase, 'Plea Book', dd. 1934, in re Amma Mmurossa versus Amma Akwaa, where plaintiff and defendant argued over the possession of 'country cloths' going back to the mid-nineteenth century. In the course of this case (at pp. 19–20) Amma Mmurossa stated that 'King Agyeman [i.e. the Asantehene Kwaku Dua Panin, 1834–67] felt us so much [sic] that he prepared food for us every day through the cook [soodoni] Kwaakye Nto'; otherwise, she stated, 'we would have starved and perished of hunger'. The tone of this, and similar statements, is such as to suggest their highly unusual – indeed aberrant – nature.

32 Bowdich, Mission, 31.

33 Ibid., 325.

34 Dupuis, Journal, 63.

35 Ibid., 65.

36 Hutton, Voyage, 198 ff.

37 Freeman, 'Life and Travels', 82.

38 Travel accounts on the area south of Kumase are critically summarized in G.

Austin, 'Rural Capitalism', 76–222.

39 WMMS, Hillard to General Secretaries, dd. Kumase, 29 May 1848.

40 *Ibid.*, West to General Secretaries, dd. Cape Coast, 9 June 1862.

41 See McCaskie, 'Paramountcy', 177 and Wilks, *Asante*, 93 ff.

42 Artefacts for the royal court were also produced in a number of the villages around Kumase; in Kurofrom (brassware); Tafo and Pankrono (pottery); Ahwiaa (wood carving); Fumesua, Bampanase and Wawase (blacksmithing); Mamponten, Gyamfi Wono, Tano Odumase, Aboaso, Kona and Ntonso (*adinkra* and *kuntunkuni* cloth); Saakora Wono, Adadwumaase and Besease (*kente* cloth); Kantinkrono (goldwork); Wawase (shields, palanquins); Adwumakaase Kɛsɛɛ (drums); and Dabaa (beads). See M. Johnson, Fieldnotes, July/August 1975, 'Craft Villages around Kumase'.

43 Bowdich, *Mission*, 323–4; see further, T.E. Bowdich, *An Essay on the Superstitions, Customs, and Arts, common to the Ancient Egyptians, Abyssinians, and Ashantees* (Paris, 1821), 55.

44 Freeman, 'Life and Travels' and *The Western Echo, Supplement*, 10 February 1886.

45 *Ibid.* See further T.C. McCaskie, Interviews: *Sodohene* Kwasi Anane, dd. Kumase, December 1975. Kwasi Anane's father was Kokua Nyame, who worked in provisioning Kumase *ahenfie* in the late nineteenth century.

46 ARA, The Hague, Archief van het Ministerie van Kolonien 1814–49, no. 3965: Elmina Journal, appendix: 'Journaal van den Fabriek en Magazijn Meester J. Simons gehouden op deszelfs Missie naar den Konig van Assiantijn te Koemasie', entries, for example, dd. Kumase, 13–15, 17–21 and 23 February 1832. I am most grateful to Larry Yarak for providing me with a copy of his draft English translation of this source.

47 NAG, Accra, ADM 1/2/4, Winniet's 'Journal', entry dd. Kumase, 15 October 1848.

48 T.C. McCaskie, Interviews: ɔkyeame Boakye Tenten (Kofi Apea Agyei), dd. Kumase, 3 and 4 January 1976. For the dread reputation of Kumase among non-Asante – as the seat of the *Asantehene* – see, for example, *Der Evangelische Heidenbote* (Basel, April 1882), 4, 26, citing a report from Mohr on a mission to Asante in 1881, and BMA, Basel, D/20, 4, 5. N.V. Asare, *Asante Abasem (Twi Kasamu)*. For the 'purchase' of the site of Kumase by the *Oyoko Kɔkɔɔ* see, HA, 'Oti Akenten: 1631–1662'.

49 J. Gros, *Voyages, aventures et captivité de J. Bonnat chez les Achantis* (Paris, 1884), 194–5. See further NAG, Kumase, Item 2912, Native Customary Law, 'Definition of Ahinkwa, 1925' and the judgement in MRO, Kumase, Palaver File 1948–9, Yaw Assuoman (*afenasoani*) *versus* Opanin Yaw Berkye (*afenasoani*), dd. Kumase, 1 February 1949. See too the remarks (1930) on *nhenkwaa* by the Kumase *Domakwaehene/Akyeamehene* Kwasi Apea Nuama in E.E. Kurankyi-Taylor, 'Ashanti Indigenous Legal Institutions and their Present Role', Ph.D., 2 vols. (Cambridge, 1951), II, 490, and those of the Kumase *Bantamahene/Krontihene* Kwame Kyem in NAG, Kumase, File 216/5, Correspondence on 'Slavery', 1910s–20s, encl. in 'Tribal Histories' series. (I am most grateful to W. Tordoff for allowing me access to his extensive notes, taken in the 1950s, on a number of the Files that are presently recorded as being in NAG, Kumase, but

that I have been unable to locate.) For a popular, folk Asante view of the character of royal *nhenkwaa* see Asare, *Asante Abasem.*

50 See Bowdich, *Mission*, 324 for the 'about sixty stalls or sheds' in the main Kumase market and 330 ff. for the luxury and other trades. No first-hand account known to me suggests that the population of Kumase could have been provisioned by the foodstuffs available for sale in *dwaberem.*

51 Freeman, 'Life and Travels' and *The Western Echo, Supplement*, 24 February 1886.

52 Gros, *Voyages*, 195.

53 See MRO, Kumase, Kumasihene's Tribunal, CRB 17, November 1932 to March 1933, Kofi Manu and others *versus* Yaw Britwum, commenced 3 December 1932.

54 Chapman, 'Journal', entry dd. Kumase, 13 March 1845. At the same place Chapman recorded a similar such case. A person was 'detected' in the practice of illicitly 'in the King's name (i.e. acting as an *ahenkwaa*) ... levying a contribution in Gold' from villagers 'at a distance from Kumasi.' This offender was arrested, publicly humiliated, and detained at the pleasure of the *Asantehene* Kwaku Dua Panin.

55 For general historical description see Wilks, 'Land, Labour, Capital', 490 ff. There is detailed, illuminating material in ASSM, 7: Kasei: Farm Survey; 24: Land Tenure; 32: Agriculture; 42: Dept. of Agriculture (Correspondence). My own understanding of the agricultural (foodstuff) cycle, and the techniques deployed in the precolonial period, benefited greatly from conversations in the 1970s/1980s with farmers in Afrantwo, Daaso, Tepa, Suponso, Nyameani and Kuntanase; I am most grateful to the late Anthony Doku for his patience and expertise in explaining matters to a non-farmer. The context of 'rural' agricultural life – i.e. not in the immediate environs of Kumase – is richly caught, for the very early colonial period, in Kyei, *My Memoir*, I. The best general analysis of Asante agriculture in its West African regional context is K. Hart, *The Political Economy of West African Agriculture* (Cambridge, 1982).

56 See T.C. McCaskie, 'The History of the Manwere *nkoa* at Drobonso', *Asante Seminar*, 6 (December 1976), 33–8; *ibid.*, 'Office, Land and Subjects in the History of the Manwere *Fekuo* of Kumase: An Essay in the Political Economy of the Asante State', *JAH*, 21, 2 (1980), 189–208; *ibid.*, 'State and Society, Marriage and Adultery: Some Considerations towards a Social History of Precolonial Asante', *JAH*, 22, 4 (1981), 477–94; *ibid.*, 'Accumulation, Wealth and Belief ... I' and 'Accumulation, Wealth and Belief in Asante History. II. The twentieth century', *Africa*, 56, 1 (1986), 3–23; *ibid.*, 'Politics in 19th Century Asante', paper presented at the Conference on the City of Kumase, Kumase, Ghana, December 1990; I. Wilks, 'The Golden Stool and the Elephant Tail: An Essay on Wealth in Asante', in G. Dalton (ed.), *Research in Economic Anthropology*, II (Greenwich, 1979), 1–36; K. Arhin, 'Some Asante Views on Colonial Rule: As Seen in the Controversy Relating to Death Duties', *THSG*, 15, 1 (1974), 63–84; *ibid.*, 'Rank and Class'; *ibid.*, 'Trade, Accumulation and the State'; and, for an interesting recent intervention, G. Austin, 'Kinship, Coercion and the Market: Human Pawning in Asante', paper presented at the Annual Meeting of the ASAUSA, Seattle, 1992. An

interesting and unusual treatment is M. Nyaggah, 'Social Origins of the Asante Traditional Administrators: 1700–1900', Ph.D. (Berkeley, 1974).

57 There is, as yet, no detailed treatment of the Asante export trade in gold in the nineteenth century. However, all sources suggest that gold was endemically in short supply in nineteenth-century Asante. State laws against the retention of rock gold – as for example in the well-documented case, in the early 1860s, of the Manso Nkwanta *sikani* Kwasi Gyani – may have been prompted by strictly economic considerations as well as by socio-legal or sumptuary norms.

58 See McLeod, *The Asante*, 87 ff. See too C. Fox, *Asante Brass Casting: Lost-Wax Casting of Gold-Weights, Ritual Vessels and Sculptures, with Handmade Equipment* (Cambridge, 1988).

59 See for example OMP, Kumase, 'Notes of the Working Party on Contributions to the War Effort', 1940–2; RH, Oxford, CRP, MSS Brit. Emp. s.344, Papers of Sir Charles Henry Harper, 'The Effects of British Rule in Asante', Memorandum, dd. 1922; TOR, Notes and MSS, File on 'Money and Politics'; H.J. Bevin, MSS, 'The Economy of Ashanti in the Early Colonial Period', unpublished draft, (?) *c.* 1963; excellent on background is K. Arhin, 'The Pressure of Cash and Its Political Consequences in Asante in the Colonial Period', *Journal of African Studies*, 3, 4 (Winter 1976–7), 453–68.

60 Bowdich, *Mission*, 257 and Hutton, *Voyage*, 318.

61 RAI, Rattray MSS, 203, GC no. 314, dd. 24 June 1908, encl. C.H. Armitage, 'Native Laws and Customs [in] Ashanti', 27 May 1908. See too RCS, London, Gold Coast, Box 2, Fuller to Secretary for Native Affairs, dd. Kumase, 1 July 1907.

62 See Gold Coast Colony, 1945: *Report of the Commission of Inquiry (C.R. Havers, Q.C.) into Expenses incurred by Litigants in the Courts of the Gold Coast and Indebtedness caused thereby*, 25.

63 *Ibid.* See too Gold Coast and Ashanti, Loans Recovery Ordinance (cap. 146), 1918 and Moneylenders Ordinance (cap. 779), 1940.

64 GCC, 1945: *Inquiry (Havers)*, 25 ff. Compare H.C. Belfield, *Report on the Legislation Governing the Alienation of Native Lands in the Gold Coast Colony and Ashanti: with some Observations on the 'Forest Ordinance', 1911* (London, 1912) and LO, Kumase, Files on 'Individual' and 'Stool' Debt. For an instance of an individual trapped in escalating debt, and unable to escape, see MRO, Kumase, 'Letter Book on the Affairs of Donyina', M.O. Bonsu *versus Donyinahene*, dd. Donyina and Kumase, 1934–5.

65 This is a famous – and widely recounted – case. See HA for the authoritative traditional account. See too, from an immense volume of documentation, RAI, Rattray MSS, 'Enquiry into the Adonten Stool, conducted by C. Furness-Smith, Ag. Crown Counsel', dd. Kumase, 24 March 1925 (there are copies of this in MRO, Kumase; ASC, Cambridge, Fortes MSS; and TOR, Notes and MSS); MRO, Kumase, *Proceedings of the Meeting of the Committee of Privileges held at Kumasi at (from) 10 a.m. on Tuesday the 18th June 1935*, 68 ff.; *ibid.*, Civil Enquiry on Disputes, 4 April 1935 to 22 February 1939, *obaapanin* Akua Kwaadu and J.P.K. Appiah *versus* E.O. Asafu Adjaye, commenced 9 May 1938 (and ancillary correspondence); *ibid.*, Record Files of the Kumase Traditional Council, Agyeman Badu *versus*

Kwaku Mensah, commenced 16 November 1964 (a transcript of the hearing – but without the accompanying correspondence – was reproduced as IAS/AS/CR 41); MFU, 'Notabilities and Personalities: J.K. Frimpon, the Asafo Agyeis, and the Adonten Stool', dd. Kumase, 1946; *ibid.*, 'Some Conversations with and Observations on "George", Kumase *Adontenhene*', dd. New Town, Kumase, January 1946. See further the highly circumspect account given by the Kumase *Adontenhene* Kofi Adonten in IAS/AS 95: Adonten Stool History, recorded by J. Agyeman-Duah, 17 July 1963. For a summary reconstruction see ACBP/52: Kwaaten Pɛtɛ, *Asantesɛm*, 10 (1979), 31–6. I am grateful to the *wirempofoɔ* of *Adonten* for various conversations (1970s–80s) and to J. Rice for transcripts of court cases relevant to the broader history of the Kumase *Adonten fekuo*.

66 MFU, 'Discussions with Individuals at Obogu', 1946 and *ibid.* J.C. Frimpong to M. Fortes, dd. English Church Mission, Bekwai, 20 January 1946.

67 GCC, 1945: *Inquiry (Havers)*, 25 ff. Customary practice was compounded and disfigured – in its monetary effects – by the need to meet legal fees in the cash economy of the British colonial dispensation. See Arhin, 'The Pressure of Cash'. An Amendment (1906) to the Asante Administrative Ordinance (1901) excluded lawyers from practising in Asante (although Asante clients had open access to the legal and appellate court machinery of the Gold Coast Colony), but this ban was reviewed in the early 1920s and thereafter revoked; see RH, Oxford, CRP, MSS Brit. Emp. s.344, Papers of Sir Charles Henry Harper, 'Lawyers in Asante: A Memorandum', n.d. (but 1922). As is well known, in this century the resort to (traditionally) high-interest loans – commonly secured against land – to underwrite repeated litigation trapped many Asante stools in debt and impoverishment. Thus, GCC, 1945: *Inquiry (Havers)*, 32 cites the case of *Donyinahene versus Nyameanihene* ('settled' by British arbitration in 1907, but systematically litigated thereafter, and appealed all the way up to the Privy Council in 1935, where judgement was finally given in favour of Donyina). But by 1935 the Donyina stool had incurred legal costs from this case alone of £1,700. Land had been pledged to secure a loan for this amount, 'upon which interest was charged', so Havers noted, 'at 50%. Part of the debt has not yet [1945] been repaid'. For pertinent discussion of this very case – in relation to 'exorbitant' interest rates, 'sometimes being as high as 100%' – see A.A.Y. Kyerematen, *Inter-State Boundary Litigation in Ashanti* (Cambridge and Leiden, n.d.), 67. Kyerematen notes some of the 'knock-on' consequences for stools enmeshed in such debts: 'Stool lands or other property mortgaged in security of the loans might be sold by the money-lender. Action might be taken in court by the money-lender for the redemption of the loan, thus involving the chiefdom in further litigation and further expense.' Of course, Donyina and Nyameani were both concurrently involved in much other litigation; see for example MRO, Kumase, CRB 14, 28 December 1931 to 25 April 1932, Kwame Fosu of Hamabenase *versus* Osei Kwame of Donyina, commenced 29 February 1932 (and see evidence of *Donyinahene* Yaw Nimo on 13 October 1932); *ibid.*, CRB 3, 24 October 1927 to 22 June 1928, *Kwasohene* Kwadwo Nketia *versus Nyameanihene* Kwabena Dumfe, commenced 14

June 1928. An indication of the sheer longevity of outstanding stool debts is given in *ibid.*, File 183/35: Dadease Native Affairs, 17 October 1950 to 18 August 1954. Evidence of the penalties incurred by individuals standing guarantee for stool loans is to be found in MLC, Minutes of the Mampon Literary Club (*kontonkyi*), dd. Mampon, 1941–4. The lives of some of the most prominent moneylenders of colonial Asante are well documented – e.g. Kwame Kyem, 'Papa' Sraha, Amankwaa Tia, John Kwame Frimpon, and various citizens of Saawua – but their financial affairs have yet to be investigated in detail.

68 For some discussion see Rattray, *Ashanti Law and Constitution*, 285 ff.

69 The jural formula of *atitɔdeɛ* was that the *Asantehene* sent an ɔkyeame to announce to the miscreant, *mɛ dɛ wo tiri kyɛ wo* ('I make you a present of your head'); the offender then agreed to pay over whatever had been set as *atitɔdeɛ*, and supplied a sacrificial sheep to purify the *sika dwa kofi*. For the introduction of *atitɔdeɛ* by the *Asantehene* Kusi Obodom see the oral testimony recorded in Kurankyi-Taylor, 'Legal Institutions', I, 28–9. A more circumspect account is in HA, where Kusi Obodom is credited with commuting the death penalty – albeit only temporarily – on demographic grounds (the payment of a sheep is mentioned). Oral traditions current in the nineteenth century led Reindorf, *History*, 137, to characterize Kusi Obodom as 'the most humane' of all Asante rulers, and – most suggestively – to assert that he 'forbade the human sacrifices'.

70 Kurankyi-Taylor, 'Legal Institutions', I, 29. For the illustrative case of the Domaase *odekuro* Yaw Nti 'buying his head' from the financially embarrassed Kofi Kakari, after arraignment for the capital offence of impugning the royal ancestry, see MRO, Kumase, 'Papers on the Kumase Akyempem', Domaase *odekuro* Yaw Bese *versus* Abena Kyi, Kwame Donkoh, and others, commenced 22 August 1932.

71 The *Asantehene* Kwaku Dua Panin is credited with extensive use of this mechanism.

72 Kurankyi-Taylor, 'Legal Institutions', I, 114. Compare Rattray, *Ashanti Law and Constitution*, 111, and the general remarks on 'Penalties' in RAI, Rattray MSS, 203, GC no. 314, dd. 24 June 1908, encl. C.H. Armitage, 'Native Laws and Customs [in] Ashanti', 27 May 1908.

73 This essentializing tendency is evident in both Rattray and Fortes, and most especially so in work that built upon their findings. See K.A. Busia, *The Position of the Chief in the Modern Political System of Ashanti: A Study of the Influence of Contemporary Social Changes on Ashanti Political Institutions* (London, 1951); for Busia's debt to Rattray and Fortes see *ibid.*, x and xii.

74 For *abirɛmpɔn* among the Akan, prior to the emergence of the Asante state, see R.A. Kea, *Settlements, Trade, and Politics in the Seventeenth-Century Gold Coast* (Baltimore, 1982), 98 ff.; A. Jones, *German Sources for West African History 1599–1669* (Wiesbaden, 1983), 298 (citing W.J. Müller's Fetu wordlist from the 1660s). For discussion in the Asante context see McCaskie, 'Accumulation, Wealth and Belief ... I', 27 ff. and Wilks, 'The Golden Stool and the Elephant Tail', 12 ff.

75 On military reorganization and the elevation of deserving persons by the *Asantehene* Osei Tutu see HA; on incorporation see HA, and especially

traditions concerning Osei Tutu's subjugation of Tafo, Kaase, Amakom and Wonoo, and on the creation of Asankare; compare IAS/AS unclassified: 'The History of the Baworo Stool and the Baworo People', recorded by J. Agyeman-Duah, 24 April 1975, 6, for a representative case from this early period. For the *Asantehene* Osei Agyeman Prempeh II's thoughts on *abirɛmpɔn* see MRO, Kumase, *Proceedings of the Meeting of the Committee of Privileges ... 1935*, 48.

76 RAI, Rattray MSS, 'Enquiry into the Adonten Stool', evidence of Kumase *Akyeamehene/Domakwaehene* Kwasi Apea Nuama. Wilks, 'The Golden Stool and the Elephant Tail', 13 (citing a copy of the 'Enquiry' deposited in NAG, Accra, ADM 11/1338), justly observes that Kwasi Apea Nuama's statement 'is the only account of the full admission procedures [to *ɔbirɛmpɔn* status] known to be extant'. A different but shorter variant (derived from Kwasi Apea Nuama?) is in MFU, 'Notes and Documents by and on R.S. Rattray'.

77 On *sasa* in trees see Rattray, *Religion and Art*, 185–6. Kyei, *My Memoir*, I, 53 ff. gives an excellent account, based on the writer's childhood memories, of the various uses and meanings of trees, including *sasa*. For the most exalted ritual use of the *nsa* see Komfo Anokye's instructions that the *sika dwa kofi* should never rest on the ground, but always on *nsa* or *banwoma* (skin cut from an elephant's ear or back) in HA.

78 *Ibid.* Tafo is now within Kumase; see conveniently Arhin and Afari-Gyan (eds.), *City of Kumasi Handbook*. For the seizure of Tafo lands around Kumase by the *Asantehene* see Lewin, 'The Structure of Political Conflict', II, 287–8; see too MRO, Kumase, CRB, Divisional Court 'B', no. 30, *Apagyahene* Owusu Afriyie *versus Tafohene* Yaw Dabanka, commenced 9 March 1944.

79 Rattray, *Ashanti*, 121. See the authoritative account of the significance of Asantemanso in 'The Seven Families and the Place of Assumya Ashantimansu', in AK; see too Asare, *Asante Abasem*. On Asumegya see Rattray, *Ashanti Law and Constitution*, 131–47 and B.A. Firempong (ed.), *Asumagya-Asantemanso Mpaninsɛm* (Legon, 1976).

80 Simons, 'Journaal', entry for 9 February 1832; Rattray, *Ashanti*, 121–2.

81 J.G. Christaller, *Twi Mmebusɛm; mpensā-ahansīa mmoaano. A Collection of Three Thousand and Six Hundred Tshi Proverbs* (Basel, 1879), 19; Rattray, *Ashanti Proverbs*, 60. Compare for example, *ɛsono akyii aboa ne bɔmmɔfo* ('After the elephant is a [yet greater] animal, the hunter'); and, *nea ɛsono wu n'afikyiri no, ɛhɔ ahabaŋ nhina sae* ('Where an elephant died, all the leaves in his backyard were spoiled'), which at p. 58, is suggestively glossed by Rattray as meaning that the 'leaves' were flattened 'by people coming to cut up the meat'. By the mid-nineteenth century elephants were relatively rare in the Asante heartland; but for an account of the killing and consumption of two of them at Ansa and Praso (respectively 48 and 62 miles south of Kumase), see Chapman, 'Journal', entries dd. Ansa and Praso, 21, 22 and 23 November 1844. For the survival into this century of the *nnaŋso* (a hunting camp with sleeping huts) for elephant tracking in Agogo and Asante Akyem (in eastern Asante) see MFU, 'Miscellaneous Papers on Agogo'; for the 'last recorded account of elephant on the Kwahu portion of the Afram Plain' in August 1941 see GPRL, Accra, J.R. Wallis, 'The Kwahu Afram Plain ...', 4. For the elephant in the context of *sasa*

see McCaskie, 'People and Animals', 231 ff.

82 See Wilks, 'The Golden Stool and the Elephant Tail', 51. For a crucial instance of the 'capture' of an elephant's *mena/mmra* – by the *Asantehene*-to-be Osei Tutu on his journey home from Akwamu to Kumase – see HA and Asare, *Asante Abasem.*

83 McCaskie, 'Accumulation, Wealth and Belief ... I', especially 31. It is very difficult to elicit oral data in direct confirmation of this association. The Asante are fastidious, and *ɛsono* is a much diminished physical and cognitive presence in twentieth-century Asante. I remain grateful to those who have discussed this matter with me – including those whose denials of any such association were voiced with a vehemence that was itself suggestive. Much work remains to be done on the range of Asante attitudes towards substance shifting – dryness, wetness, viscosity, fluidity, solidity, *et al.* – for the evidence implies that the Asante were (and are) concerned with the nature of all such transformations and with the cognate question of defining boundaries. Thus, for example, both Fortes (1940s) and myself (1980s), in confidential conversations relating to (male) sexuality, detected a range of concepts and attitudes that had much to do, generally speaking, with boundaries and substance shifting. Of course, all this is very far from being culturally specific to the Asante, but – as is the case elsewhere – understanding is difficult to achieve (and properly so) in any direct or interrogative way. I take the opportunity here to set down my gratitude to all those Asante who have enlarged my comprehension over many years in adventitious or contingent exchanges; incremental gleanings of this sort, of course, are not produced by formal fieldwork, but their insightful value is inestimable.

84 Wealth – in money or goods – is volatile in extremely complex and diverse ways. For an anthropological perspective see J. Parry and M. Bloch (eds.), *Money and the Morality of Exchange* (Cambridge, 1989). A powerfully argued sociological analysis, dealing with the work of Simmel and others, is N.B. Dodd, 'Money in Social Theory', Ph.D. (Cambridge, 1992).

85 WMMS, W. West to General Secretaries, dd. Cape Coast, 9 June 1862 (with an account of his residence in Kumase, 17 March to 22 April 1862).

86 *Ibid.*

87 See MRO, Kumase, Kumasihene's Tribunal, CRB 6, 22 January to 8 May 1929, and 7, 8 May to 13 September 1929, *odekuro* Kwaku Addai of Atasumansu *versus odekuro* Kofi Aidoo of Adeambra, commenced 13 February 1929. For context see ACBP/51: Kwasi Brantuo, *Asantesɛm*, 7 (1977), 14–17 and McCaskie, 'Office, Land and Subjects', especially 198–9. For the chronology, which corrects that offered in *ibid.*, 198, see Chapman, 'Journal', entry dd. Kumase, 15 July 1844.

88 T.C. McCaskie, Interviews: *Manwerehene* Nana Kwabena Boaten and *Asabihene* Asabi Boakye II, dd. Kumase, December 1975–January 1976; *ibid.*: Anthony Kwadwo, dd. Manhyia Akuropon and Kumase, January 1976 and March–April 1983; MRO, Kumase, Kumase Village Affairs: Letters on the Affairs of Adiebeba, *Manwerehene* Kwasi Brantuo IV to *Asantehene* Osei Agyeman Prempeh II, dd. Kumase, 19 February 1951.

89 MRO, Kumase, Kumasihene's Tribunal, CRB 10, 5 June to 1 October 1930,

Ankobeahene Kwame Kusi *versus* Komfo Akwasi Kobi, commenced 23 June 1930; *ibid.*, Kwaku Addai *versus* Kofi Aidoo, evidence of the Kumase *Akwamuhene/Asafohene* Kwame Akwawua, 13 May 1929; *ibid.*, Akwamu Tribunal, File 12, *odekuro* Kwame Tawia of Aboabo *versus* Yaw Tia, commenced 25 June 1938.

90 WMMS, W. West to General Secretaries, dd. Cape Coast, 9 June 1862 (with an account of his residence in Kumase, 17 March to 22 April 1862).

91 Hutchison's Diary, dd. Kumase, 14 November 1817, in Bowdich, *Mission*, 395; see further *ibid.*, 396.

92 MRO, Kumase, Gyase Clan Affairs, 163/35: File 48/1, 16 March 1935 to 22 January 1944, *Gyaasewa Mmammahene* Joseph Kwesi Edubofuor *versus* Charles E. Osei, commenced 21 December 1939 (a transcript of this same case, drawn from elsewhere in MRO, Kumase, was kindly supplied to me by Ivor Wilks; there is no significant difference between the copies). See too *ibid.*, HA, and *ibid.*, Native Tribunal, CRB 17, 21 November 1932 to 8 March 1933, *Pinanko obaapanin* Akua Afriyie *versus Gyaasewahene* Kwadwo Poku, commenced 6 February 1933. In *ibid.*, Kwaku Addai *versus* Kofi Aidoo, evidence of the Kumase *Akwamuhene/Asafohene* Kwame Akwawua, 13 May 1929, it is stated that Opoku Frɛfrɛ 'displayed himself' (i.e. 'hunted the elephant') at 'Darkwadwam' (now Dakojom?), a piece of land in the Adeɛbeba-Adeɛmbra area that was granted to him for this purpose by the then *Akwamuhene/Asafohene* Kwaakye Kofi. For a reconstruction of the complex events surrounding Opoku Frɛfrɛ's display of wealth (*yi nɛ ho adi*) and the award to him of the *mena/mmra* see para. 56.03 in ACBP/1: Opoku Frɛfrɛ, *Asantesɛm*, 11 (1979), 38–53.

93 Chapman, 'Journal', entry dd. Kumase, 15 July 1844. 'Brentu' is, of course, *Manwerehene* Kwasi Brantuo; 'Afarqua' is presently unidentified, at least in as much as a number of possible identifications exist.

94 McCaskie, 'Office, Land and Subjects', 196–9 for this and other acquisitions of land and *nkoa*; see *ibid.*, 'Manwere *nkoa* at Drobonso' for the detailed history of one such group of *nkoa*.

95 Kyerematen, *Kingship and Ceremony*, 21. For Opoku Ware's childhood link with *pampaso* see HA and AK. Boa Kwatia's branch of the *Oyoko Kɔkɔɔ* was likewise associated with *asaaman*; for a confused – but suggestive –tradition that, following Opoku Ware's accession as *Asantehene*, *asaaman* became known as *asaaman kwaadane* ('the enslaved *asaaman*'), to signify that no royal from there should ever again contest for the *sika dwa kofi*, see Asare, *Asante Abasem*.

96 Hutchison's Diary, dd. Kumase, 14 November 1817, in Bowdich, *Mission*, 395. It would seem that Opoku Frɛfrɛ (uniquely?) displayed his wealth twice, and was awarded the elephant tail on two separate occasions; first, *c.* 1790, when he was *Fotosanfoɔhene* under the *Asantehene* Osei Kwame; second, 1817 when he was *Gyaasewahene* under the *Asantehene* Osei Tutu Kwame. See ACBP/1: Opoku Frɛfrɛ, *Asantesɛm*, 11 (1979), 40 and 48.

97 See MRO, Kumase, 'Plea Book', dd. 1934, 'Affairs of Nyinahin', *Nyinahinhene* Yaw Dwema *versus* (representatives of) the Bantama and Akyempem stools, 1933 (this is a précis; I have been unable to locate the original case documents).

Compare the observations on Ntim Panin (who may have committed suicide c. 1780 because of revelations concerning his despoliation, while acting as caretaker, of the Gyaasewa stool) in ACBP/1: Opoku Frɛfrɛ, *Asantesɛm*, 11 (1979), 46–7, with the traditional, exculpatory account in A.C. Denteh, 'History of Gyaasewa', unpublished MS (1965), 5–6.

98 T.C. McCaskie, Interviews: *Manwerehene* Nana Kwabena Boaten, dd. Kumase, December 1975–January 1976; *ibid.*, 'Office, Land and Subjects', 197. Compare the evidence in MRO, Kumase, Kumasihene's Tribunal, CRB 1, 29 November 1926 to 19 April 1927, Osei Yaw *versus* Kofi Asamoa, commenced 18 December 1926.

99 Wilks, 'The Golden Stool and the Elephant Tail', 18; and see McCaskie, 'Accumulation, Wealth and Belief ... I', 30 ff.

100 Some account of the differences between *awunnyadeɛ* and *ayibuadeɛ* is in RAI, Rattray MSS, Bundle 107, Notebook 7, 1925, 33 ff. See further Bowdich, *Mission*, 254 and 319; Bonnat MSS, Cahier 15, *Mœurs et Coutumes de l'Achanty*, dd. Kumase, 19 September 1871, especially 13–14. For a range of detailed comments see MFU, 'Notes and Documents by and on R.S. Rattray'.

101 An account of tax evasion from the 1880s – by the Kumase *Apesemakahene ɔheneba* Kofi Bayeyere, a son of the *Asantehene* Osei Yaw Akoto – is in MRO, Kumase, Kumasihene's Tribunal, CRB 8, 12 September 1929 to 27 February 1930, and 9, 27 February to 2 June 1930, Penin Kwame Enin *versus Sodohene* Kofi Mainoo, commenced 3 November 1929; a summary of this is in ACBP/70: Adwowa Akosua, *Asantesɛm*, 10 (1979), 42–5.

102 See Arhin, 'Some Asante Views on Colonial Rule'; *ibid.*, 'A Note on the Asante *akonkofo*: A Non-literate Sub-elite, 1900–1930', *Africa*, 56, 1 (1986), 25–31; Wilks, 'Dissidence in Asante Politics'; McCaskie, 'Accumulation, Wealth and Belief ... II'. The possible revival of historic forms of appropriation was debated by the 'intelligentsia' of the Asante Kotoko Union Society (AKUS) in the 1920s. This needs fuller investigation. Regrettably, I have only once consulted (some) volumes of the proceedings of the AKUS (1976; kindly loaned to me by the late I.K. Agyeman – the present whereabouts of these volumes is unknown). For materials on the AKUS see NAG, Kumase, Files on Shelves 14 and 15, no. 401 (Ash MP 85/23); RH, Oxford, CRP, MSS Afr. s.593, Papers of Lt. Col. A.C. Duncan-Johnstone, Box 4, File 1, 'The Repatriation of ex-King Prempeh'; TOR, Notes and MSS, Miscellaneous Items. I am grateful to Gareth Austin and Wilhelmina Donkoh for materials on, or discussions about, the AKUS.

103 Reindorf, *History*, 75. For Opoku Ware's general reputation as an innovator see HA.

104 McCaskie, 'Office, Land and Subjects'; *ibid.*, 'Accumulation, Wealth and Belief ... I'. The relevant careers are summarized in ACBP/60: Yamoa Ponko, *Asantesɛm*, 9 (1978), 28–32, and ACBP/51: Kwasi Brantuo, *Asantesɛm*, 7 (1977), 14–17.

105 *Ibid.* and ACBP/1: Opoku Frɛfrɛ, *Asantesɛm*, 11 (1979), 43–6 (but the 1811 campaign was a political failure, in part because of Opoku Frɛfrɛ's rapacity). Opoku Frɛfrɛ's comment (which is susceptible of wider interpretation than

that offered here) is in Hutchison's Diary, dd. Kumase, 26 September 1817, in Bowdich, *Mission*, 381. Akuapem and Danish accounts of the 1811 war are in M.A. Kwamena-Poh, *Government and Politics in the Akuapem State 1730–1850* (London, 1973), 86–8, 146; R.A. Kea, 'A Provisional Translation of Two Danish Documents on the Asante Expedition of 1811', *Asante Seminar*, 6 (1976), 39–50, and *ibid.*, 'More Danish Accounts of the 1811 Asante Expedition', *Asantesɛm*, 11 (1979), 60–71. See further Reindorf, *History*, 160 ff. and H. Meredith, *An Account of the Gold Coast of Africa with a Brief History of the African Company* (London, 1812), 229–33. Very circumspect Mampon accounts of events in the 1780s are in Rattray, *Ashanti Law and Constitution*, 239 and J. Agyeman-Duah, 'Traditional History of Ashanti Mampong', MS, dd. Kumase State Council, April 1959. In general see HA.

106 See IAS/AS 154: Hia Stool History, recorded by J. Agyeman-Duah, 2 February 1965, 7, for Yamoa Ponko's trading in Gonja; for background, Wilks, Levtzion and Haight, *Chronicles from Gonja, passim*. On the southern trade see, conveniently, Wilks, 'The Golden Stool and the Elephant Tail', 24 ff.

107 See MRO, Kumase, Gyase Clan Affairs, 163/35: File 48/1, 16 March 1935 to 22 January 1944, *Gyaasewa Mmammahene* Joseph Kwesi Edubofuor *versus* Charles E. Osei, commenced 21 December 1939; A.C. Denteh, 'History of Gyaasewa', unpublished MS (1965), 9–10.

108 T.C. McCaskie, Interviews: *Manwerehene* Nana Kwabena Boaten and *Asabihene* Asabi Boakye II, dd. Kumase, December 1975–January 1976; see too MRO, Kumase, Asantehene's Divisional Court 'B', CRB 52, 26 June to 31 October 1950, *Manwerehene* Kwasi Brantuo *versus* Kyei Tra, commenced 6 September 1950; for discussion, McCaskie, 'Office, Land and Subjects', 196.

109 Asare, *Asante Abasem*. Compare the remarks in MRO, Kumase, 'Letters and Petitions', 31B, *Beposohene* Kwadwo Boadi to (?) *Asantehene*, dd. Kumase, March 1937.

110 Bowdich, *Mission*, 295.

111 HA.

112 Asare, *Asante Abasem*.

113 HA.

114 McCaskie, 'Office, Land and Subjects'; *ibid.*, 'Accumulation, Wealth and Belief ... I'; *ibid.*, '*Ahyiamu*'; and for a misreading of my argument see Arhin, 'Rank and Class', 12.

115 The best discussions of this are in the detailed work of Gareth Austin on Amansie. See, accessibly, G. Austin, 'The Emergence of Capitalist Relations in South Asante Cocoa-Farming, c.1916–33', *JAH*, 28, 2 (1987), 259–79; *ibid.*, 'Capitalists and Chiefs in the Cocoa Hold-Ups in South Asante, 1927–1938', *IJAHS*, 21, 1 (1988), 63–95; and see also *ibid.*, 'Class Struggle and Rural Capitalism in Asante History', unpublished draft paper, n.d.

116 RAI, Rattray MSS, 'Enquiry into the Adonten Stool, conducted by C. Furness-Smith, Ag. Crown Counsel', dd. Kumase, 24 March 1925.

117 Starting with McCaskie, 'Paramountcy', I have explored different aspects of this feature of the reign of the *Asantehene* Kwaku Dua Panin in a number of articles already cited. My most recent view of Kwaku Dua Panin's personal and political motivation is set out in *ibid.*, '*Konnurokusɛm*'. Although I have

never undertaken a relevant content analysis for all of the very many cases I have read from MRO, Kumase, I am certain that any such effort would reveal a (statistically?) significant redistribution of *nkoa* and land under Kwaku Dua Panin. For other, suggestive perspectives on Kwaku Dua Panin's impress on Asante history and memory see Kurankyi-Taylor, 'Legal Institutions', I, 127, and MFU, 'Files on the Histories of Kuntanase, Kaase, Deduako, *et al.*', 1946.

118 See ASSM, Unnumbered Files on 'Land Use', 1945–6; *ibid.*, T.[E.] K[yei?], 'Notes on Farming in Ashanti', n.d. but 1946; Wilks, 'Land, Labour, Capital', especially 500–1. For the modification and use of *abusa* in this century (and notably in cocoa farming) the fullest treatment is A.F. Robertson, 'Abusa: The Structural History of an Economic Contract', *The Journal of Development Studies*, 18, 4 (1982), 447–78.

119 Bowdich, *Mission*, 335–6.

120 *Ibid.*, 324.

121 See, for example, the debates recounted in MRO, Kumase, *Proceedings of the Meeting of the Committee of Privileges ... 1935*. The importance of rights in subjects and land is also reflected in authoritative tradition; thus, the history of such matters forms a central theme in HA.

122 By way of illustration see MRO, Kumase, 'Enquiry into the Relations between the Stools of Bantama and Nkawe, held before the Chief Commissioner (Ashanti)', commenced 11 June 1920. This single file (from the many hundreds in MRO) has 125 pages of sworn evidence, supplied by ten witnesses; the testimony ranges across two centuries of Asante history. I have never looked systematically, but MRO contains at least another five case files dealing with rights (in land, in people) disputed between these two stools. Embedded in such documents is, arguably, the most detailed historical material available for any precolonial African polity.

123 My general account of Yamoa Ponko's career is drawn from the files of the ACBP and from the biographical reconstruction published as ACBP/60: Yamoa Ponko, *Asantesɛm*, 9 (1978), 28–32. I record here my debt to Ivor Wilks for furnishing me with materials (including field interviews), and for conversations about his work on Yamoa Ponko.

124 See, for example, HA, and numbers of the stool histories in the series IAS/AS (Legon).

125 RAI, Rattray MSS, Bundle 107, Book 9, 'History of Tekiman', commenced 27 August 1925, and D.M. Warren and K.O. Brempong, *Techiman Traditional State, Part I: Stool and Town Histories* (IAS Legon, 1971) for Takyiman traditions. See too MRO, Kumase, *Proceedings of the Meeting of the Committee of Privileges ... 1935*, 94 (evidence of *Ntwiraahene*).

126 HA; IAS/AS 137: Ahenkro Stool History, recorded by J. Agyeman-Duah, 10 October 1964, is – predictably – silent on this matter; see also MRO, Kumase, File 76/35: Oyoko Atutue Stool Affairs, I, 1933–4, and II, 1935.

127 HA; IAS/AS 115: Sekyedomase Stool History, recorded by J. Agyeman-Duah, 25 February 1964, has a version of this tradition.

128 See K. Arhin, 'The Financing of the Ashanti Expansion (1700–1820)', *Africa*, 37, 3 (1967), 283–91 for *apeatoɔ* in its military context; *apeatoɔ* was a discretionary tax, customarily (but not always) levied *ex post facto* to meet

expenditure already incurred. See also ASSM, 'Notebook on Miscellaneous Customs', n.d.

129 For Yamoa Ponko's elevation to the office of *Kyidomhene* see HA. A detailed variant (with a predictably different slant) is in IAS/AS 154: Hia Stool History, recorded by J. Agyeman-Duah, 2 February 1965. IAS/AS 158: Kyidom Stool History, recorded by J. Agyeman-Duah, 16 February 1966, 6 for the tradition about Yamoa Ponko's guardianship of Osei Kwame. For the *nkoa* and the promotion see MRO, Kumase, Kumasihene's Tribunal, CRB 14, 28 December 1931 to 25 April 1932, Kwame Fosu of Hamabenase *versus* Osei Kwame of Donyina, commenced 29 February 1932; *ibid.*, CRB 9, 27 February to 2 June 1930, *Atipinhene* Kwaku Dua *versus odekuro* Kwasi Kyi of Paakoso, commenced 1 May 1930; *ibid.*, 'Kyidom Affairs, 1925–1928', File K/20, Drobon *odekuro* Kwabena Dapaa to Chief Commissioner Asante, dd. Kumase, 1 and 15 February and 22 April 1926. The son in question was Gyesi Kwame, Yamoa Ponko's favourite (*obayeyere*).

130 HA; the *Asantehene* Osei Kwame gave Yamoa Ponko a 'grand funeral', and assigned Opoku Frɛfrɛ to assess the estate. Compare IAS/AS 158: Kyidom Stool History, recorded by J. Agyeman-Duah, 16 February 1966, 6: 'Nana Yamoah is described as a man of opulence and a person of property qualification and did enhance and enrich the Kyidom stool with all available jewellery.'

131 MRO, Kumase, *Committee of Privileges ... 1935*, 35–6.

132 Asare, *Asante Abasem*. Yamoa Ponko contracted a marriage with a sister of the *Agogohene* Kwasi Tutu; the union produced Kyei Panin (who became *Agogohene*), and Kyei (Kofi) Kuma (who became Agogo *Kyidomhene*). Thus, Yamoa Ponko is well remembered in the traditions of Agogo (50 miles east of Kumase) as being so rich that 'he hung gold nuggets on the boughs of an orange tree' in front of his dwelling. As a result, he had a horn call that played: *Afrifa Yamoa Ponko, merebɛko mekurom Ankaase, daamerɛ ankaa gyedua se mpɔ.* 'Afrifa Yamoa Ponko, I shall be going into my town Ankaase, where orange shade trees grow gold nuggets.' Another horn call commemorated the throwing of gold by Yamoa Ponko into the – notoriously dangerous– Kyirade river, accompanied by the arrogant instruction that the river should not drown any of *his* descendants. See Kyei, *My Memoir*, I, 16–17; MFU, 'Agogo Genealogies'; MRO, Kumase, Bompata (Asante Akyem) Native Tribunal, 20 October 1917, *in re* Kwabena Tando *versus* Afua Yeboa of Offinso. Compare the horn call of the *ɔbirɛmpɔn Manwerehene* Kwasi Brantuo: *Akyampon Akwasi ei, yɛ sere wo twetwe, yɛ sere wo twe twetwe twe* ('Akyampon Akwasi, you are the subject of mockery, of mockery'); i.e., 'I was once mocked because I was poor, but now I am wallowing in wealth.'

133 Similarly, the term *mfaso* (profit, gain), used of Yamoa Ponko's dealings, connotes an admired skill in self-advancement *and* a form of self-serving greed.

134 HA; IAS/AS 199: Akropong Stool History, recorded by J. Agyeman-Duah, 13 March 1967, makes no mention of Kwadwo Gyamfi's disgrace. It is sometimes said that the Akuropon stool is 'unlucky' – a reference, presumably, to the disgrace of Kwadwo Gyamfi, to the execution (*c.* 1839) of his successor Ansere Tepa by the *Asantehene* Kwaku Dua Panin, and to the destoolment (*c.* 1875) of

Ansere Tepa's successor Kwame Agyepon by the *Asantehene* Mensa Bonsu.

135 See MRO, Kumase, Gyase Clan Affairs, 163/35: File 48/1, 16 March 1935 to 22 January 1944, *Gyaasewa Mmammahene* Joseph Kwesi Edubofuor *versus* Charles E. Osei, commenced 21 December 1939; A.C. Denteh, 'History of Gyaasewa', unpublished MS, 1965, especially 26–7. The genealogical materials are summarized in ACBP/1: Opoku Frɛfrɛ, *Asantesɛm*, 11 (1979), 38–53.

136 On the corporate identity of the Gyaasewa *mmamma* descended from Opoku Frɛfrɛ – as shown by their collective role in forcing the removal of the usurpatory (British-appointed) *Gyaasewahene* Kwame Tua in 1906 – see Asare, *Asante Abasem*; BMA, Basel, D/1, 84. N.V. Asare, 'Annual Report of Kumase to the Home Committee', dd. Kumase, 12 February 1906; see too NAG, Kumase, File D.681, 'Deposition of Chief Kwame Tua by his Subjects', 1905, and File D.118, 'Petition of Kwame Tua to be reinstated as Pinanko Chief', 1919; ASC, Cambridge, Fortes Papers, File 12, 'Interview with Mr. Edubofo, Mmamahene of Kumasi Gyasewa', 26 September 1945. For discussion see McCaskie, '"You Must Dis/Miss/Mis/Re/Member This" ...'.

137 It is said that the Sekyedumase *nkoa* were gratified at the transfer, since numbers of them had already been killed by the Ankaase people to mark the death (and funeral) of Yamoa Ponko.

138 MRO, Kumase, Kumasihene's Tribunal, CRB 9, 27 February to 2 June 1930, *Atipinhene* Kwaku Dua *versus odekuro* Kwasi Kyi of Paakoso, commenced 1 May 1930; *ibid.*, 'Kyidom Affairs, 1925–1928'. The Atipin *ɔkyeame* Gyesi Kwame, son of Yamoa Ponko, died in the Gyaman war of 1818–19. Atipin was created by the *Asantehene* Osei Kwame out of the villages and *nkoa* impounded from the *Adontenhene* Kwaaten Pɛtɛ and the Adonten *fekuo* (see p. 40 and note 65 above); *atipini* means 'a closing of the avenues of mercy', for Osei Kwame is said to have remarked of the sequestration that permitted the creation of Atipin, *sɛ mampini me tirim a, anka mantumi manye sika yi* ('If I had not closed all the avenues of mercy [to the Adonten *fekuo*], I could not have collected this amount'). See HA, and IAS/AS 9: Atipin, recorded by J. Agyeman-Duah, 28 October 1962.

139 Bowdich, *Mission*, 319.

140 For the calculations of (gold) density in relation to (flagon) capacity see Wilks, *Asante*, 693 fn 102. Wilks' reckoning is based on estimates given him by 'a number of chemists'. It should be emphasized that, in following Wilks here, I am giving figures that must be regarded as tending towards the upper levels of possibility. Thus, Tim Garrard (personal communication, 5 May 1985) has pointed out that if the *apem brontɔa* literally contained 1,000 *mperedwan*, then it would have weighed some 140 (very unwieldy) lb (a standard 'headload', by comparison, ranged between about 50 and 70 lb). He also argues, with some justice, that *apem* was a sort of Asante 'optimum number'. Thus, a given *apem brontɔa* might indeed contain 1,000 *mperedwan* (2,250 oz), but another might contain, for example, 1,000 *suru* (283 oz); therefore, it is possible that the (talismanic?) number *apem* led to the generic designation *apem brontɔa* being used to describe a container holding 1,000 units of gold dust – but measured out in a range of standard Asante goldweights. To this must be added the frank admission that direct evidence is lacking for levels of adulteration, density of

packing, and a mixing of unit sizes in any specific historical case. All that said, the *cultural* valorization of gold must be taken into account. Many discussions in Kumase about this matter have led me to three general conclusions: (*a*) wealthy individuals favoured the *peredwan* as *the* unit of measurement that proclaimed their status; (*b*) adulteration carried draconian penalties and fearful personal disgrace ('a bad name'), and the Asante state had, in 'death duties', an inescapable (posthumous) mechanism for assaying individual wealth and social worth; (*c*) the *peredwan* was the preferred unit of measurement in most financial transactions involving the state and its office holders. In sum, I feel a considered confidence (like Wilks) in adducing the figures given here – and a firm belief that they reflect general accuracy as a scale of magnitude. I stand to be corrected, but cannot see where precise corrective data are to be found.

141 Bowdich, *Mission*, 319. For the events that led to Apea Nyanyo's trial, disgrace and suicide see *ibid.*, 129, 244, 258; Huydecoper, *Diary*, entries dd. 'Asante Camp' (Fante), 3 and 7 May, and Kumase, 10 and 13 August 1816. For discussion McCaskie, 'Paramountcy', 38–40.

142 See pp. 45–6 (note 91). For discussion McLeod, *The Asante*, 72–86.

143 Bowdich, *Mission*, 254.

144 *Ibid.*, 258.

145 Thus – to confine comparison to a single leading instance – the Duke of Wellington's reward from parliament for his epochal victory at Waterloo (1815) was an *ex gratia* gift of £200,000.

146 Again, I have followed the calculations in Wilks, *Asante*, 418–19, and again I must emphasize that these computations tend towards the upper levels of possibility. A much smaller capacity (of 70,000 oz; £248,888) for the *adaka kɛsɛɛ* is claimed by Garrard, *Akan Weights*, 190. Tim Garrard (personal communication, 5 May 1985) has since refined his argument, field research persuading him to the view that the great chest was structured to contain 1,000 *kotoko* (68,000 oz; the *kotoko* being the largest goldweight possessed by the *Asantehene*, weighing approximately 2,112 grams or 68 oz, and so being equivalent to 30 *mperedwan*). The *adaka kɛsɛɛ*, as both scholars correctly note, was sub-divided into three compartments. Thus, following Garrard's argument, an equal distribution of the contents would give three sub-divisions of 10,000 *mperedwan* in each compartment; this arrangement would mean that the contents of each compartment were themselves a complete 'thousand' (*apem*), being 1,000 *mperedwan du*, the largest of all goldweights (equal to 10 *mperedwan*) permitted for use to the most senior office holders under the *Asantehene*. Garrard's speculative inferences are well taken – and 68,000 oz, as he says, 'is still a very impressive amount' – but all of my own field research in this area still persuades me towards the higher estimates given by Wilks. Once more, and regrettably, this is a debate that is unlikely to be resolved by any access of new and/or precise empirical evidence.

147 The genealogical details are set out in ACPB/60: Yamoa Ponko, *Asantesɛm*, 9 (1978), 28–32. Nti Kusi was certainly a paternal – and possibly a full – brother of Yamoa Ponko. Gyesi Tenten was the child of a marriage between Yamoa Ponko and a sister (name not yet known) of the *Nsutahene* Oduro Panin (who

was himself the father of, *inter alios*, the Kumase *Adontenhene* Kwaaten Pɛtɛ).
148 In earlier life Owusu Bannahene was called Owusu Nsemfo. This outline of his career is drawn from the files of the ACBP. For discussion see McCaskie, 'Paramountcy', 66–7, and Wilks, *Asante*, 139 (and fn. 78 for references by Bowdich and Dupuis to Owusu Bannahene). See too R.A. Kea, 'Four Asante Officials in the South-East Gold Coast (1808)', *GNQ*, 11 (1970), 42–7. The traditional account is in IAS/AS 158: Kyidom Stool History, recorded by J. Agyeman-Duah, 16 February 1966, 6. For his death – 'Bundahin ... the King's uncle' – see H.J. Ricketts, *Narrative of the Ashantee War* (London, 1831), 124–5. Okine – *Adomasahene* (immediately?) prior to Owusu Bannahene – was raised to ɔbirɛmpɔn status by the *Asantehene* Opoku Ware; see IAS/AS 131: Ofoase Adomasa Stool History, recorded by J. Agyeman-Duah, May 1964.
149 See ACBP/39: Owusu Dome, *Asantesɛm*, 10 (1979), 9–15. It is presumed that Owusu Dome is to be identified with Owusu Ansa Ntitraa, first *Atene Akotenhene* and titular head of the palace torch-bearers; see HA for the very complex history of office creation prior to the Gyaman war of 1818–19. Owusu Dome's death occurred in Kumase on or about 2 August 1837, and thirty-two people (at least) were immolated at his funeral custom; see, conveniently, A. van Dantzig, 'The Dutch Military Recruitment Agency in Kumasi', *GNQ*, 8 (1966), 21–4, especially 24. An engraving of Owusu Dome in Cape Coast (1820) is in Hutton, *Voyage*, facing 214.
150 See MRO, Kumase, Kumasihene's Tribunal, CRB 14, 28 December 1931 to 25 April 1932, Kwame Fosu of Hamabenase *versus* Osei Kwame of Donyina, commenced 29 February 1932. For context see McCaskie, 'Office, Land and Subjects', 198.
151 For different aspects of the reign of the *Asantehene* Kwaku Dua Panin see a succession of my own writings: 'Paramountcy'; 'Office, Land and Subjects'; 'Accumulation, Wealth and Belief ... I'; 'Death and the *Asantehene*'; '*Konnurokusɛm*'; 'Politics in 19th Century Asante'. See too Yarak, 'State, Society and Politics'.
152 McCaskie, 'Office, Land and Subjects'. See further IAS/AS 143: Ahubrafoɔ Stool History, recorded by J. Agyeman-Duah, 30 November 1964 for a very cursory account of the titular (but long dormant) headship of the *ahoprafoɔ* group. Compare the evidence on Kwaku Dua Panin and the *ahoprafoɔ* in MRO, Kumase, Kumasihene's Tribunal, CRB 1, 29 November 1926 to 19 April 1927, Osei Yaw *versus* Kofi Asamoa, commenced 18 December 1926.
153 I thank here – but cannot possibly list – all of those in Asante who have provided (and continue to provide) relevant insights. See, in brief, T.C. McCaskie, Interviews: *Manwerehene* Nana Kwabena Boaten and *Asabihene* Asabi Boakye II, dd. Kumase, December 1975–January 1976; I.K. Agyeman, dd. Kumase, 3, 6 and 11 January 1976; ɔkyeame Boakye Tenten (Kofi Apea Agyei), dd. Kumase, 3 and 4 January 1976: Anthony Kwadwo *et al.*, dd. Manhyia Akuropon, January 1976; Yaw Twimsai *et al.*, dd. Nkontonko, 13 March 1983; Osei Bekere, dd. Ayija (Kumase), April 1988. I also thank C. Osei-Bonsu for responding to written queries.
154 See McCaskie, '*Konnurokusɛm*'.
155 See T.C. McCaskie, Interviews: I.K. Agyeman, dd. Kumase, 3, 6 and 11

January 1976.

156 See MRO, Kumase, Asantehene's Divisional Court 'B', CRB 52, 26 June to 31 October 1950, *Manwerehene* Kwasi Brantuo *versus* Kyei Tra, commenced 6 September 1950; for context and further details see McCaskie, 'Office, Land and Subjects', 196–7.

157 See McCaskie, 'Manwere *nkoa* at Drobonso' for details. See further 'Kumawu's Claims to Drobonso' in MRO, Kumase, *Committee of Privileges ... 1935*, 107–14; MRO, Kumase, File AC/C1/54, 'Kumawu Stool Lands: Drobonso, Affram Plains', 1954.

158 *Ibid.*, Asantehene's Divisional Court 'B', CRB 54B, 3 April to 25 July 1951, *Akyempemhene* Boakye Dankwa *versus* Kwame Kobi of Apaaso, commenced 22 June 1951; T.C. McCaskie, Interviews: I.K. Agyeman, dd. Kumase, 3, 6 and 11 January 1976; McCaskie, '*Konnurokusɛm*' has a detailed analysis of the disgrace of Osei Kwadwo.

159 *Ibid.* See too MRO, Kumase, Kronti Tribunal, File 2, 1935–9, Toase *obaapanin* Akua Kobi *et al.* to *Asantehene*, dd. Kumase, 27 September and 11 November 1938.

160 MRO, Kumase, Asantehene's Divisional Court 'B', CRB 13, 31 March to 7 July 1938, Boakye Yam Kuma *ɔkyeame* Yaw Mensa (Boakye Dankwa) *versus* Kwadwo Apea Agyei, commenced 19 May 1938.

161 *Ibid.*, Palaver Book, 1940–3, *in re* Yaw Sekyere *versus* Kwaku Wuo, 1942 (original case not found); *ibid.*, Kumase Village Affairs, File 73, 1950–1; McCaskie, 'Manwere *nkoa* at Drobonso'. It is probable that the transaction involving Nyameani, Sobonkuo and Deduaku had something to do with the execution of the wealthy twins Ata Panin and Ata Kuma (of Kwaso Deduaku) in February 1844. They were tried for murdering one of their own slaves, for which offence the *Asantehene* Kwaku Dua Panin wished to show clemency, but then – in anger – they swore an oath on the *Asantehene's* life; they were beheaded, and their very considerable estates were confiscated and redistributed. For their death see Chapman, 'Journal', entry dd. Kumase, 14 February 1844, and for Kwaku Dua Panin's foreclosure on debts owed to them see *ibid.*, entry dd. Kumase, 11 April 1844. The wealth and heinous offence of Ata Panin and Ata Kuma are well remembered; see MRO, Kumase, Kumasihene's Tribunal, CRB 3, 24 October 1927 to 22 June 1928, *Kwasohene* Kwadwo Nketia *versus Nyameanihene* Kwabena Dumfe, commenced 14 June 1928; ASC, Cambridge, Fortes Papers, File 17, 'Discussions at Nyameani', 15 January 1946.

162 See Christaller, *Twi Mmebusɛm*, 38, and Rattray, *Ashanti Proverbs*, 162.

163 PRO, London, CO 96/58, Pine to Newcastle, dd. Cape Coast, 10 December 1862; *ibid.*, the *Asantehene* Kwaku Dua Panin to Pine, dd. Kumase, 9 February 1863; WMMS, West to Boyce, dd. Cape Coast, 11 March 1863; ARA, The Hague, NBKG 721, the *Asantehene* Kwaku Dua Panin to Elias, dd. Kumase, 19 December 1865. HA states bluntly that Kwasi Gyani was an office holder from Manso Nkwanta who claimed that he was wealthy, thereby exciting the avarice of Kwaku Dua Panin who wanted him killed so that his property might be seized.

164 Bowdich, *Mission*, 249.

165 For a survey of British diplomacy see W.E.F. Ward, 'Britain and Ashanti,

1874–1896', *THSG*, 15, 2 (1974), 131–64.

166 Compare W.G. Beasley, *The Meiji Restoration* (Stanford, 1972).

167 The civil war is recounted in detail in Lewin, *Asante before the British*, 69–134 and in Wilks, *Asante*, 549–665. A brief but interesting reading is in A. Akosua Aidoo, 'The Asante Succession Crisis of 1883–88', *THSG*, 13, 2 (1972), 163–80.

168 See McCaskie, 'Accumulation, Wealth and Belief ... I', 37–9.

169 Kofi Kakari's actions are richly documented and thoroughly explored. For his profligacy, bynames, and (alleged) observation see HA and Asare, *Asante Abasem*. See too 'Asantehene Kofi Karikari ho nsentia bi', in *Sika-Mpoano Kristofo a wokasa Twi no Senkekafo (The Christian Reporter for the Natives of the Gold Coast ...)*, Basel, February 1913, 14–15.

170 For Mensa Bonsu's behaviour see HA. A key illustration is explored in ACBP/47: Kwabena Awua, *Asantesɛm*, 10 (1979), 21–30.

171 Asare, *Asante Abasem*.

172 BMA, Basel, D/1, 95, N.V. Asare, 'Annual Report of Kumase to the Home Committee', dd. Kumase, 24 February 1911.

173 McCaskie, 'Accumulation, Wealth and Belief ... I', 38 for my argument. Evidence adduced in many of the court cases in MRO, Kumase shows just how chaotically disruptive, materially and cognitively, the 1880s were for many Asante. For one type of response to this see T.C. McCaskie, 'Social Rebellion and the Inchoate Rejection of History: Some Reflections on the Career of Opon Asibe Tutu', *Asante Seminar*, 4 (1976), 34–8 and *ibid.*, 'Anti-witchcraft Cults in Asante: An Essay in the Social History of an African People', *HA*, 8 (1981), 125–54.

174 C.7917, 1896, *Further Correspondence relating to Affairs in Ashanti* (Accounts and Papers LVIII), 'The Ashantis in the Western Protectorate' to Governor (Brandford Griffith), dd. Cape Coast, 1 October 1894, and NAG, Accra, ADM 11/1483, 'The Ashantis' to Governor (Brandford Griffith), dd. Cape Coast, 15 December 1894. Both documents are discussed in detail in Wilks, 'Dissidence in Asante Politics'.

175 The most succinct treatment is Arhin, 'A Note on the Asante *akonkofo*'.

176 MRO, Kumase, Kyidom Clan Tribunal, Minute Book 1, 11 January 1928 to 28 August 1929, *Kwasohene* Kwadwo Nketia *versus Nyameanihene* Kwabena Dumfe, commenced 27 March 1928.

177 For the history of one group of refugees – those led by the *Kokofuhene* Osei Asibe – see TOR, Notes and MSS, File on 'Repatriation' (extracted from ANA/1/24 of 1924 in Regional Office, Kumase).

178 See McCaskie, '*Ahyiamu*' for an extended discussion.

179 *Ibid.*, 184.

180 For Kyidom at this time see ACBP/26: Kwame Boaten, *Asantesɛm*, 8 (1978), 12–21.

181 MRO, Kumase, Kumasihene's Tribunal, CRB 3, 24 October 1927 to 22 June 1928, *Kwasohene* Kwadwo Nketia *versus Nyameanihene* Kwabena Dumfe, commenced 14 June 1928, evidence of Boankra *odekuro* Kwabena Gyima. The contracting parties listed here are those mentioned in HA. However, others were seemingly present in an 'official' capacity; thus, in *ibid., Proceedings of the Committee of Privileges ... 1935*, 63–4, the sometime Kyerema Kobia *ɔkyeame*

Kwaku Safo stated that those who 'drank fetish' also included Akua Fokuo and (the future *Asantehemaa* and mother of the *Asantehene* Osei Agyeman Prempeh II) Akua Abakoma – the senior surviving children of the *Asantehemaa* Yaa Kyaa, and maternal half-sisters to Agyeman Prempe.

182 NAG, Kumase, File 113/1908, Kofi Sraha and others to Chief Commissioner (Ashanti), dd. Kumase, 11 October 1930. (Akua Afriyie was the younger full sister of Akua Fokuo and Akua Abakoma; compare note 181 above). For discussion see Arhin, 'Some Asante Views on Colonial Rule', 65 and 77–9.

3   SOCIETY AND STATE IN ASANTE HISTORY

1 Various facets of this antagonism are explored in McCaskie, 'Accumulation, Wealth and Belief ... I', 'Komfo Anokye', '*Asantesɛm*', 'Armah's *The Healers*', and 'People and Animals'.

2 Thus, AK is a narrative account of human increase among the *Oyoko Kɔkɔɔ* – from the time of the single 'great ancestress' Ankyewa Nyame (great great grandmother of the first *Asantehene* Osei Tutu) to the early twentieth century – with a proleptic confidence in the face of the (open-ended) future. This genealogical continuum is hedged about with sub-texts that memorialize achievement and proclaim intention; from the opening sequence – 'The Hunter in the Forest' – the thrust of the argument is about the ongoing maximization of Asante culture. Compare the text and argument in T.C. McCaskie, '*Asantehene* Agyeman Prempe's Account to the *Asantemaŋ* of His Exile from Kumase (1896–1924): A Document with Commentary', *Asantesɛm*, 7 (1977), 32–42.

3 The most accessible summary is Fortes, *Kinship and the Social Order*, 154 ff.

4 *Ibid.* For Fortes' project (and notably his construction of 'descent') see *ibid.*, 'Custom and Conscience', 'An Anthropologist's Apprenticeship', and 'Descent, Filiation and Affinity: A Rejoinder to Dr. Leach', *Man*, 59, 309 (1959), 193–7 and 59, 311 (1959), 206–12. See too Rattray, *Ashanti Law and Constitution*, 1–6. An interesting intervention is K. Akwabi-Ameyaw, 'Ashanti Social Organization: Some Ethnographic Clarifications', *Ethnology*, 21 (1982), 325–33.

5 For an explicit statement of this perplexity see, for example, H.W. Basehart, 'Ashanti', in D.M. Schneider and K. Gough (eds.), *Matrilineal Kinship* (Berkeley and Los Angeles, 1961), 270–97.

6 Geertz, *Works and Lives*, 16.

7 See the contrast between the late nineteenth-century full siblings and refugees Yaw Sapon and Adoma Penya (originally subjects of the Kumase *Akyeremadeɛhene* at Esaase), as recounted in ASSM, *Asafo Agyei Ko*, MS, compiled from interviews with 'elders of Juabin, Asokore, Konongo, etc.' by M. Fortes, 1946.

8 See Christaller, *Tŵi Mmebusɛm*, 36 and Rattray, *Ashanti Proverbs*, 118.

9 Bowdich, *Mission*, 144–5 and 255. Safie ('Assaphi') – one of the four – probably occupied one or other of the Wirempi stools from (originally) the Manso Nkwanta area; he was disgraced by the *Asantehene* Osei Tutu Kwame for the (presumably desperate?) theft of funeral donations: four *mperedwan* and 'a quantity of expensive cloths'.

10 For the traditions concerning *Dako ne Dako* (Dako Panin and Dako Kuma), and on the death of Kwame Agyem, see Asare, *Asante Abasem*. Asare's informants conflated two traditions, stating that *Dako ne Dako* had contested for the *sika dwa kofi* with Opoku Ware (in *c.* 1712 or 1717–20). In fact, Boa Kwatia – also identified with the *asaaman* ward (see chapter 2 note 95) – contested with Opoku Ware, while *Dako ne Dako* fought unsuccessfully for the *sika dwa kofi* against Kusi Obodom (in *c.* 1750). Thus, variant accounts associate the name *asaaman kwaadane* with the eclipse of either Boa Kwatia or *Dako ne Dako* – all three being members of that *Oyoko Kɔkɔɔ* lineage segment that traced royal descent from the 'great ancestress' Ankyewa Nyame, but through her granddaughter Otiwa Kese rather than her granddaughter Abena Gyapa, the maternal grandmother of Osei Tutu. It is possible that Kusi Obodom formally reconfirmed Opoku Ware's earlier excoriation of *asaaman kwaadane* in order to underscore the final defeat and permanent exclusion from the highest offices (of *Asantehene* and *Asantehemaa*) of any future aspirants from this now collateral branch of the Kumase dynasty. Whatever the strictly *historical* facts of the case, however, Asare's informants clearly understood the *ideological* crux of the matter. They conceded the indubitable 'nobility' (of descent) of *Dako ne Dako* as well as Opoku Ware, the maternal grandson of Osei Tutu's own sister Bonafie, but asserted the superior claims of the latter to the *sika dwa kofi* on the grounds of meritorious achievement as well as birth; that is, they argued that the *sika dwa kofi* had been awarded to Opoku Ware because it was *his* lineage segment (in the august personage of the first *Asantehene* Osei Tutu) that had 'enhanced the prominence of the state', and therefore it would have been 'a travesty of justice if one [Osei Tutu] had laboured so that another [*Dako ne Dako*] might enjoy the fruits'. Thus, the 'noble kin' of Obiri Yeboa – Osei Tutu's predecessor as ruler of Kwaman-Kumase – were set aside because of Osei Tutu's unprecedented achievements in liberating Asante from Denkyira control and in enlarging the Asante polity.

11 Little has been published thus far on *mpoatwa*. See Arhin, 'Trade, Accumulation and the State', especially 532 and McCaskie, '*Konnurokusεm*'.

12 For discussions of the concept of *mpoatwa* I am grateful to Kwame Arhin, Yaw Safo, Michael Adjei, P.I. Boateng and Ernest Gyimah. I should also like to thank Kwesi Yankah for some insightful remarks made to me in Accra in 1990. Yankah is an expert in the constitutive role played by the Twi language in the framing of Akan culture, and he is also – as the satirist of 'Abonsam Fireman' and the author of the bitingly sardonic *Woes of a Kwatriot: Reflections on the Ghanaian Situation* (Accra, 1990) – a skilful practitioner of resonant forms of traditional verbal defiance translated to contemporary cultural idioms.

13 ASSM, 'The Ownership of Houses in Kumase', 1946 (a version of this is in ASC, Cambridge, Fortes Papers, File 3, 'Houses at Kumase'). Fortes recorded that, for example, the then incumbent Kumase *Mmentiahene* Kofi Nyame regarded ownership of a house in Kumase as 'an indispensable necessity', *inter alia* as a means of commanding the respect of stool subjects. ASSM, 'Notes on House D.B. 477, Kumasi, built by Chief Kwasi Nuama in ca. 1907' records that, after the death of *Domakwaehene* and *Akyeamehene* Kwasi Apea Nuama in 1937, the title of this house – an acknowledged source of 'prestige' as well as

revenue – was hotly disputed between his successor ('his mother's sister's daughter's son') Kofi Amankwa and other lineage members; the matter was still unresolved in 1945.

14 See, for example, the intense disputes over burial rights in MRO, Kumase, File 166/32/V2, 'Mampong Native Affairs' and File 18/46, 'Tena Family, Mampong'. For context see T.C. McCaskie, 'Power and Dynastic Conflict in Mampon', *HA*, 12 (1985), 167–85.

15 Behaviour that was *di bakoma* (and otherwise extremely arrogant) was sometimes practised by those of undistinguished or obscure lineage who wished to simulate – to this extreme degree – the mannerisms of the well born. Thus, the great military office of the Kumase *Bantamahene* and *Krontihene* was in the gift of the *Asantehene*, and appointees to it were commonly men of humble, lowly, or even 'unknown' origin. The *Bantamahene/Krontihene* Adu Gyamera – who may have been (a Bron?) from Ahafo – was arraigned and executed by the *Asantehene* Osei Kwadwo in the 1760s for his insupportable pretensions and overweening 'arrogance' of behaviour. See HA, for Adu Gyamera's behaviour and downfall; NAG, Kumase, File D.102, 'Succession to Coomassie Stools', Kwame Kyem to Chief Commissioner (Ashanti), dd. Kumase, 19 June 1916, for some account of the origins of occupants of the Bantama stool; and IAS/AS 39 and 40: Bantama Stool History I and II, recorded by J. Agyeman-Duah, November–December 1962, which, understandably, glosses over Adu Gyamera's origins and misdemeanours.

16 For examples of the exposition of Asante moral seriousness within the framework of ludic narrative see Rattray, *Folk Tales*.

17 RAI, Rattray MSS, Bundle 107, Notebook 3, pp. 1801–1900 (this case is recorded at 1823). It is said that the *Asantehene* sometimes used the *ɔbodiasɛm sumaŋ* to 'stir up' *mpoatwa* (and any other manifestation of conflict or ill-feeling) so as to profit from any resulting litigation.

18 Bowdich, *Mission*, 253; compare *ibid.*, 40 and 281 for Bowdich's views of the 'interesting vanity' affected by children who were conscious of their own status and importance.

19 *Ibid.*, 252–3.

20 The remark quoted concerning Amankwatia (Amankwa Tenteŋ) is in Wilks, *Asante*, 404 (citing Bonnat's views as given in *L'Explorateur*, 1875–6, II, 622; I have been unable to locate this precise observation in the Bonnat MSS); F. Boyle, *Through Fanteeland to Coomassie: A Narrative of the Ashantee Expedition* (London, 1874), 276–7 states – on the authority of the long-term (1869–74) Asante captive J. Kühne – that Amankwatia was 'a mere creature of the king, whose ancestry no one knows, or, at least, troubles about'; for Amankwatia and Akrofuom see NAG, Kumase, File D.102, 'Succession to Coomassie Stools', Kwame Kyem to Chief Commissioner (Ashanti), dd. Kumase, 19 June 1916. For Amankwatia's career see ACBP/14: Amankwatia, *Asante Seminar*, 3 (1975), 10–12.

21 On Bantama see note 15 above. Both Ivor Wilks (Interview with the *Asantehene* Osei Agyeman Prempeh II, dd. Kumase, 22 December 1958) and myself (Discussions with the *Akyempemhene ɔheneba* Boakye Dankwa, dd. Kumase, December 1975–January 1976) have been admonished for inferring

that the occupant of the Bantama stool was anything other than a 'slave' of the *Asantehene* (that is, for assuming that any *Bantamahene* 'had a lineage'). These dismissals – unsurprisingly, in terms of their exalted sources – are extremely blunt, and go beyond any of the conventions embraced or described by *mpoatwa*.

22 See the correspondence in NAG, Kumase, File D.94, 'New Chidom Hene [*Kyidomhene*]', 1915 for instances of competitiveness among *ahenemma* over rank and precedence; see McCaskie, 'Death and the *Asantehene*' for some discussion of the *ahenemma* as a corporate status group.

23 Again I record my indebtedness to all those many Asante who have contributed over the years to my understanding of these matters; the late Jack Berry, an outstanding scholar of the Twi language, once gave me invaluable pointers to (and demonstrations of) 'dry' and 'wet' speech on a flight between Chicago and London.

24 These developments form a central theme of Asante historiography; for a useful summary of much of the relevant literature (Aidoo, Lewin, McCaskie, Wilks) see Yarak, 'State, Society and Politics in Nineteenth Century Asante'. See too *ibid.*, *Asante and the Dutch*, 1–28 and McCaskie, 'Empire State'.

25 Coercive potential might be realized in a variety of prescribed ways. Thus – depending on the circumstances – execution was carried out by *ɔsekaŋ* (beheading with the knife of the *abrafoɔ*), by *bu kon(mu)* (strangling – mandatory in the case of *adehyeɛ*), by *abaporowa* (clubbing), by *twa asua* (drowning, or 'crossing the river'), or by *atɔperɛ* (the 'dance of death'). Draconian punishments have passed into folk memory. Thus, I have severally been informed that the *Asantehene* Kwaku Dua Panin detained one youth for so many years that he eventually died of old age; RAI, Rattray MSS, Bundle 107, Notebook 3, 1837 records a variant – that a boy was detained 'in log' by Kwaku Dua Panin until 'he had grown a beard'. See too the generic comment (from a tradition written down by an Akuropon man in 1893) in T.C. McCaskie and J.E. Wiafe, 'A Contemporary Account in Twi of the *Akompi Sa* of 1863: A Document with Commentary', *Asantesɛm*, 11 (1979), 72–8 that the *Asantehene* Kwaku Dua Panin detained people until 'their fingernails have grown like those of an animal, and their hair has reached their neck'.

26 In some traditions it is said that the head was concealed in the stomach of a pregnant corpse.

27 The authoritative account is in HA. For the Gyaman traditions see Terray, 'Une Histoire du Royaume Abron du Gyaman', III, 1150 ff. The *Gyamanhene* Kwadwo Adinkra's death was a notable event, and it features in the traditions of numbers of peoples in the Ivory Coast and Ghana. Perrot, *Les Anyi-Ndenye*, 308 records an Ndenye tradition (1965) which mentions the concealment of Kwadwo Adinkra's head under a pile of corpses; L. Brydon and T.C. McCaskie, Interviews: Elders of Gbadzeme, April 1988 confirms that the death of Kwadwo Adinkra is remembered among the Ewe and Avatime of Volta Region, Eastern Ghana. Interestingly, the Ndenye, Ewe and Avatime informants all erroneously associated the prosecution of the Gyaman war with the *Gyaasewahene* Adu Bofoɔ rather than with his father the *Gyaasewahene* Opoku Frɛfrɛ.

28 Compare Bowdich, *Mission*, 255–6 with the traditions recorded in Asare,

Asante Abasem, and with the cases noted in Chapman, 'Journal', entry dd. Kumase, 13 March 1845.

29 Ramseyer and Kühne, *Four Years*, 143. BMA, Basel, Jenkins (Ramseyer MS *et al.*), entry dd. Kumase, 21 November 1871 adds only that the man was an Asante-born 'slave' (of the *Asantehene*, as he himself remarked, i.e. an *ahenkwaa*). He had been condemned to death, was fearful that he would be executed in the impending funeral custom for the *Kokofuhene*, but was pardoned by the *Asantehene* Kofi Kakari following pleas from the European captives; see Bonnat MSS, Cahier 7, entries dd. Kumase, 20 (marginal note) and 26 November 1871.

30 *The Western Echo, Supplement*, 30 June 1886; Freeman, 'Life and Travels', 161.

31 Christaller, *Twi Mmebusem*, 54 and Rattray, *Ashanti Proverbs*, 116. By corollary, to insult or to harm a royal *ahenkwaa* was to offer a direct challenge to the *Asantehene*. Traditions recount that the calculated amputation of the fingers of visiting royal *nhenkwaa* was a common symbolic formula for rejecting Kumase's authority and for declaring war on Asante; see MFU, 'In Mr. Nyantakyi's House, with Notes on Various Asante Customs', n.d. (but 1946).

32 Asare, *Asante Abasem*. Sampanne was subsequently promoted, and perhaps is to be identified with 'Samponday' or 'Sampane, chief captain, Adum host' (i.e. the Kumase *Adumhene* Kwadwo Sanpanin) who was killed in 1826 at the battle of Katamanso; see Ricketts, *Narrative*, 124–5; Reindorf, *History*, Appendix C, 352; and McCaskie, 'Politics in 19th Century Asante'. If this identification is correct, then Sampanne's (Asante) father was the Kumase *Adumhene* Agyei Keseε; see IAS/AS 5: Adum Stool History, recorded by J. Agyeman-Duah, 13 February 1963.

33 Asare, *Asante Abasem*.

34 For succinct discussion see Arhin, 'Peasants', 474–5.

35 These indices are to be distinguished from instances of political disaffection on the part of elite divisional or provincial office holders. Asante traditions record nothing that might be confidently identified with the features listed here, and nothing that is comparable with events reported from the southern Gold Coast. See Klein, 'Inequality in Asante'; Kea '"I am here to plunder on the general road"'; and compare, more generally, R.A. Austen, 'Social Bandits and Other Heroic Criminals: Western Models of Resistance and their Relevance for Africa', in Crummey (ed.), *Banditry, Rebellion and Social Protest*, 89–108.

36 See the extended study by E. Terray, 'Contribution à une étude de l'armée asante', *CEA*, 61–2, XVI–1–2 (1976), 297–356.

37 The *Asantehene* Kwaku Dua Panin, for example, stockpiled 'the stores and munitions of war' in a 'royal arsenal' near to his 'country palace' at Eburaso, some $3\frac{1}{2}$ miles outside of Kumase; see Freeman, 'Life and Travels', 128. It is highly likely that military stores were also kept in the outlying royal residences at Breman, Besehenease, Amanhia and Atwereboanna; on these buildings see McCaskie, 'Paramountcy', 161–6, to which should be added – on Breman – MRO, Kumase, Asantehene's Divisional Court 'B', Record of Proceedings *in re Apagyahene* Owusu Afriyie III *versus Tafohene* Yaw Dabanka, commenced 9 March 1944. On types of guns and their distribution see M. Johnson,

Fieldnotes, July/August 1975, 'Craft Villages around Kumase'.

38 WMMS, W. West to General Secretaries, dd. Cape Coast, 9 June 1862 (with an account of his residence in Kumase, 17 March to 22 April 1862). For context see ACBP/20: Owusu Koko, *Asante Seminar*, 4 (1976), 5–10.

39 Informants often cite 'carrying a gun' as a male 'equivalent' to the formalized nubility rites undergone by females; for some account see P. Sarpong, *Girls' Nubility Rites in Ashanti* (Accra and Tema, 1977), and especially 11. An evocative insight into the matter is afforded by the photograph of 'Owusu Sekyere, Omanhene (Paramount Chief) of Mampon [i.e. the *Mamponhene* Owusu Sekyere Kuma], and His Sons' – all holding guns – published as the Frontispiece to Rattray, *Ashanti Proverbs*.

40 MFU, 'In Mr. Nyantakyi's House, with Notes on Various Asante Customs', n.d. (but 1946).

41 Fortes, *Kinship and the Social Order* has the fullest discussion of his views on the jural dimension in Asante; for historical discussion see McCaskie, '*Konnurokusɛm*'.

42 See, typically, Freeman, 'Life and Travels', 119 on the *Asantehene* Kwaku Dua Panin's burdensome judicial role: 'Day after day consecutively, with the exception of birth-days, fetish-days and periods of custom, he sits in the Palace for many hours hearing and deciding cases.' Compare Bonnat MSS, Cahier 15, *Mœurs et coutumes de l'Achanty*, dd. Kumase, 19 September 1871 on the – reputedly indolent – *Asantehene* Kofi Kakari; 'il consacre la majeure partie de son temps', noted Bonnat, to presiding over the administration of justice. In addition to his duties with respect to formal litigation, the *Asantehene* also conducted – generally in the evenings, and into the night – a great deal of informal arbitration (*ŋkurobo*). In HA, Komfo Anokye invests Osei Tutu with the role of judge (father *and* ruler) over the Asante; and immediately following the manifestation of the *sika dwa kofi*, Komfo Anokye announces his 'Seventy-seven National Laws' and charges Osei Tutu, as *Asantehene*, with impartiality in their enforcement.

43 For some discussion see Kurankyi-Taylor, 'Legal Institutions', I, 19 ff. and OMP, Kumase, 'The Chief and Chiefship in Ashanti', a memorandum prepared for the Ashanti Confederacy Council, dd. Kumase, 14 February 1941. I have been informed that the Committee of Traditional Authorities charged with assembling materials for inclusion in HA also produced a series of drafts, including one on the subject of *amaŋ mmu* and *amaŋ bre*; I have been unable to locate any such MS, and it is not among the letters and accompanying notes (many of which are of an administrative nature) originally filed with HA.

44 Kurankyi-Taylor, 'Legal Institutions', I, 80, fn. 1 and 92, fn. 1. See MRO, Kumase, File D 17/39, 'Correspondence on the Affairs of Denyase', 1939–40 for a case involving discussion of the principle of *pae abusua*.

45 Historical aspects are discussed in Wilks, 'Land, Labour, Capital' and McCaskie, 'State and Society, Marriage and Adultery'. Relevant here is one well-documented case. Anihemaa of Mampon of the *Tana (Atena)* matriclan was wife to the *Asantehene* Opoku Ware (*c.* 1720–50). She physically assaulted him; she and her relatives were executed, the Mampon *ɔman* was heavily fined,

and the *Tana (Atena)* matriclan was abolished throughout Asante. It was amalgamated into the *Bretuo (Biretuo)* matriclan by Opoku Ware, and two centuries later, in 1946, the *Asantehene* Osei Agyeman Prempeh II reconfirmed his predecessor's ruling. For a full discussion see McCaskie, 'Power and Dynastic Conflict in Mampon', especially 173.

46 See Rattray, *Ashanti Law and Constitution*, 19 and Fortes, *Kinship and the Social Order*, 185. For details of the consequences of *pae abusua* and the severance of lineage ties for the individual see the case of Akua Brenya of Mamponten in MRO, Kumase, Correspondence File JKA/7, Petitions of Yaw Nsia *et al.* to the *Asantehene* and the *Oyokohene*, dd. Kumase, 17 March and 6 June 1938.

47 See, for example, ACBP/20: Owusu Koko, *Asante Seminar*, 4 (1976), 5–10 and T.C. McCaskie, 'A Note on the Career of *Akyempemhene ɔheneba* Owusu Koko', *Asante Seminar*, 6 (1976), 21.

48 Dupuis, *Journal*, xxxi.

49 MFU, 'A Schedule of Interviews and Conversations in the Lake Bosomtwe Villages and Mponua Towns', 1946, and especially materials from Ajiman, Anyatiase, Brodekwano, Brodwum, Detieso (Dɔteɛso), Nkawe, Pepia 1 and 2, and Wawase. For context on the Lake Bosomtwe area see I. Boakye, 'Some Aspects of the Social Organization of the Fishing Villages on Lake Bosumtwi', M.A. (Ghana-Legon, 1965).

50 These issues are addressed – but with insufficient attention to historical detail – in Klein, 'Inequality in Asante'.

51 The voluminous records of civil (and criminal?) proceedings deposited in MRO, Kumase, supplemented by historical materials and appropriate fieldwork, could be deployed to generate literally hundreds of such illustrative instances.

52 For an impressive introduction to a huge range of scholarship see J. Goody, *The Oriental, the Ancient and the Primitive: Systems of Marriage and the Family in the Pre-industrial Societies of Eurasia* (Cambridge, 1990).

53 The bulk of the evidence deployed comes from MRO, Kumase, Kumasihene's Tribunal, CRB 4, 1928, *Pampasohene* Osei Yaw *versus Atene Akotenhene* Yaw Bredwa, commenced 5 July 1928; supplementary biographical materials are drawn from the files of the ACBP; in particular see ACBP/34: Yaw Nkyera, *Asante Seminar*, 5 (1976), 10–13 and ACBP/16: Kwame Agyepon, unpublished. See further McCaskie, 'State and Society, Marriage and Adultery'.

54 The principal sources used include ASSM, *Asafo Agyei Ko*, MS compiled from interviews with 'elders of Juabin, Asokore, Konongo, etc.' by M. Fortes, 1946; *ibid.*, 'Asokore Town: The History of the Asokore Stool, with Notes on Talks with Lineage and Household Heads, and Others (Panin Bɔm, Nana Owusu Firempong, etc.)', n.d. (incomplete); ASC, Cambridge, 'The Asafo Agyei War; Talk with Panin Bɔm of Asokore', n.d. Supplementary materials include NAG, Kumase, D.1423, 'Reports from Commissioners of Districts in North and East Ashanti' (selected), 1905–6, 1911–12, 1913–14, 1923–4, 1929–30; MRO, Kumase, File 6/35, 'Correspondence on Matters Arising from the Committee of Privileges' (on Asokore and on Ananta, 1935–6); *ibid.*, *Committee of Privileges ... 1935, passim* (several entries); and HA. On the

politics of the Dwaben war (1875) compare ACBP/74: Kofi Kato, *Asantesɛm*, 10 (1979), 49–52.

55 Klein, 'Inequality in Asante', I, 52 puts the matter acutely, if in the service of ideas and arguments other than those addressed here: 'The state, like the lineage, monopolized all avenues to corporateness. It monopolized the genealogical future tense.' Distinct but relevant aspects of Asante selfhood – an understudied subject – are analysed in McCaskie, 'People and Animals'.

56 See Kurankyi-Taylor, 'Legal Institutions', II, 490.

57 Slaves from the north were, of course, part of a larger political economy and history. For overviews see Wilks, *Asante*, 243–309 and K. Arhin, 'Savanna Contributions to the Asante Political Economy', in Schildkrout (ed.), *The Golden Stool*, 51–9. Surprisingly, there is as yet no comprehensive treatment of the Asante slave trade.

58 See, for example, S.A. Winsnes (trans. and ed.), *Letters on West Africa and the Slave Trade: Paul Erdmann Isert's 'Journey to Guinea and the Caribbean Islands in Columbia' (1788)* (Oxford, 1992), 83; compare Bowdich, *Mission*, 182–3.

59 Rattray, *Ashanti Law and Constitution*, 35–6; RAI, Rattray MSS, Notebook 4, 'Ashanti Law and Constitution', commenced 4 June 1925.

60 Asante informants still give conflicting derivations of *ɔdɔnkɔ/nnɔnkɔfoɔ*. For the argument that *ɔdɔnkɔ* derives from the Mande, *dyõnko*, see I. Wilks, 'The Mande Loan Element in Twi', *GNQ*, 4 (1962), 26–8.

61 WMMS, 'Journals of the Rev. Thomas B. Freeman', entry dd. Kumase, 23 December 1841; compare the *Asantehene* Kwaku Dua Panin's views on the slave trade in Chapman, 'Journal', entry dd. Kumase, 18 July 1844, and those of the *Asantehene* Osei Tutu Kwame in Dupuis, *Journal*, 162–3.

62 McLeod, *The Asante*, 36–7 lists all of those who were cast, at death, upon a midden (*sumina; suminaso*) rather than being interred in a burial ground, because they were less than complete Asante persons (citizens): 'they were, in some sense, damaged or incomplete beings'. See Rattray, *Religion and Art*, 147–66 for the rites surrounding the burial of Asante citizens. Slaves who had outlived their usefulness were sometimes simply abandoned to die in the bush.

63 See Yarak, *Asante and the Dutch*, 109.

64 For some discussion see J. LaTorre, 'Birthplaces of Dutch East Indies Troops "Recruited" in Kumase, 1837–1842', *Asante Seminar*, 5 (1976), 31–42.

65 Gramsci, of course, reflected upon these problems at length in the Italian context and in other historical situations. A now classic discussion, seminal in its influence upon many scholars, is E.J. Hobsbawm, *Primitive Rebels: Studies in Archaic Forms of Social Movement in the 19th and 20th Centuries* (Manchester, 1959); in the African context see D. Crummey, 'Introduction: "The Great Beast"', in *ibid.* (ed.), *Banditry, Rebellion and Social Protest*, 1–29.

66 For some account of cicatrization see Bowdich, *Mission*, 183; RAI, Rattray MSS, Notebook 4, 'Ashanti Law and Constitution', commenced 4 June 1925 states that Asante informants told the author that 'tribal marks' were a distinctive feature of *nnɔnkɔfoɔ* (the Asante, of course, did not scarify themselves); see too Rattray, *Ashanti Law and Constitution*, 35, fn. 2. See in general A.W. Cardinall, *The Natives of the Northern Territories of the Gold Coast: Their Customs, Religion and Folklore* (London, 1920); *ibid., In Ashanti;*

and Rattray, *Tribes of the Ashanti Hinterland*. A sense of the uncertainty and disorientation felt by such slaves emerges from the (very rare) autobiographical testimony of one such individual – Musa Datari of Nkoransa (born late 1840s–early 1850s); see 'Mose der Koransier', from a letter of Br. Wilh. Rottmann (Gold Coast) in *Der Evangelische Heidenbote* (Basel, 1892), 76–8; for some discussion see McCaskie, 'Death and the *Asantehene*', 418–19.

67 See Rattray, *Ashanti Law and Constitution*, 43.

68 BMA, Basel, Begoro Station Correspondence, II.85, Dilger's Report of a Journey: Obogu-Konongo-Agogo, dd. 17 March 1884; see too *ibid.*, II.94, Dilger to Basel, dd. 26 October 1883.

69 Rattray, *Ashanti Law and Constitution*, 44.

70 Jural definition (of rights in property, etc.) was surely the reason why the terminology of slave status by precise type was so developed – if rarely used in everyday speech; see RAI, Rattray MSS, Notebook 4, 'Ashanti Law and Constitution', commenced 4 June 1925. The contradictions between a given slave's seemingly benign daily life and ultimate jural status were the subject of much inconclusive debate in the early colonial period (1904–5); see NAG, Kumase, File D.234, 'Slaves and Pawns'. Similar themes underpin the discussion in A.N. Klein, 'The Two Asantes: Competing Interpretations of "Slavery" in Akan-Asante Culture and Society', *IASRR*, 12, 1 (1980), 37–51.

71 On bynames ('answer names') see Rattray, *Ashanti Law and Constitution*, 46. Compare the remarks in E. Terray, 'The Political Economy of the Abron Kingdom of Gyaman', *IASRR*, 12, 1 (1980), 1–36, and especially 8.

72 For some account see Rattray, *Ashanti Law and Constitution*, 123–4; such persons were named *asansafoɔ* (sing. *ɔsansani*), which denoted the unarmed members of a military force, but which also, significantly, carried the sense of 'worthless' people.

73 *Ibid.*, 42. I note but eschew extended discussion of the lengthy, inconclusive debate over the possible existence of an Asante 'slave mode of production'. This has focused on the issue of whether gold mining was carried out by slave or free labour, and it has deployed often ambiguous evidence in the service of either endorsing or refuting sectarian Marxist ideas from the 1970s; see, for example, R. Dumett, 'Precolonial Goldmining and the State in the Akan Region, with a Critique of the Terray Hypothesis', in G. Dalton (ed.), *Research in Economic Anthropology*, II (Greenwich, 1979), 37–68; *ibid.*, 'Traditional Slavery in the Akan Region in the Nineteenth Century: Sources, Issues and Interpretations', in D. Henige and T.C. McCaskie (eds.), *West African Economic and Social History: Studies in Memory of Marion Johnson* (Madison, 1990), 7–22; and E. Terray, 'Gold Production, Slave Labor, and State Intervention in Precolonial Akan Societies: A Reply to Raymond Dumett', in G. Dalton (ed.), *Research in Economic Anthropology*, V (Greenwich, 1983), 95–129. My own view, argued here, is that the Asante state depended upon the sectoral mobilization of both free *and* unfree labour. On the specific point, all my own research in Asante leads me tentatively to agree with Terray – but without endorsing his ideological presuppositions – at *ibid.*, 121, that Asante gold mining was done principally by slaves with little participation by free *nkoa*. This is certainly the recollection of most Asante informants. It is also

borne out by certain unequivocal traditions. In RH, Oxford, CRP, MSS Brit. Emp s.344, Papers of Sir Charles Henry Harper, 'The Traditional History of Denkera and Ashanti collected from Native Stories told to Jan H. Koens at Dunkwa', n.d., accounts are given of 'slave villages' being established by the Asante along the Offin River in the eighteenth century to 'dig and wash for gold'; 'much cruelty was practised here', it was said, 'on unwilling slaves or prisoners sent down from Coomassie'.

74 On the *Dwabenhemaa*, Konongo and *ŋkyere* see Kurankyi-Taylor, 'Legal Institutions', II, 469, fn. 2.; ASSM, *Asafo Agyei Ko*, MS compiled from interviews with 'elders of Juabin, Asokore, Konongo, etc.' by M. Fortes, 1946; and Rattray, *Ashanti Law and Constitution*, 42–3.

75 See Fortes, *Kinship and the Social Order*, 263. In RAI, Rattray MSS, 203, GC No. 314, dd. 24 June 1908, encl. C.H. Armitage, 'Native Laws and Customs [in] Ashanti', 27 May 1908, 12, it is noted that, 'The Ashantis were partial to marrying "slaves" for in such a case the children became the husband's property and could not be taken away from them [*sic*] by an uncle' (i.e. by the matrilineage).

76 For some discussion see McCaskie, 'Power and Dynastic Conflict in Mampon', 169–70. See too the remarks about primordial seating arrangements by 'family' on the right and left hands of the 'great ancestress' Ankyewa Nyame in AK.

77 Rattray, *Ashanti Law and Constitution*, 40. Compare Poku, 'Traditional Roles and People of Slave Origin in Modern Ashanti'.

78 This applies even if we grant validity to extreme or idiosyncratic readings. Thus, Klein, 'Inequality in Asante', I, 99 ff., constructs a case that 'Asante state slavery' reached critical mass in terms of numbers (and the potential for insurrection) *c.* 1810–20; that no rebellion took place is then ascribed to the *Asantehene* Osei Tutu Kwame's deployment of 'domestic servitude' as a 'legitimizing doorway into Akan matriliny' for huge numbers of *nnɔnkɔfoɔ*. In other words, 'Asante state slavery' was not benign – but the potential for rebellion produced by its oppressive nature was controlled by the state's use of the jural mechanisms that defined social identity. Klein's argument is highly questionable, but at least it engages with historical evidence. Others, in an understandable but wrong-headed quest to asseverate the complex virtues of Asante society, throw the historical baby out with the cultural-nationalist bathwater; see, representatively, A.Y. Yansane, 'Cultural, Political, and Economic Universals in West Africa', in M.K. and K.W. Asante (eds.), *African Culture: The Rhythms of Unity* (Trenton, 1990), 39–68, and especially 61, where we are led – astonishingly – to understand that Asante represented 'most explicitly the dialectical growth of a state society whose economic base was not exploitation of labor'.

79 See Rattray, *Ashanti Law and Constitution*, 35, fn. 2. This draconian prohibition against *amaŋfrafoɔ yɛbea* in the precolonial period is perhaps one reason why fashion innovators – in housing, furnishings, clothing, hairstyling, music, behaviour – in the early colonial era were seen as being so 'daring'. I am grateful to Wilhelmina Donkoh for discussions of these matters.

80 NAG, Kumase, File D.234, 'Slaves and Pawns', F.A. Ramseyer to Governor,

dd. Kumase, 31 October 1904; *ibid.*, F.C. Fuller (Chief Commissioner, Ashanti) to the Acting Colonial Secretary (Accra), dd. Kumase, 5 August 1905, with a 'Memorandum on Domestic Slavery in Ashanti'. This file is extensive and, predictably, it contains contradictory claims; its contents are discussed in depth in G. Austin, 'Kinship, Coercion and the Market'. For Ramseyer, the Basel Mission and the issue of slavery in early colonial Asante see copies of the periodical *Das Sklavenheim. Kollekteblat des bern. Hülfsvereins für das Missionswerk und Sklavenheim in Asante*, Basel, 1 (July 1898), *et seq.*

81 Emancipated slaves puzzled their benefactors by being 'ungrateful', and by seeking to forge new relations of dependence (and security). This was especially if predictably true of adolescents; see BMA, Basel, 'About the Slave Children', in D/1, 88, N.V. Asare, 'Annual Report of Kumase to the Home Committee', dd. Kumase, 29 February 1908. For the British view see NAG, Kumase, File D.234, 'Slaves and Pawns', C.H. Armitage to Chief Commissioner (Ashanti), dd. Obuasi, 13 September 1907 and Fuller, *A Vanished Dynasty*, 219.

82 See McCaskie, 'Social Rebellion and the Inchoate Rejection of History' for the radical reading of history and the moral order proposed, in the 1920s, by one phenomenally successful Christian Asante evangelist.

83 Thus, the seminal Rattray, *Religion and Art* is characterized by analytical perspectives that oscillate uncertainly between the individual and the social. The reading produced is unsatisfactory *per se*, and its equivocations are compounded, sometimes jarringly, by an insistently confessional tone. This last is the key. The sensibility displayed throughout the text is cued by an intimate identification, with Rattray urging upon himself the idea that any quintessential understanding of the *social* dimensions of Asante belief is to be obtained primarily by interactive empathy with *individual* aspirations to the ethical (to put matters plainly, there is altogether too much desirous participation, and not enough disengaged observation). Rattray's construction of Asante belief as an ethical yearning – for the harmonies of the integrated self, mediated by a striving towards a fully realized monotheism – was taken up and rehearsed by Akan commentators. See, almost canonically, J.B. Danquah, *The Akan Doctrine of God* (London, 1944), and C.A. Ackah, *Akan Ethics: A Study of the Moral Ideas and the Moral Behaviour of the Akan Tribes of Ghana* (Accra, 1988), in which Akan 'godliness' is given a sharper focus, and cast as a communitarian ethics (allowing for the self-realization of the individual in the communal sociabilities of ritual practices). Fatally, however, all such readings blankly omit the historical impress of power; *pace* Rattray, Danquah, Ackah and the celebrants of an Akan belief system of dedicated communitarianism – in which hierarchy is naturalized to the neutral performance of an agreed ethics – the *history* of Asante belief (at *all* points along the continuum described) is one of endless ideological interventions by the wielders of state power. Belief was not epiphenomenal to power, an item that could be abandoned to the ethical musings of 'tender consciences'; as an idiom of belonging – a pervasive reference to 'Asante-ness' – it irresistibly commanded the (self-)interest of the Asante state. Akan philosophers have gone some way towards acknowledging this, albeit from a viewpoint that is insufficiently explicit about historical

causes. So Wiredu, *Philosophy and an African Culture*, 3–4, talks of traditional society in terms of 'grass-roots authoritarianism' and 'the principle of unquestioning obedience to superiors'; but these arguments about the culture – by one of its most acute inheritors – are still ethical (and puzzled) rather than historical (and documented).

84 See, illustratively, the terms and names in BMA, Basel, D-10.2, 6. *Gottesnamen der Tschi-Neger der Goldküste*, n.d. (but probably compiled in this form in the 1910s/1920s); this should be compared with some of the materials in *ibid.*, D-20, Sch. 4, 3. 'Aspects of Twi Culture', n.d. (in Twi). See further the appropriate verbal and nominal entries in the unsuperseded and invaluable Christaller, *A Dictionary of the Asante and Fante Language* and, for some technical explication, P. Boakye, *Syntaxe de l'Achanti: du phonéme à la phrase segmentée* (Berne, Frankfurt and New York, 1982).

85 This *obiter scriptum* is by K.A. Opoku, and it is cited in K. Gyekye, *An Essay on African Philosophical Thought: The Akan Conceptual Scheme* (Cambridge, 1987), 129. Here Gyekye is arguing – *contra* Opoku, Danquah and Sarpong – for a consideration of 'basic existential conditions' (i.e. lived historical experience) in the shaping of Akan ethics, as against the simplistic supposition that the Akan moral order was generated, somehow, by religious belief *tout court*; compare the opinions on 'African communalist doctrine' [*sic*] in *ibid.*, *The Unexamined Life: Philosophy and the African Experience* (Accra, 1988), 24–5. It should be noted that there is much interesting detail in K.A. Opoku, *West African Traditional Religion* (Accra, 1978), not least concerned with axiological issues, but this author's propositional framework is ahistorical – and often deontological, with (religious) duty prior to (historical) value; and, at *ibid.*, 6, Rattray is applauded, symptomatically, for his 'sympathetic disposition' towards Asante religion.

86 This is a complex matter. Thus, in his cultural commentaries the (Asante) Roman Catholic Bishop of Kumase is somewhat reticent on the subject of human sacrifice; see P. Sarpong, *The Sacred Stools of the Akan* (Accra and Tema, 1971) and *ibid.*, *Ghana in Retrospect: Some Aspects of Ghanaian Culture* (Accra and Tema, 1974). The Wesleyan-Methodist S.G. Williamson, *Akan Religion and the Christian Faith: A Comparative Study of the Impact of Two Religions* (Accra, 1965), 46, simply observes that 'educated, enlightened Akans deplore even the historical record' of human sacrifice 'as a blot upon their tribal dignity'. This is far too sanguine. Some Christian Asante simply refuse to discuss human sacrifice. Others are prepared to talk freely. In conversation these latter tend to identify human sacrifice with the lamentable absence of (revealed Christian) 'enlightenment' in the precolonial era; on the other hand, the same people – when discoursing in nationalist vein upon the glories of Asante culture and the historic power of the *Asantehene* – include the fact of human sacrifice, without any embarrassment, in their celebratory remarks.

87 I include here the Fregean understanding of idea as the subjective associations of a word, contrasted with its meaning, as well as the Kantian (and Platonic) concept of idea as a representation of something that cannot be experienced.

88 Peel, 'History, Culture and the Comparative Method', 108.

89 Compare the discussion of the 'medieval tradition' in J. Van Engen, 'The Christian Middle Ages as an Historiographical Problem', *AHR*, 91 (1986), 519–52 and B. Stock, *Listening for the Text: On the Uses of the Past* (Baltimore, 1990).

90 R. Horton, 'Tradition and Modernity Revisited', in M. Hollis and S. Lukes (eds.), *Rationality and Relativism* (Oxford, 1982), especially 227–38. Horton's work is deservedly influential – but also diverse and contentious; for the evolution of ideas relevant here see *ibid.*, 'African Traditional Thought and Western Science, I and II', *Africa*, 37, 1 and 2 (1967), 50–71 and 155–87; 'African Conversion', *Africa*, 41, 2 (1971), 85–108; 'On the rationality of conversion, I and II', *Africa*, 45, 3 and 4 (1975), 219–35 and 373–99. For a critique of Horton's intellectualist stance see J. Skorupski, *Symbol and Theory: A Philosophical Study of Theories of Religion in Social Anthropology* (Cambridge, 1976), 189 ff.

91 Horton, in for example 'African Traditional Thought', expresses himself as being aware of the lack of 'historical depth' for the study of 'traditional African thought'. The point is well taken, but Horton's own empirical work – on the Kalabari of the Niger Delta – has been conducted in a society for which the historical record is markedly disadvantaged by comparison with Asante.

92 These parallels are drawn, implicitly and explicitly, throughout Rattray's works; he used comparative hierarchies of order to articulate what he regarded as the inseparability of 'religion' from 'almost any aspect of social life' (including the political).

93 See McCaskie, 'Komfo Anokye', '*Asantesɛm*' and 'People and Animals'.

94 See the childhood reminiscences of Agogo in Kyei, *My Memoir*, I and MFU, 'Talk with Panyin Bewuowu (Wobewu a wawu) of Bekwai', 1946.

95 BMA, Basel, D-10.2, 6. *Gottesnamen der Tschi-Neger der Goldküste*.

96 See Gyekye, *An Essay*, 221–2, fn. 9 for clarification of the etymology of this term.

97 See Danquah, *The Akan Doctrine of God*, 55 for the construction and reading of this term.

98 Chapman, 'Journal', entry dd. Dwaben, 13 February 1844.

99 As is well understood, the phenomenon of the 'withdrawn God' appears to be especially prevalent in West Africa.

100 Rattray, *Ashanti Proverbs*, 20–1 for the full account in Twi.

101 For discussion from a variety of perspectives see McCaskie, 'Accumulation, Wealth and Belief ... I', 'Komfo Anokye', 'Death and the *Asantehene*' and 'People and Animals'.

102 For details on divination see Asare, *Asante Abasem*; ASSM, 'A Pot of Herbs at Jaachi (Gyakye)', n.d.; MRO, Kumase, CRRB, Kyidom Clan Tribunal, *in re* Bosomfo Kobina, heard before Osei Yaw *et al.*, 1940–1. I am grateful to A.S. Koranteng and 'Papa' Manu of Suame, Kumase, for discussions of divining.

103 See HA. Compare the pessimistic testimony recorded in Chapman, 'Journal', entry dd. Kumase, 13 January 1844.

104 Bowdich, *Mission*, 261–2. Compare J. Beecham, *Ashantee and the Gold Coast* (London, 1841), 172–3 (based on information supplied by the Asante *ahenemma* Owusu Nkwantabisa and Owusu Ansa, and by T.B. Freeman). For versions of this account from among the Fante of Cape Coast see A.J.N.

Tremearne, 'Extracts from Diary of the late Rev. John Martin, Wesleyan Missionary in West Africa, 1843–48', *Man*, 73–4 (1912), 141.

105 Rattray, *Ashanti*, frontispiece ('A temple and priest of 'Nyame, the god of the sky'), 94, 141–4 and 175 does seem to suggest the existence of such temples and priests; however, as McLeod, *The Asante*, 57 correctly points out, 'there is no other record of them'.

106 There are numerous references to such shrines. See, for example, Bowdich, *Mission*, 308, and the illustration of the exterior of the *Asantehene* Osei Tutu Kwame's bedchamber ('The King's Sleeping Room'), reproduced as No. 10 between 312 and 313. For contextual discussion see L. Prussin, 'Traditional Asante Architecture', *AfAr*, 13, 2 (1980), 57–65, 78–82 and 83–7.

107 The concepts of *nkrabea* and *hyɛbea* have inspired various readings. My discussants lead me to agree with Gyekye – and *contra* Hagan, Danquah and Sarpong, who argue in different ways for a conceptual separation between *nkrabea* and *hyɛbea* – that 'the two [terms] are identical in their referent'; see Gyekye, *An Essay*, 108–19 for an extended discussion of the issues involved.

108 Bowdich, *Mission*, 262. Compare the views of ''De Gowu, a man who has access to the King', as reported in Chapman, 'Journal', entry dd. Kumase, 13 October 1843.

109 See ASC, Cambridge, Fortes Papers, 'The Origin of the "Abosom": A Talk with Kwasi Broni, Fetish Priest of Taa Kojo of Asokwa', 1946; MFU, 'The Fetish Priest Adu Anwona of Eduadin at Sipe', n.d.; *ibid.*, 'Akua Wasaa the Witch', n.d.; T.C. McCaskie, Interviews: Immanuel Donkoh and Kofi Adjaye, dd. Bogyawase and Kumase, April 1988. For folklore about the origin of the *abosom* see Rattray, *Folk-Tales*, 190–7 and 244–7.

110 ASC, Cambridge, Fortes Papers, 'Kwasi Broni, Fetish Priest, Speaks', 1946; see too *ibid.*, 'A Talk with Kobina Affum of Adeɛbeba on how Nsuman are Made', 1946.

111 Personalized *asuman* might be acquired for a variety of purposes; for example, *ayera suman* was used by hunters for concealing themselves; *konya suman* was used by women to sway men's affections; *abamo suman* was used to protect twins and ninth- and tenth-born children from malign influences; and *ntɔkwa suman* – commonly comprising bangles, poisonous ants, wasp stings, roots from a crossroads, leopard skin, threads, cowrie shells and 'medicine' from a squeezed leaf (*asɔso duro*) – was used by men going forth to war.

112 ASC, Cambridge, Fortes Papers, 'Origin of *akɔm* or 'Fetishism' (*sɛ Twumasi [Chwumasi] ammɔ dam ante aŋka 'akɔm' amma*)', n.d. For descriptions of dancing *akɔm* at Goaso (Ahafo) see Cardinall, *In Ashanti*, 233–4, at Adwira (Mampon) see Rattray, *Ashanti*, 209–10, and at Agogo see Kyei, *My Memoir*, I.

113 Rattray, *Religion and Art*, 38–47 gives details of the training involved (but erroneously limits the 'novitiate', as he terms it, to three years); compare MFU, 'The Fetish Priest Adu Anwona of Eduadin at Sipe', n.d. For discussion from a different perspective see P.A. Twumasi, *Medical Systems in Ghana: A Study in Medical Sociology* (Accra and Tema, 1975). An account of the training of 'priestesses' in recent times at the *Akonnedi* shrine (Larteh, Akuapem) is in Opoku, *West African Traditional Religion*, 75–90.

114 ASC, Cambridge, Fortes Papers, and MFU, 'A History of the Descent of a

Fetish, Kwabena of Adɛbeba', 1945; I have quoted the former, but the latter version has more details on the composition of *Taa Kwabena Bena*, and on its 'worship' in this century.

115 *Ibid.*, 'List (incomplete) of Fetishes visited in the Kwawuma Area Court Division', n.d.; 'Fetish Shrines at Saawua, Toase, etc.', n.d.

116 *Ibid.* Similarly, for example, the eighteenth-century shrine of *Taa Kora* at Safo in Kwabre had, and still has, a more than local reputation; see Nana Akwasi Abayie Boaten I, *An Economic Survey of Kwabre District: A Study in Rural Development* (Legon, 1990). A shrine might acquire a reputation for efficacy in dealing with specific problems. Thus, that of Tano at Heman was consulted by childless women; it is said that the *Asantehene* Kwaku Dua Panin was conceived after his mother had eaten an egg on the orders of the Heman *ɔbosom*. It was also the case that, after appropriate measures had been taken, certain shrines might be relocated; for the removal of the shrines of *Taa Toa, Aframso, Dwantua, Nkwaboa* and *Benaa* to Drobonso in the 1840s–50s see McCaskie, 'Manwere *nkoa* at Drobonso', 35.

117 Hutchison's Diary, dd. Kumase, 21 and 22 December 1817, in Bowdich, *Mission*, 412.

118 HA. The reputation of certain *abosom* was so entrenched that their shrines were consulted on a 'national' basis. On the history of one such shrine, that of *Dente* at Krakye, see D.J.E. Maier, *Priests and Power: The Case of the Dente Shrine in Nineteenth-Century Ghana* (Bloomington, 1983); and for *Dente* in Asante see Rattray, *Ashanti Proverbs*, 52–3. The *abosom* might be variously identified with places and/or with kin groups. Thus, Kyei, *My Memoir*, I, lists the following *abosom* in Agogo: 1. *Taa Kofi* (the oldest; a 'state' *ɔbosom*, consulted by the *Agogohene*; associated with the *Aduana abusua*); 2. *Afram* (the other 'state' *ɔbosom*; associated with the *Aduana abusua*); 3. *Anokye* (manifested itself temp. *Asantehene* Mensa Bonsu; associated with the *Asona abusua*); 4. *Antwiaa Tano* (associated with the *Oyoko abusua*); 5. *ɔdomaŋkama* (associated with the *Asona abusua*); 6. *Akogya* (the spirit of a small stream; 'patron *ɔbosom* of the *Agogoman*'); 7. *Kurowire Abena* (the spirit of a small stream). By the 1980s some of the Agogo *abosom* were 'dormant', but at least two (1, 2) still played a very active part in the town's affairs. For some general idea of the range of *abosom* see Christaller, *A Dictionary of the Asante and Fante Language*, Appendix B, 598–9.

119 BMA, Basel, 'The Worship of Tanno, the Great and Celebrated Fetish of the Whole Country', in D/1, 82, N.V. Asare, 'Annual Report of Kumase to the Home Committee', dd. Kumase, 14 February 1905. Compare Freeman, *Travels and Life in Ashanti and Jaman*, 144–5. For context see R.A. Silverman, 'Historical Dimensions of Tano Worship Among the Asante and Bono', in Schildkrout (ed.), *The Golden Stool*, 272–88.

120 This account has been compiled from the sometimes contradictory evidence in MFU, 'A Schedule of Interviews and Conversations in the Lake Bosomtwe Villages and Mponua Towns', 1946; ASC, Cambridge, Fortes Papers, 'Report from Akyenakrom', 24 August 1945; and *ibid.*, 'Tɔnwora (a pool) and Abrafia (a stream) in Akyenakrom', 1945.

121 On *sasabonsam* see, in brief, Rattray, *Ashanti Proverbs*, 47–8 and *Religion and*

Art, 28. I am grateful to all those, including the schoolchildren at Edweso, who have talked to me about *sasabonsam*.

122 On *mmoatia* see ASC, Cambridge, Fortes Papers, 'The Mmoatia or Fairies', 1945 (encl. 'Do You Believe in the Existence of Mmoatia?', *Ashanti Pioneer*, Kumase, 22 December 1945); Rattray, *Religion and Art*, 25–7. Compare the account of men and 'monkeys' (interpreted as a form of transmigration) in Chapman, 'Journal', entry dd. Kumase, 9 January 1844.

123 ASC, Cambridge, Fortes Papers, 'Statement by Kwame Sarpong, ex-*Krontihene* of Goaso', n.d. (but 1945).

124 *Ibid.* and MFU, 'A History of the Descent of a Fetish, Kwabena of Adɛbeba', 1945 (and see attached sketches).

125 This was also the area in which *akɔmfoɔ* were customarily buried, separately from others, in their own burial grounds; see ASC, Cambridge, Fortes Papers, File 3 on 'Funerals and Funeral Customs', in which it is also noted that such interments were conducted in an atmosphere of 'gravity and grandeur'.

126 Swithenbank, *Ashanti Fetish Houses*, 23–24. Since the 1920s Abirimu village has grown, and it now encompasses the old shrine complex.

127 Freeman, *Travels in Ashanti and Jaman*, 148, and in general 148–55. For *Sakara Bounou* see R.A. Bravmann, *Islam and Tribal Art in West Africa* (Cambridge, 1974), 100 ff.

128 On the Akan pharmacopoeia compare J. Petiver, 'A Catalogue of some Guinea Plants, with their Native Names and Virtues, etc.', *Philosophical Transactions (Royal Society)*, 19 (1697), 677–86, and H. Tedlie, '*Materia Medica* and Diseases', ch. 11 in Bowdich, *Mission*. Supernatural and natural explanations for illness were combined by Asante diagnosticians. Rattray, *Religion and Art*, 40 is correct when he distinguishes *akɔmfoɔ* from those persons who had a practical knowledge of specific drugs, or who trafficked only in *asumaŋ*. The *ɔkɔmfɔ* had a vocation that simultaneously embraced and superseded all of these subsidiary skills. See MFU, 'The Fetish Priest Adu Anwona of Eduadin at Sipe', n.d., and – for some discussion of these issues at Mampon and Kumawu – K. Ampratwum, 'Traditional Medical Centres', M.Sc. (UST Kumase, 1969).

129 This is the distinctive hairstyle that Bowdich, *Mission*, 40 termed 'a thrum mop' and that Freeman, *The Western Echo, Supplement*, 24 March 1886 (in describing the state executioners) said was 'twisted into numerous small cords, very much like an English mop', and was 'rusty' coloured from lack of grooming and exposure to the elements. See the portrait of the *ɔkɔmfɔ* in McLeod, *The Asante*, 63.

130 Asante discussants are understandably reticent about this matter. Unfortunately, European commentators have sometimes tended to schematize the 'psychological' in this relationship into a crudely explanatory *gestalt*; see G. Tooth, *Studies in Mental Illness in the Gold Coast* (London, 1950) and M.J. Field, *Search for Security: An Ethno-Psychiatric Study of Rural Ghana* (London, 1960).

131 Chapman, 'Journal', entry dd. Kumase, 3 November 1843.

132 See the sentiments expressed in Rattray, *Ashanti Proverbs*, 33–6.

133 *Ibid.*, 31.

134 Cardinall, *In Ashanti*, 53–4. From 1936 until 1947 there was an 'epidemic' of

'money-doubling' in Asante; see Kurankyi-Taylor, 'Legal Institutions', I, 209. In the early colonial period the British fancifully pictured fraudulent $akɔmfoɔ$ operating through 'the many secret societies which still flourish in Ashanti'; see C. Armitage, 'The Fetish-Worship of Ashanti', *Wide World Magazine*, 15 (April 1905), 62–7.

135 See, for example, the implications of the account of the death of Kwamena Bwa in Bowdich, *Mission*, 116.

136 See Chapman, 'Journal', entries dd. Kumase, 13 October, 24 November and 29 December 1843 and 17 and 24 January 1844 for clues to unknowing and anxiety. At *ibid.*, 13 October 1843 the afterlife is portrayed as a court of judgement; compare McCaskie, 'Komfo Anokye'. See too Bowdich, *Mission*, 262–3.

137 MFU, 'A Schedule of Interviews and Conversations in the Lake Bosomtwe Villages and Mponua Towns', 1946.

138 For explorations see McCaskie, 'Social Rebellion and the Inchoate Rejection of History', 'Anti-witchcraft Cults in Asante' and 'Komfo Anokye'. See too J.G. Platvoet, 'The Return of Anokye: The Use of a Political Myth by an Asante 'Puritan' Movement', draft paper, 1984.

139 ASC, Cambridge, Fortes Papers, 'The Custom of Witch Finding; Witch Finding Fetishes Mere Extortion; Brogya Could not be Tolerated', 1945. In variant versions the $ɔkɔmfɔ$ fails the test, and is executed. But the stratagem of entrapment is common to all versions.

140 Bowdich, *Mission*, 263–4.

141 See MFU, 'Statement by the Goldsmith Osei Kwame', n.d. and ASC, Cambridge, 'How Fetishes Read Oracles', 1945. The $nkɔntwima$ of an $ɔbosom$ was customarily borne by a servitor known as $pɔnkɔ$ ('horse').

142 *Ibid.* and see T.C. McCaskie, Interviews: Immanuel Donkoh and Kofi Adjaye, dd. Bogyawase and Kumase, April 1988. An $ɔkɔmfɔ$ found guilty by poison ordeal was not simply killed; he also suffered ritualized dismemberment.

143 In some references to this widely remembered case it is said that females were among the $akɔmfoɔ$ summoned before the *Asantehene*, and that these were condemned at *apremoso* after having been detected in the surreptitious act of trying to remove poisonous snakes from their genitals; see MFU, 'A Conversation About Female Witches with R.A.', n.d.

144 See McCaskie, 'Komfo Anokye' and '*Asantesɛm*'.

145 See G. Vattimo and P.A. Rovatti (eds.), *Il Pensiero Debole* (Milan, 1983).

146 See, for example, the *Asantehene* Agyeman Prempe's words when he physically repossessed the *sika dwa kofi* after his return from exile in the Seychelles: 'I have the stool ... nothing can stop me now from being restored to my rightful position as head of all Ashanti', reported in RH, Oxford, CRP, MSS Afr. s.593, Papers of Lt. Col. A.C. Duncan-Johnstone, Box 4, File 1, 'The Repatriation of ex-King Prempeh'. See further J. Agyeman-Duah, 'Golden Stool: Soul of the Ashanti Nation', n.d.

147 HA. The chronology of these events is summarized in ACBP/28: Kwaadu (Konadu) Yaadom, *Asantesɛm*, 11 (1979), especially 10–11.

148 At one extreme moment (August 1883) it was reported that the *Akyempemhene* $ɔheneba$ Owusu Kɔkɔɔ even contemplated the destruction of the *sika dwa kofi*

in order to forestall any attempt to seize it by his arch-rival the ex-*Asantehene* Kofi Kakari; for context see Wilks, *Asante*, 550–1.

149 See, for example, Asare, *Asante Abasem*. There are innumerable popular accounts; see for example K.O. Bonsu Kyeretwie, *Ashanti Heroes* (Accra, 1972) and the final speech by Komfo Anokye (Act III: Scene 3) in M. Dei-Anang, *Okomfo Anokye's Golden Stool: A Ghanaian Play in Three Acts* (Accra, 1963).

150 HA.

151 For a useful survey see G. Feeley-Harnik, 'Issues in Divine Kingship', *ARA*, 14 (1985), 273–313. Interesting in the Akan context is M. Gilbert, 'The Person of the King: Ritual and Power in a Ghanaian State', in D. Cannadine and S. Price (eds.), *Rituals of Royalty: Power and Ceremonial in Traditional Societies* (Cambridge, 1987), 298–330.

152 HA.

153 *Ibid.* See too the relevant – if somewhat disjointed – passages in AK.

154 McCaskie, 'Komfo Anokye'.

155 *Ibid.* Thus, for example, the appellation *ananse* ('the wise') accorded to the *Asantehene* Kwaku Dua Panin commemorates the understanding that 'he was the greatest of Asante law-givers *after* Anokye'. Rattray, *Ashanti Law and Constitution*, 279–80 catches something of the issues involved in his own reading of Komfo Anokye: 'The student of Ashanti law and custom, however, continually receives in answer to the question, "Why is such and such a rule observed?" the reply, "We do not know; Komfo Anotche made this a law."'

156 HA.

157 See, for example, BMA, Basel, 'Legend About Tula the Fetishman' in D/1, 84, N.V. Asare, 'Annual Report of Kumase to the Home Committee', dd. Kumase, 12 February 1906; Asare, *Asante Abasem*; compare the account of Komfo Anokye in *ibid.*, D/1, 79, N.V. Asare, 'Annual Report of Kumase to the Home Committee', dd. Kumase, 20 February 1904. See too MFU, 'Conversations with Nsuta People in Kumasi', n.d. and the account of Tuuda (although he is not actually named) in *ibid.*, 'The Fetish Priest Adu Anwona of Eduadin at Sipe', n.d. For a popular recounting see Bonsu Kyeretwie, *Ashanti Heroes*, 18–22. Tuuda first came to my attention in Asante in 1975, but my understanding has been deepened by general conversations with I. Donkoh, J.F. Opoku and others (1988), and by information supplied in writing (14 May 1990) by J.E. Gyimah. For the praise poem see K. Arhin, 'Asante Military Institutions', *JAS*, 7, 1 (1980), 22–30 and *ibid.*, 'The Asante Praise Poems', 194.

158 For discussion see McCaskie, 'Komfo Anokye'.

159 *Ibid.*, 329 for some discussion of the 'Laws'. The fullest written accounting of the 'Laws' is in HA. European observers were greatly baffled (and horrified) by the strict enforcement of 'The Seventy Seven Laws of Komfo Anokye'. Thus, for example, *ibid.*, 'Law 22' states: 'A pot containing oil must not be broken in any street in Kumasi'; Chapman, 'Journal', entry dd. Kumase, 12 August 1844 records: 'Yesterday a young female happening to let fall a small pot of palm oil in one of the streets, was immediately punished with the loss of her ears, nose and lips. Last week a woman was killed on account of a similar accident. It appears, there is a law in force the penalty of which is death, to any person who

either through accident or carelessness pours palm oil upon the ground in any of the streets.'

160 The seventy-seven wards are listed by name in Asare, *Asante Abasem*.

161 For a brief description see Rattray, *Religion and Art*, 89, 113 and Fig. 45. Modern Asante sometimes refer to the shrine and its location as '(being) where the King swallowed up evil men'.

162 See Rattray, *Religion and Art*, 29–30 for the testimony of Yaw Adawua, a sometime member of *ɔdomaŋkama*, and 'a famous witch-finder'. For discussion see McCaskie, 'Anti-witchcraft Cults in Asante' and 'Komfo Anokye', and Platvoet, 'The Return of Anokye'.

163 BMA, Basel, D-1, 32–159, F. Ramseyer to the Home Committee, dd. Abetifi, 19 June 1880. (I am most grateful to P. Jenkins and to J.G. Platvoet for providing me with copies of their translations of this very important letter to check against my own.) A published summary in French, with other relevant letters, is in 'Au Comité des Missions de Neuchâtel', *Bulletin de la Mission Achantie*, Neuchâtel, 3, 1 (1880), 1–16.

164 There is a vivid (eyewitness?) reminiscence of the suppression of *ɔdomaŋkama* by the (British-appointed) Kumase *Atipinhene* and subsequently *Mamponhene* Kwaku Dua Agyeman in ASC, Cambridge, Fortes Papers, 'The Biography of Nana Mansu [*sic*] Bonsu', n.d. (and an extended version of the whole biography in MFU); see McCaskie, 'Komfo Anokye', 332–3 for the crucial passage. See too MRO, Kumase, File A/77, 'Supernaturalism in Ashanti' and the documentation recorded in McCaskie, 'Anti-witchcraft Cults in Asante', 132–3.

165 ASC, Cambridge, Fortes Papers, 'The Custom of Witch Finding: Witch Finding Fetishes Mere Extortion: Brogya Could not be Tolerated', 1945. (The account is annotated as an 'episode in the unwritten History of Ashanti'.) According to information supplied (by the Kumase envoys *Asabihene* Asabi Antwi and *Akomfodehene* Kwaku Bosommuru Dwira) to the *ɔheneba* Owusu Ansa in Cape Coast, the *abonsamkɔmfoɔ* 'gradually became so impudent, that one morning they forced their way into the palace, allowed themselves all sorts of liberties there at first ... then, suddenly, one of them fired a shot at the King, but failed to hit him ... You know the Ashanti. You know how they honour their King. Everyone threw themselves upon the evil-doers who were killed. The others were arrested'; see Owusu Ansa to Ramseyer, Cape Coast, n.d., encl. in BMA, Basel, D-1, 32–159, F. Ramseyer to the Home Committee, dd. Abetifi, 19 June 1880. Whatever the 'evil-doers' did or did not do in Kumase *ahenfie*, it is clear that the Asante construed the mêlée as a confrontation between right order (as exemplified by the *Asantehene*, custodian of the *sika dwa kofi* 'authored' by Komfo Anokye) and its antithesis.

166 See, in summary, B.M. Haight, 'Bole and Gonja: Contributions to the History of Northern Ghana', Ph.D. (Northwestern, 1981); P. Ferguson, 'Islamization in Dagbon: A Study of the Alfanema of Yendi', Ph.D. (Cambridge, 1973); S. Drucker Brown, *Ritual Aspects of the Mamprusi Kingship* (Cambridge and Leiden, 1975) (on the *alfadima* of Nalerigu); Izard, *Gens du pouvoir, Gens de la terre*; Terray, 'Une Histoire du Royaume Abron du Gyaman'.

167 This is not to argue that the impulse to *jihād* did not exist. But it is to argue that

it was individual rather than societal, intellectual rather than popular; see, succinctly and representatively, the failure of the mid-nineteenth-century *jihād* of Al-Hājj Maḥmūd Karantaw to gain mass support, or to persuade the conservative *'ulamā'* of 'the older Suwarian tradition' in the northern Asante hinterland, as recounted in I. Wilks, *Wa and the Wala: Islam and Polity in Northwestern Ghana* (Cambridge, 1989), especially 100–3. Militant Islam did play a more prominent role in the Asante hinterland in the period of anarchic disruption that accompanied the colonial conquest at the end of the nineteenth century; see J. Holden, 'The Zabarima Conquest of North-West Ghana, Part I', *THSG*, 8 (1965), 60–86 and Y. Person, *Samori: une révolution dyula* (Dakar, 1968–75), 3 vols.

168 See, for example, the comments of the learned (and orthodox) *sharīf* Ibrāhīm al-Barnawī on the Muslim community in Kumase in Hutchison's Diary, dd. Kumase, 20 November 1817, in Bowdich, *Mission*, 397–8; see too the reservations expressed by leaders of that community – the *imām* Muḥammad al-Ghamba' and Abū Bakr Turay – in (the pro-Muslim) Dupuis, *Journal*, 128. Muḥammad al-Ghamba' was forced to a crisis of conscience in the Gyaman war (1818–19). He deserted from the Asante army when he could no longer accommodate himself to fighting for 'unbelievers' against (some) Muslims, or reconcile himself to 'the horrid butcheries' perpetrated by Asante troops; the *Asantehene* Osei Tutu Kwame was reportedly 'enraged' at this perfidy, and 'swore that had he [Muḥammad al-Ghamba'] not been a holy man, he would have put him to death'. See *ibid.*, 98, fn. Notwithstanding this extreme expression of his doctrinal reservations, however, Muḥammad al-Ghamba' returned to live in Kumase, where he resumed his position as titular *imām* of the 'stranger' community there, becoming a friend and confidant of Dupuis in 1820.

169 See McCaskie, 'Innovational Eclecticism'; D.J.E. Maier, 'Nineteenth-Century Asante Medical Practices', *CSSH*, 21, 1 (1979), 63–81; Owusu-Ansah, *Talismanic Tradition*, 183 ff., where Asante-Muslim relations in Kumase are characterized (following Gramsci) as conforming to a 'Dominant-Subaltern' typology; and, in similar vein, the judicious R.A. Bravmann and R.A. Silverman, 'Painted Incantations: The Closeness of Allah and Kings in 19th-Century Asante', in Schildkrout (ed.), *The Golden Stool*, 93–108. Bravmann and Silverman sensibly conclude that the *Asantehenes* – their exemplars being Osei Tutu Kwame and Kofi Kakari – viewed Islam as 'a system of belief capable of preserving themselves and their citizenry' (via 'painted incantations' on cloth or sandals), but on terms set out by the ('dominant') Asante themselves, for 'neither of these rulers swerved from the ancient deities, shrines, and ancestral forces that had long sustained Asante'. Wilks, *Asante*, 250–1 draws attention to the *Asante Nkramo* – a group of Muslims who were (possibly) first introduced into Kumase via Mampon in the late eighteenth century, and who were attached to the *nsumaŋkwaafoɔ* under the authority of the Kumase *Nsumaŋkwaahene*. By definition the *nsumaŋkwaafoɔ* were 'the *asumaŋ* people'; they practised supernatural 'medicine' on behalf of the *Asantehene*, and also medicine *per se* (hence their designation as 'court physicians'). The *Asante Nkramo* simply added their own particular skills to

this enterprise, and in a markedly syncretistic way. For the roles of the *nsumaŋkwaafoɔ* see T.C. McCaskie, Interviews: *Nsumaŋkwaahene* Domfe Gyeabuo, dd. Kumase, 5–6 January 1976, and the same individual's testimony in Owusu-Ansah, *Talismanic Tradition*, 124.

170 Wilks, *Asante*, 253–4 advances the case for the *Asantehene* Osei Kwame being 'strongly inclined towards Islam', and for the part that opposition to Islam (and its egalitarian tendencies) played in his deposition; Wilks goes on to suggest that Osei Kwame's removal as (a pro-Muslim) *Asantehene* 'may explain' why there ensued various 'uprisings in the northwest intended to achieve his restoration to power'. Apart from reservations about what might be termed the cultural logic of this argument in the Asante context, note needs to be taken of the fact that Wilks' direct evidence that Osei Kwame was 'a believer at heart' (in Islam) comes from a single, highly partisan witness – the *imām* Muḥammad al-Ghamba' – and his speculations about events in the aftermath of Osei Kwame's removal from office are also derived from Muslim testimony; see Dupuis, *Journal*, 245–6. By contrast, Bowdich, *Mission*, 238–40 gives a detailed account of Osei Kwame's deposition, but without mentioning Islam; likewise, HA enumerates the detailed causes of Osei Kwame's deposition, but again without mentioning Islam. Wilks does provide a more considered view of the deposition (and death) of Osei Kwame – emphasizing dynastic politics and his erratic behaviour (the failure to hold the Kumase *odwira* of 1802), and putting his supposed 'leanings towards Islam' in a more speculative perspective – in ACBP/28: Konadu (Kwaadu) Yaadom, *Asantesɛm*, 11 (1979), 10–11 (another, fuller discussion is in McCaskie, '*Konnurokusɛm*'). I have pursued this matter here, because Wilks' symptomatic conjectures about Osei Kwame bear directly upon the larger issue of how he has constructed his reading of the significance of Islam in Asante (and has directly influenced subsequent scholarship on the subject). In all of his writings on Islam in Asante – as in the case of Osei Kwame – Wilks has consistently given the strength of Muslim influence the benefit of any evidential doubt. In this he might be compared with Dupuis, whose intellectual interest in Islam (a world religion, a literary tradition), and personal empathy with the Muslims in Kumase (as friends, as informants), led him to overstate, at the least, the *religious* impact of Islam on the Asante, as opposed to the *instrumental* incorporation by the Asante of items of Islamic religious practice into the pre-existing framework of indigenous beliefs. Muslims in Kumase were politically and commercially valuable to the Asante state, but their faith was acceptable only in as much as its adherents were prepared syncretically to adjust its doctrines to Asante demands and desires. Unsurprisingly, therefore, Muslims in Kumase, whatever their private sentiments, lived public lives that extended along a spectrum from compromise to apostasy.

171 On the *Asante Adimɛm* see Wilks, *Asante*, 316–18. See also *ibid.*, 'A Letter of 1888 from Abū Bakr b. 'Uthmān Kamaghatay', 43, which quotes, from 3 December 1928, the *Asantehene* (but at that time the British-appointed *Kumasihene*) Agyeman Prempe writing as follows to the D.C. (Kumase): 'When I was enstooled [in 1888] I sent for the Priest Arbooba [Abū Bakr b. 'Uthmān Kamaghatay] – and the writer [i.e. Agyeman Prempe] enstooled him

as Safoohene [i.e. appointed him as an Asante office holder with the title and rank of *asafohene*].'

172 In 1839, following the Wesleyan-Methodist T.B. Freeman's first visit to Kumase, the Basel Mission sent A. Riis there to assess the possibilities on its behalf. The visit was not a success. The Basel Mission then effectively left Kumase to the Wesleyan-Methodists, until it finally came to establish a permanent presence there in 1896; it contented itself, in the interim, with proselytizing in Asante Akyem (after 1874), and with reconnaissances to Kumase (Huppenbauer and Buck, 1881; Ramseyer and Mohr, 1881; Ramseyer and Asante, 1882). See A. Riis, 'Reise des Missionars in Akropong nach dem Aschantee-Lande im Winter 1839 bis 1840', *Magazin für die Neueste Geschichte der Evangelischen Missions- und Bibel-Gesellschaften* (Basel, 1840), Pt III, 92 ff. and 216–35; see too WMMS, Rev. Hoffmann to Sir Thomas Fowell Buxton, dd. Basel, 15 September 1840. For the visits to Kumase in the 1880s see BMA, Basel, General Correspondence, 'Reports of the Journey to Kumase of Buck and Huppenbauer' (comprising letters of 7 and 26 February and 1 March 1881); 'Reports of the Journey to Kumase of Ramseyer and Mohr' (comprising letters of 7 and 28 September, and 5 and 25 October 1881); Ramseyer to Basel, dd. Abetifi, ? October 1882; and see too D. Huppenbauer, *Von Kyebi nach Kumase: Eine Reise ins Hinterland der Goldküste* (Basel, 1914).

173 See, for example, Chapman, 'Journal', entries dd. Kumase, 16, 17 and 18 November 1844, and WMMS, Chapman to General Secretaries, dd. Cape Coast, 11 December 1844 (with addenda of 6 January 1845) and ? July 1845 for Asante attempts to use the Wesleyan-Methodists as a diplomatic conduit to the British during a crisis of relations between the two governments (and for cautious missionary acceptance of this role); and Chapman, 'Journal', entry dd. Kumase, 16 February 1844, for the *Asantehene* Kwaku Dua Panin's understanding of the relationship between the missionaries and British officialdom.

174 For a contemporary account of this trade see Cruickshank, *Eighteen Years*, II, 30–46. For brief overviews from the Asante and Fante points of view respectively see Wilks, 'The Golden Stool and the Elephant Tail', 24 ff. and M. McCarthy, *Social Change and the Growth of British Power in the Gold Coast: The Fante States 1807–1874* (Lanham, 1983), 125 ff. Wesleyan-Methodist converts among the coastal Akan were prominent among the ultimate economic beneficiaries of the Asante trade; see the names listed in E. Reynolds, *Trade and Economic Change on the Gold Coast, 1807–1874* (London, 1974), 80.

175 The Asante clung fitfully to this aspiration, but became circumspect about discussing it; see the conversation of the *Asantehene* Kwaku Dua Panin in Chapman, 'Journal', entry dd. Kumase, 18 July 1844.

176 See *inter alia* WMMS, Chapman to General Secretaries, dd. Kumase, 24 March 1844; Brooking to General Secretaries, dd. Anomabo, 25 April 1844; Freeman, 'The Progress of the Kumasi Mission', 28 September 1844; Chapman to General Secretaries, dd. Kumase, 8 October 1844; Wharton to General Secretaries, dd. Kumase, 31 May and 9 November 1846, and 18 October 1847; Hillard to General Secretaries, dd. Kumase, 29 May 1848; Hart

to General Secretaries, dd. Kumase, 13 May 1850; Laing to Freeman, dd. Kumase, 20 February 1852. For a summary overview see McCaskie, 'Paramountcy'.

177 The most prominent Wesleyan-Methodist missionary 'converts' in Kumase were Opoku Ahoni and Opoku Awusi; both were *Oyoko Kɔkɔɔ adehyeɛ*, and the former was 'second heir-apparent' to the *Asantehene* Kwaku Dua Panin. Their adherence to Christianity was (for the most part) clandestine, and both were executed *c.* 1847 or early 1848. Freeman thought that their deaths were 'not without strong suspicions that their attachment to Christianity had been a means, though not ostensibly shown, of shortening their earthly existence'; see *The Western Echo, Supplement*, 8 May 1886. However, in the same place, Freeman noted that 'both of these princes had perished in politico-domestic excitements of the palace', and the balance of the evidence is such as to suggest that dynastic politics played at least as large a part in their execution as did the profession of Christianity; see McCaskie, '*Konnurokusɛm*'. It is exceedingly hard to gauge the Christian sincerity of these two 'princes' (or, indeed, of any other Asante who expressed an interest in Christian doctrines). Thus, Opoku Ahoni's acquisition of some skills in reading and writing may have been instrumental; and the Wesleyan-Methodist correspondence makes it abundantly clear that many Asante approached the missionaries as a source of imported goods. The Wesleyan-Methodists themselves, understandably, always chose to cast Asante inquiries about Christianity in the most optimistic light. Wesleyan-Methodist optimism led the missionaries to hopeful – but often errant – readings of Asante behaviour. Thus, Chapman, 'Journal', entry dd. Kumase, 19 February 1844 recorded, with deep satisfaction, the public burning by Opoku Awusi of 'his fetish'. But the account itself is deeply ambiguous in its details of the proceedings; what Chapman chose to construe as evidence of 'Christian principles' conformed in fact to standard Asante rituals for disposing of a *suman* with waning or lost powers. (See MFU, 'The Power of Juju of Kobina Efum', n.d. for an account of the disposal of *pim san* – 'push and go back' – a *suman* dedicated to maintaining personal 'stability', but no longer efficacious.) Typical of Wesleyan-Methodist reading is the fact that with each successive retelling the story of the destruction of Opoku Awusi's 'fetish' became more slanted towards interpretation as an act inspired by Christian revelation and grace. (See, for its ultimate apotheosis, 'In the Footsteps of Thomas Birch Freeman', *The Foreign Field* (London, June 1929), 220–1: 'A youth of royal blood became a Christian and publicly burned his fetiches – and soon after was murdered!') It should also be added that the voluminous writings of Wesleyan-Methodist missionaries in Asante, with their clutching need to believe in even the very faintest hint of success, need to be understood in strict context; these men were mostly alone, often ill, frequently frightened – isolated, as they saw, in an alien world.

178 The Asante state had reason for these concerns. Reflections and personal asides expressed throughout all of the Wesleyan-Methodist writings from, and about, Kumase show a keenness to promote the enhanced empowerment of the individual – defined through responsibilities for the self, to be undertaken morally and educationally – and a concomitant questioning of the established

order in the light of these criteria for personal salvation.

179 See WMMS, 'Journals of the Rev. Thomas B. Freeman', entry dd. Kumase, 17 January 1842.

180 WMMS, Hillard to Beecham, dd. Kumase, 16 January 1849.

181 Chapman, 'Journal', entry dd. Kumase, 18 June 1844. It would be tedious to document the many attempts made by the Wesleyan-Methodists to secure permission to establish a school in Kumase, as opposed to their (very intermittent) tutoring of one or two individuals. By 1852, after thirteen years of mission work, there were only four probationary members of the mission in Asante, and three of these were sojourners from the coast (the single Asante, optimistically counted, was from a rural area and rarely seen). See WMMS, Laing to Freeman, dd. Kumase, 20 February 1852; Laing resignedly concluded that 'We have toiled here, like Peter with his fellow Fishermen, all night and have caught nothing.'

182 Chapman, 'Journal', entry dd. Kumase, 10 September 1844.

183 For the text of the treaty of 1831 see J.J. Crooks, *Records relating to the Gold Coast Settlements: From 1750 to 1874* (Dublin, 1923), 262–4. The two youths were handed over to the British as 'security' for the *Asantehene* Osei Yaw Akoto keeping the peace. The British had stipulated the surrender of 'two young men of the royal family of Ashantee' – and the Asante seemingly complied; however, the British thought that they were taking custody of potential future rulers of Asante, i.e. *adehyeε* rather than *ahenemma*, and they persisted in this confusion for some time thereafter. Baptized and educated as Anglicans, the two *ahenemma* were then put into the hands of the Wesleyan-Methodists; in 1841 they returned with T.B. Freeman to Kumase, where, it was hoped, they would advance Christianity among their countrymen by preaching and example; see WMMS, 'Maclean's Instructions to the Ashanti Princes on the Eve of their Departure for Kumasi, 1841, with Comments by the Rev. B. Tregaskis'. For (John) Owusu Ansa and (William) Owusu Nkwantabisa in summary see Owusu-Mensa, 'Prince Owusu Ansa'; Metcalfe, *Maclean of the Gold Coast*, especially 88, 204 and 270–5; and Wilks, *Asante*, 190 and 203–4.

184 See Chapman, 'Journal', entry dd. Kumase, 5 October 1844; *ibid.*, 6 October 1844, for the contrite acknowledgement, by the two *ahenemma*, that 'the complaints of the King were not without foundation', and for Chapman's view that Owusu Nkwantabisa was a more persistent offender than Owusu Ansa; and see too WMMS, Chapman to Freeman, dd. Kumase, 7 October 1844. Charges of this sort had been levelled before. In August 1842, Owusu Nkwantabisa and a married woman were convicted before the *Asantehene* of committing adultery. The woman was executed. Owusu Nkwantabisa – who said that the woman entered his room while drunk, and that no adultery occurred – only escaped a heavy fine through missionary intervention on his behalf. Interestingly, the affair took place during *odwira* – but if the mitigating factor of sanctioned licence was even entertained, it failed to save the woman; see *ibid.*, Brooking to Beecham, dd. Kumase, n.d. (but January 1843), and Owusu Nkwantabisa to the Rev. C. Pine, dd. Kumase, 20 January 1843. Owusu Nkwantabisa was apparently never able to adjust to his situation; he

died prematurely on the Gold Coast, evidently from addiction to alcohol, in 1859. Owusu Ansa, as is well known, went on to play a major political role in Asante–British relations, but progressively, throughout the 1850s–60s, he too distanced himself from his earlier, intimate identification with the Wesleyan-Methodists.

185 *Ibid.*, T.B. Picot to the Rev. W.B. Boyce, dd. Cape Coast, 3 May 1876 (with an account of his residence in Kumase, 10 to 21 April 1876).

186 For summary careers see ACBP/2: Adu Bofɔɔ, *Asante Seminar*, 1 (1975), 10–14, and ACBP/47: Kwabena Awua, *Asantesɛm*, 10 (1979), 21–30.

187 WMMS, London, T.B. Picot to the Rev. W.B. Boyce, dd. Cape Coast, 3 May 1876, 14–15.

188 *Ibid.*, 15.

189 *Ibid.*, 15–16. This meeting commenced at 11 a.m. on 21 April, and Picot 'left Kumasi the same afternoon'. His summary recommendation, following his visit to Kumase, was that the cause of Christianity in Asante seemed hopeless *pro tem*, and that the Wesleyan-Methodist effort should be concentrated henceforth (among the Assin) in areas 'within the [British] protectorate' (of the Gold Coast). After 1876, the Wesleyan-Methodists had no permanent – or even sustained – presence in Kumase until after the British occupied the city in 1896; until then, they contented themselves with brief reconnaissance visits, or with itinerary preaching by peripatetic agents in Adanse (and, to some extent, Bekwai). See for example, *ibid.*, Mountford to Osborn, dd. Cape Coast, 8 February 1883; W. Terry Coppin, 'Journal (including a Visit to Ashanti)', MS dd. 1885; Terry Coppin to Osborn, dd. Cape Coast, 24 March 1886; and Somerville to Hartley, dd. 'King Prempeh's Palace, Kumasi', 23 May 1896. In 1913, the *Asantehene* Agyeman Prempe, in exile in the Seychelles, recalled that Mensa Bonsu and his office holders had rejected 'the institutions [*sic*] of school buildings for training at Kumasi'; see NAS, C/SS/2 vol. II, 'Political Exiles, Ashanti: Ex-King Prempeh and Others', 1906–15, E. Prempeh *et al.* to Governor, Seychelles Islands, dd. Ashanti Camp, Le Rocher, Mahé, 16 October 1913. (There is a transcribed version of this MS, dd. 7 August 1922, in GPRL, Accra.)

190 Compare, for example, the Wesleyan-Methodist and Congregationalist enterprises among the Tswana as recounted in J. and J. Comaroff, *Of Revelation*, and especially 252 ff.; and see too the succinct discussion of the meaning(s) of conversion to Islam in West Africa in M. Hiskett, *The Development of Islam in West Africa* (London and New York, 1984), 302–19.

191 Compare here the ideological-historical terms of the *Asantehene* Mensa Bonsu's rejection of 'liberty of conscience' (in 1876) with the discussion of *tiboa* – given as 'conscience' – in Gyekye, *An Essay*, especially 142–3. Here Gyekye makes an important general point, albeit from an ethical rather than a historical perspective: 'I maintain that *tiboa* is not innate to man ... It is the cumulative result of the individual's response to past moral situations. Thus, I interpret *tiboa* as nothing mysterious or supernatural in its origins. This interpretation appears consonant with the generally empirical orientation of Akan philosophy.' That is, *tiboa* is 'acquired through socialization, through habituation, through moral experience', and so Asante 'conscience' – socially

contextualized, individually practised – is a negotiable adjustment to history rather than a non-negotiable property of belief.

192 The terms used here deliberately echo the early Heidegger, not least because the Asante present particular difficulties for any phenomenologist in the post-Husserlian European tradition. An argument might be made for the Asante as Heideggerian 'beings-in-the-world' inhabiting life through a constitutive *Dasein*; but the phenomenological dedication to the individual (of European modernity), and the atomized, person-specific concept of *'Sorge'* ('care'), in Heideggerian terms the prevailing attitude of *Dasein*, are poorly developed in and perhaps alien to what is understood of the Asante conceptualization of a person. Furthermore, the Heideggerian construction(s) of knowledge as becoming – and particularly, following Kierkegaard, the identification of 'anxiety' as a recognition of the being of the world – apply to the Asante in terms of their experience of the inescapable presence of being but *not* its meaninglessness. Quite unlike Heidegger (and the Western Christian tradition), the Asante had no investment in the fact of physical death as either the root of 'anxiety' or (individually experienced, as realization) the key to authenticity. See M. Heidegger, *Being and Time* (*Sein und Zeit*, 1927), trans. J. Macquarrie and E. Robinson (Oxford, 1962), especially Part I, Divisions I, II. My own reading of the terms of Asante 'anxiety' – as experience of the inescapable presence of being (in the Heideggerian sense described here) – is explored, most recently, in McCaskie, 'People and Animals'. Absent from Asante in the sense used here, iconography has of course played a crucial and often contentious role as argument in the representation of Christian beliefs (the extreme case being in the Byzantine Empire in the eight to ninth centuries, during and after the reign of the iconoclast Emperor Leo III).

193 WMMS, T.B. Picot to the Rev. W.B. Boyce, dd. Cape Coast, 3 May 1876. The Victorian Christian Fante view was, unsurprisingly, somewhat different; see, by way of illustration, the opinions informing the (English common law) arguments in J.M. Sarbah, *Fanti National Constitution* (London, 1906).

194 See the (con)textual framework in, for example, MRO, Kumase, 'Papers and Report on the Funeral Custom of the late Kumasihene', (from) 21 May 1932. The twentieth-century impact of Christianity, at least in this context, has been to reinforce the understanding of the 'immortality' of ancestors; for some very good discussion, but concerning the Akan of Akuapem, see M. Gilbert, 'The Sudden Death of a Millionaire: Conversion and Consensus in a Ghanaian Kingdom', *Africa*, 58, 3 (1988), 291–314. In Christian Asante ephemera (of a huge variety of sectarian persuasions) the traditional construction of the link between the living and the dead is maintained, and celebrated, within a biblical framework; see E.K. Braffi, *The Esoteric Significance of the Asante Nation* (Kumase, 1984).

195 See, from a range of affirmations, one possible interrogation of the appropriateness of this structuration, as reported in Chapman, 'Journal', entry dd. Kumase, 24 January 1844.

196 For some account of responses to the marginalization of the individual ego see McCaskie, 'People and Animals'. Another view is given in Gyekye, *An Essay*, especially 154–62.

197 For very different ventures in tackling the legacy of Lévy-Bruhl throughout Africa – and most especially the incautious refutation of that inheritance by the 'philosophers' of an African 'democratic' communalism – see Hountondji, *Sur la philosophie africaine*; T. Okere, *African Philosophy: A Historico-Hermeneutical Investigation of the Conditions of its Possibility* (Lanham, 1983); and, on 'ethnophilosophy', Mudimbe, *The Invention of Africa*, 135 ff. A challenge to Lévy-Bruhl – but very much of its period and intellectual milieu in its idealization (and valorization) of an ethical Akan communalism – is in Danquah, *The Akan Doctrine of God*, especially 104 ff.

198 The very recent (1980s) insertion into Asante life of novel varieties of fundamentalist and/or charismatic Christianity is a significant case in point. This needs to be studied in detail; the appeal of glossolalia is of particular interest, I think, to the student of Asante culture, and I am grateful to Rosalind Hackett for some conversation on this matter.

4   ASANTE *ODWIRA*: EXPERIENCE INTERPRETED, HISTORY CONSTRUCTED

1 Bowdich, *Mission*, 274, for example, goes on to compare *odwira* to the ancient Roman *Saturnalia* in an attempt to domesticate its excesses to the understanding of educated Europeans. Interestingly, Bowdich's (older) contemporary, Goethe, who travelled twice to Italy in the 1780s in pursuit of the classical ideal formulated by Winckelmann, observed the Roman *carnevale*, the direct if remote Christian descendant of *Saturnalia*. Goethe's account is more self-consciously 'literary' than Bowdich's, but the two share in an exasperation at the inadequacy of words in distilling any overall description from the sheer confusion of events; see J.W. Goethe, *The Italian Journey (1786–1788)*, trans. W.H. Auden and E. Meyer (London, 1970), 446–70.

2 Compare the account of the annual 'general feast' held along the Gold Coast in July, in P. de Marees, *Description and Historical Account of the Gold Kingdom of Guinea (1602)*, trans. from the Dutch and ed. A. van Dantzig and A. Jones (Oxford, 1987), 170; W.J. Müller's 1660s description of the yearly 'great festival' held in Fetu, in Jones, *German Sources*, 167–9; and Bosman's 1690s report of the annual ritual of 'driving out the devil' in Axim, in W. Bosman, *A New and Accurate Description of the Coast of Guinea, Divided into the Gold, the Slave, and the Ivory Coasts* (London, 1705), 158–9. On Bosman see too A. van Dantzig, 'English Bosman and Dutch Bosman: A Comparison of Texts – III', *HA*, 4 (1977), 253. For useful discussions see Kea, *Settlements, Trade, and Politics*, 291–2, and for a popular ethnographic account see A.A. Opoku, *Festivals of Ghana* (Accra, 1970).

3 On the prime significances of 'purification and thanksgiving' at *odwira*, and for the profound historical sense that informed its celebration, see *Address by Otumfuo, Opoku Ware II, Asantehene, at the Golden Jubilee Odwira Durbar, Kumasi, Saturday, November 16, 1985* (Kumase, 1985).

4 See, in brief, the list in Kyei, *My Memoir*, I, 'Appendix 8: Crops I saw Grown in My Grandmother's and My Mother's "Nfikyi-Fuo" (Foodcrop Farms) in my Childhood Days'.

5 The exception, discussed below, was in 1871. On the agricultural cycle, and its modern adaptation to European calendrical time, see, conveniently, MRO, Kumase, Misc. Files, 'Asranna – Day, Month Calendars', 1983, 1985, etc. See too T.C. McCaskie, Interviews: A.K. (Osei) Nana Boateng, 'Chief Farmer', et al., dd. Adwira Market, April 1979.

6 The ritual significance of yam is referenced throughout Rattray, Ashanti, and see ibid., Religion and Art, 66, for a very specific ritual use; ASSM, Farming Records (File 37) has some account of the 'celebrated' farmers 'Baa Maanu' and 'Dinkyi' of Kokofu; RAI, Rattray MSS, MS Bundle 107, Notebook 3, 1809–10, has details on the sexual division of labour in agriculture, etc.; The Western Echo, Supplement, 24 March 1886, for the 'pain of severe punishment by public authority' for the unauthorized consumption of yam (which Freeman here attributes – accurately, but secondarily – to health concerns about the consumption of unripe yam); MRO, Kumase, 'The King Anim of Adanse', n.d. (but ? 1942), for materials on the 'personalization' of types of yam, and Rattray, Folk-Tales, 72–7, for a folk account of a competition set by onyaŋkopɔŋ to name one particular yam.

7 See AK. Compare HA.

8 Compare here in particular the excellent M. Gilbert, 'Aesthetic Strategies: The Politics of a Royal Ritual', revised draft paper, August 1990, on the odwira in Akuropon, capital of the Akan state of Akuapem; Gilbert's subtle analysis is primarily ethnographic, with a contemporary rather than a historical focus, for, as she notes at fn 3, there 'are no early travellers' reports of odwira in Akuropon as there are of the Kumase celebration'. I am most grateful to Michelle Gilbert for generously allowing me access to her unpublished work, and for discussions on the subject of odwira.

9 The authoritative account is in HA.

10 The Asantemaŋhyiamu presided over by the Asantehene was also the highest court of first instance and of appeal. Many of the historic decisions taken by it are still widely remembered. It is severally recounted, for example, that the Kumawuhene Kwaatrafani was sentenced to death by the Asantemaŋhyiamu in the reign of the Asantehene Osei Kwadwo for cowardice in the war against Banna (1773–4). To ensure the victory over the Bannahene Worosa, Osei Kwadwo reportedly 'sacrificed' a cow by releasing it before the Asante army, with instructions that no one should harm it. But subjects of the Offinsohene allegedly found Kwaatrafani's men flaying the butchered animal, and a sword (domfo ansian) and hunting pouch (apretwa) belonging to Kwaatrafani were certainly found by the carcass; Kwaatrafani (who was named for an ɔbosom) denied the 'supernatural' offence, and claimed he had simply dropped his accoutrements in battle. But his men were found with some of the beef, and because of the loss of the sword and pouch Kwaatrafani was convicted of being adufo (a coward). The latter conviction alone carried a mandatory death sentence. However, Kwaatrafani's sentence was commuted on appeal to a massive fine (mperedwan oha nwɔtwɛ, plus court fees – nearly £1,000), as Komfo Anokye had decreed that no Kumawu royal might ever suffer execution, in token of the nation's gratitude for the Kumawuhene Tweneboa Kodia's voluntary sacrifice of his life to secure victory in the Asante war of

liberation against Denkyira; Kwaatrafani was then destooled. By contrast to such major constitutional cases, the hearing of criminal charges against private individuals by the *Asantemaŋhyiamu* was comparatively rare; it is said that the last such trial concerned a man who was convicted of having had sexual intercourse with a wife of the *Asantehene* Mensa Bonsu, and who perished by *atɔperɛ*.

11 Wilks, *Asante*, 387–413, for an overall survey of the history of relations between the two bodies. At *ibid.*, 413, Wilks justly remarks that jurisdictional conflict between the *Asantemaŋhyiamu* and the Kumase assembly 'was never fully resolved'. An adequately detailed history of this relationship has yet to be written. My own view is a commonsensical one. That is, power came increasingly to be centred in Kumase, but – on certain issues, and at different times – given provincial office holders might (and did) play a major role in decision making. Equally, any *Asantehene* who failed to cultivate or otherwise to manage relations with the *Asantemaŋhyiamu* did so at his peril, because the latter possessed the supreme constitutional authority to instigate destoolment procedures against the former. Some insight into the acknowledged framework of relations between the ruler and 'the assembly of the nation' – underlining the ultimate subordination of *all* political actors, the *Asantehene* included, to custom and law – is afforded by traditions that vividly recall those occasions on which the former was disciplined by the latter for normative transgressions; see Kurankyi-Taylor, 'Legal Institutions', I, 30 and 124–7, and Rattray, *Religion and Art*, 212. The unprecedented levels of scheming interference and piecemeal coercion practised by the *Asantehene* Kwaku Dua Panin against leading members of the *Asantemaŋhyiamu* – for which see, McCaskie, 'Paramountcy', 90–151 – was exceptional, and, significantly, it was matched by an equivalent authoritarianism in that ruler's dealings with the office holders of Kumase themselves. A related issue – but one that is also underexplored in any systematic historical way – is the shifting dynamic of power *within* the Kumase council itself, and most particularly the degree to which the individual personality of a given *Asantehene* (rather, say, than any putative principle of 'bureaucratic' continuity) might shape or determine events. The Asante themselves accord a crucial significance to this last factor. Discussants will often expatiate – at length, if discretely – upon the directions followed by Asante in this century, for example, in the light of the identifiably different, highly individualized character traits specific to successive *Asantehenes*; for analysis of these matters in a nineteenth-century context, see McCaskie, '*Konnurokusɛm*'.

12 Historical mnemonics that took their cue from the lives of successive *Asantehenes* formed, and form, the key enabling articulations in rituals other than the *odwira*. The intensely emotional atmosphere generated by, and through, the performed referencing of the past on such occasions has an undeniable power to involve participants and spectators alike in willing identification. At a Kumase *akwasidae* in 1990, for example, the Asante who were seated by me were visibly stirred and clearly moved by the rehearsal of the past produced by the contrapuntal interplay between horns (*ntahera* and *nkofe*) and panegyric recitation (*apaeɛ*). This performance, so I was informed,

was appropriately 'driven' or executed. The *Asantehene* Opoku Ware II signalled his own feelings by electing to dance at the close of this particular ceremony – a mark of approbation at the fitness of things that heightened engagement to the point of cathartic cheering, shouting and weeping acclamation. There is some useful account of the (con)textual mnemonics deployed in Arhin, 'The Asante Praise Poems', and in P.K. Sarpong, *The Ceremonial Horns of the Ashanti* (Accra, 1990), but – and here I can only echo Bowdich – no words can convey the overwhelming sense of participant belonging in and identification with history that is so palpably *present* at a ritual like the *akwasidae*.

13 To numerous Asante – in 1935, as today – the British 'restoration' of the *Asantehene* is a manifest contradiction in terms; colonial fiat, by its own alien definitions, 'abolished' (1896–1901) and 'restored' (1935) something that could be neither abolished nor restored! Thus, even after long years of exile (1896–1924), and final repatriation to Kumase as the anomalous private citizen 'Mr. Edward Prempeh', Agyeman Prempe was still considered, by his people and by himself, as the *Asantehene*; British awareness of this is a major theme in, for example, the confidential memoranda in RH, Oxford, CRP, MSS Afr. s.593, Papers of Lt. Col. A.C. Duncan-Johnstone. Significantly, opposition to the 'restoration' of 1935 was spearheaded by non-Asante West African nationalists, and supported, but briefly, by a very few *amanhene* (led by the *Mamponhene*), who feared erosion of their own provincial authority by a reinvigorated central power. The motives and programme of the mainly non-Asante opposition 'Ashanti Freedom Society' were ambiguous, and still remain so. See I.T.A. Wallace-Johnson, *Restoration of the Ashanti Confederacy: January 31 – February 4, 1935* (Accra, 1935); compare 'Asante Kotoko Society (60th Anniversary), 1916–1976', MS, 1976 (compiled by authorization of the Society); and for discussion, W. Tordoff, *Ashanti Under the Prempehs 1888–1935* (Oxford, 1965), 322–51, and A. Triulzi, 'The *Asantehene*-in-Council: Ashanti Politics under Colonial Rule, 1935–50', *Africa*, 42, 2 (1972), 98–111. For a revealing if partisan account of the sources of Mampon opposition to the 'restoration' of 1935 see HA; and for the Mampon context see McCaskie, 'Power and Dynastic Conflict in Mampon', 178–9.

14 See *Address by Otumfuo, Opoku Ware II ... November 16, 1985*, and the remarks on the *odwira* broadsheet calendar *Asantefoɔ Asranna 1985*, printed to accompany the celebration.

15 McCaskie, 'Time and the Calendar'.

16 *Ibid.*, 181. Compare P.F.W. Bartle, 'Forty Days: The Akan Calendar', *Africa*, 48, 1 (1978), 80–4, and Gilbert, 'Aesthetic Strategies'. Today, *nawotwe* is often used interchangeably with *dapɛŋ*, which is literally 'a series of days', but which is now equated, for obvious reasons, with the European 'week'. Literally translated, *nanson* and *nawotwe* – six- and seven-day cycles arithmetically – are respectively 'seven days' (cf. *ɛson/soŋ*; seven) and 'eight days' (cf. *ŋwotwe/awotwe*; eight). This is because *nanson* and *nawotwe* are reckoned inclusively. Thus, for example, *dapɛŋ* (*nawotwe*) – translated to the European 'week' – is sequentially understood, in every successive instance, as Sunday to Sunday inclusive; of course, these reckonings are not to be understood as arithmetical (daily)

chronology.

17 The term *adaduanan* is literally 'forty days' (cf. *aduanan/aduanaŋ*; forty). In the Asante sources, 'forty days' is often used symbolically to indicate a short period of time (e.g. such-and-such an office holder 'died after forty days on the stool'). The term is clearly – if oddly, and ambiguously – related to the Asante understanding of inclusive reckoning. However, the arithmetical multipliers are unequivocal; *adaduanan* is a concurrent counting of *nanson* with *nawotwe*, that is an aggregated compound of 42 (6×7) days.

18 McCaskie, 'Time and the Calendar', 182, Table 3, gives a summary list of sixteen *awukudae* (1816–74) and sixteen *akwasidae* (1816–88) recorded by Europeans in Kumase; this is by no means an exhaustive enumeration. For the *adae* in general see Rattray, *Ashanti*, 86–120.

19 Bowdich, *Mission*, 266. Dupuis, *Journal*, 213, fn. remarked, on the testimony of the *imām* Muḥammad al-Ghamba', that in the European year of 365 days, 'the proportion of good or lucky days [by Asante reckoning] ... is no more than 150 or 160'. In McCaskie, 'Time and the Calendar', 184, I fear that I placed overmuch faith in the literal accuracy of this estimation of the proportional ratio of *nnabɔne* to *nnapaa*.

20 MFU, 'Notes and Comments on "Bad Days" in Agogo, compiled by M.F.', n.d.; contrast here the modern account given in Kyei, *My Memoir*, I, 'Appendix 3: A 1983 Calendar (*Asranna*) of "Nna-Bonee" (Sacred Days)'.

21 MFU, 'Auspicious Days of Ashanti: Bad Days of the Ashanti Calendar. At an Interview with Yaw Mensah, Caretaker of the Obosom Kwabena Bena of Adeebeba under Manwerehene, 1 January 1946'.

22 *Ibid.* McCaskie, 'Time and the Calendar', 185–9 discusses the details of Asante diplomatic protocols and practices in the light of *nnabɔne* and *nnapaa*. Calendrical complexities were often exacerbated by an overlay of other considerations – local, occupational, personal, etc. Some sense of this may be gleaned from the testimony regarding variations in fishing and farming periodicity among the settlements (and among the kin groups composing each of those settlements) situated around the 'sacred' lake Bosomtwe. See, MFU, 'A Schedule of Interviews and Conversations in the Lake Bosomtwe Villages and Mponua Towns', 1946; and for context see, Rattray, *Ashanti*, 54–76, and ASC, Cambridge, Fortes Papers, 'A Talk with the *Asantehene* about Lake Bosomtwe', 1946. Individual life passages were punctuated by a series of time reckonings that were important, but with which I am not concerned here. An Asante woman, for example, counted her pregnancy by the cycle of the moon (*ɔsram*); *ɔsram* also denoted a lunar 'month', and the term is often used now to mean a calendrical month.

23 This account of the *ewim Anokye* at Agogo is mainly based upon disparate materials and annotations filed in MFU, 'Notes and Comments on "Bad Days" in Agogo, compiled by M.F.', n.d. There is a much condensed variant in Kyei, *My Memoir*, I.

24 Thus, *monodwo* was the preferred day for the formal reception of visitors into Kumase; see McCaskie, 'Time and the Calendar', 186–8. Equally, *monodwo* was the preferred day for the enstoolment of an *Asantehene*; thus, for example, Kwaku Dua Panin (25 August 1834), Kofi Kakari (26 August 1867), Kwaku

Dua Kuma (28 April 1884), Agyeman Prempe (11 June 1894), Osei Agyeman Prempeh II (24 April 1933) and Opoku Ware II (27 July 1970) were all at last formally enstooled – after protracted ritual preliminaries and sometimes unwelcome delays – as *Asantehene* (occupant and custodian of the *sika dwa kofi*) on *monodwo* (41: Monday). See, indicatively, C.7917, 1896, *Further Correspondence relating to Affairs in Ashanti* (Accounts and Papers LVIII), *Asantehene* Agyeman Prempe to Governor, dd. Kumase, 28 June 1894; and, for a useful discussion, L. Yarak and I. Wilks, 'A Further Note on the Death of *Asantehene* Osei Yaw Akoto and on the Enstoolment of Kwaku Dua Panin', *Asantesɛm*, 9 (1978), 56–7.

25 For a chronological summary see Wilks, *Asante*, 235–42 and 497–509.

26 See Christaller, *Twi Mmebusɛm*, 134–5, and Rattray, *Ashanti Proverbs*, 189–90. There were numbers of generic folk terms that served to demarcate loose categorical subdivisions of historical time; *firi tɛtɛ* (lit. 'from the very beginning') was applied to the remote or distant past; *kane no* (lit. 'at first, firstly') was used flexibly of the past ten years or of the past two centuries; *nnansa yi* (lit. 'three days ago') was employed to denote the senses of lately, recently or 'nowadays'. 'History' was itself literally *abakosɛm* ('past things'). Some terms were understood as implicating the mythical in the historical, and the spatial in the temporal; see the discussion of *ho/ɛhɔ* ('that place, there, thither ... sometimes applied to time') in McCaskie, 'Komfo Anokye', 336–7.

27 Modern calendars use different orthographies – *afrihyia, afirihyia, afenhyia, afrinhyia, afirin(n)hyia*. The basic root terms are *afe* + *(n)hyia* (inf. 'a meeting with, a coming together, a joining, a converging'); hence, in one felicitious Asante English usage, 'the edges of the year are come together', i.e. the anniversary of the year (*afe*), and so New Year. Thus, the greeting *afirin(n)hyia pa* ('a happy return of the year', i.e. Happy New Year), and cognately *afe nkɔ nsan mmɛto yɛn mfeɛ so* ('many happy returns'). Discussants say that Western New Year and Christmas cards first came into widespread use in Kumase in the 1930s.

28 The word *afedaŋ* is *afe* + *daŋ* (lit. 'turning, altering, changing'); *afefoforo* is elided in speech to *afeforo*, and is *afe* + *fo(fo)ro* (lit. 'new, different, fresh') – so, *afefo(fo)ro da* (New Year's Day). The envelope of time in question was circumscribed, at its extremes, by *akitawonsa* (i.e. *a kita wo nsa*, 'hold your hand': this refers to pain and tiredness in the hands, brought on by the arduous task of removing weeds, occasioned by the heavy rains, from farms) and by *obubuo* (der. *bu*, 'to break off', i.e. to reap: this refers to the concluding period of harvesting). In modern calendars, *akitawonsa* is commonly equated with July, and *obubuo* with November. Christaller, *A Dictionary of the Asante and Fante Language*, 51 and 237 is more accurate, acknowledging a general (and shifting) concordance between the Akan agricultural cycle and the Gregorian calendar, rather than a precise fit; so, *akitawonsa* ('name of a month, *about* July'), and *obubuo* (ditto, '*about* November').

29 Discussants have told me (1990) that the procedures for scheduling *odwira* were secret and complex, but that they were all directed to the identification of the appropriate *nkyidwo* (20: Monday) within the appropriate (upcoming) *adaduanan* cycle; in addition, *akwasidae* in the *adaduanan* cycle two before *odwira* (i.e. seventy-two days, inclusive, before *odwira nkyidwo*) was denoted *butuw* (lit. 'to overturn, to turn upside down'), because the blackened stools of

the *Oyoko Kɔkɔɔ* were left lying on their sides throughout this particular celebration of the 'big' *adae*; see too HA; ACBP/1: Opoku Frɛfrɛ, *Asantesɛm*, 11 (1979), 38–53. Asante citizens clearly had a general idea, based on the natural and agricultural cycles, of when, roughly, the annual *odwira* was due for celebration; on folk perceptions of this sort, but in relation to the *adae*, see Bowdich, *Mission*, 280–1.

30 For the 'dry roads' argument see Wilks, *Asante*, 389. The term *ɔpɛnimma* is *ɔpɛ* (drought; associated with the dry, cool, seasonal northeasterlies from the Sahara, i.e. the *harmattan*) + *nimma* (lit. 'small, immature'); *ɔpɛpɔŋ* is *ɔpɛ* + *pɔŋ* (lit. 'big, large, great').

31 For the expenses incurred by the *Asantehene* during *odwira* see HA; and compare *The Western Echo, Supplement*, 24 March 1886, for the 'heavy expenditure' by the *Asantehene* on gifts to office holders at *odwira*, 'far exceeding anything he may receive' in return.

32 See the preliminary remarks in McCaskie, 'Time and the Calendar', 192–3; see too Gilbert, 'Aesthetic Strategies', for the 'ideal' model *odwira* in Akuropon, Akuapem (1977), which occupied one (Gregorian) week, and then three succeeding weeks, during which 'lesser *rites de passage* are concluded'.

33 State control over provisioning was enforced on all those occasions when, as at *odwira*, the resident population of Kumase was augmented by large numbers of visitors. On this see Chapman, 'Journal', entry dd. Kumase, 31 May 1844, when a law was promulgated to control food supplies in anticipation of the numbers expected – 'much greater', it was surmised, than at the 1843 *odwira* – to attend the reception of the *Anantahene* Asamoa Nkwanta's army into Kumase on *monodwo* (41: Monday) 3 June. Asante government awareness of food shortages and inflationary prices is a recurrent theme in the writings of the Europeans – Bonnat, Ramseyer, Kühne – held captive in Kumase (1869–74), and particularly during the crisis years 1872–3.

34 See MRO, Kumase, D/35, 'Donyina Affairs' (containing an abstract of the case *in re* Kwasi Abankwa *et al. versus* Ntim Bediako, 1936–7).

35 See, for example, Chapman, 'Journal', entry dd. Kumase, 8 September 1844; WMMS, Brooking to Freeman, dd. Kumase, 21 June 1842, and, for the timing of the 1842 *odwira*, *ibid.*, Brooking to General Secretaries, dd. Kumase, 23 August 1842. Food was relatively scarce at various, if predictable, periods throughout the natural and agricultural cycles, e.g. in *ɔbɛnem* (? 'the ripening of palm fruit'; der (?). *abɛ*, palm fruit + *nem*, to mature, ripen) and in *oforisuo* ('calling out for rain'; der. *frɛ*/*frɛ*, to summon, call + *(o)suo*, rain) – roughly March–April; see *ibid.*, Chapman to General Secretaries, dd. Kumase, 31 March 1845.

36 For some account see HA and IAS/AS 87: Sawua Stool History, recorded by J. Agyeman-Duah, 10 September 1963. Some of the new yam – wrapped in white cloth in a brass basin, and borne under a canopy – was carried from Saawua to the palace in Kumase by a train of attendants, so I have been told, 'worthy of a chief'. *Saawuahene* or his representative presided over the distribution and preparation of the new yam in Kumase, and then returned to Saawua.

37 In Kumase (1990) I was severally told that *nkyidwo* (20: Monday) was the *dapaa* customarily preferred, but that other *nnapaa* were also deemed to be appropriate; the reasoning behind this remains opaque.

38 For the *baamu* see Rattray, *Religion and Art*, 117–21; Kyerematen, 'Ashanti

Royal Regalia'; *ibid.*, 'The Royal Stools of Ashanti', *Africa*, 39, 1 (1969), 1–10; McCaskie, 'Death and the *Asantehene*'.

39 On *kuduo* (? *puduo*) see R.A. Silverman, 'Akan *Kuduo*: Form and Function', in D.H. Ross and T.F. Garrard (eds.), *Akan Transformations: Problems in Ghanaian Art History* (Los Angeles, 1983), 10–29; on *ntɔrɔ* generally see Rattray, *Ashanti*, 45–76.

40 HA; Asare, *Asante Abasem*.

41 The oblatory use of sheep was so widespread that the term *oguaŋ* was often used to signify any kind of 'payment' or 'offering'.

42 HA gives this conventional estimate. There exists a (fugitive) tradition that at the *odwira* of, presumably, 1774, immediately after the Banna war (dry season, 1773–4), the *Asantehene* Osei Kwadwo, pleading necessity, was allowed to borrow twice from the Bantama *sika futuro*; see OMP, Kumase, 'A Notebook on Office Holding', prepared for (and by?) the *Asantehene* Agyeman Prempe, dd. Kumase, 1927.

43 For Kofi Kakari's weeping gratitude, and sheer disbelief, at the amount of gold that he eventually inherited from Kwaku Dua Panin see the vivid traditional account recorded in Asare, *Asante Abasem*; on this see further HA, which also states that Brantuo Kuma – Kwasi Brantuo's successor as *Manwerehene* – was executed for remonstrating with the *Asantehene* Kofi Kakari about his profligacy. The *Asantehemaa* Afua Kobi's reluctant transfer of these revenues to Kofi Kakari seemingly took place between *kurukwasie/akwasidae* (33: Sunday) 16 June and *kwakwasie* (40: Sunday) 23 June 1872. See Bonnat MSS, Cahier 12, entries dd. Kumase, 16 and 23 June 1872; Ramseyer and Kühne, *Four Years*, 171 (compare BMA, Basel, *Tagebuch Ramseyer: 1869–1874*, entry dd. Kumase (? erroneously) 14 June 1872; but on this document see A. Jones, '*Four Years in Asante*: One Source or Several?', *HA*, 18 (1991), 173–203). In the event, Afua Kobi's reservations were justified. Thus, as early as 3–5 August 1872, Kofi Kakari alienated many by recklessly expending gold and disbursing valuables in order to invest his personal favourites with elevated rank and office; for the promotion of Kwaku Bosommuru Dwira (to *Akomfodehene/Nyameanihene*), Yaw Bosommuru Tia (to *Manwere Mmagyegyefuɔhene*), Saben (to *Atipinhene*), and Mensa Kukuo (to *Pampasohene*), see Bonnat MSS, Cahier 12, entries dd. Kumase, 3 and 5 August 1872; compare Bowdich, *Mission*, 295; and, for context, see McCaskie, '*Ahyiamu*', especially 178–9.

44 See McCaskie, 'Death and the *Asantehene*'. Compare J.G. Platvoet, 'In de koelte van de "ontvangstboom": de politieke functie van een akan godsdienstig symbool', in H. Manschot, H. van Reisen and W. Veldhuis (eds.), *Van Gerechtigheid tot Liturgie* (Hilversum, 1984), 61–91. On umbrellas see conveniently S.F. Patton, 'The Asante Umbrella', *AfAr*, 7, 4 (1984), 64–73 and 93–4. For *kyiniɛhyia(mu)* ('the whirlpool') see Rattray, *Religion and Art*, 128.

45 MRO, Kumase, Agyeman Prempe to DC (Kumase), dd. Kumase, 26 October 1927; compare OMP, Kumase, 'A Notebook on Office Holding', prepared for (and by?) the *Asantehene* Agyeman Prempe, dd. Kumase, 1927.

46 Bowdich, *Mission*, 279.

47 See HA. There are many accounts of *sumpene* being used on ritual and state occasions; see, for example, WMMS, W. West to General Secretaries, dd.

Cape Coast, 9 June 1862 (with an account of his residence in Kumase, 17 March to 22 April 1862), on the *Asantehene* Kwaku Dua Panin's celebrations of *akwasidae* (23 March) and *awukudae* (16 April); and, for a physical description of *sumpene* see *ibid.*, Freeman, 'Life and Travels', 83–4. Some distinction, but not a hard and fast one, was evidently made between the *sumpene* at *dwaberem* and *apremoso/bogyawe*. The former was the larger of the two – *sumpeε kεsεε* – and was reportedly used for 'festal occasions', such as the *akwasidae*; the latter and smaller – *sumpeε kuma* – was used for 'funerals and other serious or mournful occasions', but also for drinking parties (*sadwa*); for this, and their current location, see Kyerematen, *Kingship and Ceremony in Ashanti*, 1. Asante informants emphasize the ritual pre-eminence of *dwaberem* and *apremoso/bogyawe* among the numerous Kumase *sumpene*, but questions posed (1988, 1990) about which of the two was used during particular passages of *odwira* have yielded inconclusive and contradictory answers. Accordingly, in the text I have indicated 'either ... or' (of the two *sumpene*) where direct evidence is lacking, but have given *dwaberem* or *apremoso/bogyawe* where the sources permit clear identification. I have used *apremoso/bogyawe* to refer to the smaller of the two, as informants employ both terms (together and separately); in fact, it was located within the *bogyawe* ward of Kumase, but hard by the eastern side of the *apremoso* ward where this abutted on *bogyawe* (and on the *kete* and *ntahera* wards). Tradition asserts that *dwaberem*, the 'most senior'of all Kumase *sumpene*, was built on the orders of Komfo Anokye (? after the Takyiman war, *c.* 1723), and that he buried 'medicine' under the raised mound or dais to enable Asante to prosper.

48 See BMA, Basel, Jenkins (Ramseyer MS *et al.*), annotations, December 1871; Ramseyer and Kühne, *Four Years*, 147 is accessible but incomplete. Compare Bonnat MSS, Cahier 7, entry dd. Kumase, 10 December 1872, on the refurbishment of 'tous les grands socles en terre dans les différentes parties de la ville ... avant l'Apafram'.

49 *Ibid.* Wilks, *Asante*, 382, draws an odd, strained, but entirely typical parallel: 'The immaculately ochred floors and elaborate bas-reliefs [of the *adampaŋ*] were the equivalent of the present day executive's carefully tended carpets and murals.'

50 Anticipation, quickening and excitement (aural and visual) are integral features of festival; see here J. Le Goff and J.-C. Schmitt (eds.), *Le Charivari* (Paris and The Hague, 1981). In Asante, as all sources testify, the preliminaries were a promiscuous mixture of the aural (drumming, shouting, firing) and the visual (decorating, colouring, cleaning); for some leading remarks, following Febvre and Elias, on the aural-visual nexus (in the *commedia dell'arte*) see F. Braudel, *Le Modèle italien, 1450–1650* (Paris, 1989). Dance (aural and visual) featured in Asante preparations, but little historical work has been done on this; compare P. Spencer (ed.), *Society and the Dance: The Social Anthropology of Process and Performance* (Cambridge, 1985). Anticipation of *odwira* addressed, at one level, the problems of shifting, negotiable identity, the Bakhtinian 'exit from the self' into a temporary, purposeful structuration of community, highlighted in certain ways and directed to particular ends; for some insight see T. Todorov, *Michail Bakhtine: le principe dialogique suivi de*

Écrits du Cercle de Bakhtine (Paris, 1981). I cannot pretend to have captured the myriad references – the allusive signifiers – that intend and 'mean' *odwira* (festival, celebration). Thus, for example, I have encountered the term (?) *ɔwɔntomanu* ('beneath the cloth') used in the context of *odwira*; the reference is to the knee and waist beads worn ('beneath the cloth') by Asante office holders on festive occasions. The range of such references, could they be recovered, would furnish detailed understandings of how, and in what ways, *odwira* impacted on Asante consciousness(es), and also provide some indexing of the spectrum of possible/plausible 'readings'. On this compare McCaskie, 'People and Animals', on the anamorphic and anaphoric in Asante ways of seeing.

51 WMMS, 'Journals of the Rev. Thomas B. Freeman', entry dd. Kumase, 20 December 1841. For further instances, and a discussion of the chronology, see McCaskie, 'Time and the Calendar', 190–2. The conspicuous waste of palm wine (running down Kwaku Dua Panin's beard) was a mark of great status; palm wine – all the time fermenting, and so unstable – was a luxury, in as much as there was a brief optimum period of 'sweetness' when it was best drunk, and because tapping for it often killed the tree.

52 See Dupuis, *Journal*, especially 128–50. Some flexibility was permitted, and practised, in these withdrawal rituals. For example, the *Asantehene* might elect to quit Kumase over the period of seclusion. Thus, on *nwonabena* (7: Tuesday) 21 February 1832, the *Asantehene* Osei Yaw Akoto – admittedly remembered for his erratic behaviour – left Kumase for his country residence at Breman. There he secluded himself in anticipation of the impending *awukudae* (15: Wednesday) on 29 February. He received some invited visitors with pressing business, and, presumably, transacted some scaled-down version of the appropriate formalities on *kuruyawo* (9: Thursday) 23 February. See Simons, 'Journaal', entries dd. Kumase, 21–5 February 1832.

53 A. Riis, 'Reise des Missionars in Akropong nach dem Aschantee-Lande', 92 ff. and 216–35.

54 See, conveniently, Ramseyer and Kühne, *Four Years*, 226. Compare the remarks in Bonnat MSS, Cahier 13, entry dd. Kumase, 28 May 1873. (For parts of this period Bonnat's journal entries are consolidated. That is, they cover events before and sometimes after the actual date of inscription. He was busy farming and building at this time, and was intermittently ill.)

55 See C.3687, 1883, *Further Correspondence regarding the Affairs of the Gold Coast* (Accounts and Papers XLVIII), 'Report by Capt. R. La T. Lonsdale, C.M.G., of his Mission to Ashanti and Gaman ... April to July 1882', encl. in Lonsdale to Derby, dd. London, 14 April 1883.

56 There are numerous descriptions of this ceremony. For references to over thirty accounts from the nineteenth century see McCaskie, 'Time and the Calendar', 197, fn. 16.

57 Again, there are numerous descriptions. Thus, for example, for accounts of the *Asantehene* Kwaku Dua Panin's visits to the Bantama *baamu* – on *kwayawo* (16: Thursday), 20 January 1842, and 23 April 1846; on *kwadwo* (34: Monday), 27 December 1841, 9 January and 18 September 1843, and 30 March and 11 May 1846 – see, under the dates given, WMMS, 'Journals of the Rev. Thomas B. Freeman' (for 1841–3); *ibid.*, Wharton to General Secretaries, dd. Kumase,

31 May 1846 (for 1846).

58 Chapman, 'Journal', entry dd. Kumase, 12 September 1844.

59 Ramseyer and Kühne, *Four Years*, 147. BMA, Basel, Jenkins (Ramseyer MS *et al.*), annotations, December 1871, adds the detail that Ramseyer, Kühne and Bonnat watched the *Asantehene* Kofi Kakari's progress from one of the *adampaŋ* near 'the market square'.

60 Bonnat MSS, Cahier 12, entry dd. Kumase, 23 August 1872: 'Mercredi était le jour du petit Adé, le dernier Adé avant "L'Appaframe". Jeudi [i.e. the *odwira kwayawo*, 22 August 1872] en revenant de Bantama le roi avec toute sa suite a fait le tour de la ville pour inspecter les galeries ou "Dampan". C'était là le commencement ou le prélude de leur grande fête...'.

61 *Ibid.*, Cahier 7, entry dd. Kumase, 14 December 1871. Bonnat added: 'cette promenade du roi est pour voir si l'ordre qu'il avait donné de badigeonner et refaire les galeries ainsi que de refaire les grands socles en terre, sur lesquels il s'assoit en publique, ont [*sic*] été exécuté...'. Compare *ibid.*, Cahier 15, *Mœurs et coutumes de l'Achanty*, 52–9 ('L'Adé des Achantys').

62 See HA; MFU, 'Conversations with Nsuta people in Kumasi', n.d. Komfo Anokye is said, for example, to have buried a most potent *aduru* at the *ŋkwaŋtanaŋ* where the Kumase–Mampon path crossed the Kumase–Akyem path in the *adum* ward, another at the crossroads on the same route in the *akyeremade* ward, and yet another at the intersection of a branch of the Mampon road with the routes to Akyem and Lake Bosomtwe in the *dadeεsoaba* ward.

63 Bonnat MSS, Cahier 7, entry dd. Kumase, 14 December 1871. Bonnat referred to *anowu (ntannosuo)* as 'Anau', and identified the house as being at the end of the street that led through the *anowu* ward towards *dwaberem*. In BMA, Basel, Jenkins (Ramseyer MS *et al.*), annotations, December 1871, this dwelling is identified as being the birthplace of an earlier *Asantehene*; Ramseyer may simply be in error, but the *Asantehene* Osei Yaw Akoto was, in fact, the son of the *Anowuhene* Owusu Yaw.

64 For the genealogy see AK, and MRO, Kumase, 'Ashanti Families', unsigned typescript, n.d. (but 1920s or 1930s). The evidence for Kofi Nti's recent death is indirect, and based on inference about the nature of the ritual (celebrated in his honour?) by Kofi Kakari on *fomemene* (18: Saturday) 10 September 1870; see Bonnat MSS, Cahier 3, entry dd. Kumase, 10 September 1870, and, yet more elliptically, Ramseyer and Kühne, *Four Years*, 85. Kofi Nti may have died as early as *c.* 1850–5; see ACBP/4: Boakye Tenten, *Asante Seminar*, 6 (1976), 5–13. Kofi Nti, himself a grandson of the *Asantehene* Osei Kwadwo, was father of Kofi Kakari by his marriage to the future *Asantehemaa* Afua Kobi. Boakye Tenten, who succeeded Kofi Nti as *Boakye Yam Panin ɔkyeame*, also married his widow Afua Kobi. This marriage was opposed by Kofi Kakari, reportedly on the grounds of dislike for Boakye Tenten's self-seeking ambition.

65 HA. Asante informants emphasize the signal importance of the blackened personal stool of the *Asantehemaa* Nyaako Kusi Amoa. Clearly, this item of regalia is of national significance. However, oral testimony also suggests, if discreetly, a further consideration. It is said that Nyaako Kusi Amoa's stool is symbolic of the pact that confirmed the seniority of Osei Tutu's descent line

among all those comprising the Kumase *Oyoko Kɔkɔɔ* dynasty (notably including the 'older' line of Osei Tutu's predecessor Obiri Yeboa), and that vested the two offices of *Asantehene* and *Asantehemaa* in the line of Osei Tutu and his niece (his mother's uterine granddaughter) Nyaako Kusi Amoa. Komfo Anokye is said to have spared Nyaako Kusi Amoa's stool at the appearance of the *sika dwa kofi*, ordering that it be preserved and blackened after her death. It is also said by some informants that Komfo Anokye presided over the blackening of the stool of Ofobiri Odeneho – the senior female royal *temp*. Obiri Yeboa, and hence Nyaako Kusi Amoa's 'predecessor' – but ordered it preserved in its own *baamu* at *kwadaso*, entirely separate from any other succeeding royal artefact.

66 *Ibid.*, for a detailed enumeration of these sites and artefacts; compare Rattray, *Religion and Art*, 129.

67 See AK for the basic genealogical data. The life histories of the persons listed are known in some detail, but from sources much too numerous and diverse to catalogue here. See, for the representative case of the father of the *Asantehene* Opoku Fofie, ACBP/71: Adu Twum Kaakyire, *Asantesɛm*, 10 (1979), 46–8.

68 Amakom (in the Kwaman area) was older than Kumase. It was a separate village throughout the precolonial period, lying about 1 mile southeast of the Kumase *asafo* ward, and is now incorporated into the city (the University of Science and Technology is built on Amakom land). For the complexities of Amakom–Kumase relations in the seventeenth century, and the parenthood of Opoku Ware, see HA and AK. A basic account is IAS/AS 77: Amakom Stool History, recorded by J. Agyeman-Duah, 15 June 1963. Amakom is in the Adonten *fekuo*, but its relations with the other Adonten stools was, and is, complex and contentious. See *ibid.*, Records of the Adonten Tribunal, which contains many cases involving Amakom; and see further RAI, Rattray MSS, 'Enquiry into the Adonten Stool', *passim*.

69 For a somewhat circumspect account of royal burial grounds, other than at Bantama, see Rattray, *Religion and Art*, 144–6; see too Kyerematen, *Kingship and Ceremony in Ashanti*, 11–12. The Bantama *baamu* was destroyed by the British in 1896, but after its relics had been removed to safety by the Asante. The *Asantehene (Kumasihene)* Agyeman Prempe built a new royal *baamu* at Breman after his return from exile in 1924; the remains from Bantama were formally (re)interred there, as was Agyeman Prempe himself; see TOR, Notes and MSS, 'A Report of the Observance of the Funeral Custom of the late Kumasihene, died 12 May 1931', prepared by J.W.K. Appiah for the Asst Chief Commissioner (Ashanti), with notes and letters by F.W. Applegate, 1931–2.

70 According to HA, the aged Kusi Obodom went blind (an 'abomination' to the *sika dwa kofi*), was forced to abdicate, and then lived in retirement for three years in the Kumase *akyeremade* ward until his death, which occurred in 1764; for discussion, *inter alia* of the European sources, see J.K. Fynn, 'The Reign and Times of Kusi Obodum, 1750–64', *THSG*, 8 (1965), 24–32, and Wilks, *Asante*, 332. The most recent treatment of the complex events surrounding the abdication and death of Osei Kwame is McCaskie, '*Konnurokusɛm*'.

71 Wilks, *Asante*, 509–13 and 534–43, for convenient summaries of the political

events of 1874 and 1883.

72 Rattray, *Religion and Art*, 127 and 131. See further E.K. Braffi, *Otumfuo Opoku Ware II (Asantehene) Celebrates Odwira Festival* (Kumase, 1985), 11, for a modern view, but with an occult interpretation, of 'the general and moral significance of this Asante Odwira Festival'; and compare Gilbert, 'Aesthetic Strategies', for Akuapem measures to address the ancestors.

73 M. Fortes – in conversation, as in his writings – was much concerned with the exploration of Asante kinship in relation to such propositions. In long discussions (1979–80), it was made clear to me that his abiding interest in such matters arose from (and was congruent with) his unswerving commitment to defining Asante jural personhood, and to delineating the arena of amity, and its obverse, with ultimate reference to Asante understandings of relational positioning within kinship structures.

74 Thus, and famously, Gramsci made recurrent reference to the Italy of his day in just such terms; the early twentieth-century Italian state, however, was manifestly less successful than its eighteenth- and nineteenth-century Asante counterpart in subsuming conflicts and contradictions in any coherent ideological (re)presentation of itself.

75 In McCaskie, 'Accumulation, Wealth and Belief ... II', 13–17, there is a summary analysis of the desecration of the *sika dwa kofi* in 1921, and of the motives of the perpetrators. In that treatment I paid little attention to the expressive details – verbal, emotional – of the overwhelming senses of repugnance and despair articulated by, or reported of, the mass of Asante in response to this act. Contemporary testimony, Asante and British, makes it abundantly clear that desecration was experienced as fear and anomie, and that it was construed as being a harbinger of social dissolution (in pathological terms, transcending the politics of the outrageous event itself). From a plethora of evidence see RH, Oxford, CRP, MSS Brit. Emp. s.344. Papers of Sir Charles Henry Harper (including a transcript of the trial proceedings against the desecrators); Rattray, *Ashanti*, 287–93; OMP, Kumase, 'Dark Days of Seniagya', typescript prepared by J.W.K.A[ppiah], *c.* 1935; TOR, Notes and MSS, 'Notes on the Ashanti Kotoko Union Society'. My understanding of these matters was sharpened by an incident at a Kumase *adae* in the 1980s, when I noticed an extremely frail old woman being virtually carried towards the palace. I enquired who she was, and was told she travelled regularly to *adae* from Buokrom (about 2 miles away), and came 'to check the wellbeing and continued good health of the nation'.

76 For a summary see McCaskie, 'Power and Dynastic Conflict in Mampon'.

77 My understanding of *kra*, *sunsum*, *mogya* and *ntɔrɔ* has benefited from countless exchanges with Asante discussants, in Europe and the USA, as well as in Asante itself; I owe a particular debt in this regard to the late I.K. Agyeman, not only for his own views (and particularly on *ntɔrɔ*), but also for directing me to discussions with Dominic Ansah and others (at Danyaase), and with B.A. Bobie Serwaah and others (at Krapa). The literature on this subject is large, diverse and sometimes contradictory in its emphases and interpretations. The most stimulating recent discussion is in Gyekye, *An Essay*, 85 ff. But Gyekye's reading, like my own, is incomplete, at least in the very important

sense of acknowledging the elusive resistance of *all* aspects of this subject to formal analysis. This is as it must be, for the lacunae inhere directly in those blanknesses where the Asante interrogation of being itself breaks down in mystery.

78 Asante discussants are concerned to show symmetry and balance – and so completeness – in the representation of these four constituent elements. They often convey this by drawing a circle (a person), internally subdivided by a simple cross into quadrants, each one of these being assigned an element. Of itself this basic morphology invites to speculative pairings and oppositions. But there is more to the matter than that, for people do dwell upon aspectual consonances and dissonances between given pairs.

79 See Rattray, *Religion and Art*, 29–30; ASC, Cambridge, Fortes Papers, 'The Effect, on the Gold Coast "Abusua Ties", of the Belief [in Witchcraft]', n.d.

80 Thus, for example, the ethical vocabulary of Twi is well developed, but little priority is afforded to assigning rigorous causal absolutes to antithetically conceived elements of being; the pairings or linkages in question are complex but diverse. See the treatment of selected terms in Ackah, *Akan Ethics*, 25 ff.; compare here the curious juxtaposition of situational ethics with technical casuistry about types of cases in Danquah, *The Akan Doctrine of God.*

81 Women, I have been told by men, are capable of concealing venomous snakes in their genitals, and some of them deliberately leave a room before intercourse so as to remove these reptiles. The perception is that all women are potentially witches, or that some women envy men to the point of wishing to harm or destroy them. Women's own perceptions can imply that men are faithlessly vain and 'alien'. I am duly cautious in recording this, because the bases of these assertions are different; I have talked to men in groups and individually, but I have never discussed these matters with women on any basis other than the individual. The literature on gender in Asante commonly lacks a historical dimension. Admittedly, this is a difficult area to research. See McCaskie, 'State and Society, Marriage and Adultery'; J. Allman, 'Of "Spinsters", "Concubines" and "Wicked Women": Reflections on Gender and Social Change in Colonial Asante', *Gender and History*, 3, 2 (1991), 176–89; for some of the general problems, A. Jones, 'Prostitution, Polyandrie oder Vergewaltigung? Zur Mehrdeutigkeit europäischer Quellen über die Küste Westafrikas zwischen 1660 und 1860', in *ibid.* (ed.), *Aussereuropäische Frauengeschichte: Probleme der Forschung* (Pfaffenweiler, 1990), 123–58; and – better on diplomacy than on gender – I. Wilks, 'She Who Blazed a Trail: Akyaawa Yikwan of Asante', in P.W. Romero (ed.), *Life Histories of African Women* (London, 1988), 113–39.

82 For one list of twelve – possibly derived from J.B. Danquah, *Ɔkanniba Abotafowa* (London, 1954) – see Opoku, *West African Traditional Religion*, 98. Compare Rattray, *Ashanti*, 47–8, and MRO, Kumase, 'Ashanti Families', unsigned typescript, n.d. (but 1920s or 1930s). In AK, no less than eighteen *ntɔrɔ* are listed by name. However, this total is achieved by enumerating discrete sub-divisions; thus, *Adufudeɛ* ('Adufoodier') and *Asafodeɛ* ('Assafoodie') are counted separately, and not as sub-divisions of *Bosommuru* (which itself is not named).

83 This tabulation has been compiled from a mass of oral and written sources. I would argue for its overall validity, but not for each and every one of its specifics. In AK, the *Asantehene* Agyeman Prempe wisely cautioned that aspects of *ntɔrɔ* organization are 'a bit complicated to understand'. Thus, the discussion of the original 'twelve [Akan] tribes or families' in Bowdich, *Mission*, 229–31, is couched in ways such as to suggest that the author compounded, in his own understanding, information that he had been given on the *ntɔrɔ* as well as the *abusua*. All these difficulties are now intensified by the impact of modernity. Few, indeed, are the contemporary Asante who can talk comprehensively about the detailed arcana of the *ntɔrɔ* system.

84 See generally Kyei, *Marriage and Divorce among the Ashanti*.

85 For some insight into the historical importance of *aboadenfoɔ* see Asare, *Asante Abasem*; and for the relationship between the *Asantehenes* Kwaku Dua Panin and Kwaku Dua Kuma in this regard see McCaskie, '*Konnurokusɛm*'.

86 AK.

87 MRO, Kumase, 'Ashanti Families', unsigned typescript, n.d. (but 1920s or 1930s), for *Bosommuru* as the paragon of 'nobility'.

88 That is to say, the ideal model of the *kra pa* was conceived of as being produced by an arrangement that was marked by the transmission of male names (in alternative generations, and via cross-cousin marriage).

89 Wilks, *Asante*, 327–73. At *ibid.*, 371, Wilks – acutely aware of the errant conclusion that the incautious might draw from the evidence as presented – sensibly moots the idea of an Asante double descent system, but only in order to dismiss it. The logic of Wilks' reconstruction of the 'highly compact' Kumase dynasty is quite exemplary here, but once again he all but neglects ideology *qua* belief; the argument is driven by instrumental political considerations, and, ironically, it reaches the right conclusions, but offers only formal justifications for them. The *deus ex machina* favoured as explanation by Wilks is a tautological acceptance of a principle of dynastic identity, but taken on the generalized surface level proposed by its self-interested authors. The result is hermetic ('this is how it is', because ... 'this is how it is'); the narrative slides towards a version of medieval chronicle, in which the court historian celebrates the authorized biography of a royal family (and shows skill in dealing with the awkward – see the phrasing at *ibid.*, 371. fn. 174).

90 AK; Reindorf, *History*, Appendix B, 'Kings and the Royal Family of Asante'; and, predictably in terms of naming practices, see HA for Kusi Obodom's son, the *ɔheneba* Apaw of Apeboso and Gyakye.

91 Reference has already been made to the complexity of this matter; see ACBP/28: Kwaadu Yaadom, *Asantesɛm*, 11 (1979), 5–13; and McCaskie, '*Konnurokusɛm*'. RAI, Rattray MSS, Bundle 107, Notebook 3, 1860, records that Safo Katanka was a member in fact of *Bosommuru Asafodeɛ*; see further MRO, Kumase, 'Notes Taken at the Enquiry held at Jamasi on August 28th 1933, when Certain Charges were Laid by Certain Persons against the Omanhene Kweku Dua of Mampong Ashanti'. Safo Katanka's own father was the *Dwabenhene* Osei Hwidie.

92 HA for details of the personnel who conspired to remove Osei Kwame from office (including Kwaadu Yaadom's fifth, and last, husband, the *Anowuhene*

Owusu Yaw).

93 This reconstruction from the Asante perspective is based upon a wide range of traditional sources. Indispensable among them are HA; *ibid.*, 'Ashanti Families', unsigned typescript, n.d. (but 1920s or 1930s); Asare, *Asante Abasem*; and, for cross-checking, the biographical data files of the ACBP. Compare here chapter 3 note 10, for Asare's chronological error, and for further possibilities in the reading of *asaaman kwaadane*.

94 See HA.

95 See, for example, McCaskie, 'Death and the *Asantehene*', on events in 1867. There are many accounts of the qualities – physical, moral, behavioural – required of candidates for the *sika dwa kofi*. A revealing ideological feature of tradition is the argument (clearly made *ex post facto*) that some of the most successful *Asantehenes* were guilty of irresponsible derelictions in their youth, but that the prospect of becoming the incumbent of the *sika dwa kofi* – and/or consequent enstoolment – wrought within them appropriate reformations of character. The argument here about agency is reciprocal; the individual 'becomes' the *Asantehene* as the *sika dwa kofi* 'acts' to construct him as such. In this context, see the accounts of the *Asantehenes* Osei Tutu and Osei Kwadwo in HA and AK, and for some analysis of the life of the former in this regard see McCaskie, 'People and Animals'.

96 Selfhood and individual agency are understudied in precolonial African history. Paucity of source materials is a valid reason for this, but it has developed into something of an excuse. The value of such a perspective is incontrovertible, and this – in variable ways, and with suggestive results – is recognized by some historians of the colonial era, and by others working on the twentieth century. See, specifically on the Akan, R. Rathbone, *Murder and Politics in Colonial Ghana* (New Haven and London, 1993); and Gilbert, 'The Sudden Death of a Millionaire'. The significance of Asante individuals making themselves, and so 'making' history, is brilliantly conveyed in Appiah, *In My Father's House*, 294–313; this account of negotiations around the funeral of the writer's father strikes chords – mostly absent from the work of historians – that have an immediately vivid resonance for anyone familiar with Asante people.

97 This point is as obvious as it is neglected. Ideological distancing of the sort described has gone on throughout Asante history, and goes on still. Contrast here the two portraits of the *Asantehene* Agyeman Prempe II in, for example, A.A.Y. Kyerematen, *Daasebre Osei Tutu Agyeman Prempeh II, Asantehene: A Distinguished Traditional Ruler of Contemporary Ghana* (Kumase, n.d.), and MFU, 'Conversations in His House with the Ashantihene Prempeh', 1946. When an *Asantehene* made public utterance on the state's behalf, his subjective self was absented. He became the inhabitant of the continuous present of his public role. 'The King', it was said, 'always spoke of the acts of all his ancestors as his own'; Bowdich, *Mission*, 71, fn. But each *Asantehene* also had an identity that was rooted in subjective personality traits (and all that these terms imply). Thus, the *Asantehenes* Osei Tutu Kwame, Kwaku Dua Panin and Kofi Kakari all had favourite wives (and children); see, *ibid.*, 76; Freeman, 'Life and Travels', 123; Owusu Ansa, 'The King of Ashantee', *The Times*, London, 29

July 1873. The matter that commands exploration is the nexus of interactions between emblematic role and individual persona. The historiography all but ignores the latter. From the Asante point of view this is odd. That is, much of the traditional history of the Kumase dynasty is framed as an allegory of perfection (the role of *Asantehene*) in dialogue with an aspirational narrative of events (the persons of successive *Asantehenes*). The tensions between the two arise from the completed status of the former and the idiosyncrasies of the latter. After all, there is one strand in Asante understanding that proposes, for example, that the *Asantehene* Osei Kwame authored his own downfall by his wilful refusal to abandon his liaison (which was incestuous by the Asante rules of exogamy) with the seductive Dwaben *Oyoko ɔdehyeɛ* Agyeiwaa Badu, by whom he had a son named Sikayepena. Love may not conquer all, so to speak, but it, and other personal emotions, played an evident part in Asante history. On the theme of emotion generally see R. Rosaldo, 'Putting Culture in Motion', in *ibid., Culture and Truth: The Remaking of Social Analysis* (London, 1993), 91–108.

 98 BMA, Basel, 'The Funeral Custom for Late King Mensa Bonsu of Kumase who Died 1900 at Praso', in D/1, 95, N.V. Asare, 'Annual Report of Kumase to the Home Committee', dd. Kumase, 24 February 1911. It is said that the usurpatory *Gyaasewahene* Kwame Tua – a British collaborator, but also a noted musician and satirist – used daringly to mimic the inflections of *adehyeɛ kasa*.

 99 Asante Twi is rich in such verbal modes of expression; see McCaskie, '"You Must Dis/Miss/Mis/Re/Member This"' on Kwame Tua's character.

100 Miscreants might be submitted for judgement to *otoro bo* ('the slander stone'); ridicule, disgrace or execution followed conviction, depending upon the gravity of the offence.

101 Disputes between, for example, the *Asantehene* and the *Asantehemaa* were (and are) settled privately as *afisɛm*. Asante will make reference to matters at issue between members of the *Oyoko Kɔkɔɔ*, but are markedly reluctant to discuss details or to offer speculations. For some comment on the relationship between the *Asantehene* Osei Agyeman Prempeh II and the *Asantehemaa* Kwaadu Yaadom II (born Ama Adusa) see MFU, annotations to 'Conversations in His House with the Ashantihene Prempeh', 1946.

102 See, for example, the special issue 'The History of the Family in Africa', *JAH*, 24, 2 (1983), 145–283.

103 See McCaskie, '*Konnurokusɛm*' for discussion, and for an extended analysis of the specific case, dealt with here in summary, of the *Asantehene* Kwaku Dua Panin. In the version of the reconstruction offered here I have restricted notes mainly to primary sources, for reasons of space. That said, I wish to record that the sorting out of chronology and genealogy, and the two in relation to one another, is indispensably grounded in intensive work carried out in the 1970s under the auspices of the ACBP by Ivor Wilks and myself. I acknowledge here my debt to Ivor Wilks for this period in which, as co-directors of the ACBP, we researched, argued and laboured our way to a new level of understanding of the nuts and bolts of Asante political history. Equally, my understanding of the kinship relations examined in this reconstruction owes much to Meyer Fortes.

I have also mined, as appropriate, the previously published work of, particularly, Wilks, Yarak and myself. I can only add that my reconstruction is built, with gratitude, upon the diverse labours of that community of scholars who have contributed to an understanding in detail of key aspects of the Asante past.

104 AK for the received version.

105 The crucial review and analysis of the available evidence is in I. Wilks, 'A Note on Career Sheet ACBP/28: Kwaadu Yaadom', *Asantesɛm*, 11 (1979), 54–6; this should be read in conjunction with the earlier discussion in *ibid.*, *Asante*, 336 ff. Immediately relevant ACBP reconstructions are ACBP/28: Kwaadu Yaadom and ACBP/71: Adu Twum Kaakyire, in respectively, *Asantesɛm*, 11 (1979), 5–13 and 10 (1979), 46–8.

106 AK records of Kwaadu Yaadom that 'she conceived again and bore one more and died as the child was laid down'. British reports of her death date it to the first half of 1809; for the references see Wilks, 'A Note', 54.

107 The evidence is summarized in ACBP/28: Kwaadu Yaadom, *Asantesɛm*, 11 (1979), 5–13.

108 HA has a circumspect but suggestive account of this transfer, stating *inter alia* that the *Asantehene* Osei Kwadwo 'somehow managed to obtain' this stool from the collateral *Oyoko* royals at Kokofu; the stool was brought to Kumase where Kwaadu Yaadom was 'installed' upon it, and a replacement stool was 'made for Kokofu'. Interesting supplementary evidence is in NAG, Accra, ANA 1/24, Minuted Petitions enclosed in SNA Correspondence, 1924–6, 'Ex-King of Kokofu George Asibi' [i.e. *Kokofuhene* Osei Asibe Kuma], George Asibi to (Ag.) Colonial Secretary, dd. Kokofu, 4 September 1926. In this petition, the ex-*Kokofuhene* complained at length about his treatment at the hands of the British and the Asante since his repatriation from exile in the Seychelles. In his rambling list of grievances, this 'sad figure' (as the British minuted) included examples of slights that Kokofu had allegedly suffered because of the bad faith and duplicity of Kumase; 'even one King of Kumasi, Osai Kojo Okooaweea', he complained, 'took away from Kokofu the ancient stool of our queen mother protectress of our families [*sic*]'.

109 Wilks, 'A Note', 54–5, for the source references.

110 I follow Wilks' reasoning here. All attempts by myself (1988, 1990) to gather further information on 'Akjaanba' (Akyaama) have thus far failed. However, one discussant – who specifically asked that no attribution be made to him – did venture the opinion, without elaboration, that some people (of whom he clearly disapproved) did suggest that Kwaadu Yaadom was the 'first' *Asantehemaa* (by implication, it must be presumed, on the 'new' Kokofu stool). It was then made clear to me that enquiries along these lines were unwelcome. In Wilks, 'A Note', 55–6, the speculation is ventured, but with appropriate caution, that the stool of the disgraced Akyaama may have been attached to *Oyoko Pampaso* (which does indeed contain a stool – named for an 'Akyiaa-Ama' – that is used in the enstoolment rituals of an *Asantehene*).

111 *Ibid.*, 56, for the British source that indicates that the reclassification following the 'cancellation' of Akyaama was already in force by 1780.

112 HA; and see J. Agyeman-Duah, 'Uproar in the Kumase Council of Chiefs,

1777', *Asantesɛm*, 7 (1977), 43–4.
113 HA, although the account is admittedly both confused and confusing.
114 On the status of widows generally see Kyei, *Marriage and Divorce among the Ashanti*.
115 AK.
116 For discussion see McCaskie, 'Paramountcy'; *ibid.*, 'Office, Land and Subjects', 196–7; Wilks, *Asante*, 356–7; and Yarak, *Asante and the Dutch*, 252 ff.
117 AK; for the birth of Kwaku Dua Panin see McCaskie, 'Paramountcy', 9, fn. 4.
118 See Yarak, *Asante and the Dutch*, 257–60.
119 See ACBP/28: Kwaadu Yaadom, *Asantesɛm*, 11 (1979), 5–13.
120 Suggestively, Kyenkyenhene, Kwame Kusi, Oti Akenten and Akyampon Kwasi all simply vanish from the sources at this point.
121 Osei Kwame's intentions in this regard may well have contributed to the tensions between Dwaben and Kumase that are reported throughout Bowdich, *Mission*. Certainly, the rebellion of Dwaben against the *Asantehene* Osei Yaw Akoto in 1832 resulted from an immediate crisis that was rooted in long-term antagonisms.
122 For an analysis of the circumstances surrounding Opoku Fofie's death see McCaskie, 'Death and the *Asantehene*', 429.
123 AK.
124 See the discussion at pp. 66 ff.
125 See AK; HA; Asare, *Asante Abasem*; and, on the death of Owusu Afriyie ('Gamadooah'), Ricketts, *Narrative*, 124–5. For some discussion see McCaskie, 'Paramountcy' and Yarak, *Asante and the Dutch*, 260 ff.
126 HA; compare Reindorf, *History*, 148. It is said that these catastrophic deaths gave rise to the oath, *mekɔeɛ deɛ nanso mante* ('I was there, but did not hear [what happened]'). It is possible that Amma Sewaa and her children were in fact repatriated to Kumase immediately following these events.
127 For one estimation of Osei Yaw Akoto as heir-apparent see Bowdich, *Mission*, 246. Wilks, *Asante*, 355, Fig. 11, summarizes the patrilineal descent of Osei Yaw Akoto. Relevant here is the history of the heir-apparency and of the *ahenemma* in relation to the Kumase Akyempem stool; for some discussion see McCaskie, 'Death and the *Asantehene*', 439–40.
128 Kwaadu Yaadom was accorded a lavish funeral. For a telling, if exaggerated, account see Bowdich, *Mission*, 289. At *ibid.*, 240–1, Bowdich reported that Kwaadu Yaadom was sexually very active – 'a second Messalina' – up until her death (in childbirth).
129 See ACBP/54: Adoma Akosua, *Asantesɛm*, 11 (1979), 14–17; for discussion of this conspiracy see McCaskie, 'Anti-Witchcraft Cults in Asante', 126–9.
130 AK, supported by most traditions, lists Amma Sewaa, Yaa Dufi and Afua Sapon consecutively as Adoma Akosua's successors; but HA records Adoma Akosua's successors as being Yaa Dufi, and then Afua Sapon – with no mention of Amma Sewaa.
131 See IAS/AS 72: Mamesene Stool History, recorded by J. Agyeman-Duah, 22 April 1966.
132 See Asare, *Asante Abasem*; HA. For context see McCaskie, 'Paramountcy', especially 8–9.

133 HA; compare Reindorf, *History*, 198.

134 HA on the retreat and the Saawua oath. For resentment against Osei Yaw Akoto after Katamanso (and possibly more than that) see C.4052, 1884, *Further Correspondence regarding the Affairs of the Gold Coast* (Accounts and Papers LVI), Report by Capt. K. Barrow of his Mission to Ashanti, dd. 5 July 1883.

135 *Ibid*. On Osei Yaw Akoto's drinking see Kea, 'The Danes and the Gold Coast', 66.

136 These details of Osei Yaw Akoto's behaviour are described in HA; compare Reindorf, *History*, 216 and 285 ff. Another view of the death of Kwadwo Adusei Kyakya – which accepts Osei Yaw Akoto's charge that the *Gyakye ɔkyeame* 'knowingly betrayed the country for love of money' – is in MRO, Kumase, 6:00/2, Gyaakyi Stool Affairs, Kwabena Wireku of Gyakye to Kumase Divisional Council, dd. 1 July 1935.

137 *The West African Herald*, Accra, 2nd Series, 4/7, 13 June 1871. This newspaper was edited by Charles Bannerman (d. 1872). He was a son of the marriage between the James Town (Accra) merchant James Bannerman (1790–1858) and the *ɔheneba* Yaa Hom (a daughter of the *Asantehene* Osei Yaw Akoto), who had been taken captive at Katamanso in 1826. HA simply records the capture of Yaa Hom, and her subsequent marriage to 'an Accra man'. On the Bannerman family, and its ongoing links with Asante in the nineteenth century, see R.G. Jenkins, 'Gold Coast Historians and their Pursuit of the Gold Coast Pasts, 1882–1917', 2 vols., Ph.D. (Birmingham, 1985). I must record my gratitude to Larry Yarak, who first drew my attention to this intimate (Bannerman and *Oyoko Kɔkɔɔ*) family tradition.

138 The precise date remains speculative. See Asare, *Asante Abasem*. Afua Sapon was certainly *Asantehemaa* by February 1832. At his official reception into Kumase, J. Simons noted that 'Effua Sapon' – 'cousin of the King' – was seated immediately next to the *Asantehene* Osei Yaw Akoto, in the place customarily occupied on all such occasions by the *Asantehemaa*; see Simons, 'Journaal', entry dd. Kumase, 13 February 1832.

139 See McCaskie, '*Konnurokusɛm*' for an extended discussion of these relationships.

140 The nexus of relations described here is crucially important in the Asante understanding of kinship – and most especially in terms of the parameters of affect and/or alienation. The structural problems involved (exacerbated by personal emotion) remain conflicted and highly charged among the Asante, and other Akan, to the present day. Thus, to take one single related aspect, attempts by the Ghana government in the mid-1980s to legislate, following English common law, for the security of inheritance of widows and children *contra* the dispositional claims of Akan orthodoxy in such matters generated much heated debate.

141 *The West African Herald*, Accra, 2nd Series, 4/7, 13 June 1871.

142 On the chronology see R.A. Kea, 'The Chronology of the Asante Kings: A Note on the Death of the *Asantehene* Osei Yaw Akoto', and L. Yarak and I. Wilks, 'A Further Note on the Death of *Asantehene* Osei Yaw Akoto and on the Enstoolment of Kwaku Dua Panin', *Asantesɛm*, 9 (1978), 55 and 56–7 respectively.

143 Asare, *Asante Abasem*. In his prefatory remarks to the traditions he collected,

Asare noted, in a strikingly modern way, the importance of securing the trust of informants. He continued: 'I lived in Kumasi for a long time [1902–13] and ... I made numerous knowledgeable and influential friends... Besides, I was not informed by just one person. To ensure the truth [of my account], I approached several well-informed elderly people.'

144 Rattray, *Religion and Art*, 325.

145 For Opoku Ahoni see McCaskie, 'Paramountcy', 219–21, and Wilks, *Asante*, 353 ff. For his execution for dynastic reasons *c*. 1847–8 (but by some accounts because of his interest in Christianity) see further, chapter 3 note 177 above.

146 McCaskie, 'Paramountcy'. For the 'sultanist' and patrimonial reading see Arhin, 'Trade, Accumulation and the State', 531; see too Yarak, *Asante and the Dutch*, 285.

147 I am arguing here, of course, for an exploration of these factors in the life of *every Asantehene*, and generally in *all* relevant Asante historical contexts.

148 ARA, The Hague: KvG, 716: Elmina Journal, entries dd. 25 January, 10 May and 12 July 1859.

149 WMMS, Owusu Ansa to General Secretaries, dd. Cape Coast, 11 April 1860.

150 ARA, The Hague: KvG, 716: Elmina Journal, entry dd. 12 July 1859.

151 WMMS, Owusu Ansa to General Secretaries, dd. Cape Coast, 13 June 1862.

152 Wilks, *Asante*, 491–2. It is impossible to date the rebellion of the *Akwaboahene* Adu Tutu from the sources used by Wilks; see IAS/AS 17: Akwaboa Stool History, and IAS/AS 39 and 40: Bantama Stool History, I and II, recorded by J. Agyeman-Duah, 7 March 1963, ? November and 7 December 1962 respectively.

153 See, for example, Chapman, 'Journal', entry dd. Kumase, 18 November 1844; WMMS, 'Journals of the Rev. Thomas B. Freeman', entry dd. Kumase, 30 January 1842.

154 Ramseyer and Kühne, *Four Years*, Appendix III, 'The Government of Ashantee', 309. (This passage, so far as I can judge, does not appear in my copy of the Ramseyer MS from BMA, Basel; the source of this information may well have been Owusu Ansa, who was on intimate terms with the missionaries during their captivity in Kumase.)

155 The blood of a royal might not be spilled; see Bowdich, *Mission*, 256. Preferred methods for executing *adehyeɛ* included, as in Osei Kwadwo's case, ritual strangulation (*bu kon*) and drowning (*twa asua*; 'crossing the river').

156 Fuller, *A Vanished Dynasty: Ashanti*, lviii. Kwasi Apea Nuama, a British collaborator and full brother of the *Gyaasewahene* Kwame Tua, appears in many sources (British and Asante) as an expert witness on Asante historical tradition. In part this was due to the function of his office (traditional head of the *akyeame* to the *Asantehene*), but also because of a keen personal interest that he took in historical matters. This interest of his is still today widely remembered in Kumase.

157 *Ibid.*, 87.

158 HA.

159 Asare, *Asante Abasem*. Asante discussants have assisted me to a fuller understanding of the *konnurokusɛm* in the reign of Kwaku Dua Panin, and to them I am extremely grateful. I earnestly trust I have not abused any confidences in the historical analysis offered here. That said, I must record that

most of my enquiries about this matter have been met by head-shaking, silence or denial. One discussant (in Ashanti New Town, Kumase) bluntly asked me where I had heard of *konnurokusɛm*, which I had mentioned with reference to Kwaku Dua Panin; he then went on immediately to say that, 'such things are not for talking over'. By contrast, a friend – an Asante musician – was able to discuss and to offer interpretations of the term, but he had no knowledge of the historical context in which I was interested.

160 Comparable indirections or avoidances were famously employed in the verbal conventions of Asante oaths. The 'great oath' (*ntam kɛsɛɛ*) of the *Asantehene* was simply sworn as such. That is, no one swearing by verbalizing this mnemonic couplet would ever make any direct allusion to the event(s) that gave rise to it (and which it memorialized); that is, no reference was made (on pain of execution) to the death of the *Asantehene* Osei Tutu while campaigning against the Akyem (*adaka gyeaboɔ, ɛno na wawu na n'amu di ako*: 'the coffin that receives bullets, he is the dead one whose corpse yet fights'). Similarly, when a person was tried for cursing the *Asantehene*, the actual words constituting the offence were never repeated in court; instead, understood euphemisms were employed – e.g. *wase biribi* ('he has said something').

161 Compare chapter 3 note 177 above.

162 The basic narrative framework used here is taken from Asare, *Asante Abasem*, amplified and supplemented by the comments of discussants on it. The interpretation is, of course, my own.

163 *The West African Herald*, Accra, 2nd Series, 4/7, 13 June 1871. Compare here Freeman's portrait of the measured, controlled, somewhat austere person of Kwaku Dua Panin in *The Western Echo, Supplements*, 30 January and 10 February 1886. Conversations I have had in Asante, going back over two decades, suggest an *Asantehene* who was all at once admired for his sagacity, celebrated for his long life, respected for his lawgiving and feared for his exercise of power, but who was not much liked in person. In McCaskie, 'Paramountcy' (and in publications on aspects of his reign), the written and oral sources allowed me to document the authoritarian, sometimes arbitrary, violence of Kwaku Dua Panin's tenure of office; I was also able to identify his key lieutenants – notably, the *Akyeamehene/Domakwaehene* Kwame Poku Agyeman and the *Manwerehene* Kwasi Brantuo – and to present these men as being the creations (and creatures) of royal patronage. But what I failed to address systematically, though the evidence lay before me, was the signal part played by kinship, family and personality in the shaping of his or any other reign.

164 Fortes, 'Kinship and Marriage among the Ashanti', 276.

165 See *The West African Herald*, Accra, 2nd Series, 4/7, 13 June 1871 for an assessment of the relationship between Akyampon Yaw and Kwaku Dua Panin. For the careers see ACBP/8: Akyampon Yaw, and ACBP/61: Akyampon Tia, *Asantesɛm*, 9 (1978), 5–14 and 33–6 respectively. Aspects of the careers of both men are discussed throughout Yarak, *Asante and the Dutch*; and see further R. Baesjou, *An Asante Embassy on the Gold Coast: The Mission of Akyempon Yaw to Elmina, 1869–1872* (Leiden, 1979).

166 For more on this theme see chapter 5 below.

167 See McCaskie, 'Office, Land and Subjects', 199.

168 See Rattray, *Religion and Art*, 249.

169 See McCaskie, 'Paramountcy', 226–9; Wilks, *Asante*, 360–5; and, for a different perspective, McCaskie, 'Office, Land and Subjects', 199–201.

170 C.4052, 1884, *Further Correspondence regarding the Affairs of the Gold Coast* (Accounts and Papers LVI), Statement of C. Asanti to Barrow, dd. Kumase, 30 May 1883, enclosed in Report by Capt. K. Barrow of his Mission to Ashanti, dd. 5 July 1883.

171 See McCaskie, 'Death and the *Asantehene*', 441–2. At *ibid.*, 442, fn. 93, I stated that in 1867 Kwabena Anin was still alive, and was simply passed over in favour of Kofi Kakari. I now think, on balance, that he was dead by this date, but the evidence is ambiguous and I stand to be corrected.

172 'Agyeman' is *nea ogye ɔman*, 'defender or saviour of the nation'.

173 Added to the individual case were general character traits that were held to be specific to each *ntɔrɔ*. These were associated with the *akrammoa*. Thus, for example, one of the *akrammoa* of *Bosommuru* was *enini* (python); hence, members of that *ntɔrɔ* were understood to share in the elusive, predatory and dangerous nature ascribed to that snake.

174 Compare the observations in Fortes, *Kinship and the Social Order*, 191–216, and especially 194 and 199, fn. 15.

175 See, for example (following Durkheim, and Granet on China), work carried out on ritual in ancient Greece; see representatively, L. Gernet, *Anthropologie de la Grèce antique* (Paris, 1968); M. Detienne, *Les Jardins d'Adonis* (Paris, 1972); J.-P. Vernant, *Mythe et société en Grèce ancienne* (Paris, 1974); J.-P. Vernant and P. Vidal-Naquet, *Mythe et tragédie en Grèce ancienne* (Paris, 1972).

176 A more parsimonious, atomized view of the force of emotion in relation to selfhood – that is, personally direct rather than ideologically mediated – is R. Rosaldo, 'Grief and a Headhunter's Rage: On the Cultural Force of Emotions', in E.M. Bruner (ed.), *Text, Play, and Story: The Construction and Reconstruction of Self and Society* (Washington, 1984), 178–95. In *odwira* the articulation of representations worked to conduce an emotive response to (and in) history, but the individual person, as in Rosaldo's argument, brought to this arena his/her own emotional baggage; in the 'emoting' of Asante history, individuals might find spaces in which engagement was, at least temporarily, direct. Oscillation and overlapping between the two responsive modes was a crucial expressive component of what observers registered as 'anarchy'.

177 Bonnat MSS, Cahier 7, entry dd. Kumase, 14 December 1871; compare Ramseyer and Kühne, *Four Years*, 148.

178 *Ibid.*, Appendix III, 'The Government of Ashantee', 309.

179 See the *Bosompra akyiwadeɛ* listed at pp. 170–2 above, and Rattray, *Ashanti*, 47.

180 Huydecoper, *Diary*, entry dd. Kumase, 22 August 1816.

181 Bonnat MSS, Cahier 7, entry dd. Kumase, 14 December 1871. For Sanwi see Valsecchi, 'Il Sanwi e l'Impero Asante', and R.A. Horovitz, 'Trade between Sanwi and her Neighbours, 1843–93', paper presented to the Conference on the Akan, Bondoukou, 1974.

182 Bonnat MSS, Cahier 7, entry dd. Kumase, 14 December 1871; for the funeral custom of the *Kokofuhemaa* ('the sister of the King of Cocofoo'), with Kofi

Kakari in attendance at Kokofu, see *ibid.*, Cahier 6, *Mœurs et coutumes, Achanty (une partie en anglais)*.

183 Chapman, 'Journal', entry dd. Kumase, 1 September 1843; Bowdich, *Mission*, 274.

184 This listing is a composite derived from all of the primary sources; for a schematic account of attendance see HA.

185 Bowdich, *Mission*, 274.

186 Chapman, 'Journal', entries dd. Kumase, 14 and 15 September 1844.

187 See McCaskie, 'Paramountcy', 113–51.

188 See WMMS, Freeman, 'Life and Travels'.

189 Bowdich, *Mission*, 323; NAG, Accra, ADM 1/2/4, Winniet, 'Journal', entry dd. Kumase, 9 October 1848.

190 Inferences drawn from the nineteenth-century sources are confirmed by discussants. It is said that during *odwira* people slept everywhere and almost anywhere, and especially in the *adum* ward hard by the palace; the reputation of *adum*, for disorderly celebration, has been maintained to the present day.

191 Bonnat MSS, Cahier 7, entry dd. Kumase, 15 December 1871.

192 *Ibid.*, Cahier 7, entry dd. Kumase, 15 December 1871; Cahier 12, entry dd. Kumase, 23 August 1872: 'ils [the executioners] sont en train de danser . . . autour d'"Apeteseni" . . . appelant et maudissant les "Assamanfo"'. Bonnat's 1872 account is less full – with composite entries, and consequent chronological errors – than its 1871 equivalent. Compare HA, and Bowdich, *Mission*, 323.

193 *Ibid.*, 293.

194 Red, black and white are fundamental to many cultures; see J.R. Goody, *The Culture of Flowers* (Cambridge, 1993).

195 See G.P. Hagan, 'A Note on Akan Colour Symbolism', *IASRR*, 7, 1 (1970), 8–14.

196 For discussion, in different contexts, see McCaskie, 'Armah's *The Healers*' and 'People and Animals'.

197 On menstruation, for example, see McLeod, *The Asante*, 35–6.

198 Compare Rattray, *Ashanti*, 287, fn. 2.

199 European sensory response, even when recollected in tranquillity, tended to cast events in terms of individual subjective experience; the 'I' of the interpreter registered sheer horror, not only at the presumed assault upon its own integrity, but also at the breaking down of the individual 'I' in participants. For a subtle and suggestive analysis of this post-Enlightenment sensibility, of which Goethe was an ambivalent precursor, see Bakhtin, *Rabelais and His World*, especially 244 ff. By the nineteenth century this point of view was a European middle-class universal; the loss of the 'I' (of observer and observed) was a fearful presence, whether the customs described were those of the 'savages' of the French countryside or of Flaubert's and Du Camp's Egypt. I leave aside here (for there are no instances in Asante) that deformation of this point of view that, with ambiguous but excited trepidation, sought to cancel or annihilate the 'I' of self in the customs of the exotic mass; Bowdich and his successors were manifestly not Rimbaud.

200 Bowdich, *Mission*, 275.

201 Rattray, *Religion and Art*, 127.

202 See, for example, H.M. Cole, 'The Art of Festival in Ghana', *AfAr*, 8, 3 (1975),

12–23 and 60–2. Compare here the now classic J. Huizinga, *Homo Ludens: A Study of the Play Element in Culture* (London, 1950).

203 In focusing my argument here I have found recent discussions in art history helpful. See S. Alpers, *The Art of Describing* (Chicago, 1983); N. Bryson, *Vision in Painting: The Logic of the Gaze* (New Haven, 1983); C. Ginzburg, *The Enigma of Piero: Piero della Francesco (The Baptism, the Arezzo Cycle, the Flagellation)* (London, 1985); D. Preziosi, *Rethinking Art History: Meditations on a Coy Science* (New Haven, 1989); and N. Bryson, M.A. Holly and K. Moxey (eds.), *Visual Theory: Painting and Interpretation* (Oxford, 1991).

204 Bowdich, *Mission*, 322. See too HA, and the remarks of Owusu Ansa in 'The King of Ashantee', *The Times*, London, 29 July 1873.

205 *The Western Echo*, *Supplement*, 24 March 1886.

206 This is still the case. Anyone approaching the *Asantehene* on formal occasions must pick a way along a narrow approach. The sensation is of being lost amidst a press of seated *gyaasefoɔ*. Photographs convey this well, for, taken from a distance, they show the *Asantehene* in seeming isolation on the far side of what appears to be an impenetrable screen of bodies.

207 Bonnat MSS, Cahier 7, entries dd. Kumase, 2, 3 and 4 September 1871 (with accompanying sketch and drawings).

208 WMMS, Freeman, 'Life and Travels', 89–90.

209 Chapman, 'Journal', entry dd. Kumase, 2 September 1843; see further WMMS, 'Journals of the Rev. Thomas B. Freeman', entry dd. Kumase, 2 September 1843.

210 Reverse order of precedence was (and is) standard in all formal exchanges of greetings.

211 *The Western Echo*, *Supplement*, 24 March 1886. A useful discussion of types and uses of swords is in M.J. Ehrlich, 'A Catalogue of Ashanti Art taken from Kumasi in the Anglo-Ashanti War of 1874', Ph.D. (Indiana, 1981), 40 ff.

212 Chapman, 'Journal', entry dd. Kumase, 2 September 1843.

213 See Patton, 'The Asante Umbrella', 64–73.

214 For discussion see McCaskie, 'Death and the *Asantehene*', 422–5.

215 Bowdich, *Mission*, 275. On *odwira fomemene* 2 September 1843, Freeman estimated that 175 'large umbrellas' were present; see WMMS, 'Journals of the Rev. Thomas B. Freeman', entry dd. Kumase, 2 September 1843.

216 Chapman, 'Journal', entry dd. Kumase, 2 September 1843.

217 *The Western Echo*, *Supplement*, 24 March 1886.

218 See Kyerematen, 'Ashanti Royal Regalia', 81 ff.; Bowdich, *Mission*, 38 and 288–91. An interesting, if odd, account is in Ehrlich, 'A Catalogue of Art', 137 ff. For a general treatment of the aesthetics of *puruw/puruo* see K. Antubam, *Ghana's Heritage of Culture* (Leipzig, 1963), 105–6.

219 See, for example, Chapman, 'Journal', entry dd. Kumase, 2 September 1843.

220 See Asare, *Asante Abasem*, and MRO, Kumase, File on 'Regalia', n.d. (but 1940s). Compare Bowdich, *Mission*, 299–300. There are innumerable 'strong names'; thus, for example, *ɔbuabasa* ('breaker of arms') was a customary honorific used of occupants of the Kumase *Gyaasewa* stool (Opoku Frɛfrɛ, Adu Bofoɔ *et al.*).

221 Voluntary motion by the *Asantehene* when he was seated in this way was

termed 'dancing in the palanquin', and it was a sign of royal approbation; see Chapman, 'Journal', entry dd. Kumase, 3 September 1843, for 'dancing in the basket'.

222 HA; Asare, *Asante Abasem*; J.H. Nketia, *Drumming in Akan Communities of Ghana* (London, 1963), especially 124–5 and 196; E.O. Aboagye, 'Some Traditional Drums of Ghana', B.A. thesis (UST Kumasi, 1968). I have followed Asante tradition in identifying Ataara Finam, but I am aware that the name is often used eponymously of early rulers of the Kwawu-Afram plains area.

223 BMA, Basel, Jenkins (Ramseyer MS *et al.*), entry dd. Kumase, 16 December 1871; see too Ramseyer and Kühne, *Four Years*, 148. Bonnat MSS, Cahier 7, entry dd. Kumase, 17 December 1871: '... femmes du roi [at the reception of the 16th] dans les pagnes de soie, la buste poudré d'un poudre grise jaune – la tête ... surmonti d'espèce de petit Diadème ... et la figure garnie de dessins ... les huit premières entourés d'eunuques, marchaient en baissant la tête, tenant chacune de la main gauche, une petite arme (? pistolet) ... les sept autres qui suivaient n'avaient point de Diadème, mais portaient chacune un riche cofret du bois ou en argent – toutes avaient au cou et au main des bijoux de toutes espèces et en grande abondance'. (The text here is difficult to read, and Bonnat's sentence structure, grammar and spelling are somewhat erratic.)

224 Chapman, 'Journal', entry dd. Kumase, 2 September 1843; Bonnat MSS, Cahier 12, entry dd. Kumase, 24 August 1872.

225 *Ibid.*, Cahier 7, entry dd. Kumase, 17 December 1871: 'Hier [16 December] au soir ... la grande réception (au flambeau) ... finit les 10 ou 11 heures du soir.' BMA, Basel, Jenkins (Ramseyer MS *et al.*), entry dd. Kumase, 16 December 1871, states that the reception lasted for three hours into the night, and that the crowd was so dense that office holders had difficulty in finding their allotted places. See Bowdich, *Mission*, 275, for 6 September 1817 (note the comparison with a 'large fair').

226 *Ibid.*, 300. For a popular account, A.A. Anti, *The Ancient Asante King* (Accra, 1974), 18. The horns in question were *ntahera* and *nkofe*. Similarly, the playing of the *kwakrannya* horns around dawn signalled that the *Asantehene* was awake.

227 The European observer who came closest to understanding the production of identification and catharsis was T.B. Freeman. See *The Western Echo*, *Supplements*, 24 March and 30 June 1886.

228 These factors are implicit in the phrasing used to describe *odwira* in HA. Cole, 'Art of Festival' situates these successive episodes with reference to levels and intensities of 'energy flow'. This is useful – as far as it goes – but Cole's account is ideologically somewhat innocent. Gilbert, 'Aesthetic Strategies', 24, catches some of the ideological issues at stake in bald assertions made by her Akuropon informants (in response to questions about flexibility and change in transacting *odwira*): 'I was told, sometimes heatedly, that I was mistaken: the ritual is unchanging and immaculate. However, I *was* told that were the King to be ill, *Odwira* would not be performed, or only minimally; and if that were to happen, then disaster, drought, famine and pestilence would surely follow.' Compare the structurations and periodicities described in Geertz, *Negara*.

229 The anthropological literature – going back as far as A. Van Gennep, *Les Rites*

de passage (Paris, 1908) – is huge. Mauss, Hertz, Gluckman, Turner, Douglas and numerous others have done much to explore and refine the concept (broadly speaking) of liminality. Historians of popular culture – Febvre, Le Roy Ladurie, Baroja, Ginzburg, Darnton and others – have variously used insights gleaned from anthropology (and given further insights back to the anthropologists). The overall contribution of Bakhtin is indispensable. In focusing ideas and reading on this subject, the work of Maurice Bloch proved especially suggestive. See, most recently, M. Bloch, *Ritual, History and Power: Selected Papers in Anthropology* (London, 1989).

230 *The Western Echo, Supplement*, 10 April 1886. See too WMMS, Freeman to General Secretaries, dd. Kumase, 7 September 1843. For 'the shouting and screaming' on the *odwira nwonakwasie* of 23 October 1870, see Ramseyer and Kühne, *Four Years*, 92; compare Bonnat MSS, Cahier 3, entry dd. ? 'Ebenezer', 23 October 1870.

231 Chapman, 'Journal', entry dd. Kumase, 3 September 1843.

232 Rattray, *Religion and Art*, 139–43. HA is reticent on the sacrificial component of the ritual. Discussants have variously told me that the numbers killed were not fixed, but depended on contingencies such as the wishes of the *abosom* and *Asantehene*. Bowdich, *Mission*, 279, and Ramseyer and Kühne, *Four Years*, 148–9, give only general (and confused) accounts. The difficulty with the sources is that Europeans saw the *Asantehene* depart for, and return from, Bantama, but they themselves were disbarred from accompanying him to the *baamu*.

233 HA. See the remarks in Chapman, 'Journal', entry dd. Kumase, 15 September 1844.

234 *Ibid.* Bonnat MSS, Cahier 12, entry dd. Kumase, 24 August 1872 (Bonnat gets the date wrong here, but correctly identifies the day as 'Dimanche'); this individual, noted Bonnat, was the third *ɔkɔmfɔ* to be executed in the space of four months. See too Ramseyer and Kühne, *Four Years*, 179.

235 Horrified Europeans reported this dismemberment in grisly – but great – detail. See, for example, Chapman, 'Journal', entries dd. Kumase, 3 September 1843 and 15 September 1844; Bonnat MSS, Cahier 7, entry dd. Kumase, 17 December 1871, reported that the executioners simulated eating portions of the corpse, and distributed the severed head and limbs, and pieces of the flesh, among themselves. Compare Chapman, 'Journal', entry dd. Kumase, 24 January 1844.

236 *Ibid.*, entry dd. Kumase, 24 November 1843, for a suggestive account (by a youthful member of the *adumfoɔ*) of the ambiguities attaching to the role of executioner. See M.F.C. Bourdillon and M. Fortes (eds.), *Sacrifice* (London, 1980), for the equivocal complexities inhering in all sacrificial acts.

237 HA. Offenders' names are catalogued in the *apaeɛ* of the *Asantehene*; see Arhin, 'The Asante Praise Poems'.

238 HA forms the basis of this minimal list. I have footnoted those entries where amplification is provided by tradition or scholarship.

239 See C.-H. Perrot, 'Le Raid d'Ebiri Moro contre Kumasi, la capitale Ashanti (1718)', *Cultures et Développement*, 16, 3/4 (1984), 537–52; *ibid.*, *Les Anyi Ndenye*.

240 Reindorf, *History*, 76–7, for an interesting tradition that the captive Ameyaw

Kwaakye instructed Opoku Ware in various facets of government, and that his death was brought about by a conspiracy of Kumase office holders as a result of his 'persistent endeavours in advocating despotic rule'.

241 For problems of dating and reconstruction see Terray, 'Une Histoire du Royaume Abron'.

242 For the chronology see L. Yarak, 'Dating Asantehene Osei Kwadwo's Campaign against the Banna', *Asantesɛm*, 10 (1979), 58.

243 Chapman, 'Journal', entries dd. Kumase, 3 September 1843 and 15 September 1844; WMMS, Freeman to General Secretaries, dd. Kumase, 7 September 1843; *ibid.*, 'Journals of the Rev. Thomas B. Freeman', entry dd. Kumase, 3 September 1843.

244 In addition to the materials already cited see, for some present day insights, R. Da Matta, 'Constraint and License: A Preliminary Study of Two Brazilian National Rituals', in S.F. Moore and B.G. Meyerhoof (eds.), *Secular Rituals* (Amsterdam, 1977), 244–64. Interesting on the balance between the myriad inscriptions of licence and control in a modern state – Castro's Cuba – is J. Bettelheim, 'Negotiations of Power in Carnaval [*sic*] Culture in Santiago de Cuba', *AfAr*, 24, 2 (1991), 66–75 and 91–2. Compare too D. Birmingham, 'Carnival at Luanda', *JAH*, 29, 1 (1988), 93–103.

245 Ramseyer and Kühne, *Four Years*, 148; Bonnat MSS, Cahier 7, entry dd. Kumase, 17 December 1871.

246 Bowdich, *Mission*, 278. Bowdich compared the scene with 'les scènes les plus honteuses et les plus destructives de la subordination et de la discipline', recorded by Voltaire in his moralizing account of the siege of Pondicherry.

247 Chapman, 'Journal', entry dd. Kumase, 15 September 1844.

248 BMA, Basel, Jenkins (Ramseyer MS *et al.*). According to Ramseyer, the 'high day' when this occurred was Sunday, 23 October 1870, which was indeed 19: *nwonakwasie* by the Asante calendar. Compare Bonnat MSS, Cahier 3, entry dd. Kumase, 23 October 1870: 'Aujourd'hui (dimanche) tout le monde jouer' – drinking spirits and palm wine, but not eating. See too Ramseyer and Kühne, *Four Years*, 92. In his MS account, Ramseyer adds that the Europeans, held captive just outside Kumase at 'Ebenezer', heard noise from the *odwira* celebrations in the capital every day from 23 October until at least 6 November, which was the *odwira akwasidae* (33: *kurukwasie*).

249 It is said by some that in the 1880s Kwame Tua greatly offended the *Edwesohene* Kwasi Afrane Kɛsɛɛ by lampooning that office holder's self-importance. For some discussion of music as social critique see J.H. Kwabena Nketia, 'The Musician in Akan Society', in W.L. d'Azevedo (ed.), *The Traditional Artist in African Societies* (Bloomington, 1975), 79–100.

250 See MRO, Kumase, Correspondence File 1937, Kwame Kwabea *et al.* to *Asantehene*, dd. Kumase, 2 January 1937 (in explanation of a Petition concerning the Properties of Akua Marbua, July 1935; encl. and minuted by (?) J.W.K. Appiah).

251 Bowdich, *Essay*, 49. For context see McCaskie, 'State and Society, Marriage and Adultery'.

252 Compare Kea, *Settlements, Trade, and Politics*, 291–2, on 'rituals of rebellion' amongst the coastal Akan in the seventeenth century.

253 For this (Bakhtinian point) in one very specific historical context see M. Ozouf, *La Fête révolutionnaire, 1789–1799* (Paris, 1980); on act and metaphor as predictions of closure, in an orchestrated licensing of participation in violence, see D. Arasse, *La Guillotine et l'imaginaire de la Terreur* (Paris, 1987).

254 Asare, *Asante Abasem*. For some royal wives life was a matter of *yɛbɔfa no saraa* ('taking it as it is'; i.e. enduring a status that could never be changed).

255 Anti, *Ancient Asante King*, 51, and 7 (on sources). Versions of this account, but without its lurid phrasing, are widespread. It is commonly said that the last Asante to suffer execution by *atɔperɛ* was a man convicted of having had sexual intercourse with a wife of the *Asantehene* Mensa Bonsu.

256 Chapman, 'Journal', entry dd. Kumase, 3 September 1843. On Sir Charles McCarthy's skull see too Ramseyer and Kühne, *Four Years*, 149.

257 Bonnat MSS, Cahier 7, entry dd. Kumase, 17 December 1871.

258 *Ibid.*, Cahier 12, entry dd. Kumase, 24 August 1872 (correctly identified as Sunday, but wrongly dated; Sunday, 19: *nwonakwasie* was 25 August. The second part of this composite entry is in Cahier 13).

259 *Ibid.*, Cahier 7, entry dd. Kumase, 17 December 1871.

260 Chapman, 'Journal', entry dd. Kumase, 15 September 1844.

261 *Ibid.*, entry dd. Kumase, 3 September 1843. Compare the reference to the *Asantehene* Kofi Kakari dancing on *odwira nwonakwasie* 25 August 1872 in Ramseyer and Kühne, *Four Years*, 179.

262 Bowdich, *Mission*, 275. Was Bowdich mistaken? I have argued so here. First, because the authoritative HA, together with all of the European sources other than Bowdich, assigns the events described to 19: *nwonakwasie*. Second, because by his own account – *ibid.*, 89 – Bowdich kept only a 'rude diary', which he abridged in dealing with events after July 1817. It is possible that the *Asantehene* Osei Tutu Kwame had the enemy skulls paraded on *odwira fomemene*, but – in the absence of any documented reason of any sort – the likelihood is that Bowdich simply made a mistake. Presumably, the 'rude diary' itself was written rather haphazardly during the confusions of September.

263 Chapman, 'Journal', entry dd. Kumase, 15 September 1844.

264 For the formulaic insults see BMA, Basel, Jenkins (Ramseyer MS *et al.*), entry dd. Kumase, 17 December 1871. On the historical pedagogy involved see Bonnat MSS, Cahier 7, entry dd. Kumase, 17 December 1871. Bonnat observed that these skulls – each belonging to a major offender (killed in war or executed at Kumase) – were deposited at Bantama, and 'confié a des gens [*barimfoɔ*] qui ont la charge spéciale de les distinguer les unes des autres et de se rappeller leur nom et l'histoire de leur crime ou de leur défaite et capture ... selon si c'est un grand criminel ou un roi ou chef défait en bataille ils sont toujours ... connaître la meme tête, de sort (?) qui l'histoire (?) conserver très bien depuis ... des generations'. Compare *ibid.*, Cahier 13, entry dd. Kumase, 24 August 1872, in which Bonnat comments on the historical knowledge of the *barimfoɔ*, and prophesies that 'leur Histoire serait un jour un des principaux matériaux pour la construction de l'Histoire de ce pays'. It is said that the Bantama skulls were 'fed' with the left hand, to indicate contempt.

265 *Ibid.* More work needs to be done on the biographies of malefactors named in the *apaeɛ* of the *Asantehenes*.

266 Bowdich, *Mission*, 278.

267 Huydecoper, *Diary*, entry dd. Kumase, 25 August 1816.

268 *The Western Echo, Supplement*, 10 April 1886.

269 Asante tradition records the use of sword and shield in early warfare (*temp.* Obiri Yeboa) – and notably in encounters between heroic individuals.

270 Owusu Ansa, 'The King of Ashantee', *The Times*, London, 29 July 1873; compare Chapman, 'Journal', entry dd. Kumase, 9 March 1844, for a description of 'a "field day" among the Aristocracy'.

271 HA. Compare Rattray, *Religion and Art*, 132 and 135.

272 HA and AK particularly emphasize that the *odwira suman* was brought into Asante from outside – and in historical time. Asante discussants overwhelmingly assert its northern origins. However, Asante has long been the recipient of anti-witchcraft cults of northern origin, and in this century the 'north' has come to be regarded as the generic source of alien supernatural powers. AK unequivocally states that it was brought into Asante from Akyem.

273 HA asserts that Barikorang (Bre Kuran) – son of the Kumase *Akwamuhene* Awere, and the traveller who brought the *odwira suman* back to Kumase – handed it over to Osei Tutu, because 'he found that only the King could keep it'; that is, only the *Asantehene* could successfully mediate and deploy its enormous power(s).

274 Cardinall, *In Ashanti*, 153–4; see McCaskie, 'People and Animals', for a fuller analysis of *ɔtrommo*, and of kindred animals possessed of *sasa*. Rattray, *Religion and Art*, 135, states that the contents of the *suman* were placed within the horn(s), of *ɔtrommo*.

275 On barkcloth see McCleod, *The Asante*, 148–9.

276 On the decorated skulls see Bowdich, *Mission*, 275, and Rattray, *Religion and Art*, 132. On 17 December 1871, there were some forty skulls present, each with 'a red rag' around its forehead; see Ramseyer and Kühne, *Four Years*, 149. Compare Rattray, *Ashanti Proverbs*, 43, *ɔsamene ahoofwam ne nunum* ('the smell of a ghost is the smell of the *nunum* shrub').

277 For the placing of the left foot on the skulls see HA; for the *Asantehene* Kwaku Dua Panin placing his foot on McCarthy's skull see Chapman, 'Journal', entry dd. Kumase, 3 September 1843. With his foot on each skull in turn, the *Asantehene* addressed it as follows: *Me Nana Asumasi na okuu wo, ohene biara a obesore atia me no. Ma me nya ne ti mentwa, me ka wo die yi ho* ('My Great Grand Uncle so-and-so killed you. If any other ruler [alt. substitute "person"] rebels against me, let me get his head to cut off and put beside yours').

278 They were sited in *kurotia*; see HA.

279 Bonnat MSS, Cahier 7, entry dd. Kumase, 17 December 1871: the enemy skulls 'seraient au milieu de la nuit porter, vers l'eau ... par la route de Cape Coast'. *Ibid.*, Cahier 13, entry dd. Kumase, 24 August 1872: 'ils sont porté près du "Soubin" au Sud de la ville'. See too Rattray, *Religion and Art*, 134.

280 *Ibid.*, 135; MFU, 'Ashanti Deities (Some Notes On)', n.d.

281 I have been told that during 'the *awo* ceremony' every year a person was killed in honour of *asase yaa*, the earth (construed as female); other discussants, in line with Rattray's and Fortes' informants, urge that only one human sacrifice – the original one – was ever made. For the puzzling etymology of *apafram* see

Rattray, *Religion and Art*, 127, fn. 1. I am unable to improve on Rattray, for the derivations of the term that I have been offered are diverse, speculative and contradictory. That said, *apafram* was understood to refer to (and at some level to embody?) the general conceptual sense of being Asante. It was an articulation of belonging and identity that was expressed in *odwira*. However, the precise status of *apafram* remains obscure. Authoritative traditions equate it with – or collapse it into – the *odwira sumaŋ*; AK and HA both give *apafram* as being the original name of the *odwira sumaŋ*. Other sources, oral and written, imply that *apafram* was distinct from the *odwira suman*; that it was an *ɔbosom* in its own right, albeit of a unique (pre-Asante?) kind; and that it was conduced to manifest itself at *odwira* as the distillation of a sense of 'Asante-ness'; see, for example, the reading of *apafram* (if not the occult interpretation placed upon it) in Braffi, *Esoteric Significance*, 15–16 ('The Race-God, "Apafram"'). While I follow two *Asantehenes* in equating *apafram* with the *odwira sumaŋ*, and in associating it with Asante identity, I am aware that this is a vexed issue. Thus far, further details have eluded me, and these may now be unrecoverable. It should be added that the nineteenth-century European sources habitually use *apafram* and *odwira* as synonyms.

282 See MFU, 'Ashanti Deities (Some Notes On)', n.d.

283 Danquah, *The Akan Doctrine of God*, 156. Danquah emphasized that this distinction 'is not merely a splitting of hairs'.

284 See Bonnat MSS, Cahier 7, entry dd. Kumase, 17 December 1871: 'cette cérémonie dure depuis minuit jusqu'au chant du coq. Pendant ce temps là un calme de mort est gardé par tout le monde, excepte les "fétiche" prêtres et si un homme (n'importe qui) riait ou baillait, ou éternuait, ou crachait par terre, il serait decapité sur place.' See too, *ibid.*, Cahier 13, entry dd. Kumase, 24 August 1872. Compare the authoritative account in HA: 'Every one of them turns about and runs homeward in perfect silence. If any body falls down, he is killed on the spot.'

285 For a vivid popular account see Anti, *The Ancient Asante King*, 18–19. When the *Asantehene* was in mourning, he would go out into Kumase at night; on such occasions, he would put on a plain red cloth (*kɔbene*), under which he wore – tied around his body – the knife that was kept in the scabbard of the *mponponsuo* sword.

286 Asare, *Asante Abasem*.

287 The address to *awo* and the *asamanfoɔ* was: '*Awo ee! Awo ee! Awo ee!* [then *awo* 'replied' and the *ɔkyeame* continued] *Afe ano aghia, Yerebetwa Odwira, Begye odie yi di, Obiara a ompe se osom Asantehene no, Ma yen nsa nku no nku no, Sedie yekuu wo ne mfefuo atofuo no*' ('The edges of the year are come together, we are about to celebrate the Odwira. Come and take this yam and eat it. If anyone does not want to serve the *Asantehene*, let us get him and kill him, just as we killed you and all your fellow condemned criminals').

288 Note the unspoken part played in all this by narrativity. In *odwira* the Asante 'lived' a (re)presented or 'criticized' past in a continuous present enabled by the hermeneutic. The narrative thereby produced depended upon belief as figuration, but upon ideology as refiguration. It was the centrality and strength of acceptance (*vide* Peel) that underlay the capacity to derive other statements;

that this derivation was ideological is evident throughout *odwira*. The range of articulations between acceptance and derivation can only be understood historically. The failure to address this adequately is the weakest part of – for example – Ricoeur, *Le Temps raconte*, and of many other attempts to practise a 'questioning back' (*Rückfrage*) from the epistemological to the ontological – but without referencing actual histories. The hermeneutic, in short, is not inscribed, but rather is brought into play historically.

289 It is interesting that in, for example, Danquah, *The Akan Doctrine of God*, or Ackah, *Akan Ethics*, the modelling of the moral individual takes place in an idealized vacuum outside of history. This timelessness is an attempt to evade history, or rather to circumvent its masterful embrace by situating the 'good' in agreed communitarian values. Appeals to such a yardstick generate possible models of living – but only in the abstract, or in dialogue between similarly (and impossibly) detached autonomies. The paradoxes involved are to be seen perhaps, and poignantly, in the contrast between Danquah's writings and his life.

290 The *Asantehene* was both himself in present time and the continuous present of all of his predecessors in office in historical time. He was also, all at once, an embodiment of his role and a metaphor for it. As actor, he performed his part, but this performance was the subject of constant comment. Everything he did was an action that was also proclaimed by sanctioned observers, using the third person 'he'; that is, for instance, an embodiment named Osei Tutu Kwame presided over the *odwira* of 1817, but in so doing 'he' enacted and fulfilled expectations vested in an office of which he was temporarily the incumbent. The performative 'he' that conduced commentary belonged to the role, not the player.

291 Thus, in the text of HA, the categorization of enemies (and their listing by name) is referenced exclusively to their offence against, and due punishment by, an *Asantehene*.

292 See *The Western Echo*, *Supplement*, 10 April 1886, on sanctioned mourning in the night of *odwira fomemene/nwonakwasie*.

293 Bowdich, *Mission*, 279.

294 Ramseyer and Kühne, *Four Years*, Appendix III, 'The Government of Ashantee', 305–6. The competencies of the *Asantemaŋhyiamu* are well described in *The Western Echo*, *Supplements*, 24 March and 10 April 1886. Compare AK: 'when Ossai Tutu got the suman, he published it all through his districts and counties and told them that a day once in a year will be appointed for every one under Ashanti Kingdom to celebrate the suman'.

295 Bowdich, *Essay*, 27; see too *ibid.*, *Mission*, 274.

296 *The Western Echo*, *Supplement*, 10 April 1886.

297 See WMMS, Wharton to General Secretaries, dd. Kumase, 9 November 1846, and Rattray, *Ashanti Law and Constitution*, 240. For the full context see McCaskie, 'Power and Dynastic Conflict in Mampon'.

298 Bonnat MSS, Cahier 13, entry dd. Kumase, 20 September 1872. Bonnat specifically states that the Asante Akyem office holders had been unsuspecting participants in *odwira* when they were tried and executed.

299 The military commands and dispositions are described throughout Huydecoper, *Diary*. For the individuals I have used the files of the ACBP.

300 *Ibid.*
301 Huydecoper, *Diary*, entry dd. Kumase, 14 August 1816; Bowdich, *Mission*, 73.
302 Huydecoper, *Diary*, entry dd. Kumase, 1 September 1816.
303 Bowdich, *Mission*, 73. On Bariki's previous military record see *ibid.*, 237.
304 Huydecoper, *Diary*, entries dd. Kumase, 2 September and 28 October 1816; Bowdich, *Mission*, 73.
305 Huydecoper, *Diary*, entry dd. Kumase, 3 March 1817; Bowdich, *Mission*, 129.
306 Bonnat MSS, Cahier 7, entry dd. Kumase, 29 December 1871. Bonnat described the case of 'Nto-bi' as being 'assez singulier'. For the prosecution of Owusu Ntobi, although he is not actually named, see too Ramseyer and Kühne, *Four Years*, 147, which records that 'the prince was to be killed'. For Owusu Ntobi's role in the conflicted aftermath of Kwaku Dua Panin's death in 1867 see McCaskie, 'Death and the *Asantehene*', 436–7.
307 Bonnat MSS, Cahier 15, *Mœurs et coutumes de l'Achanty*, for public announcements of such judgements; see too Kurankyi-Taylor, 'Legal Institutions', I, 122 ff.
308 See HA and Rattray, *Religion and Art*, 136–7. There are various chronological confusions in the ethnographic accounts. These have doubtless arisen because of the different observance days of the two *ntɔrɔ*. By contrast, the historical sources give some chronological fix, but in an uncomprehending and partial way (Europeans being disbarred from private rituals). The matter is simpler than it might first appear to be, so long as all accounts are reconciled together using the fixed bases provided by the two historically relevant *ntɔrɔ* observance days: *kurubena* (21: Tuesday) and *kwawukuo* (22: Wednesday). As the *Asantehene* struck the *akyiwadeε* animal he addressed the sword he was holding: *wukyi, nso mede mereka wo* ('This is your taboo, but I am now touching you with it'). When he cleansed the sword from defilement he (or an appointed proxy) concluded: *ohene bosom kεsεε bosommuru* [or *bosompra*], *mebo wo nsu oo!* ('The King's great sword *Bosommuru* [or *Bosompra*], I sprinkle water on you to sanctify you').
309 *The Western Echo, Supplement*, 10 April 1886.
310 Bonnat MSS, Cahier 7, entry dd. Kumase, 22 December 1871: 'un jour de cadeau ... toute la nuit nous avons entendu des coups de fusil ... tiré par des hommes qui accompagne leur chef respectif aux différentes points de l'eau qui entoure Coumassie, portant avec eux leurs (?) maisons pour être lavée...'.
311 *Ibid.*; *The Western Echo, Supplement*, 10 April 1886.
312 Bowdich, *Mission*, 280; Ramseyer and Kühne, *Four Years*, 151; Chapman, 'Journal', entry dd. Kumase, 12 September 1843. Bowdich's chronology is once again vague, but there is no doubt that he is talking about the *odwira fofie*. Chapman's account of the 8th was set down on the 12th, because he had been ill during the intervening days.
313 Ramseyer and Kühne, *Four Years*, 149; BMA, Basel, Jenkins (Ramseyer MS *et al.*) adds that the water in 1871 had been brought from 'a special Tano cult site'; Chapman, 'Journal', entry dd. Kumase, 20 September 1844.
314 Bonnat MSS, Cahier 7, entry dd. Kumase, 22 December 1871; Ramseyer and Kühne, *Four Years*, 150–1; Chapman, 'Journal', entry dd. Kumase, 12 September 1843; compare WMMS, 'Journals of the Rev. Thomas B.

Freeman', entry dd. Kumase, 8 September 1843.

315 *The Western Echo, Supplement*, 10 April 1886; BMA, Basel, Jenkins (Ramseyer MS *et al.*) for the objects, including the two mirrors, that were carried in 1871; compare Ramseyer and Kühne, *Four Years*, 151.

316 Versions of the Twi texts, with English translations, are to be found in HA, and in Rattray, *Religion and Art*, 138. I am grateful to those who have taken time to go through these texts with me.

317 See Bowdich, *Mission*, 280.

318 *Ibid.*

319 *Ibid.*, 279.

320 Hutton, *Voyage*, 201.

321 See HA, and MFU, 'Ashanti Deities (Some Notes On)', n.d.

322 Bowdich, *Mission*, 280; HA.

323 Bowdich, *Mission*, 280.

324 Ramseyer and Kühne, *Four Years*, 93.

325 Bonnat MSS, Cahier 15, *Mœurs et coutumes de l'Achanty*; *The Western Echo, Supplement*, 10 April 1886.

326 Chapman, 'Journal', entry dd. Kumase, 20 September 1844.

327 Bowdich, *Mission*, 274; compare *ibid.*, *Essay*, 49.

328 Bonnat MSS, Cahier 7, entry dd. Kumase, 22 December 1871.

329 Rattray, *Religion and Art*, 143. Compare HA.

330 See BMA, Basel, D/1, 82, N.V. Asare, 'Annual Report of Kumase to the Home Committee', dd. Kumase, 14 February 1905; D/1, 86, 20 March 1907; D/1, 95, 24 February 1911.

331 *Ibid.*; Asare, *Asante Abasem*. Further materials are doubtless awaiting recovery from MRO, Kumase, Criminal Case Records Books; thus far, I have only sampled this rich source of evidence. Riotous behaviour has continued to be a feature of Christmas and New Year in Asante. Thus, for example, on Christmas Day 1951 a pitched battle took place between the villagers of Akyerekurom and Fumesua; in the same holiday period there was public concern about the 'degrading' behaviour of the young in the unlicensed bars and dance halls of Kumase. See *The Ashanti Pioneer*, Kumase, 28 and 29 December 1951. Riotous conduct was certainly an observable feature of Christmas and New Year in Kumase as recently as 1975–6.

332 Bowdich, *Mission*, 274; compare Le Roy Ladurie, *Le Carnaval de Romans*.

333 Chapman, 'Journal', entry dd. Kumase, 14 September 1843.

334 See Bonnat MSS, Cahier 7, entry dd. Kumase, 29 December 1871. The date of this entry (29 December 1871) was *nwonafie* (31: Friday), and looking back from it to his previous journal entry (22 December) on *fofie* (24: Friday), Bonnat noted the following concerning the intervening days: 'Dans ces journées le roi et les grands chefs étrangers se sont réuni pour parler des affaires importantes de l'état et pour juger les grandes affaires...'.

335 Chapman, 'Journal', entry dd. Kumase, 28 September 1844.

336 Rattray, *Religion and Art*, 139.

337 Chapman, 'Journal', entry dd. Kumase, 28 September 1844.

338 *Ibid.*, entry dd. Kumase, 15 September 1843; see too HA. During *odwira* the *Bantamahene* shaved his hair in the manner of the stool carriers (*ogya mpram*)

to commemorate the first *Bantamahene* Amankwatia's service to Osei Tutu before he became the *Asantehene*.

339 Chapman, 'Journal', entry dd. Kumase, 29 September 1844.

340 See Nketia, *Drumming in Akan Communities*, 128 ff. for some discussion.

341 Chapman, 'Journal', entry dd. Kumase, 17 September 1843.

342 Bonnat MSS, Cahier 13, entry dd. Kumase, 8 September 1872; HA.

343 Chapman, 'Journal', entry dd. Kumase, 18 September 1843; WMMS, 'Journals of the Rev. Thomas B. Freeman', entry dd. Kumase, 18 September 1843.

344 *The Western Echo, Supplement*, 10 April 1886.

345 Thus, a theme running through Chapman's 'Journal' is of his being importuned for European clothes by the Asante elite; for the *Asantehene* Osei Tutu Kwame in European dress see Bowdich, *Mission*, 122. For context see McCaskie, 'Innovational Eclecticism'.

346 Chapman, 'Journal', entry dd. Kumase, 27 September 1843.

347 Hutchison's Diary, entry dd. Kumase, 30 September 1817, in Bowdich, *Mission*, 384.

348 WMMS, 'Journals of the Rev. Thomas B. Freeman', entry dd. Kumase, 27 September 1843.

349 Bonnat MSS, Cahier 7, entry dd. Kumase, 9 January 1872; BMA, Basel, Jenkins (Ramseyer MS *et al.*), entry dd. Kumase, 9 January 1872; Ramseyer and Kühne, *Four Years*, 154.

350 See MFU, 'Ashanti Deities (Some Notes On)', n.d.; Kyerematen, 'Ashanti Royal Regalia'.

351 Bowdich, *Mission*, 291.

352 Bonnat MSS, Cahier 7, entry dd. Kumase, 9 January 1872; Ramseyer and Kühne, *Four Years*, 154; and on Kwaku Bosommuru Dwira's career see McCaskie, 'Office, Land and Subjects', 201–2.

353 HA; Bonnat MSS, Cahier 15, *Mœurs et coutumes de l'Achanty*. Compare Bowdich, *Mission*, 288–9; and, on the status and roles of *ŋkradwarefoɔ*, see *The African Times*, London, III, 29, 23 November 1863.

354 Hutchison's Diary, entry dd. Kumase, 30 September 1817, in Bowdich, *Mission*, 385.

355 Bowdich, *Essay*, 34.

356 Bonnat MSS, Cahier 7, entry dd. Kumase, 12 January 1872; for the *asumaŋ nnɔrɔ* ('the dance of charms') see MFU, 'Ashanti Deities (Some Notes On)', n.d.

357 Hutchison's Diary, entry dd. Kumase, 3 October 1817, in Bowdich, *Mission*, 387.

358 Ramseyer and Kühne, *Four Years*, 154–5 (the text mistakenly refers to 'Friday, January 13th' instead of the 12th).

359 HA. BMA, Basel, Jenkins (Ramseyer MS *et al.*) entry dd. Kumase, 12 January 1872, specifically points out that this 'purification ceremony', though similar to ones that had recently occurred (during *odwira*), was 'especially in honour of the King's soul'; chief among the *asumaŋ* containers carried from the palace was a 'silver urn'. Also carried from the palace on this occasion (as on all such) was the reigning *Asantehene's* personal stool. Kofi Kakari's personal stool was the *kotoko dwa* (a 'porcupine' stool, embossed with gold discs), and it was destined to be 'blackened' in due course after his death. But this never occurred, for Kofi Kakari was removed from office. The stool was instead kept

as a 'white' stool, and it was named *damu dwa* ('two-penny' stool), in derisive memory of the penurious disgrace that Kofi Kakari brought upon himself through his profligacy.

360 Huydecoper, *Diary*, entry dd. Kumase, 19 September 1816.

361 WMMS, 'Journals of the Rev. Thomas B. Freeman', entry dd. Kumase, 19 September 1843.

362 Bowdich, *Essay*, 21.

363 Chapman, 'Journal', entry dd. Kumase, 13 October 1844.

364 Bonnat MSS, Cahier 7, entry dd. Kumase, 18 January 1872; HA. On *fodwo* 30 March 1891 – 'an unfortunate evil day' – see McCaskie, 'Time and the Calendar', 183.

365 Rattray, *Religion and Art*, 127, for example, is echoed in Cole, 'Art of Festival', in Gilbert, 'Aesthetic Strategies', and in H.M. Cole and D.H. Ross, *The Arts of Ghana* (Los Angeles, 1977), especially 200–9. Compare here the issues addressed in J.M. Borgatti, 'The Festival as Art Event – Form and Iconography: Olimi Festival in Okpella (Midwest State, Nigeria)', Ph.D. (UCLA, 1976).

366 Bowdich, *Mission*, reproduced between 274 and 275.

367 Alert readers will be aware that my reading of Bowdich has been influenced by recent work in art history, and notably by discussions of Goodman's concept of 'density'. This argues, in paraphrase, that images are 'dense' in that their entire worked surface area is continuously significant, for all the 'marks' present are necessarily interdependent; the written text, by contrast, is basically discontinuous and fractured, and hence lacking in 'density'. *The First Day of the Yam Custom* and the analogies cited differ enormously in painterly skills of execution, but all are attempts to confer a satisfactory 'density' in place of the representational inadequacy of written description. When Goodman goes on to argue that reference is not defined by resemblance, and that denotation is the core of representation ('almost anything may stand for anything else'), I follow his prompting – at least in as much as it says something about what Bowdich brought (of himself?) to his engraving. The *odwira* is the 'subject', but it is Bowdich who selects, emphasizes, orders and valorizes the register of denotation. In grappling with representation, Bowdich is in unacknowledged juxtaposition with the 'meaning' he intends, for it is his desire to know that is privileged over what is to be known. His filling of the space is a hierarchical imposition on Asante experience, a metaphorical wash over that which he cannot explain to himself in words – and not least because it cannot be explained to him. See N. Goodman, *Languages of Art: An Approach to a Theory of Symbols* (Indianapolis, 1976); *ibid.*, *Of Mind and Other Matters* (Cambridge and London, 1984); N. Goodman and C.Z. Elgin, *Reconceptions in Philosophy and Other Arts and Sciences* (London, 1988). The critical literature is too large to cite, but, for a useful art historical contextualization of Goodman's ideas, see D. Summers, 'Real Metaphor: Towards a Redefinition of the "Conceptual" Image', in Bryson, Holly and Moxey (eds.), *Visual Theory*, 231–59.

368 Bowdich viewed Asante as a society whose admirable qualities and barbaric impulses alike stemmed from a much diluted remembrance of its remote

origins in the Abyssinian highlands and ancient Egypt. This was most fully expressed in the *Essay on the Superstitions*, which was written amidst the circle of *savants* gathered around Baron Cuvier in Paris, and which was definitively shaped by Bowdich's eclectic, autodidactic reading in the huge library of the Hôtel Cuvier. It would be the work of another book to disentangle the complex (but reasonably well-documented) skein of Bowdich's intellectual influences. Prominent among these, however, were Cuvier's (or Banks', or Von Humboldt's) imperative to a taxonomy of the natural world, including man, and the excited 'rediscovery' of ancient Egypt by both the French and the English in the less than thirty years between Napoleon's expedition there and Champollion's decipherment of hieroglyphics. See – a revealing panegyric – Mrs R. Lee (formerly Mrs T.E. Bowdich), *Memoirs of Baron Cuvier* (London, 1833). The scholarly literature is simply too vast and too diverse to list. But anyone seriously interested in Bowdich's intellectual formation would need to consider, *inter alia*, 'orientalism' and related matters (Said, Bernal, Schwab, etc.), early nineteenth-century science (Outram, Coleman, Bowler, Moravia, etc.), the politics of intellectual life (Agulhon, Appel, Cahn, Crosland, Gillispie, etc.), and, of course, African exploration (Curtin, Hallett, etc.).

369 N. Goodman, *Ways of Worldmaking* (Indianapolis, 1978). Goodman's argument is wide ranging, influential and contentious. Here I make use only of its fertile discussion of discretion in ordering and reordering. Important critical responses to Goodman (with some of which I agree) include, on radical relativism, H. Putnam, 'Reflections on Goodman's *Ways of Worldmaking*', *JPhil*, 76, 4 (1979), 603–18; on found criteria, C.G. Hempel, 'Comments on Goodman's *Ways of Worldmaking*', *Synthèse*, 45 (1980), 193–9; and, on versions of the world, I. Scheffler, 'The Wonderful Worlds of Goodman', *Synthèse*, 45 (1980), 201–9.

5   THE ASANTE PAST CONSIDERED

1 WMMS, W. West to General Secretaries, dd. Cape Coast, 9 June 1862 (with an account of his residence in Kumase, 17 March to 22 April 1862). West's MS is composed of forty-five pages of handwritten foolscap. Other documents relevant to West's journey to Asante include *ibid.*, Wharton to Osborne, dd. Cape Coast, 13 February 1862; W. West to General Secretaries, dd. Cape Coast, 3 March 1862; W. West to Osborne, dd. Kumase, 5 April 1862; Owusu Ansa to General Secretaries, dd. Cape Coast, 13 June 1862; and W. West to General Secretaries, dd. Cape Coast, 12 July 1862. West's travelling companion R.J. Ghartey (subsequently King Ghartey IV of Winneba) published a gazetteer of the villages passed through on the road to Kumase in 1862. See the *Guide, for Strangers Travelling to Coomassie, the Capital City of Ashantee* (1862), reprinted as an Appendix in Boyle, *Through Fanteeland to Coomassie*.

2 For the relevant sources on Eduabin, Baaman and succession to the Adonten stool see chapter 2 note 65. The decline of Eduabin was, of course, relative. It remained a comparatively substantial settlement, for it was well supplied with water, and advantageously situated for the transit trade of the 1830s–40s.

However, its air of neglect and lack of systemic upkeep reflected its diminished status; simply, its political significance had vanished. Indeed, some of the sources suggest that Kwaaten Pɛtɛ was the first *Adontenhene* to reside more or less permanently in Kumase, one implication being that his predecessors from the *Aseneɛ abusua* of Agyeiwaa Badu had dignified Eduabin by living there for extended periods of time. On Eduabin in 1832, see Simons. 'Journaal', entry dd. 12 February 1832; in 1839, WMMS, 'Journals of the Rev. Thomas B. Freeman', entry dd. 29 March 1839; in 1841, *ibid.*, entry dd. 9 December 1841; in 1843, *ibid.*, entry dd. 31 August 1843, and Chapman, 'Journal', entry dd. 31 August 1843; and in 1846, WMMS, Wharton to General Secretaries, dd. Kumase, 31 May 1846 (excerpts from this journal in letter form are reprinted in W. Moister, *Henry Wharton, the Story of His Life and Missionary Labours* (London, 1875)).

3 WMMS, W. West to General Secretaries, dd. Cape Coast, 9 June 1862 (with an account of his residence in Kumase, 17 March to 22 April 1862), MS p. 12.

4 *Ibid.*, MS p. 13.

5 Thus, amongst all of the folk paeans to the honour due to 'grey hairs' are some notably ambiguous items. Indicative is the proverb *ɔpanyin to asa a, na ɛwɔ mmofra de mu* ('When the old man's bottom is flat, its fat has gone to the children'), which succinctly makes allusion to duty and obligation, but allows for the conflicted emotions of affection and due deference on the one hand, and resentment and disrespect on the other. As previously noted (in the case of the *Asantehene* Kwaku Dua Panin) Asante kinship relations – within the *ɔyafunu koro*, and between genitor and genetrix (and what each represents) in relation to children – possessed inbuilt potential for conflict as well as harmony. Much depended on the individuals involved, and on their circumstances. Certainly, in Asante, as in other societies, there is a countervailing perception of old age that runs against the grain of presumptive orthodoxies about its ineffable virtues. Old women are the Asante 'witches' *par excellence*, and old men are often held to be cantankerous, spiteful and vengeful (and particularly where relatives and money are concerned). Asante will talk relatively freely about these negative features of old age, but generally to cast them as lapses from the desired norms of behaviour. Significantly, exemplification in such cases is personalized ('so-and-so's actions'), for discussants recognize the crucial place of individuals, and of specific relationships, in framing behavioural excesses. As West found in Eduabin, and Fortes later found in Agogo, the tranquillity of communal village life might be threatened by the disruptive, even reckless, words and deeds of the aged.

6 For *ohyira ɔhene* see Rattray, *Ashanti Law and Constitution, passim* but especially 311–12. Revealingly, in the present context, Rattray records that he once asked an Asante why any individual would choose to commit *ohyira ɔhene*, when the penalty was certain death: 'He replied that a man might have become exasperated beyond all measure at another's conduct and declare, "I call upon such and such a god to kill the King, and do so on your head, and after I am killed may you pay one hundred *pereguan*, i.e. £800, to buy the Bongo's skin with which I shall be strangled."' (Note here the use of the skin of *ɔtrommo* to administer the final extinction of life; see p. 220. Euphemism

surrounded everything to do with *ohyira ɔhene*. Thus, the crime itself was sometimes called *ode ne nsa asi fam* ('touching the earth with a finger') or *bo ɔhene dua* ('hitting the King with a stick'). It was a crime of the utmost gravity. Thus, any Asante who proclaimed before witnesses *mennidi bio* ('I shall not eat') was arraigned on a 'murder' charge, the clear presumption in law being that the speaker intended either actual homicide or the act of *ohyira ɔhene*. Condemned criminals had their cheeks and tongue skewered by *sɛpɔ* knives, expressly to prevent them practising *ohyira ɔhene* when *in extremis*. Significantly too, in the present context, *ibid.*, 302, fn. 4 points out that neither drunkenness nor insanity were accepted as pleas in mitigation or excuse in cases of *ohyira ɔhene*.

7 For all those individuals or groups implicated by name in *ohyira ɔhene*, innocence of complicity in intention might only be established by meeting the conditions imposed by the swearer. Moreover, it was the duty of the perpetrator's kin and community to report the matter to immediate political authority, and for all involved – relatives, friends, neighbours, fellow citizens, local office holders – it was mandatory both to inform the *Asantehene* in Kumase, *and* to keep the malefactor alive to suffer prescribed punishment at the hands of the *Asantehene's* agents. The old man of Eduabin lived to meet his appointed fate. Other malefactors did not. Thus, in a case that was still remembered by the royal *akyeame* in this century, a Mampon *Sanaahene* committed *ohyira ɔhene* against the *Asantehene* Kwaku Dua Panin, and then took his own life. The *Mamponhene* Oduro Firikyi (1833–45), as the political authority responsible, was charged with having failed to prevent the man's suicide. This was adjudged to be complicity, and some urged that the *Mamponhene* should pay the full penalty. However (and doubtless for political reasons to do with his exalted rank) the *Mamponhene* was allowed 'to buy his head', but Kwaku Dua Panin imposed upon him the swingeing fine of 100 *mperedwan* (£800) and thirty sheep to cleanse Kumase (*bo Kumase asu*: 'to sprinkle Kumase with water'). Mampon tradition asserts that the *Mamponfoɔ* had to pawn (*awowa*) and even sell (*ton ate tramma*) their relatives and children to realize this sum. The *Asantehene* also confiscated 'whole families of men, women and children' of the *Mamponhene's* subjects resident at Kodiekurom. There are versions of this story in *ibid.*, 302; in RAI, Rattray MSS, Bundle 107, Notebook 3, 1849; in Kurankyi-Taylor 'Legal Institutions', I, 30–2; in OMP, Kumase, 'A Notebook on Office Holding', prepared for (and by ?) the *Asantehene* Agyeman Prempe, dd. Kumase, 1927; and in MRO, Kumase, Appeal from Ashantihene's Native Court 'A' *in re* Jamasi and other claims against the *Mamponhene* (Owusu Sekyere Abonyawa), heard before G.P.H. Bewes, Ag. Chief Commissioner, 1936.

8 Africanist discourse is too ready to cover the aporetic cracks with *a priori* paint (using the narrative brush). A reason may be the unsustainable burden habitually placed on 'oral tradition'. This has been fetishized by Africanists in its sources, its gathering and its codification. Its deployment is another, rather less reflective matter. It is parcelled into gobbets that go to fuel a narrative engine designed to equate action with intention. The consequence is that Africanists constantly risk hypostatizing the contexts of 'oral tradition' by

grasping after *a* meaning as that meaning which acting and planning human beings really intended. This implies a Collingwood-like unexamined faith in people saying only what they mean, and meaning only what they say, with the two legislating intention and so action. But the historical resolution of intention is not so easily adjudicated. See Gadamer, *Wahrheit und Methode*, 350 ff. (*Truth and Method*, 334 ff.); and, for another, 'tropological' view of the same problem, H. White, 'The Historical Text as Literary Artifact', in *Tropics of Discourse*, 81–100, and especially 83–5. In McCaskie, '*Asantesɛm*' too little attention was paid, I fear, to the individual and interpersonal capacity to generate unintended consequences.

9 M. Hollis, *The Cunning of Reason* (Cambridge, 1987), 184. Hollis adds, pointedly and very aptly: 'We need to understand both the legitimating reasons and the real reasons [of actors]. (I do not call them "motives", because that would suggest something different in kind from "reasons" and essentially private in some philosophical sense.)' Compare here the serio-comic framing of the argument in 'Truth: A Dialogue', in Wiredu, *Philosophy and an African Culture*, 189–232. This begins with Wiredu's (Akan?) 'Critic' loading the dice to some effect: 'The view that truth is nothing but belief or opinion is open to so many objections that I hardly know where to start.'

10 I use 'simple' to point to the contrast with knottier problems of cultural engagement in African history. If the field of inquiry was, for example, Sokoto in early 1903, and the protagonists were the Englishman Frederick Lugard and the Hausa-Fulani Muḥammad Attahiru b. Aḥmad, then two (even three?) discrete sets of cultural referents would need to be accommodated to the grid. The grid itself, of course, remains the same.

11 See Chapter 1 *passim*, but especially pp. 12–18.

12 The approaches of Yarak and Wilks are compared in McCaskie, 'Empire State'. Briefly to reiterate: Yarak, *Asante and the Dutch*, 22 calls attention to Wilks' 'peculiar use of Weber'; *ibid.*, 25–7 points out, with polite but quite deadly effect, Wilks' fundamental misreading of Weber, and his subsequent egregious misappropriation of Marx.

13 Wilks, *Preamble*, xliv–xlv, *Asante in the Nineteenth Century* (reprint, 1989). In McCaskie, 'Empire State', 474, I described this passage as an 'astonishing statement'. The epithet was intended to convey two things; a sense of wonderment at Wilks' attempt to evade and finesse scholarly criticism by 'simply shifting the goalposts'; and a feeling of being witness to a sleight of hand so barefaced as to suggest a clumsily perpetrated attempt at irony. Be that as it may, I have little to add here to what I said in 1992. Then I noted, *ibid.*, 473, that 'the central concerns' of *Asante* 'dissipate and are lost in a vast quarry of empirical detail'. This juxtaposition was unfortunate, for it might be read as a condemnation of the (theoretical) building, but as an argument for the salvaging of (empirical) bricks from the rubble. *Mea culpa*, for I meant to point no such easy contrast, to suggest no such simple choice. In *Asante* the 'theoretical' and the 'factual' are imbricated to a point where rejection of the former enjoins, at the very least, a degree of sceptical care in the handling of the latter. As I said in conclusion in *ibid.*, 476, Wilks 'fetishizes "facts"', but as I also said, history 'is not factually "true" in a positivist sense'. That is, Wilks

might choose to cling to the fantasy that 'facts' speak for themselves, but they do not. The manufacturer bears ultimate responsibility for the manufacture, and doubly so in the case of defective or shoddy goods.

14 See, for example, the conclusion on 'the patrimonial quality of Asante office' in Yarak, *Asante and the Dutch*, 283–4. The 'patrimonial' theme runs through a range of recent work by Arhin, and it is to be hoped that some of his findings – and conversational insights – can soon be translated into an extended treatment.

15 The original, severally translated into English, is in M. Weber, *Gesammelte Aufsatze zur Wissenschaftslehre*, 3rd edn, ed. J. Winckelmann (Tübingen, 1968), 195; see E.A. Shils and H.A. Finch (eds.), *The Methodology of the Social Sciences* (New York, 1949), 94.

16 These, again severally translated into English, are, of course, the opening words of *Wirtschaft und Gesellschaft*. A succinct but trenchant reading of the place of *Verstehen* (and *Erklären*) in Weber's work is in Käsler, *Max Weber*, 175–80. Attention should also be paid to Collins, *Weberian Sociological Theory*, and to Hennis, *Max Weber* – not least for their mastery of an extremely large literature. Simmel's place in prompting Weber's views about these matters is well known, complex and contested, and is noted here rather than explored.

17 To my own mind the most intellectually satisfying discussion of all of these matters is Scaff, *Fleeing the Iron Cage*. Weber's views of the construction of historical reality are perhaps exemplified in his attitude towards the 'developmental laws' created by Marx. He proposed treating these concepts as being themselves 'ideal types' with a great heuristic value if – and only if – they were used for *comparison* with historical reality. The same Marxist concepts Weber thought pernicious, however, as soon as they were considered to be empirically valid or even real. See 'Die "Objektivität" sozialwissenschaftlicher und sozialpolitischer Erkenntnis', in Weber, *Gesammelte Aufsatze . . .*, 204–5. Tenbruck, 'Wie gut kennen wir Max Weber?' may be taken as representative of that writer's now widely accepted argument (formulated since the 1950s, and *contra* Parsons and other seekers after a Weberian 'system') that Weber was primarily an empirical researcher with only a secondary interest in methodology. In the English-speaking world in the mid-twentieth century Weber's essays in interpretative modelling were accorded an explanatory weight or value far beyond their heuristic intent, not least because the reception of Weber's work into English was haphazard and full of lacunae. It is perhaps this oddly fragmented and now discredited construction of the Weberian problematic that has allowed historians of Asante, and of course many others, to isolate and to deform 'ideal types' ('bureaucracy', 'patrimonialism'), and in the case of Wilks blithely to attempt to substitute Marx for Weber, as if both were proponents of explanatory 'laws'.

18 Scaff, *Fleeing the Iron Cage*, 55. Simpler than Scaff, but certainly not simplistic, is the analysis of 'ideal types' in Albrow, *Max Weber's Construction of Social Theory*, 149–53; in plain language, this underlines the point that Weber himself never confused 'ideal types' with historical reality.

19 Wiredu, *Philosophy and an African Culture*, 213–14.

20 See the enormously influential W.V. Quine, 'Two Dogmas of Empiricism'

(1951), reprinted in his *From a Logical Point of View* (New York, 1961). Since the publication of Quine's paper, as one critic concedes, 'there has been a steady erosion in philosophical confidence in the notion of an "*a priori*" truth'; H. Putnam, *Reason, Truth and History* (Cambridge, 1981), 82–3. At *ibid.*, 128, the important consequential point is advanced that 'truth is not a simple notion. The idea that truth is a passive copy of what is "really" (mind-independently, discourse-independently) "there" has collapsed ... even if it continues to have a deep hold on our thinking.' Compare the arguments in Wiredu, *Philosophy and an African Culture*, 228.

21 Ackah, *Akan Ethics*, 50–1 inadvertently makes the same point, for his discussion of truth is articulated through situational ethical examples; and, at 105, *nokware* is located very firmly among the behavioural parameters of Akan socialization, as being one among a range of ethical 'labels' that 'become associated in the child's mind, as it grows, with reward or praise and punishment or blame'. In Gramscian terms we might say that this 'truth' is ideology as habitual behaviour rather than conscious thought – a fertile field indeed for the structurations effected by power. The disfiguring insertions of a later colonial and neo-colonial power into ideology as habitual behaviour elsewhere in Africa is one of the subjects acutely, and passionately, addressed in Mudimbe, *The Invention of Africa*; see McCaskie, '*Asantesɛm*', 70–2, for a discussion of why this is so, and Mudimbe's response to it. It is much to be regretted that scholars of the African past who are interested in the 'truth–power' conjuncture (however qualified) seem more deeply engaged by external manipulations of it than by articulations of its internal dynamic; see in this regard J. and J. Comaroff, *Of Revelation*, in which Southern Tswana society is less fully realized historically than is its missionary 'converted' (in both senses) representation.

22 Gyekye, *An Essay*, 168.

23 *Ibid.*, Table 11.2, 167 provides a quite fascinating enumeration of 'expressions that are mentalistic in English but physicalistic in Akan'. Of the items listed – and I paraphrase – seven are referenced to the chest and heart; six to the eyes; three to the stomach; two each to the ears, the face, the head, and the body; and one each to the skin, and the arm. To take one example, 'satisfaction, contentment, composure' are referenced to the chest, heart and stomach. Appropriate integrities defined wholeness. Thus – and no doubt unusually – *busufuo* (hermaphrodites) were buried alive at birth.

24 The complexity of Asante readings of the body ranges far beyond ethnographic commonplaces about apposite wholeness – about birth, living, dying and burial successfully negotiated in relation to a prescriptive corporeal integrity. Any student of the literature must be struck immediately by the density of Asante interrogation (and classification) of any and all forms of physical exceptionalism. By corollary, discretionary mapping of the physical is dedicated, elaborate and discursive (teeth and digits, for example, have names, roles *and* 'social' relationships). Gyekye argues that the Akan conception of the person is both 'dualistic and interactionist', and while I dissent from his choice of terms I appreciate the difficulty he is trying to address at *ibid.*, 99–103. This is the Akan understanding of the relationship between the immaterial (the

'soul', in his terms) and the material (the body), which, as he rightly says, 'bristles with difficulties'. Asante perceptions of the body's wholeness, or lack of it, require fuller investigation in the light of the evident importance of the subject. Fortes did some suggestive work on this, but in a very unsystematic way; McCaskie, 'Death and the *Asantehene*' is only a beginning in looking at one important aspect of this subject historically.

25 Rattray, *Religion and Art*, 87–9, for example, has a detailed account of *atɔperɛ* practices ('from the lips of an old friend of mine, who had been a king's executioner, and had taken a leading part on several occasions...'); another such description is in Bonnat MSS, Cahier 15, *Mœurs et Coutumes de l'Achanty*. There are many historical references; thus, KITLV, Leiden, MS H. 509, 'Aanhangsel: Extract uit het journaal gehouden te Comassie door eenen tapoeier' (P. de Heer), entries dd. Kumase, 19 December 1866 and 1 February 1867, has accounts of the protracted deaths (six and nine hours respectively) of two convicted murderers at the hands of the 'Atoepieree people'. Two very detailed eyewitness accounts of *atɔperɛ* are in Chapman, 'Journal', entry dd. Kumase, 9 July 1844 (the death of an executioner who had murdered five people, and who underwent *atɔperɛ* for more than eight hours); and in WMMS, W. West to General Secretaries, dd. Cape Coast, 9 June 1862 (with an account of his residence in Kumase, 17 March to 22 April 1862), on 24 March 1862 (the death of a murderer, who underwent *atɔperɛ* for more than ten hours). For *atɔperɛ* drum playing (and *adaban*, the accompanying dance movements) see Nketia, *Drumming in Akan Communities of Ghana*, 131–2.

26 Rattray, *Religion and Art*, 88, has some account. Chapman, 'Journal', entry dd. Kumase, 9 July 1844, has uncomprehending comments on the condemned victim being 'conducted to the house of every Chief in the Town', details of the progressive dismemberment, and a record of some of the taunts and insults uttered by the executioners. Similarly, but with an equally horrified bewilderment, WMMS, W. West to General Secretaries, dd. Cape Coast, 9 June 1862 (with an account of his residence in Kumase, 17 March to 22 April 1862), on 24 March 1862, commented: 'they led him [the condemned man] to the residence of one chief after another, and made him dance before them; while at every place at which he stopped, some fresh torture awaited him. At the house of one his right ear was cut off; at that of another his shin was scraped to the bone, with a knife, from the knee down to the ankles, while at the house of another large gashes were cut down the front of his thighs.' At the conclusion of these events in 1862, the *Asantehene* Kwaku Dua Panin spoke to the assembled *Kumasefoɔ* about *atɔperɛ* being the just punishment for murder. The victim was then 'taken to the street called "Blood never dry", and literally cut to pieces'.

27 T. Eagleton, *Ideology: An Introduction* (London, 1991), 116. This is an unexceptional and neutral summary of Gramsci's views, and I cite it as such without necessarily subscribing to Eagleton's overall perspective. His framing of the general problem of 'ideology' is an interested, partisan contribution to a very contentious debate; on this see the review of Eagleton's book by R. Rorty, 'We Anti-Representationalists', *RP*, 60 (1992), 40–2.

28 Hegemony in Asante worked to monopolize the past. Its authors (and

servitors) occupied a place akin to that of Nietzsche's 'genealogist'. Their purpose was not the discernment of truth, but rather the decipherment (and reinforcement) of value. That is, they critically 're-read' Asante history from the perspective of the values inscribed at its origin, in an attempt to control the conditions of the re-inscription of those values over time. One crucial feature of this was the exclusion of all other 'genealogists'. The analogy can be carried forward to include Foucault's 'archaeology' (as a reading of Nietzsche), but only if we direct a sceptical eye at this particular construction of 'genealogy'. Foucault's relentless 'archaeological' pursuit of the historical origins of power in its discursive rules and strategies has been profoundly influential, but it (deliberately?) works to the end of dissolving histories in texts. In precolonial Asante, if not in the late twentieth-century *Collège de France*, the now much derided 'subject' was the articulating hinge that linked (lived) history and (meditated, hegemonic) text. In this regard, I find Nietzsche both more accurate and more congenial than Foucault (in whom a singularly self-conscious and privileged status as a late twentieth-century Western 'subject' is projected *de haut en bas* onto the histories of all 'subjects'), for while the former's 'genealogy' is sited in history, the latter's 'archaeology' hovers above it.

29 That is, an *Asantehene* was a continuously reported figuration in the landscape of his own public being. By primary definition all of the royal *nhenkwaa*, whatever their functional specialization, simultaneously served, reflected and explicated this figuration. That is to say, their deeds and words proclaimed an *Asantehene* in all of the very many aspects of his public life. A systematic study of all such forms of 'commentary' is long overdue, as is a complementary consideration of its structural setting in the culture of the 'court' in Kumase. The kinds of themes pursued in, for example, Elias, *Die höfische Gesellschaft*, are present in Asante materials; one place to start would be with the royal *akyeame* (seen in terms of the rhetoric of their relationship to the *Asantehene*).

30 I am grateful to those Asante who have afforded me insights into *anibɔne*. The *Asantehene* embodied such powers that he had to be approached indirectly with care and/or through the offices of a sanctioned mediator. The matter of royal power(s) is to be taken literally; the look, touch, slap, censure or curse of an *Asantehene*, so it is said, could occasion illness, madness and death in their recipient. Even today, in court proceedings, those adjudged guilty can sometimes be seen shaking as the *ɔkyeame* speaks the verdict on behalf of the *Asantehene*; such people, as they listen, never look at the *Asantehene*. Once when I observed this (the speaker in the case being the Kwame Butuakwa *ɔkyeame* Baffuor Akoto), I commented on the obvious distress of the guilty to my Asante companions. With a unanimous seriousness they apprised me of the fact that the visible shaking and upset were caused by the metaphysical rather than the physical power(s) of the *Asantehene*; one friend said 'these people are afraid because they cannot withstand the King's look'. Deeper insights into such issues can be expected from Kwesi Yankah's ongoing work on politics, rhetoric and oratory.

31 Bowdich, *Mission*, 71, fn. (and 69, fn. for the speech context).

32 MFU, 'In Mr. Nyantakyi's House, with Notes on Various Asante Customs', n.d. (but 1946).

33 Asare, *Asante Abasem*.

34 Eagleton, *Ideology*, 223, puts the issue in terms that, so to speak, any *Asantehene* would have been happy to endorse: 'Ideology is a matter of "discourse" rather than of "language" – of certain concrete discursive effects, rather than of signification as such. It represents the points where power impacts upon certain utterances and inscribes itself tacitly within them.' Standing squarely in the Marxist tradition, Eagleton offers 'active political struggle' as a response to the 'death-dealing beliefs' (the control of history) inhering in the ideologies of state power. Again, our notional *Asantehene* would have nodded agreement at this oppositional juxtaposition, but of course with the contrary deduction that 'active political struggle' (in its broadest sense) was precisely what had to be suppressed. Let us pursue this a little further. The *Asantehene* reads in the now vast radical-relativist literature on 'ideology', and pays particular attention to the seminal L. Althusser, *Philosophie et philosophie spontanée des savants* (Paris, 1967). In this Althusser proposes (to enormously wide-ranging effect subsequently) that 'ideology' cannot be 'rational', and so can be just or unjust but not true or false. The *Asantehene* is puzzled – for 'ideology' is both 'rational' and just because it is true. This mastery over history is triumphalist, and brooks no rivals. In this century, as I have discussed in McCaskie, 'Inventing Asante', mastery struggles to reinvent (and reinscribe) itself in changed conditions, using the weapon of a 'nationalist' cultural exceptionalism. Its success has been mixed, and arguably it *may* have had to confront 'active political struggle' (Nkrumah's CPP), but certainly, thus far, it has faced no concerted challenge to the idea that it is ideologically 'rational'.

35 See P. Ricoeur, *Hermeneutics and the Human Sciences: Essays on Language, Action and Interpretation*, trans. and ed. J.B. Thompson (Cambridge, 1981), 227.

36 Inscription is constitutive *of* the subject, but it requires response *from* the subject. In effect, when Gramsci talks of 'consent' or Weber of 'legitimation' they are situating the conditions of that response. Ideology and its discursive effects produce such conditions. But (and both thinkers recognized this) power is never entirely explicit. Thus, the Asante state elicited response by direction, but also by being clothed, in Ricoeur's terminology, in 'opaqueness'. This opacity that resides in power is at once constructed (as dissimulation) and inherent (as undecidability). However, it is an errant, even perverse, and particularly Western and postmodern, satire to equate the undecidability *in* power with the textual autonomy *of* power. Power is everywhere and always historicized (and dissimulation and undecidability are both produced by specific conjunctural relationships between power and history). There is no (in)script(ion) beyond power, no superordinate reference manual that instructs power or authorizes decidability on its behalf.

37 N. Elias, *Was ist Soziologie?* (Munich, 1970), trans. S. Mennell and G. Morrissey as *What is Sociology?* (London, 1978), 130. For contextual discussion of the concept of 'figuration' see Mennell, *Norbert Elias*, and

Chartier, 'Social Figuration and Habitus: Reading Elias', in *Cultural History*, 71–94. Compare here Hollis, *The Cunning of Reason*, especially 153.
38 McCaskie, 'Accumulation, Wealth and Belief ... I', 38.

APPENDIX I

1 That is, *apremoso/bogyawe*; see chapter 4 note 47.
2 For Kumase-Dwaben relations at this time and subsequently see McCaskie, 'Paramountcy', 116–32.
3 See pp. 206–12 above.
4 Compare Bowdich, *Mission*, 31–2.
5 Bells were commonly attached to stools. Their ringing, when a stool was being carried in procession, summoned ancestors by attracting their attention. See, for example, Rattray, *Ashanti*, 289–90, fn. 4.
6 See ACBP/25: Adum Ata, *Asante Seminar*, 4 (1976), 14–19.
7 An umbrella finial (*ntuatiri*; *kyini akyi*) might be representational (as in this case) or abstract. See McLeod, *The Asante*, 109–11.
8 Compare Bowdich, *Mission*, 33.
9 Oti Panin was the son of Boakye Yam and his successor in office; for Boakye Yam's wealth, and Oti Panin's (partly illicit?) access to it see p. 62–3, and Bowdich, *Mission*, 254. For the death of Kwasi Kankam – 'Karcum, chief linguist' – see Ricketts, *Narrative*, 124–5. See too ACBP/602: Oti Panin, 1979, unpublished; and ACBP/72: Kwasi Kankam (*aka* Kwasi Patom), 1984, unpublished.
10 See ACBP/22: Kwadwo Adusei, *Asante Seminar*, 5 (1976), 5–9.
11 See ACBP/6: Asante Agyei, *Asante Seminar*, 3 (1975), 5–7.
12 See Rattray, *Religion and Art*, 278–9 for deformity and the *nsenieɛfoɔ*.
13 Compare Bowdich, *Mission*, 38–9.
14 The *Asantehenes* frequently solicited national flags from the European powers on the Gold Coast, and displayed them (not least to proclaim the extent of Asante foreign relations).
15 See chapter 4 notes 262 and 276.
16 Compare Bowdich, *Mission*, 294–5. As a boy, during the reign of the *Asantehene* Osei Kwame, the youthful *ɔdehyeɛ*, and future *Asantehene*, Osei Tutu Kwame served as *ahoprani* (elephant tail bearer) to Opoku Frɛfrɛ. For the affection then established between the two, and for its consequences in their later lives, see ACBP/1: Opoku Frɛfrɛ, *Asantesɛm*, 11 (1979), 40.
17 See Sarpong, *Ceremonial Horns*.
18 Frederick James (the original head of the British mission of 1817) and Bowdich quarrelled over policy, and were rivalrous and antipathetic to one another. Bowdich was supported by Hutchison and Tedlie, and assumed *de facto* headship of the mission. James was recalled by letter to the coast, and he quit Kumase on 12 July 1817. For African Company politics and the 1817 mission to Kumase see W.E.F. Ward, 'Introduction to Third Edition', in Bowdich, *Mission* (London, 1966), 11–59; a still unsurpassed account of the mission's attitudes and behaviour while in Kumase is E. Collins, 'The Panic Element in Nineteenth-Century British Relations with Ashanti', *THSG*, 5, 2 (1962), 79–144.

19 See ACBP/31: Kwaakye Kofi, 1985, unpublished.
20 For the 'monumental confusion' in Asante tradition about the campaigns of this period see Wilks, *Asante*, 351, fn. 95.
21 Compare chapter 4 note 51.
22 For *ɔsaŋku* ('sanko') see Christaller, *Dictionary of the Asante and Fante Language*, 427.
23 Compare Bowdich, *Mission*, 31–41.

Guide to sources and materials consulted

PRINTED WORKS: BOOKS, BOOK PARTS, ETC.

Ackah, C.A., *Akan Ethics: A Study of the Moral Ideas and the Moral Behaviour of the Akan Tribes of Ghana*. Accra, 1988

Adamson, W.L., *Hegemony and Revolution: A Study of Antonio Gramsci's Political and Cultural Theory*. Berkeley, 1980

Adjaye, J.K., *Diplomacy and Diplomats in Nineteenth Century Asante*. Lanham, 1984

Albrow, M., *Bureaucracy*. London, 1970
  Max Weber's Construction of Social Theory. London, 1990

al-Khalil, S., *The Monument: Art, Vulgarity and Responsibility in Iraq*. London, 1991

Alpers, S., *The Art of Describing*. Chicago, 1983

Althusser, L., *Philosophie et philosophie spontanée des savants*. Paris, 1967

Andoh, A.S.Y., 'The Asante National Liberation Movement of the 1950s in Retrospect', in E. Schildkrout (ed.), *The Golden Stool: Studies of the Asante Center and Periphery*, 173–83. New York, 1987

Anti, A.A., *The Ancient Asante King*. Accra, 1974

Antubam, K., *Ghana's Heritage of Culture*. Leipzig, 1963

Appiah, J., *Joe Appiah: The Autobiography of an African Patriot*. Westport, 1990

Appiah, K.A., *In My Father's House: Africa in the Philosophy of Culture*. London, 1992

Arasse, D., *La Guillotine et l'imaginaire de la terreur*. Paris, 1987

Arhin, K., *West African Traders in Ghana in the Nineteenth and Twentieth Centuries*. London, 1979
  'Savanna Contributions to the Asante Political Economy', in E. Schildkrout (ed.), *The Golden Stool*, 51–9. New York, 1987

Arhin, K. (ed.), *Brong Kyempim: Essays on the Society, History and Politics of the Brong People*. Accra, 1979

Arhin, K. and Afari-Gyan, K. (eds.), *The City of Kumasi Handbook: Past, Present and Future*. Legon, 1992

Armah, A.K., *The Healers: An Historical Novel*. Nairobi, 1978

Austen, R.A., 'Social Bandits and Other Heroic Criminals: Western Models of Resistance and Their Relevance for Africa', in D. Crummey (ed.), *Banditry*, 89–108. London, 1986

Ayer, A.J., 'Replies', in G.F. Macdonald (ed.), *Perception and Identity*, 277–333. London, 1979

Baden-Powell, R.S.S., *The Downfall of Prempeh: A Diary of Life with the Native Levy in Ashanti, 1895–96*. London, 1896

Baesjou, R., *An Asante Embassy on the Gold Coast: The Mission of Akyempon Yaw to Elmina, 1869–1872*. Leiden, 1979

Baker, G.P. and Hacker, P.M.S., *Language, Sense and Nonsense*. Oxford, 1984

Baker, Jr, H.A., *Afro-American Poetics: Revisions of Harlem and the Black Aesthetic*. Madison, 1988

Bakhtin, M., *Tvorchestvo Fransua Rable*. Moscow, 1965. Trans. H. Iswolsky, *Rabelais and His World*. Bloomington, 1984

Barber, K., *I Could Speak Until Tomorrow: Oriki, Women and the Past in a Yoruba Town*. Edinburgh, 1991

Barber, K. and de Moraes Farias, P.F. (eds.), *Discourse and Its Disguises: The Interpretation of African Oral Texts*. Birmingham, 1989

Self-Assertion and Brokerage: Early Cultural Nationalism in West Africa. Birmingham, 1990

Barnes, J.A., *Three Styles in the Study of Kinship*. London, 1971

Basehart, H.W., 'Ashanti', in D.M. Schneider and K. Gough (eds.), *Matrilineal Kinship*, 270–97. Berkeley and Los Angeles, 1961

Beasley, W.G., *The Meiji Restoration*. Stanford, 1972

Beecham, J., *Ashantee and the Gold Coast: Being a Sketch of the History, Social State and Superstitions of the Inhabitants of those Countries with a Notice of the State and Prospects of Christianity among Them*. London, 1841

Bendix, R., *Max Weber: An Intellectual Portrait*. London, 1966 edn

Benjamin, W., *Parigi: capitale del XIX secolo*. Turin, 1986

Bernstein, R.J., *The New Constellation: The Ethical-Political Horizons of Modernity/Postmodernity*. Oxford, 1991

Bhabha, H.K., 'Foreword: Remembering Fanon: Self, Psyche and the Colonial Condition', in F. Fanon, *Black Skin, White Masks*, trans. C. Lam Markmann, 1–17. London, 1986

Bhabha, H.K. (ed.), *Nation and Narration*. London, 1990

Bhaskar, R., *Philosophy and the Idea of Freedom*. Oxford, 1991

Bloch, Marc, *Les Rois thaumaturges: études sur le caractère surnaturel attribué à la puissance royale, particulièrement en France et Angleterre*. Strasbourg, 1924 (new edn, Paris, 1983)

Apologie pour l'histoire, ou Métier d'historien. Paris, 1949

Bloch, Maurice, *Ritual, History and Power: Selected Papers in Anthropology*. London, 1989

'What Goes Without Saying: The Conceptualization of Zafimaniry Society', in A. Kuper (ed.), *Conceptualizing Society*, 127–46. London, 1992

Boakye, P., *Syntaxe de l'Achanti: du phonéme à la phrase segmentée*. Berne, Frankfurt and New York, 1982

Bobbio, N., 'Gramsci and the Conception of Civil Society', in C. Mouffe (ed.), *Gramsci and Marxist Theory*, 21–47. London, 1979

Bonsu Kyeretwie, K.O., *Ashanti Heroes*. Accra, 1972

Bosman, W., *A New and Accurate Description of the Coast of Guinea, Divided into the Gold, the Slave, and the Ivory Coasts*. London, 1705

Boucher, D., *Texts in Context*. Dordrecht, 1985

Bourdillon, M.F.C. and Fortes, M. (eds.), *Sacrifice*. London, 1980

Bowdich, T.E., *Mission from Cape Coast Castle to Ashantee, with a Statistical*

Account of that Kingdom, and Geographical Notices of Other Parts of the Interior of Africa. London, 1819

An Essay on the Superstitions, Customs, and Arts, common to the Ancient Egyptians, Abyssinians, and Ashantees. Paris, 1821

Boyle, F., *Through Fanteeland to Coomassie: A Narrative of the Ashantee Expedition.* London, 1874

Brackenbury, H., *The Ashanti War: A Narrative.* 2 vols., London, 1874

Braffi, E.K., *The Esoteric Significance of the Asante Nation.* Kumasi, 1984

Braudel, F., *Le Modèle italien, 1450–1650.* Paris, 1989

Bravmann, R.A., *Islam and Tribal Art in West Africa.* Cambridge, 1974

Bravmann, R.A. and Silverman, R.A., 'Painted Incantations: The Closeness of Allah and Kings in 19th-Century Asante', in E. Schildkrout (ed.), *The Golden Stool,* 93–108. New York, 1987

Bristol, M., *Carnival and Theater: Plebeian Culture and the Structure of Authority in Renaissance England.* New York, 1985

Brown, R.H., *Social Science as Civic Discourse: Essays on the Invention, Legitimation, and Uses of Social Theory.* Chicago, 1989

Bruner, E.M. (ed.), *Text, Play, and Story: The Construction and Reconstruction of Self and Society.* Washington, 1984

Bruzina, R. and Wilshire, B. (eds.), *Phenomenology: Dialogues and Bridges.* Albany, 1982

Bryson, N., *Vision in Painting: The Logic of the Gaze.* New Haven, 1983

Bryson, N., Holly, M.A. and Moxey, K. (eds.), *Visual Theory: Painting and Interpretation.* Oxford, 1991

Buci-Glucksmann, C., *Gramsci et l'état.* Paris, 1975

Burke, P., *The Historical Anthropology of Early Modern Italy: Essays on Perception and Communication.* Cambridge, 1987

Busia, K.A., *The Position of the Chief in the Modern Political System of Ashanti: A Study of the Influence of Contemporary Social Changes on Ashanti Political Institutions.* London, 1951

Cameron, A. (ed.), *History as Text: The Writing of Ancient History.* London, 1989

Cannadine, D. and Price, S. (eds.), *Rituals of Royalty: Power and Ceremonial in Traditional Societies.* Cambridge, 1987

Cardinall, A.W., *The Natives of the Northern Territories of the Gold Coast: Their Customs, Religion and Folklore.* London, 1920

In Ashanti and Beyond. London and Philadelphia, 1927

Carruthers, M., *The Book of Memory: A Study of Memory in Medieval Culture.* Cambridge, 1990

Chartier, R., *Cultural History: Between Practices and Representations,* trans. L.G. Cochrane. Oxford, 1988

Les Origines culturelles de la révolution française. Paris, 1990

Chaunu, P., 'Un Nouveau Champ pour l'histoire sérielle: le quantitatif au troisième niveau', *Histoire quantitative, histoire sérielle,* 216–30. Paris, 1978

Chipp, T.F., *The Forest Officers' Handbook of the Gold Coast, Ashanti and the Northern Territories.* London, 1922

Christaller, J.G., *A Grammar of the Asante and Fante Language.* Basel, 1875

Tŵi Mmebusɛm: mpensā-ahansīa mmoaano. A Collection of Three Thousand and

Six Hundred Tshi Proverbs. Basel, 1879

A Dictionary of the Asante and Fante Language, Called Tschi. Basel, 1881, 2nd edn, revised and enlarged, Basel, 1933

Clark, S.H., *Paul Ricoeur.* London, 1990

Clendinnen, I., *Ambivalent Conquests: Maya and Spaniards in Yucatan, 1517–1570.* Cambridge, 1987

Clifford, J., *The Predicament of Culture: Twentieth-Century Ethnography, Literature, and Art.* Cambridge, 1988

Clifford, J. and Marcus, G. (eds.), *Writing Culture: The Poetics and Politics of Ethnography.* Berkeley, 1986

Cohen, D.W. and Atieno Odhiambo, E.S., *Siaya: The Historical Anthropology of an African Landscape.* London, 1988

Cole, H.M. and Ross, D.H., *The Arts of Ghana.* Los Angeles, 1977

Collins, R., *Weberian Sociological Theory.* Cambridge, 1986

Comaroff, Jean and John, *Of Revelation and Revolution: Christianity, Colonialism and Consciousness in South Africa,* I (of 2 vols.). Chicago, 1991

Connah, G., *African Civilizations. Precolonial Cities and States in Tropical Africa: An Archaeological Perspective.* Cambridge, 1987

Connerton, P., *How Societies Remember.* Cambridge, 1989

Coquery-Vidrovitch, C., *Afrique noire: permanences et ruptures.* Paris, 1985

Corbin, A., *Le Miasme et la jonquille.* Paris, 1983

Couteau-Begarie, H., *Le Phenomène 'nouvelle histoire': stratégie et idéologie des nouveaux historiens.* Paris, 1983

Crapanzano, V., *Hermes' Dilemma and Hamlet's Desire: On the Epistemology of Interpretation.* Cambridge, 1992

Crooks, J.J., *Records relating to the Gold Coast Settlements: From 1750 to 1874.* Dublin, 1923

Cruickshank, B., *Eighteen Years on the Gold Coast of Africa, including an Account of the Native Tribes, and their intercourse with Europeans,* 2 vols. London, 1853

Crummey, D. (ed.), *Banditry, Rebellion and Social Protest in Africa.* London, 1986

'Introduction: "The great beast"', in D. Crummey (ed.), *Banditry,* 1–29. London, 1986

Cuoq, J.M., *Recueil des sources arabes concernant l'Afrique occidentale du VIIIe siècle.* Paris, 1975

Da Matta, R., 'Constraint and License: A Preliminary Study of Two Brazilian National Rituals', in S.F. Moore and B.G. Meyerhoof (eds.), *Secular Rituals,* 244–64. Amsterdam, 1977

Danquah, J.B., *The Akan Doctrine of God: A Fragment of Gold Coast Ethics and Religion.* London, 1944

Ɔkanniba Abotafowa. London, 1954

Darnton, R., *The Great Cat Massacre and Other Episodes in French Cultural History.* New York, 1984

The Kiss of Lamourette: Reflections on Cultural History. London, 1990

d'Azevedo, W.L. (ed.), *The Traditional Artist in African Societies.* Bloomington, 1975

de Certeau, M., *L'Ecriture de l'histoire.* Paris, 1975

L'Invention du quotidien: I. Arts de faire. Paris, 1980

La Fable mystique, XVI–XVIIe siècle. Paris, 1982

Heterologies: The Discourse of the Other. Minneapolis, 1986

Dei-Anang, M., *Okomfo Anokye's Golden Stool: a Ghanaian Play in Three Acts.* Accra, 1963

Delumeau, J., *L'Histoire de la peur.* Paris, 1979

de Marees, P., *Description and Historical Account of the Gold Kingdom of Guinea (1602)*, trans. (from the Dutch) and ed. A. Van Dantzig and A. Jones. Oxford, 1987

de ste. Croix, G.E.M., *The Origins of the Peloponnesian War.* London, 1972
The Class Struggle in the Ancient Greek World. London, 1981

Detienne, M., *Les Jardins d'Adonis.* Paris, 1972

Dickson, K.A., *A Historical Geography of Ghana.* Cambridge, 1971

Doku, E.V., *Cassava in Ghana.* Accra, 1969

Dollimore, J. and Sinfield, A. (eds.), *Political Shakespeare: New Essays in Cultural Materialism.* Manchester, 1985

Douglas, M., 'Is Matriliny Doomed in Africa?', in M. Douglas and P.M. Kaberry (eds.), *Man in Africa*, 121–35. London, 1969
Evans-Pritchard. London, 1980

Douglas, M. and Kaberry, P.M. (eds.), *Man in Africa.* London, 1969

Drah, F.K. 'The Brong Political Movement', in K. Arhin (ed.), *Brong Kyempim: Essays on the Society, History and Politics of the Brong People*, 119–62. Accra, 1979

Drucker-Brown, S., *Ritual Aspects of the Mamprusi Kingship.* Cambridge and Leiden, 1975

Dumett, R., 'Traditional Slavery in the Akan Region in the Nineteenth Century: Sources, Issues and Interpretations', in *West African Economic and Social History*, eds. D. Henige and T.C. McCaskie, 7–22. Madison, 1990

Dunn, J. and Robertson, A.F., *Dependence and Opportunity: Political Change in Ahafo.* Cambridge, 1973

Dupuis, J., *Journal of a Residence in Ashantee.* London, 1824

Eagleton, T., *Ideology: An Introduction.* London, 1991

Eisenstadt, S.N., *The Political Systems of Empires: The Rise and Fall of the Historical Bureaucratic Societies.* 2nd edn, New York, 1969

Elias, N., *Über den Prozess der Zivilisation: Soziogenetische und psychogenetische Untersuchungen.* 2 vols. Basel, 1939. Trans. E. Jephcott, with revisions by N. Elias, *The Civilizing Process: Sociogenetic and Psychogenetic Investigations. I. The History of Manners.* Oxford, 1978; *II. State Formation and Civilization.* Oxford, 1984
Die höfische Gesellschaft, Untersuchungen zur Soziologie des Königtums und der höfischen Aristokratie mit einer Einleitung: Soziologie und Geschichtswissenschaft. Berlin, 1969. Revised edns 1975. 1983; trans. E. Jephcott, with revisions by N. Elias, *The Court Society.* Oxford, 1985
Was ist Soziologie? Munich, 1970. Trans. S. Mennell and G. Morrissey, *What is Sociology?* London, 1978
Involvement and Detachment, trans. E. Jephcott (from the German edn of 1956). Oxford, 1987
The Society of Individuals, essays ed. M. Schroter and trans. E. Jephcott. Oxford, 1991

Elton, G.R., *The Tudor Revolution in Government: Administrative Changes in the Reign of Henry VIII*. Cambridge, 1953

Evans-Pritchard, E.E., *Anthropology and History*. Manchester, 1961
The Azande: History and Political Institutions. Oxford, 1971
A History of Anthropological Thought, ed. A. Singer. London, 1981

Fage, J.D., *A History of Africa*. London, 1978

Febvre, L., *Le Problème de l'incroyance au XVIe siècle: la religion de Rabelais*. Paris, 1942; reprinted 1968
Amour sacré, amour profane: autour de l'Heptaméron. Paris, 1944; reprinted 1971
Combats pour l'histoire. Paris, 1953

Femia, J.V., *Gramsci's Political Thought: Hegemony, Consciousness, and the Revolutionary Process*. Oxford, 1981

Fentress, J. and Wickham, C., *Social Memory*. Oxford, 1992

Fernandez, J.W., *Bwiti: An Ethnography of the Religious Imagination in Africa*. Princeton, 1982

Field, M.J., *Search for Security: An Ethno-Psychiatric Study of Rural Ghana*. London, 1960

Fink, C., *Marc Bloch: A Life in History*. Cambridge, 1989

Finley, M.I., *The Ancient Economy*. 2nd edn, London, 1985
Ancient History: Evidence and Models. London, 1985

Finnochiaro, M.A., *Gramsci and the History of Dialectical Thought*. Cambridge, 1988

Firempong, B.A., *Asumagya-Asantemanso Mpaninsɛm*. Legon, 1976

Forgacs, D. (ed.), *A Gramsci Reader, 1916–1935*. London, 1988

Forgacs, D. and Nowell Smith, G. (eds.), *Antonio Gramsci: Selections from Cultural Writings*. London, 1985

Fortes, M., *The Dynamics of Clanship among the Tallensi*. London, 1945; reprinted 1967
'Kinship and Marriage among the Ashanti', in A.R. Radcliffe-Brown and D. Forde (eds.), *African Systems of Kinship and Marriage*, 252–84. London, 1950
Oedipus and Job in West African Religion. Cambridge, 1959; reprinted 1983, with an essay by R. Horton
'The "submerged descent line" in Ashanti', in I. Schapera (ed.), *Studies in Kinship and Marriage*, 58–67. London, 1963
Kinship and the Social Order: The Legacy of Lewis Henry Morgan. London, 1969
Time and Social Structure and Other Essays. London, 1970
'Prologue: Family Studies in Ghana 1920–1970', in C. Oppong (ed.), *Domestic Rights and Duties in Southern Ghana. Legon Family Research Papers I*, 1–27. Legon, 1974

Fortes, M. and Dieterlen, G. (eds.), *African Systems of Thought*. London, 1965

Fortes, M. and Evans-Pritchard, E.E. (eds.), *African Political Systems*. London, 1940

Fox, C., *Asante Brass Castings: Lost-wax Casting of Gold-weights, Ritual Vessels and Sculptures, with Handmade Equipment*. Cambridge, 1988

Fraser, N., *Unruly Practices: Power, Discourse and Gender in Contemporary Social Theory*. Cambridge, 1989

Freedman, M., *Main Trends in Social and Cultural Anthropology*. New York, 1978

Freeman, R.A., *Travels and Life in Ashanti and Jaman*. London, 1898

Freeman, T.B., *Journal of Various Visits to the Kingdoms of Ashanti, Aku, and*

Dahomi in Western Africa. London, 1844

Fuller, Sir Francis, *A Vanished Dynasty: Ashanti.* London, 1921

Fyfe, C. (ed.), *African Studies since 1945.* London, 1976

Gadamer, H.-G., *Wahrheit und Methode.* 4th edn, Tübingen, 1975. 2nd edn trans. G. Burden and J. Cumming, *Truth and Method.* London, 1975

Gadamer, H.-G. and Ricoeur, P., 'The Conflict of Interpretations' (with a discussion), in R. Bruzina and B. Wilshire (eds.), *Phenomenology: Dialogues and Bridges*, 299–320. Albany, 1982

Garnsey, P.D.A., *Famine and Food Supply in the Graeco-Roman World: Responses to Risk and Crisis.* Cambridge, 1988

Garnsey, P.D.A. and Saller, R.P., *The Roman Empire: Economy, Society and Culture.* London, 1987

Garrard, T.F., *Akan Weights and the Gold Trade.* London, 1980

Geertz, C., *The Interpretation of Cultures.* New York, 1973
  Negara: The Theatre State in Nineteenth-Century Bali. Princeton, 1980
  Works and Lives: The Anthropologist as Author. Stanford, 1988

Geiss, I., *The Pan-African Movement.* London, 1974

Gellner, E., 'Introduction', in E.E. Evans-Pritchard, *A History of Anthropological Thought*, ed. A. Singer, xiii–xxxvi. London, 1981

Gernet, L., *Anthropologie de la Grèce antique.* Paris, 1968

Gerth, H.H. and Mills, C.W., *From Max Weber: Essays in Sociology.* London, 1948

Ghartey, R.J., *Guide, for Strangers Travelling to Coomassie, the Capital City of Ashantee.* 1862. Reprinted as an Appendix in F. Boyle, *Through Fanteeland to Coomassie: A Narrative of the Ashantee Expedition.* London, 1874

Gilbert, M., 'The Person of the King: Ritual and Power in a Ghanaian State', in D. Cannadine and S. Price (eds.), *Rituals of Royalty: Power and Ceremonial in Traditional Societies*, 298–330. Cambridge, 1987

Ginzburg, C., *Il formaggio e i vermi: il cosmo di un mugnaio del 1500.* Turin, 1976
  The Enigma of Piero: Piero della Francesco (The Baptism, the Arezzo Cycle, the Flagellation). London, 1985

Goethe, J.W., *The Italian Journey (1786–1788)*, trans. W.H. Auden and E. Meyer. London, 1970

Goldstein, L.J., 'Collingwood on the Construction of the Historical Past', in M. Krausz (ed.), *Critical Essays on the Philosophy of R.G. Collingwood*, 241–67. Oxford, 1972

Goodman, N., *Languages of Art: An Approach to a Theory of Symbols.* Indianapolis, 1976
  Ways of Worldmaking. Indianapolis, 1978
  Of Mind and Other Matters. Cambridge and London, 1984

Goodman, N. and Elgin, C.Z., *Reconceptions in Philosophy and Other Arts and Sciences.* London, 1988.

Goody, J.R., *Technology, Tradition and the State in Africa.* Oxford and London, 1971
  The Oriental, the Ancient and the Primitive: Systems of Marriage and the Family in the Pre-industrial Societies of Eurasia. Cambridge, 1990
  The Culture of Flowers. Cambridge, 1993

Gramsci, A., *Opere di Antonio Gramsci*, ed. F. Platone *et al.*, 12 vols. Turin, 1947–1972. (*Quaderni del Carcere*, II-VII. 1949–51. Most relevant are vol. IV,

Il Risorgimento. 1949; vol. V, *Note sul Machiavelli, sulla politica, e sulla stato moderno.* 1949; vol. VII, *Passato e presente.* 1951)

Scritti politici, ed. P. Spriano, 3 vols. Rome, 1973

Quaderni del Carcere, ed. V. Gerratana (Istituto Antonio Gramsci), 4 vols. Turin, 1975

Greenblatt, S.J., *Shakespearean Negotiations: The Circulation of Social Energy in Renaissance England.* Berkeley, 1988

Gros, J., *Voyages, aventures et captivité de J. Bonnat chez les Achantis.* Paris, 1884

Gruppi, L., *Il concetto di egemonia in Gramsci.* Rome, 1977

Guha, R. (ed.), *Subaltern Studies,* I-VI. Delhi, 1982–9

Guha, R. and Spivak, G. Chakravorty (eds.), *Selected Subaltern Studies,* Foreword by E.W. Said. New York, 1988

Gyekye, K., *An Essay on African Philosophical Thought: The Akan Conceptual Scheme.* Cambridge, 1987

The Unexamined Life: Philosophy and the African Experience. Accra, 1988

Habermas, J., *Der philosophische Diskurs der Moderne: Zwölf Vorlesungen.* Frankfurt-am-Main, 1985

Hart, K., *The Political Economy of West African Agriculture.* Cambridge, 1982

Heidegger, M., *Sein und Zeit.* 1927. Trans. J. Macquarrie and E. Robinson, *Being and Time.* Oxford, 1962

Henderson, H. (trans. and ed.), *Antonio Gramsci: Gramsci's Prison Letters.* Edinburgh, 1988.

Henige, D. and McCaskie, T.C. (eds.), *West African Economic and Social History: Studies in Memory of Marion Johnson.* Madison, 1990

Hennis, W., *Max Weber: Essays in Reconstruction.* London, 1988

Hiskett, M., *The Development of Islam in West Africa.* London and New York, 1984

Hoare, Q. and Nowell Smith, G. (eds.), *Selections from the Prison Notebooks of Antonio Gramsci.* London, 1971

Hobart, M., *Ideas of Identity: The Interpretation of Kinship in Bali.* Denpasar, 1980

'Summer's Days and Salad Days: The Coming of Age of Anthropology', in *Comparative Anthropology,* ed. L. Holy, 22–51. Oxford, 1987

Hobsbawm, E.J., *Primitive Rebels: Studies in Archaic Forms of Social Movement in the 19th and 20th Centuries.* Manchester, 1959

Hofmann, J., *The Gramscian Challenge: Coercion and Consent in Marxist Political Theory.* New York, 1984

Hollis, M., *The Cunning of Reason.* Cambridge, 1987

Hollis, M. and Lukes, S. (eds.), *Rationality and Relativism.* Oxford, 1982

Holub, R., *Antonio Gramsci: Beyond Marxism and Postmodernism.* London, 1992

Holy, L. (ed.), *Comparative Anthropology.* Oxford, 1987

Home, R., *On the Engineering Operations in the Gold Coast during the Recent Expedition.* R.E. Papers, Chatham, 1876

Horton, R., 'Tradition and Modernity Revisited', in *Rationality and Relativism,* eds. M. Hollis and S. Lukes, 227–38. Oxford, 1982

'Social Psychologies: African and Western', in M. Fortes, *Oedipus and Job in West African Religion,* 41–82. Cambridge, 1983 reprint

Hountondji, P.J., *Sur la philosophie africaine.* Paris, 1976

Huizinga, J., *Homo Ludens: A Study of the Play Element in Culture.* London, 1950

Hume, D., 'Of the Origins of Government', 'Of the First Principles of Government', 'Of Civil Liberty', essays IV, V, XII, *Essays: Moral, Political, Literary*, ed. E.F. Miller. Indianapolis, 1985

Huppenbauer, D., *Von Kyebi nach Kumase: Eine Reise ins Hinterland der Goldküste*. Basel, 1914

Hutchinson, R.A., 'Diseases and Pests of Stock', in J.B. Wills (ed.), *Agriculture and Land Use in Ghana*, 437–40. Accra, 1962

Hutchison, W., 'Diary', in T.E. Bowdich, *Mission from Cape Coast Castle to Ashantee*, 381–421. London, 1819

Hutton, W., *A Voyage to Africa*. London, 1821

Huydecoper, W., *Huydecoper's Diary: Journey from Elmina to Kumasi 28 April 1816 to 18 May 1817*, trans. G. Irwin. Legon, 1962

Iliffe, J., *The African Poor: A History*. Cambridge, 1987

Irvine, F.R., *West African Crops*. Oxford, 1969

Izard, M., *Gens du pouvoir, gens de la terre: les institutions politiques de l'ancien royaume du Yatenga (Bassin de la Volta Blanche)*. Cambridge and Paris, 1985

Jackson, M., *Paths Towards a Clearing: Radical Empiricism and Ethnographic Inquiry*. Bloomington, 1989

Jewsiewicki, B. and Newbury, D. (eds.), *African Historiographies*. Beverly Hills, 1985

Joll, J., *Gramsci*. London, 1977

Jones, A., *German Sources for West African History 1599–1669*. Wiesbaden, 1983
 'Prostitution, Polyandrie oder Vergewaltigung? Zur Mehrdeutigkeit europäischer Quellen über die Küste Westafrikas zwischen 1660 und 1860', in *Aussereuropäische Frauengeschichte: Probleme der Forschung*, ed. A. Jones, 123–58. Pfaffenweiler, 1990

July, R.W., *The Origins of Modern African Thought*. London, 1968
 An African Voice: The Role of the Humanities in African Independence. Durham, 1987

Käsler, D., *Max Weber: An Introduction to his Life and Work*. Oxford, 1988

Kaye, H.J., *The British Marxist Historians*. Oxford, 1984

Kaye, H.J. and McClelland, K. (eds.), *E.P. Thompson: Critical Perspectives*. Oxford, 1990

Kea, R.A., *Settlements, Trade, and Politics in the Seventeenth-Century Gold Coast*. Baltimore, 1982
 '"I am here to plunder on the general road": Bandits and Banditry in the pre-nineteenth century Gold Coast', in *Banditry, Rebellion and Social Protest in Africa*, ed. D. Crummey, 109–32. London, 1986

Krausz, M. (ed.), *Critical Essays on the Philosophy of R.G. Collingwood*. Oxford, 1972

Kuper, A., *Anthropology and Anthropologists: The Modern British School*. London, 1983

Kuper, A. (ed.), *Conceptualizing Society*. London, 1992

Kwamena-Poh, M.A., *Government and Politics in the Akuapem State 1730–1850*. London, 1973

Kyerematen, A.A.Y., *Kingship and Ceremony in Ashanti*. Kumase, n.d.
 Daasebre Osei Tutu Agyeman Prempeh II, Asantehene: A Distinguished Traditional Ruler of Contemporary Ghana. Kumase, n.d.
 Inter-State Boundary Litigation in Ashanti. Cambridge and Leiden, n.d.

LaCapra, D., *Rethinking Intellectual History: Texts, Contexts, Language*. Ithaca, 1983
History and Criticism. Ithaca, 1985
Laitin, D., *Hegemony and Culture: Politics and Religious Change among the Yoruba*. Chicago, 1986
Law, R., *The Horse in African History*. London, 1980
Lee, Mrs R. (formerly Mrs T.E. Bowdich), *Memoirs of Baron Cuvier*. London, 1833
Le Goff, J., *L'Imaginaire médiéval: essais*. Paris, 1990
Le Goff, J. and Nora, P. (eds.), *Faire de l'histoire*, 3 vols. Paris, 1974
Le Goff, J. and Schmitt, J.-C. (eds.), *Le Charivari*. Paris and The Hague, 1981
Le Roy Ladurie, E., *Montaillou: village occitan de 1294 à 1324*. Paris, 1975
Le Carnaval de Romans: de la Chandeleur au mercredi des Cendres, 1579–1580. Paris, 1979
Levtzion, N., *Ancient Ghana and Mali*. London, 1973
Lewin, T.J., *Asante before the British: The Prempean Years, 1875–1900*. Lawrence, 1978
Lintott, A.W., *Violence, Revolution and Civil Strife in the Classical City*. London, 1982
Lycan, W. (ed.), *Mind and Cognition*. Oxford, 1990
McCarthy, M., *Social Change and the Growth of British Power in the Gold Coast: The Fante States 1807–1874*. Lanham, 1983
McCaskie, T.C., 'Asantesɛm: Reflections on Discourse and Text in Africa', in *Discourse and Its Disguises: The Interpretation of African Oral Texts*, eds. K. Barber and P.F. de Moraes Farias, 70–86. Birmingham, 1989
'Nananom Mpow of Mankessim: An Essay in Fante History', in *West African Economic and Social History: Studies in Memory of Marion Johnson*, eds. D. Henige and T.C. McCaskie, 133–50. Madison, 1990
'Armah's *The Healers* and Asante History', in *Images of Africa: The Depiction of Pre-Colonial Africa in Creative Literature*, ed. M. Gray and R. Law, 42–60. Stirling, 1990
'Inventing Asante', in *Self-Assertion and Brokerage: Early Cultural Nationalism in West Africa*, eds. K. Barber and P.F. de Moraes Farias, 55–67. Birmingham, 1990
Macdonald, G.F. (ed.), *Perception and Identity: Essays Presented to A.J. Ayer and his Replies to Them*. London, 1979
MacGaffey, W., *Religion and Society in Central Africa: The BaKongo of Lower Zaire*. Chicago, 1986
McLeod, M.D., *The Asante*. London, 1981
Maier, D.J.E., *Priests and Power: The Case of the Dente Shrine in Nineteenth-Century Ghana*. Bloomington, 1983
Mann, H.-D., *Lucien Febvre: la pensée vivante d'un historien*. Paris, 1971
Margolis, J., *The Truth About Relativism*. Oxford, 1991
Mennell, S., *Norbert Elias: Civilization and the Human Self-Image*. Oxford, 1989
Meredith, H., *An Account of the Gold Coast of Africa with a Brief History of the African Company*. London, 1812
Metcalfe, G.E., *Maclean of the Gold Coast: The Life and Times of George Maclean, 1801–1847*. Oxford, 1962
Mink, L.O., *Mind, History and Dialectics: The Philosophy of R.G. Collingwood*. Bloomington, 1969

Moister, W., *Henry Wharton, the Story of His Life and Missionary Labours.* London, 1875

Mommsen, W.J., *The Age of Bureaucracy: Perspectives on the Political Sociology of Max Weber.* Oxford, 1974

The Political and Social Theory of Max Weber: Collected Essays. Chicago, 1989

Mommsen, W.J. and Osterhammel, J. (eds.), *Max Weber and His Contemporaries.* London, 1987

Morera, E., *Gramsci's Historicism: A Realist Interpretation.* London, 1990

Mouffe, C., 'Hegemony and Ideology in Gramsci', in *Gramsci and Marxist Theory*, ed. C. Mouffe, 168–204. London, 1979

Mudimbe, V.Y., *The Invention of Africa: Gnosis, Philosophy and the Order of Knowledge.* Bloomington, 1988

Muir, E. and Ruggiero, G. (eds.), *Microhistory and the Lost Peoples of Europe.* Baltimore, 1992

Nadel, L., Cooper, P., Culicover, P. and Harnish, R. (eds.), *Neural Connections, Mental Computations.* Cambridge, 1989

Nketia, J.H. Kwabena, *Drumming in Akan Communities of Ghana.* London, 1963

'The Musician in Akan Society', in *The Traditional Artist in African Societies*, ed. W.L. d'Azevedo, 79–100. Bloomington, 1975

Norris, C., *Uncritical Theory: Postmodernism, Intellectuals and the Gulf War.* London, 1992

Okere, T., *African Philosophy: A Historico-Hermeneutical Investigation of the Conditions of its Possibility*, Lanham, 1983

Opoku, A.A., *Festivals of Ghana.* Accra, 1970

Opoku, K.A., *West Africa Traditional Religion.* Accra, 1978

Owusu-Ansah, D., 'Power or Prestige? Muslims in 19th Century Kumase', in *The Golden Stool*, ed. E. Schildkrout, 80–92. New York, 1987

Islamic Talismanic Tradition in Nineteenth-Century Asante. Lewiston, 1991

Ozouf, M., *La Fête révolutionnaire, 1789–1799.* Paris, 1980

Pagden, A. (ed.), *The Languages of Political Theory in Early Modern Europe.* Cambridge, 1987

Parker, N., *Portrayals of Revolution: Images, Debates and Patterns of Thought on the French Revolution.* London, 1990

Parry, J. and Bloch, M. (eds.), *Money and the Morality of Exchange.* Cambridge, 1989

Passmore, J., *A Hundred Years of Philosophy.* London, 1966

Recent Philosophers. London, 1985

Pears, D., 'A Comparison between Ayer's Views about the Privileges of Sense-Datum Statements and the Views of Russell and Austin', in *Perception and Identity: Essays Presented to A.J. Ayer and his Replies to Them*, ed. G.F. Macdonald, 61–83. London, 1979

Peel, J.D.Y., *Aladura: A Religious Movement among the Yoruba.* London, 1968

Ijeshas and Nigerians: The Incorporation of a Yoruba Kingdom, 1890s–1970s. Cambridge, 1983

'History, Culture and the Comparative Method: A West African Puzzle', in *Comparative Anthropology*, ed. L. Holy, 88–118. Oxford, 1987

Perrot, C.-H., *Les Anyi-Ndenye et le pouvoir aux 18e et 19e siècles.* Paris, 1982

Person, Y., *Samori: une révolution Dyula*, 3 vols. Dakar, 1968–75

Platvoet, J.G., 'In de koelte van de "ontvangstboom": de politieke functie van een akan godsdienstig symbool', in *Van Gerechtigheid tot Liturgie*, eds. H. Manschot, H. van Reisen and W. Veldhuis, 61–91. Hilversum, 1984

Pocock, J.G.A., *The Machiavellian Moment: Florentine Political Thought and the Atlantic Republican Tradition*. Princeton, 1975

Pratt, M.L., *Imperial Eyes: Travel Writing and Transculturation*. London, 1992

Preziosi, D., *Rethinking Art History: Meditations on a Coy Science*. New Haven, 1989

Putnam, H., *Reason, Truth and History*. Cambridge, 1981

Quine, W.V., *From a Logical Point of View*. New York, 1961

Radcliffe-Brown, A.R. and Forde, D. (eds.), *African Systems of Kinship and Marriage*. London, 1950

Ramseyer, F.A. and Kühne, J., *Four Years in Ashantee*. London, 1875

Rathbone, R., *Murder and Politics in Colonial Ghana*. New Haven and London, 1993

Rattray, R.S., *Ashanti Proverbs: The Primitive Ethics of a Savage People*. Oxford, 1916
Ashanti. Oxford, 1923
A Short Manual of the Gold Coast. Accra, 1924
Religion and Art in Ashanti. Oxford, 1927
Ashanti Law and Constitution. Oxford, 1929
Akan-Ashanti Folk Tales. Oxford, 1930
Tribes of the Ashanti Hinterland. Oxford, 1932
The Leopard Priestess. Oxford, 1934

Reindorf, C.C., *History of the Gold Coast and Asante, based on Traditions, and Historical Facts ... from about 1500 to 1860*. Basel, 1895

Revel, J., 'Mentalités', in *Dictionnaire des sciences historiques*, ed. A. Burguière, 449–56. Paris, 1985

Reynolds, E., *Trade and Economic Change on the Gold Coast, 1807–1874*. London, 1974

Ricketts, H.J., *Narrative of the Ashantee War*. London, 1831

Ricoeur, P., *Hermeneutics and the Human Sciences: Essays on Language, Action and Interpretation*, trans. and ed. J.B. Thompson. Cambridge, 1981
Temps et récit, I. Paris, 1983
II. La Configuration dans le récit. Paris, 1984
III. Le Temps raconte. Paris, 1986

Rorty, R., *Philosophy and the Mirror of Nature*. Oxford, 1980
Consequences of Pragmatism: Essays 1972–80. Minneapolis, 1982
Objectivity, Relativism and Truth: Philosophical Papers Vol. 1. Cambridge, 1991
Essays on Heidegger and Others: Philosophical Papers Vol. 2. Cambridge, 1991

Rosaldo, R., 'Grief and a Headhunter's Rage: On the Cultural Force of Emotions', in *Text, Play, and Story: The Construction and Reconstruction of Self and Society*, ed. E.M. Bruner, 178–95. Washington, 1984
Culture and Truth: The Remaking of Social Analysis. London, 1993

Ross, D.H. and Garrard, T.F. (eds.), *Akan Transformations: Problems in Ghanaian Art History*. Los Angeles, 1983

Roth, G. and Wittich, C. (eds.), *Economy and Society: An Outline of Interpretive Sociology*, 3 vols. New York, 1968

Sahlins, M., *Historical Metaphors and Mythical Realities: Structure in the Early History of the Sandwich Islands Kingdom*. Ann Arbor, 1981

'Supplement to the Voyage of Cook: or *le calcul sauvage*', M. Sahlins, in *Islands of History*, 1–31. Chicago, 1985

Said, E.W., *Orientalism*. London, 1978

Salamini, L., *The Sociology of Political Praxis: An Introduction to Gramsci's Theory*. London, 1981

Sarbah, J.M., *Fanti National Constitution*. London, 1906

Sarpong, P.K., *The Sacred Stools of the Akan*. Accra and Tema, 1971
   Ghana in Retrospect: Some Aspects of Ghanaian Culture. Accra and Tema, 1974
   Girls' Nubility Rites in Ashanti. Accra and Tema, 1977
   The Ceremonial Horns of the Ashanti. Accra, 1990

Scaff, L.A., *Fleeing the Iron Cage: Culture, Politics and Modernity in the Thought of Max Weber*. Berkeley, 1989

Schama, S., *Dead Certainties (Unwarranted Speculations)*. London, 1991

Schildkrout, E. (ed.), *The Golden Stool: Studies of the Asante Center and Periphery*. New York, 1987

Schneider, D.M. and Gough, K. (eds.), *Matrilineal Kinship*. Berkeley and Los Angeles, 1961

Shils, E.A. and Finch, H.A. (eds.), *The Methodology of the Social Sciences*. New York, 1949

Silverman, R.A., 'Akan *Kuduo*: Form and Function', in *Akan Transformations: Problems in Ghanaian Art History*, eds. D.H. Ross and T.F. Garrard, 10–29. Los Angeles, 1983
   'Historical Dimensions of Tano Worship Among the Asante and Bono', in *The Golden Stool*, ed. E. Schildkrout, 272–88. New York, 1987

Skorupski, J., *Symbol and Theory: A Philosophical Study of Theories of Religion in Social Anthropology*. Cambridge, 1976

Spence, J.D., *The Memory Palace of Matteo Ricci*. London, 1985

Spencer, P. (ed.), *Society and the Dance: The Social Anthropology of Process and Performance*. Cambridge, 1985

Spivak, G. Chakravorty, *In Other Worlds: Essays in Cultural Politics*. New York, 1987

Squire, F.A., 'Tsetse Flies', in *Agriculture and Land Use in Ghana*, ed. J.B. Wills, 441–4. Accra, 1962

Starobinski, J., *Jean-Jacques Rousseau: la transparence et l'obstacle*. Paris, 1971

Stock, B., *Listening for the Text: On the Uses of the Past*. Baltimore, 1990

Stocking, G.W., *Functionalism Historicized: Essays on British Social Anthropology*. (History of Anthropology 2). Madison, 1984

Stoianovich, T., *French Historical Method: The* Annales *Paradigm*. Ithaca, 1976

Summers, D., 'Real Metaphor: Towards a Redefinition of the "Conceptual" Image', in *Visual Theory: Painting and Interpretation*, eds. N. Bryson, M.A. Holly and K. Moxey, 231–59. Oxford, 1991

Suskind, P., *Das Parfüm*. Zurich, 1985

Swithenbank, M., *Ashanti Fetish Houses*. Accra, 1969

Taussig, M., *Shamanism, Colonialism, and the Wild Man: A Study in Terror and Healing*. Chicago, 1987

Tedlie, H., '*Materia Medica* and Diseases', in T.E. Bowdich, *Mission from Cape Coast Castle to Ashantee*, 370–80. London, 1819

Temu, A. and Swai, B., *Historians and Africanist History: A Critique. Post-Colonial*

Historiography Examined. London, 1981

Thompson, E.P., *The Making of the English Working Class.* London, 1963
   The Poverty of Theory and Other Essays. London, 1978

Tipple, A.G., *The Development of Housing Policy in Kumasi, Ghana, 1901 to 1981.* Newcastle, 1987

Todorov, T., *Michail Bakhtine: le principe dialogique suivi de Ecrits du cercle de Bakhtine.* Paris, 1981

Tooth, G., *Studies in Mental Illness in the Gold Coast.* London, 1950

Tordoff, W., *Ashanti Under the Prempehs 1888–1935.* Oxford, 1965

Toulmin, S., 'Conceptual Change and the Problem of Relativity', in *Critical Essays on the Philosophy of R.G. Collingwood,* ed. M. Krausz, 201–21. Oxford, 1972

Trautmann, T.R., *Lewis Henry Morgan and the Invention of Kinship.* Berkeley, 1987

Trevor-Roper, H.R., *The Rise of Christian Europe.* London, 1965

Turner, V., *The Forest of Symbols: Aspects of Ndembu Ritual.* Ithaca, 1967
   Revelation and Divination in Ndembu Ritual. Ithaca, 1975
   On the Edge of the Bush: Anthropology as Experience. Tucson, 1985

Twumasi, P.A., *Medical Systems in Ghana: A Study in Medical Sociology.* Accra and Tema, 1975

Tyler, S.A., *The Unspeakable: Discourse, Dialogue and Rhetoric in the Postmodern World.* Madison, 1987

Valeri, V., *Kingship and Sacrifice: Ritual and Society in Ancient Hawaii.* Chicago, 1985

Van Der Dussen, W.J., *History as a Science: The Philosophy of R.G. Collingwood.* The Hague, 1981

Van Gennep, A., *Les Rites de passage.* Paris, 1908

Vattimo, G. and Rovatti, P.A. (eds.), *Il pensiero debole.* Milan, 1983

Venturi, R., Scott Brown, D. and Izenour, S., *Learning from Las Vegas: The Forgotten Symbolism of Architectural Form,* revised edn. Cambridge, 1977

Vernant, J.-P., *Mythe et société en Grèce ancienne.* Paris, 1974

Vernant, J.-P. and Vidal-Naquet, P., *Mythe et tragédie en Grèce ancienne.* Paris, 1972

Veyne, P., *Le Pain et le cirque.* Paris, 1976
   Comment on écrit l'histoire: suivi de Foucault révolutionne l'histoire. Paris, 1978

Vickers, A., *Bali: A Paradise Created.* Victoria, 1989

Vovelle, M., *Piété baroque et déchristianisation en Provençe au XVIIIe siècle.* Paris, 1973

Wallace-Johnson, I.T.A., *Restoration of the Ashanti Confederacy: January 31–February 4, 1935.* Accra, 1935

Ward, W.E.F., 'Introduction to Third Edition', in T.E. Bowdich, *Mission from Cape Coast Castle to Ashantee,* 11–59. London, 1966

Warnke, G., *Gadamer: Hermeneutics, Tradition and Reason.* Oxford, 1987

Warren, D.M. and Brempong, K.O., *Techiman Traditional State, Part I: Stool and Town Histories.* Legon, 1971

Weber, M., *Wirtschaft und Gesellschaft,* ed. J. Winckelmann, Tübingen, 1976 (earlier edns 1922, 1925, 1947, ed. Marianne Weber; 1956, 1972, ed. J. Winckelmann)
   Gesammelte Aufsatze zur Wissenschaftslehre, ed. J. Winckelmann, 3rd edn. Tübingen, 1968

Weiskel, T.C., 'Asante and the Akan Periphery: The Baule on the Western Akan Frontier', in *The Golden Stool,* ed. E. Schildkrout, 260–71. New York, 1987

White, H., *Tropics of Discourse: Essays in Cultural Criticism*. Baltimore, 1978

Whittaker, C.R. (ed.), *Pastoral Economies in Classical Antiquity*. Cambridge, 1988

Wilks, I., *The Northern Factor in Ashanti History*. Legon, 1961

'The Position of Muslims in Metropolitan Ashanti in the Early Nineteenth Century', in *Islam in Tropical Africa*, ed. I.M. Lewis, 318–41. London, 1966

'Ashanti Government', in *West African Kingdoms in the Nineteenth Century*, ed. D. Forde and P.M. Kaberry, 206–38. London, 1967

'Asante Policy towards the Hausa Trade in the 19th Century', in *The Development of Indigenous Trade and Markets in West Africa*, ed. C. Meillassoux, 124–41. London, 1971

Asante in the Nineteenth Century: The Structure and Evolution of a Political Order. Cambridge, 1975; reprinted with a new *Preamble*, 1989

'Dissidence in Asante Politics: Two Tracts from the Late Nineteenth Century', in *African Themes: Northwestern University Studies in Honor of Gwendolen M. Carter*, ed. I. Abu-Lughod, 47–63. Evanston, 1975

'Land, Labour, Capital and the Forest Kingdom of Asante: A Model of Early Change', in *The Evolution of Social Systems*, eds. J. Friedman and M.J. Rowlands, 487–534. London, 1977

South Wales and the Rising of 1839. London, 1984

'What Manner of Persons were These? Some Reflections on Asante Officialdom', in *The Golden Stool*, ed. E. Schildkrout, 109–29. New York, 1987

'She Who Blazed A Trail: Akyaawa Yikwan of Asante', in *Life Histories of African Women*, ed. P.W. Romero, 113–39. London, 1988

Wa and the Wala: Islam and Polity in Northwestern Ghana. Cambridge, 1989

Wilks, I., Levtzion, N. and Haight, B.M., *Chronicles from Gonja: A Tradition of West African Muslim Historiography*. Cambridge, 1986

Williams, R., *Keywords: A Vocabulary of Culture and Society*. Glasgow, 1976

Marxism and Literature. London, 1977

Williamson, S.G., *Akan Religion and the Christian Faith: A Comparative Study of the Impact of Two Religions*. Accra, 1965

Wills, J.B. (ed.), *Agriculture and Land Use in Ghana*. Accra, 1962

Winkler, J.J., *The Constraints of Desire: The Anthropology of Sex and Gender in Ancient Greece*. New York, 1990

Winsnes, S.A. (trans. and ed.), *Letters on West Africa and the Slave Trade: Paul Erdmann Isert's 'Journey to Guinea and the Caribbean Islands in Columbia' (1788)*, Oxford, 1992

Wiredu, K., *Philosophy and an African Culture*. Cambridge, 1980

World Bank, The, *Ghana: Policies and Program for Adjustment: A World Bank Country Study*. Washington, 1984

Wyse, A.J.G., *H.C. Bankole-Bright and Politics in Colonial Sierra Leone, 1919–1958*. Cambridge, 1990

Yankah, K., *Woes of a Kwatriot: Reflections on the Ghanaian Situation*. Accra, 1990

Yansane, A.Y., 'Cultural, Political, and Economic Universals in West Africa', in *African Culture: The Rhythms of Unity*, eds. M.K. and K.W. Asante, 39–68. Trenton, 1990

Yarak, L.W., 'Kwasi Boakye and Kwaku Poku: Dutch-Educated Asante "Princes"', in *The Golden Stool*, ed. E. Schildkrout, 131–45. New York, 1987

Asante and the Dutch 1744–1873. Oxford, 1990
Young, R., *White Mythologies: Writing History and the West*. London, 1990
Zemon Davis, N., *The Return of Martin Guerre*. Cambridge, 1983
  Fiction in the Archives: Pardon Tales and their Tellers in Sixteenth-Century France. Stanford, 1987

PRINTED WORKS: JOURNAL ARTICLES, PERIODICAL LITERATURE, ETC.

Adamson, W.L., 'Gramsci and the Politics of Civil Society', *Praxis International* (Oct. 1987/Jan. 1988), 320–39
Addo-Fening, R., 'Asante Refugees in Akyem Abuakwa, 1875–1912', *Transactions of the Historical Society of Ghana*, 14, 1 (1973), 39–64
  'The Background to the Deportation of King Asafo Agyei and the Foundation of New Juaben', *Transactions of the Historical Society of Ghana*, 14, 2 (1973), 213–28
Agyeman-Duah, J., 'Uproar in the Kumase Council of Chiefs, 1777', *Asantesɛm*, 7 (1977), 43–4
Aidoo, A. Akosua, 'The Asante Succession Crisis of 1883–8', *Transactions of the Historical Society of Ghana*, 13, 2 (1972), 163–80
Akwabi-Ameyaw, K., 'Ashanti Social Organization: Some Ethnographic Clarifications', *Ethnology*, 21 (1982), 325–33
Allman, J.M., 'The Youngmen and the Porcupine: Class, Nationalism and Asante's Struggle for Self-Determination, 1954–57', *Journal of African History*, 31, 2 (1990), 263–79
  'Of "Spinsters", "Concubines" and "Wicked Women": Reflections on Gender and Social Change in Colonial Asante', *Gender and History*, 3, 2 (1991), 176–89
Anderson, P., 'The Antinomies of Antonio Gramsci', *New Left Review*, 100 (1976–7), 5–78
Ankersmit, F.R., 'Historical Representation', *History and Theory*, 27 (1988), 205–28
  'Historiography and Postmodernism', *History and Theory*, 28 (1989), 137–53
  'Reply to Professor Zagorin', *History and Theory*, 29 (1990), 275–96
Arhin, K., 'The Financing of the Ashanti Expansion (1700–1820)', *Africa*, 37, 3 (1967), 283–91
  'Some Asante Views on Colonial Rule: As Seen in the Controversy Relating to Death Duties', *Transactions of the Historical Society of Ghana*, 15, 1 (1974), 63–84
  'The Pressure of Cash and Its Political Consequences in Asante in the Colonial Period', *Journal of African Studies* (Winter 1976–7), 453–68
  'Asante Military Institutions', *Journal of African Studies*, 7, 1 (1980), 22–30
  'Rank and Class among the Asante and Fante in the Nineteenth Century', *Africa*, 53, 1 (1983), 2–22
  'Peasants in Nineteenth Century Asante', *Current Anthropology*, 24, 4 (1983), 471–80
  'A Note on the Asante *akonkofo*: A Non-literate Sub-elite, 1900–1930', *Africa*, 56, 1 (1986), 25–31
  'The Asante Praise Poems: The Ideology of Patrimonialism', *Paideuma*, 32 (1986), 163–97
  'Trade, Accumulation and the State in Asante in the Nineteenth Century', *Africa*, 60, 4 (1990), 524–37

Armitage, C., 'The Fetish-Worship of Ashanti', *Wide World Magazine*, 15 (April 1905), 62–7

Austin, G., 'The Emergence of Capitalist Relations in South Asante Cocoa-Farming, c. 1916–1933', *Journal of African History*, 28, 2 (1987), 259–79

'Capitalists and Chiefs in the Cocoa Hold-Ups in South Asante, 1927–1938', *International Journal of African Historical Studies*, 21, 1 (1988), 63–95

Bartle, P.F.W., 'Forty Days: The Akan Calendar', *Africa*, 48, 1 (1978), 80–4

Bates, T.R., 'Gramsci and the Theory of Hegemony', *Journal of the History of Ideas*, 36 (1975), 351–66

Benedict, P. and Levi, G., 'Robert Darnton e il massacro dei gatti', *Quaderni Storici*, 58 (1985), 257–77

Berman, R.A., 'Troping to Pretoria: The Rise and Fall of Deconstruction', *Telos*, 85 (Fall 1990), 4–16

Bernstein, H. and Depelchin, J., 'The Object of African History: A Materialist Perspective', *History in Africa*, V (1978), 1–19 and VI (1979), 17–43

Bettelheim, J., 'Negotiations of Power in Carnaval Culture in Santiago de Cuba', *African Arts*, 24, 2 (1991), 66–75 and 91–2

Bhabha, H.K., 'Signs Taken for Wonders: Questions of Ambivalence and Authority under a Tree outside Delhi, May 1817', *Critical Inquiry*, 12, 1 (1985), 144–65

Birmingham, D., 'Carnival at Luanda', *Journal of African History*, 29, 1 (1988), 93–103

Boureau, A., 'Propositions pour une histoire restreinte des Mentalités', *Annales: Economies, Sociétés, Civilisations*, 44, 6 (1989), 1491–1504

Censer, J.R., 'Review Article: Revitalizing the Intellectual History of the French Revolution', *Journal of the History of Ideas*, 50, 4 (1989), 652–66

Chartier, R., 'Le Monde comme représentation', *Annales: Economies, Sociétés, Civilisations*, 44, 6 (1989), 1505–20

Cheal, D.J., 'Hegemony, Ideology and Contradictory Consciousness', *Sociological Quarterly*, 20 (Winter 1979), 109–18

Cole, H.M., 'The Art of Festival in Ghana', *African Arts*, 8, 3 (1975), 12–23 and 60–2

Collins, E., 'The Panic Element in Nineteenth-Century British Relations with Ashanti', *Transactions of the Historical Society of Ghana*, 5, 2 (1962), 79–144

Depelchin, J., 'Review' (of I. Wilks, *Asante in the Nineteenth Century*, 1975), *Africa Development*, 2, 4 (1977), 97–106

Dumett, R., 'Precolonial Goldmining and the State in the Akan Region, with a Critique of the Terray Hypothesis', *Research in Economic Anthropology*, 2 (1979), 37–68

Ekeh, P.P., 'Social Anthropology and the Contrasting Uses of Tribalism in Africa', *Comparative Studies in Society and History*, 32, 4 (1990), 660–700

Feeley-Harnik, G., 'Issues in Divine Kingship', *Annual Review of Anthropology*, 14 (1985), 273–313

Ferrarotti, F., 'Civil Society and State Structures in Creative Tension: Ferguson, Hegel, Gramsci', *State, Culture and Society*, 1 (1984), 3–25

Fortes, M., 'The Ashanti Social Survey: A Preliminary Report', *Rhodes-Livingstone Journal*, 6 (1948), 1–36

'Descent, Filiation and Affinity: A Rejoinder to Dr. Leach', *Man*, 59, 309 and 331 (1959), 193–7 and 206–12

'Kinship and the Social Order: The Legacy of L.H. Morgan', *Current Anthropology*, 13, 2 (1972), 285–96

'Custom and Conscience in Anthropological Perspective', *International Review of Psycho-Analysis*, 4 (1977), 127–54 (a reworking of the Ernest Jones Memorial Lecture of the British Psychoanalytical Society, London, 1973)

'An Anthropologist's Apprenticeship', *Annual Review of Anthropology*, 7 (1978), 1–30

Fortes, M., Steel, R.W. and Ady, P., 'Ashanti Survey, 1945–6: An Experiment in Social Research', *Geographical Journal*, 110 (1948), 149–79

Friedman, J., 'Review' (of M. Sahlins, *Islands of History*, 1985), *History and Theory*, 26, 1 (1987), 72–99

'Beyond Otherness or: The Spectacularization of Anthropology', *Telos*, 71 (Spring 1987), 161–70

Fynn, J.K., 'The Reign and Times of Kusi Obodum, 1750–64', *Transactions of Historical Society of Ghana*, 8 (1965), 24–32

Gilbert, M., 'The Sudden Death of a Millionaire: Conversion and Consensus in a Ghanaian Kingdom', *Africa*, 58, 3 (1988), 291–314

Gruppi, L., 'Le Concept d'égemonie chez Antonio Gramsci', *Dialectiques*, 4/5 (1974), 4–54

Hagan, G.P., 'A Note on Akan Colour Symbolism', *Institute of African Studies Research Review* (Legon), 7, 1 (1970), 8–14

Hall, S., 'Gramsci's Relevance for the Study of Race and Ethnicity', *Journal of Communication Inquiries*, 10 (1986), 5–27

Hart, K., 'The Social Anthropology of West Africa', *Annual Review of Anthropology*, 14 (1985), 243–72

Hempel, C.G., 'Comments on Goodman's *Ways of Worldmaking*', *Synthèse*, 45 (1980), 193–9

Holden, J., 'The Zabarima Conquest of North-West Ghana, Part I', *Transactions of the Historical Society of Ghana*, 8 (1965), 60–86

Horton, R., 'African Traditional Thought and Western Science, I and II', *Africa*, 37, 1 and 2 (1967), 50–71 and 155–87

'African Conversion', *Africa*, 41, 2 (1971), 85–108

'On the Rationality of Conversion, I and II', *Africa*, 45, 3 and 4 (1975), 219–35 and 373–99

Hountondji, P., 'Que peut la philosophie?', *Présence Africaine*, 119 (1981), 47–71

Jacobitti, E.E., 'Hegemony before Gramsci: The Case of Benedetto Croce', *Journal of Modern History*, 52 (March 1980), 66–84

Johnson, M., 'The Population of Asante, 1817–1921: A Reconsideration', *Asantesɛm*, 8 (1978), 22–8

Jones, A., '*Four Years in Asante*: One Source or Several?', *History in Africa*, 18 (1991), 173–203

Kea, R.A., 'Four Asante Officials in the South-East Gold Coast (1808)', *Ghana Notes and Queries*, 11 (1970), 42–7

'A Provisional Translation of Two Danish Documents on the Asante Expedition of 1811', *Asante Seminar*, 6 (1976), 39–50

'The Chronology of the Asante Kings: A Note on the Death of the *Asantehene* Osei Yaw Akoto', *Asantesɛm*, 9 (1978), 55

'The Danes and the Gold Coast: Ten Danish Documents of the Early 1830s', *Asantesɛm*, 10 (1979), 64–70

'More Danish Accounts of the 1811 Asante Expedition', *Asantesɛm*, 11 (1979), 60–71

Kelley, D.R., 'What is Happening to the History of Ideas?', *Journal of the History of Ideas*, 51, 1 (1990), 3–26

Kellner, H., *Narrativity in History: Post-Structuralism and Since, History and Theory Beiheft*, 26 (1987)

Kiser, E. and Hechter, M., 'The Role of General Theory in Comparative Historical Sociology', *American Journal of Sociology*, 97, 1 (1991), 1–30

Klein, A.N., 'The Two Asantes: Competing Interpretations of "Slavery" in Akan-Asante Culture and Society', *Institute of African Studies Research Review* (Legon), 12, 1 (1980), 37–51

Kyerematen, A.A.Y., 'The Royal Stools of Ashanti', *Africa*, 39, 1 (1969), 1–10

LaTorre, J., 'Birthplaces of Dutch East Indies Troops "Recruited" in Kumase, 1837–1842', *Asante Seminar*, 5 (1976), 31–42

Law, R., 'Wheeled Transport in Pre-colonial West Africa', *Africa*, 50, 3 (1980), 249–62

'For Marx, But With Reservations about Althusser: A Comment on Bernstein and Depelchin', *History in Africa*, 8 (1981), 247–51

'Human Sacrifice in Pre-colonial West Africa', *African Affairs*, 84 (1985), 53–87

Lears, T.J.J., 'The Concept of Cultural Hegemony: Problems and Possibilities', *American Historical Review*, 90 (June 1985), 567–93

Le Goff, J., 'Is Politics Still the Backbone of History?', *Daedalus*, 100, 1 (1971), 1–19

Levtzion, N., 'Early Nineteenth Century Arabic Manuscripts from Kumase', *Transactions of the Historical Society of Ghana*, 8 (1965), 99–119

Lindenfeld, D., 'On Systems and Embodiments as Categories for Intellectual History', *History and Theory*, 27, 1 (1988), 30–50

Lonsdale, J., 'States and Social Processes in Africa: A Historiographical Survey', *African Studies Review*, 24, 2/3 (1981), 139–225

McCaskie, T.C., 'Innovational Eclecticism: The Asante Empire and Europe in the Nineteenth Century', *Comparative Studies in Society and History*, 14, 1 (1972), 30–45

'Social Rebellion and the Inchoate Rejection of History: Some Reflections on the Career of Opon Asibe Tutu', *Asante Seminar*, 4 (1976), 34–8

'A Note on the Career of *Akyempemhene ɔheneba* Owusu Koko', *Asante Seminar*, 6 (1976), 21

'The History of the Manwere *nkoa* at Drobonso', *Asante Seminar*, 6 (1976), 33–8

'*Asantehene* Agyeman Prempe's Account to the *Asanteman* of His Exile from Kumase (1896–1924): A Document with Commentary', *Asantesɛm*, 7 (1977), 32–42

'Office, Land and Subjects in the History of the Manwere *Fekuo* of Kumase: An Essay in the Political Economy of the Asante State', *Journal of African History*, 21, 2 (1980), 189–208

'Time and the Calendar in Nineteenth Century Asante: An Exploratory Essay', *History in Africa*, 7 (1980), 179–200

'State and Society, Marriage and Adultery: Some Considerations towards a Social History of Precolonial Asante', *Journal of African History*, 22, 4 (1981),

477–94
'Anti-witchcraft Cults in Asante: An Essay in the Social History of an African People', *History in Africa*, 8 (1981), 125–54
'Accumulation, Wealth and Belief in Asante History. I. To the Close of the Nineteenth Century', *Africa*, 53, 1 (1983), 23–43
'R.S. Rattray and the Construction of Asante History: An Appraisal', *History in Africa*, 10 (1983), 187–206
'*Ahyiamu* – "A Place of Meeting": An Essay on Process and Event in the History of the Asante State', *Journal of African History*, 25, 2 (1984), 169–88
'Power and Dynastic Conflict in Mampon', *History in Africa*, 12 (1985), 167–85
'Accumulation, Wealth and Belief in Asante History. II. The Twentieth Century', *Africa*, 56, 1 (1986), 3–23
'Komfo Anokye of Asante: Meaning, History and Philosophy in an African Society', *Journal of African History*, 27, 2 (1986), 315–39
'Death and the *Asantehene*: A Historical Meditation', *Journal of African History*, 30, 3 (1989), 417–44
'People and Animals: Constru(ct)ing the Asante Experience', *Africa*, 62, 2 (1992), 221–47
'Empire State: Asante and the Historians', *Journal of African History*, 33, 3 (1992), 467–76
'*Konnurokusɛm*: An Essay on Kinship and Family in the History of the *Oyoko Kɔkɔɔ* Dynasty of Kumase', *Journal of African History*, forthcoming
McCaskie, T.C. and Wiafe, J.E., 'A Contemporary Account in Twi of the *Akompi Sa* of 1863: A Document with Commentary', *Asantesɛm*, 11 (1979), 72–8
Maier, D.J.E., 'Nineteenth-Century Asante Medical Practices', *Comparative Studies in Society and History*, 21, 1 (1979), 63–81
Modood, T., 'The Later Collingwood's Alleged Historicism and Relativism', *Journal of the History of Philosophy*, 27, 1 (1989), 101–26
O'Hanlon, R. and Washbrook, D., 'After Orientalism: Culture, Criticism and Politics in the Third World', *Comparative Studies in Society and History*, 34, 1 (1992), 141–67
Owusu-Ansah, D., 'Islamization Reconsidered: An Examination of Asante Responses to Muslim Influence in the Nineteenth Century', *Asian and African Studies*, 21, 2 (1987), 145–63
'The State and Islamization in 19th Century Africa: Buganda Absolutism *versus* Asante Constitutionalism', *Journal: Institute of Muslim Minority Affairs*, 8, 1 (1987), 132–43
Patton, S.F., 'The Asante Umbrella', *African Arts*, 7, 4 (1984), 64–73 and 93–4
Perregaux, E., 'Chez les Achanti', *Bulletin de la Société Neuchâteloise de Géographie*, 17 (1906), 7–312
Perrot, C.-H., 'Le Raid d'Ebiri Moro contre Kumasi, la capitale Ashanti (1718)', *Cultures et Développement*, 16, 3/4 (1984), 537–52
Petiver, J., 'A Catalogue of Some Guinea Plants, with their Native Names and Virtues, etc.', *Philosophical Transactions (Royal Society)*, 19 (1697), 677–86
Poku, K., 'Traditional Roles and People of Slave Origin in Modern Ashanti – A Few Impressions', *Ghana Journal of Sociology*, 5, 1 (1969), 34–8
Prakash, G., 'Writing Post-Orientalist Histories of the Third World: Perspectives

from Indian Historiography', *Comparative Studies in Society and History*, 32, 2 (1990), 383–408

'Can the "Subaltern" Ride?: A Reply to O'Hanlon and Washbrook', *Comparative Studies in Society and History*, 34, 1 (1992), 168–84

Prussin, L., 'Traditional Asante Architecture', *African Arts*, 13, 2 (1980), 57–65, 78–82 and 85–7

Putnam, H., 'Reflections on Goodman's *Ways of Worldmaking*', *Journal of Philosophy*, 76, 4 (1979), 603–18

Rathbone, R. and Allman, J.M., 'Discussion: The Youngmen and the Porcupine', *Journal of African History*, 32, 3 (1991), 333–8

Rattray, R.S., 'The Drum Language of West Africa', *Journal of the Royal African Society*, 22 (1923), 226–36 and 302–16

'The Arts and Crafts of Ashanti', *Journal of the Royal African Society*, 23 (1924), 265–70

'A Wembley Idol', *Blackwood's Magazine*, 1325 (1926), 395–402

'Some Aspects of West African Folklore', *Journal of the Royal African Society*, 28 (1928), 1–11

'The Mausoleum of Ampong Agyei', *Blackwood's Magazine*, n.s. 233 (June 1928), 842–53

'The African Child in Proverb, Folklore and Fact', *Africa*, 6 (1933), 456–71

'The Golden Stool of Ashanti', *The Illustrated London News* (2 March 1935), 333–5

Rattray, R.S. with Buxton, L.H.D., 'Cross-Cousin Marriages', *Journal of the Royal African Society*, 24 (1925), 83–91

Riis, A., 'Reise des Missionars in Akropong nach dem Aschantee-Lande im Winter 1839 bis 1840', *Magazin für die Neueste Geschichte der Evangelischen Missions-und Bibel-Gesellschaften*, Basel (1840), Pt III, 92 ff. and 216–35

Robertson, A.F., 'Abusa: The Structural History of an Economic Contract', *The Journal of Development Studies*, 18, 4 (1982), 447–78

Rorty, R., 'We Anti-Representationalists', *Radical Philosophy*, 60 (1992), 40–2

Said, E.W., 'Intellectuals in the Post-Colonial World', *Salmagundi*, 70–1 (1986), 44–81

Schama, S., 'The Many Deaths of General Wolfe', *Granta*, 32 (1990), 15–56

Scheffler, I., 'The Wonderful Worlds of Goodman', *Synthèse*, 45 (1980), 201–9

Schurmann, R., 'On Constituting Oneself an Anarchic Subject', *Praxis International*, 6 (1986), 294–310

Sereque Berhan, T., 'Karl Marx and African Emancipatory Thought: A Critique of Marx's Euro-Centric Metaphysics', *Praxis International*, 10, 1–2 (1990), 161–81

Shafir, G., 'Interpretative Sociology and the Philosophy of Praxis: Comparing Max Weber and Antonio Gramsci', *Praxis International* (April 1985), 63–74

Stahl, A.B., 'Ethnic Style and Ethnic Boundaries: A Diachronic Case Study from West-Central Ghana', *Ethnohistory*, 38, 3 (1991), 250–75

Tenbruck, F.H., 'Wie gut kennen wir Max Weber?', *Zeitschrift für die gesamte Staatswissenschaft*, 131 (1975), 719–42

'Abschied von *Wirtschaft und Gesellschaft*', *Zeitschrift für die gesamte Staatswissenschaft*, 133 (1977), 703–36

'The Problem of Thematic Unity in the Work of Max Weber', *British Journal of Sociology*, 31, 3 (1980), 316–51

Terray, E., 'Review' (of I. Wilks, *Asante in the Nineteenth Century*, 1975), *Annales:*

Économies, Sociétés, Civilisations, 32, 2 (1977), 311–25

'Contribution à une étude de l'armée asante', *Cahiers d'Etudes Africaines,* 61–2, XVI–1–2 (1976), 297–356

'The Political Economy of the Abron Kingdom of Gyaman', *Institute of African Studies Research Review* (Legon), 12, 1 (1980), 1–36

'Gold Production, Slave Labor, and State Intervention in Precolonial Akan Societies: A Reply to Raymond Dumett', *Research in Economic Anthropology,* 5 (1983), 95–129

Tremearne, A.J.N., 'Extracts from Diary of the late Rev. John Martin, Wesleyan Missionary in West Africa, 1843–48', *Man,* 73–4 (1912), 138–43

Triulzi, A., 'The *Asantehene*-in-Council: Ashanti Politics under Colonial Rule, 1935–50', *Africa,* 42, 2 (1972), 98–111

Valsecchi, P., 'Lo Nzema fra Egemonia Asante ed Espansione Europea nella prima metà del XIX secolo', *Africa: Rivista Trimestrale di Studi e Documentazione dell' Istituto Italo-Africano,* 41, 4 (1986), 507–44

'Il Sanwi e l'Impero Asante: dati e ipotesi per una storia della relazioni politiche', *Africa: Rivista Trimestrale di Studi e Documentazione dell' Istituto Italo-Africano,* 44, 2 (1989), 175–210

Van Dantzig, A., 'The Dutch Military Recruitment Agency in Kumasi', *Ghana Notes and Queries,* 8 (1966), 21–4

'English Bosman and Dutch Bosman: A Comparison of Texts – III', *History in Africa,* 4 (1977), 247–73

Van Engen, J., 'The Christian Middle Ages as an Historiographical Problem', *American Historical Review,* 91, 3 (1986), 519–52

Vickers, A., 'Balinese Texts and Historiography', *History and Theory,* 29, 2 (1990), 158–78

Von Laue, T.H., 'Transubstantiation in the Study of African Reality', *African Affairs,* 74 (1975), 401–19

'Anthropology and Power: R.S. Rattray among the Ashanti', *African Affairs,* 75 (1976), 33–54

Ward, W.E.F., 'Britain and Ashanti, 1874–1896', *Transactions of the Historical Society of Ghana,* 15, 2 (1974), 131–64

Wilks, I., 'The Mande Loan Element in Twi', *Ghana Notes and Queries,* 4 (1962), 26–8

'Aspects of Bureaucratization in Ashanti in the Nineteenth Century', *Journal of African History,* 7, 2 (1966), 215–32

'A Letter of 1888 from Abū Bakr b. 'Uthmān Kamaghatay to Asantehene Agyeman Prempe', *Asante Seminar,* 4 (1976), 42–4

'The Population of Asante, 1817–1921: A Rejoinder', *Asantesεm,* 8 (1978), 28–35

'A Note on Career Sheet ACBP/28: Kwaadu Yaadom', *Asantesεm,* 11 (1979), 54–6

'The Golden Stool and the Elephant Tail: An Essay on Wealth in Asante', *Research in Economic Anthropology,* 2 (1979), 1–36

'Portuguese, Wangara and Akan in the Fifteenth and Sixteenth Centuries: The Matter of Bitu', *Journal of African History,* 23, 2 (1982), 333–49

'The Struggle for Trade', *Journal of African History,* 23, 3 (1982), 463–72

'Asante: Human Sacrifice or Capital Punishment? A Rejoinder', *International Journal of African Historical Studies,* 21, 3 (1988), 443–52

Wilks, Ivor G. Hughes, 'Insurrections in Texas and Wales: The Careers of John

Rees', *The Welsh History Review: Cylchgrawn Hanes Cymru*, 11, 1 (1982), 67–91

Williams, C., 'Asante: Human Sacrifice or Capital Punishment? An Assessment of the Period 1807–1874', *International Journal of African Historical Studies*, 21, 3 (1988), 433–41

Yankah, K., 'To Praise or Not to Praise the King: The Akan *Apae* in the Context of Referential Poetry', *Research in African Literatures*, 14, 3 (1983), 381–400

Yarak, L.W., 'Asante Interest in Europe in the Reign of Opoku Ware I', *Asantesɛm*, 9 (1978), 70–1

  'Dating Asantehene Osei Kwadwo's Campaign against the Banna', *Asantesɛm*, 10 (1979), 58

Yarak, L.W. and Wilks, I., 'A Further Note on the Death of *Asantehene* Osei Yaw Akoto and on the Enstoolment of Kwaku Dua Panin', *Asantesɛm*, 9 (1978), 56–7

Zagorin, P., 'Historiography and Postmodernism: A Reconsideration', *History and Theory*, 29, 2 (1990), 263–74

PRINTED WORKS: MISCELLANEA

Address by Otumfuo, Opoku Ware II, Asantehene, at the Golden Jubilee Odwira Durbar, Kumasi, Saturday, November 16, 1985. Kumase, 1985

Akwasi Abayie Boaten I, Nana, *An Economic Survey of Kwabre District: A Study in Rural Development*. IAS, Legon, 1990

Braffi, E.K., *Otumfuo Opoku Ware II (Asantehene) Celebrates Odwira Festival*. Kumase, 1985

Fortes, M. *et al.*, 'A Demographic Field Study in Ashanti', in *Culture and Human Fertility*, ed. F. Lorimer, UNESCO Report, Paris, 1954

Owusu Ansa, 'The King of Ashantee', *The Times*, London, 29 July 1873

Wilks, I., *Political Bi-Polarity in Nineteenth Century Asante*, Ninth M.J. Herskovits Memorial Lecture, Edinburgh University. Edinburgh, 1970

UNPUBLISHED WORKS: DRAFT PAPERS, MANUSCRIPTS, ETC.

Agyeman-Duah, J., 'Traditional History of Ashanti Mampong', MS dd. Kumase State Council, April 1959

  'Golden Stool: Soul of the Ashanti Nation', n.d.

'Asante Kotoko Society (60th Anniversary), 1916–1976', MS 1976. Compiled by Authorization of the Society

Austin, G., 'Class Struggle and Rural Capitalism in Asante History', draft paper. n.d.

  'Kinship, Coercion and the Market: Human Pawning in Asante', draft paper, presented at the Annual Meeting of the ASAUSA, Seattle, 1992

Denteh, A.C., 'History of Gyaasewa', MS (from information gathered since 1928). Legon, 1965

Gilbert, M., 'Aesthetic Strategies: The Politics of a Royal Ritual', revised draft paper, August 1990

Horovitz, R.A., 'Trade between Sanwi and her Neighbours, 1843–93', draft paper presented at the Conference on the Akan, Bondoukou, 1974

Kyei, T.E., *My Memoir*, 6 vols. Kumase, n.d.

Marriage and Divorce among the Ashanti. Forthcoming from the African Studies Centre, Cambridge

McCaskie, T.C., 'Politics in 19th Century Asante', draft paper presented at the Conference on the City of Kumase, Kumase, December 1990

'"You Must Dis/Miss/Re/Member This": Kwame Tua in Time, and Other Passages from Asante History', draft paper presented at the Red Lion Seminar (Northwestern University/University of Chicago), Chicago, 1992

Machin, N.P.F., '"Understanding the Natives": The Life of R.S. Rattray, 1881–1938', MS, 277 pp., 1973

Platvoet, J.G., 'The Return of Anokye: The Use of a Political Myth by an Asante "Puritan" Movement', draft paper, 1984

Yarak, L.W., 'State, Society and Politics in Nineteenth Century Asante', draft paper presented at the Conference on the City of Kumase, Kumase, December 1990

UNPUBLISHED WORKS; THESES, DISSERTATIONS, ETC.

Aboagye, E.O., 'Some Traditional Drums of Ghana', B.A. thesis (UST, Kumasi), 1968

Adjaye, J.K., 'Asante and Britain in the Nineteenth Century: A Study in Asante Diplomatic Practice', Ph.D. (Northwestern), 1981

Aidoo, A.A., 'Political Crisis and Social Change in the Asante Kingdom, 1867–1901', Ph.D. (California-Los Angeles), 1975

Allman, J.M., 'The National Liberation Movement and the Asante Struggle for Self-Determination, 1954–1957', Ph.D. (Northwestern), 1987

Ampratwum, K., 'Traditional Medical Centres', M.Sc. thesis (UST, Kumasi), 1969

Austin, G., 'Rural Capitalism and the Growth of Cocoa-Farming in South Ashanti, to 1914', Ph.D. (Birmingham), 1984

Boakye, I., 'Some Aspects of the Social Organization of the Fishing Villages on Lake Bosumtwi', M.A. thesis (Ghana-Legon), 1965

Borgatti, J.M., 'The Festival as Art Event – Form and Iconography: Olimi Festival in Okpella (Midwest State, Nigeria)', Ph.D. (California-Los Angeles), 1976

Brown, J.W., 'Kumasi, 1896–1923: Urban Africa during the Early Colonial Period', Ph.D. (Wisconsin-Madison), 1972

Dodd, N.B., 'Money in Social Theory', Ph.D. (Cambridge), 1992

Ehrlich, M.J., 'A Catalogue of Ashanti Art taken from Kumasi in the Anglo-Ashanti War of 1874', Ph.D. (Indiana-Bloomington), 1981

Ferguson, P., 'Islamization in Dagbon: A Study of the Alfanema of Yendi', Ph.D. (Cambridge), 1973

Haight, B.M., 'Bole and Gonja: Contributions to the History of Northern Ghana', Ph.D. (Northwestern), 1981

Jenkins, R.G., 'Gold Coast Historians and their pursuit of the Gold Coast Pasts, 1882–1917', Ph.D., 2 vols. (Birmingham), 1985

Kea, R.A., 'Trade, State Formation and Warfare on the Gold Coast 1600–1826', Ph.D. (London), 1974

Klein, A.N., 'Inequality in Asante: A Study of the Forms and Meanings of Slavery and Social Servitude in Pre- and Early Colonial Akan-Asante Society and Culture', Ph.D., 2 vols. (Michigan-Ann Arbor), 1981

Kurankyi-Taylor, E.E., 'Ashanti Indigenous Legal Institutions and their Present Role', Ph.D., 2 vols. (Cambridge), 1951

Kyerematen, A.A.Y., 'Ashanti Royal Regalia: Their History and Functions', D.Phil. (Oxford), 1966

LaTorre, J.R., 'Wealth Surpasses Everything: An Economic History of Asante, 1750–1874', Ph.D. (California-Berkeley), 1978

Lewin, T.J., 'The Structure of Political Conflict in Asante, 1875–1900', Ph.D., 2 vols. (Northwestern), 1974

McCaskie, T.C., 'The Paramountcy of the *Asantehene* Kwaku Dua (1834–1867): A Study in Asante Political Culture', Ph.D. (Cambridge), 1974

Mikell, G., 'Cocoa and Social Change in Ghana: A Study of Development in the Sunyani District', Ph.D. (Columbia), 1975

Nyaggah, M., 'Social Origins of the Asante Traditional Administrators: 1700–1900', Ph.D. (California-Berkeley), 1974

Okai, K.A., 'The Juaben Revolt and the Founding of New Juaben in Akim Abuakwa', B.A. dissertation (Ghana-Legon), 1972

Owusu-Ansah, D., 'A Talismanic Tradition: Muslims in Early Nineteenth Century Kumase', Ph.D. (Northwestern), 1986

Owusu-Mensa, K., 'Prince Owusu Ansa and Asante-British Diplomacy, 1841–1884', Ph.D. (Wisconsin-Madison), 1974

Porter, R., 'European Activity on the Gold Coast, 1620–1667', D.Litt. (University of South Africa), 1975

Quarcoo, A.B., 'Cocoyam Cultivation in Asante: History and Prospects', B.A. dissertation. (Institute of Administration, Greenhill (Ghana)), 1968

Terray, E., 'Une Histoire du Royaume Abron du Gyaman: des origines à la conquête coloniale', Doctorat d'Etat, 5 vols. (Paris), 1984

Yankah, K., 'The Proverb in the Context of Akan Rhetoric', Ph.D. (Indiana-Bloomington), 1985

Yarak, L.W., 'Asante and the Dutch: A Case Study in the History of Asante Administration, 1744–1873', Ph.D. (Northwestern), 1983

ARCHIVES, FIELD MATERIALS, ETC.

ACBP: ASANTE COLLECTIVE BIOGRAPHY PROJECT (1973–9)

The ACBP was co-directed by Ivor Wilks and T.C. McCaskie. It was dedicated to the production and publication of life histories (in the form of pre-code sheets) of individual Asante, *fl.* late seventeenth to twentieth centuries. Thirty-six of these were published in eleven issues of the ACBP Bulletin (*Asante Seminar*, 1–6 (1975–6); *Asantesɛm*, 7–11 (1977–9)), together with documentary materials and other items on Asante history. By 1979, pre-code sheet numbers had been assigned to some 1,000 named persons, and numbers of pre-code sheets were in preliminary or draft form. It was intended eventually to computerize the pre-code sheet data base, but when ACBP ceased publication in 1979 this goal was still unrealized. Wilks has since attempted to resurrect the ACBP, but lack of funding has prevented this (see I. Wilks, *Asante in the Nineteenth Century*, 1989 reprint, *Preamble*, xxxii–xxxiii). The data base is in the form of some 20,000 typed or handwritten $8'' \times 5''$ file cards. Full references to ACBP/pcs items are given in the notes, as are references to all other materials published in *Asante Seminar* and *Asantesɛm*. I have made only the most limited use of unpublished ACBP materials, largely confining myself to noting items in the public domain.

ARA: ALGEMEEN RIJKSARCHIEF (THE HAGUE, NETHERLANDS)

Full references to ARA items are given in the notes. The original MS of W. Huydecoper's journal of 1816–17 (see Printed works: books, book parts, etc.) is in NBKG (Archief van de Nederlandsche Bezittingen ter Kuste van Guinea), 349. Special mention should be made here of one further item. This is catalogued at Archief van het Ministerie van Kolonien 1814–49, no. 3965: Elmina Journal, Appendix: 'Journaal van den Fabriek en Magazijn Meester J. Simons gehouden op deszelfs Missie naar den Konig van Assiantijn te Koemasie'. This is the 44-page foolscap MS journal (dd. 27 December 1831 to 11 March 1832) kept by the Dutch agent J. Simons during his visit to Kumase. An annotated English translation of this by L.W. Yarak is being prepared for publication. I thank Larry Yarak for making his draft translation of the text available to me.

ASC: AFRICAN STUDIES CENTRE (CAMBRIDGE, UK), FORTES PAPERS

These are the publicly deposited papers of the late Meyer Fortes (sometime William Wyse Professor of Social Anthropology, Cambridge University). They are drawn from and chiefly relate to the work of the Ashanti Social Survey, 1945–6 (see ASSM), of which Fortes was a principal co-researcher. This deposit grew out of an SSRC Project ('Kinship Organisation in Cocoa Production among the Ashanti, 1945 to the Present') undertaken by Fortes and V. Ebin in 1979–80, and it includes selected materials relevant to that Project, as well as some of Fortes' other Asante fieldwork materials. A Catalogue of this deposit was included in the Final Report of the Project to the SSRC. This gives a listing of the materials by broad, and sometimes confusing, categories. I have cited all items by individual nominal reference, and these are fully given in the notes.

ASSM: ASHANTI SOCIAL SURVEY MSS (PRIVATE DEPOSIT)

The ASSM materials are in the form of manuscripts and papers held by Professor R.W. Steel, M. Fortes' principal co-researcher in Asante in 1945–6. Some of these items are organized in categorical files. Others are completely unclassified (being single sheets, notes, letters or other fugitive items). They are variously by Steel, Fortes or their Asante assistants, and they cover a very broad range of subjects. I am most grateful to Robert Steel for approaching me, for placing the ASSM materials at my disposal, and for discussing them with me. I intend to catalogue this archive for consultation at the Centre of West African Studies, University of Birmingham, by interested scholars. Full references to all items cited are given in the notes.

BALME LIBRARY, UNIVERSITY OF GHANA (LEGON, GHANA)

I have made use of a few items deposited in the Pamphlets and MSS Boxes that are adjunct to the Furley MSS Collection. Full references are given in the notes.

BMA: BASEL MISSION ARCHIVES (BASEL, SWITZERLAND)

All references to the Gold Coast Correspondence are cited in full in the notes. I have consulted the originals, but have made use of the extensive (and indispensable) draft English translations made by Paul Jenkins, the Basel Mission archivist. Two further items require specific mention. First: the BMA contains an 825-page foolscap MS diary entitled 'Tagebuch Ramseyer, 1869–1874', covering the Asante captivity of F.A. Ramseyer and J. Kühne. There are as yet unresolved textual problems with this diary (for which see below). I have consulted my copy of this diary in conjunction with the published English and German versions of Ramseyer and Kühne. Very importantly, I have had access to P. Jenkins' draft collations, annotations and English translations from the 'Tagebuch Ramseyer', the two published German editions of Ramseyer and Kühne, and the published English and French translations. Jenkins' labours have produced a usable if provisional 'master text' in note form for the period from June 1869 to March 1872. Although as yet uncompleted, this is invaluable. I am hugely in Paul Jenkins' debt, and acknowledge this with gratitude. I have cited the familiar 1875 English edition of Ramseyer and Kühne where this seems complete and reliable for my immediate purposes (and after cross-checking it with the other versions available to me). I have also cited Jenkins' work (BMA, Jenkins, Ramseyer MS *et al.*) where appropriate, and used it as a base guide and reference point. The disparate Ramseyer (and Kühne) materials need authoritative scholarly treatment. This is acknowledged in A. Jones, '*Four Years in Asante*: One Source or Several?', *HA*, 18 (1991), 173–203, which is a most useful outline of the history and problems of these various texts. Unfortunately, but I fear accurately, Jones concludes (*ibid.*, 198) that it would take four years of undivided work to produce a scholarly edition of the 'Tagebuch Ramseyer'! Second: the BMA contains N.V. Asare, *Asante Abasem (Twi Kasamu)*, a 124 (variously sized) page MS in Twi (dd. 1915). This episodic History of Asante was compiled from oral traditions collected by Asare when serving with the Basel Mission in Kumase between 1902 and 1912. It is an extremely valuable source, in places unique, but hitherto neglected. While I was writing this book, my student W. Donkoh was simultaneously engaged in translating this MS as part of an M.A. degree at the University of Birmingham. I am most grateful to her for extended discussions of the text and its translation. Ms Donkoh's completed M.A. is not yet available for public consultation, pending publication of it in full or excerpted part. I have used both of our drafts and notes, and re-checked my copy of the original, when citing or quoting Asare. All other materials cited from the BMA are fully referenced in the notes.

H.J. BEVIN MSS (PRIVATE DEPOSIT)

I have made only the most limited use of these manuscripts and papers, which were collected or compiled in Ghana in the 1950s and 1960s by the late H.J. Bevin. These are currently held at the Centre of West African Studies, University of Birmingham, and I am most grateful to Mrs H.J. Bevin for placing them in my care. There is as yet no Catalogue. Full references are given in the notes.

GPRL: GEORGE PADMORE RESEARCH LIBRARY (ACCRA, GHANA)

This library has since been renamed the Library of African Affairs. Full references to all materials cited are given in the notes.

IAS: INSTITUTE OF AFRICAN STUDIES, UNIVERSITY OF GHANA (LEGON, GHANA)

Full references to items from the Asante Stool Histories series (IAS/AS), the Asante Court Records series (IAS/CR), and to all other materials are given in the notes.

M. JOHNSON, FIELDNOTES AND MSS (PRIVATE DEPOSIT)

The late Marion Johnson's fieldnotes and manuscripts were administered after her death by the Centre of West African Studies, University of Birmingham. I have made use here of materials gathered from Asante informants in 1975. Full references are given in the notes.

KITLV: KONINKLIJK INSTITUUT VOOR TAAL-, LAND-, EN VOLKENKUNDE (LEIDEN, NETHERLANDS)

I have made use of MS H. 509: 'Aanhangsel: Extract uit het journaal gehouden te Comassie door eenen tapoeier'. This is the Kumase journal of the Dutch agent P. de Heer for 1866–7. A subsequent part of this journal – which I have read but not cited here – is in the University of Amsterdam Library, MS ES. 44: '[Journaal van] de agent van het Nederlandsche gouvernement bij den vorst van Ashantijn'. I thank René Baesjou and Larry Yarak for providing me with copies of their draft English translations of, respectively, the first and second of these MSS. Full references are given in the notes.

KTC: KUMASE TOWN COUNCIL (KUMASE, GHANA)

I have made use of a few manuscript materials from the KTC, and I am grateful for assistance provided by its officials. Full references are given in the notes.

LO: LANDS OFFICE, MANHYIA (KUMASE, GHANA)

I have made use of a very few manuscript materials from LO on land and ancillary matters. In all cases these were made available to me on an individual basis by document, for LO is not an archive with a Catalogue to consult. It is a working part of the *Asantemaŋ* administration. LO also contains a variety of useful maps and drawings. Full references are given in the notes.

T.C. MCCASKIE: INTERVIEWS, FIELDNOTES, ETC. (PRIVATE DEPOSIT)

I have made use of materials that I collected in Ghana (1968–90). Full references are given to all formal interviews in the notes. In addition, I have used the Diaries and Notebooks that I kept during field trips (1975–90). These record, *inter alia*, informal discussions or conversations with many Asante on a variety of topics, together with my observations made at the time of writing. Some of this material was supplied in confidence, and I have observed this restriction where appropriate. I have also used formal interview materials that I collected with Lynne Brydon in the Volta Region (1988), and I am greatly indebted to her, not least for her command of spoken Avatime and Ewe. My field materials have been supplemented over the years by letters from Asante informants in answer to specific queries, and by countless talks with Asante resident in the UK. A variety of taped materials still await transcription and/or translation into English.

MFU: MEYER FORTES, UNACCESSIONED MSS, NOTES, ETC.

In 1979–80 in Cambridge I had lengthy discussions with the late Meyer Fortes about his work and about Asante matters generally. He kindly supplied me with copies of manuscripts or notes made by himself and by his Asante research assistants or correspondents, but proscribed use of all such materials during his lifetime. The originals (and/or variant versions) of some of these items are on deposit in ASC, Cambridge. Others are not. But I have not as yet made a systematic comparison between the ASC holdings and my own copies. It has been agreed with K. Hart, Director of ASC, Cambridge, that this will be done, and that my copies, as relevant, will be deposited in ASC. Full nominal references are given in the notes (together with notations indicating my present awareness of variant or duplicate copies in ASC).

MLC: MAMPON LITERARY CLUB (PRIVATE DEPOSIT)

I have cited only the Minutes of the MLC, 1941–4. I intend to explore this resource fully on a future visit to Mampon.

MRO: MANHYIA RECORD OFFICE (KUMASE, GHANA)

Since I first worked in this archive it has been reorganized under the auspices of IAS Legon (Director, Professor K. Arhin), on behalf of the *Asantehene* and the *Asanteman* Council. The resources of this archive are of the first importance for the student of Asante. I have used it extensively. All references to civil and criminal court records, miscellaneous files, etc. have been given in the notes. Two items require specific mention. First, 'The History of Ashanti Kings and the Whole Country Itself, Written by me, F.A. Prempeh, and was Dictated by E. Prempeh, Commence [*sic*] on 6th August 1907' (referred to in my text as AK). AK is a MS of 87 handwritten foolscap pages, begun in 1907 in the Seychelles at the dictation of the then exiled *Asantehene* Agyeman Prempe. A supplement to this (covering the period *c.* 1867–96) is in NAS (see below), with at least one known transcription in GPRL. I was fortunate enough to secure a *verbatim* transcription of AK, but in *c.* 1980 the original was removed from MRO for rebinding. It is not now (1990) in MRO, and its present whereabouts are unknown, at least to me. Happily, there is at least one copy other than mine in circulation, and I understand that Professors Adu Boahen and Ivor Wilks intend to produce a published version of it. Second, 'The

History of Ashanti,' MS (with letters and accompanying notes) prepared by a Committee of Traditional Authorities under the Chairmanship of *Ashantihene* Osei Agyeman Prempeh II, n.d. (but in the 1940s), referred to in my text as HA. HA is a single-spaced, heavily annotated foolscap typescript of 261 pages, and it was written at the behest of the *Asantehene* Osei Agyeman Prempeh II (see Kurankyi-Taylor, 'Ashanti Indigenous Legal Institutions', I, 89–90, fn. 2). The accompanying documentation is mainly of an administrative nature (but includes some original testimonies, e.g. a 28-page typescript 'History of Edweso'). Again, I was fortunate enough to secure a *verbatim* transcription of HA (and have since taken extensive notes on the accompanying MS documents). In the 1970s, there circulated in Kumase at least one shortened and 'corrected' typed version of HA (but of a draft, rather than the full original). A number of identifiable abstracts are also in circulation. In a paper prepared in early 1990 ('Inventing Asante', in K. Barber and P. de Moraes Farias (eds.), *Self-Assertion and Brokerage*, 55–67 (1990), see Printed works: books, book parts, etc.), I reported that as of 1988 HA (like AK) was no longer in MRO. In October 1990, however, following an audience with the *Asantehene*, I learned that HA (and all of its ancillary documentation) was still in Kumase, but that it had been removed during the 1980s from MRO to the New Manhyia Palace. This is fortunate, for, despite interpolations from European sources, HA is a uniquely detailed document.

NAG: NATIONAL ARCHIVES OF GHANA (ACCRA, KOFORIDUA, KUMASE, SUNYANI)

Full references to all items cited from branches of the NAG are given in the notes.

NAS: NATIONAL ARCHIVES OF THE SEYCHELLES (VICTORIA, MAHE)

I am most grateful to H.J. McGaw, Director, National Archives of the Seychelles, for copies of all documents ('Political Exiles: Ashanti') that pertain to the Seychelles exile (1896–1924) of the *Asantehene* Agyeman Prempe and his fellow detainees. There are 5 vols. of these documents (totalling 374 typed and handwritten foolscap pages). I have made only the most cursory of direct references to NAS, but reading these documents has informed the contents of this book. Specific note is made here of NAS, C/SS/2, vol. II, E. Prempeh *et al.* to Governor, Seychelles Islands, dd. Ashanti Camp, Le Rocher, Mahé, 16 October 1913 (which is clearly a supplement to AK: see MRO). A transcribed version of this (dd. 1922) is in GPRL, Accra. Adu Boahen, I understand, has secured copies of the NAS materials for GPRL and MRO (see J.K. Adjaye, '*Asantehene* Agyeman Prempe I and British Colonization of Asante: A Reassessment', *IJAHS*, 22, 2 (1989), 223–49, esp. 224, fn. 3).

OMP: OLD MANHYIA PALACE (KUMASE, GHANA)

A small collection of manuscripts and documents assembled by the late *Asantehene* Osei Agyeman Prempe II (while presiding over the writing of HA?) is held in OMP, which was formerly the principal private residence of the *Asantehene*. I have consulted some, but by no means all, of these. Full references to all items cited are given in the notes.

PD: PRIVATE DEPOSIT, BONNAT MSS

This extremely important source, entitled 'Manuscrits de M.-J. Bonnat (copié par M. L'Abbé Bonnat)', was recovered by Claude-Hélène Perrot, University of Paris, in the 1970s. It is composed of fifteen separate 'Cahiers', the great majority being a chronological diary covering the period June 1869 to January 1874; two of the 'Cahiers', however, are general ethnographic accounts of Asante customs (part of one being transcribed in English); one 'Cahier', moreover, contains a confessional novel ('La Chimère') written by Bonnat in captivity. I am extremely grateful to C.-H. Perrot for furnishing me with a complete copy of this source (which has been photographically enlarged in the interests of clarity). The Centre of West African Studies, University of Birmingham, was to participate with French colleagues in producing a published version of this massive manuscript, but the death of Marion Johnson aborted this plan. I understand that C.-H. Perrot (together with A. Van Dantzig) still hopes to publish the Bonnat MSS in whole or in part. Full references to all items cited are given in the notes by 'Cahier' number, and by date of entry. My reconstruction of the *odwira* would have been much less full without the Bonnat MSS.

PRM: PITT-RIVERS MUSEUM (OXFORD, UK)

I have consulted PRM, 1941.3.177–219. This is the R.S. Rattray Collection of Photographs. It contains some 1,300 items, of which about 1,000 are photographs taken in Asante. Rattray's notes and ascriptions on some of the photographs are of independent interest.

PRO: PUBLIC RECORD OFFICE (KEW, LONDON, UK)

Full references to all items cited are given in the notes.

RAI: ROYAL ANTHROPOLOGICAL INSTITUTE (LONDON, UK)

I have used the collected Manuscripts and Papers of R.S. Rattray. Full references to items cited are given in the notes.

RCS: ROYAL COMMONWEALTH SOCIETY (LONDON, UK)

I have used the Gold Coast Boxes and Files. These contain a small quantity of original and/or unique materials. Full references to items cited are given in the notes.

RH: RHODES HOUSE (OXFORD, UK)

I have consulted manuscripts and papers in the Colonial Records Project. Most useful for my purposes have been CRP, MSS Brit. Emp. s.344 (Papers of Sir Charles Henry Harper) and CRP, MSS Afr. s.593 (Papers of Lt. Col. A.C. Duncan-Johnstone). Full references to all items cited are given in the notes.

RU: RHODES UNIVERSITY LIBRARY (GRAHAMSTOWN, SOUTH AFRICA)

I have used Cory MS 15, 104, 'Journal of the Rev. George Chapman, 1843–1857'. Full references to all items cited from Chapman's 'Journal' are given in the notes. With the permission of Rhodes University, I am currently engaged in preparing this manuscript for publication.

TOR: PAPERS AND MSS OF W. TORDOFF (PRIVATE DEPOSIT)

I am most grateful to William Tordoff for making available to me notes and materials that he collected in Kumase in the 1950s. The particular value of TOR is that it contains detailed notes on manuscripts that, sadly, are no longer to be found in the original in NAG, Kumase. Full references to all items cited from TOR are given in the notes.

WMMS: WESLEYAN-METHODIST MISSIONARY SOCIETY ARCHIVES (LONDON, UK)

I have made very extensive use of the Gold Coast Correspondence, of the Journals of Thomas B. Freeman (and of his unpublished book-length text: 'Life and Travels: Gold Coast, Ashantee, Dahomey', MS n.d. but c. 1860), and of various other journals and miscellaneous items. When I worked in the WMMS archive it was located in Methodist House, Marylebone Road, London, and it was haphazardly indexed and catalogued. It has since that time been removed to the School of Oriental and African Studies, London, and it is now comprehensively indexed and catalogued. References to all items cited are given in the notes.

Note: I do not list in this Guide such items as the printed British Parliamentary Papers, various newspapers, etc. To do so would be repetitious as well as tedious. Full references to each and every one of these items is given in the notes in which they are cited.

Index

Figures in italics indicate illustrations

474

OTHER BOOKS IN THE SERIES

T.C. MCCASKIE lectures on the social history of West Africa at the Centre of West African Studies, University of Birmingham.